Handbook of Research on Software Quality Innovation in Interactive Systems

Francisco Vicente Cipolla-Ficarra
Latin Association of Human-Computer Interaction, Spain & International Association of Interactive Communication, Italy

A volume in the Advances in Systems Analysis, Software Engineering, and High Performance Computing (ASASEHPC) Book Series

Published in the United States of America by
IGI Global
Engineering Science Reference (an imprint of IGI Global)
701 E. Chocolate Avenue
Hershey PA, USA 17033
Tel: 717-533-8845
Fax: 717-533-8661
E-mail: cust@igi-global.com
Web site: http://www.igi-global.com

Library of Congress Cataloging-in-Publication Data

Names: Cipolla-Ficarra, Francisco V. (Francisco Vicente) editor.
Title: Handbook of research on software quality innovation in interactive systems / Francisco Vicente Cipolla Ficarra, editor.
Description: Hershey : Engineering Science Reference, [2021] | Includes bibliographical references and index. | Summary: "This book looks at the constant evolution of the software to keep pace with the hardware revolution and discusses a host of new horizons to maintain and increase the quality of the interactive systems, following a set of standardized norms and rules for the production of interactive software"-- Provided by publisher.
Identifiers: LCCN 2020036431 (print) | LCCN 2020036432 (ebook) | ISBN 9781799870104 (h/c) | ISBN 9781799870128 (eISBN)
Subjects: LCSH: Computer software--Quality control.
Classification: LCC QA76.76.Q35 S657 2021 (print) | LCC QA76.76.Q35 (ebook) | DDC 005.3028/7--dc23
LC record available at https://lccn.loc.gov/2020036431
LC ebook record available at https://lccn.loc.gov/2020036432

This book is published in the IGI Global book series Advances in Systems Analysis, Software Engineering, and High Performance Computing (ASASEHPC) (ISSN: 2327-3453; eISSN: 2327-3461)

British Cataloguing in Publication Data
A Cataloguing in Publication record for this book is available from the British Library.

Advances in Systems Analysis, Software Engineering, and High Performance Computing (ASASEHPC) Book Series

Vijayan Sugumaran
Oakland University, USA

ISSN:2327-3453
EISSN:2327-3461

Mission

The theory and practice of computing applications and distributed systems has emerged as one of the key areas of research driving innovations in business, engineering, and science. The fields of software engineering, systems analysis, and high performance computing offer a wide range of applications and solutions in solving computational problems for any modern organization.

The **Advances in Systems Analysis, Software Engineering, and High Performance Computing (ASASEHPC) Book Series** brings together research in the areas of distributed computing, systems and software engineering, high performance computing, and service science. This collection of publications is useful for academics, researchers, and practitioners seeking the latest practices and knowledge in this field.

Coverage

- Distributed Cloud Computing
- Computer System Analysis
- Engineering Environments
- Enterprise Information Systems
- Human-Computer Interaction
- Virtual Data Systems
- Network Management
- Performance Modelling
- Storage Systems
- Computer Networking

IGI Global is currently accepting manuscripts for publication within this series. To submit a proposal for a volume in this series, please contact our Acquisition Editors at Acquisitions@igi-global.com or visit: http://www.igi-global.com/publish/.

The Advances in Systems Analysis, Software Engineering, and High Performance Computing (ASASEHPC) Book Series (ISSN 2327-3453) is published by IGI Global, 701 E. Chocolate Avenue, Hershey, PA 17033-1240, USA, www.igi-global.com. This series is composed of titles available for purchase individually; each title is edited to be contextually exclusive from any other title within the series. For pricing and ordering information please visit http://www.igi-global.com/book-series/advances-systems-analysis-software-engineering/73689. Postmaster: Send all address changes to above address.

Titles in this Series

For a list of additional titles in this series, please visit:
http://www.igi-global.com/book-series/advances-systems-analysis-software-engineering/73689

Impacts and Challenges of Cloud Business Inelligence
Shadi Aljawarneh (Jordan University of Science and Technology, Jordan) and Manisha Malhotra (Chandigarh University, India)
Business Science Reference • © 2021 • 263pp • H/C (ISBN: 9781799850403) • US $195.00

Handbook of Research on Modeling, Analysis, and Control of Complex Systems
Ahmad Taher Azar (Faculty of Computers and Artificial Intelligence, Benha University, Benha, Egypt & College of Computer and Information Sciences, Prince Sultan University, Riyadh, Saudi Arabia) and Nashwa Ahmad Kamal (Faculty of Engineering, Cairo University, Giza, Egypt)
Engineering Science Reference • © 2021 • 685pp • H/C (ISBN: 9781799857884) • US $295.00

Artificial Intelligence Paradigms for Smart Cyber-Physical Systems
Ashish Kumar Luhach (The PNG University of Technology, Papua New Guinea) and Atilla Elçi (Hasan Kalyoncu University, Turkey)
Engineering Science Reference • © 2021 • 392pp • H/C (ISBN: 9781799851011) • US $225.00

Advancements in Model-Driven Architecture in Software Engineering
Yassine Rhazali (Moulay Ismail University of Meknes, Morocco)
Engineering Science Reference • © 2021 • 287pp • H/C (ISBN: 9781799836612) • US $215.00

Cloud-Based Big Data Analytics in Vehicular Ad-Hoc Networks
Ram Shringar Rao (Ambedkar Institute of Advanced Communication Technologies and Research, India) Nanhay Singh (Ambedkar Institute of Advanced Communication Technologies and Research, India) Omprakash Kaiwartya (School of Science and Technology, Nottingham Trent University, UK) and Sanjoy Das (Indira Gandhi National Tribal University, India)
Engineering Science Reference • © 2021 • 312pp • H/C (ISBN: 9781799827641) • US $245.00

Formal and Adaptive Methods for Automation of Parallel Programs Construction Emerging Research and Opportunities
Anatoliy Doroshenko (Institute of Software Systems, Ukraine) and Olena Yatsenko (Institute of Software Systems, Ukraine)
Engineering Science Reference • © 2021 • 279pp • H/C (ISBN: 9781522593843) • US $195.00

701 East Chocolate Avenue, Hershey, PA 17033, USA
Tel: 717-533-8845 x100 • Fax: 717-533-8661
E-Mail: cust@igi-global.com • www.igi-global.com

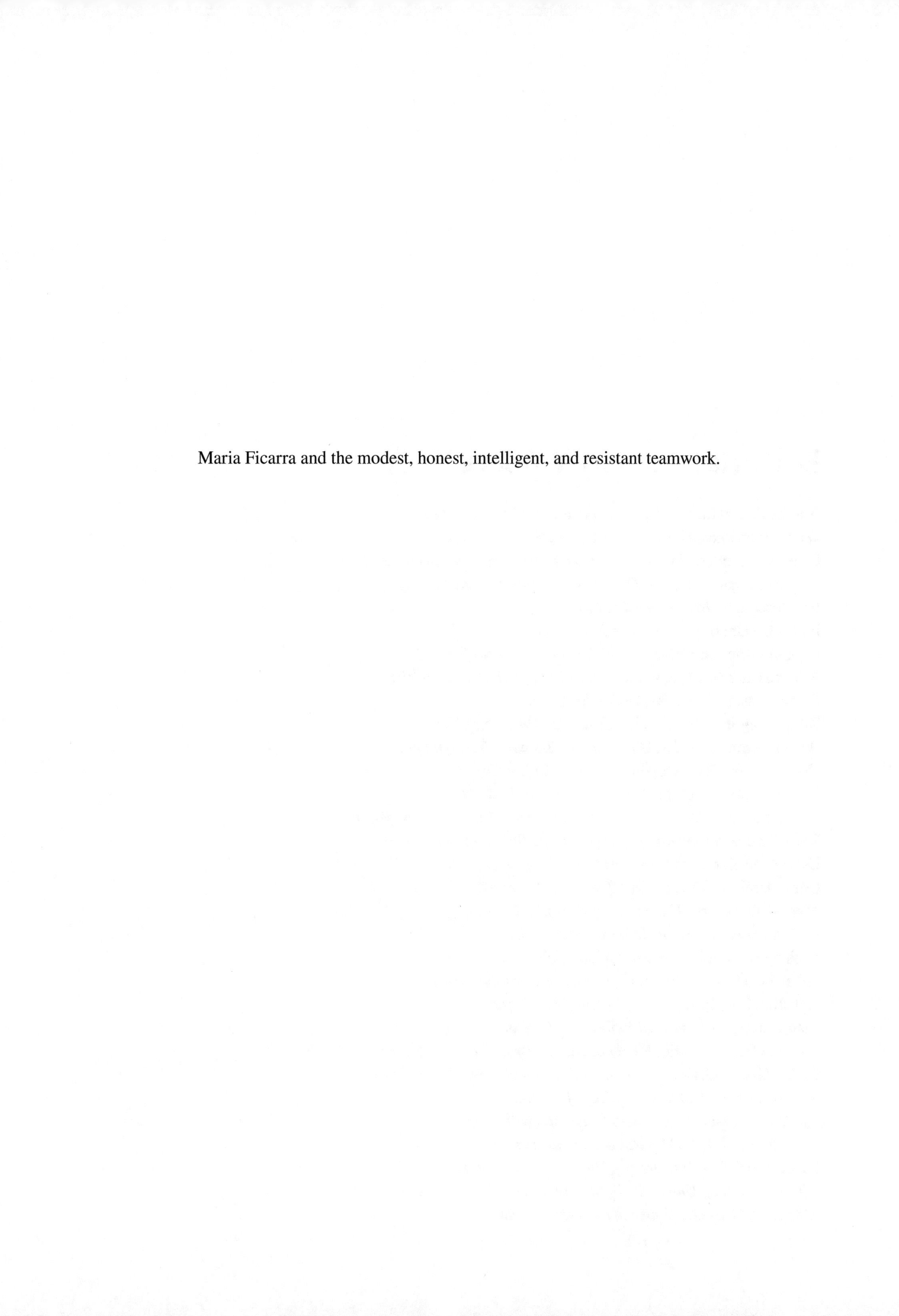

Maria Ficarra and the modest, honest, intelligent, and resistant teamwork.

Editorial Advisory Board

List of Contributors

Agrawal, Rohit / *University Institute of Technology, Rajiv Gandhi Proudyogiki Vishwavidyalaya, India* 359
Ansari, Saif / *University Institute of Technology, Rajiv Gandhi Proudyogiki Vishwavidyalaya, India* 359
Budan, Paola Daniela / *Universidad Nacional de Santiago del Estero, Argentina* 371
Castañeira, Veronica / *Facultad de Tecnología Informática, Universidad Abierta Interamericana, Argentina* 304
Cheliadin, Olexander / *Kharkiv Aviation Institute, Ukraine* 154
Cipolla-Ficarra, Francisco V. / *Latin Association of Human-Computer Interaction, Spain & International Association of Interactive Communication, Italy* 1, 41
Dergachov, Konstantin / *Kharkiv Aviation Institute, Ukraine* 154
Doğanay, Pelin Şerefhan / *Korkmaz Kitchen and Small Home Appliances, Turkey* 285
Eren Erdoğmuş, İrem / *Faculty of Business Administration, Marmara University, Turkey* 285
Ficarra, Miguel Cipolla / *Latin Association of Human-Computer Interaction, Spain & International Association of Interactive Communication, Italy* 41
Garino, Carlos Gabriel García / *ITIC, Facultad de Ingeniería, Universidad Nacional de Cuyo, Argentina* 133
Godoy, Pablo Daniel / *ITIC, Facultad de Ingeniería, FCEN, Universidad Nacional de Cuyo, Argentina* 133
Haurech, Hugo Rolando / *Department of Management Technologies, Misiones National University, Argentina* 267
Herrera, Susana Isabel / *Universidad Nacional de Santiago del Estero, Argentina* 371
Krasnov, Leonid / *Kharkiv Aviation Institute, Ukraine* 154
Maldonado, Marilena del Valle / *Universidad Nacional de Santiago del Estero, Argentina* 371
Marianetti, Osvaldo Lucio / *Facultad de Ingeniería, Universidad Nacional de Cuyo, Argentina* ... 133
Martinez, David Luis la Red / *Northeast National University, Argentina* 267
Marzorati, Diego E. / *Facultad de Tecnología Informática, Universidad Abierta Interamericana, Argentina* 304
Morales, María Inés / *Universidad Nacional de Santiago del Estero, Argentina* 371
Ontiveros, José Daniel / *Facultad de Ingeniería, Universidad Nacional de Jujuy, Argentina* 338
Pandey, Rajeev / *University Institute of Technology, Rajiv Gandhi Proudyogiki Vishwavidyalaya, India* 359
Plakhotnyi, Olexander / *National Aerospace University KhAI, Ukraine* 154
Poli, Annamaria / *Università degli Studi di Milano-Bicocca, Italy* 324

Poncio, Silvia Victoria / *Facultad de Tecnología Informática, Universidad Abierta Interamericana, Argentina* 304
Quiroga, Alejandra / *The University of Sydney, Australia* 41
Quispe, Gloria Lola / *Facultad de Ingeniería, Universidad Nacional de Jujuy, Argentina* 338
Radley, Alan / *Kim Veltman Perspective Institute, UK* 102, 213
Rodríguez, Maria Fernanda / *Facultad de Ciencias Económicas, Argentina* 338
Rosenzvaig, Federico / *Universidad Nacional de Santiago del Estero, Argentina* 371
Roth, Eric Hermán / *Facultad de Tecnología Informática, Universidad Abierta Interamericana, Argentina* 304
Ruiz, Pablo Javier Najar / *Universidad Nacional de Santiago del Estero, Argentina* 371
Salinas, Sergio Ariel / *ITIC, Universidad Nacional de Cuyo, Argentina* 192, 252
Sánchez, Carlos Antonio / *Universidad Nacional de Santiago del Estero, Argentina* 371
Shukla, Piyush Kumar / *University Institute of Technology, Rajiv Gandhi Proudyogiki Vishwavidyalaya, India* 359
Tamburini, Daniela / *Sperimenta – Centro Studi Cinema e Formazione, Italy* 324
Tedaldi, Marco / *University of Bologna, Italy* 391
Tedini, Daniel / *Facultad de Tecnología Informática, Universidad Abierta Interamericana, Argentina* 304
van Till, Jaap / *Tildro Research, The Netherlands* 83
Vural, Görkem / *Marmara University, Turkey* 285

Table of Contents

Preface xx

Acknowledgment xxx

Introduction xxxi

Chapter 1
Software and Innovation: Detecting Invisible High-Quality Factors 1
Francisco V. Cipolla-Ficarra, Latin Association of Human-Computer Interaction, Spain & International Association of Interactive Communication, Italy

Chapter 2
Quality and Web Software Engineering Advances 41
Francisco V. Cipolla-Ficarra, Latin Association of Human-Computer Interaction, Spain & International Association of Interactive Communication, Italy
Alejandra Quiroga, The University of Sydney, Australia
Miguel Cipolla Ficarra, Latin Association of Human-Computer Interaction, Spain & International Association of Interactive Communication, Italy

Chapter 3
Masters of Imagination: From Hierarchies to Connected Swarms 83
Jaap van Till, Tildro Research, The Netherlands

Chapter 4
The Universal Knowledge Machine 102
Alan Radley, Kim Veltman Perspective Institute, UK

Chapter 5
Experiences With Computer Architecture Remote Laboratories 133
Pablo Daniel Godoy, ITIC, Facultad de Ingeniería, FCEN, Universidad Nacional de Cuyo, Argentina
Osvaldo Lucio Marianetti, Facultad de Ingeniería, Universidad Nacional de Cuyo, Argentina
Carlos Gabriel García Garino, ITIC, Facultad de Ingeniería, Universidad Nacional de Cuyo, Argentina

Chapter 6
The Method and Tools Development for Web-Cameras Color Correction in Binocular Vision Systems 154
Konstantin Dergachov, Kharkiv Aviation Institute, Ukraine
Leonid Krasnov, Kharkiv Aviation Institute, Ukraine
Olexander Cheliadin, Kharkiv Aviation Institute, Ukraine
Olexander Plakhotnyi, National Aerospace University KhAI, Ukraine

Chapter 7
A Communication Model Based on Fractal Geometry for Internet of Things 192
Sergio Ariel Salinas, ITIC, Universidad Nacional de Cuyo, Argentina

Chapter 8
The Science of Smart Things 213
Alan Radley, Kim Veltman Perspective Institute, UK

Chapter 9
Autonomous Communication Model for Internet of Things 252
Sergio Ariel Salinas, Universidad Nacional de Cuyo, Argentina

Chapter 10
The Analytic Hierarchy Process as a Method for the Selection of Resources in the Cloud 267
Hugo Rolando Haurech, Department of Management Technologies, Misiones National University, Argentina
David Luis la Red Martinez, Northeast National University, Argentina

Chapter 11
Exploring Antecedents to Adopt Mobile Augmented Reality Applications: A Uses and Gratifications Approach 285
İrem Eren Erdoğmuş, Faculty of Business Administration, Marmara University, Turkey
Pelin Şerefhan Doğanay, Korkmaz Kitchen and Small Home Appliances, Turkey
Görkem Vural, Marmara University, Turkey

Chapter 12
Students in Socially Vulnerable Contexts: Discovering Their Entrepreneurial Potential 304
Silvia Victoria Poncio, Facultad de Tecnología Informática, Universidad Abierta Interamericana, Argentina
Daniel Tedini, Facultad de Tecnología Informática, Universidad Abierta Interamericana, Argentina
Veronica Castañeira, Facultad de Tecnología Informática, Universidad Abierta Interamericana, Argentina
Diego E. Marzorati, Facultad de Tecnología Informática, Universidad Abierta Interamericana, Argentina
Eric Hermán Roth, Facultad de Tecnología Informática, Universidad Abierta Interamericana, Argentina

Chapter 13
The Language of Cinema Fosters the Development of Soft Skills for Inclusion and Interdisciplinary Learning 324
Annamaria Poli, Università degli Studi di Milano-Bicocca, Italy
Daniela Tamburini, Sperimenta – Centro Studi Cinema e Formazione, Italy

Chapter 14
Comparative Analysis of ACO Algorithms for the Solution of the Travelling Salesman Problem.... 338
Gloria Lola Quispe, Facultad de Ingeniería, Universidad Nacional de Jujuy, Argentina
Maria Fernanda Rodríguez, Facultad de Ciencias Económicas, Argentina
José Daniel Ontiveros, Facultad de Ingeniería, Universidad Nacional de Jujuy, Argentina

Chapter 15
A Survey on the Techniques to Improve the Visibility of Geospatial Resources on the Web............ 359
Saif Ansari, University Institute of Technology, Rajiv Gandhi Proudyogiki Vishwavidyalaya, India
Piyush Kumar Shukla, University Institute of Technology, Rajiv Gandhi Proudyogiki Vishwavidyalaya, India
Rajeev Pandey, University Institute of Technology, Rajiv Gandhi Proudyogiki Vishwavidyalaya, India
Rohit Agrawal, University Institute of Technology, Rajiv Gandhi Proudyogiki Vishwavidyalaya, India

Chapter 16
Developing Augmented Reality Multi-Platform Mobile Applications........ 371
Susana Isabel Herrera, Universidad Nacional de Santiago del Estero, Argentina
Paola Daniela Budan, Universidad Nacional de Santiago del Estero, Argentina
Federico Rosenzvaig, Universidad Nacional de Santiago del Estero, Argentina
Pablo Javier Najar Ruiz, Universidad Nacional de Santiago del Estero, Argentina
María Inés Morales, Universidad Nacional de Santiago del Estero, Argentina
Marilena del Valle Maldonado, Universidad Nacional de Santiago del Estero, Argentina
Carlos Antonio Sánchez, Universidad Nacional de Santiago del Estero, Argentina

Chapter 17
Results of the Research in the Comparison and Analysis of Historical Artifacts' Photographic Images Catalogued in Online Databases: The Case of a Roman Stele From Ravenna 391
Marco Tedaldi, University of Bologna, Italy

Conclusion 430

Appendix: The "G" Factor in the Web, New Technologies, and Education........ 437

Compilation of References 464

About the Contributors 489

Index........ 498

Detailed Table of Contents

Preface xx

Acknowledgment xxx

Introduction xxxi

Chapter 1
Software and Innovation: Detecting Invisible High-Quality Factors 1
Francisco V. Cipolla-Ficarra, Latin Association of Human-Computer Interaction, Spain & International Association of Interactive Communication, Italy

The study analyzes the invisible factors that influence the innovation and quality of the software of the 21st century, through natural language and programming languages. The analysis of languages shows how technological evolution influences the innate and acquired skills of human beings, especially those who are dedicated to software engineering and all its derivations in the field of ICTs. There is a detailed list of internal and external factors affecting the qualitative and reliable software industry. It also examines the relationships between innovative and creative education of experts in new technologies, programming over time, and the role of social networks. Finally, a state of the art on the myths and realities of the software profession in the new millennium is presented, which together with a group of rhetorical questions allows generating new lines of research within the formal and factual sciences, starting from the inquiries and conclusions of this work.

Chapter 2
Quality and Web Software Engineering Advances 41
Francisco V. Cipolla-Ficarra, Latin Association of Human-Computer Interaction, Spain & International Association of Interactive Communication, Italy
Alejandra Quiroga, The University of Sydney, Australia
Miguel Cipolla Ficarra, Latin Association of Human-Computer Interaction, Spain & International Association of Interactive Communication, Italy

In this chapter, the main avant-garde components that favor quality on the web are disclosed, especially from the perspectives of software and design. At the same time, the deviations of these components that slow down these processes from the technical-human point of view are presented. In this dualistic perspective, the role of education is included in each of the generations of users, programmers, and publishers of digital content on the web, as well as the context in which they are immersed. A triadic vision of past, present and future is presented in each of the aspects and components, directly and indirectly related, with the development of operations, models, and methods, which converge in obtaining a high quality of the web. Finally, parallels are drawn between the formal science professions and infinite semiosis in web engineering.

Chapter 3
Masters of Imagination: From Hierarchies to Connected Swarms 83
Jaap van Till, Tildro Research, The Netherlands

This chapter is about some observations of the social and economic impact of ICT and ICT digital infrastructures and more specifically what users do with processing and telecommunication power tools. Network architects should be aware of those. Computer systems are no longer neutral tools, but they influence companies, public policies for control and institutions, and civil society cooperatives. Even the internet architecture board (IAB) has issued a directive about these effects. Electronic and network surveillance of users and what they do is growing with effects on elections. ICT is at the core of several large-scale transitions identified in this chapter. Groups of people who are immune to social media propaganda and alternative truth are discovered. And the chapter is rounded off with a hopeful vision about constructive value creation in cooperatives and science teams, making use of liberty of though and diversity of backgrounds. Making swarms and micro grids makes society alive again. Social super resolution is an interesting direction to pursue together.

Chapter 4
The Universal Knowledge Machine 102
Alan Radley, Kim Veltman Perspective Institute, UK

The chapter introduces a technical prescription for a universal knowledge machine (UKM), or World-Brain, a proposed global media system with the capability to encapsulate/organize/index and provide user-friendly access to all human knowledge. The goal is not to develop an artificial brain or any kind of Artificial Intelligence (AI) so-to-speak. Rather, the authors wish to build a collective intelligence repository, a vast ‘living’ memory bank for everything known and in terms of a totality of knowledge emanating from each of the three worlds of physical, mental, and objective knowledge. Envisaged is a place for humanity to come together collectively and to create, capture, record, link, search, sort, filter, classify, map, granulate, aggregate, chunk, window, overview, catalogue plus communicate a vast number, and great variety, of ideas, facts, claims, variants, data, texts, theories, images, happenings, and opinions. The goal is nothing less than a grand unification of all knowledge such that items are endlessly visible, explorable, linkable, navigable, etc.

Chapter 5
Experiences With Computer Architecture Remote Laboratories 133
Pablo Daniel Godoy, ITIC, Facultad de Ingeniería, FCEN, Universidad Nacional de Cuyo, Argentina
Osvaldo Lucio Marianetti, Facultad de Ingeniería, Universidad Nacional de Cuyo, Argentina
Carlos Gabriel García Garino, ITIC, Facultad de Ingeniería, Universidad Nacional de Cuyo, Argentina

This chapter resumes several experiences about using a remote laboratory based on Raspberry Pi computers and Arduino microcontrollers. The remote laboratory has been used to teach computer architecture, parallel programming, and computer networks on computer sciences and telecommunications careers. The laboratory is aimed at students with medium level of programming knowledge, which require flexible access to the computers being able to implement their own solutions. Students can explore the software and hardware of the laboratory computers, deploy, and run their codes, perform input and output operations, and configure the computers. Four different architectures are described, based on cloud computing and remote procedure calls, IoT platforms, VPN, and remote desktop. On the other hand, practical activities performed by students are summarized. Advantages and disadvantages of these architectures, problems that arose during the teaching experiences, and future work are described.

Chapter 6
The Method and Tools Development for Web-Cameras Color Correction in Binocular Vision Systems 154
Konstantin Dergachov, Kharkiv Aviation Institute, Ukraine
Leonid Krasnov, Kharkiv Aviation Institute, Ukraine
Olexander Cheliadin, Kharkiv Aviation Institute, Ukraine
Olexander Plakhotnyi, National Aerospace University KhAI, Ukraine

The possibilities of using an adaptation principle in application for organizing the close-loop life circuit of autonomous fly vehicles (FV) are discussed in chapter. The uncertainties arising at each stage of the life cycle of an autonomous fly vehicles (FV) are considered. To solve a problem, the approach using intelligent, rational objects, and using knowledge database tool is proposed. The main theses of rational adaptation control system (CS) are represented. The preliminary designing tools for constructing rational adaptation algorithms for motion control system (CS) are considered. The practical applications of the proposed approach at the stage of preliminary design of control systems for autonomous fly vehicles are presented.

Chapter 7
A Communication Model Based on Fractal Geometry for Internet of Things 192
Sergio Ariel Salinas, ITIC, Universidad Nacional de Cuyo, Argentina

Internet of things (IoT) is a paradigm that involves an increasing number of human activities. IoT fuses heterogeneous electronic devices and processes into cyber physical system (CPS) to improve conventional processes efficiency in terms of performance and resource usage. The Institute of Electrical and Electronics Engineering (IEEE) has polled more than 150 IoT scenarios based on CPSs to be developed in the next years. A CPS is strongly coupled to a communication system for interchanging data among devices that orchestrate actions in certain environments such as a factory. In general, a decentralized communication model is more resilient and efficient in data traffic management than centralized model. A problem with decentralized models is how to keep track of nodes location without a centralized service that keeps updated data of nodes. This work describes a decentralized model where any node is able to be located based on its identification in the system.

Chapter 8
The Science of Smart Things 213
Alan Radley, Kim Veltman Perspective Institute, UK

An ontological analysis of the application of the key concept of synergy to the internet of things (IoT) is presented. The authors begin by defining synergy as it applies to all types of human-made objects, and in particular to connected things, along the way developing a new theory of synergetic accommodation that provides a detailed aetiology of smart technology. A presentation of the history, routes, plus a complete definition of smart technology is given before looking at how the IoT is developing today and might progress in the future for the benefit of all humankind. Accordingly, the authors develop two new concepts, situated and distributed intelligence, that may be used to develop practically useful smart technology that fully meets the needs of the future in terms of providing efficient, magnified, reliable, safe, automated, and economical services.

Chapter 9
Autonomous Communication Model for Internet of Things 252
Sergio Ariel Salinas, Universidad Nacional de Cuyo, Argentina

The internet has changed the way human activities are performed. In a few years, this communication infrastructure evolved to leverage a new technological paradigm named internet of things (IoT). This technology fuses processes and devices to create multipurpose cyber-physical systems (CFS) that improve human quality of life. These systems rely on internet availability, which can be affected by natural phenomena such as earthquakes carrying out economic and social consequences. In this work, an autonomous communication model for IoT domains is proposed. The main goal of this model is to set the basis for the development of a communication system capable of operating independently of the internet. This communication autonomy is critical in catastrophe scenarios where information broadcasts can support disaster management. According to simulation results, the proposed model can be implemented in different IoT scenarios including cities developed under this technology.

Chapter 10
The Analytic Hierarchy Process as a Method for the Selection of Resources in the Cloud 267
Hugo Rolando Haurech, Department of Management Technologies, Misiones National University, Argentina
David Luis la Red Martinez, Northeast National University, Argentina

Due to technological advances, organizations have to face many challenges in providing support through the use of information technologies (IT) to carry out tasks that require computing skills. It is important to adopt adequate resources with the aim of developing processing skills that meet actual needs. Cloud computing (CC) represents an alternative that offers many opportunities to be exploited. This chapter introduces characteristics of CC, the technologies that enable its deployment, and a model of selection based on qualifications and mathematical development.

Chapter 11
Exploring Antecedents to Adopt Mobile Augmented Reality Applications: A Uses and Gratifications Approach 285
İrem Eren Erdoğmuş, Faculty of Business Administration, Marmara University, Turkey
Pelin Şerefhan Doğanay, Korkmaz Kitchen and Small Home Appliances, Turkey
Görkem Vural, Marmara University, Turkey

The concept of augmented reality (AR) is a topic of increasing importance for the future of marketing. Research, especially on AR in mobile devices, is still in its infancy; therefore, this study explored the user motivations to employ mobile augmented reality applications against the hindrance of perceived risks and tried to understand user acceptance and willingness to use this technology and possible marketing-related outcomes. In-depth interviews were carried on with 16 participants as well as three mini focus group interviews with 12 participants. The underlying theories utilized were the technology acceptance model (TAM) and the uses and gratifications (U&G). The results showed that entertainment, obtaining information, experiential qualities, socialization, and personal motivations acted as gratifications in the adoption of AR applications, which exerted positive influence on brand interest, image, and purchase intention of the users.

Chapter 12
Students in Socially Vulnerable Contexts: Discovering Their Entrepreneurial Potential.................. 304
Silvia Victoria Poncio, Facultad de Tecnología Informática, Universidad Abierta Interamericana, Argentina
Daniel Tedini, Facultad de Tecnología Informática, Universidad Abierta Interamericana, Argentina
Veronica Castañeira, Facultad de Tecnología Informática, Universidad Abierta Interamericana, Argentina
Diego E. Marzorati, Facultad de Tecnología Informática, Universidad Abierta Interamericana, Argentina
Eric Hermán Roth, Facultad de Tecnología Informática, Universidad Abierta Interamericana, Argentina

A survey was developed based on an adaptation of the resource used by the Association for Training, Research and Development of Entrepreneurship (AFIDE: Asociación para la Formación, Investigación y Desarrollo del Emprendimiento, in Spanish) in the project for the Entrepreneurial Potential of Latin American Undergraduates (PEUL: Potencial Emprendedor de los Universitarios de Latinoamérica, in Spanish). The results showed that more than three-quarters of the students acknowledged having initiative, being creative and innovative, and obtaining and managing information in order to make their own decisions. They also identified that they value flexibility and time management, and they feel confident and motivated by making uncertainty a tool that allows them to recognize mistakes and continue to pursue their projects.

Chapter 13
The Language of Cinema Fosters the Development of Soft Skills for Inclusion and Interdisciplinary Learning 324
Annamaria Poli, Università degli Studi di Milano-Bicocca, Italy
Daniela Tamburini, Sperimenta – Centro Studi Cinema e Formazione, Italy

This chapter presents research on an Italian education project implemented with immigrant students attending C.P.I.A. courses in Bergamo (Centro Provinciale Istruzione Adulti – Provincial Adult Education Center). This contribution proposes an educational experience characterized by an interactive approach among different disciplines. The title of the project was Cinema as a resource for enhancing interdisciplinary teaching and learning by harnessing knowledge and skills from across different subject areas: from Italian language to geography and history, and from science and maths to the visual arts. Over the four years of the project, film was used in multiple ways as a tool/resource for teaching-learning focused on developing school inclusion. The overall aims of the project were to incorporate the cinema into the construction of an interdisciplinary teaching/learning path, while seeking to integrate theory and praxis within a collaborative professional development and research model. The project activities were designed in keeping with EU recommendations on core competences for ongoing learning. From 2006 to 2018, the European Parliament and Council approved a set of "Recommendations on Key Competences for Lifelong Learning," that is to say, knowledge, skills, and attitudes that will help learners find personal fulfilment and, later in life, find work and take part in society. The project was also informed by recent Italian legislation encouraging the use of cinema in education, particularly Law 14 November 2016, No. 220, containing "Discipline of Cinema and Audiovisual" and the Law 13 July 2015, No. 107, the school reform framework "La BuonaScuola."

Chapter 14
Comparative Analysis of ACO Algorithms for the Solution of the Travelling Salesman Problem.... 338
Gloria Lola Quispe, Facultad de Ingeniería, Universidad Nacional de Jujuy, Argentina
Maria Fernanda Rodríguez, Facultad de Ciencias Económicas, Argentina
José Daniel Ontiveros, Facultad de Ingeniería, Universidad Nacional de Jujuy, Argentina

Metaheuristics are non-deterministic algorithms. Metaheuristic strategies are related to design. This chapter presents an introduction on metaheuristics, from the point of view of its theoretical study and the foundations for its use. Likewise, a description and comparative study of the ant colony-based algorithms is carried out. These are ant system (AS), ant colony system (ACS), and max-min ant system (MMAS). These results serve to deliver solutions to complex problems and generally with a high degree of combinatorics for those there is no way to find the best reasonable time. An experimentation and analysis of the results of the ACO algorithms (optimization by ants colonies) is also carried out. For the evaluation of the algorithms, comparisons are made for instances of the TSPLIB test instance library. Therefore, it is deepened in the resolution of the travelling salesman problem (TSP), and a comparative analysis of the different algorithms is carried out in order to see which one adjusts better.

Chapter 15
A Survey on the Techniques to Improve the Visibility of Geospatial Resources on the Web............ 359
Saif Ansari, University Institute of Technology, Rajiv Gandhi Proudyogiki Vishwavidyalaya, India
Piyush Kumar Shukla, University Institute of Technology, Rajiv Gandhi Proudyogiki Vishwavidyalaya, India
Rajeev Pandey, University Institute of Technology, Rajiv Gandhi Proudyogiki Vishwavidyalaya, India
Rohit Agrawal, University Institute of Technology, Rajiv Gandhi Proudyogiki Vishwavidyalaya, India

Geographical information has become ubiquitous. The demand to access geospatial data on the web is growing in numerous knowledge domains and disciplines. For the sharing of geospatial data, geoportals acts as entryways to the SDI (spatial data infrastructure) from where the data is disseminated. Because these geoportals are limited to geoinformation communities only, they exhibit challenges in terms of indexing by web search engines. Thus, the geospatial resources need a boost in terms of visibility over the internet (web). In this chapter, a discussion on the present state of geospatial resources on the web and comparison of various methods that have been employed for increasing the discoverability of geographical resources is presented. Therefrom, by discussion, the chapter concludes with a conjecture regarding scope for the further improvement in the methods that have been reviewed, along with depicting the need for the presence of geospatial resources on the internet.

Chapter 16
Developing Augmented Reality Multi-Platform Mobile Applications 371
Susana Isabel Herrera, Universidad Nacional de Santiago del Estero, Argentina
Paola Daniela Budan, Universidad Nacional de Santiago del Estero, Argentina
Federico Rosenzvaig, Universidad Nacional de Santiago del Estero, Argentina
Pablo Javier Najar Ruiz, Universidad Nacional de Santiago del Estero, Argentina
María Inés Morales, Universidad Nacional de Santiago del Estero, Argentina
Marilena del Valle Maldonado, Universidad Nacional de Santiago del Estero, Argentina
Carlos Antonio Sánchez, Universidad Nacional de Santiago del Estero, Argentina

This chapter presents advances in the software engineering field related to the efficient development of multi-platform mobile applications that require access to the device hardware for 3D marker-based augmented reality functions. After presenting the theoretical background that supports the proposed solutions, the complex problem of the development of AR multi-platform mobile applications is introduced. The problem about how to choose a framework for developing multi-platform applications is described, and a general model for developing mobile applications with AR is proposed. The advances were applied to the field of m-learning. A linear algebra educational practice was designed using MADE-mlearn, and an augmented reality mobile app called AlgeRA was developed using MobileRA methodology. The instantiation of the general model for the development of AlgeRA is reported. It includes the development environment, the programming libraries (to manage 3D objects repositories, patterns readers, rendering of images) and the 3D model.

Chapter 17
Results of the Research in the Comparison and Analysis of Historical Artifacts' Photographic Images Catalogued in Online Databases: The Case of a Roman Stele From Ravenna 391
Marco Tedaldi, University of Bologna, Italy

In the field of archaeology, when a discovery is made, the comparison of images is often used to catalogue a find and give it an interpretation. The image on an exhibit is always subject to analysis, comparisons, graphic reconstructions, which can define it, classify it, and most of all, understand it as a whole. The problem arises when the discovered find proposes a completely new and unpublished image. It therefore requires an in-depth study in all its elements. Photographic images, online databases, and archive collections of museums provide some valid help for solutions or interpretations; and the theories that come out of this comparison can then shed light on the meaning of an image present in a find, when there is no direct confirmation.

Conclusion 430

Appendix: The "G" Factor in the Web, New Technologies, and Education 437

Compilation of References 464

About the Contributors 489

Index 498

Preface

Quality is an attribute that increases over time in users who interact daily with interactive systems. The quality is usually associated with the notion of beauty. That is, something that people like and that is easier to detect in its absence than in its presence, because it is currently considered as something implicit and essential in the software of the new millennium.

If these people interact with other people through interactive systems, they require not only speed and precision in the interaction process but also a qualitative communication with multiple addresses between users (grouped or isolated), traditional computing devices, latest generation hardware, etc.

In the generation of interactive systems, software engineering plays an essential role in including, evaluating, increasing and maintaining quality levels so that the associated hardware works in the best possible way. That's the reason why the professionals of the social sciences were included in this domain since the '90s. At that time, the main theorists of software engineering expressed the need to include sociologists, psychologists, pedagogues, among others, in the programming of the computer systems. However, with the boom and democratization of the hypertext, multimedia and hypermedia systems and hardware, together with the democratization of the Internet, other, broader needs were generated in software engineering, from the design, evaluation, tuning, production, etc. of interactive systems in augmented / mixed / virtual / extended reality, etc.

The new interactive systems began to incorporate texts, video, audio, computer animations, etc. In other words, it was necessary to meet the growing demand of users with dynamic media rather than static media, such as text, photographs, drawings, etc. Dynamic media where the notion of quality was not always present in commercial interactive systems and with international distribution, for programming reasons, as for example, synchronizing audio with moving images. As the multimedia information supports were evolving in storage capacity (CD-Rom, CD-Interactive, DVD, HD-DVD, etc.), access to information, development of new algorithms in indexing the records of the databases, etc., went from the usability of the systems to the communicability in the interaction.

It is in communicability, that is, the quality of interactive communication, where software engineering has its greatest challenge for the coming years, especially for new generations of users of interactive systems. At the end of the 20th century and the beginning of the 21st century, the foundations were laid for generating a new expert in communicability, with the purpose of enhancing software programming of new interactive devices (hardware), ranging from multimedia mobile telephony, the microinformatics, to interactive robotic systems that use artificial intelligence.

In this wide range of rapidly evolving hardware, the software must accelerate its development, so as not to be left behind for reasons of poor quality or programming failures of the systems that allow the operation of new hardware. A quality whose presence the end user senses from the interfaces down to the timing of the answers and precision of the operations carried out with the computers, irrespective of the device that he/she is using, whether or not it is connected to the network, whether it has artificial intelligence or not, among many other aspects related to information and communication technologies.

The timing of the development of the software has been reduced by the constant advances of hardware, which make the hardware go ahead of the software. The inclusion of experts in communicability in the software industry has allowed to speed up the timeframes in the commercialization of new technological products worldwide. However, this constant evolution of the software in face of the hardware revolution opens up a host of new horizons to maintain and increase the quality of the interactive systems, following a set of standardized norms and rules for the production of interactive software. Currently, we can see some efforts towards this goal, but they are still partial solutions, incomplete and flawed from the theoretical as well as practical point of view, if the quality of the interactive design is analyzed down to the training of the professionals in order to generate systems that are efficient, reliable and user-friendly, cutting-edge.

Reliability, efficiency and acceptability are some of the attributes of the traditional software applications, and therefore, of the interactive systems. In the process of generating new software for new interactive systems, the fundamental stages such as requirements, design, development, verification, validation, and production, properly speaking, are maintained. In each of them, the human factor and social factors are present. That is, it is necessary for the software developer to understand that his/her responsibilities extend to the whole of society. This is another area where there are gaps, both theoretical and practical, with regard to the context for which the quality of products and services must be developed, maintained and increased, as well as oriented towards new interactive systems.

In this sense, in our days, it is easy to detect an endless number of professionals in the formal sciences, such as physicists, mathematicians, industrial engineers, etc. who strive to understand the psychological, sociological, anthropological, etc., aspects of the potential users of the multimedia systems in mobile telephony, for the ergonomic development of new electronic devices linked to information technology and telecommunications, and also to offer them high quality services in the interrelationships between people and computing devices.

In short, what is intended is that software engineering can offer the potential users of interactive systems high quality services, with reduced costs and with reduced production times to the maximum. It is a triadic relation nonexistent at present, if one considers the communicability or the stages necessary to generate innovative software, taking into account the real context of the users. There is no style guide such as the steps to follow to develop an intercultural interface for the operating systems of the late twentieth century, in keeping with the principles derived from the notion of usability in the software.

Nor is there a set of theoretical and/or practical works that can constitute a kind of model with regard to the dynamic and static medias of the modern interactive systems. We continue to use a group of experts or professionals from the formal sciences and factual sciences to solve the classic problems of interactive design flaws, belonging to the exclusive field of usability, and software engineering of the '90s. In other words, there is no evolution but rather an involution from the point of view of interactive design, for example.

In the '90s, with the rise of the notion of software quality, especially with the dissemination of off-line interactive systems, there was a growing need to incorporate social science professionals in the software industry. Subsequently, with the democratization of the internet and the transfer of audiovisual content to the network in the transition from the old to the new millennium, there was a need to incorporate computer technicians in the context of the social sciences, especially those oriented towards the digitized information online.

Until then, interactive systems were programmed, evaluated and produced by interdisciplinary teams, where quality was evaluated, without an accurate methodology or style guide, especially in the context of the commercial interactive systems for education, entertainment, public information, etc. One proof of this assertion is to be found in the style guides for programming the interfaces of those applications that worked with two of the main personal computers of that time: those compatible with IBM/PC, that is, Windows, and Apple computers, in other words, Macintosh Operating System (MacOS). In both cases, there were some interface designers who tried to generate a synergy between those components that were common between the two.

Now, when we talk about interfaces and information architecture, they are important components of software quality, and they are directly and indirectly related to the notion of beauty, but the latter depends on other components of the software, particularly, in the field of the interactive systems. In this regards, it is possible to mention, among others, the types of access to the databases, the programming language used, the compatibility of the different operating systems, and the ideal data processor for the best functioning of the interactive applications.

That is to say, the presentation of the information in the interface, that the new generations of users of interactive systems or generation Z consider intrinsic for the quality in the interaction, in reality is only one among the group of components of the different categories that make up the interactive application, from the moment of conception of the system until the verification of its correct functioning.

In this sense, there is no reference to the possibility of carefully dividing and analyzing the quality of the software, from the perspectives of interactive design, for example, covering, navigation through content, the structure of interactive information in database, the synchronization of dynamic and static media, the compatibility of multimedia content, among the various devices of last generation, among other categories.

Nor is there a set of works that can serve as references for future lines of education and research, concentrating human and financial resources towards progressive sectors, in the short, medium and long term. Moreover, there is no vademecum or guide of technologies related to communication and interactive information, which focuses the attention of students and future professional on the constant inventions and discoveries of those components related to hardware, in order to increase the quality of the software.

Simultaneously, there is no ideal model of knowledge that should be gathered by future experts in the software quality of interactive systems, given the existing chaos in the field of design, evaluation and fine-tuning of systems, with professionals who lack the necessary theoretical bases, since many of them come from areas of knowledge unrelated to the academic training in computer science, software engineering and systems, multimedia engineering, telecommunications engineering, to mention some disciplines related to the programming of interactive systems of last generation.

Our intention is to generate a first guideline to be consulted and considered at the moment that the subject of the quality of the software and human factors applied to the interactive systems is approached. The selection of works that are included has a theoretical-practical vision and excludes the chaos coming from the use of the notion of interdisciplinarity with commercial, pseudo-educational purposes that lack scientific foundations. Simultaneously, the present work aims to correct the aspects that distort the dissemination of progressive scientific knowledge in the interactive applications, in light of of the constant revaluation of notions overcome by the passage of time, in the field of software engineering.

This objective implies an in-depth selection of those technologies, current and future, that will continue to establish milestones in the constant democratic evolution of information societies. That is, there is a review of the past and present of information and communication technologies, with a projection towards the future, indicating the paths to be followed by the current and future generations of teachers, researchers, software producers, etc. Furthermore, the quality of the software is analyzed, from the design phases to the use, irrespective of whether the objective of the end users is leisure (e.g., videogames), information (the map of the main touristic places of a city, the schedules of public transport services, etc.) or education (consultations of online books of a digital library, downloads of practical exercises in computer science, electronic, chemistry, languages, geometry, etc.).

This establishes a first set of links between the basic components of software quality and interactive systems, which will be immutable in the coming years, and which serve as a guideline in R&D projects, transfer of knowledge between universities and industry, creation of new companies, demand for new professionals, implementation of new masters, generation of continuing education courses, etc.

The main ideal contexts/professionals are: students, professors, researchers, programmers, analysists of systems, computer engineering, interactive designers, managers of software quality, human-social factors experts and evaluators of interactive systems. Besides, professionals working in education management, R&D projects, management in the field of software industry (e.g., design, evaluation, programming, users satisfaction, system and software engineering, usability engineering, web engineering, etc.), among others interested in locating trends in software quality oriented to interactive systems.

Many of the chapters have been presented orally and compiled in the following international conferences, symposiums and workshops (2018-2020): Advances in New Technologies, Interactive Interfaces and Communicability (ADNTIIC), Communicability, Computer Graphics and Innovative Design for Interactive Systems (CCGIDIS), Evolution of the Sciences, Informatics, Human Integration and Scientific Education (ESIHISE), Horizons for Information Architecture, Security and Cloud Intelligent Technology (HIASCIT), Human-Computer Interaction, High Education, Augmented Reality and Technologies (HCIHEART), Human-Computer Interaction, Telecommunications, Informatics and Scientific Information (HCITISI), Human-Computer Interaction, Tourism and Cultural Heritage (HCITOCH), Multimedia, Scientific Information and Visualization for Information Systems and Metrics (MSIVISM), Quantum Information Technologies Applied to Nature and Society (QUITANS), Research and Development in Imaging, Nanotechnology, Industrial Design and Robotics (RDINIDR), and Software and Emerging Technologies for Education, Culture, Entertainment, and Commerce (SETECEC). Some presentations whose times range between 45 and 75 minutes, depending on the type of work to be presented. That is, the authors have to fully explain the works developed, both from a theoretical and a practical point of view. Consequently, these are unplanned international events for the fleeting mini-presentations of their authors, following the commercial model, of door-to-door sellers of goods and / or services. Now, a brief description found in each of the chapters:

Chapter 1. The first chapter, "Software and Innovation: Discovering Invisible High-Quality Factors", describes those fundamental elements that from the origins of the Internet have been shaping new academic and work areas, such as web engineering. Focusing on the point of view of software and design, it examines how in the educational and scientific field the exact limits of the disciplines have been expanded, until practically eliminating the pre-existing borders that respected the epistemology of the sciences, when referring to the current HCI and UX. There is also research on the evolution of software, interactive systems, the emergence of new professions related to the web, and their future, where the role of university training centers is highlighted. Finally, Francisco V. Cipolla Ficarra presents each of the components inside and outside the network have been transforming the democratic or horizontal principles that the Internet had in the '90s is disclosed in detail, until the appearance of authoritarian or vertical structures in the new millennium.

Chapter 2. The authors of the research work "Quality and Web Software Engineering Advances" are Francisco V. Cipolla Ficarra, Alejandra Quiroga and Miguel Cipolla Ficarra. They have focused on presenting the invisible factors that enhance or slow down the software industry, oriented to the development of interactive systems, in the most varied supports of digital information, from the end of the 20th century to the present day. The study begins by highlighting the importance of language, as a natural communicative process of the human being, until it reaches the languages of computers. The diachronic vision in time allows to establish parallels and projections towards the future, especially within internal, external, temporal, geographical, human and social factors, which directly and indirectly affect the quality of software and innovation. There is constantly a call for attention to the distorted elements of software that affect the evolution or revolution of hardware, such as the example of inversion of the communicative pyramid, belonging to the model established by Lasswel and Shannon, or the notion of linguistic ambiguity. Finally, the myths and realities are summarized, focused on the new professionals in the software sector and all its derivations, within the context of ICTs.

Chapter 3. In this research, "Masters of Imagination: From Hierarchies to Connected Swarms", Jaap van Till, TheConnectivist, describes crucial drivers and incentives behind the recent huge success of Internet and ICT. Imagine Covid lockdowns without them. And he shows the directions in which use of those technologies can lead economy and society. Cooperation of diverse & unique people and new 'Digital Democracy. Early days Internet was 'sold' to managers a way to share expensive computer centers of universities, while in reality it was used on a massive scale for email and cooperation between scientists. More recently Internet & ICT is misused for mass advertising consumer stuff and propaganda & election influencing. Jaap shows however that this misuse is only based on the first of five network effects. Communication and Cooperation between people are more powerful in the sense that instead of 'value extraction' for the few, they are resulting in 'value creation' for all participants and synergy. This chapter is hopeful, but we must go through huge transitions in mindsets and new priorities. ICT and Internet use will shift to handling of images and patterns and will require imagination. Some extraordinary people, immune to propaganda, who can lead the way in those transitions are described. And the successor to AI.

Chapter 4. The author of this chapter, "The Universal Knowledge Machine", is Alan S. Radley (scientific director of the Kim Veltman Institute of Perspective). He has examined a technical prescription for a Universal Knowledge Machine (UKM) – or World-Brain – the same being a proposed global media system with the capability to encapsulate/organise/index – and provide userfriendly access to – all human knowledge. This key topic encapsulates several widely-felt end-user needs of great interest currently for the educational context such as how ubiquitous mobile technologies can be employed to build/access a collective knowledge repository – a vast 'living 'memory bank – for everything known. Accordingly, we present a review of all those research, commercial and didactic resources linked to concepts of the 'World-Brain' technology to boost or foster learning in the classrooms (and also in wider real-world contexts(s)). An interesting historic vision of current and past attempts to build a 'World-Brain' has been included by the authors. Said vision(s) can quickly place the reader in context with respect to the evolution of the 'World-Brain' and Internet technologies that have been used with didactical purposes in the classrooms of high schools and universities (to mention two examples in the last several decades).

There is also a bibliography which may be looked up by those interested in widening the 'WorldBrain' concepts that the author present's in the chapter.

Chapter 5. The authors of the work "Experiences With Computer Architecture Remote Laboratories" are Pablo Godoy, Osvaldo Marianetti and Carlos García Garino. They have used remote and nomadic laboratories to teach and research issues related with computer architectures and networks at Universidad Nacional de Cuyo and Universidad de Mendoza during several years. Four architectures have been used to build the remote laboratories presented in this chapter: remote procedure calls, IoT platforms, VPNs and remote desktops. The chapter begins with an introduction to remote and nomadic laboratories. Advantages and disadvantages of this tool against simulations and experiments over real equipment are discussed. After, block diagrams, advantages, disadvantages, problems, and usage experiences of the remote laboratories deployed by the authors are presented. These remote laboratories are based on Raspberry Pi computers and Arduino microcontrollers, both technologies widely known by computer and electronic researchers and students. Bibliography which may be looked up by those interested in further knowledge about these architectures and implementation details are provided. Finally, two promising future research directions are presented.

Chapter 6. Under the title of "The Method and Tools Development for Web-Cameras Color Correction in Binocular Vision Systems", its authors Konstantin Dergachov, Leonid Krasnov, Olexander Cheliadin, and Olexander Plakhotnyi present us a complete research about the fundamental and primary possibilities of using an adaptation principle in application for organizing the close-loop life circuit of autonomous fly vehicles. They have focused on the Stereoscopic Vision Systems; Video Stream Images, Color Correction, Web-Cameras Stereo-System; Joint Rectification and Color Balance of the Left and Right Chambers. The main areas of the chapter are: Theoretical framework; Construction of a separate camera color correction algorithms; Essence of the proposed color correction method; Calibration and rectification of web cameras stereo pair; Efficiency assessment of the used color correction algorithm; Laboratory stand and stereo vision research program: Experimental research and main results; Conclusions and Future research directions. The excellent figures enrich each one of the different sections. In this research we can see that the good quality and convenience of the procedure for calibrating the stereopair cameras and the rectification of channel images provides high accuracy of distance measurement and the construction of maps of the depth of the scene. This creates prerequisites for solving a wide range of applied tasks in the field of mobile robots navigation, 3D scene reconstruction, pattern recognition, etc., taking into account the volumetric characteristics of objects.

Chapter 7. The author of the chapter "A Communication Model Based on Fractal Geometry for Internet of Things" is Sergio A. Salinas. He presents a communication model based on fractal geometry for IoT applications. Communication systems will play a fundamental role in the development of IoT scenarios where a large number of devices will constantly exchange information to perform in some cases critical tasks. The work describes a decentralized model where any node is able to be located based on its identification in the system. Besides, this work describes a new model and define the equations to measure the performance of unicast and broadcast services. Some main concepts defined by the author are: Fractal Geometry (it is a geometry structure composed of unlimited number of nested substructures with the same shape); Broadcast Service (it is an algorithm to send a message from one node to all other nodes in a communication network); Unicast Service (it is an algorithm to send a message from one node to another node in a communication network); Scalable Communication System (it is an infrastructure capable to include a growing number of nodes without affecting significantly the quality of communication services); Smart City (it is an urban area where different cyber-physical systems interact to provide services to citizens based on the Internet of Thing infrastructure); Smart Grid (it is a electrical networks managed by cyber-physical systems supported by the Internet of Things infrastructure), among many other words.

Chapter 8. The author of the chapter called "The Science of Smart Things" is Alan S. Radley –scientific director of the Kim Veltman Institute of Perspective. He has examined a theoretical prescription for a new Science of Smart Things – whereby it is claimed that within 20-30 years, over 1 billion Things will be connected to the Internet. Henceforth provided is a foundational framework for the entire field of: the Internet of Things (IoT); and by means of logical, integrated and holistic perspective(s) –combined with use of the scientific method. However the IoT has come to mean more than just connected Things –but rather relates to Things that are imbued– at the same time, with useful abilities surrounding the concept of 'Smartness' and/or with what are named here as 'Situated and Distributed Intelligence(s)'. Accordingly, the author examines key aspects of how to embed intelligence in the environment –both in a moving and also in a stationary sense– and hence the developed theory is of great interest currently for educational context(s) such as the use of ubiquitous mobile technologies by people going about their daily business in a wide range of contexts. The work presents a review of all those didactic resources linked to the IoT to boost or foster learning both inside and outside of the classrooms. In parallel, the author has developed n comprehensive series of tests with the goal of verifying the impact of the discussed IoT Framework for ubiquitous mobile technologies in the classrooms. An interesting summed-up historic vision of the IoT has been included by the author.

Chapter 9. In this chapter, "Autonomous Communication Model for Internet of Things", a new communication model is presented by Sergio A. Salinas to create an autonomous communication area that can be implemented in different domains of IoT as a smart city or industrial zone. It is a representation of a communication structure where nodes can exchange messages autonomously independently of the Internet infrastructure, and IoT is a communication infrastructure based on the Internet to connect heterogeneous devices utilized by cyber physical systems to assist diverse human activities. The new model enables access to a message exchange service between two nodes. A Cartesian plane is defined where the nodes' position depends on their geographical positioning information. The positioning data in the plane makes it possible to create a communication path between two nodes. The exchange of messages is done through a selective routing algorithm that uses a mark value to select the nodes that define a communication route. The main areas of the research are dynamic routing algorithm, ranking of neighboring nodes, analysis of operational feasibility and analysis of communication routes. Although the results obtained are preliminary, they provide evidence on the feasibility of creating a communication system independent of the Internet that can operate in certain cities in emergency scenarios.

Chapter 10. In the research work "The Analytic Hierarchy Process as a Method for the Selection of Resources in the Cloud", the authors –Hugo R. Haurech and David L. la Red Martinez, have examined a paradigm that is constantly evolving and therefore of great interest to organizations, such as the use of ubiquitous technologies and how the resources that are part of them can be selected. The work presents a review of the main aspects of cloud computing, which highlights the models that offer services and that can be accessed with any device and from anywhere. In addition, they have presented the technology that, among others, is considered of major importance for cloud computing to achieve elasticity and scalability. Those services, resources and now providers are part of the analysis to determine which best fit an activity. Accordingly, they have intensively developed a selection method based on weight assignments and equations as an alternative for decision making and selection, known as the Hierarchical Analytical Process. A real case of resource selection has been developed with the objective of knowing the alternatives of providers and infrastructure resources, in order to understand the procedure of the model. The authors have paid attention to present the details of the use of this model so that it can be taken as an example for readers. It also includes the bibliography that was part of the chapter and that can be consulted by interested parties to expand the concepts that the authors have presented.

Chapter 11. The research titled "Exploring Antecedents to Adopt Mobile Augmented Reality Applications: A Uses and Gratifications Approach" has been developed by the following authors: Irem Eren Erdogmus, Pelin Serefhan Doganay, and Görkem Vural. The work explored the user motivations to employ mobile augmented reality applications against the hindrance of perceived risks, and tried to understand user acceptance and willingness to use this technology, and possible marketing-related outcomes. Some main keywords of the research work are: Augmented Reality; Virtual Reality; Uses and Gratifications; Technology Acceptance Model; Perceived Ease of Use; Perceived Usefullness; Brand Loyalty; In-depth Interview; and Focus Group Interview. The authors highlighted the importance of AR applications for the future of consumer-brand relationships. Besides, the relevant research showed that information-providing, practical and enjoyable experience should be blended together to provide a usefull AR application, that will create a difference for the brands, and lead to positive consumer reactions. Finally, in a didactic way the authors present tables to demonstrate the transcendence of the heuristic evaluation (profiles and interviews) as well as the obtained results.

Chapter 12. The chapter "Students in Socially Vulnerable Contexts: Discovering Their Entrepreneurial Potential" is a research carried out to assess the entrepreneurial potential of students who attend the Job Training Institute from Cuatro Vientos Educational Center (*Instituto de Capacitación Laboral del Centro Educativo Cuatro Vientos*, in Spanish), where those who participate in its activities are prepared for a quick insertion into the world of work. A survey was developed by Silvia V. Poncio, Daniel Tedini, Veronica Castañeira, Diego E. Marzorati, and Eric H. Roth (authors) that based on an adaptation of the resource used by the Association for Training, Research and Development of Entrepreneurship (AFIDE –*Asociación para la Formación, Investigación y Desarrollo del Emprendimiento*, in Spanish), in the research project for the Entrepreneurial Potential of Latin American Undergraduates (PEUL –*Potencial Emprendedor de los Universitarios de Latinoamérica*, in Spanish). Despite growing up in contexts of vulnerability and in times of uncertainty, it was identified that most of these young people belonging to the "Millennials" and "Z" generations would like to have their own business or entrepreneurship as a future opportunity for employment. Furthermore, in coincidence with the characterization found for these generations, all of them present skills indicating that they have entrepreneurial potential, which can facilitate an improvement in their quality of life, reduce the possibility of economic and social vulnerability and develop tools and attitudes to meet the demands of the society.

Chapter 13. "The Language of Cinema Fosters the Development of Soft Skills for Inclusion and Interdisciplinary Learning" is a chapter that presents research on an Italian education project implemented with immigrant students. The authors are Annamaria Poli and Daniela Tamburini. This research proposes an educational experience characterized by an interactive approach among different disciplines. The film was used in multiple ways as a tool and/or resource for the teaching-learning process focused on developing school inclusion students (cinema is present in Italian educational and school settings to a very limited extent). The primary objective of the authors were to incorporate the cinema into the construction of an interdisciplinary teaching/learning process, while seeking to integrate theory and praxis within a collaborative professional development and research model. In other words, the virtuous relationship to be established between cinema and vocational secondary education also underpinned our project from a pedagogical viewpoint, especially in terms of identifying connections between the aesthetic dimension characterizing film and the educational/didactic dimension of schooling. The use of cinema has allowed the design of activities for an interactive learning and teaching system in which digital technologies have played a decisive role. The project activities were designed in keeping with European Union recommendations on core competences for ongoing learning.

Chapter 14. The work "Comparative Analysis of ACO Algorithms for the Solution of the Travelling Salesman Problem" presents the results that were reached during the research process and the authors are Gloria L. Quispe, Maria F. Rodríguez, and José D. Ontiveros. Yes, variants of the original ACO algorithms have been proposed, some of them being more successful than others. Ant colony-based optimization is a relatively young methodology compared to other stories such as evolutionary computing, taboo search, or simulated annealing. But it has been shown that these algorithms are quite flexible and efficient. For this reason, the objective was to analyze the algorithms based on ant colonies applied to the problem of the Commercial Traveler. To achieve this objective, the information related to these algorithms was collected and analyzed, to then compare their characteristics and understand the operation of each one of them, as well as evaluate the efficiency of each one with respect to the traveling salesman problem, it was tested with three instances of problems from the TSPLIB library, obtaining solutions very close to the optimum. So the authors of this work have come to conclude as future contributions: Analyze the operation of other algorithms based on ant colonies and identify characteristics that can be incorporated into the proposed algorithm; Apply other techniques of Artificial Intelligence regarding the proposed algorithm, and Identify problems from different areas that can be treated as optimization problems to apply algorithms based on ant colonies for their resolution.

Chapter 15. The authors of the work titled "A Survey on the Techniques to Improve the Visibility of Geospatial Resources on the Web" are Saif Ansari, Piyush Kumar Shukla, Rajeev Pandey, and Rohit Agrawal. They present a state-of-the-art about Geospatial resources on the web. The study starts with the detailed definition of the terminologies in the research (e.g., Search Engine Optimization Techniques for increasing the discoverability of websites; SKOS, Ontologies and Thesauri; Web Map Services; Folksonomy, Logsonomy and Semantic annotations; Georesource Crawler and GSE) until the comparison of various methods that have been employed for increasing the discoverability of geographical resources. Furthermore, throughout the work the authors explain in a gradual and thorough way each one of the presented concepts: spatial data, geospatial metadata, spatial data infrastructure (sdis), geo portals, geospatial data discoverability, surface web, deep web, search engine optimization, etc. In this chapter, they can appreciate that requirement for geospatial data is increasing but the availability of geospatial resources is limited to geo communities. Comparion tables are explained in the literature review to promote future lines of research.

Chapter 16. The authors of the chapter "Developing M-Learning and Augmented Reality Multi-Platform Applications" are Susana I. Herrera, Paola D. Budan, Federico Rosenzvaig, Javier Najar Ruiz, María I. Morales, Marilena del Valle Maldonado, and Carlos A. Sánchez. They examined the problem of the development of multi-platform mobile applications that uses augmented reality. In this complex problem many aspects are involved: Multi-platform software development frameworks; Hardware access libraries; 3D objects repositories access libraries; Image-rendering libraries; 3D objects characteristics for AR, among others. A general conceptual model that makes it easy to consider all the components that participate in this type of applications was produced. This model provides a map that shows which are the main elements to be considered while developing multi-platforms mobile applications with AR. To give an example of how to instantiate that general model into a concrete model, an m-learning practice for Linear Algebra was designed using MADE-mlearn and a multi-platform mobile app, AlgeRA, was developed. Also shows the characteristics of the 3D model created for AlgeRA. The findings are considered useful for software engineering practitioners developing these types of applications, mainly in the field of education.

Chapter 17. "Results of the Research in the Comparison and Analysis of Historical Artifacts' Photographic Images Catalogued in Online Databases: The Case of a Roman Stele From Ravenna" is the title of the work submitted by its author: Marco Tedaldi. It is a valid example of a study of cultural heritage with modest technological resources but with an exceptional use of the technique of direct observation, traditionally used in the social sciences, usability engineering, human-computer communication, etc. A technique that can be a source of important discoveries as is the case analyzed. This indicates the high professionalism of the analyst who uses it, since he previously has extensive theoretical knowledge of the subject analyzed and has the necessary technological instruments to verify the hypotheses, which he formulated at the beginning of the study. In this heuristic work, the importance of the analysis of the images stored in the databases is highlighted, as well as the value of digital photography. The author explains in a detailed way, in each of the sections, the steps that he has followed for the magnificent discovery that Marco Tedaldi has made in the archaeological field of Roman culture. In short, archeology continues to be a constant source of inspiration for future research, thanks to the development of new technologies but coupled with the high professionalism of cultural heritage researchers, as can be seen in this chapter.

Francisco V. Cipolla Ficarra
Latin Association of Human-Computer Interaction, Spain & International Association of Interactive Communication, Italy

Acknowledgment

Now, it is the moment of showing our exceptional gratitude for all the people who have helped us in this arduous task, such as collecting all this material, in the midst of the pandemic. The word thank you is insignificant for all the displays of affection, sympathy and disinterested help that we have received from those who gave us a lifeguard in August 2012, from Chocolate Ave., in Hershey, USA: "IGI Global."

For that lifeline launched quickly from the American continent, an infinite thank you, from the depths of our hearts, to that exceptional group of workers, whose headquarters are in a very sweet city. Through that kindness, courtesy, professionalism and beautiful person that is Jan Travers, special thanks go to all the rest of the wonderful team in IGI Global.

An deep appreciation goes to Maria Ficarra for her infinite nobleness, wisdom and spirituality.

Thanks a lot to Miguel C. Ficarra, Ir. J.W. Jaap baron van Till, Mary Brie, Amélie Bordeaux, Luisa Varela, Silvia Fernández, Julia Ruíz, Alicia Martín, Graciete Amaro, James Brewer, and Carlos Albert.

I really appreciate everything you've done.

Introduction

Quality as well as beauty is intrinsic to the manifest and/or latent wishes of the purchasers or users of goods and services, related to new technologies. From democratization, to access, to interactive systems, since the last decade of the 20th century.

Historically, quality is a notion that bi-directionally interrelates with beauty. When there is beauty there is quality, and vice versa. In other words, quality is a kind of psychic imprint, which activates various sensory channels in the human being, consciously or unconsciously, in its presence or absence, for centuries. In its presence it goes unnoticed as a natural feeling of pleasure, acceptance and serenity, but

Figure 1. Photography of the 20th century, in black and white, take inside photographic studios. Black and white photography has always had an added value of visual impact, veracity and simplicity to powerfully attract attention in the written press. The composition is very important, since the lines, the textures, the light contrasts jump to the light and become more evident

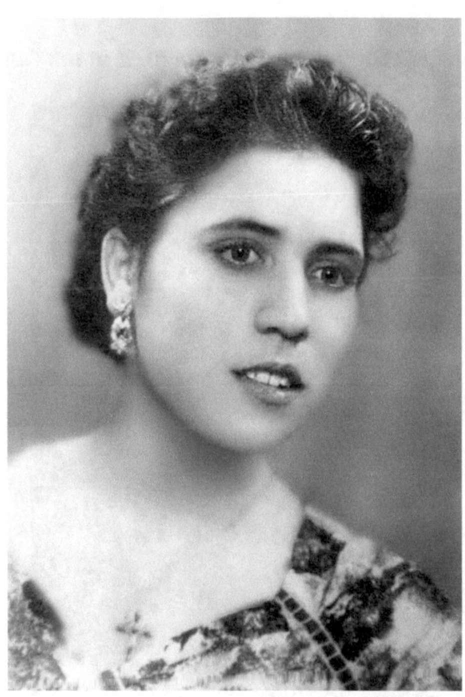

Figure 2. Photographs of the 20th century, in black and white are silent witnesses of the ways, uses and customs of the population through time. Today, many photography professionals are returning to it to make their works and express harmony, tranquility, purity, etc. For example, high contrast enhances visual strength, especially if they have the full tonal range, from white through all grays to absolute black

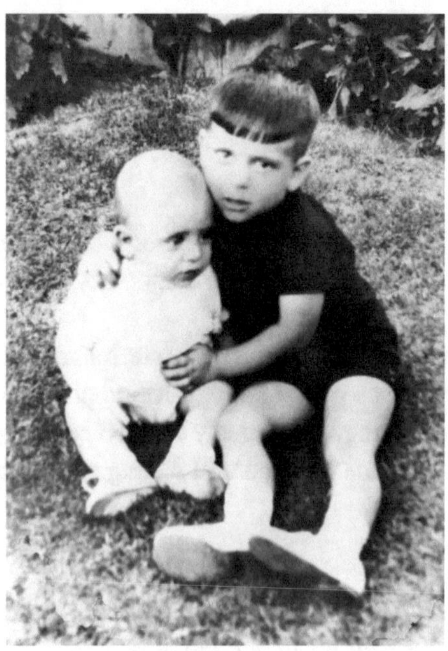

Figure 3. La Gioconda –Leonardo Da Vinci, which is located in the Louvre Museum (Paris, France)

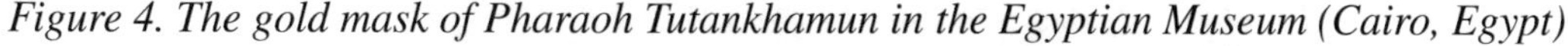

Figure 4. The gold mask of Pharaoh Tutankhamun in the Egyptian Museum (Cairo, Egypt)

in the absence, it can cause anxiety, disorientation and rebellion. Beauty and quality are related to what is well or is good. And what is good is longed for in our daily life and in the context that surrounds us.

Over time, beauty has manifested itself through art. Black and white photographs, a painting, a sculpture, an architectural work, etc. are objects where beauty and therefore quality are present. Architects, painters, sculptors and poets for centuries have been in charge of transmitting the notion of beauty, to this day. Some examples in the following figures:

Some of these works have reached an incalculable level from the economic point of view for their aesthetic value. Aesthetics, beauty and quality make up a two-way interrelated triad, which can be found in the current interfaces of interactive systems, aimed at health, education, hobbies, among others. It is a triad that depends on the historical period, the culture and the public or user, if we refer to an interactive system, for example. Therefore, it is feasible to establish isotopic lines of the triad from a synchronous and diachronic perspective.

From a synchronous perspective, that is, in the current temporal space, what is beautiful within painting may not be beautiful within literature, for example. This denotes the independence of the arts. Furthermore, from a diachronic perspective, already in ancient Greece, beauty was associated with measurement. In classical Greece the Greek term "kalón" which can be translated as beautiful, in literary texts it could be read that: Kalón is what is pleasant, generates admiration and attracts attention. With Plato two origins of the notion of beauty originate that would develop through time: beauty as harmony

Figure 5. Art Nouveau: Palau de la Música (Barcelona, Spain)

and proportion of the parts (derived from Pythagoras) and beauty as splendor. He maintained that beauty has an autonomous existence, irrespective of the support that contains it (Cooper 1997).

In this Greek and western context, beauty maintains a distance between the object and the observer. That is, the visual and auditory senses prevail with reference to touch, taste and smell. These last three, historically, were located more in the oriental culture than in the western one. Audiovisual communication channels represented 80% for the capture of messages between human beings at the beginning of the emergence of the Internet. Maintaining the attention of users in audiovisual communication will depend not only on the aesthetic triad, beauty and quality, but also on other components related to the quality of the content of the messages, such as creative innovation.

In today's western culture, belief in genius continues to be held as the origin of creative innovation in the sciences (formal and factual) or in the arts. A genius with exceptional intellectual processes, together with an extraordinary personality, favors the creative and original imagination (i.e., figure 6). In other words, an innovative and original genius is able to make sense from somethings in which other people see nothing.

However, the old popular saying: "There is nothing new under the Sun" may refer to the behaviorism of John Watson (Buckley, 1998). He maintained that nothing a person can do will be authentically creative. There are two reasons for his claims: The new situation could resemble an old, already known situation. Now the new situation was not related to any known situation and is the result of a random or fortuitous combination. This dichotomous situation of behaviorism has its anthropological parallelism with the notions of discovery and invention (Herskovits, 1948), for example. The first is something that already exists but nobody knew it and its knowledge is produced through search. While the second is something that does not exist and its knowledge is generated from experiments.

In both cases there is a common denominator that is the constant and persevering work of the human being. The dysfunction of that work leads to plagiarism and negative behaviors, in the workplace: mobbing, bullyng, stalking, pseudo feminism, etc. These patterns of behaviour can be included within the set of human and social factors in software engineering. Behaviors that in the 21st century are promoted through the social networks and eternal international legal immunity. The aim is to marginalize and destroy creative innovation in its main pillars of avant-garde societies, and from the human perspective, such as education and health.

With the passing of time, the societies and the parameters derived from it to determine genius are dynamic. Genius is a characteristic that society grants the scientist, expert, artist, etc., for the result of their works. Consequently, in the history of creative innovators, it is easy to detect how many of those who achieved the status of geniuses have been forgotten by posterity. As a rule, this happens when it is discovered that their unpublished works, innovative personal actions, etc., are the result of "copying and pasting" (Cipolla-Ficarra, 2010), exaggerated narcissism (Hirigoyen, 2019), or the illegal appropriation of third-party professional career (Cipolla-Ficarra, 2010),, among others. This new phenomenon can be called "dynamics persuaders" (Cipolla-Ficarra, 2010), or "pseudo genius." (Kemper, 2005).

Now, between these two positions, between genius and those presented by behaviorism, it is necessary to establish a third alternative, where the experience and studies of the social sciences intervene, especially in the framework of communication, social psychology, sociology and cultural systems. This third way is also necessary to evaluate the reliability of an endless number of advanced courses, master's degrees, doctoral students, post doctorates, etc., in the "Mercantilist training industry", related to: innovation and design management; audiovisual innovation and interactive environments; creative programming; technologies such as creative and narrative tools, to name a few examples (Cipolla-Ficarra, 2018). That is to say, a miscellany of words, that although they have a great impact for global marketing, they entail little or no scientific seriousness, innovative training and impactful individual experience, specifically, when it comes to joining the workforce.

The education and training industry in creative thinking was developed in the mid-20th century and aside from scientific psychology. Back then, there were few specialists interested in creative problem solving concerning the workplace. They were not in a position to help corporate managers, who were eager to increase creative thinking skills in their employees. The exception was psychologists interested in tests to measure human creativity, highlighting the figure of Joy Paul Guilford (Guilford, 1986). He presented his own theory, through a set of hypotheses, with regard to the capacities, competences and fundamental knowledge in creative thinking. From that set of ideas, he would develop a series of tests, based on the principle that a creative thinker produces new ideas, which are called original ideas. This

Figure 6. Mafalda, a comic strip character created by Joaquín Lavado (Quino –www.quino.com.ar)

consideration led him to postulate that in the creative invention are the notions of convergent and divergent thinking, as well as the ability to evaluate information and draw conclusions.

Guilford's work was essential for the theoretical formulation of creativity education and training courses within the industrial field and which are currently still in force in European schools, institutes, academies, universities, etc. although using an unprecedented multitude of synonyms and neologisms related to ICTs. In parallel, there was an interest within the social sciences, especially in social psychology. These first investigations were very important because their conclusions coincided at the same time with the entry of technology into institutions. Municipalities, tax agencies, large financial and banking groups, state universities and libraries, mass public transport industries (cars, railways, aviation, etc.), are some of the public and private institutions, where large computers are installed, which they operated with vacuum valves. Until the appearance of the integrated circuit (microchip) that allowed the minicomputers and PC's to be manufactured and interconnected.

The users of these devices were experts in systems and/or computing. Moreover, in that historical period, there was already a presence of female staff in the calculation centers, with roles that ranged from computer system operators to system programming and analysis. They were highly appreciated for their quality and precision in their job functions. The staff did not interact directly with the computer, but did so through its input and output peripherals, such as punched paper cards readers and ribbons, printed listings, etc. That is, data that was processed in batches, in order to obtain information. Information that, through system feedback, could be converted back into data for a new process. Processing that computers carried out for hours and hours. ALGOL (Algorithmic Language), BASIC (Beginners' All-purpose

Figure 7. 20th century creativity can mark historic milestones in social media applications. An example is Steve Barron's –www.steve-barron.com, animated video clip "Take On Me", made for the Norwegian musical group "a-ha." A work done in 1985 and that has been resmatered. On YouTube it has exceeded one billion views in February 2020 (uploaded to the network, 06.01.2010). All this denotes that moving images, with a high imagination and originality, through the intersection of comic, music and video, achieve an innovative effect on the viewer, by mixing the real (video characters) and the virtual (2D animation of the comic, which in some frames manages to emulate 3D).

Symbolic Instruction Code), COBOL (COmmon Business-Oriented Language), FORTRAN (FORmula TRANslation), are some of the languages used by computer manufacturers and programmers at the time: IBM, Digital Equipment, Hewlett Packard, among others.

Programming tasks involved a high level of creativity to get the most out of the hardware and software people were using, due to memory limitations, the need to make as few errors as possible in data entry tasks when feeding the computer, the impossibility of repeating the prints in a listed format, given the high volumes of printed paper, etc. At this time, creative innovation is non-existent when resorting to commercial software or open software. This loss of skills of the users of interactive devices in the third millennium, such as compression, memory, arithmetic calculation, reading, writing, etc., derives from a canned and mercantile education that uses the best style of graphic design and packaging technologies to attract its students, or rather, consumers or clients.

Faced with the loss of innate or acquired abilities of the human being, it is necessary to look towards the origins of computing, revaluing the original functions of education in software and hardware (Cipolla-Ficarra, 2018). Those functions can be improved or enhanced. However, they should not lose the human being and the good of the local and global community as the central axis of all the processes of interactive communication, whether they are processes of an evolutionary or revolutionary nature. Regardless of certain geographical and temporal contexts, communicability must seek excellence in beauty, creativity, innovation, simplicity and universality. In figure 7, we have an excellent example from an audio-visual bridge between 1985 (videoclip) and 2020 (social networking).

REFERENCES

Buckley, K. W. (1989). *Mechanical Man: John B. Watson and the Beginnings of Behaviorism*. Guilford Publications.

Cipolla-Ficarra, F. (2010). *Persuasion On-Line and Communicability: The Destruction of Credibility in the Virtual Community and Cognitive Models*. Nova Science.

Cipolla-Ficarra, F. (2018). *Technology-Enhanced Human Interaction in Modern Society*. IGI Global. doi:10.4018/978-1-5225-3437-2

Cooper, J. M., & Hutchinson, D. S. (1997). *Plato Complete Works*. Hackett Publishing.

Guilford, J. P. (1986). *Creative Talents: Their Nature Uses and Development*. Bearly Limited.

Herskovits, M. J. (1948). *Man and His Works: The Science of Cultural Anthropology*. Alfred A. Knopf.

Hirigoyen, M. F. (2019). *Les Narcisse: Ils ont pris le pouvoir*. La Découverte.

Kemper, S. (2005). *Reinventing The Wheel: A Story of Genius, Innovation, and Grand Ambition*. HarperCollins.

Chapter 1
Software and Innovation:
Detecting Invisible High-Quality Factors

Francisco V. Cipolla-Ficarra
Latin Association of Human-Computer Interaction, Spain & International Association of Interactive Communication, Italy

ABSTRACT

The study analyzes the invisible factors that influence the innovation and quality of the software of the 21st century, through natural language and programming languages. The analysis of languages shows how technological evolution influences the innate and acquired skills of human beings, especially those who are dedicated to software engineering and all its derivations in the field of ICTs. There is a detailed list of internal and external factors affecting the qualitative and reliable software industry. It also examines the relationships between innovative and creative education of experts in new technologies, programming over time, and the role of social networks. Finally, a state of the art on the myths and realities of the software profession in the new millennium is presented, which together with a group of rhetorical questions allows generating new lines of research within the formal and factual sciences, starting from the inquiries and conclusions of this work.

INTRODUCTION

Human face-to-face communication remains a key element in the evolution of information technology. Technologies that for a long time have tried to displace almost all the human knowledge that has been accumulating for centuries, on the Internet (Crocker, 2019; Chang, 2018; Cipolla-Ficarra, 2017). The purpose is to structure a kind of great collective memory, as a legacy for future generations. In this legacy are the uses and customs, for example, transmitted through oral communication, in the different cultures of the world. It is the great analog and digital baggage of knowledge that testifies to the wealth of the human being when it comes to solving the problems of everyday life. This communication practice still persists, in numerous communities, far from the great cities of the planet.

With the daily technological advance, this oral knowledge has been digitized and stored on various magnetic supports, such as: magnetic tape, hard disk, floppy disk, compact disk, DVD, USB flash drive,

DOI: 10.4018/978-1-7998-7010-4.ch001

etc. These are data that is to be accessed online, through software applications. However, these interactive systems have also evolved over time from hypertexts, multimedia, etc. until reaching mixed reality. However, with the breakthroughs in information technologies, many creative and innovative contents have become obsolete, due to the change in the operating system, although the associated hardware and the rest of the applications on personal computers, tablet PCs, servers, etc., have always functioned correctly (Appuswamy, 2019; Egyed, et al., 2018; Allu, 2017).

Technologically, today, there is no single device to read or interact with them. Therefore, in the era of the expansion of communicability, there are retrograde technological factors, derived from human decisions, which thus belong to the set of human factors in software engineering. In this case, these factors act as real barriers or filters, since they prevent the population's access to a part of the universal historical knowledge, whose origin is in the diffusion of computer science in the homes of millions of users. However, there are masterful exceptions in the field of human communication.

Without resorting to the latest technologies, messages can be emitted and received, between humans and across the distance, for instance by whistling, on one of the islands of the Canary archipelago: La Gomera. "*Silbo gomero*" –gomero whistling, declared an intangible cultural heritage by UNESCO, is a whistled language practiced since the time of the local indigenous people (*Guanches,* in Spanish) or First Nations, to communicate from several kilometers away (Classe, 1957; Meyer, 2008).

In our days, that can be an example of ancestral creativity or linguistic innovation. In addition, it continues to surprise many, if it is analyzed from a sociological point of view, since it allows creating personal interrelationships at a distance in a rural context, and without using personal computers, tablet PCs, smartphones, etc., derived from international projects unfinished or unsuccessful, such as the One Laptop per Child –OLPC (Kramer, Dedrick & Sharma, 2009).

Although we are dealing with two language systems, one natural (whistling) and the other artificial (computing), both are governed by a set of rules. These rules must be known and respected by each component (human or technological), in the communication process. A greater mutual and shared knowledge of the science is related to each other, with a high level of communicative quality. In other words, *communicability* is included (Cipolla-Ficarra, 2017). In addition, innovation in an artificial system occurs when the initial product evolves towards something different and new, and this innovation occurs on the basis of small evolutions or transformations, and not of a great revolution. Frequently, hardware revolutions make software evolutions drag behind.

Our main objective in this chapter is to discover the interrelationships of the factors that increase quality within software, traditional creativity and modern innovation in programming through the languages of computers and human language. We consider that the analysis of language and communicability continue to be an interesting starting point in the software industry, to establish new methods, techniques, skills, procedures, etc., among the agents who are changing the structural components of daily human coexistence in the great global village, defined by McLuhan, in 20th century (McLuhan & Powers, 1989). In short we intend to provide answers to questions, such as: What few visible factors boost the quality of software today? What programmer skills last and disappear over time? What sociological contexts enhance the qualitative increase of interactive systems? Are there strategies to promote precision in the use of natural and artificial language? Is there a fluctuation in the interest of programmers towards innovation and quality? How can education influence the training of motivated programmers? What is the role of social networks in fluctuating software quality and maintaining professionalism in this sector?

COMPUTERS, QUALITY AND NEW GENERATIONS

With the democratization of the Internet, there is a great trend to develop quality metrics (Gregory, 2019; Pressman & Maxim, 2015; Hoftman, R., Marx, M. & Hancock, 2008; Fenton, 1994). The purpose is to evaluate computer programs with methods and techniques, from an endless number of professional groups, who define themselves as experts. Although, in fact, neither by educational background and / or experience, do they belong to that set. Moreover, they belong to a diverse set of disciplines, which have not been in great demand in the traditional labor market since the 20th century, such as anthropologists, physicists, mathematicians, chemists, nuclear engineers, graduates in fine arts, industrial engineers, etc.

Of course, this statement requires a geographical-temporal appreciation beforehand, because an industrial engineer in the American or Asian continent, for example, is not the same as in the European Mediterranean. In the first geographical area, large heavy, semilight and light industries persist, which are associated with top-notch or mature technology. While in the second context, the vast majority of these industries have been transferred to other areas of the planet, where human capital, which works manually and / or intellectually, has lower costs.

In this scenario, computing has been a kind of job panacea for professions with very little demand in the national job market. Today, they, through the social networks, define themselves as experts in software, hardware, telecommunications, human-computer interaction (HCI), usability engineering, user experience (UX), innovative creativity and digital entrepreneurship, virtual reality and a long etcetera (Cipolla-Ficarra, 2010b; Cipolla-Ficara, 2017), although when left to themselves they don't know how to program in Logo or Python (Papert, 1993; Kanetkar & Kanetkar, 2020). The reliability of online information is practically zero, if you seriously consider computer knowledge and all its derivations (Cipolla-Ficarra, 2010a; Cipolla-Ficarra, 2017).

Which is why labor-educational indexes have been developed in the software sector, which allow us to extract information online, about the most used languages nowadays. From these indexes and their specific evaluation methodologies, it is easy to extrapolate data from the Internet so that not only the programming specialist knows what the state of the art is, but also knows what their position is in the labor market, based on knowledge of languages. Some examples are: Programming languages that have a higher demand for information from users; What are the courses of the most requested programming languages, in their various stages (initial, intermediate and advanced), and the total number of professionals with university studies, specialized in the different languages.

Quantifying quality based on online information may not be very accurate and valuable for making strategic decisions, whether personal, business and/or industrial, specifically, in the case of the pseudo experts. Or if a critical-analytical review of the evolution of science and interactive systems online and offline is made, from the mid-1980s to the present day.

An expanded vision between new technologies and formal and factual sciences allows us to answer two fundamental questions:

1) Where are we?
2) Where are we going?

The audiovisual industry that represents interactive systems is an interesting sector to start with the analysis of the evolution of software, the hardware revolution, and the eternal metamorphosis of the imaginary innovation of the human being, based on the science literature fiction and daily progress in the

ICT sector. Today, that collective imaginary can be reflected in content related to artificial intelligence, robotics, science data, computer graphics, mixed reality, videogames, etc. A priori, such content may be trivial. However, each of them constitutes a kind of epicyclic or planetary gears, in the software industry, today and for the future, whether in the short, medium and long term (Basili, et al., 2018; Cipolla-Ficarra, 2014). The energy that boosts the operation of each of these gears, within the mechanism of software, hardware, innovation and communicability, is called "quality".

To better understand some of these scientific components, the content of a recent film, with international diffusion, such as "Ready Player One" (Cline, 2011), by Steven Spielberg, can be put as a primary example. This cinematographic product denotes the potential of software, ranging from interface design to web engineering, through artificial intelligence to mixed reality. This film represents a wealth of technological content and involves an unprecedented transformation in the audiovisual context, from the linguistic perspective. In a mixed reality context, the speech is intermingled with an endless number of technological neologisms, by real and virtual characters, linked to black / white and color scenes. Not only must the viewer adapt mentally, to the constant change between real and virtual images, but also, to the use of a technological terminology, real or fictitious, which forces him to resort to online search engines (Baidu, Bing, Google, etc.), continuously, to know the meaning of the words, whether they are neologisms or not.

This new phenomenon opens a new gap between generations or "Gen" (Seemiller & Grace, 2018). In short: X (social researchers typically use birth years around 1961 to 1981), Y (1982 – 1995), Z (1995 – 2010) and Alpha (a new period between 2010 as the starting birth year to 2025). That is, to the loss of the ability to perform mental arithmetic operations, at the end of the XX century, or the concentration on reading, at the beginning of the XXI century, derived from the democratization of the Internet, now, we add recurrence or appeal to the online databases in order to know the meaning of the words, colloquial or not, and within the mother tongue or native language. Apart from the sociological, psychological, anthropological, economic, educational, semiological, etc., aspect of this situation, which affects the human being, as "social animal, in the global village", the film represents, exceptionally, the intersection of a diverse range of programming languages and technological devices.

The Importance of Resorting to a Correct and Logical Terminology in Computing

In our days, through a set of words related to software creation, we can find notions such as: project, analysis, planning, design, model, evaluation, development, programming, reuse, validation, management, maintenance, costs etc. (Sommerville, 2016; Pressman & Maxim, 2015). From the point of view of a programming language, terms such as: didactics, diffusion, efficiency, standardization, expandability, flexibility, generality, integrability, readability, modularity, portability, robustness, etc. refer to the internal and external characteristics of the language. Each of these terms is characterized by a precise definition in software engineering, for example (Ingeno, 2018; Pressman & Maxim, 2015; Sebesta, 2016; Valiron, et al., 2015; Westfall, 2010). The use of correct language is one of the main characteristics to reduce the timing and therefore, the costs in the production of current software. In addition, it allows the team of analysts, engineers, programmers, etc. of interactive systems **not** to make serious mistakes in each of the phases of its elaboration.

Accuracy and structuring are two common denominators, which have remained constant over time, in software professionals, who do not belong to the so-called Z generation (Seemiller & Grace, 2018).

Figure 1. The film "Ready Player One" denotes the potential of software, ranging from advanced interface design to web engineering, through artificial intelligence to mixed reality

Those who have developed systems with unstructured programming languages (BASIC, FORTRAN, Assembler, etc.) and structured programming languages (C, COBOL, dBASE, PASCAL, etc.) have been able to naturally develop logical and empathetic skills, which they have been able to apply in an endless number of occasions in everyday life and the workplace (Bergin & Gibson, 1996; Sebesta, 2016). Skills that are not easily visible in "ad hoc" computer applications, developed in the new millennium, for example. This is a sign of the failure of interdisciplinarity, transdisciplinarity, multidisciplinarity, pluridisciplinarity, extradisciplinary, intradisciplinary, etc. education promoted by anthropologists and pedagogues, to name two examples.

Consequently, these notions added to others, such as: transhumanism, hyperhumanism, posthumanism, etc., illogically related to the new technologies, and whose genesis can be located in an anthropological or sociological elite, lead to negative results. Negativity is reached when the human being is not considered, in a dignified, free and independent way, at the time he carries out his main activities within the computer field. That is, without constantly relying on intergroup communication, as can happen in outsourcing services. In the last decade of the 20th century, the inclusion of anthropologists, sociologists, psychologists, etc., in the software development stages responded to advice from software engineering experts in USA (Basili, et al., 2018; Basili & Musa, 1991) to improve the quality of the first applications of commercial multimedia, intended for education, culture, tourism, hobby, etc. (Cipolla-Ficarra, et al., 2010; Cipolla-Ficarra, 2010).

With the arrival of the new millennium, the era of communicability was inaugurated. In the field of interactive systems, a new professional figure called an expert in communicability appeared (Cipolla-Ficarra, 2010b). It was the result of the intersection between the formal and factual sciences. A professional with knowledge in unstructured, structured, functional, imperative programming languages, etc., who, together with linguistics, semiotics or semiology, among other areas of information technology knowledge, can continue to maintain the theoretical and practical importance of 20th century precision, in the 21st century software industry (Cipolla-Ficarra, et al., 2012).

A precision that arises in the writing from the first programs aimed at administrative management, for example, where rudimentary menus grouped operations such as: data registration, information modification, record cancellation, list printing, file duplication, etc. Using with information input and output hardware: cathode ray screens, keyboard, printer, magnetic tapes, hard drives, floppy disks, etc. Some programs carried out in high-level languages, such as: BASIC, COBOL, PASCAL, etc., all of which had to go through the compilation phase (detection of syntax errors) until obtaining the executing program (file with the .exe). In other words, the programmer wrote in a high-level language, that is, closer to the human being, until obtaining the executable program through compilation (Kit, 1995; Godbolt, 2020). The programmer's ability was to make as few errors as possible from the point of view of syntax and logic. However, the intellectual advantages of these skills were contained or delimited, given the need to compile these programs, by the various operating systems and hardware of the time. In other words, the portability of the application came into play.

In the past century, these limitations derived from the software and the hardware made the creativity of the IT staff superior to find solutions to the problems of memory space of the personal computers or the dimension that the executable programs occupied in the portable supports, such as floppy disks or floppy drives. Where storage capacity was limited and high inventiveness was required in the solutions, to make the most of the available hardware resources. For example, an 8-inch floppy disks, IBM 43FD model, in 1976, had a capacity of 512 Kilobytes; the 5¼-inch (QD) floppy disks with a 1.2 Megabyte capacity, in 1984; and a 3½-inch (HD) floppy, in 1987, had a capacity of 1.44 Megabytes.

Although there was a tendency to decrease the size of said disks, and increase the storage capacity, it is necessary to remember that these magnetic supports should not only contain the programs, but also small databases, for the execution of scheduled tasks. In these days, these information carriers could not store a black and white photograph made with an actual smartphone. This shows the creative, innovative and inventive capacity of the original solutions of the programmers of the 80s, derived from the precise use of the language and the quality of the applications.

Today, these training and professional skills are difficult to find not only in university study plans, related to the computing environment or human-computer interaction, but also in masters, specialization courses, doctorates or post-doctorates, where innovation and creativity are its main axes. Studies that respond to the temporary fads of global marketing rather than to the solid and timeless structure of quality software (Cipolla-Ficarra, 2010; Cipolla-Ficara, 2014; Cipolla-Ficara, 2017; Koutroumpis, Leiponen & Thomas, 2017).

Computer Precision Versus Linguistic and Semiotic Elasticity

The rigor of a language in software engineering of the late twentieth century has an excellent example when differentiating four words: *mistake* (a human action that produces an incorrect result), *fault* (an incorrect step, process, or data defintion in a computer program), *failure* (an incorrect result) and *error* (the amount by which the result is incorrect): as Edward Kit does, at the time of reviewing the terminology used (Kit, 1995), through the Standard Glossary of Software Engineering Terminology (IEEE – Institute of Electrical and Electronics Engineers / ANSI – American National Standards Institute). Today, in colloquial language, those four notions would be used as synonyms. However, in the context of

Figure 2. The listing of a COBOL program, with 04/01/1985 date, where the personal data of all the participants in its development were included and identified. A correct way to protect the rights and duties of all. That is, not only was identified the company for which the programmer was working (Micro Systems) and the client (Vespasiani's motor vehicles), including his initials, but there was also respect for the employee's intellectual property towards the software company, and vice versa. Something non-existent on the 21st century web and social networking applications, although there is an infinity of international treaties, national laws, ethical and / or professional codes of associations, organizations, and institutes related to computing and all its derivations

```
x=======================x
 IDENTIFICATION DIVISION.
x=======================x
 PROGRAM-ID.    VALMOV.
 AUTHOR.        MICRO SISTEMAS S. A.
xxxxxxxxxxxxxxxxxxxxxxxxxxxxxxxxxxxxxxxxxxxxxxxxxxxxx
x
x  PROGRAMA:    VALMOV.COB  (Validacion de movimiento
x
x  CLIENTE:     Vespasiani Autotomotores S. A.
x
xxxxxxxxxxxxxxxxxxxxxxxxxxxxxxxxxxxxxxxxxxxxxxxxxxxxx
x
x  Autor  Fecha  Version  Modific.  Fecha  ---- Comen
x  Prog.  esc.            por:      mod.
xxxxxxxxxxxxxxxxxxxxxxxxxxxxxxxxxxxxxxxxxxxxxxxxxxxxx
x
x F.V.C.F 010485  1.00     ---      ---        -----
xxxxxxxxxxxxxxxxxxxxxxxxxxxxxxxxxxxxxxxxxxxxxxxxxxxxx)
x
x
x===================x
 ENVIRONMENT DIVISION.
x===================x
 CONFIGURATION SECTION.
 SPECIAL-NAMES.
                DECIMAL-POINT IS COMMA.
 INPUT-OUTPUT SECTION.
 FILE-CONTROL.
                SELECT IMPRESORA ASSIGN TO PRINTER.
                SELECT CLIENTES  ASSIGN TO DISK
                       ORGANIZATION IS RELATIVE
                       FILE STATUS IS ERROR-1
                       RELATIVE KEY IS RELCLI
                       ACCESS MODE IS DYNAMIC.
                SELECT MOVIM ASSIGN TO DISK
                       ORGANIZATION IS LINE SEQUENTIAl
                       FILE STATUS IS ERROR-3
                       ACCESS MODE IS SEQUENTIAL.
/
x=============x
 DATA DIVISION.
x=============x
 FILE SECTION.
 FD   CLIENTES
                     RECORD 165
                     LABEL RECORD IS STANDARD
                     VALUE OF FILE-ID 'C:CLIENTES.RL'
                     DATA RECORD IS REG-MAE.
 01   REG-MAE.
      02  NUMCLI     PIC 9(5).
      02  FILLER     PIC X(05).
      02  CONTUA     PIC 9.
```

communicability, the transparency of meaning is one of the quality attributes of the interactive systems, starting with the graphical user interface (GUI).

The transparency of meaning analyzes the use of terms (principally), images and sounds –statics or dynamics media, within the interface that do not produce ambiguities between the levels of expression and content. These two levels are related to the notion of signifier and signified. The transparency of meaning has a direct relation with five quality atributes of the interactive systems: accesibility, motivation, predicion, self-evidence and reusability (Cipolla-Ficarra, 2010). Signifier and Signified have their origin in linguistics and have consequently been studied in semiotics or semiology (Nöth, 1995; Holdcroft, 1991).

Semiotics or semiology is the science that studies signs in general; whether these are coded or not, systematic or not, eventual or stable, natural or cultural. The two terms, semiotics (supported by Charles Sanders Peirce) and semiology (defined by Ferdinand de Saussure), are considered as synonyms today, although the use of one and the other is variable, depending on the cultural field and the historical moment (De Saussure, 2011; Deledalle, 2001).

The fundamental difference between Pierce and Saussure is that Peirce focused on the character and logical function of the sign (pragmatism), while Saussure focused on the psychological or social aspect (structuralism), but as both aspects are in the sign semiology and semiotics belong to the same discipline (De Saussure, 2011; Nöth, 1995; Holdcroft, 1991; Eco, 1979; Cobley & Jancz, 1999). With the passage of time, they were going to establish two parallel lines of research, with several authors in each of them:

a) In the first are the followers of Saussure with Claude Lévi-Strauss, Julia Kristeva, Roland Barthes, Paul-Michel Foucault, Jacques Derrida, among others (Nöth, 1995; Holdcroft, 1991). They were oriented towards human signs and discourse.
b) In the second line, established by Pierce, scholars such as Charles William Morris, Thomas Sebeok, Ivor Armstrong Richards, etc. are located (Nöth, 1995; Cobley & Jancz, 1999). All of them guided by the premise of an universe perfused with signs. Both lines would tend to converge in the works of Roman Osipovich Jakobson and Umberto Eco (Eco, 1979).

Obviously, linguistics, being a new discipline for university study, in the context of the social sciences of the 20th century, would generate various points of convergence and divergence between the diverse authors of these two main lines, and those from the predominant philosophical movements. For example, the basic notion of arbitrariness of relations in the Saussurean sign was questioned in the mid-20th century, through the post-structuralism movement (Cobley & Jancz, 1999; Nöth, 1995).

A representative of this movement, the French Emile Benveniste claims that "the connection between the signifier (the material notation) and the signified (mental concept engendered by the signifier) is so comprehensively learned at an early age by sign users that virtually no separation between the two is ever experienced" (Cobley & Jancz, 1999; Nöth, 1995). That observation is valid with the simplest users who experiment for the first time, before the icons of the interfaces on smartphones, for example.

However, it is important that the notions established by Saussure have facilitated the precision of language, through the concept of sign, the components of the sign, and the evolution of the sign concept (figures 3 and 4). The following bibliographical references allow us to broaden these concepts (Saussure, 2011; Cobley & Jancz, 1999; Bouissac, 1998; Nöth, 1995; Holdcroft, 1991; Deledalle, 2001; Eco, 1979).

Furthermore, it is necessary to focus on the transparency of the Saussurian concept or meaning, or the content of Hjemlslevian meaning to avoid ambiguity (Bouissac, 1998; Nöth, 1995). Precisely, ambiguity

Figure 3. The components of the sign according to Saussure

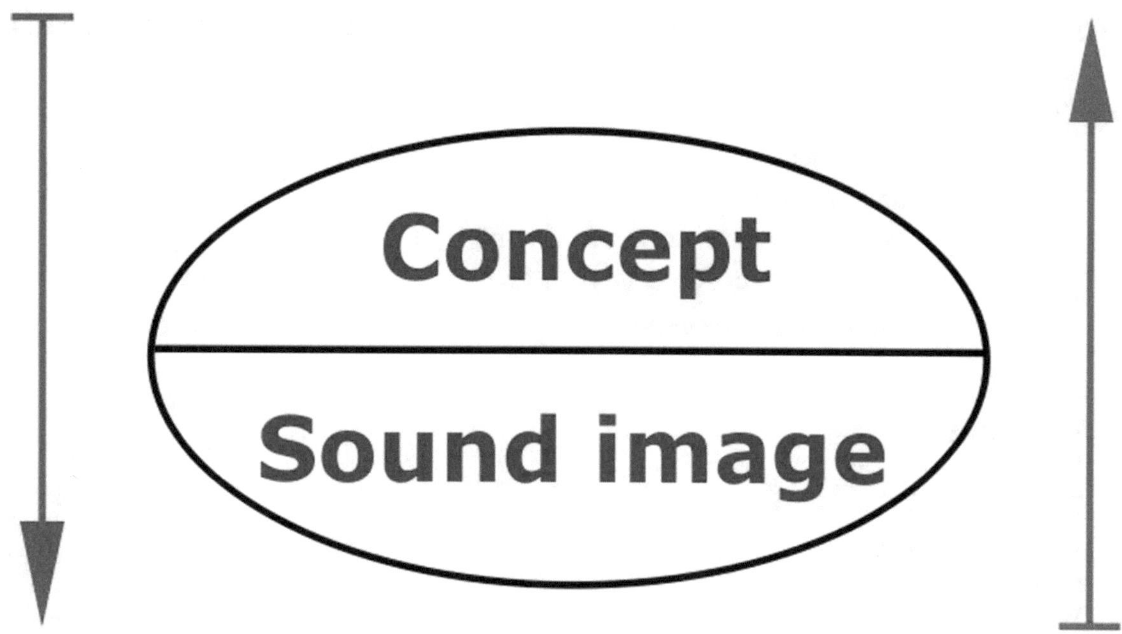

is one of the negative human factors, in the cost-time equation for the realization of an interactive application, using the latest hardware, working in an interdisciplinary and multicultural team. Therefore, the greater the ambiguity, the greater the time taken to obtain a system that works perfectly and with a high level of communicability for the end user, and the project costs are also higher. Graphically this equation is represented in figure 5.

An ambiguous content is one to which outside of any context it is possible to assign two or more interpretations. This phenomenon of connotations is related to Pierce's notion of unlimited semiosis (Eco, 1979; Nöth, 1995; Deledalle, 2001) but that depending on the geographical context could seriously affect the usability of an interactive system in the 1990s, or communicability in the 21st century. Baldinger's triangle serves to observe a case of ambiguity –different meaning, with the term "piano" on Italian (this word has the same pronunciation and written form, in Spanish, Portuguese, French, Finnish, English, and Italian):

Figure 4. Metamorphosis of the sign concept

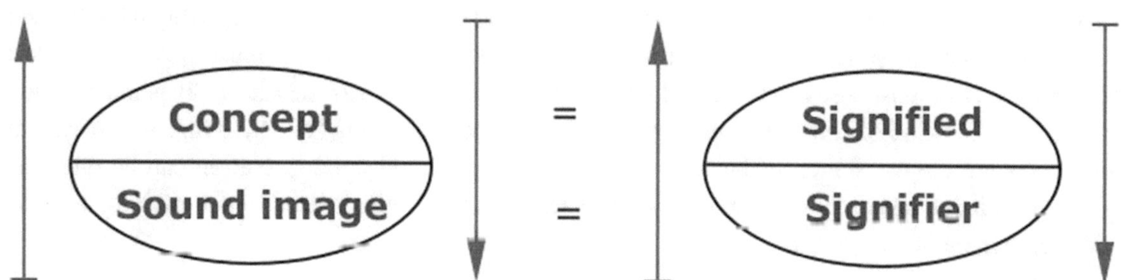

Figure 5. Main variables affected by the lack of linguistic precision in an international software project

Ambiguity in the Cost Equation for International Software Project

Ambiguity = < Communicability,
> Time,
> Costs,
> Negative Human Factors,
< Multicultural Team,and
< Interdisciplinarity.

1. Walk slowly.
2. Work plan.
3. Plan of a building.
4. Floor of a building.
5. Plain surface.
6. Whisper.

Subsequently, there is a bidirectional triadic interrelation of its components, with a process of production of meanings, in a constant and infinite way. The sign (representation), its object and an interpreter, are present in the process of elaborating a meaning and in the construction of reality. He asserts that there is no power of thought without signs. Thought is continuous and in it are the signs, in a constant flow, that is, one thought leads to another and this in turn to another, and so on indefinitely (Deledalle, 2001; Bouissac, 1998; Nöth, 1995).

In the continuity of thought lies not only one of the bases for the understanding of the triadic structure, but also the key to find innovative solutions to the most varied aspects in the phase of software production. For example, in the evaluation phase of interactive devices, such as the use of think-aloud (Nielsen & Mack, 1994). The user uses the system, and continually makes "value judgments" about it. Thinking is the main way to represent and interpret a sign, that is, to clarify or discover its meaning. Here, a differentiation should be included between the creative thinking of the isolated individual, in the 20th century, from the less original collective thinking, derived from social networks in the 21st century.

Now, knowing the sign, its meaning is inferred. That ability to inference is one of the key elements of communicability. The people or interpreters derived from current artificial intelligence, for example, carry in themselves interpretations. The sign elaborates "something" in the person's mind or in the artificial intelligence system. That "something" elaborated by the sign, has also been created in an indirect and relative way by the object of the sign, in the human being, and which is replicated in artificial intelligence.

If the processes of significance are accepted as processes of inference, it must also be considered that inference is in most cases hypothetical or abductive. In other words, that it involves interpretation and that there is a kind of conjecture, as in Natural Language Processing (NLP), in interactive systems, whose tasks are the translation of languages. This is the reason why interpretation can be uncertain, and therefore it can be corrected, improved and enriched as the methods used in natural languages and automated translation systems do.

Figure 6. Triadic relationship between signified, signifier and object

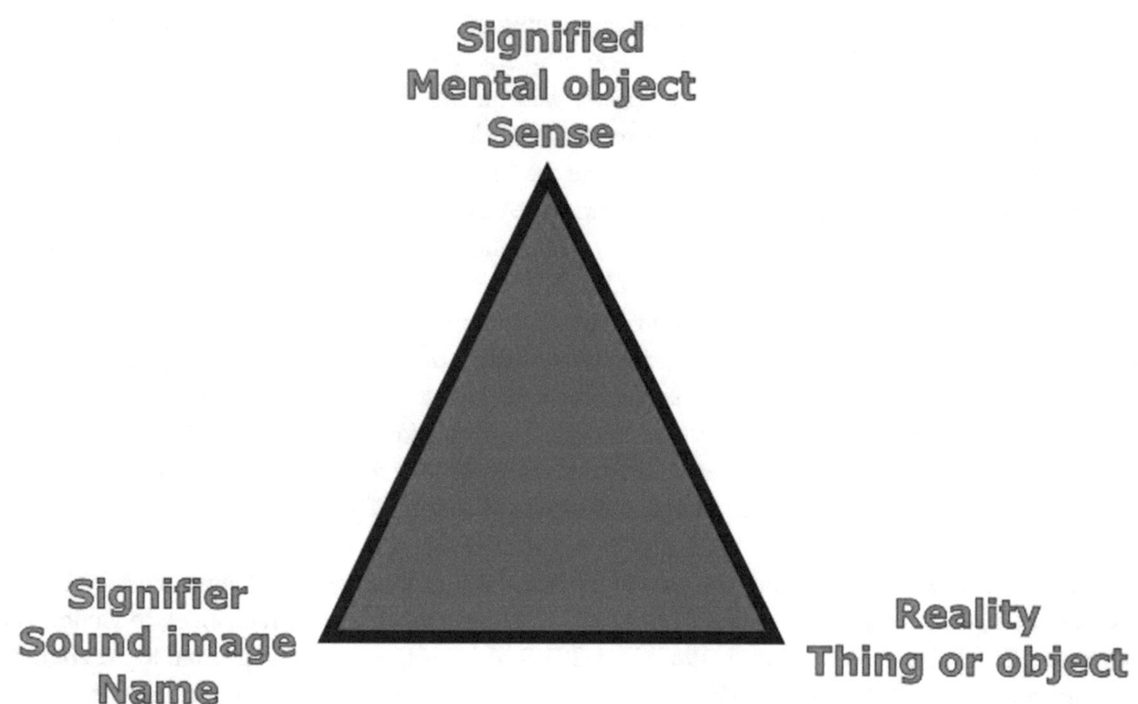

Communication and Context in Software Quality

The two-way relationship of the sign defined by Saussure, like the two states of a bit (off and on), in traditional computing, allow to establish dichotomous links (positive and negative), specifically in the software industry, with the human factors. Simultaneously, Pierce's triadic relationship (Deledalle, 2001; Bouissac, 1998; Nöth, 1995) serves as a link between internal, external, temporal and geographical factors in the evolution of the use of software and hardware. These are some of the main reasons, why it is necessary to delve into the notions of the sign, in the field of semiotics or semiology. These two words refer to the difference between Europeans and Americans, always placing Saussure and Pierce as their main representatives (Deledalle, 2001; Cobley & Jancz, 1999; Eco, 1979).

Europeans dedicated their research not only to explaining sign systems, but also to participating in the study of cultural systems, communication, and the media. The semiologist representatives from the USA and Canada came from the information theory, mass communication theory and cybernetics (Bouissac, 1998; Nöth, 1995; McLuhan & Powers, 1989; Eco, 1979). These differentiations are very important to consider how they establish historical links with current reality, from the point of view of professionals dedicated to quality and innovation in software and hardware for interactive systems.

For example, this differentiation is one of the reasons why there is a tendency to name the studies of mass communication in the USA and social communication in Europe and in much of Latin America. The influences and the creation of lines of research and action in the field of computing can be summarized as: "*Americans do*" and "*Europeans explain what the Americans did.*"

In addition, there is another two-way reality, and that continues since the origins of the first large computers, until the democratization of online multimedia content, that is, that hardware is always ahead of software. This one-to-one and timeless reality fundamentally influences the achievement of final quality in interactive systems, such as the educational training of professional teams, aimed at supervising the quality of products and services, in the context of interactive communications.

Already in the 1950s, two historical milestones were marked in the context of message transmission: distance communications and the definition of models for the emission and reception of messages. The first is related to the start of the space race and the inauguration of the ARPA agency (Advanced Research Projects Agency) in the USA to counteract the advance of the former USSR, in space, from the launch of the first artificial satellite (Sputnik). Later, those activities would go to NASA (Crocker, 2019; Cipolla-Ficarra, et al., 2010; Nelson, 1993).

Consequently, ARPA researchers began to study computers, and especially communication among them, throughout the United States, giving rise to the ARPANET in 1969, in order to join computers and university researchers, so as to help them in common research related to computers and communication networks, and start using computers in research. Undeniably, the potential for other network purposes, such as security, had since been anticipated. However, the Internet was conceived at that time as a network to share resources and exchange information (Crocker, 2019; Jirotka, et al., 2017; Cipolla-Ficarra, et al., 2010).

In this context, and in relation to the second historical event, it is the model enunciated by Harold Lasswell, in 1948, who based on rhetoric question: "Who says what, in which channel, to whom, and with what effect? (Shannon & Weaver, 1963; Poe, 2010). A basic question fundamental to the communication process, but which from the point of view of qualitative communication, should include perhaps the most important rhetoric question: What is the purpose of communication?

Today, the rhetorical question technique continues to be used in endless literature related to software quality (Cipolla-Ficarra, 2010b), where the author or authors mostly raise questions related to internal or external factors of the software, for example (Gregory, 2019; Koutroumpis, Leiponen, & Thomas, 2017; Baker & Wallace, 2007; Jackson, 2006).

In 1949, Claude Shannon and Warren Weaver presented another model (Shannon & Weaver, 1963). A model where Shannon dealt with the mathematical transmission of signals and Weaver with the use of signals in human communication. It is a model where the information is encoded in signals that will be decoded by the receiver. In this last phase lies the human comprehensibility to capture the messages, as reliably as possible at the time of emission.

This mathematical model of the transmission of information has influenced the social sciences, since its enunciation to the present through the infinity of professionals not related to computer science, but who are dedicated to human-computer interaction, human-computer communication, children-computer interaction, human-robot interaction, etc. (Xu, 2019; Chang, 2018; Cipolla-Ficarra, et al., 2017).

Lasswell, Shannon and Weaver would transfer to the present day a highly influential professional triangle for obtaining qualitative results in the process of human communication with new technologies: mathematicians, communicators and politicians. Wherein, the "authentic" communicators occupy the bottom of that triad (figure 7). Consequently, an unnatural metamorphosis process in the triad is verified, depending on the temporal and geographical context. For example, in mathematics and logic, its results are systematic and verifiable, from the point of view of scientific research analysis.

However, these investigations are not objective, and do not provide information on the reality because they do not deal with the facts, as Mario Bunge maintains (Bunge, 1981). Both disciplines deal with ideal entities. That is, some abstract or interpreted entities that exist in the human mind (Bunge, 1981). Hypothetically, its members and experts should build their own objects of study, resorting to creativity and innovation, from the abstraction of real objects, which are in nature and / or in society. In other words, the raw material used by mathematicians and logicians is not factual but ideal, and they should meet the needs of technologists, ecologists, and sociologists, to name three examples, occupying a place of subordination, in the face of such needs.

In reality and with the advancement of new technologies, mathematicians and politicians tend to come together as one. The strength that this union generates comes from religion or other types of organizations, groups, etc. akin to it, to gain the power and control of the triad. The primary purpose is to occupy the apex of the triangle and to maintain themselves over time. This union is one of the sources of communication noise on social networks, in the classic Shannon-Weaver model (Shannon & Weaver, 1963).

Currently, one way to reduce that noise from language is through the operations of anchoring the sense (Nöth, 1995; Bouissac, 1998). For example, in an interactive system whose objective is to learn several languages if you do not insert images of the object you are referring to, a term in isolation can lead to confusion at the time of user interaction (Cipolla-Ficarra, 2017). The image in this case fulfills the function of anchoring the sense. Furthermore, the ambiguity of meaning in interactive systems is presented to the user as a disjunction between two or more different interpretations and there is no orientation. It is important to note that ambiguity is basically a problem of meaning rather than of the signifier.

Disorientation in navigation decreases the quality of the system (Cipolla-Ficarra, 2010). That loss of orientation, depending on the type of user and the type of the interactive application. For example, augmented or mixed reality, abundant or rich from the perspective of content (combination of texts, graphics, animations, photos, videos, music, etc.), can discourage the end user from continuing to enjoy the system (Cipolla-Ficarra, 2017). This behavior occurs regardless of whether or not the user belongs to generation Z.

Programming languages like human or natural language, have a structure or syntax, and a meaning or semantics, specifically related to English, in the computer context and all its derivations. The different languages, dialects, etc. are governed by a set of norms that are elaborated within a spatio temporal community. With the passage of time, a natural evolution is observed in syntax and semantics. In other cases, technological advances under the domain of the edge "mathematics + politics + religion" within the triangle of figure 19, disadvantage the universal use of English terms, software and hardware, even if both have been accepted within the Dictionary of the Spanish Royal Academy (www.rae.es), because they are translated into Catalan, as "*programari*" and "*maquinari*", respectively (www.diccionari.cat).

This is not a process of natural evolution within a langue (a system of differences between signs), language or dialect, as Saussure argued (De Saussure, 2011). Rather, it reflects a vertical and unidirectional structure. That is, a small elitist and enlightened group that from above decides and imposes its linguistic rules on the majority, that is, on millions of people, who occupy the base of the population pyramid. The case of "machinery –*maquinari* (hardware) and programming –*programari* (software)" is a great exception to the norms of international linguistics, oriented to new technologies. Usually, the rules or norms define the different ways to combine the various types of words, either to constitute sentences or phrases, which are accepted within a certain language.

The Disadvantages of Natural Language in Programming Languages

In programming languages there is no wealth of vocabulary or lexicon, semantics, syntax, etc., as in natural languages. Although there are fewer possible combinations, they must be respected and used correctly in order to avoid mistakes. These languages offer a set of instructions with a certain syntax

Figure 7. The Shannon and Weaver model and its involution in time through distorting agents, which ruin and destroy the field of new technologies, education, health, computing, interactive communications, research in formal and factual sciences, the paradigm of the common good in societies, future generations, etc.

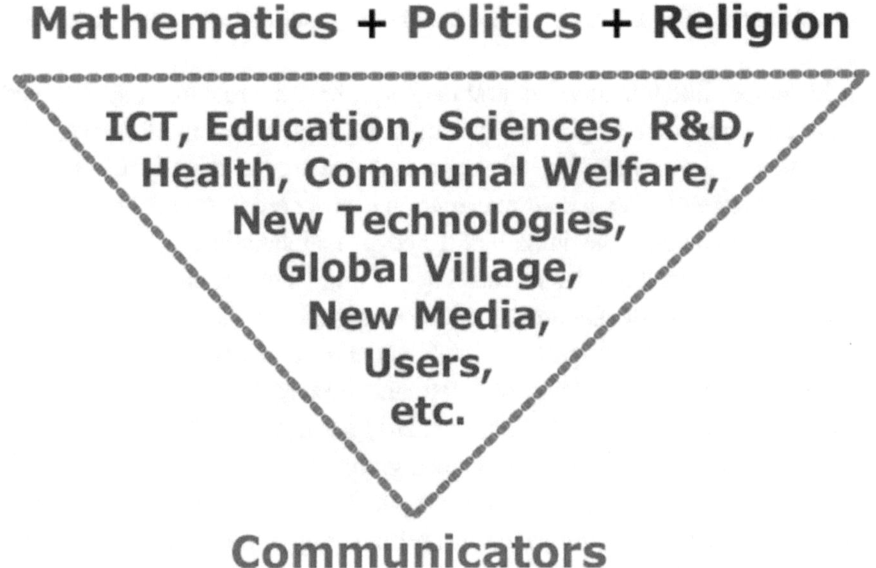

to execute a function. In other words, they use a set of characters that constitute a kind of alphabet or lexicon to communicate with computers. The first systems were binary, that is, 1 or 0.

Undoubtedly, it was a very complex task to use for the first programmers. With the passing of time, the evolution of writing systems would bring them closer to human language, as can be seen in the ASCII code (American Standard Code for Information Interchange) or EBCDIC (Extended Binary Coded Decimal Interchange Code). For example, one of the 256 characters inside the ASCII table is the at sign "@", and within several text applications (Notepad, Word, etc.) you can get it by holding down the ALT key and typing number 64 on the numeric keypad.

The first programmers knew these tables by heart, as well as the conversion operations between the binary, octal, hexadecimal decimal, etc., among many other skills, which enriched the intellectual capacities of these professionals, and which considerably reduced costs. in the development of pioneering systems, in the field of industry, commerce, health, education, etc. (Cipolla-Ficarra, 2017).

In reference to the richness of the content, two situations are observed: one positive and the other negative. On the one hand, it can complicate the "decoding" of the message given the abundance of data in various formats (sounds, texts, graphics, illustrations, photographs, 2D, 3D reconstructions, etc.) in front of the user, and on the other hand, it facilitates decoding by reducing the number of performances. Despite this, the user is faced with various interpretations and does not know what sense to choose. The context provided by a natural metaphor makes it easier for the end user to choose the most appropriate interpretation among the various alternatives that have been presented.

There is a type of ambiguity called phonics (Cipolla-Ficarra, 2017) that affects the dynamic media of interactive systems (Cipolla-Ficarra, et al., 2010). They are those audio elements (sememes) in which the synchronization of the emission of the slowed down locution produces incomprehension on the part of the user. It was a frequent error in commercial interactive systems, in off-line support from the 90s, or when the network speed is slow. These sememes constitute a set formed by messages, which although they may occasionally receive the same phonetic articulation, have different phonological descriptions. Finally, related to ambiguity are also these two notions: Vagueness and indeterminacy.

- **Vagueness:** A term is vague when its designation limits are imprecise. For example, the Polish translation of acronym 5GL in Wikipedia: "5th – generation programming language" (figure 10). The other classical example is the following definition of the "C" language from a multimedia system off-line: "It is a more widespread programming language" (Cipolla-Ficarra, 2017). The term "widespread" by itself does not establish exactly the reason for the extension, such as the following factors: due to the ease of use, compatibility with other programming languages, flexibility with different operating systems, labor demand in the computer and telecommunications market, etc.

In this case, it is a definition that comes from a classic Spanish interactive system off-line called "*Enciclopedia Universal*" –Universal Encyclopedia (Micronet, 2004). In addition, it does not refer to whether it is a structured language or not or to which level and generation that language belongs, to mention some examples. Programming languages are feasible to be classified as either structured or unstructured languages, that is, when we refer to the way instructions are written and grouped. In addition, there are low, intermediate and higher level languages depending on the degree of communication with the CPU (Central Processing Unit) and the degree of complexity of the instructions. The "C" belongs to the set of structured languages with a high level or higher.

Historically, and with regard to generations (Cipolla-Ficarra, et al., 2012; Bergin & Gibson, 1996), we find that the first generation are machine languages (instructions that can be executed directly by computer's CPU; the second generation are assemblers or ASM (a strong correspondence between the instructions in the language and the architecture's machine code instructions); the third generation are procedural symbolic languages, such as C, BASIC, ADA, PASCAL, LISP, PROGOL, SIMULA, RPG, etc., and the fourth generation are relational languages, such as SQL, for example, whose main

Figure 8. An example of the high computer creativity of the 1980s, through the use of ASCII code and dot matrix printing or impact matrix printing. Today it is called "ASCII Art"

function is to write queries or questions, to modify or select data from a database. However, more than languages they are tools, and therefore, object-oriented programming could be included in this area, with languages such as: C++, Delphi, Power Builder, Visual Basic, etc. Finally, the fifth generation is related to artificial intelligence and neural networks, such as the Japanese project called 5GL, but with a low quorum of programmers.

Perhaps, such a concise, vague and imprecise definition was an advance to the current times, where the new generation of users of interactive systems must constantly access the Internet, to know the meanings of words or to expand the definitions of words, technical terms, colloquial expressions, etc.

In the example of the definition of "C" language –digital encyclopedia online (figure 11) and off-line (Micronet, 2004), it has been found that there are realities that can be denoted by both the term and neighboring signs in the system. Vagueness is a phenomenon of designation, not of significance (for example, the differentiation existing within the fourth generation of languages). This phenomenon has its origin in the inaccurate limits that possess the designative class of signs of a language or a natural language. The meanings within it are established from oppositions of concepts. The signs of natural languages show a high degree of vagueness.

Figure 9. Detail of the printed artistic image, where you can see the combination of letters, punctuation marks, mathematics, etc.

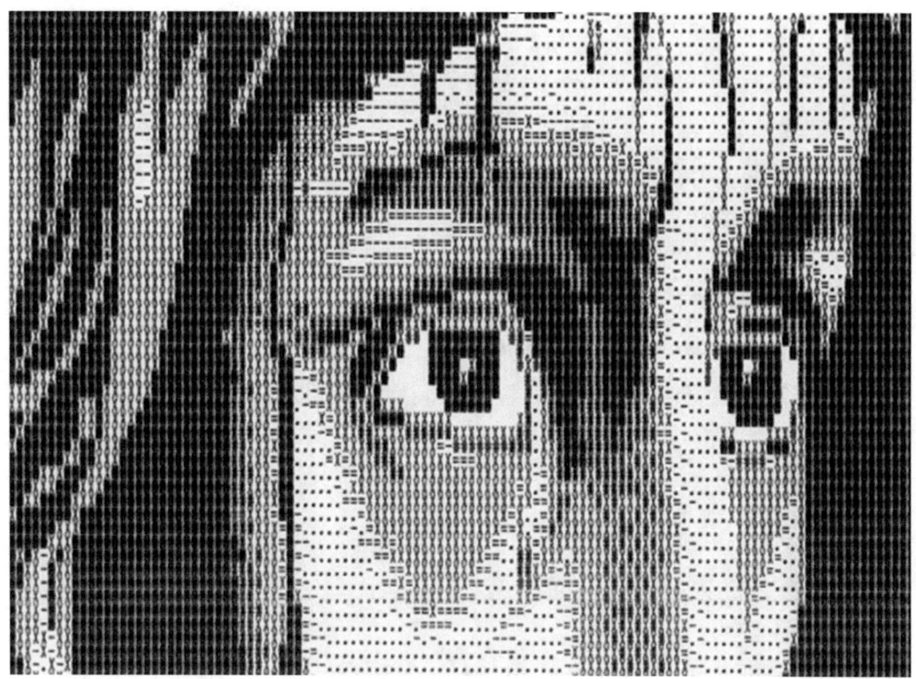

Scientific language that claims to be precise and exact should avoid it as much as possible. This precision is an objective to be met and that has its drawbacks when you achieve it, since natural language terms are used in the definitions of scientific language (Bunge, 1981). One of the ways to achieve precision in science is by defining concepts. Definitions are not selected randomly or whimsically. They must be appropriate and consistent with the speech. Once selected, the rest of the content must be congruent to it, in order to avoid indeterminacy or loss of textual quality.

- **Indeterminacy**: It is the lack or poverty of information. The end user wants to know more information (static or dynamics contents) than what is transmitted through the interactive system. In indeterminacy the meaning is always unique. In short, there is no significant duplication or a semiosis infinity, and it is a classical resource used to motivate progress in a computer-assisted education (CAE) system based on HCI, for example (Cipolla-Ficarra, 2010b). The content is presented to the student, in a fractional, sequential and progressive way (figure 12).

In the example in figures 13 and 14, it can be observed how indeterminate information or interface design reduces motivation to a final user or student. The failure about indeterminacy generally occurs in some encyclopedia-type systems that have been translated from other foreign languages but which do not contemplate all the alternatives of Baldinger's triangle (Bouissac, 1998; Nöth, 1995). In retrospect, it is a frequent failure in the first European and commercial off-line multimedia systems. Exceptionally, this failure is non-existent in the Dictionary of the Spanish language (*Diccionario de la Real Academia Española –D.R.A.E.*), either in the digital format or off-line multimedia system (Espasa-Calpe, 1998). In

Figure 10. A multilingual online encyclopedia (Wikipedia) that defines the 5GL in Polish language using vague terminology

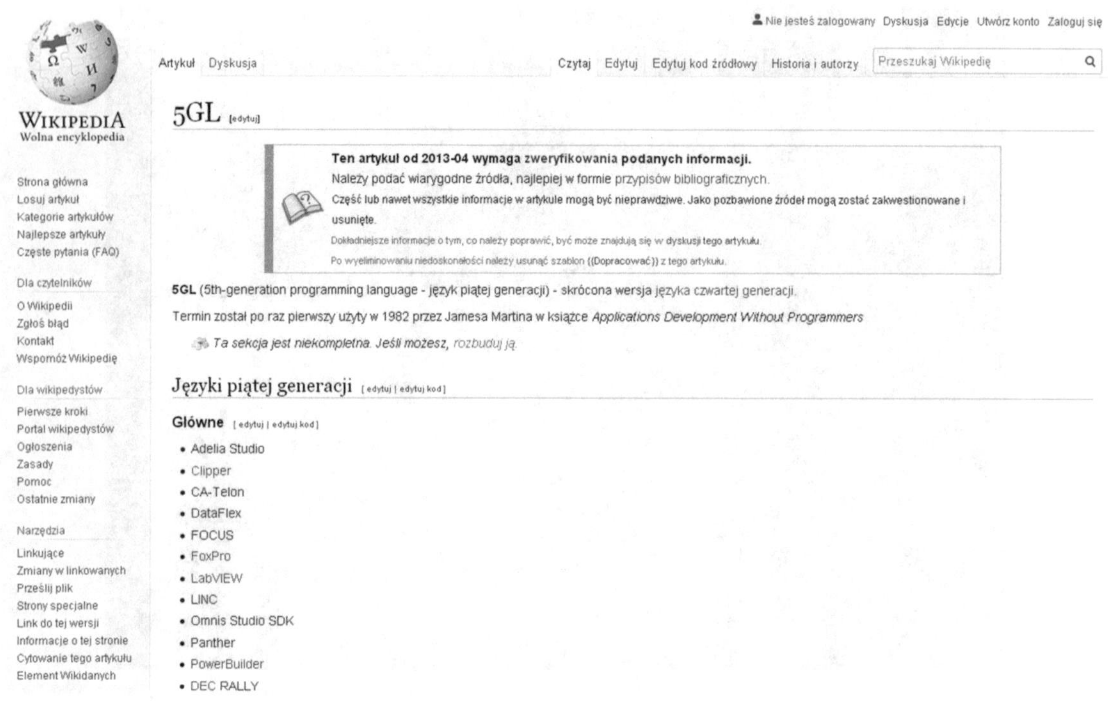

addition, it contained functions in the search within the database that still do not exist in Google Search, today. For example, when searching, the words in rounded, bold, italic and small capitals it could be differentiated in the typographic format. However, these options are not available in D.R.A.E. online (www.drae.es –figure 18, in the upper right hand box).

These two notions, ambiguity and indeterminacy, in the scientific and educational field, diminish the quality of training in the local community and in the global village. In other words, it is a "glocal" (global + local) and "classic" error in the quality of the interactive systems. The notion of "classic" refers to the diachronic aspect of the failure. In other words, it has endured over time.

Failures and errors that have verified its existence, from the '90s usability engineer, oriented to personal computers, with CD-Rom / DVD players, to the era of expansion of communicability, through smartphones, of the latest technological generation (Nielsen & Mack, 1994; Cipolla-Ficarra, 2010b). These glocal and timeless errors, in the interactive systems of encyclopedias, manuals, etc., denote a high rate of access by students, and therefore, should be eradicated from the design stage, through methods and techniques of evaluation of the quality (Cipolla-Ficarra, 2010b).

Now, science creates artificial languages, through the invention of symbols, be they words, electronic symbols, mathematical signs, etc. Each of these signs is given a meaning, depending on the rules of the designation. For example, in the design of interfaces, you can follow the rules of the signaling system, many of its symbols are internationally recognized and accepted. In the universal classification of sign types and within Pierce's triad, three components are distinguished: symbols (arbitrarily related to their object), icons (similar to their object) and indexes (physically related to their object). The symbol is a word that comes from the Greek "*simbolon*", as a sign of recognition.

Figure 11. Wikipedia and the very poor definition of "C" language in Aragonese dialect (Spain)

The etymology of the term determines that a symbol is something compound, that is, it is the union

Figure 12. Example of an excellent solution to the indeterminacy of meaning on various screens or menus

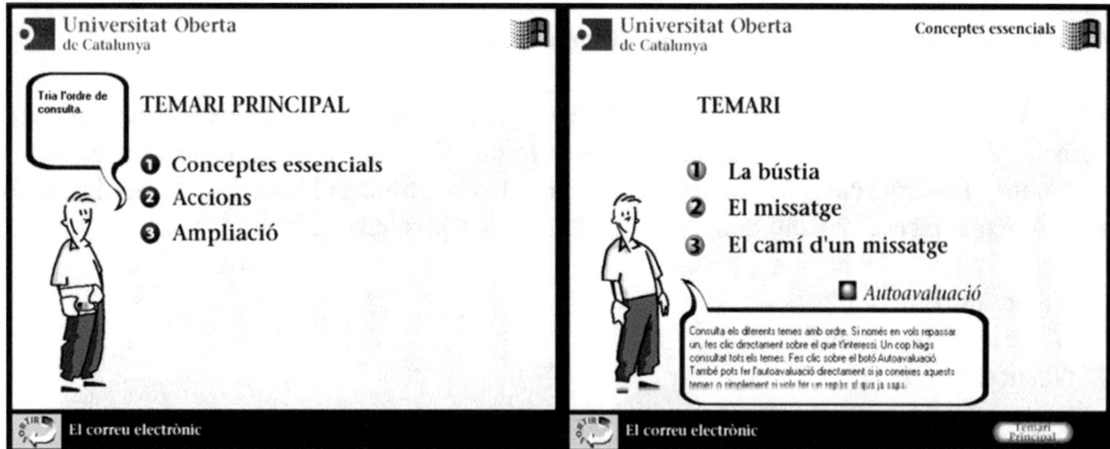

Figure 13. A classic example of mistakes in user interface design such as the Garden Encyclopedia (Book-that-Work, 1996) where it is impossible to read the contents, due to an overlap of the windows or dialog boxes

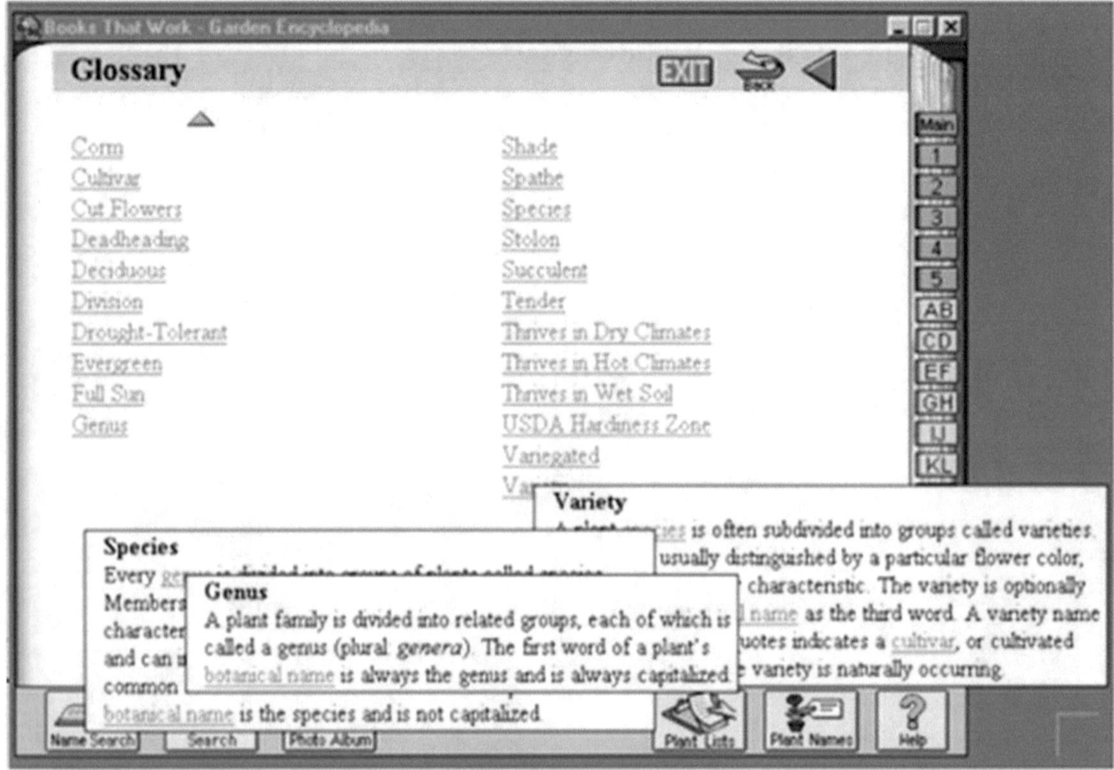

of two or more elements. When you try to interpret a symbol, you look for the invisible reality below the visible one, and the way they are related. Except for the notion of symbols, icons and indexes are considered as "passepartout" categories or "wildcard concepts" that function due to their vagueness, as Umberto Eco maintains (Eco, 1979). He corrected the common use of the notions of icons and indexes and he would establish some limitations to Pierce's infinite semiosis.

Evolution of Internal Factors in Software Quality

The basic symbols will be as simple as possible, however they can be combined according to certain pre-established and conventionally accepted rules to form configurations as complex as necessary. In the evolution of educational software, starting with the quality attribute of the orientation of interactive systems (Cipolla-Ficarra, 2010b), and answering three basic questions, such as:

- Where am I?
- Where do I come from?
- Where can I go?

Figure 14. Very short definition about Franklin symbol (physical unit for electrical charge): "Fr symbol of franklin" (Zanichelli, 1997)

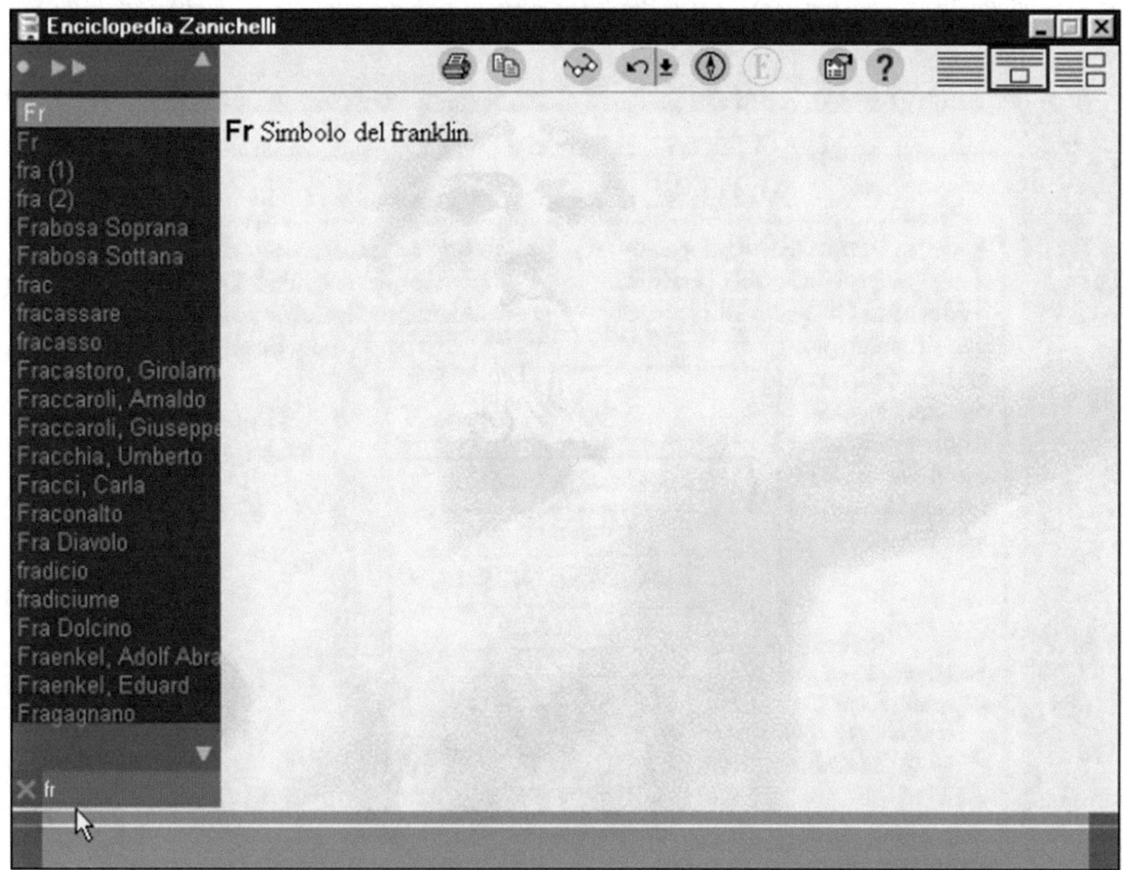

Programming commands or instructions were created for didactic purposes and related to "the movement." For example, go forward, backward, turn, turn left, etc. of a cursor (turtle icon), were basic commands or instructions of the programming language called LOGO (Papert, 1993). Created in 1967, by Seymour Papert, Wally Feurzeig, Danny Bobrow, and Cynthia Solomon. This programming language was based on some of the pre-established principles of the LISP language (Berk, 1985).

LOGO emerges as an ideal language to promote interest in children's and youth programming (Ito, 2009). Some commands are:

- *FORWARD 500* (the turtle walks forward 500 steps).
- *BACK 100* (back 100 units).
- *LEFT 90* (turns left 90º).
- *RIGHT 45* (Turns 45 degrees to the right).

They denote the ease of use towards the first personal computers, and connote the creative capacity, at an early age to program. LOGO is a high-level, functional and structured language (Ito, 2009). Another example is the BASIC (Beginner's All-purpose Symbolic Instruction Code), developed in 1964 by two

Figure 15. An excellent example from another encyclopaedia of science (Dorling-Kindersley & Zeta, 1998), with regard to Lithium, where there is the possibility of hearing its name (audio), information about the chemical symbol, but also the type (alkali metal), the atomic number (3) and its atomic mass (7)

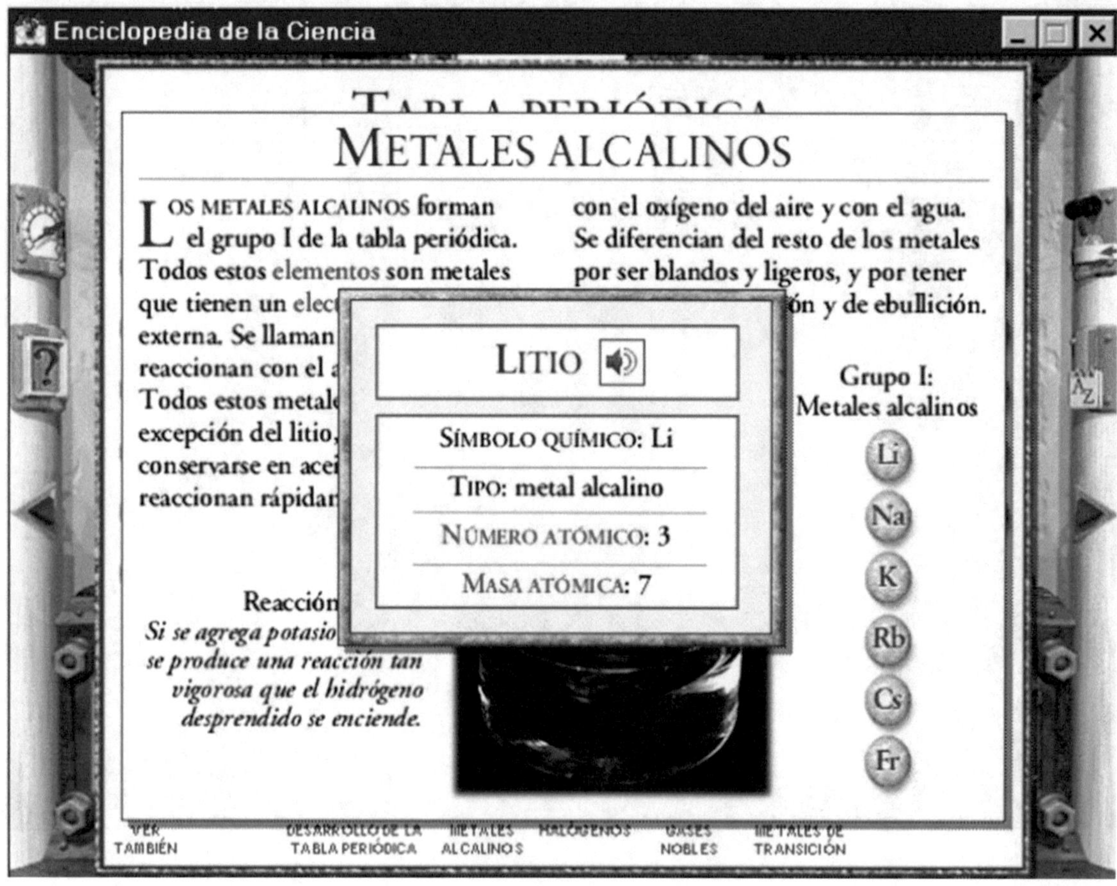

mathematics teachers John George Kemeny and Thomas Eugene Kurtz (Lorenzo, 2017), considered "the first user-friendly computer programming language." Kurtz had developed it for his students, at Dartmouth College (Hanover, USA). Some move and decision making commands are:

- *GOTO*,
- *GOSUB – RETURN*,
- *IF – THEN – ELSE*, etc.

The programs, in their source code, had a high goto number and when they were extensive (called "*spaghetti*"), finding the compilation errors could require many hours of human control (Cipolla-Ficarra, 2012). The *GOSUB – RETURN* command allowed to better structure the execution of the subroutines. In the decision structures (*IF – THEN – ELSE*) the creative logic of the programmer could be glimpsed. Over the decades, several versions emerged, which were adapting to the evolution of software, such as operating systems and hardware, with the various models of computers. These "movement" commands would be repeated in languages such as Fortran, Cobol, Visual Basic, SQL Server, etc. As the language

Figure 16. The text in Spanish defines BASIC as follows: "Acronym of the English expression 'Beginners Allpurpose Symbolic Instruction Code'. It is a symbolic conversational language without a specific application used in computers" (Micronet, 2004). This definition indicates some of the existing errors in various classical and commercial offline encyclopedias of the 20th century, in southern Europe

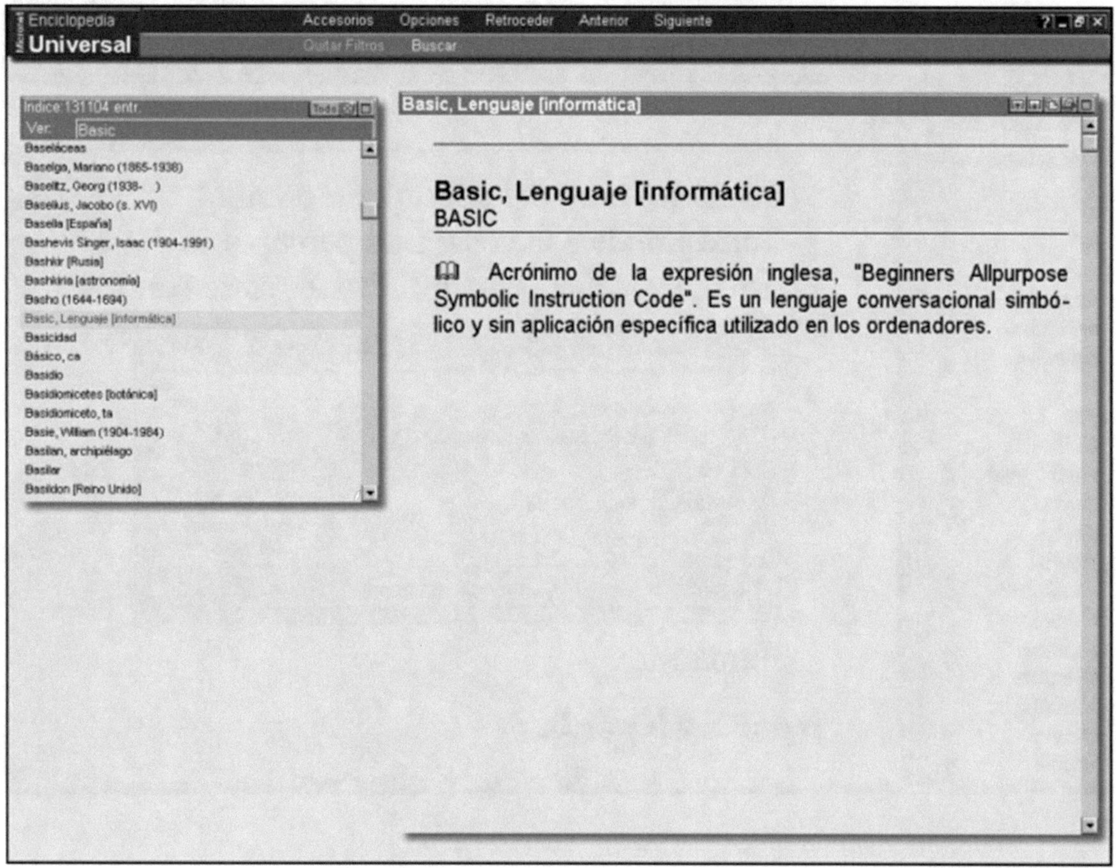

level rises it is simpler from a programming point of view but they are less efficient from the perspective of their execution, for example.

Through these first programming languages oriented to education and some of its commands, it has been possible to verify the existence of laws or common agreements reached in the combination of the signs, which intervene in the production of complex expressions, such as a mathematical formula within a program, and which are called: "training rules" in science and its research method. Rules that have served as the basis for the growth of the software industry since the mid-20th century (Harper, 2016). Currently the main programming languages, in alphabetical order are:

- C,
- C ++,
- C#,
- Java,
- JavaScript,

Figure 17. The D.R.A.E. off-line multimedia system is an excellent example of access to information in off-line databases, with cutting-edge functions in queries –distinguish upper / lower case, differentiate between formats: bold, italic, rounded, etc.

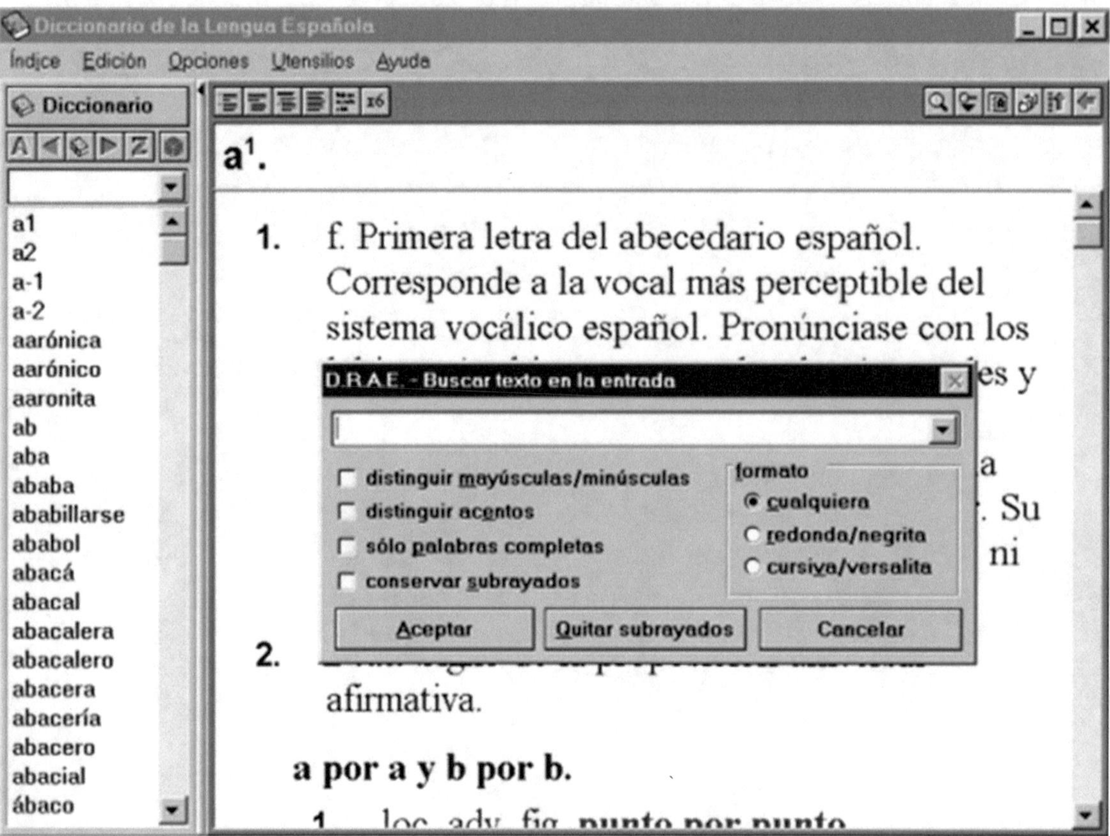

- PHP,
- Python,
- SQL,
- SWIFT, and
- Visual Basic .NET.

When faced with the rhetorical question: What is the best of them all? Here, it is necessary to present in response a couple of rhetorical questions, such as:

- In which context will they be applied?
- What are the internal and external characteristics of each of the programming languages?

The last question establishes an indirect relationship with the internal and external factors of software engineering, if we consider it metaphorically as a kind of island that emerges from the ocean and where each element of the context influences it –temporal and geographical, as can be seen in figure 19.

Figure 18. The online version of D.R.A.E. has not an access to information that analyze upper / lower case, divide between formats: bold, italic, rounded, etc.

The internal characteristics are directly related to the work that the programmer has to carry out, regardless of the operating system, compiler, hardware, etc. That is, the constitutional quality of the language, derived from its architecture or the way in which it is structured, and the syntax. Many notions are intrinsic to linguistics, semiotics or semiology, etc., since we are considering natural languages and their transfer to programming languages (Pressman & Maxim, 2015; Valiron, 2015; Sommerville, 2016; Sebesta, 2016; Cipolla-Ficarra, et al., 2012; Cipolla-Ficarra, et al., 2010). Some of the main internal characteristics, alphabetically ordered, and using terminology of greater diffusion nowadays, can be summarized as follows:

- **Simplicity:** It is the facility to write an algorithm and the operations related to them. It can be stated that if the language allows an algorithm to be written with few instructions and as close to scientific language as possible (mathematical, physical, electronic, chemical, etc.), the simplicity index will be high.
- **Learnability:** A programming language has a high level of learnability, when the time used to use it is less, compared to other similar languages. A classic example is BASIC, with its few but precise commands or instructions that indicate what can and cannot be done through its use. BASIC has served to program videogames, in the first 8-bit computers and with wide diffusion at home, such as the C64 (Commodore 64) or CBM 64 (short for its business name, Commodore Business Machines Inc.).
- **Readability:** It is the ability to understand the operation of a program, by reading the source code. This requires from the programmer an excellent ability to structure and explain with precise comments each of the sections that make up the program. In other words, the less time it takes to understand the intrinsic logical structure, the greater the readability.
- **Robusticity:** It is an attribute that refers to the prevention of errors in programming, through the type and control of the data that may contain its variables, and the rigidity of the syntax to avoid

Figure 19. A representative island of quality in software engineering in the 21st century. In the graphic representation are internal and external factors of the software (methods of access to the database, metaphor used in the interface, etc.), temporal and geographical contexts (it is not the same to evaluate the speed of access to the media dynamics of the off-line supports of the 20th century, than the current ones on-line, as well as the possible problems derived from Internet connections in a rural area rather than in a large city). Furthermore, like all of them, they are directly and indirectly under the influence of the G Factor (G = Garduña)

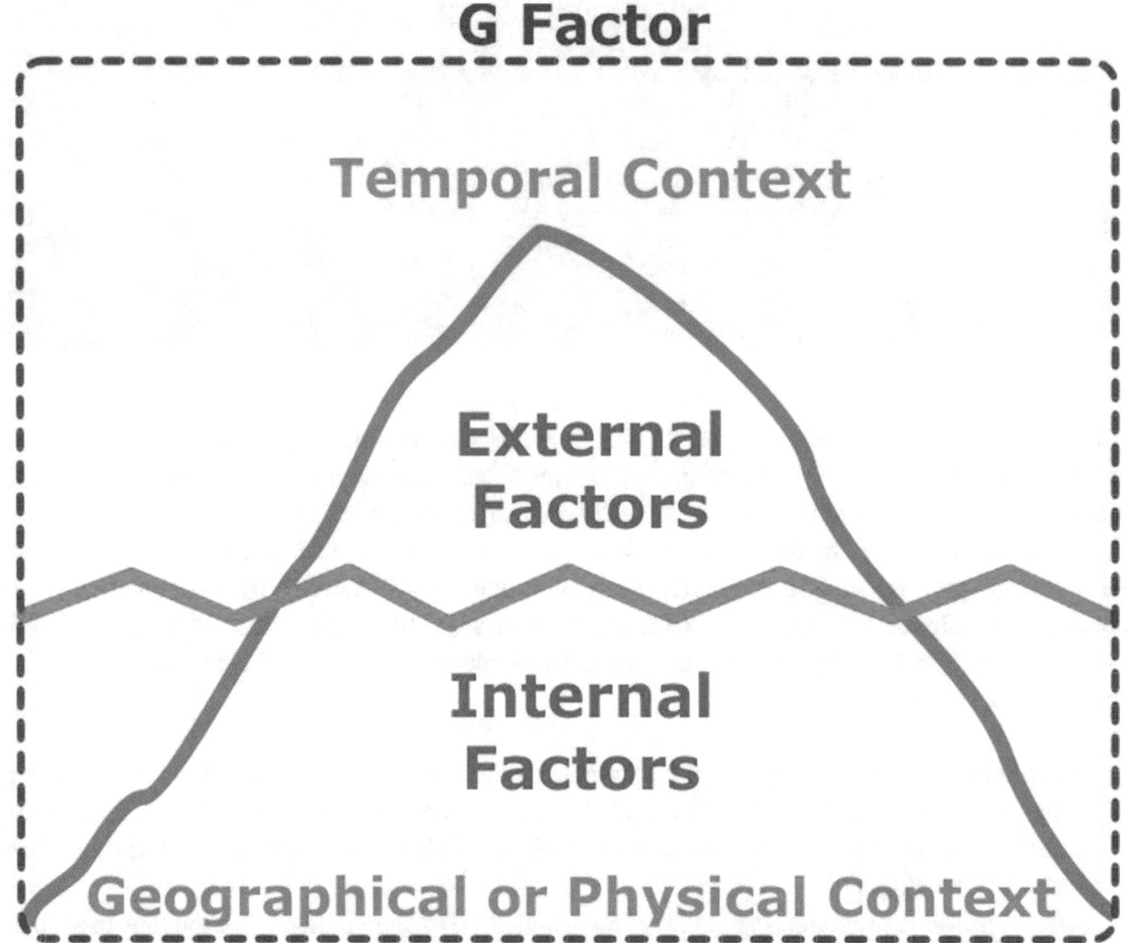

errors at the time of program execution, related to memory use, recording the results of operations in files, etc. In work practice, programmers usually find greater robustness in COBOL and Pascal than in C or ASM (Assembly). The latter, also called symbolic machine code, that is, it works at a more hardware and / or operating system level, using pointers. A program carried out efficiently using the ASM language can be faster and use fewer system resources, such as RAM, compared to a similar program but compiled from a high-level language.

- **Modularity:** It is the ability to decompose a complex system. It is one of the main features of object-oriented programming, and it consists of dividing a program into modules that can be compiled separately, although it maintains interconnections with other modules. The same can be accomplished outside of object programming through the use of applets (subprograms) that use subroutines, procedures, functions, etc. In other words, the structure of the program is divided into modules to streamline updating tasks, error detection, among others.

- **Flexibility:** It is detectable in those programming languages where it is feasible to adapt it to new commands or operators, such as Java. In other words, in most modern programming languages, from object-oriented programming. Another example is in the evolution of C, that is, C ++.
- **Universability:** Perhaps, it is the most important quality attribute within this group, since it denotes the ability of language to adapt to new requirements, which ranges from the adaptation of algorithms to the syntax of mathematical logical operators, for example. The C language and its evolution has been a valid example, since it has demonstrated its universality over time, from programs aimed at controlling peripherals connected to computers or servers, to graphic computing or 3D printing.
- **Productivity:** It is the qualitative analysis of the temporal equation in the best use of all the devices that are accessed from the program, such as the time in the execution of said devices. Generally, when there is programmer excellence, low-level programs (for example, Assembly, since it operates with instructions that control each bit of the CPU - Central Processing Unit) are faster than high-level programs, for example, the SQL, dBase, Pascal, among others. We refer to the excellence of the programmer, such as can be their training or work experience because although these programs work at the hardware level, it is necessary to have a special development skill, in the shortest possible time and with few errors, in the definitive version of the programs.
- **Intelligibility:** It is resorting to a set of basic and uniform strategies that remain constant, in each of its parts, establishing a kind of isotopies, which generate in the programmer a kind of empathy towards the overall functionality of the program. Therefore, they facilitate learning and eventual detection of errors or failures, since knowing some fundamental principles, said principles will be similar and / or will be repeated in the various sections that make up the program.

This is a first group of internal factors, where some of the quality attributes play an important role in the quality of the software, applied to other areas of computing, such as computer animations, for example. Where simplicity and universability are two of the four key elements for the success of a 3D animation, aimed at all humanity, along with originality and humor (Cipolla-Ficarra, 2014). Consequently, it is verified how the quality is transversal, in the software industry, having the human being, in this case the programmer, as the central axis. Obviously, that together with all these qualitative attributes of language, it is necessary to consider the technological context in which they work, that is, the hardware. Being understood as such, from personal computers, tablet PCs, smartphones, etc., down to the servers in universities, 3D printers in building construction companies, robots in industry, etc. Therefore, these hardware elements must also be considered when writing a program.

The Importance of External Factors in Quality

At the design stage of a new system, the team of developers, generally made up mainly of computer engineers, systems analysts, and programmers, must evaluate and weigh each of the pros and cons of the programming languages that they will use, depending on the type of programs, interfaces, databases, etc. that make up the system to be generated (Basili, et al., 2018; Pressman & Maxim, 2015; Sommerville, 2016; Sebesta, 2016; Cipolla-Ficarra, et al., 2012; Westfall, 2010; Basili & Musa, 1991). In addition, programming languages must be easily understood by the professionals in the sector, so that they can be quickly and efficiently modified later, if there are new requirements. The set of qualitative attributes that affect the final product, in the software industry, are called external factors, which we briefly describe, in alphabetical order:

- **Globality:** It is that group of programming languages that have a wide acceptance by the computer community worldwide. This globalization will depend on the new hardware requirements, at a certain moment in time and those that are maintained through the years. That is, in the set of programming languages, which have expanded in the community of programmers, you can have a synchronous, diachronic, and "symbionic" vision. The latter is the combination of the previous two, with languages that go back decades and are still in force today, as in the case of C. Now, with greater expansion or globalization, there is a greater number of libraries available to programmers, manuals and online courses for learning, forum for discussing eventual problems and their solutions, etc., and vice versa. This criterion has been one of the bases of open-source software (OSS), since the democratization of the Internet in 1990.
- **Compatibility:** It is one of the special characteristics that exists in the OSS. In commercial languages, there is a tendency to generate variables so that the language is better adapted to certain projects, since the number of formulas that can be found in a program for quality control in a chemical laboratory is not the same as in control of the inventory of the components stored in an industrial plant of automobiles. This entails that the programmers tend to generate a kind of dialects within the main language. One way to avoid this phenomenon is the ISO (International Organization for Standardization, based in Geneva - Switzerland) and ANSI (American National Standards Institute, whose headquarters are in Washington - USA). Both international organizations are non-profit, and establish norms, rules, common models, etc., standardized and global in scope.
- **Adaptability:** It is the possibility of reusing sections of previously written programs that work without problems, such as the printing routines of lists, elaboration of interfaces, etc., in other languages or not, within new programs of greater dimension, resorting in some cases to language converters. Obviously, this adaptability to the reusability of the code previously implies that this option, from the syntactic point of view such as semantics, is present in the most recent versions of the programming language where the source code emigration will take place.
- **Transportability:** It is when a program works immediately from the operating system and the used hardware. That is, it is independent of the platform. Such advantages exist in the C or the Delphi. For example, the Delphi language has allowed for decades the simulation of fabrics on computer screens and their corresponding color printers. Portability depends on the degree of globalization or standardization of the language.

Each of these notions can be expanded or redefined over time, adjusting to the new needs of end users of interactive systems, current or future. That conversion is related to natural linguistic evolution, through time. However, under the label of creativity, innovation, digital entrepreneurship, etc., there is a tendency to use each of the synonyms that indicate quality, and use them for commercial purposes in the global village and by western private or religious education.

This contemporary reality is affecting the precision that boosts quality, in the workplace context of the software industry, although this also happens in the social sciences, for example, with the term *empathy*.

One of the fundamental words in the human communication process of the 20th century. Now it is used in a trivial way in the social networks and in scientific communication, becoming a kind of new aura of the human being and a fundamental quality attribute, ranging from artificial intelligence, applied to robotics at home and in public spaces, even politics.

Deviations in Software Quality

The origin of these deviations is to be found in the interactive design within the human-computer interaction and / or user experience, which are governed by the top of the pyramid in figure 19. They not only aim at controlling the design and use of the interactive systems, but also their contents. That is, making emotional design and the cognitive system the great set of domination, where the UX is a subset. It would include the subset of the HCI. In short, an illogical situation in the era of the expansion of communicability.

Consequently, the HCI has lost its exact limits as a discipline and has become a great container for diverse professionals, who work with loose notions among themselves, as happened with usability engineering in the 1990s and the beginning of the new millennium. This phenomenon of inaccuracy also expands into what is called user experience.

These are the consequences when the programming languages are not studied by certain self-appointed experts, within the global computing context, which can have high indexes in h-index (Hirsch index) and / or i10-index (publications cited by at least 10 sources). Both indices do not reflect the individual and autonomous computer reality of the person who is being quantified by their research references, nor the group strategies followed in the field of ITCs, to increase said value fraudulently and in such a short period of time.

Therefore, it is a very easy value to manipulate in ICTs publications related to: software engineering, web engineering, usability engineering, human-computer interaction, embodied interaction, information retrieval, graphical user interface, recommended systems, education, and a long etcetera, and they also stray away from human reality.

In an endless number of cases, these Google indices and other scientific databases point to an anomalous situation, since even the automatons equipped with the best artificial intelligence programs cannot reach them even if they are working 24 hours a day, throughout each of the days of the week. Therefore, today, it is not a reliable value.

In addition, quantifying the quality of the software through these indices is wrong because the human factor is present, which transforms behaviors or behaviors to achieve certain results, as occurs with the G factor (G = Garduña), in the educational-scientific-productive fields (Cipolla-Ficarra, 2010).

From a mercantile education point of view (read private, public, and hybrid universities, governed directly or indirectly by religious-business groups), advertising campaigns on social media and in the traditional media promote the study of programming, based on a set of slogans and sterile clichés, whose contents are devoid of truthfulness, on the perimeter of honesty. Using the rhetoric of persuasion and argumentation. Some examples are:

- Why should you study advanced programming in our modern R&D labs?
- Did you know that studying programming with us can ensure you a job forever and a profitable salary?

- Would you quickly occupy a privileged place in the organization's structure that would allow you to travel around the world for free?
- Could you use and experience the latest technological innovations at no cost?
- Would you have the opportunity to activate your own spin off or startup, without business risks?
- Can you maintain a high level of consumerism in your family and friends without major problems?

These are some questions from the pseudo experts in innovation and digital entrepreneurship in many university study institutions, whose common denominator can be summarized in two acronyms: HCI and UX. In short, they are in command, and the rest of the people are mere apprentices to operators, with poor working conditions, compared to part-time jobs, such as IBM card punching, in the '80s.

It is evident that the collaboration in social networks, the design of web pages, the programming of the apps, the security in the multimedia mobile telephony, the improvement of the mixed reality, the optimization of the telecommunications in the videoconferences, the development of tools for cloud computing, the application of robotics in the industry, the development of applications for quantum computing, among others (Appuswamy, et al., 2019; Basili, et al., 2018; Chang, 2018; Valiron, et al., 2015; Stubbs & Hinds, 2007), are topics that attract the attention of potential programmers, system analysts, software engineers, etc., of the new generations (Walrad, 2017; Koutroumpis, Leiponen & Thomas, 2017; Zyda, 2009; Selfridge, 2006). They seek or pursue the possibility of continuous technical and professional growth. However, the constant inclusion of quality and the exclusion of obsolete cliches and persuasive communication are necessary, as can be seen in the table 1.

Lessons Learned

In the diagram of figure 20, lessons learned can be verified in the set of elements that directly and indirectly influence the quality of software, oriented towards innovation.

The dotted lines in orange represent positive internal and external factors to the development of qualitative and innovative software. The same type of dotted lines but in light blue those coming from the context / temporal or geographical factors. In some cases, these factors can favor or slow down this development, depending on the endogenous and exogenous circumstances of the context and which are related to the natural evolutionary process of an R&D project, in software, for example. Also, with dotted lines but in gray, is the hardware and everything related to technological aspects, which are usually ahead of the evolution or revolution of software.

Instead, the solid red line coming from human and social factors should be avoided because they represent negative elements. In purple, another continuous line that refers to the G factor, that is, the absolute destruction of quality in innovation oriented software development, nowadays.

Finally, the central green line with dots and dashes indicates that each of these factors are interrelated, enhancing or weakening the quality of software and innovation in the 21st century.

From the observation and examination of the graph it is easy to see how human and social factors play a fundamental role in the evolution of software and in the technological revolution, beginning with hardware.

Quality disappears in the face of savage commercialism and educational narcissism in the computing of the new millennium, for example. The natural process of learning in the programming languages of the 20th century, and all the mental skills that programmers developed, have disappeared in our day, beginning with logic programming, mathematics, and low-level language learning.

Table 1. Didactic mirage versus professional reality of the software

Persuasive Mirage in Education	Reality in the Software Industry
Being at the forefront of technology	In many institutions, the renewal of hardware / software is slow, after the world financial crisis, in the first decade of the 21st century. There are laboratories, centers, departments, etc., in universities that do not pay their software licenses, for example. This has boosted the rise of open software.
Periodically participate in updating courses on software and hardware news.	This possibility will depend on the size of the organization, the type of structure, the policies of the managers and / or the staff department, among other variables.
Enhancing creativity, thanks to the inclusion and development of the own initiatives.	Sometimes, negative human factors outweigh positive ones, within the computer science workgroup, thus preventing the incorporation of your own ideas or improvements in developing systems, current procedures, techniques and methodologies of quality control, etc.
Working as a freelance in ICT	When a programmer, analyst, computer engineer, etc. works as a freelance, it means a loss of status to the work that is done. In addition, it reliably indicates the equivalence of designing interfaces, creating web pages, writing programs, verifying the correct operation of the system, etc., to the tasks of writing an article, taking photographs, etc., for a newspaper or magazine.
Developing applications remotely	It is the most recurring strategy to hire cheap labor, outside the industrialized states. That is, the projects are signed and financed in developed countries, while the executors of the project (read programmers, analysts, engineers, etc.) are located in nations, in the process of economic development.
Independently select specialization topics, for example: apps, enhanced reality, big data, 3D printers, IoT, networks, servers, robotics, video games, etc.	Each of the "fashionable" subjects requires time for specialization, due to constant changes in hardware and software. In addition, if the computer scientist is within a stable work structure, he or she has already been assigned his/her duties and specific topics, which is why they receive a salary.
Periodically increasing salary	Currently, in large computer companies, those who are dedicated to sales, marketing, human resource management, have better salaries than programming, for example. Only with the G factor, in the universities of southern Europe, the salary increases dramatically, through extracurricular activities and without teaching, but which are highly profitable and allow you to achieve a life-long job.
Activating a personal company	In many large international companies, it is considered an unfair and unethical practice. So much so, that in some legislations it is prohibited to use public structures for the own mercantile purposes. However, it is the common denominator in southern Europe to open a spin off or startup, having free programmers available or at very low cost (students).

However, there are cases in which the use of language escapes any logic, within the academic and computer context, such as when evaluating papers for national and international events, for example. Some members of the evaluation committees, with a high presence on the social networks but with a lack of knowledge of the topics to be evaluated, often resort to language as an unfortunate solution to reject research, experimentation, etc., through control of semantic, syntactic, typographical, etc. errors, and without giving them opportunities for further revision.

Sometimes they are works that are very valid from a scientific point of view but have not been considered for their other implicit qualities, such as: *innovation*, *novelty*, *originality*, *pertinence*, *relevance*, and *transcendence*. The semiotic examinations of the motivations of the evaluators' rejection denote the presence of the young heirs of the traditional pressure groups or parochialism in the sciences, whose purpose is not only to discourage future computer professionals, but also to reduce potential job competitors, within the field of the new technologies.

Currently, graduates and doctors in mathematics, physics, chemistry, and many other formal science disciplines, instead of collaborating in innovative and creative development within quantum computing, nanotechnology, bioinformatics, robotics, cybersecurity, etc., are dedicated to tasks outside their areas of knowledge and with non-demanding users of high reliability and high interactive quality, such as: children, the elderly, blind, deaf, dumb, autistic, down syndrome, dysleptics, and a long etc. of disabilities, handicaps and diseases. All this related to software engineering from interface design, HCI, and UX.

They also cover other banal or low intellectual effort topics, for example: the introduction to computer science for beginners, didactics and special education, including technology and education, programming of pages in HTML, teaching of Excel, Word, etc. The ultimate goal of these individuals is to obtain, in the shortest possible time, the maximum visibility online, within online search engines, such as Google, Yahoo, etc.

Also, that low intellectual profile allows them to constantly publish in closed circles of their international friends, to see the h-index increase, the references in Google Scholar, etc., together with frivolous reviews in the applications of social networks (Facebook, Instagram, LinkedIn, Twitter, etc.) and added to other techniques and strategies of the G factor. This is a reality already described at the bottom of figure 20, which negatively influences the invisible high-quality factors.

Therefore, it has to be eradicated immediately, to avoid demotivation and the permanent lack of programmers and computer professionals, with a qualitative, reliable and truthful experience in the various languages, applications and systems. In short, it is necessary to return to achieving a high professional and ethical profile (aseptic of religions or corruptions), for current and future challenges, within the framework of communication and information technologies, interrelated with the common well-being of the population, like those existing at the beginning of the democratization of computing and internet use, in the 20th century.

CONCLUSION

Through the conceptual exploration of language and communicability, it has been verified how there are classic and modern factors that influence the qualitative results of the software industry. A software industry that together with that of hardware, in the 21st century and for mercantilist reasons, are unable to establish a generational technological bridge, with creative and innovative content, stored on a variegated wide range of supports and platforms. For example, in the context of medicine in highly industrialized countries, many radiographs, scanners, computed tomography scans, etc. still use the CD or DVD format to store digital images, although these readers are no longer incorporated into computers.

Consequently, users are forced to buy these information access devices as an external peripheral to them, that is, as if it were a printer, scanner, microphone, speakers, etc. All this constitutes an example of technological involution since the patient continues to have the right to see his images.

In this race to change the digital support on the various platforms, the human being gradually loses the wealth of natural language, whether spoken and / or written. This is one of the reasons why high-level programming languages are also becoming a kind of low-level language, if the Internet is not used, to clarify the relationships between meaning and signifier, in an endless number of terms of daily use.

Just as language is a natural process, in the studies of linguistics and semiotics, the same should happen in the learning of programming languages by new generations. Within the components of human language, the boundaries between phonology, semantics, morphology, syntax and pragmatics remain well

Figure 20. The dotted lines whose colors are orange, blue and gray are positive and bidirectional, while the solid lines in red and violet, are negative, unidirectional, and should be eliminated quickly in engineering projects of software, informatics, systems, web, and all its derivations. The dotted and dashed line in green, originated under the heading "software quality and innovation" indicates that there is an interrelation between each of the factors

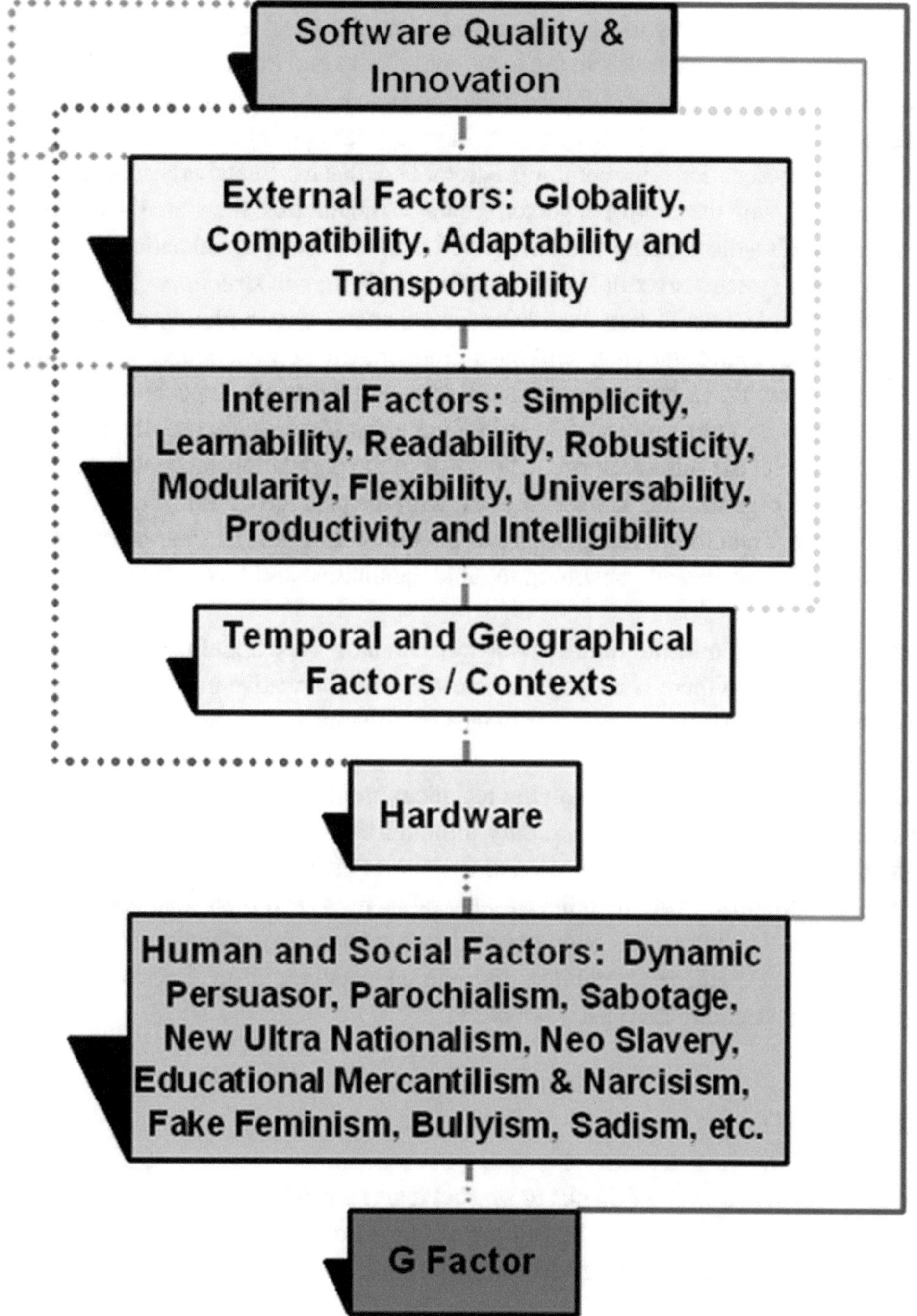

defined. In programming languages, syntax rules must be respected to avoid multiple errors in compilation and to speed up the correct operation of the various applications that make up the system, for example.

The establishment of these rules must be studied and shared by the agents who intervene in the qualitative process from the production of technological devices to communication and interaction between users. It is a dynamic process that requires constant precision and accuracy. These two qualities, among other qualitative attributes of interactive design, narrow the gap between software evolution and hardware revolution. It is also an effective way to cut costs in spreading the latest technological breakthroughs, among the widest range of potential users, in the local community and in the global village.

Innovation, the *qualitative factors of software and of the human being* is not something that can be bought in a study center or is inherited due to questions of social status. It is the result of a long procedure. The cost-quality-reliability equation is the common denominator that has linked each milestone in the history of computing. Today, with the control of personal data on the Internet, there are those who maintain that we are moving towards a dictatorship of data, derived from the use of social networks. Others argue that changes in computer systems are still faster than *changes in human structures*. When we speak of people, we refer directly to human factors. People or system users, who implicitly or explicitly tend to resist change. This change implies studying, thinking and adapting to new challenges derived from ICTs.

Consequently, they slow down the progress of software and hardware, especially in those private structures (read, religious, in Latin culture). These hierarchical structures are usually exempt from the respect and compliance with the rules or norms, of the rest of the population, since they occupy a superior position in the social organization. Universally and with the passage of time, human roles in these structures are immutable. Therefore, these groups can interact with a host of state-of-the-art computer systems, but the human factor prevents obtaining reliable, qualitative and low-cost services from these structures.

Despite these two observations, the future of software remains very hopeful, from the point of research and development, when there is an original, creative and innovative context. In this context, it is necessary that the high-level programming languages be combined with the low-level languages, in order to have real computer experts again.

In a few words, *new experts* capable of solving technical problems (software and hardware), in an autonomous way, and *specialized in communicability*, although they do not have high university degrees. For example, the hardware of the latest generation smartphones gives enormous potential for the functionalities that can be developed from the point of view of software and the social context. Therefore, it is necessary to recover the skills of autonomous and independent programming from the 1980s, to take full advantage of mini computers, mobiles, and interconnected with the network, generating an invulnerable and resistant structure for quality software.

ACKNOWLEDGMENT

We should also like to extend a word of thanks to Maria Ficarra and Miguel C. Ficarra. Besides, a special acknowledgements to Alicia Ruiz, Amélie Bordeaux, Doris Edison, Jacqueline Alma, Luisa Varela, Mary Brie, Pamela Fulton, Silvia Fernández Moreno, Jim Carré, Donald Nilson, Roberta, Riccardo and Carlos for the valuable collaboration.

REFERENCES

Allu, Y., Douglis, F., Kamat, M., Shilane, P., Patterson, H., & Zhu, B. (2017). Backup to the Future: How Workload and Hardware Changes Continually Redefine Data Domain File Systems. *IEEE Computer*, *50*(7), 64–72. doi:10.1109/MC.2017.187

Appuswamy, R., Graefe, G., Borovica-Gajic, R., & Ailamaki, A. (2019). The Five-Minute Rule 30 Years Later and Its Impact on the Storage Hierarchy. *Communications of the ACM*, *82*(11), 114–120. doi:10.1145/3318163

Baker, W. H., & Fallace, L. (2007). Is Information Security Under Control? Investigating Quality in Information Security Management. *IEEE Security and Privacy*, *5*(1), 36–44. doi:10.1109/MSP.2007.11

Basili, V. R., Briand, L., Bianculli, D., Nejati, S., Pastore, F., & Sabetzadeh, M. (2018). Software Engineering Research and Industry: A Symbiotic Relationship to Foster Impact. *IEEE Software*, *35*(5), 44–49. doi:10.1109/MS.2018.290110216

Basili, V. R., & Musa, J. D. (1991). The Future Engineering of Software: A Management Perspective. *IEEE Computer*, *24*(9), 90–96. doi:10.1109/2.84903

Bergin, T. J., & Gibson, R. G. (1996). *History of Programming Languages*. ACM Press. doi:10.1145/234286

Berk, A. (1985). *LISP: Language of Artificial Intelligence*. Cengage Learning publisher.

Book-that-Work. (1996). *CD-Rom Garden Encyclopedia*. Bellevue: Book That *Work*.

Bouissac, P. (1998). *Encyclopedia of Semiotics*. Oxford University Press.

Bunge, M. (1981). *The science: your method and your philosophy*. Siglo XXI.

Chang, S. (2018). *Frontiers of Multimedia Research*. ACM and Morgan & Claypool.

Cipolla-Ficarra, F. (2010). *Advances in Dynamic and Static Media for Interactive Systems: Communicability, Computer Science and Design*. Blue Herons.

Cipolla-Ficarra, F. (2010a). *Persuasion On-Line and Communicability: The Destruction of Credibility in the Virtual Community and Cognitive Models*. Nova Science.

Cipolla-Ficarra, F. (2010b). *Quality and Communicability for Interactive Hypermedia Systems: Concepts and Practices for Design*. IGI Global. doi:10.4018/978-1-61520-763-3

Cipolla-Ficarra, F. (2012). *New Horizons in Creative Open Software, Multimedia, Human Factors and Software Engineering*. Blue Herons.

Cipolla-Ficarra, F. (2014). *Handbook of Research on Interactive Information Quality in Expanding Social Network Communications*. IGI Global.

Cipolla-Ficarra, F. (2017). *Technology-Enhanced Human Interaction in Modern Society*. IGI Global.

Classe, A. (1957). The whistled language of La Gomera. *Scientific American*, *196*(4), 111–124. doi:10.1038cientificamerican0457-111

Cline, E. (2011). *Ready Player One*. Crown Publishing Group.

Cobley, P., & Jancz, L. (1999). Introducing Semiotics. Crows Nest: Allen & Unwin Pty.

Crocker, S. D. (2019). The Arpanet and Its Impact on the State of Networking. *IEEE Computer*, *52*(10), 14–23. doi:10.1109/MC.2019.2931601

De Saussure, F. (2011). *Course in General Linguistics*. Columbia University Press.

Deledalle, G. (2001). *Charles S. Peirce's Philosophy of Signs: Essays in Comparative Semiotics*. Indiana University Press.

Dorling-Kindersley & Zeta. (1998). *CD-Rom Enciclopedia de la Ciencia*. Dorling Kindersley-Zeta.

Eco, U. (1979). *Theory of Semiotics*. Indiana University Press.

Egyed, A., Zeman, K., Hehenberger, P., & Demuth, A. (2018). Maintaining Consistency Across Engineering Artifacts. *IEEE Computer*, *51*(2), 28–35. doi:10.1109/MC.2018.1451666

Espasa-Calpe. (1998). *CD-Rom Diccionario de la Lengua Española*. Espasa-Calpe.

Fenton, N. (1994). Software Measurement: A Necessary Scientific Basis. *IEEE Transactions on Software Engineering*, *20*(3), 199–206. doi:10.1109/32.268921

Godbolt, M. (2020). Optimizations in C++ Compilers. *Communications of the ACM*, *63*(2), 41–49. doi:10.1145/3369754

Gregory, S. (2019). Requirements Engineering: The Quest for Meaningful Metrics: Time for a Change? *IEEE Software*, *36*(6), 7–11. doi:10.1109/MS.2019.2933685

Harper, R. (2016). *Practical Foundations for Programming Languages*. Cambridge University Press. doi:10.1017/CBO9781316576892

Hoftman, R., Marx, M., & Hancock, P. (2008). Metrics, Metrics, Metrics: Negative Hedonicity. *IEEE Intelligent Systems*, *23*(2), 69–73. doi:10.1109/MIS.2008.31

Holdcroft, D. (1991). *Saussure: Signs, System and Arbitrariness*. Cambridge University Press. doi:10.1017/CBO9780511624599

Ito, M. (2009). *Engineering Play: A Cultural History of Children's Software*. The MIT Press. doi:10.7551/mitpress/7939.001.0001

Jackson, M. (2006). What Can We Expect from Program Verification? *IEEE Computer*, *39*(10), 65–71. doi:10.1109/MC.2006.363

Jirotka, M., Grimpe, B., Stahl, B., Eden, G., & Hartswood, M. (2017). Responsible Research and Innovation in the Digital Age. *Communications of the ACM*, *60*(5), 62–68. doi:10.1145/3064940

Kanetkar, Y., & Kanetkar, A. (2020). *Let Us Python Solutions*. BPB Publications.

Kaptelinin, V., & Czerwinski, M. (2007). *Beyond the Desktop Metaphor: Designing Integrated Digital Work Environments*. The MIT Press. doi:10.7551/mitpress/1584.001.0001

Kit, E. (1995). *Software Testing in the Real World: Improving the Process*. ACM Press & Addison-Wesley.

Koutroumpis, P., Leiponen, A., & Thomas, L. (2017). How Important is IT? *Communications of the ACM, 60*(7), 62–68. doi:10.1145/3019940

Kramer, K., Dedrick, J., & Sharma, P. (2009). One Laptop Per Child: Vision vs. Reality. *Communications of the ACM, 52*(6), 66–73. doi:10.1145/1516046.1516063

Lee, Y. (2009). *Journey to Data Quality*. The MIT Press.

Lorenzo, M. J. (2017). *Endless Loop: The History of the BASIC Programming Language (Beginner's All-purpose Symbolic Instruction Code)*. SE Books.

McLuhan, M., & Powers, B. (1989). *The Global Village: Transformations in World Life and Media in the 21st Century*. Oxford University Press.

Meyer, J. (2008). Typology and acoustic strategies of whistled languages: Phonetic comparison and perceptual cues of whistled vowels. *Journal of the International Phonetic Association, 38*(1), 69–94. doi:10.1017/S0025100308003277

Micronet. (2004). *CD-Rom Enciclopedia Universal*. Madrid: Micronet.

Nelson, T. (1993). *Literary Machines*. Mindful Press.

Nielsen, J., & Mack, R. (1994). *Usability Inspection Methods*. Willey. doi:10.1145/259963.260531

Nöth, W. (1995). *Handbook of Semiotics*. Indiana University Press.

Papert, S. (1993). *Mindstorms Children Computers and Powerful Ideas*. Basic Books.

Poe, M. (2010). *History of Communication Media & Society from the Evolution of Speech to the Internet*. Cambridge University Press. doi:10.1017/CBO9780511976919

Pressman, R., & Maxim, B. (2015). *Software Engineering: A Practitioner's Approach*. McGraw Hill Education.

Sebesta, R. (2016). *Concepts of Programming Languages*. Pearson Education.

Seemiller, C., & Grace, M. (2018). *Generation Z: A Century in the Making*. Routledge. doi:10.4324/9780429442476

Selfridge, O. (2006). Learning and Education: A Continuing Frontier for AI. *IEEE Intelligent Systems, 21*(3), 16–23. doi:10.1109/MIS.2006.54

Shannon, C. E., & Weaver, W. (1963). *Mathematical Theory of Communication*. University of Illinois Press.

Sommerville, I. (2016). *Software Engineering*. Pearson Education.

Stubbs, K., Hinds, P., & Wettergreen, D. (2007). Autonomy and Common Ground in Human-Robot Interaction: A Field Study. *IEEE Intelligent Systems, 22*(2), 42–50. doi:10.1109/MIS.2007.21

Valiron, B., Ross, N. J., Selinger, P., Alexander, D. S., & Smith, J. M. (2015). Programming the Quantum Future. *Communications of the ACM*, *58*(8), 52–61. doi:10.1145/2699415

Walrad, C. (2017). Standards for the Enterprise IT Profession. *IEEE Computer*, *50*(3), 70–73. doi:10.1109/MC.2017.68

Westfall, L. (2010). *The Certified Software Quality Engineer Handbook*. Quality Press.

Xu, W. (2019). Toward Human-Centered AI: A Perspective from Human-Computer Interaction. *Interaction*, *26*(4), 42–46. doi:10.1145/3328485

Zanichelli. (1997). *CD-Rom Enciclopedia Zanichelli.* Bologna: Zanichelli.

Zhuge, H. (2015). The Future Interconnection Environment. *IEEE Computer*, *38*(4), 27–33. doi:10.1109/MC.2005.142

Zyda, M. (2009). Computer Science in the Conceptual Age. *Communications of the ACM*, *52*(12), 66–72. doi:10.1145/1610252.1610272

ADDITIONAL READING

Ananthanarayan, S., & Boll, S. (2020). Physical Computing for Children: Shifting the Pendulum Back to Papertian Ideals. *Interaction*, *27*(3), 40–45. doi:10.1145/3386235

Bal, H., & Grune, D. (1994). *Programming Language Essentials*. Addison-Wesley.

Botto, F. (1992). *Multimedia, CD-ROM & Compatc Disc*. Sigma Press.

Bruderer, H. (2017). Computing History Beyond the U.K. and U.S.: Selected Landmarks from Continental Europe. *Communications of the ACM*, *60*(2), 76–84. doi:10.1145/2959085

Dunn, R. (1990). *Software Quality: Concepts and Plans*. Prentice Hall.

Eco, U. (1986). *Semiotics and the Philosophy of Language*. Indiana University Press.

Fenton, N. (1991). *Software Metrics: A Rigorous Approach*. Chapman & Hall.

Harel, D. (2008). Can Programming Be Liberated, Period? *IEEE Computer*, *41*(1), 28–37. doi:10.1109/MC.2008.10

Jagadish, H., Gehrke, J., Labrinidis, A., Papakonstantinou, Y., Patel, J. M., Ramakrishnan, R., & Shahabi, C. (2014). Big Data and Its Technical Chanllenges. *Communications of the ACM*, *57*(7), 86–94. doi:10.1145/2611567

Lanigan, R. (1991). *Speaking and Semiology*. Walter de Gruyter. doi:10.1515/9783110877113

Leigh, J., & Brown, M. (2008). Cyber-Commons: Merging Real and Virtual Worlds. *Communications of the ACM*, *51*(1), 82–85. doi:10.1145/1327452.1327488

Mehlenbacher, B. (2010). *Instruction and Technology: Designs for Everday Learning*. The MIT Press. doi:10.7551/mitpress/9780262013949.001.0001

Moore, R. J., & Arar, R. (2019). *Conversational UX Design: A Practitioner's Guide to the Natural Conversation Framework*. ACM. doi:10.1145/3304087

Pierce, B. (2005). *Advanced Topics in Types and Programming Languages*. The MIT Press.

Quizon, N. (2010). Social Change: Women, Networks, and Technology. *Interaction*, *17*(1), 36–39. doi:10.1145/1649475.1649484

Radley, A. S. (2015). *Self As Computer: Blueprints*. Visions and Dreams of Technopia. doi:10.4018/978-1-4666-7377-9.ch011

Sebeok, T. (2001). *Global Semiotics*. Indiana University Press.

Steels, L. (2006). Semiotic Dynamics Embodied Agents. *IEEE Intelligent Systems*, *21*(3), 32–38. doi:10.1109/MIS.2006.58

Thibault, P. (1996). *Re-reading Saussure: The Dynamics of Signs in Social Life*. Routledge.

Thomas, J. C., Lee, A., & Danis, C. (2002). Enhancing Creative Design via Software Tools. *Communications of the ACM*, *45*(10), 112–115. doi:10.1145/570907.570944

Veltman, K. H. (2014). *Alphabets of Life*. Virtual Maastricht McLuhan Institute.

Zahran, M. (2019). *Heterogeneous Computing: Hardware and Software Perspectives*. ACM. doi:10.1145/3281649

KEY TERMS & DEFINITIONS

Innovation: It is something that generates breakthroughs, based on human or technological action (for example, through artificial intelligence), based on pre-existing objects or knowledge. These developments may or may not be tangible, that is, goods or services. The primary purpose is to improve the productivity of goods and services.

Invisible High-Quality Factors: It is the intersection of all the elements that enhance the benefits of interactive systems (software & hardware), based on the internal and external qualitative criteria of programming languages, and with a convergent human factor.

Software Engineering: It is a discipline of formal sciences, related to development methodologies and production processes for the generation of software systems. The equation "quality, reliability and reduced cost" is one of the common denominators that each of the members of this discipline pursue.

Natural Languages: They are those languages born from the interrelationships between human beings, in order to communicate between them, and form a common identity within a certain territory.

Programming Languages: It is a set of commands and instructions, where according to a pre-established syntax, the programmer can write programs, for the execution of tasks, through the computer and the various peripherals connected to it.

Human Factors: It is a broad and diverse group of communicational, linguistic, sociological, psychological, cultural and anthropological components that positively or negatively influence human behavior, in the context of the new technologies and all their derivations.

Creativity: It is the innate or acquired ability of the human being for original invention. That human ability must be differentiated from that derived from artificial intelligence.

Chapter 2
Quality and Web Software Engineering Advances

Francisco V. Cipolla-Ficarra
Latin Association of Human-Computer Interaction, Spain & International Association of Interactive Communication, Italy

Alejandra Quiroga
The University of Sydney, Australia

Miguel Cipolla Ficarra
Latin Association of Human-Computer Interaction, Spain & International Association of Interactive Communication, Italy

ABSTRACT

In this chapter, the main avant-garde components that favor quality on the web are disclosed, especially from the perspectives of software and design. At the same time, the deviations of these components that slow down these processes from the technical-human point of view are presented. In this dualistic perspective, the role of education is included in each of the generations of users, programmers, and publishers of digital content on the web, as well as the context in which they are immersed. A triadic vision of past, present and future is presented in each of the aspects and components, directly and indirectly related, with the development of operations, models, and methods, which converge in obtaining a high quality of the web. Finally, parallels are drawn between the formal science professions and infinite semiosis in web engineering.

INTRODUCTION

In the late 1990s, Tim Berners-Lee and Robert Cailliau developed the bases for the World Wide Web in order to exchange information in the academic-scientific field (Berners-Lee, 1996; Savage, 2017; McCullough, 2018). However, very few predicted that the term web would end up being engineering. Traditionally, the word engineering denotes the action of transforming knowledge into something useful or practical (Hehn, et al., 2020; Cipolla-Ficarra, et al., 2018b). The problem is determining the purpose

DOI: 10.4018/978-1-7998-7010-4.ch002

of that usefulness and who ends up governing or controlling it. In endless inventions it is something observed and verified historically speaking, from the industrial revolution in the 19th century to the present day, with all its effects or consequences, from the social, economic and technological perspective.

A priori, the task of web engineering experts is the use of systematic, organized and quantifiable methodologies for the efficient development of commercial or non-high quality systems or applications on the web (Bagchi, et al., 2020; Schermann, Cito & Leitner, 2018; Pressman & Lowe, 2009; Suh, 2005). Taking into account, in addition, that almost everything that is not found on the web, is practically non-existent for the digital born and online artificial intelligence.

A classic example of this last observation is the evaluations with negative results of the scientific works for the conferences, workshops, symposium, doctoral consortium, demonstrations, posters, etc., when their bibliographic references are not online. These tasks are generally carried out by individuals, whose ages range between 25/30 and 45/50 years, considering them experts in the use of new technologies, but inexperienced in consulting the archived material in real libraries.

Thus, automatically and unfairly, innovation from a huge set of theoretical investigations, results of laboratory experiments, technological prototypes for the interaction between humans and robots, etc., is discarded, because very few bother to consult paper support, in university libraries, public or private. This is a reality that is difficult to overcome in the field of scientific information, since not all human knowledge is digitized and / or has free access on the web. Here is a pending subject for human beings and eventually for artificial intelligence, since currently, people in isolation or in groups (companies, industries, schools, universities, banks, etc.) tend to carry out almost all their activities through the Web.

This new means of communication that boosts the interrelationships between humans and / or automats (Du, Liu & Hu, 2020; Sun, Staab & Kunegis, 2018) has generated, in a large part of the world population, the gradual discarding of traditional communication channels (cinema, television, press, radio, etc.) by the interactive online communication (Reeves & Nass, 1996).

Consequently, from software engineering the need to create new theoretical approaches, following a set of rules, techniques, methods, etc., was raised in a systematic and disciplined manner, although major flaws were already detected from a practical point of view. These failures are mainly due to the existing partial vision to cover the 360° required on the Internet.

The lack of imagination or creativity in the curricula of software engineering has persisted since the end of the 20th century. The same was true of engineering or computer science, systems, electronics, telecommunications, etc. The failed solution was, is and unfortunately will be, to resort to other disciplines of the factual and formal sciences.

When Tim Berners-Lee and Robert Cailliau created the World Wide Web, it was the period when computing was highly interrelated with electronics (1985-1995). Thus, the first electronic documentation systems were developed (Berners-Lee et al.,1991, Barker, 1991; Barker, 1993). Electronic books, natural language processing, databases, were areas of technological knowledge that began to exchange their knowledge. In short, there was a kind of symbiosis between computer engineering and electronic engineering. In a broader sense, software and hardware. So far a logical and practical relationship with the scientific context of that time. However, this relationship has been renewed in the last decade of the 20th century, and includes bioengineering. In other words, it goes towards life sciences or bioscience.

The theoretical purpose of this new horizon was to cover the fields of science studied by living beings, such as humans, animals, and plants, drawing on techniques and concepts from the formal sciences, especially those from mathematics and physics (Oliveira, 2017; Heule & Kullmann, 2017; Cipolla-Ficarra et al., 2018a). Originally, it was intended to find innovative solutions within life science, with the methodological analysis of engineering, in the following triangular relationship: humans, flora and fauna. In practice, these last two were sidelined from the beginning, in numerous centers for academic computing studies in the southern Mediterranean. Very few research centers were devoted to aspects of nature, and tacitly focused on people, through human-computer interaction (HCI). Starting in 1991, the exact limits of the HCI disappeared by the action of mathematicians and physicists, until it became a subset within web engineering.

Some of the topics, disciplines, professions, etc., covered by current web engineering are (Charette & King, 2018; Cipolla-Ficarra et al., 2018b; Pressman & Lowe, 2009; Suh, 2005): business processes for software / applications on the web collaborative software, computer aided software engineering for web, content management system, data models for web information systems, graphic design, human-computer communication, human-computer interaction, hypertext / multimedia / hypermedia engineering, information engineering, information indexing and retrieval, metrics and evaluation methodologies for web, mobile application for web, modeling and simulation, multimedia authoring tools and software, personalization and adaptation of web applications, project management, semantic web, software engineering, software prototyping for web, systems analysis and design, testing and evaluation of web systems and applications, ubiquitous and mobile web applications, usability of web systems, user interface, web accesibility, web content management, web content, web creative, web design, web master, web metrics, web modeling, web quality, and web services development.

In brief, software engineering would also become a subset of web engineering, as it happens with HCI or information retrieval. Summarily, new disciplines that act as a kind of infinite semiosis, damaging the organization of its contents, didactics, the training of future professionals, the databases of scientific publications, the h-Index (Hirsch's index), etc. (O'Neil, 2016).

Basically, software and web engineering are oriented to the programming and development of systems or applications, commercial or not, using the same principles. The difference between the two lies in the generation of the new models, methods, techniques, tools, etc. within the web engineering. However, for these hypothetical differentiation targets it is very easy to find anomalies. For example, those from the formal sciences, linked to the G factor (G = Garduña), for which many authors of an international workshop who were in the proceedings of the hypermedia proceedings in 1995 (IWHD –international workshop hypermedia design, in Montpellier, France), appear in 2017 in the proceedings of an international web engineering conference (ICWE), in Rome, Italy. Both international events, published by the same publisher (Springer) and indexed by the same database: Digital Bibliography and Library Project (DBLP).

This is how software engineering and HCI cease to be exemplary disciplines for many decades, and become absolute chaos. Today, HCI is a large, dark nebula in infinite space. It has lost its laws, rules or scientific norms, when addressing topics related to human health, for example. The same goes for retrieval information. This is one of the many direct consequences of the abusive use of prefixes, such as: inter, trans, intra, multi, pluri, etc., when they are linked to the term "discipline" and / or synonyms of the same. In Annex #1 there is a collection of examples in this regard.

This unlimited expansion is one of the aspects that has two dichotomous values in the organization or architecture of the web. On the one hand, free access to digitized information, the contents of which refer to the past, present and future of humanity. On the other hand, the barriers or limitations to access that information derived from the same human being or artificial intelligence online. The notion of cosmos, as it is well known, means order.

Therefore, we will try in this work to analyze the main elements that across time and currently generate chaos, trying to present them in order to eradicate them for the future. A future, where intelligent technological devices are included, from the hardware perspective (i.e., Shen & Srivastava, 2017; Raggett, 2015). However, from the point of view of software and human management of the web, they are not, as found in some examples. Positive and negative aspects are also considered, which enhance or distort Tim Berners-Lee's innovative vision, through the latest developments in software and hardware.

Web and Multimedia: Origins and Metamorphosis

In countless diverse examples related to innovation and the technological revolution throughout the centuries, it is necessary to consider the constant work of researchers to achieve their goals. In the case of the World Wide Web it has not been an exception to such reality (Reisman, 2020). Studies of it began in the 1980s, at CERN (European Organization for Nuclear Research) in Geneva, Switzerland. Berners-Lee was working on a project called "Inquire", in order to create a distributed hypermedia system. Succinctly, a system capable of managing textual documents, sounds, etc., in an organized way, among computers distributed throughout our planet (Berners-Lee, 1996).

Consequently, it surpassed the notion of hypertext, by including dynamic media such as audio, for example, and was the genesis of online interactive multimedia communication, in force to this day. In a proposal called "World Wide Web: Proposal for a Hypertext Project", which he presented to CERN executives, the three letters that would change interactive communication appear in the global village for the first time: WWW (Berners-Lee et al., 1991; Berners-Lee, 1996). However, the original proposal was rejected by CERN executives. Belgian computer scientist Robert Cailliau was the exception and he quickly realized the potential of the proposal. Tim Berners-Lee and Robert Cailliau, began to partially rewrite it. Finally, in 1990 the project was approved. Subsequently, Berners-Lee would develop a new protocol called HTTP (Hyper Text Transfer Protocol) but once again would meet resistance from CERN managers. This would lead to free Internet distribution of the software devised by Tim Berners-Lee.

Global acceptance was immediate, primarily from the USA. In 1993, the project was widely supported by the National Center for Supercomputing Applications (NCSA) in Illinois. Marc Andressen and Eric Bina, founders of the web browser, Netscape in 1994. Both worked at NCSA and based on the work of Berners-Lee, they developed an easy-to-use graphical interface for the web browser, which they called "Mosaic." Through the Mosaic it was possible to access the first documents present on the Internet. Over time, graphic interfaces have evolved to facilitate access to the web for millions of users.

In this brief historical summary it can be seen how the context influences the growth of innovative ideas and the formation of new professions. Unquestionably, it is necessary to establish the exact contexts of those who are not, such as the professionals who derive from it. For example, the nuclear context in which this proposal was presented for the first time, erroneously resulted, from then on and within some European countries, in the inclusion of nuclear engineers to carry out research, development, etc., of anything related to hypertext, multimedia, hypermedia, computer graphics, virtual reality, tangible interfaces, information retrieval, recommended systems, children education, etc.

A deviation that has continued over time invariably, until reaching the third decade of the new millennium, through user experience, interface design, didactics (from primary to university), safeguarding cultural heritage, tourism industry management, business management, health, entertainment and a long etcetera (Cipolla-Ficarra et al., 2017). Excellently, this inconsistency has been partially solved by the social sciences, in order to boost the democratic expansion of the web.

The web in the new millennium, has reached a planetary spread, thanks to the increase in human skill in the use of interfaces, the efficiency of the organization of hypertext, the ease of publishing documents on the web, and the possibility of receiving and transmitting multimedia information on the most varied types of interactive communication devices, the digital interconnection of everyday objects with the internet, that is, the Internet of things (IoT).

Subsequently, all agents involved in the growth and safeguarding of freedom of access to online information, must know the genesis of global projects that are beneficial to humanity, their challenges in transposing these ideals to tangible and sustainable development, besides, how the human and social factors that slow down the progress of interactive communication have been overcome, especially in the field of hypertext, multimedia, hypermedia, graphic computing, virtual reality, augmented reality and mixed reality (Nelson, 1993; Landow, 2006; Cipolla-Ficarra et al., 2017).

Currently, the term *multimedia* has practically disappeared in the context of human-computer interaction, user experience, web engineering, information retrieval, advanced interfaces, computer graphics, to name a few examples. Some of its main components such as the classic notion of "infographics", from the late '90s, derived from the French term, *infographie* and that included topics related to computer graphics, computer animation (2D and/or 3D), etc., have completely changed their meaning. and study topics, orienting it to a simple informative visual representation or written text diagram (Lu, et al., 2020) to simplify the task of reading and interpretation, in the online social media (newspapers, magazines, brochures, etc.). Fortunately, there are excellent examples with an universal accessibility on NASA's website, (www.jpl.nasa.gov/infographics). In figure 1, there are combinations 2D and 3D, special effects in computer graphics, representation of reality through simulation and emulation, etc.

Some exemplary content, with reference to the notion of infographics based on the French term *infographie* and the English term computer graphics, are in the figures 2, 3, 4 and 5. These articles belong to the first publication in Barcelona (Spain), oriented to creativity and digital communication, with the first fixed section of avant-garde infographics in Spain and Europe, whose contents were related to multimedia, human-computer communication, graphic computing, computer animation, special effects, new media, cinema 3D, audio-visual, computer art, artificial life, computer behaviour animation, digital cartography, electronic books, desktop publishing software, computer science, artificial intelligence, CAD (computer aided design), CAE (computer-aided engineering), information technology, industrial design, graphical user interface (GIU), interactive communication, medical image processing, scientific visualization, virtual reality, 2D / 3D computer vision, and all its derivations. Unions and / or interrelations for transferring graphic / visual arts (analogical content to digital) using the first multimedia applications, devices, interfaces for the interaction, Internet, etc.

These short-term changes, within the multimedia and its components (Landow, 1991; Nelson, 1993), denote the strong presence of agents and human factors that intervene negatively in the composition of the contents of the web structure (see Annex #2). A strategic solution is to rotate the triangle of the main areas of the web 180 degrees. In the inverted form there is a revaluation of the notion of multimedia, the intersections of its constituent elements, and technological evolution in the 21st century. In addition, the elimination of those agents and factors that directly and indirectly distort the structural components of software quality and web design.

Although the word multimedia has a distant temporal origin, as Kaprow maintains when citing the example of Tchaikovsky (Kaprow, 1991), when he presented his "multimedia" overture in 1812 where he combined music with fireworks. That is, the visual and the auditory. In our days, the human being,

Figure 1. Excellent examples of infographics. Combination of computer graphics, vision, and imaging techniques –www.jpl.nasa.gov/infographics

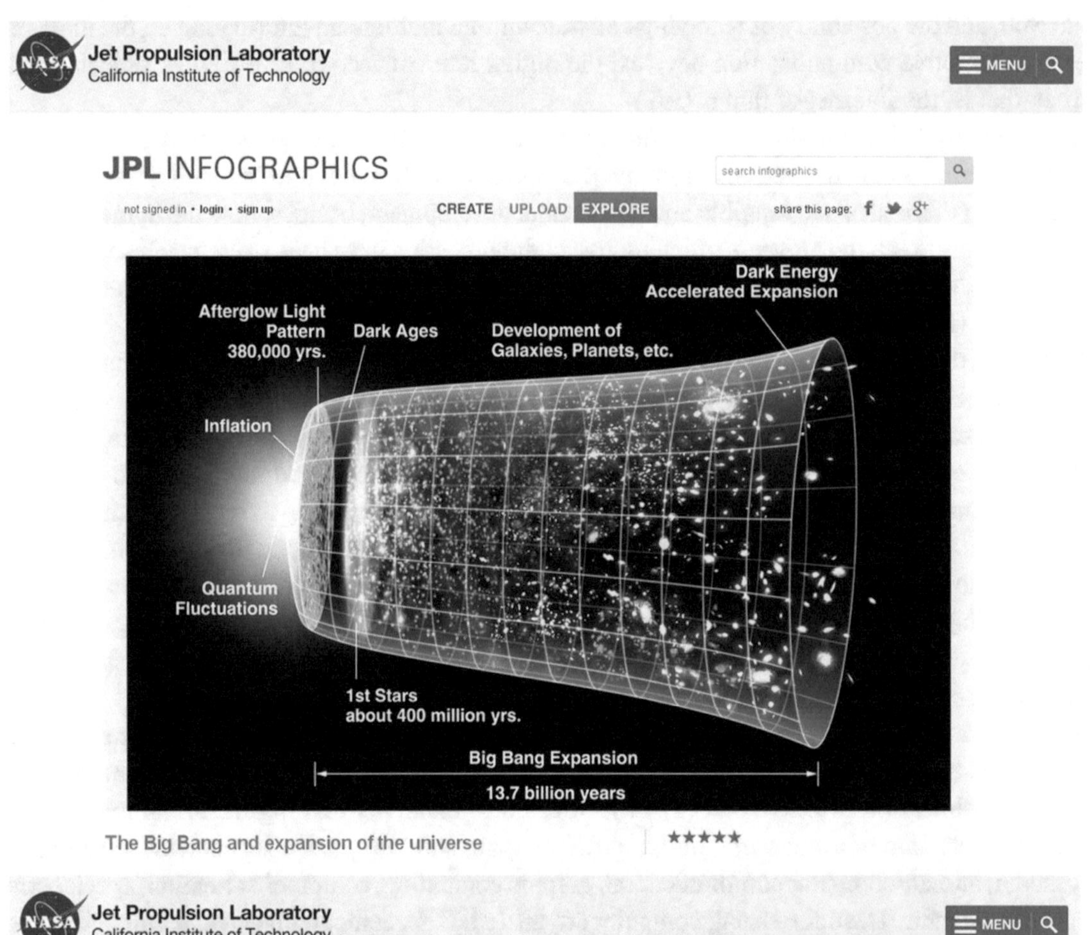

Figure 2. Traditional content of infographics: Multimedia, computer graphics, computer animation, computer aided design (CAD), software and hardware. Title of article –in Spanish: "El despertar de los PC a la infografía" –English: "The awakening of PCs to infographics" (1993).
Author: Francisco Vicente C. Ficarra. Magazine: Imaging, Vol. 7, pp. 27-35 (Barcelona, Spain) –www.pressgraph.es

Figure 3. Title of article –in Spanish: "Ciencia, comunicación científica e infografía: Una tríada exquisita, parte III" –English: "Science, scientific communication and infographics: An exquisite triad, part III" (1994)
Author: Francisco Vicente C. Ficarra. Magazine: Imaging, Vol. 16, pp. 26-31 (Barcelona, Spain). Topics: Computer animation, graphical user interface, artificial intelligence, virtual reality, computer art, sciences, scientific comunication, etc. –www.pressgraph.es

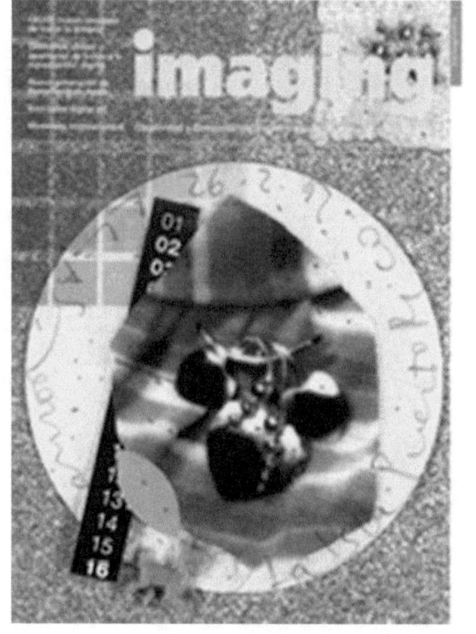

Figure 4. Title of article –in Spanish: "Ostra Delta, perla majestuosa de la infografía" –English: "Delta Oyster, majestic pearl of infographics" (1994)
Author: Francisco Vicente C. Ficarra. Magazine: Imaging-PressGraph, Vol. 227, pp. 38-45 (Barcelona, Spain). Topics: 2D, 3D, computer animation, audiovisual TV, etc. –www.pressgraph.es

imaging PressGraph

Ostra Delta,
perla majestuosa de la infografía

through smartphones, has become the largest consumer of multimedia content, through the web. Therefore, the marginality to the notion of multimedia draws attention in web engineering.

Figure 5. Title of article –in Spanish: "Entre lo real y lo virtual del diseño en Italia" –English: "Between the real and the virtual in the design in Italy" (1995)
Author: Francisco Vicente C. Ficarra. Magazine: Imaging-PressGraph, Vol. 236, pp. 76-81 (Barcelona, Spain). Topics: Industrial design, multimedia, 3D, VR, Internet, etc. –www.pressgraph.es

imaging PressGraph

Artes Gráficas y Comunicación en la Era Digital · Nº 236 · Setiembre · 1995 · 750 Ptas.

Entre lo real y lo virtual
del diseño en Italia

Una crítica positiva ayuda a tomar decisiones acertadas.
Americanos y alemanes tienden a ser efectistas en sus creaciones.
Hay un interés creciente a nivel mundial en imitar la realidad con ordenadores.
El sector industrial no puede dejar de lado a la infografía.
Los sistemas multimediales y la generación de un nuevo lenguaje.

ITALIAN DESIGN

Figure 6. Current unidirectional use of the notion of infographics from the distorted boom in the change in the relationship between meaning and signifier, from the linguistic perspective. As well as in the infinite generation of neologisms, lacking a scientific and epistemological basis in the definition from HCI, UX, educational mercantilism, etc. Besides, in this figure (The Guardian –www.theguardian.com, 08/04/08), the readers will be needing a magnifying glass in order to examine the information

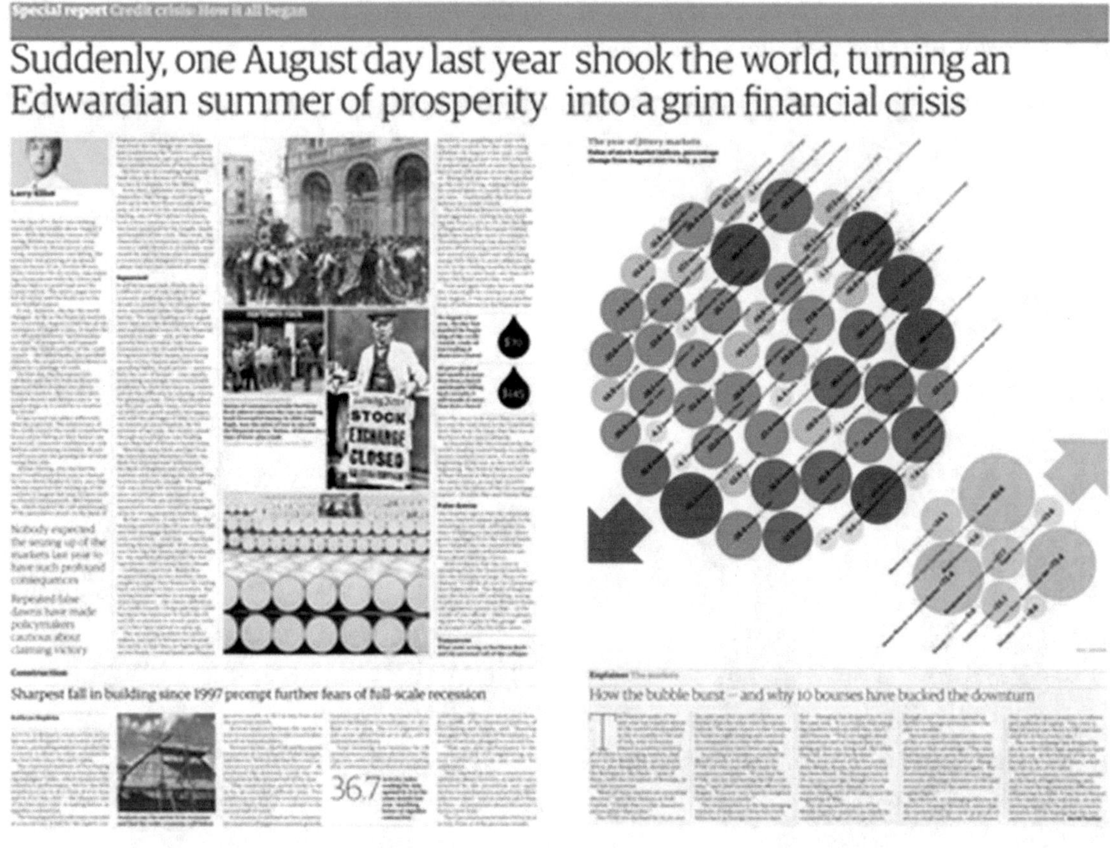

Special report Credit crisis: How it all began

Suddenly, one August day last year shook the world, turning an Edwardian summer of prosperity into a grim financial crisis

Nobody expected the seizing up of the markets last year to have such profound consequences

Repeated false dawns have made policymakers cautious about claiming victory

Sharpest fall in building since 1997 prompt further fears of full-scale recession

36.7

How the bubble burst – and why 10 bourses have bucked the downturn

In the 20th century, Nicholas Negroponte (Negroponte, 1995) stated the fusion of television, printing and computing towards a "computer-based multimedia technology." However, over time, the existence of various technologies related to multimedia and related to the computer has been found, which requires differentiation to avoid linguistic ambiguities. Depending on the degree of computer cohesion and the various degrees of interaction, historically and classically, the following classification can be made (Nielsen, 1990; Landow, 1991; Negroponte, 1995; Cipolla-Ficarra, 1996):

1) Sequential multimedia.
2) Multimedia "partially" interactive.
3) "Fully" interactive multimedia.

Nodes and links are the basic elements of a hypertextual system (Nelson, 1993; Nielsen, 1990) that has evolved to reach multimedia content that is accessible online, through mobile telephony, which con-

Figure 7. Structural and internal vision of the web in our days (origin in the classic inverted pyramid iceberg format) and how it should be inverted for a structural and systemic study of future web engineering professionals (transformation into an inverted truncated pyramid-shaped iceberg). Area #1 (surface): Amazon, eBay, Facebook, YouTube, Wikipedia, search engine results (approximately 20% of the web is indexed for Google), etc. Area #2 (deep): private networks, research papers, netbanking, medical records, abandoned sites, pay-wallet sites, research firm databases, etc. Area #3 (dark):the internet's illicit activities reside here. This area is accessible via the right online directory or hidden search site to find it. Today, all these areas under the G Factor

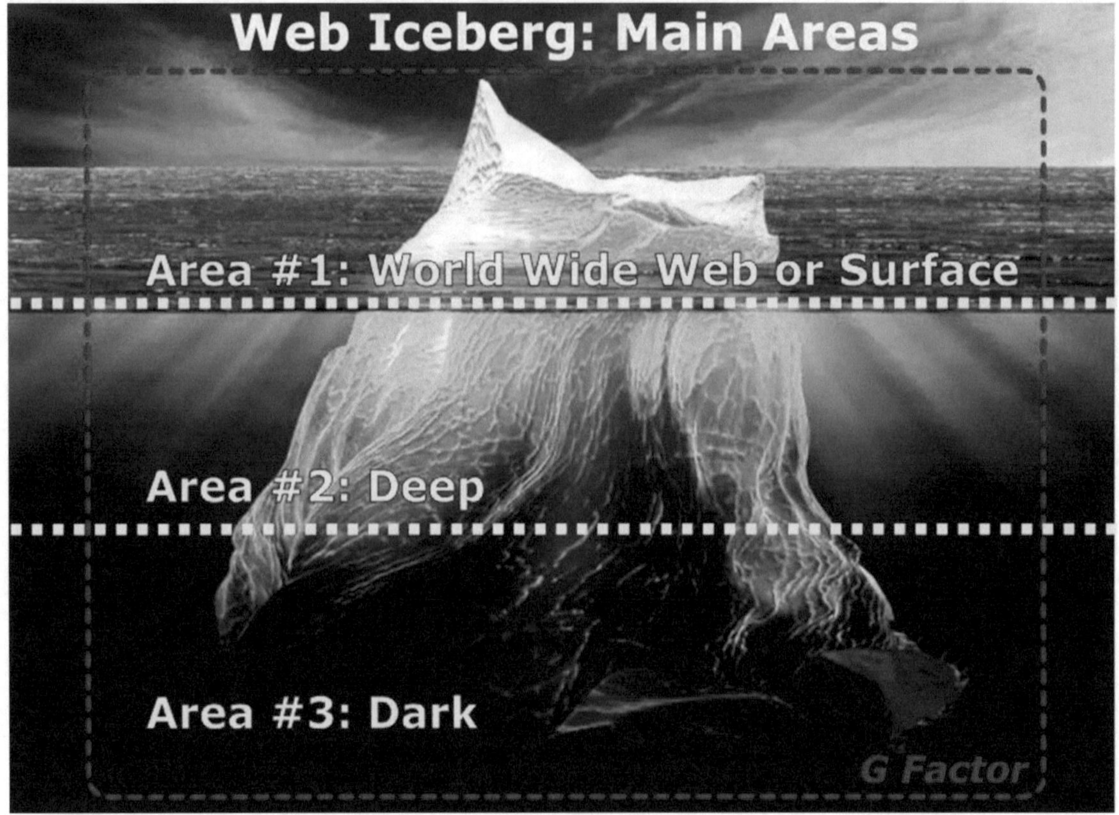

stantly requires higher speeds, in telecommunications networks, for example. The speed of connection to the network (through cable or Wi-Fi, wireless network protocols) is slow, when it does not exceed 10 Mb. per second. In the case of audiovisual content, it should be well above 50 Mb per second (Mbps). All of this depends on the geographical location where the user accesses the Internet content, as sites where connections can exceed the minimum-maximum range of 100 Mbps up to 1 Gbps. The speed from the commercial point of view refers to the download.

All this involves a brief examination of the different technologies that exist for an Internet connection, in some areas of the planet, such as southern Europe. A fiber optic connection to the home or FTTH (Fiber To The Home) by its initials, usually offers a better symmetry or upload and download speed (upload a photo to a social media application or download an attached file, for example), better latency (server response time to receive and send the information of the requested content) and jitter (unwanted

Figure 8. Externally, the web in 1990 is a normal sphere. Internally and structurally, there is an inverted pyramid with a big surface area (top), a very small deep web (middle), and practically non-existent dark area (bottom)

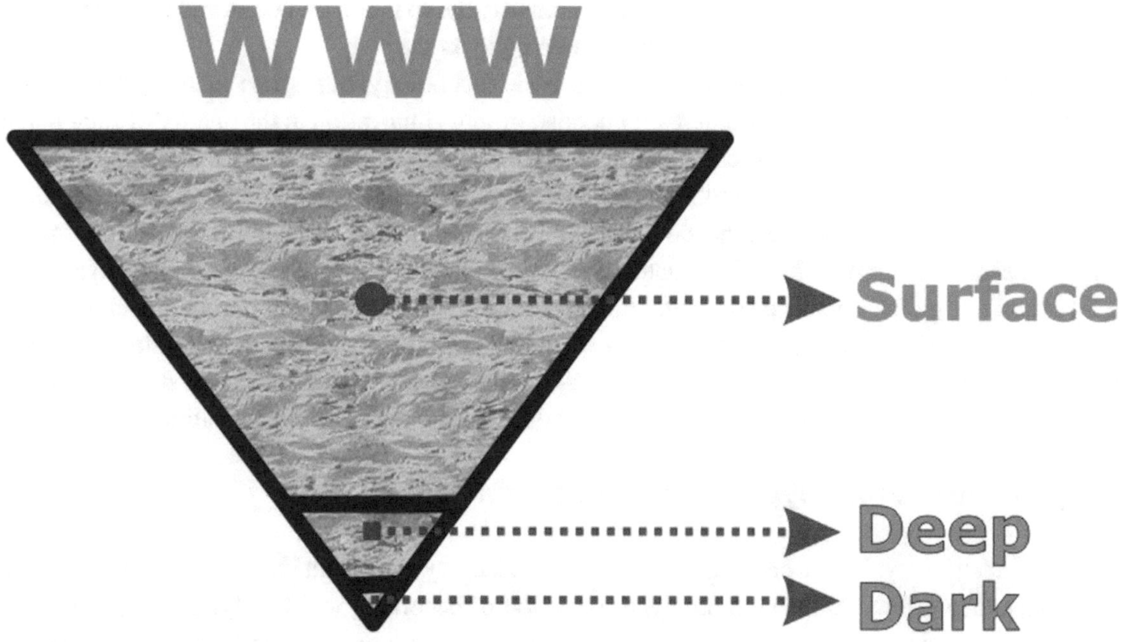

and abrupt change in the ownership of a signal) than other technologies such as 4G (fourth generation of broadband cellular network technology), or HFC (Hybrid fiber-coaxial), or ADSL (Asymmetric Digital Subscriber Line). The latter, based on copper pair technology but which is gradually being supplanted by fiber optics. Therefore, the user can access fully interactive multimedia content, using the following technologies (Dahlman, Parkvall & Skold, 2020):

- **4G and 5G**: mobile connections that propagate by waves through the air. The speed depends on parameters such as coverage, the technology used or the mobile phone device. 4G usually offers less than 100 Mbps and 5G will allow at least one Gbps.
- **FTTH**: the fiber optic cable travels from the telephone / Internet (TI) exchange to the user, ensuring maximum speed and latency. Its speed limit is unknown, and TI services companies currently offer connections of up to 1 Gbps.
- **HFC**: hybrid between fiber optics and coaxial cable used by TI companies (they are also being supplanted by FTTH). In this case, the optical fiber reaches the central node of the TI company, and from there it reaches the users by means of the coaxial cable (like that of the television antenna). Good speed and latency persist in this technology, but it is not optimal at the FTTH level.

Now, given the slow pace of renewing the network, through the various types of cables and / or fiber optics, for fixed telephony / internet, a practical solution followed by millions of users around the planet has been to resort to the latest generation multimedia mobiles, since they have higher speed and a wide range of programs. Therefore, the landlines of millions of households now have the answering machine constantly activated, since they have been supplanted by the mobile phone. Resides, in spite of the time that has elapsed since the democratization of the Internet and smartphones, there is still no single interactive multimedia technology, augmented reality, mixed reality, etc. within the digital environment. Here, the digital term refers to the information encoded numerically, so that it can be stored and manipulated by computer means, which allows random access to a node on the web.

Undeniably, great advances have been made in basic technology, but issues such as: the notion of user balance in the immersion of virtual reality persist; graphic innovation in the quality of final images (rendering) in video games; the visual and cognitive adaptation between the real and the virtual in the mixed reality; creative and original multimedia content for education (from elementary school to university studies); web engineering tools that do not yet use the full potential of the hardware; the recognition of the pioneers of the profession of evaluator, analyst and heuristic auditor of interactive systems, in the local and / or global scientific community; incorporating the profession of communicability testers into academic curricula, or into the production stages of the software industry; The latest generation multimedia systems continue to be based on partial models, that is, with primitives not unanimously accepted by all agents involved in the research and / or development of web applications.

Design Models: From Hypertext to web Engineering

Since the industrial revolution, cities have been characterized by a constant increase in the products and / or services they offered to the community, to the point of becoming an identifying element of those cities. In other words, a geographical element (city, river, sea, mountain, etc.) tends to mentally associate an object or symbol. For example, from the point of view of the tourism industry, Big Ben to London, the Tour Eiffel to Paris, the Colosseum to Rome, the Parthenon to Athens, etc. In the field of hypertext, multimedia, hypermedia, and web engineering something similar has happened with the word: "Design."

Cities like London, Amsterdam and Milan are usually related to this term. So much so, that since the end of the 1980s, some universities in these cities began to develop design models for interactive systems, following basic principles of abstraction, generalization, universality, robustness, among others, stemming from software. Some approaches or models have been developed by IT (Information Technology) professionals, in USA, UK and the Netherlands.

Others by mathematicians and nuclear engineers, for example, who worked in the computer science faculties of public/state and private (*read* mainly religious in European Union – EU) universities, in the cities of Milan (Italy), Como (Italy) and Lugano (Switzerland), which ended up being an authentic collage of concepts that were different from each other. So much so that not even the same mathematical and computer colleagues from other public universities in central and southern Europe (*read* Spain, Portugal, Switzerland, Slovenia, Croatia, Germany, Austria, etc.) understood exactly the components of these models, even if they included object-oriented programming. This is an example of how models are usually related to another term: "Fashion."

A trend in research topics that are faithfully followed by all those anomalous agents", who do not belong by training and / or experience, to the field of the disciplines in which they carry out their daily activities. However, from the abstract point of view, if the fashion is to develop models for hypermedia, then the anomalous agents, through the prefix inter / trans / multi / pluri / extra / intra / disciplinarity, will be in charge of carrying out national and international projects, even if they lack knowledge of the topics covered. These fashions make up timeless structures of people who come to supervise models that range from multimedia to education for refugee children, including health, the disabled, the elderly, feminism and a long etcetera, in Italian, French, Greek, Spanish or Portuguese HCI. In brief, the anomalous agents cross the academic field and end up imposing themselves on society, even if their proposals do not work correctly.

Only in situations of serious and real emergencies (earthquakes, tornadoes, floods, fires, pandemics, etc.), can be seen the consequences of the work of these professionals, unable to develop individually or in groups, functional models for the prevention of eventual catastrophes, safeguarding the population, custody of nature, reliable preparation of statistical information, etc., through web engineering, with all the disciplines that it incorrectly includes.

Some of the main and first design models for hypertext, multimedia and hypermedia systems are: Dexter (Dexter Hypertext Reference Model), based on the analysis of the most relevant primitives of the following systems: Augment, HyperCard, Concord, KMS (Knowledge Management System), Intermedia and NoteCards; AHM (Amsterdam Hypermedia Model) is an extension of the Dexter model and delves into the temporal aspect and semantics of navigation; RMM (Relationship Management Methodology) uses the RMDM (Relationship Management Data Model) data model to design information and links within the hypermedia system. Readers interested in the description of these models can consult the following bibliography (Cipolla-Ficarra, 2015; Cipolla-Ficarra, 2018; Cipolla-Ficarra, et al., 2018b).

The limitation of the use of some of these models, from the temporal point of view, is due to the use of a language with ambiguous notions for a designer, such as the term "*slot*", defined as "an atomic piece of information." Axiomatically, a definition from a nuclear engineering and mathematical environment, but in the context of software engineering, computing, graphic design of user interfaces, information architecture, information retrieval, ICT (Information and Communication Technology), etc. a priori, it is colloquially related to "*slot machines*" in casinos (i.e., Lugano, Monte-Carlo, Las Vegas, etc.).

This is a major failure when establishing the basis of a design model for interactive systems, since the inability to accurately select a term to define the minimum element of information, to which said model will refer, is detected. This is an obvious example of the human factor in software engineering. It obeys the cloning of personality, from the psychological point of view.

Although Tim Berners-Lee and Robert Cailliau when they presented the World Wide Web project (Berners-Lee, et al., 1991; Berners-Lee, et al., 1996), they did it in a field of nuclear research such as CERN, this does not mean that eternally the nuclear engineer or the mathematician or the physicist, is the profile for a suitable professional to project design models, from a city related to design and clothing fashion, such as Milan, in Italy.

The consequences of these failures can be seen in the lack of use within the software industry, towards those models of partial, inconsistent and non-universal design. Furthermore, the costs for the local educational and scientific community are immeasurable, over time, given the loss of competitiveness in software and hardware, for the autonomous generation of qualitative goods and services, within globalization (Oliveira, 2017; O'Neil, 2016, Pendyala, Shim & Bussler, 2015).

On the contrary, an abstract notion such as "entity", which philosophically could open an infinite semiosis (Martin & Ringham, 2006), from software engineering to epistemology of science, could be an excellent solution with the definition established by Norman Fenton and James Bieman: "An entity is an object (such as a person or a room) or an event (such as a journey or the testing phase of software project) in the real world. We want to describe the entity by identifying characteristics that are important to us in distinguishing one entity from another." (Fenton & Bieman, 2014). This is a very good example to follow, in computing and all its derivations.

Now, from the web engineering you can verify an unstoppable trend towards infinite semiosis (Martin & Ringham, 2006; Eco, & Sebeok, 1984), when it refers to the design of web pages and the quality attributes in the design of interactive systems and communicability. The beginning of this modern and erroneous phenomenon lies in the trivialization or popularization of the meaning of adjectives and nouns, such as: empathy, inclusion, cognitive, emotion, accessibility, navigability, usability, playability, friendly, security, maintainability, etc., coming in some situations, to be used as synonyms (Cipolla-Ficarra, et al. 2017; Cipolla-Ficarra, et al. 2019).

These semantic deviations are reinforced from the human-computer interaction and user experience applied to the design of the interfaces to the elaboration of the contents (Sieckenius-de-Souza, 2004). All of this contradicts many of the principles of software engineering (Pressman & Maxim, 2015). For example, in a heuristic evaluation method for interactive systems, it is necessary to have a model to efficiently analyze each of the components of the application or system to be examined. The model also serves to establish a common code or language among all participants in the evaluation process, in order to eradicate ambiguities that involve loss of time and financial resources. The main advantage of any well-defined model is that it responds to the possibility of evaluating each of the components of the applications with a high degree of precision; as can be achieved with semiotics.

Semiotics has instruments from which the components of interactive systems can be analyzed structurally or not. Basically, in the structural models of interactive systems there is a set of primitives for its modeling, establishing the structures for data and navigation. Said models contain a manifest semantics both to navigate and to present data in interactive systems (hypertext, multimedia, hypermedia, augmented reality, mixed reality, etc.). In the case of non-structural models, only the basic components of the hypertext exist, such as the nodes and the links. Within the browsing styles we find some systems for hobby or entertainment, where there is a very high freedom in browsing or enjoyment, compared to consulting multimedia educational and informative content on the web.

The lesser freedom in the enjoyment of traditional educational systems is because the path to be followed by the user is generally more predefined than in systems intended for entertainment. Contemporary, intelligent online gamification aims to change these predefined parameters, giving greater freedom to access the same content from different perspectives, as they can be obtained with the perfect combination of dynamic and static media.

The Evolutionary Development of Nodes and Links in Professions

From the earliest hypertext systems, such as Hypertext Editing System, or N-Line System (NLS) / Augment, for example, corporate work was the common element, starting in 1960, as it has been from the point of view of interactive design, nodes and links (Cipolla-Ficarra, 2015). These two elements, as hardware evolved, such as moving from large computers, workstations, etc., to personal computers, have allowed textual nodes in large computers, little by little, to include static graphics (photographs, maps, drawings, etc.), dynamic graphics (video, computer animations, etc.), audio (music, sounds, voiceovers, etc.). Consequently, nodes and links should be considered as the minimum units in hypertextual structures, from the design models to user experience (Cipolla-Ficarra, 2015; Cipolla-Ficarra, et al., 2019).

In addition, these are nodes and links that have been evolving and adapting with the various commercial, educational, scientific applications, etc., for the generation of interactive hypertext, multimedia, and hypermedia systems such as: Intermedia, NoteCards, Knowledge Management System (KMS), Hyperties, HyperCard, Toolbook, etc. Establishing generational taxonomies between the evolution of software and the hardware associated with these first interactive systems is wrong because we do not refer to human generations or types of users, such as baby boomers, generation X, millennials, and centennials (Pandit, 2015). The time limits and the purpose of use are dynamic and adaptable to the evolution of the technological context. Some of those commercial applications aimed at hypertext, multimedia and hypermedia have been used in the new millennium, such as the Toolbook, to cite an example, which denotes a high capacity to adapt to hardware and the requirements of potential users.

The use of the Toolbook implicitly involved the dilemma of who were the ideal professionals to generate electronic books. The electronic term was immediately related to electronic engineering. However, the university study plans of these engineering companies at the end of the 20th century were not designed for such tasks. Another alternative was graduates in literature, languages, etc., that is, experts in textual content. However, they lacked computer skills.

The faculties of computing, systems, software, etc., in the southern Mediterranean, for example, were governed largely by mathematicians and physicists, who were not interested in the research and development of hypertextual, multimedia, and hypermedia systems. So much so, that the design and implementation of the first interactive systems for the first Catalan virtual campus or universities (i.e., Open University of Catalonia –www.uoc.edu) were derived from the rector's office towards professionals external from those universities (Cipolla-Ficarra, 1996). Therefore, in the beginning, the Toolbook was widely used by professionals in the social sciences with computer skills. The aim was to develop the first interactive educational, artistic, tourist systems, etc. off-line, for personal computers.

As the hardware of personal computers (monitors and graphics cards) evolved and their diffusion increased, in homes, offices, schools, etc., the interfaces needed to be designed according to the potential users and the motivations for interacting with the system: distance education, search for textual information, entertainment or hobby, etc. Thus arises the need for the design of interfaces for multimedia and hypermedia systems related to science, art, history, geography, tourism, video games, etc. (Cipolla-Ficarra, et al., 2018a).

Automatically, the inclusion of graduates in fine arts was thought to solve this need in the interactive systems. However, they lacked not only computer literacy, but also the elaboration of original textual content and the establishment of principles for a universal design style guide, as would be achieved with applications running on Apple computers (Apple, 1992). This guide to interface design has made it possible to standardize universally the first metaphors used in the generation of multimedia systems in offline support, for example.

Implicitly, in the EU and UK took place a bifurcation between designers and programmers. The former would use Apple products, while the latter would use IBM or compatible personal computers, along with the Windows operating system. Subsequently, there were commercial applications for generating and editing vector and raster images, such as Photoshop or Corel Draw, on both commercial platforms. That is to say, that the operating system and the hardware on which it worked, was not a limitation for the creativity of digital artists or users, at the end of the 20th century, although the quality of a vector image is superior to the raster image.

However, since then, the commercial factor of software and hardware would influence the professional training and employment opportunities of the users of both platforms, depending on the geographical location, where they carried out their theoretical and practical studies. In other words, the designers who had theoretical knowledge and experiences, on both hardware platforms (Apple Macintosh and IBM PC or compatible), software (Windows operating system and Mac OS X), and applications to create web pages, for example, had a better chance of becoming true pioneers of digital graphic design. Those multimedia professionals who went from analog graphics to digital multimedia made the first interactive systems of the time, and without the need to be connected to an intranet, extranet or the Internet. In short, they worked autonomously although the technological possibility of group work already existed, through the various commercial software applications and the web.

The graphics or vector images that are commonly found on the World Wide Web are usually open formats SVG (Vector Markup Language) and VML (Vector Markup Language), or SWF (Scalable Vector Graphics) in proprietary format (Robbins, 2018). A brief analysis of these formats also reveals how the commercial factor and the trends of the developers of interactive systems have been influencing the context of ICTs (information communication and technology), with the need to regularize the use of the various formats of the files for images, texts, etc., either static or dynamic (animated) within the web (Cipolla-Ficarra, et al., 2018a). SVG is a two-dimensional (static or dynamic) vector graphics or image format, in XML (eXtensible Markup Language) format. It is an open standard developed by the W3C (World Wide Web Consortium) since 1999.

The W3C, is an international consortium that generates standards and a set of recommendations to ensure the long-term, organized growth and development of the World Wide Web. VML is an open programming XML language, intended for creating vector images created in 2D or 3D (static or dynamic) on web pages. Finally, the SWF (initially short for Shockwave Flash and later Small Web Format) is a vector image file format created by the Macromedia company. The latter can be viewed with Adobe Flash Player, since the company Adobe Systems bought the Macromedia company in 2007. That is, the union of Photoshop with Flash (commercial application to generate animations on web pages, such as advertising banners).

Macromedia has continued to develop commercial applications, for the main hardware platforms, in the period of the democratization of multimedia and the Internet, through a complete set of high-quality products, in the commercial software industry and related to the typography, vector images, 2D animations, multimedia systems on CD-Rom, generation of web pages, etc. Some examples are Flash, Fireworks, Freehand, Dreamweaver, Director, Authorware, Fontographer, among others. These products opened a division within the software, between the programmers that used languages like C, C ++, Visual Basic, etc. to create interactive multimedia systems, and those that used commercial applications, with high quality results.

Beginning in 1990, with the emergence of CD / DVD use among personal computer users, the demand for new interactive systems, on such media by millions of inhabitants, grew exponentially, and expert professionals were incessantly required to cover the great workplace demand. The solution was to create multimedia engineering. An engineering that in southern European countries would not have its genesis in university industrial schools, or in the faculties of computer science, systems, software, electronics, physics, mathematics, chemistry, fine arts, audiovisual, journalism, literature, telecommunications, automatic and computer architecture, etc., from public/state and hybrid universities. This engineering was planned in a new space, focused on the communicability of users with computers and telecommunications, with a constant interest in the evolution of new technologies (Cipolla-Ficarra, et al., 2019).

To achieve this objective, whoever would coordinate this new study plan should have the knowledge and experiences of the intersection between formal and factual sciences. In other words, something non-existent in a physicist, mathematician, chemist, architect, anthropologist, nuclear engineer, electronic engineer, computer science graduate, artificial intelligence graduate and a host of other professions. They only dedicated themselves to dictating strict precepts and medieval educational norms in the field of new technologies and interactive communication. Besides, the experienced coordinator in social communication should not only have a 360-degree vision, from teaching to new technologies, but also had to face the human factors derived from any revolutionary university reform, such as resistance to change inside and outside of the illuminated work environment, to collaborate in the introduction of a new study plan, in a national territory, with wide diversities –cultural, linguistic, technological, workplace, etc. (Cipolla-Ficarra, et al., 2019).

A truly innovative study plan, where some of the disciplines of the formal sciences and factual sciences would converge, for theoretical and practical purposes for the study of human-computer interaction; the realization of interactive systems with programming languages and commercial applications; quality assessment and auditing for interactive systems; analysis of the media (dynamic and static); web-oriented multimedia design; the development of 2D and / or 3D computer animations; the experimentation of virtual reality in video games, among other areas of technological and humanistic knowledge.

However, innovation and creativity do not endure when private university education is governed by a religious entity, emulating very well hybrid educational institutions. That is, between the public/state and the private, particularly when the ultimate goal pursued by that entity is profit and perennial power, through education. Therefore, the money of the students or "clients" predominates over the scientific-technological knowledge of the teachers. A perennial and unchangeable reality with the passing of decades, centuries and millennia.

The most effective solution in these types of contexts is to use instruments from commercial software or open software to develop systems. This generates in the university educational field consumers of applications or technological devices that do not require great intellectual efforts, such as knowledge and use of high and low-level programming languages, to take full advantage of the benefits of software and hardware that is available. Not for nothing these solutions would be called in educational marketing: "Producers of digital multimedia content." To some extent, there is a theoretical link to the idea of transforming computer users into content publishers, as argued by George P. Landow (Landow, 2006).

In the practice that context has not been generated because there are unnatural agents that influence it, such as physicists, mathematicians, nuclear engineers, among others. Some content producers who do not even know the existence of design patterns. Design patterns are very useful tools since they allow finding solutions to common problems in software development and other areas related to interactive design.

Those patterns are based on basic principles of software engineering such as reusability (Pressman, R. & Maxim, B., 2015). In a nutshell, it is applicable to various problems in software development, in different circumstances, and with positive results, since it solves the problems documented and analogous to previous contexts. Therefore, they are a valid and advisable instrument for solving problems, which have a common denominator, in the phases of software development. Through its use, the cost / benefit equation must always be considered by all who resort to it.

Some of the biggest benefits are that patterns provide a library or catalogs of reusable items, thus avoiding additional tasks; they generate a common vocabulary among designers; they facilitate the dissemination of knowledge or acquired solutions, and standardize the task of carrying out the design. In contrast, they can increase costs when they are intended to force its use in non-analogous situations, eliminate designer creativity, and enforce certain design guidelines, with regard to other alternatives. However, in certain elitist areas of study, future software professionals should only consume services, such as outsourcing.

The problem with studies and future professions related to the web is that you always have to consider the context available to the user and free access to the highest levels of university education, as it still persists in several countries on the American continent. So much so that in certain private and elitist training contexts, those expensive engineering, master's degrees, continuing education courses, etc., previously related to the creation of multimedia content, today are mainly based on digital photography.

The central axes of the study plan can be based on the principles of optics, light, color, movement, composition, storytelling, phototoreportage, etc. That is, the student obtains a university degree in multimedia engineering or web engineering, where they hardly need to have knowledge or experience in HTML (HyperText Markup Language), CSS (Cascading Style Sheets), JS (JavaScript), server configuration in Apache or Windows, different firewall software, to name a few examples.

Only a narcissistic presence in social networks (Pinterest, Instagram, Facebook, YouTube, Flickr, etc.) is of interest (Hirigoyen, 2019), through the latest generation photographic devices in mobile telephony, which incorporate even image self-editing functions (photography, video, audio, etc.), without resorting to the computer. Although these private universities guarantee 100% employment, those future engineers or graduates will lack both knowledge and experience, which prevents them from being autonomous throughout their professional lives, depending on third parties, even for decision-making, in the face of trivial problems which prevents them from solving the technical and / or theoretical problems of the web (Brandtzaeg & Folstad, 2017; Harrell & Lim, 2017; Allier, 2015; Pressman & Lowe, 2009).

Involution From Multimedia Publishing in Universities

Now, if to educational marketing, we add the editorial, we can find situations where the word engineering is attached to any discipline, technological device, neologism, etc., with the persuasive purpose of drawing the user's transitory attention, while browsing through the web. In this sense, it is worth noting that some qualities intrinsic to the quality of computer systems, such as the notion of usability, would also become engineering in the 1990s, based on technical publications of international scope and the commercialization of the first hypertext and multimedia systems.

Since then, the diffusion of personal computers among the population and the democratization of the use of interactive systems requires the collaboration of engineers from various branches, ranging from writing user guides for systems to teaching. Professionals in the social sciences and engineers of each specialization must have basic knowledge of other related areas, in order to solve complex problems and interrelated disciplines, within diverse work teams, for example, with the intersection of computer scientists and artists, in the first computer animations for television or cinema. It is the moment where formal science professionals join the development of interactive systems, occupying a dominant position.

This unjustified domination leads to creating illogical or implausible engineering from the point of view of the epistemology of the sciences, such as transforming the frontiers in semiotics (Deely, 1986) into engineering, based on the notion of metacommunications and presenting itself as a new theory within the HCI (Sieckenius-de-Souza, 2004). That is, the umpteenth infinite expansion of the exact limits of the HCI, resorting to notions such as: artificial intelligence, computer-mediated communication, end-user programming, graphical user interface, natural language processing, user-centered design, etc. This example is endorsed by mathematicians, anthropologists, journalists, among others. This is a serious deviation within semiotics, which has its origin in the editorial center of a university of high technological and international prestige such as MIT (Massachusetts Institute of Technology), in USA.

The use of semiotics from the first interactive systems has facilitated the generation of high-quality software, with reduced costs and in short times (Cipolla-Ficarra, 1996). It is a discipline of the social sciences, never an engineering one, as Umberto Eco said (Cipolla-Ficarra, et al., 2017), which allows the detailed analysis of the components of interactive design, once its main categories have been established, such as content, navigation, structure, connectivity, the layout, the context, etc., together with the quality attributes that the interactive system must include, and their corresponding metrics, for a heuristic evaluation, through special methodologies. Some methodologies and techniques that can speed up the evaluation process, with reliable results and spare the use of expensive usability laboratories, for example, if the person conducting the evaluation or system audit is a communicability expert. In our case, the term of communicability is not related to the erroneous vision of semiotics, turned into engineering (Sieckenius-de-Souza, 2004).

In addition, today, there is no possibility of correction in the face of such deviations in the sciences, since defense mechanisms arising from the role of women in engineering are automatically activated, with a special interest in computing, new technologies, and a long etcetera. Everything related to pseudo feminism, but which actually serves to hide the presence of the G factor. This is one of the consequences of educational quantification when you want to measure the quality of universities and establish international rankings, based on metrics, which are far from transparent. Surprisingly, universities with long centuries of existence and with former students who were Nobel prize winners today occupy lower places, compared to universities founded in the mid or late twentieth century.

The Correct use of Scientific and Technological Language

Currently, the correct use of language is something that humanity is losing as an acquired skill, due to the high diffusion of online content and its search engines, through modern smartphones. These are textual contents, once rich in the era of hypertext and the birth of the web, but which have been giving way to audiovisual content, which has gained in quality of visual and auditory reproduction, thanks to the increase in speed, in the transmission of data, whether in fixed or mobile networks, or in the development of new algorithms for the compression and decompression of this dynamic data. Today, the mixed reality is presented as the new planetary panacea for education, remote health, telework, electronic commerce, entertainment, among many other uses, although it will generate constant distortions among human beings, to distinguish between the real and the virtual, of images and sound.

The rise of certain linguistic distortions or the correct use of terms, usually has its origin in the educational field, scientific research, the media, etc. For example, in Argentina's radio communications, the topic of gender equality, inclusion, communicative empathy, etc., leads to new oral expressions in Spanish for gender equality as "*chiques*" (boys and girls, without distinction of sex), "*todes*" (indefinite adjectives that express quantity and plural, that is, all –feminine–, and all –masculine–), "*nosotres*" (the personal pronoun, first person plural, that is, we –feminine–, and us – male–).

In these three examples, the phonetic use of the "e" replaces the "a" (feminine) and the "o" (masculine). Here, a linguistic social evolution of certain Spanish-speaking geographical areas is verified. A radio phenomenon that will affect the syntax and semantics, oral and written, on the web. Similarly, some computer symbols on the network, such as the at sign (@), allow the inclusion of "all" (all different gender identities), writing as follows "*@ll*" (in English), "*tod@s*" (in Spanish), or the asterisk (*) in Italian "*tutt**", among many other examples.

The consensus begins to decrease when it comes to simplifying and abridging the written text of SMS (Short Message Service) in mobile telephony. SMS produced a considerable reduction in the costs of interpersonal communication, compared to telephone calls (1990-2005). Now, in the first models of these phones, their ergonomic design did not provide for the writing function. However, the numerical keyboard of the telephone, with the passing of time, would gradually turn into a keyboard similar to the personal computer.

Meanwhile, originally it required great skill on the part of the user to write messages with the fingers of one hand. Subsequently, these short texts would include an emoticon (it is a haplology between emotion and icon) or smiley (using punctuation marks, asterisks, parentheses, square brackets, etc., symbols of major, minor, etc.), with the objective of synthesizing the message, with a human emotion or expression.

Also, here an evolution has been verified with the passing of time, assigned unicode codes, pytograms and animated gifs (the latter in multmedia mobile telephony) until the reduction of the use of signs or textual symbols. For example: **:-)** can be represented with **:)**, and both have the same meaning: Happiness or I'm happy. Today, these emoticons are used to quickly collect the opinion of millions of users of multinationals that provide Internet services, when changing the interfaces of their portals.

In other cases, there is no social consensus and this phenomenon responds more to motivations from the context of educational marketing, where the quantitative is weighted against the qualitative. In this sense, it is enough to examine how the design of university portals has retrograded over time, moving away from educational, cultural, social information, etc. to the statistical data, as can be seen in figures 10 and 12. Statistical data which is fully manipulated because it is impossible to obtain it. Not all former students have ties to their former universities. It is also not possible to resort to other sources of student employment information, since the right to privacy would be violated.

Those statistical data of wild marketing are promoted by those who present themselves socially through social media and new media, as innovators, creatives, guarantors of individual liberties, environmental defenders, protectors of the educational and health system for all, promoters of gender equality, etc. However, when carrying out a linguistic and semiotic analysis of the messages they broadcast on Twitter, YouTube, Facebook, Pinterest, etc., certain results demonstrate the opposite. For example, a camouflaged racism and the enslavement of the "other", through the Internet. The notion of other is used as the main recipient towards which they elaborate transparent and objective, innovative, creative, etc. content, measured and apparently, including the design of everyday objects that should be free from *provocations*, as can be seen in figures 13 and 14, to attract attention and evaluate the reaction of users, on social networks.

SOFTWARE, DESIGN, EDUCATION AND PROVOCATIONS

Provocations are regarded as negative social factors in the progress of software engineering, web, computing, new technologies, telecommunications, communicability, interactive design, etc. Usually, the origin of the same come from the members of entities that have held spiritual and earthly power, for centuries, whose main objective is the profit.

Contrary to the cases of provocation presented from Herzogenaurach (Germany), in figures 13 and 14, we have excellent examples of artisans moving from analog to digital. That is, those from the graphic arts (printing) or those dedicated to the creation of moving computer images (claymation). Professionals generating creative and innovative content from the beginning of the interactive off-line systems. All of them belong to the fields of manual work based on everyday experience.

Furthermore, there is less influence of psychologists, anthropologists, graduates in fine arts, architects, industrial designers, marketing, business management, and a long etcetera, as it occurs in the Iberian and Italian peninsula, to name two examples. The context of human-computer interaction, user experience,

Figure 9. Effective use of emoticons to evaluate the changes made to a webmail in several languages (Italian, English, Spanish, etc.), using 5 smiles and a scale of 5 values, where 1 is the lowest value (anger) and 5 the highest (smile with heart eyes). The test evaluates the structure, the access speed, the modernity and liking of the design, etc.

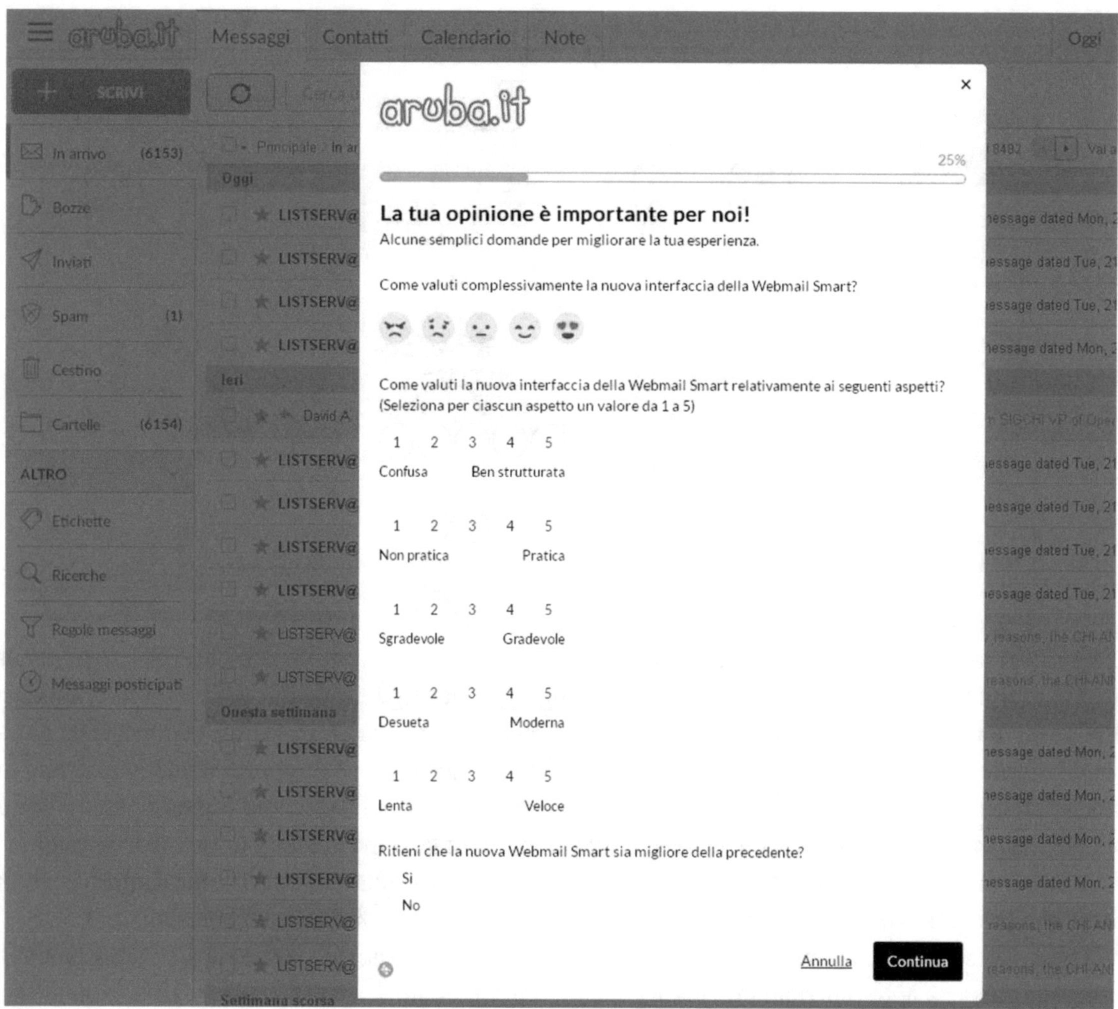

user-centered design, etc., in our day, is dominated by the G factor, fundamentally, by the interrelated triad of mathematics, politics and religion, resorting to provocation to destroy traditional knowledge.

Profit is a quantitative element that prevails over the qualitative one on the current website. The quantification of data / information has accelerated the process of protecting people's sensitive data to prevent free access to online information. For example, in figures 17 it can be seen how a portal intended for the online promotion of scientific information begins to be marketed. Although software engineering continually generates new development methodologies for project management, it is also verified that in web engineering, it has not only adopted software engineering methodologies, but also and frequently, it is creating new ones. In both processes, it is necessary that the digital information on the web can be accessed from any device that is connected to the network.

Figure 10. Educational marketing, where statistics prevail, such as the percentage of job occupation of former students (www.almalaurea.it). The mechanisms for obtaining such data are not specified, without violating people's right to privacy, since several years have passed since students have left university classrooms and / or have migrated abroad.

That is to say, those in charge of the web content, web master, web communicability, etc., insert, manage and examine the content on the portals to obtain worldwide dissemination, without inconvenience. That's why there are factors of the cultural systems, in the design together with the ethical, legal and social behavior aspects that must be respected, starting with the use of an appropriate language and the veracity of online information. Theoretically, these areas should belong to the topics of study within web engineering. In appendix #1 there are several examples of how the veracity of online information is practically non-existent, especially in certain professionals, who apparently dedicate themselves to the education, protection or dissemination of content and developments for web engineering.

Besides, a set of examples has been included of "digital metamorphosis semiosis" (constant self-referential changes in the curriculum vitae), generated by "predatory agents", and ranging from the scientific editorial context in communications, computer and information science to multinational telephone companies dedicated to health issues. It is necessary to keep in mind the differences in meaning between computer science and information science depending on the geographical location where they are used. For example, "computer science" and "information science" refer to computer science in Italy, while in Latin America the information science are related to the social sciences and the traditional media, such as: press, radio, television, cinema, etc. Another clarification is the notion of a predatory agent that we introduce in the work. It is that anomalous agent, who through the context and academic-scientific language, is dedicated to stealing and cloning personalities, from the network to real life, or vice versa.

Fundamentally, they belong to the generations (Pandit, 2015) called "Baby Boomers" (1950-1960), and others to the "Y" generation or millennials (1982-2001). The first set is made up of anomalous agents that turn into predators, either in HCI or in software engineering or in web engineering. The second group are the young people who have taken advantage of the sustained drop in the global university

Figure 11. Old university portal interface, designed and programmed by the same university students, didactically guided and that includes professional wisdom in interactive design, human-computer interaction, communicability, usability engineering, etc.

academic level and the rise of the web. On the one hand, the Bologna plan of the EU, through which in 3 years an engineering, bachelor's or doctorate degree can be obtained, rapidly increasing the statistical number of the total professionals in formal and factual sciences of the states. On the other hand, through open software, Linux, Apache HTTP server, etc., which have favored generation Y illegal actions and maintaining anonymity in cyberspace. A first and partial descriptive profile of it is to be found in Annex #2. More information about G Factor in appendix #1.

In some European legislation this cloning or theft of personality is considered a criminal offense, since actions of mobbing, bossing, bulismo, stalking, etc., coexist implicitly. This is the maximum level of loss of social consensus in the face of the diffusion of the web and the freedom of access to information, in the presence of cyberbullying, cyberterrorism, etc. In many cases they are easy to detect and point out through the analysis of information on social networks and a heuristic evaluation of online behavior. The problem lies in the ease of deleting these behaviors on the Internet, either by the same individual or by legally specialized agencies. Those crimes in the academic-scientific context are not yet stored and / or displayed on any portal of associations and / or organizations of great international prestige, such as ACM (Association for Computing Machinery – www.acm.org), IEEE (Institute of Electrical and Electronics Engineers – www.ieee.org), and IFIP (International Federation for Information Processing – www.ifip.org). Consequently, in the face of the infinite codes of ethics of associations, organizations, foundations, etc., the verifiable reality is that predatory agents have absolute immunity on the web.

Figure 12. Marketing of a multimedia engineering in a private Catalan university, where employment is guaranteed for 100% of the students. Specifically, the fact that almost all are temporary contracts (weeks, months and years), which are the common denominator of work in that region (Catalonia), and that can last a lifetime of future multimedia engineers, is not accounted for.

If the web engineer becomes aware of the unscientific implications and projections of his work, it does not mean that he will be more effective in his specialty. Perhaps, he will accumulate rational experiences but will not discover, invent more, or better. On the contrary, being in a territory of infinite semiosis, he is constantly distracted by an endless number of ICT issues, marginal to his field of study, within a subdiscipline of software engineering as it can be defined to web engineering. Furthermore, he has to get used to systematically ordering ideas and perfecting the language used, always seeking consistency, precision and maximum quality in all his activities, from planning to carrying out projects.

Advanced Technologies

Since the origins of the Internet and the web, text has always played an important role in the exchange of data that, once processed, becomes information and this, in turn, becomes new data for further processing, giving rise to the feedback loop in the communication. A communication that has gone from being passive for the recipient to active for users of computer systems. Some computer systems that together with artificial intelligence and the real objects that can be connected to it, make the home an intelligent or domotic building. A home automation that has gone from being manual or analog, through the use of buttons, keys, etc., to the human voice, with devices such as Amazon's Alexa (www.amazon.com), for example.

Figure 13. Sneakers from the same country manufacturer as the 14 figure, who commercially calls the new product "Barcelona" but incorporates the Spanish flag on the sole of the same to generate tension in social networks, due to the rise in territorial discrepancies in Spain (www.adidas.com, Herzogenaurach –Germany). El Mundo, 07.03.2020 (www.elmundo.es)

In addition, it is a ubiquitous technology that allows connection to the network at all times (internal, external, wired or wireless), regardless of the location and providing energy management, security, wellness, communication, control of automatic or robotic devices, among so many other functions. These artificial intelligence devices, such as Alexa, are based on a cloud that presents itself as a vocal assistant (interprets natural language and allows it to interact with people), which can be integrated into a speaker (with WiFi connection) or other smart devices. These new interactive communication technologies can provide information obtained from the web, carry out certain actions delegated by people or users, and control devices, apps, compatible services, and a long etcetera (Cipolla-Ficarra, et al., 2018a ; Cipolla-Ficarra, et al. 2019).

Just as personal computers, when introduced in the homes, generated a growing demand for multimedia content among users of different ages, these first ubiquitous devices, with artificial intelligence, and which operate in closed or open environments, will develop a greater diffusion and their integration in the daily life of millions of users. In some Asian communities the acceptance is such that they are already considered an essential element in the daily lives of families. In other geographical areas, such as the USA or Canada, robotics or industrial automation is expanding by companies until it reaches the

Figure 14. Sneakers reminiscent of the stylized figure of Hitler (www.puma.com, Herzogenaurach –Germany). La Vanguardia, 03.05.2020 (www.lavanguardia.com)

Figure 15. An excellent analogical, innovative and creative example, on paper. A postcard that when opened, allows the stereoscopic visualization of the 3D images that it contains, and related to the cultural heritage in the Republic of San Marino, in stamp format –www.ufn.sm

home. In other words, two paths that converge in a single highway of intelligent information and that can be interacted through tablet PCs or smartphones.

Technological devices that do not necessarily have to be constantly modernized, since connection is made through the web. Certainly, it is an interaction that requires various types of interfaces, such as: Command-Line Interface (CLI), Text-Based User Interfaces (TUI), Graphical User Interface (GUI), Voice-User Interface (VUI), Organic User Interface (OUI), Natural User Interface (NUI), etc., where web engineering can play a fundamental role, if exact limits of study are established, if a triadic vision of the past-present-future persists, and if there is a respect for the preceding or pioneering contributions in the field of software, hardware, computing, multimedia communication, etc.

From the point of view of optimizing software and hardware, it is important to know and weigh web architectures and useful methodologies for building applications and solutions, in the infinite semiosis of web engineering. Which may or may not be interrelated. In a reality of an engineer with elastic limits, it is necessary to integrate the knowledge and experiences of personal computers, servers, telematic networks, etc., towards modern multimedia smartphones, by programmers, system analysts, computer engineers, etc., belonging to generation X and Y, and vice versa. That is, from multimedia mobile telephony to personal computers, tablet PCs, servers, telematic networks, etc., by generation Z. Therefore, a first intersection of knowledge and experiences, of those three generations, related to web engineering, current and of the short-term future, can be summarized as follows:

Figure 16. A Shaun the Sheep Movie: Farmageddon (2019) –www.aardman.com. The creative vision of the commercialization of a product in DVD format, which is born from the animations with plasticine and which includes objects to enhance the recreational activities of the spectators such as puzzles (see bottom of the figure with the activity set for children). Puzzles are a successful element in content promotion, such as cultural and natural heritage, online and off-line (Cipolla-Ficarra, et al., 2018b)

- HTTP Internet protocols (the HTML standard).
- Languages and Applications (XML, eXtensible Markup Language).
- Software Architecture.
- Software Quality.
- Components and Models of Service Oriented Architecture (SOA).
- Web Applications Development.
- Interfaces and Interactive Design.
- Human and Social Factors in Multimedia Communication.
- Comunicability Evaluation.

Figure 17. Commercialization of the data registered in website aimed at the collection of scientific information. The portal promotes the transfer of the email addresses of its enrollees, to commercial companies of goods and services. ResearchGate –www.researchgate.net

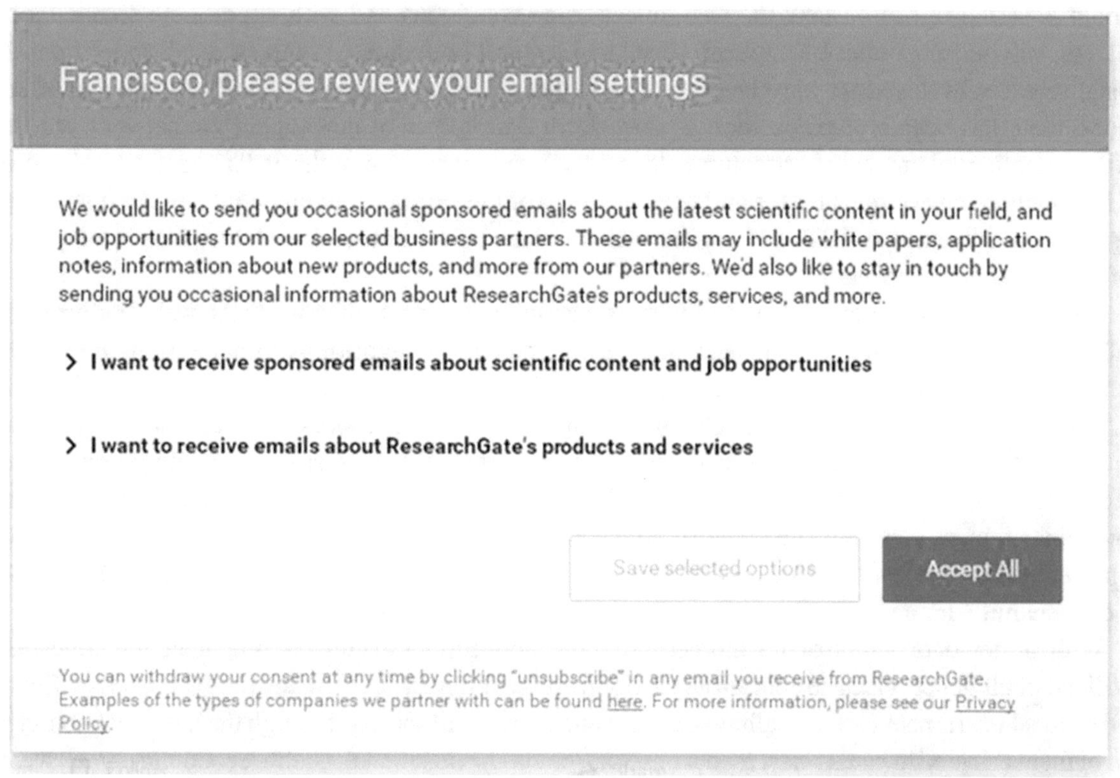

- Main Web Programming Languages (alphabetically and among others are: C #, C ++, Java, JavaScript, Perl, PHP, Python, R, Ruby, Rust, Swift).
- Frameworks for the Development of Hybrid Mobile Applications or not, on Android and iOS (iPhone Apple), for example, Ionic, React Native, Flutter, PhoneGap and Xamarin.
- Commercial Solutions for the Development of Web Portals.
- Content Management System (CMS).
- Business Applications and Solutions (ECM –Enterprise Content Management).
- e-Commerce Solutions and Implementation.
- Servers, Applications and Web Browsers.
- Privacy and Security Online.
- Cloud Intelligent Technology.
- Social Networking and Cyber Behavior.
- Corporate Networks.
- Semantic Web and Ontologies.
- Search and Positioning Technologies (SEO –Search Engine Optimization).
- Web extension in Smart Cities.
- Internet of Things (IoT).

Lessons Learned

Since the last decade of the last century and with the democratization of the Internet, all human beings should have the right to access the web, under equal conditions and with appropriate technological devices, solving economic, educational, social and cultural limitations. Progressive advances from the social sciences in this sense have been positive. However, it can be seen how, from some formal sciences, there has been a predisposition to slow down the process of developing the network, starting with promoting telematic infrastructures (long band) and interactive multimedia content (digitization of information) and original (in the authentic meaning of the word), excluding wild mercantilism, starting with the education of ICTs and engineering, masters, doctorates, and post doctorates (computing, software, systems, web, etc.).

The long band has allowed solving a host of interactive design problems for the web. For example, define suitable queries for greater speed in accessing databases, algorithms for understanding and decompressing files with audio, moving images, etc. All this due to the slowness of online multimedia (1.5 Mb. in download and 64 Kb. in upload), existing between 1995-2000. Back then, those responsible for the digitization of analog information had a certain distrust of the Internet. Especially, in circulating large volumes of information online, which could no longer be controlled by traditional means of social communication, as they could do with offline media (CD-Rom, CD-I, DVD, etc.). In short, information is power, and power fears the free dissemination of information. Something that still persists and resists in the new millennium.

With the democratization of the Internet and its first applications to human-computer communication, artificial intelligence, distance education, the digitization of libraries, etc. many thought that they finally had an ideal instrument for the qualitative advancement of world society, through the latest technologies. All of them oriented towards a new model of social, cultural, educational, health, economic organization, etc., more just and balanced. However, the human factor and the social factor corrupted the nobility of the invention until, with the rise of social networks, it generated two areas: the deep and dark web. Bipolar, negative and dark areas that have their origins in the educational and / or self-taught environment of users, with psychological and sociological problems. It is there, where the students and teachers of institutions or organizations denote a strong presence of the G factor. The goal of these individuals was, is, and will be to get the maximum personal benefit, with the minimum of effort and in the shortest possible time. The examples in the Appendix #1 attached to this research work verify this reality.

This passage from freedom of access to information, to debauchery through the anonymity of cyber behavior, is leading users of Generation X, towards a return to access to analog information, for example. That is, to re-access the daily, weekly, monthly and annual information through newspapers, magazines, books, yearbooks, catalogs, etc., or off-line multimedia / hypermedia media, such as CDs / CD-ROMs / DVDs. It is a growing phenomenon, when they verify that their personal data granted to companies of goods and services are marketed to third parties or entities, without any authorization. Sometimes, they are stolen directly through hackers.

Furthermore, in an endless number of cases, the codes of ethics in everything related to the web are totally inapplicable by the authorities dedicated to the protection of the rights of citizens. Authorities who find in software producers, online search engines, social media managers and safeguarding content, etc., an inoperative and excessive slowness to solve these problems. Problems that are located on the surface of the World Wide Web, that is, where the main search engines, free access encyclopedias, scientific databases, etc. are located.

Consequently, it is still unlikely today that a student will obtain a qualitative "theoretical-practical" qualification in web engineering in a few months, although the misleading advertising of these studies guarantees an ability to work independently in this new professional field. Learning the real structure of the web (from the surface to the dark area and vice versa), the programming languages, the server configuration, the interactive design, the correct use of the resources present in the hardware, etc., require years of studies and a high motivation for continuous training, in order to obtain fully autonomous professionals in their activities.

In this context and autonomously, web engineering and design must be 100% original in the methods, techniques, tools, models, etc., that it generates, and with minimal contributions from the other disciplines (if they are mandatorily necessary) with which it interacts, within the formal and factual sciences. In addition, you must develop a limited scope of work and avoid the phenomenon of infinite semiosis. Thus eradicating the power groups that use it to obtain short-term economic benefits, without being interested in its potential as a discipline and its scientific aspect.

Since 2000, open software has been a very positive resource, not only because of its rapid development, but also for bringing together internationally a group of young programmers, analysts, engineers, etc., interested in the continuous and original evolution of the latest information technologies. Communicability in multimedia mobile telephony, the potential of interactive audiovisual in mixed reality, the control of smart devices at a distance, the safeguard of people's online data, are some of the future challenges from the engineering of the web.

CONCLUSION

The mercantilist fashion of transforming areas of study belonging to the formal and factual sciences into engineering only allows us to achieve quantitative but not qualitative results. Even these quantitative results are partial because not all the information is on the web, despite the decades that have passed since its creation. Nor does the incorporation of anthropologists, artists, psychologists, pedagogues, etc. guarantee a higher quality of content. On the contrary, since it boosts the rise of mathematicians, physicists, chemists, nuclear engineers, management engineers, etc., to the top of the research and development projects related to web engineering. It is an immutable reality from the first hypertextual systems of the 1980s and that does not tend to change, with the passing of time.

This does not mean that these professionals should be excluded, but rather, that they carry out the activities relevant to their corresponding studies. Whenever its presence is detected in diverse fields such as information retrieval, human-computer interaction, and web engineering, to name three examples, not only do the epistemological principles of the sciences disappear, but automatically those areas of knowledge lose their exact limits, generating in addition, a great drift to the quantification of knowledge and not to quality. An example is the dire consequence of the h-index metric in times of global crisis. The objective of these professionals, in those three areas cited as examples, is to see this index increase rapidly.

Hence the constant need to review the software's past, in order to better understand the present and establish, as precisely as possible, future lines for a correct development. Well-defined and future-oriented web engineering can achieve those goals of the common good for all humanity, which were foreseen by the pioneers and developers of this new means of communication. In this sense, the inclusion of artificial intelligence is a new great challenge. However, nowadays you can assist in "the disintelligence of artificial intelligence", through automated algorithms or people, who mistakenly collect information on the web. Some examples from in Annexes #1 and #2 confirm this statement.

All this forces the user to undertake long bureaucratic paths on the surface of the web to resolve the consequences of everything that he is not an author but that refers to him on the web. The origin is usually in the deep extracts of the Internet. Now then, those negative actions that remain in the immune anonymity, leads the human being to not participate in the phenomenon of social networks, for example. Fortunately, human beings still have the power to physically isolate themselves from the network (turning off the WiFi router, disconnecting the cable from the telephone network, etc.) and working during that period with absolute security.

Necessarily, web engineering must preserve the quality of all its components, starting with analyzing the context and human factors, since they are usually the main source of insecurity on the Internet. For this reason, it must constantly search for new instruments, methods, techniques and models to promote exemplary use of the web, with high quality in the interactive communication process. Quality that must start at the time of designing the portals, interfaces, content, etc. to the use of the most suitable programs and applications to solve each of the potential problems that may arise through the web, and those computers or devices that, from a distance, can operate autonomously (artificial intelligence) or not.

A few examples, among many others, are: Interacting with household electronic devices, flying a drone with first aid kits, guiding an elderly man to his rehabilitation center, making a diagnosis of the state of health or surgical operation, moving a robot in a closed or open space, activating the irrigation system, pest control, etc. in the fields. These operations will require a new profile of professionals, accumulators of extensive knowledge and previous experiences, added to the desire to study and learn from the daily revolution, which comes from hardware and software.

ACKNOWLEDGMENT

The authors like to thank you very much to Maria Ficarra. Furthermore, special thanks to Amélie Bordeaux, Mary Brie, Gioia Giardi, Alicia Martín, Eulogia Mendoza, Luisa Varela, Jim Carré, Donald Nilson, and Carlos for the support, assistance and comments.

REFERENCES

Allier, S. (2015). Multitier Diversification in Web-Based Software Applications. *IEEE Computer*, *32*(1), 83–90.

Apple. (1992). *Macintosh Human Interface Guidelines*. Addison-Wesley.

Bagchi, S., Siddiqui, M.-B., Wood, P., & Zhang, H. (2020). Dependability in Edge Computing. *Communications of the ACM*, *63*(1), 58–66. doi:10.1145/3362068

Barker, P. (1991). Interactive Electronic Books. *Interactive Multimedia*, *2*(1), 11–28.

Barker, P. (1993). *Exploring Hypermedia*. Kogan Page.

Berners-Lee, T. (1996). WWW: Past, Present, and Future. *IEEE Computer*, *29*(10), 79–85. doi:10.1109/2.539724

Berners-Lee, T., Cailliau, R., Luotonen, A., Nielsen, H. F., & Secret, A. (1991). The World-Wide Web. *Communications of the ACM*, *37*(8), 76–82. doi:10.1145/179606.179671

Brandtzaeg, P., & Folstad, A. (2017). Trust and Distrust in Online Fact-Checking Services. *Communications of the ACM*, *60*(9), 65–71. doi:10.1145/3122803

Charette, R., & King, J. L. (2018). Winning and Losing in IT. *IEEE Computer*, *51*(10), 10–15. doi:10.1109/MC.2018.3971361

Cipolla-Ficarra, F. (1996). *Evaluation and Communication Techniques in Multimedia Product Design for On the Net University Education. In Multimedia on the Net*. Springer. doi:10.1007/978-3-7091-9472-0_14

Cipolla-Ficarra, F. (2015). *Handbook of Research on Interactive Information Quality in Expanding Social Network Communications*. IGI Global. doi:10.4018/978-1-4666-7377-9

Cipolla-Ficarra, F. (2018). *Technology-Enhanced Human Interaction in Modern Society*. IGI Global. doi:10.4018/978-1-5225-3437-2

Cipolla-Ficarra, F. (2018a). *Expanding Horizonts in Smart Cities, Software Engineering, Mobile Communicability, Cloud Technologies, and Big-data*. Blue Herons.

Cipolla-Ficarra, F. (2018b). *Technology-Enhanced Human Interaction in Modern Society*. IGI Global. doi:10.4018/978-1-5225-3437-2

Cipolla-Ficarra, F. (2019). *Examining New Points of View in Web Engineering, Visual Interfaces, Motion Graphics and Human-Computer Communicability*. Blue Herons.

Cipollla-Ficarra, F. (2017). *Cyber Destructors of the Sciences: Studies in Education, Culture, Employment and New Technologies*. Blue Herons.

Dahlman, E., Parkvall, S., & Skold, J. (2020). *5G NR: The Next Generation Wireless Access Technology*. Academic Press.

Deely, J. (1986). *Frontiers in Semiotics*. Indiana University Press.

Du, M., Liu, N., & Hu, N. (2020). Techniques for Interpretable Machine Learning. *Communications of the ACM*, *63*(1), 68–77. doi:10.1145/3359786

Eco, U., & Sebeok, T. A. (1984). *The Sign of Three: Dupin, Holmes, Peirce*. Indiana University Press.

Fenton, N., & Bieman, J. (2014). *Software Metrics: A Rigorous and Practical Approach*. CRC Press. doi:10.1201/b17461

Harrell, D., & Lim, C. (2017). Reimagining the Avatar Dream: Modeling Social Identity in Digital Media. *Communications of the ACM*, *60*(7), 50–61. doi:10.1145/3098342

Hehn, Mendez, D., Uebernickel, F., Brenner, W., & Broy, M. (2020). On Integrating Design Thinking for Human-Centered Requirements Engineering. *IEEE Software*, *37*(2), 25–31. doi:10.1109/MS.2019.2957715

Heule, M., & Kullmann, O. (2017). The Science of Brute Force. *Communications of the ACM*, *60*(8), 70–79. doi:10.1145/3107239

Hirigoyen, M. F. (2019). *Les Narcisse: Ils ont pris le pouvoir*. La Découverte.

Kaprow, A. (1991). *New Media Applications in Art and Design*. ACM Siggraph.

Landow, G. (1991). *Hypermedia and Literary Studies*. The MIT Press.

Landow, G. (2006). Hypertext 3.0: Critical Theory and New Media in an Era of Globalization. Charles Village: Johns Hopkins University Press

Lu, M. (2020). Exploring Visual Information Flows in Infographics. In *CHI 2020 - Conference on Human Factors in Computing Systems* (pp. 1-12). New York: ACM Press.

Martin, B. & Ringham, F. (2006). *Key Terms in Semiotics*. London: Bloomsbury 3PL.

McCullough, B. (2018). *How the Internet Happened From Netscape to the iPhone*. W. W. Norton.

Negroponte, N. (1995). *Being Digital*. Knopf.

Nelson, T. (1993). *Literary Machines*. Mindful Press.

Nielsen, J. (1990). *Hypertext and Hypermedia*. Academic Press.

O'Neil, C. (2016). *Weapons of Math Destruction: How Big Data Increases Inequality and Threatens Democracy*. Crown.

Oliveira, A. (2017). *The Digital Mind: How Science is Redefining Humanity*. MIT Press. doi:10.7551/mitpress/9780262036030.001.0001

Pandit, V. (2015). *We Are Generation Z: How Identity, Attitudes, and Perspectives Are Shaping Our Future*. Brown Books Publishing.

Pendyala, V., Shim, S., & Bussler, C. (2015). The Web that Extends Beyond the World. *IEEE Computer*, *48*(5), 18–25. doi:10.1109/MC.2015.150

Pressman, R., & Lowe, D. (2009). *Web Engineering: A Practitioner's Approach*. McGraw-Hill.

Pressman, R., & Maxim, B. (2015). *Software Engineering: A Practitioner's Approach*. McGraw-Hill Education.

Raggett, D. (2015). The Web of Things: Challenges and Opportunities. *IEEE Computer*, *48*(5), 26–32. doi:10.1109/MC.2015.149

Reeves, B., & Nass, C. (1996). *The Media Equation: How People Treat Computers, Television, and New Media Like Real People and Places*. Cambridge University Press.

Reisman, S. (2020). Viva la Revolucion? *IEEE Computer*, *53*(8), 71–73. doi:10.1109/MC.2020.2993622

Robbins, J. (2018). *Learning Web Design: A Beginner's Guide to HTML, CSS, JavaScript, and Web Graphics*. O'Reilly Media.

Savage, N. (2017). Weaving the Web. *Communications of the ACM*, *60*(6), 20–22. doi:10.1145/3077334

Schermann, J., Cito, J., & Leitner, P. (2018). Continuous Experimentation: Challenges, Implementation Techniques, and Current Research. *IEEE Software*, *35*(2), 26–31. doi:10.1109/MS.2018.111094748

Shen, C., & Srivastava, M. (2017). Exploring Hardware Heterogeneity to Improve Pervasive Context Inferences. *IEEE Computer*, *50*(6), 19–26. doi:10.1109/MC.2017.174

Sieckenius-de-Souza, C. (2004). *The Semiotic Engineering of Human-Computer Interaction*. MIT Press.

Suh, W. (2005). *Web Engineering: Principles and Techniques*. IGI Global. doi:10.4018/978-1-59140-432-3

Sun, J., Staab, S., & Kunegis, J. (2018). Undestanding Social Networks Using Transfer Learning. *IEEE Computer*, *51*(6), 52–60. doi:10.1109/MC.2018.2701640

ADDITIONAL READING

Bal, H., & Grune, D. (1994). *Programming Language Essentials*. Addison-Wesley.

Bau, D., Gray, J., Kelleher, C., Sheldon, J., & Turbak, F. (2017). Learnable Programming Blocks and Beyond. *Communications of the ACM*, *60*(6), 72–80. doi:10.1145/3015455

Berghel, H. (2017). Which Is More Dangerous –the Dark Web or the Deep State? *IEEE Computer*, *50*(7), 86–91. doi:10.1109/MC.2017.215

Cao, L. (2017). Data Science: Challenges and Directions. *Communications of the ACM*, *60*(8), 59–68. doi:10.1145/3015456

Chua, C., & Storey, V. (2017). Bottom-Up Enterprise Information Systems: Rethinking the Roles of Central IT Departments. *Communications of the ACM*, *60*(1), 66–72. doi:10.1145/2950044

Conklin, J. (1987). Hypertext: An Introduction and Survey. *IEEE Computer*, 17-41, 20(9),

DeBenedictis, E. (2018). A Future with Quantum Machine Learning. *IEEE Computer*, *51*(2), 68–71. doi:10.1109/MC.2018.1451646

Halasz, F., & Schwartz, M. (1994). The Dexter Hypertext Reference Model. *Communications of the ACM*, *37*(3), 30–39. doi:10.1145/175235.175237

Hardman, L., Bulterman, D., & Van Rossum, G. (1993). The Amsterdam Hypermedia Model: Extending Hypertext to Support Real Multimedia. *Hypermedia*, *5*(1), 47–69. doi:10.1080/09558543.1993.12031214

Harford, T. (2017). *Fifty Inventions that Shaped the Modern Economy*. Penguin Random House.

Heule, M., & Kullmann, O. (2017). The Science of Brute Force. *Communications of the ACM*, *60*(8), 70–79. doi:10.1145/3107239

Kaptelinin, V., & Czerwinski, M. (2007). *Beyond the Desktop Metaphor: Designing Integrated Digital Work Environments*. The MIT Press. doi:10.7551/mitpress/1584.001.0001

Mehlenbacher, B. (2010). *Instruction and Technology: Designs for Everday Learning*. The MIT Press. doi:10.7551/mitpress/9780262013949.001.0001

Rehman, M. (2019). *Human Factors in Global Software Engineering*. IGI Global. doi:10.4018/978-1-5225-9448-2

Ross, A. (2016). *The Industries of the Future*. Simon & Schuster.

Svore, K., & Troyer, M. (2016). The Quantum Future of Computation. *IEEE Computer*, *49*(9), 21–30. doi:10.1109/MC.2016.293

Tompa, F. (1989). A Data Model for Flexible Hypertext Database Systems. *ACM Transactions on Information Systems*, *7*(1), 85–100. doi:10.1145/64789.64993

Walrad, C. (2017). Standards for the Enterprise IT Profession. *IEEE Computer*, *50*(3), 70–73. doi:10.1109/MC.2017.68

Warner, J. (2009). *Human Information Retrieval*. The MIT Press. doi:10.7551/mitpress/9780262013444.001.0001

Xu, W. (2019). Toward Human-Centered AI: A Perspective from Human-Computer Interaction. *Interaction*, *26*(4), 42–46. doi:10.1145/3328485

Yadav, A., Stephenson, C., & Hong, H. (2017). Computational Thinking for Teacher Education. *Communications of the ACM*, *60*(4), 55–62. doi:10.1145/2994591

Yan, J., & Randell, B. (2009). An Investigation of Cheating in Online Games. *IEEE Security and Privacy*, *7*(3), 37–44. doi:10.1109/MSP.2009.60

KEY TERMS & DEFINITIONS

Web Engineering: It is a new branch of software engineering and consists of the use of new systematic, organized and quantifiable methodologies for the efficient development of high-quality commercial or non-commercial systems or applications on the web.

Anomalous and Predatory Agents: Professionals in the formal sciences (mathematicians, physicists, engineers and graduates who do not belong to the computer field) who exert their influence on web engineering, human-computer interaction and retrieval information and gradually develop aggressive or predatory behavior towards professionals in factual science until they transform. Cyberbullism is one of the most common practices of these agents.

Artificial Intelligence: It is the intelligence carried out by programmable machines, capable of perceiving the context, adapting in the best way to it, to carry out the tasks assigned by the programmer or user.

Web Communicability: It is the high quality of communication between the user and the components of the web. Components derived from the use of software and hardware that can be grouped by quality attributes. Each of these attributes can be evaluated heuristically, through special metrics, which make up an analysis methodology.

Semiosis of Digital Metamorphosis: They are the constant self-referential changes in social networks, websites, etc., starting with experiences and / or training in the curriculum vitae. The value of the credibility of digital information by these users is nil. Frequently, they resort to erasing information online when their lies are discovered.

Design Models: They are oriented to classic interactive systems (hypertexts, multimedia and hypermedia) or modern (augmented reality, mixed reality, etc.). They use the main components from the databases, presentation of information in the interface, programming languages, semiotics or semiology.

ENDNOTES

1 Basili, V. J. & Musa, J. (1991). The Future Engineering of Software: A Management Perspective. *IEEE Computer*, 24(9), 90-96.

2 Musa, J. (1998). Software Reliability Engineering: More Reliable Software, Faster Development and Testing. New York: McGraw-Hill.

Table 1. Unlimited expansion from formal science to medicine, through 21st century HCI. This phenomenon negatively affects interactive systems design, software quality, end-users, and the relationship of software engineering, web engineering, HCI, and UX with other disciplines.

Degree or engineering degree, together with the place of origin of said university degree	Actual university	Dept.	Topics of the first 5-10 research papers in the 20th century	International "broadcast channels"	Some keywords of the topics covered today	The relevant target audiences or study universe
Mathematics (Padova, Italy)	Polytechnic of Milan	Computer Science	Logic Programming; Hypertext; Database.	System Sciences; HCI; Design; Information Retrieval; Multimedia Tools and Applications; Visual Interfaces; Interact; Artificial Intelligence and Virtual Reality.	Language Disorders; Alzheimer's Disease; Neurodevelopment Disorders; Autism Spectrum Disorder; Cognitive Disability; Amblyopia; Intellectual Disability; Intellectual Developmental Disability; Children and People with Special Needs.	Children; Handicapped; Users.
Mathematics (Pisa, Italy)	University of Bolzano	Computer Science	Learning Automata; Data Compression; Incremental Algorithms	Recommender System; Information Retrieval; HCI; User Interfaces.	Patients in the Hospital; Patient Guidance in Day-Hospital; Model in Conversational; Mobile City Transport; User Behaviour; Music Recommendations; Food Recommender System; IT and Tourism; User Behaviour Model.	Adults; Tourists; Users.
Computer Science (Santiago, Chile)	University of Chile	Computer Science	Searching Algorithms; Similarity Queries; Text-Retrieval; Software Engineering.	World Wide Web; String Processing and Information Retrieval; Research and Development in Information Retrieval; Intelligent Data Analysis.	People with Dyslexia; Detection of Dyslexia with a Web-Based Game; Abortion Debate.	People; Lawyers; Social Media.
Industrial and Systems Engineering (Monterrey, Mexico)	Politechnical University of Catalonia	Computer Science	Algorithm for Recovering Possibilistic Causal Networks; Control-Flow Mechanism; Waste-Water Treatment Plants; Knowledge-Based Systems; Subjective Situations.	Artificial Intelligence; Environmental Modelling and Software; Computing Research Repository; Pervasive Technologies.	Alzheimer's Disease; Drosophila Pupae; Tumour Genetic; Convolutional Neural Networks; People Living with Dementia; Brain MEG Recordings in Schizophrenia; Schizophrenia Diagnostic; Elders Mobility; Human Organ for Transplantation.	Elder Population; People with Special Needs; Users.
Mathematics (La Plata, Argentina)	National University of La Plata	Computer Science	Information Models; Object-Oriented Applications; Hypermedia and the Psycho-Therapeutic.	Web Engineering; Universal Access in the Information Society.	Blind Users	Blind People; Users.
Physics (Navarra, Spain)	University of the Basque Country	Computer Architecture and Technology	Tele-communication; Artificial Intelligence; Universal Access to Mobile Telephony; Inflected Language	Computers for Handicapped Persons; Universal Access in the Information Society.	People with Dementia; Children with Cerebral Palsy. People with Motor Impairments; Memory in Deaf Users'; Deaf Signer Users; People with Physical or Cognitive Restrictions; Rehabilitation Therapy.	Handicapped; People with Disabilities; Elderly People; Children.
Mathematics (Valencia, Spain)	Pompeu Fabra University	ICT	Multichannel Radio Station Programming; Geographic Information; Structured Peer-to-Peer Grids; Indexing and Retrieval of Geo-Referenced Video.	Advanced Learning Technologies; Technology Enhanced Learning; 3D Web Technology; Intelligent Networking and Collaborative Systems.	Cardiac Dyssynchrony Assessment; Analysis of Pedestrian Behaviors; Ethnographic Study; Older People in HCI; Smarter Cities for Older People; Older People in Brazil.	Users; Old People.

APPENDIX 1

In other words, these are the first examples that will be expanded in research work over time. The table shows the destruction of the HCI discipline from the formal sciences. The profile of the authors and modus operandis are reflected in Annex #2. That is, how they extend uncontrollably and irresponsibly from the formal sciences (maths, physics, etc.) to medicine, resorting to the destruction of HCI and the relationship of with other disciplines. It is an event that damages the quality of software, communicability and scientific knowledge, for example.

The destructive mechanism used is the infinite widening of the study limits and / or distorting its epistemology as a discipline. Finally, the bipolar personality disorders of its authors, to cite just one example, are reflected in the statements in the articles in the written press. In them they maintain that they were interested in "studying medicine", instead of mathematics, physics, computer science, engineering, etc. Over time, all this material has been compiled in the format of press articles (interviews, essays, etc.), which form a corpus of study for future research.

APPENDIX #2

The list of nouns and adjectives in figure 18 can be seen as synonymous with each other, redundant, or trivial. However, when a computer security system, in a company or industry, leaks information, such as the transfer of confidential data to the competition, more than in the technical sectors of the network, software, hardware, etc., one would have to concentrate on the human factor. A human factor that surely hides among the people who manage these systems, several of the words in the list.

This list is the result of theoretical and practical experiences, in the business, industrial and university educational sectors (computer science, computer graphics, computer animation, multimedia, HCI, etc.), in almost four decades. Through it, theories from software engineering in the '90s, with the studies carried out by Basili and Musa[1], Musa[2], among others, denote a total failure of the model to include anthropologists, sociologists, psychologists, artists, physicists, mathematicians, etc. to increase the quality of the software. These and other professionals have served to reinforce the G factor and vastly expand the dark zone on the Internet, since the late 1990s.

No human structure is exempt from these negative qualities of human behavior, as well as their transfer in artificial intelligence. That is why we can already affirm the existence of "artificial misintelligence." As examples, the automatic activation of profiles on social networks (Facebook, Twitter, LinkedIn, etc.) without the actions or authorization of the people to whom they refer. Eliminating these false profiles is practically impossible in a short time, through the local instruments of the entities or government institutions that regulate the proper functioning of the Internet.

In these cases, the misintelligence artificial is a kind of mirror about the human structures that have a high vertical and unidirectional profile (from top to bottom) among their members. For example, in the automatic process of indexing scientific works, some Germanic databases (i.e., DBLP – Digital Bibliography & Library Project, www.dblp.org) have implemented as a prerequisite that calls to submit papers, posters, demos, etc., are registered on websites (i.e., WikiCFP –a Wiki for Call For Papers –www.wikicfp.com), where it is now necessary to pay a fee. In the previous decade, this requirement did not exist in that database and that event advertising portal (WikiCFP) was completely free.

Figure 18. First set of actions, modus operandis, psychological traits, etc. collected for almost 40 years. In this set are represented those aspects of the human factor that not only slow down the social technological advance of ICTs, but also destroy them from the inside, such as software engineering, web engineering, HCI, UX, etc. The detailed explanation with true examples is a future line of research.

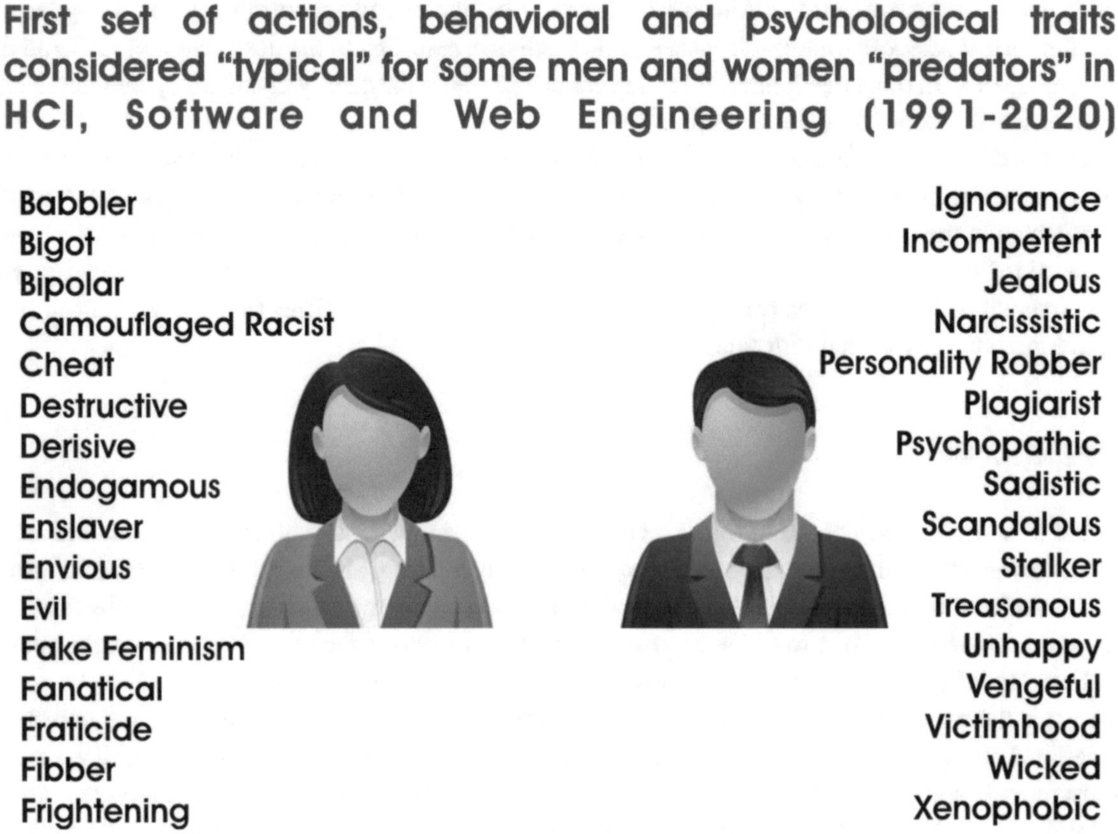

First set of actions, behavioral and psychological traits considered "typical" for some men and women "predators" in HCI, Software and Web Engineering (1991-2020)

Babbler
Bigot
Bipolar
Camouflaged Racist
Cheat
Destructive
Derisive
Endogamous
Enslaver
Envious
Evil
Fake Feminism
Fanatical
Fraticide
Fibber
Frightening

Ignorance
Incompetent
Jealous
Narcissistic
Personality Robber
Plagiarist
Psychopathic
Sadistic
Scandalous
Stalker
Treasonous
Unhappy
Vengeful
Victimhood
Wicked
Xenophobic

Fortunately, there are countless other event advertising portals, based in Asia, America, Europe and Oceania that still have a cost equal to zero euro cents, dollar, yen, yuan or other international currencies, but unfortunately they have not been considered by that Germanic database. It is the umpteenth way to verify the presence of the G factor in the new technologies.

In one-way vertical structures, each of the terms in figure 18 are promoted. In the mid-1990s, the Internet became democratized among millions of users around the planet. However, tests were not democratized to previously analyze, from a psychological / psychiatric / intellectual, etc. point of view, the degree of suitability people in HCI, UX, ICT, software engineering, web engineering, etc., who occupy key positions in daily decisions, which affect millions of local and global citizens. Future research will develop these issues that negatively distort the progressive advance of information sciences, interactive systems and communicability.

Figure 19. Link between the Germanic database DBLP and the website WikiCFP. That option was non-existent in the first decade of the new millennium.

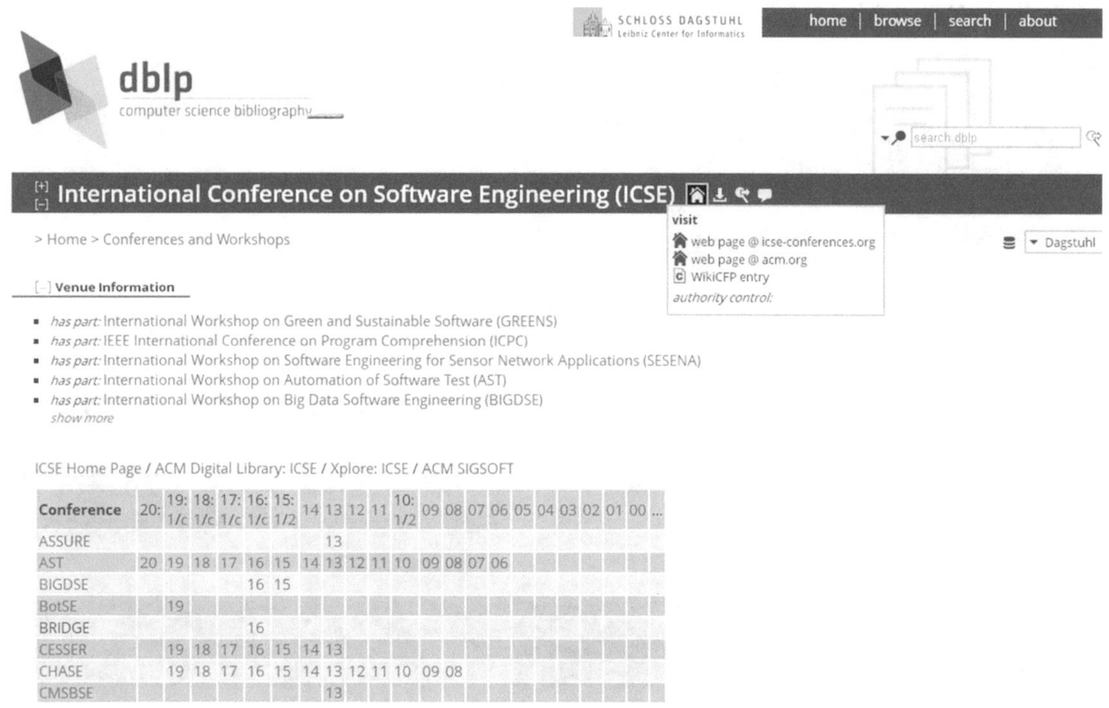

Figure 20. Excellent websites for the promotion of the international events and the cost requested to publish an event is equal to zero (it is a free service): conferencealerts.com, myhuiban.com, 10times. com, conferencemonkey.org, and siggraph.org

Add your events

Add an event to the Conference Alerts database. It's quick and free!

Promote your events

Promote your event via targeted e-mails, Conal Monthly and on the Conference Alerts website.

Conference Partner

Conference Partner » Home

3,902
CONFERENCES

1,056
JOURNALS

Find Conferences Worldwide

Chapter 3
Masters of Imagination:
From Hierarchies to Connected Swarms

Jaap van Till
Tildro Research, The Netherlands

ABSTRACT

This chapter is about some observations of the social and economic impact of ICT and ICT digital infrastructures and more specifically what users do with processing and telecommunication power tools. Network architects should be aware of those. Computer systems are no longer neutral tools, but they influence companies, public policies for control and institutions, and civil society cooperatives. Even the internet architecture board (IAB) has issued a directive about these effects. Electronic and network surveillance of users and what they do is growing with effects on elections. ICT is at the core of several large-scale transitions identified in this chapter. Groups of people who are immune to social media propaganda and alternative truth are discovered. And the chapter is rounded off with a hopeful vision about constructive value creation in cooperatives and science teams, making use of liberty of though and diversity of backgrounds. Making swarms and micro grids makes society alive again. Social super resolution is an interesting direction to pursue together.

INTRODUCTION AND SITUATION

Change is in the air. Worldwide, people, especially in the main cities, protest against the corruption and incompetence of their failing national ruling class, aka 'the rich 1%', who still treat them as slaves. The Demos finally had enough of living in a society run badly by a self-interested and self-serving Establishment (Allende, 2018). At the same time Digitalisation is changing these societies fundamentally and those who help implement the new systems to support network connected value-chains, have influence and can also see what is happening. Not only Big Brother but also the Little Brothers are watching on their screens. And they discuss that and cooperate to find solutions on social networks and billions of mobile smartphones on the Internet. People are faced with ongoing uncertainty, poverty and mass redundancy associated with the health costs for Covid-19 infections with social isolation and high social costs They

DOI: 10.4018/978-1-7998-7010-4.ch003

are living in a world plagued by ideologically influenced international conflicts, led by governments and financial institutions still firmly entrenched in the Neoliberal mindset, which is both failing and outdated.

In response to these uncertainties, governments and business managers have introduced distractions and various blame actions, to distract from their failures, playing on the national xenophobic sentiments of the population. For example: the new Tory leader in Scotland declared in his maiden speech, August 5, 2020 that the dangerous "traveling people (Gypsies) in Scotland should be brought under control". It is however now known and understood by the public that those 'vital workers' that kept our society working during the lockdowns were the very people that the managers had kept on low pay and laid off in large numbers to save money: nurses and health workers, police persons, people in the food chains, teachers and scientists, energy and water operations workers, telecom network operators, internet technicians. Their contribution needs more than rounds of applause. They need more than simply more money. They need respect, besides the satisfaction of results of what they do. Their anger is now going to expose as sham the layers and layers of zoom- meetings by managers, which add no value, and are in fact high paid obstacles.

I will not describe here what/who is causing what effects, but summarize that all over the world there is tension and anger, analogous to post-crash 1930 and pre-WWII fascism (Applebaum, A., 2020). For example: a high Pentagon official recently earmarked 'people of the Press' and 'demonstrators' as adversaries, meaning: enemies of the state. I will also not describe here what movements have started to counter that scenario and re-define and re-establish Democracy, Constitutions and The Law, such as Digital Democracy in Taiwan (Till, J.van, 2020).

The key point is that we are living post-crash 2008, which has still not ended, and that a new economic crash is around the corner. And the Cold War has resurfaced as The Information War (ICT Cyberwar). The financial crisis of 2008 was caused by an avalanche of selling of bad debts which were introduced by sophisticated capital-gambling computer systems, interconnected all over the world by computer systems and low latency optic fiber cables and microwave links. Complex networks can be shown to be unstable above a certain level of complexity (Till, J.van, 2016). Now in 2020 we are dangerously near that canyon again and the SEC people know that. Around 2000 I was approached by bankers who told me that by interconnecting their computer systems the risk of disturbances could be spread out, as was common practice in the insurance world. I warned that I could not guarantee that, because chain effects could also happen when the coupling was automatic and fast. Such avalanches happened in 2008 and have been happening in the energy grids too. Electricity systems are switched off to prevent them from overloading which cause other electricity producers to overload. In other words: computer and communication networks can also increase instability. Not all is progress everywhere. There is a USA state which has declined so fast in jobs, food and health (life expectancy) that they are now at the level of Bangladesh. Proof that the internet and especially mobile internet has deep influence on society is that on orders of Head of State of Belarus, the dictator Lukashenko did get the Internet out of operation before, during and after the elections in August 2020. Nevertheless, smart people there managed to get real-time videos out so the world could see what the security forces did to the demonstrators. And so people in Hong Kong did comment on what the factoryworkers, doctors and nurses did in Minsk. ICT networks DO have effects and are used extensively as most people have experienced during the lockdowns, working and Zooming from home.

The Underlaying Long Term Processes of Technological Innovations

All of the above is very much intertwined with ICT systems and networks, so computer scientists and technicians should be aware of their social-economic effects. They are not neutral tools and hence, I would argue, far too important to leave to those politicians. Yes, most of them have views on AI and jobs lost by automation, while in reality it is as if they have handed out AK47 machine guns at Kindergarten! Fortunately, children do know what to do with smartphones and tablets. From another angle: we should be aware that most people in the world, including remote and poor areas of Africa or Siberia do have one or more cellphones, thus improving their ability to contact, trace and communicate in and outside their country.

Formal description of the impact of mobile phones (and now also smartphones with internet access) is "lowering of transaction costs" + speeding up of finding help to solve problems and fast reaching of consensus over large distances.

Most of the above are symptoms of underlying long-term processes. To most of us so slow moving or the other extreme, striking so fast, that they go unnoticed while others are not directly interested because it seems not to influence their personal interest. Or as computer nerds live on other planets, not able to generalize small disturbances into patterns you can expect. I can. Let me show you three.

I. The brilliant financial–economic scientist Prof. Carlota Perez, (see more about her on WikiPedia), now at University College London, published (Perez, C., 2003) about her discovery of learning curves of progress repeating again and again when technological discoveries where absorbed and applied into society. As a scholar she specializes in technology and socio-economic development, researching the concept of Techno-Economic Paradigm Shifts and the theory of great surges, a further development of Schumpeter's work on Kondratieff waves.

To summarize, she found is that the growth curves of a number of key inventions/ fields of knowledge - "Technological Revolutions" can be identified:

(1) The Golden Age in the Seven Provinces of the Netherlands: 1600 - 1700 Innovative shipbuilding and worldwide maritime trading and logistics. This happened because a number of key ingredients coincided to renew: cheap energy, skilled foreign and respected local craftsmen and well-paid sailors, trusted transactions, **worldwide communications** and learning system, charts and instruments, law and trade ethics.
(2) The 'Industrial Revolution', started in England, 1771 – 1830
(3) Steam and Railways, 1830 – 1880
(4) Age of Steel, Coal, Electricity and Heavy Engineering, ca. 1880 -1920
(5) Age of Oil, The Automobile, Mass Production: 1900 - 1980

Including post WWII boom in building and "electro/mechanic/chemical" industries.

(6) The Age of Information and Telecommunications **(ICT)** 1971 – Present

Incidentally, I would argue that the German and French car industries and all the hundreds of thousands of jobs and suppliers are still stuck in the mindset of the golden ages of (5). They have difficulty in adapting to the hundreds of ICT systems inside the cars and to the electrification of cars forced on them by innovators such as Musk. Also in a number of countries the fossil fuel and chemical raw materials industries also in (5), have a lot of political influence, for instance in UK and NL, are facing slowdown due to corona, economic slump and eco crisis. They struggle to even imagine (6).

Each Technological Revolution has driven a different GREAT SURGE of development and with different ways of financing.

They are continuing and overlap but sooner or later the motor technology that drives such curve shifts to another booming field. When these different technology penetration curves over decades are superimposed the same four phases that where identified by Perez:

Installation-A. Start and Irruption (field testing)
Installation-B. Frenzy of entrepreneurs scaling up fast; with the very wealthy making serious profits, monopolies and fortunes.
Deployment-C. Synergy
Deployment-D. Maturity

The good news is that we are halfway up one such technological learning curve (6) and even more relevant here, the technological revolution driving an upcoming golden age is ICT = **Information and Communication Technologies.** The bad news however, is that between B. and C. there always is a crash and we fall into a deep hole of recession and companies collapsing. That happened in 2008 and is happening now in 2020. Covid, Economy and Ecology crashes at the same time.

A number of structural/ strategic measures must be made to be able to get us out of the hole together and continue progress for all. Most of those measures where published in 2005 (Perez, 2003), when she forecast quite accurately the financial crisis in 2008. Those urgent measures announced to be taken were repeated in 2009 (Perez, 2009) but still left unheeded even now, predominantly by bankers in Wall Street and The City, where gambling with money continues, at the expense of pension funds and government, under the pretense that money can be made with money. This does not work even with second, third and fourth derivatives of money, no longer representing actual goods or services that create value. Interestingly, a number of measures proposed by Perez are happening here and there anyway. Which means that these changes and transitions are inevitable.

This present learning curve is depicted in Fig. 1. presented here with permission of Carlota Perez. The horizontal axis is time and the vertical axis depicts the degree of diffusion of the new technological potential which is reflected in the successful growth of wealth and, let us hope, wellbeing.

Another important point to know is that after the crash, during phase C. SYNERGY and D. MATURITY the role of Finance and of the State are not vanished as some business leaders insist, but should be strengthened and must be changed fundamentally. This is shown in Fig. 2. The focus shifts to a wider rollout of the ICT technologies into the population and small business (Civil Society). The role of the Government here is to create platforms, infrastructures and conditions benefitting economy and society, while promoting and enabling "Digitalisation". You can expect the fossil fuel mega managers of learning curve (5) and the profit makers from phase B. to resist that trend, as it threatens their power and profit and sustainability. As with the transition from sailing ships to steam engines and like the film moguls in Hollywood in the "Roaring Twenties," (B.) had to wind down during the sudden Crash of 1930.

To conclude this short trend story, we can conclude the following:

- Our mindsets in society, state and business should synchronise on Further Deployment of ICT "Phase C" with Synergy at its core.

Figure 1. Present Learning Curve

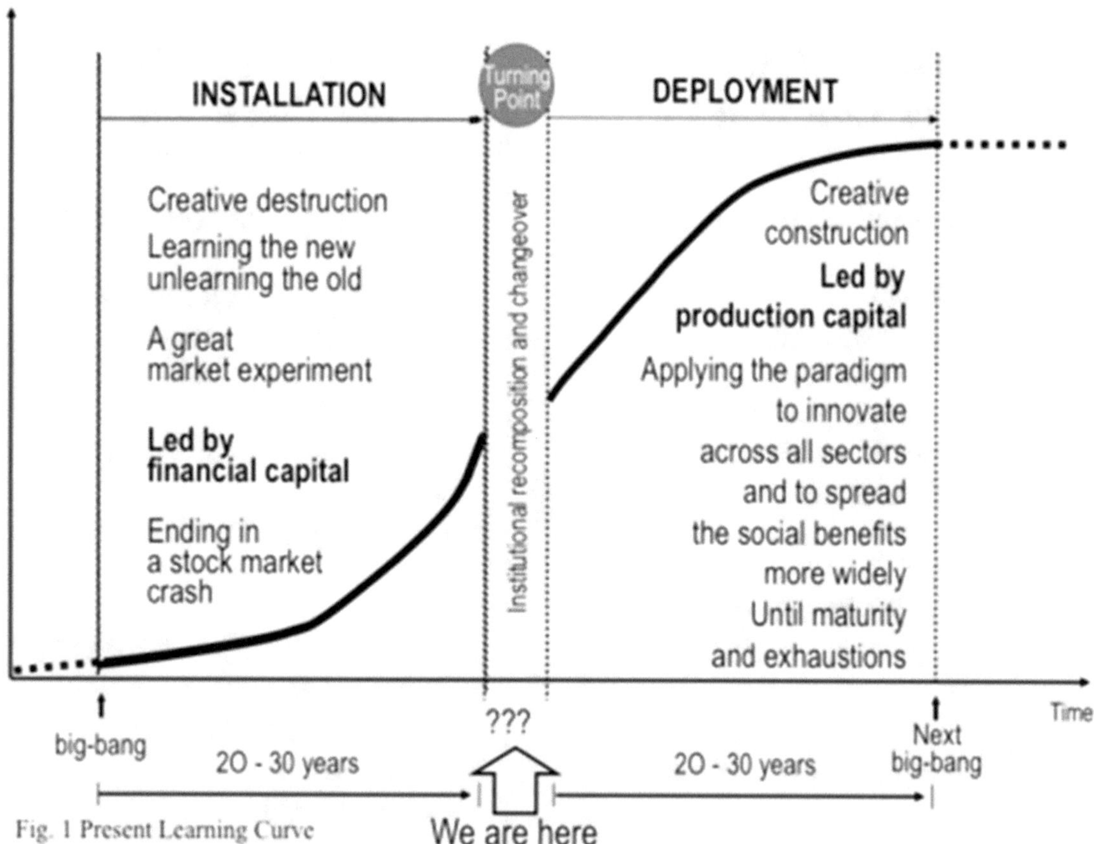

Fig. 1 Present Learning Curve

- Actions should be taken to further Digitalisation all over society. The core of that Digitalisation are systems and infrastructures that Create Value by combining a diversity of people by interconnecting, and Peer-to-Peer cooperation. I have christened this movement by the name 'Synthecracy', in ' several of my blogs and lectures. That is instead of the now too popular but crashing NeoLib phrase, Value Extraction, which is to the disadvantage of workers and nature, driving the ages of (2),(3),(4) and (5). Incentives for governments, investors and inventors for such value creation are the FIVE ICT Network Effects, see (Till, J van, 2015a) and (Till,J. van, 2019). Interestingly the Third Networking Law shows that Cooperation yields the highest value for all participants, because it unlocks Synergy, see Phase C above and (Corning, P. (2018).
- ICT technology, coding and (internet) network stuff is much more than some so-called 'geeky tech'. They are must know abilities and skills, to be educated in, applied in jobs, updated and co-created, all the way into top functions. I recommend here the books used at Polytechnics and Universities to introduce Network Science (Menczer, Fortunato & Davis; 2020) and (Barabási, 2016) as applicable in many fields and sectors.
- These movements mean that we individually and in groups will have to go through transitions towards C. And that control and execution of ICT supported tasks will be much more non-central with connected decentral authority and even internal & external cooperation. This can explain the

Figure 2. The Transition. Role of Financials and State

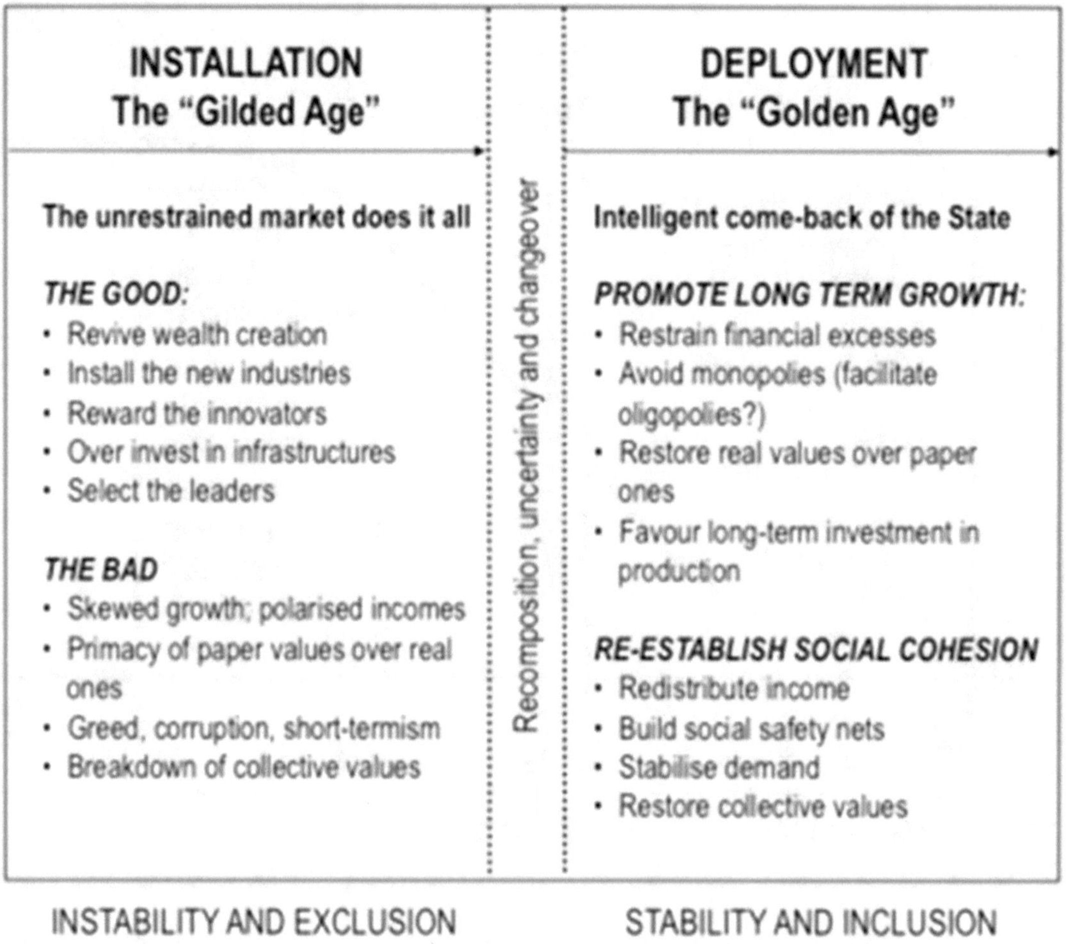

INSTALLATION The "Gilded Age"	Recomposition, uncertainty and changeover	DEPLOYMENT The "Golden Age"
The unrestrained market does it all ***THE GOOD:*** • Revive wealth creation • Install the new industries • Reward the innovators • Over invest in infrastructures • Select the leaders ***THE BAD*** • Skewed growth; polarised incomes • Primacy of paper values over real ones • Greed, corruption, short-termism • Breakdown of collective values		**Intelligent come-back of the State** ***PROMOTE LONG TERM GROWTH:*** • Restrain financial excesses • Avoid monopolies (facilitate oligopolies?) • Restore real values over paper ones • Favour long-term investment in production ***RE-ESTABLISH SOCIAL COHESION*** • Redistribute income • Build social safety nets • Stabilise demand • Restore collective values
INSTABILITY AND EXCLUSION		STABILITY AND INCLUSION

recent interest about how in nature Swarms of birds, Flocks of Birds and Anthills with emergent behaviour, are able to function. And more importantly, given the new ICT tools and network connections, how can we organize and flock ourselves in such swarms too? (See (Moffett, 2019) and below).

An interesting book from a 2017 conference describing the political implications of certain new ICT power tools is Werbach, *After the Digital Tornado –Networks, Algorithms, Humanity.*

2020. Worries in government circles about control of AI, Blockchain, Algorithms, Big Data, Internet of Things are important and I am happy that the politicians and regulators are updated on what is going on and what may happen, but I would be even more happy if they would actually start to invest in education, finance and steer these developments, which are too important to be left to the business people only focusing on their profits for shareholders. And these fields are under constant changes, so you can follow them only with the right mindsets. In this paper I do not explain the subjects of the Werbach book, but concentrate on the long lines of changes and TRANSITIONS + mindset jumps and changes. This kind of regulatory and political control conferences has grown into a real industry, although usually a lot of hot air is produced by authorities that read prepared papers about the WWW and uses of the Internet. If I may be so bold, it might be more useful if they read the formal definition of ***what Internet is****, see (Till, 2015b). "A set of voluntary bilateral agreements between owners of digital networks to interconnect. And to transport and transit each-others data packets, without payment".*

II Another pattern you can expect is the Dual Transition that Michel Bauwens, Guru of the P2P Foundation, and I discussed in a dialogue a couple of years ago. There are two seemingly rock-solid assumptions in society that have turned out not ot be so,, under pressure from scale and ICT tools.

Fossil fuels (gas, oil, coal) and minerals mineable from the Earth are abundant, inexhaustible, and can be owned by the extractor.

From the golden ages of (4) and (5) is in transition to:

Fossil fuels and minerals and ecologies in Nature from which we can harvest (and its waste used in a circular fashion) are scarce resources to be replaced as much as possible by renewable energy sources (sun, wind, waterpower), assisted by ICT, Age (6)

At the same time, we transit from the following assumption:

Information and knowledge are scarce Resources with its Intellectual Property and copyright exclusively owned by the publisher and multiplicator and distributor, which encourages and protects the Authors/ Creators.

is in transit to:

Information, knowledge and wisdom are abundancy and to be shared on the Internet.

Copying and sharing (multiplication and distribution with ICT is now costless) and does not diminish their value and can be done with Creative Commons (CC) license, which has the explicit intent that people can combine parts of CC protected publications/music/videos from different fields/sectors into further new creative art or new scientific discoveries. This is also part of Age (6).

To summarize it should be noticed that both original assumptions are no longer valid and might now be called 'outdated fairytales. Not everybody agrees and some of them even fight these transitions. Another way of putting it is that Knowledge is no longer a product but it is becoming a ICT supported process.

A further interesting further trend is that we can see the following separate platforms/layers of 'information' processing and communication developing:

- actively: taking actions in Reality, actual business processes, Nature
- imagination and patterns
- insight
- wisdom

Figure 3. Some layers of information and image use

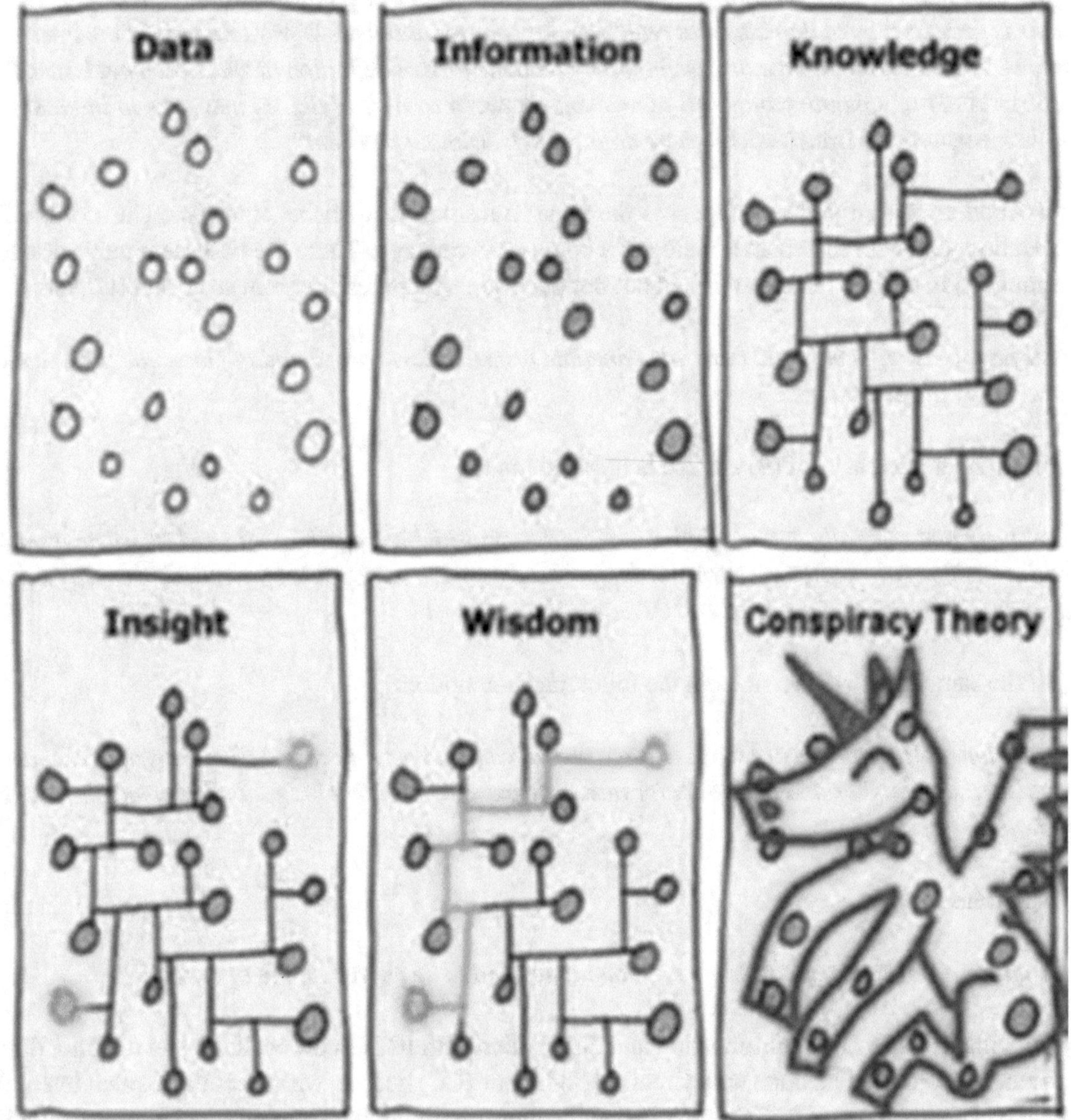

- knowledge, models
- semiosis & semantics (meaning) and image constructs 2D & 3D
- syntax and images
- data
- signs
- signals

What we effectively do to handle complexity in issues and architectures is to split them in parts that are relatively **orthogonal** to each other, meaning changes in one layer do only have a quantitative effect on other layers. So, we can constantly improve components and supplier stuff on each layer without having to re-design the whole architecture and all its infrastructures. This was the original idea behind the so called OSI-ISO layers, later implemented in the Internet protocol stack (Stuttgart Wineglass). And, more recently, in the concept of the much debated 'Network Neutrality': ie. network access and -transport providers should not have any say in the content or application of the data packets they transport. (This is for the sake of not being stuck in vertical integrated structures and services). Freedom to change and improve. Make our ICT and social infrastructures future proof and able to scale up in size. Some years ago, I introduced the 'Tillevision model' as a tool to chart the different layers of corporate ICT infrastructure, to explain this to management and internal ict support groups.

Figure 4. The Tillevision Model

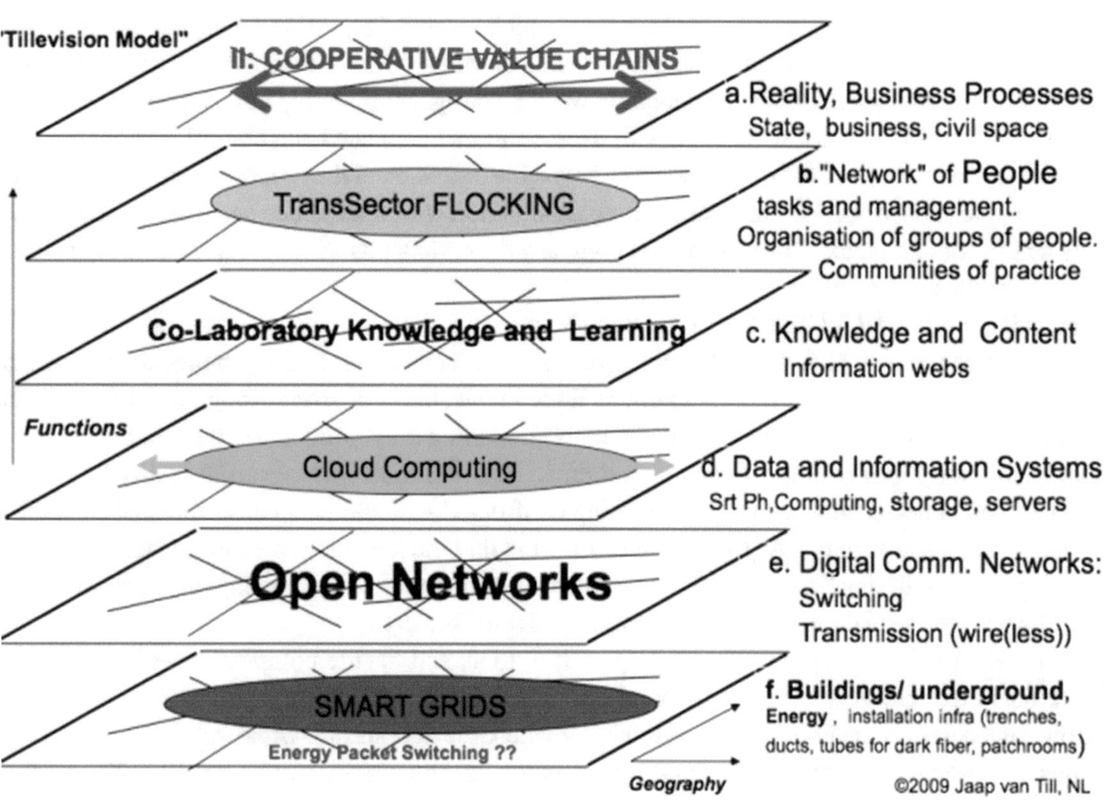

The orthogonalisation of issues can also be done in groups of people with the advantage that correlation and matching is much simpler to do and by extrapolation of the spectrum we can achieve super resolution. In the human brain there is somewhere a split at the fourth level from below between two separate structures. One for language (auditive) processing and one for processing and analysis of images (visual). It is interesting to note that efforts on AI based on the first one, mathematics and formal algorithms got stuck and AI based on deep learning of images with parallel connectivity did suddenly make fast progress. In the human brain a large part is dedicated to handling images, patterns and models.

The three uppermost ones in the above schematic are indeed still very scarce and may be supported by AI but cannot (yet) be replaced by machines or networks. They reside in humans and some animals and may also be present some day in groups of people who are organized as a collective intelligence-network supported. Imagination is scarce indeed, as the famous inventor of word processing and hypertext Ted Nelson once remarked in front of a conference room full of managers: "Imagination is scarce, some managers cannot even imagine that other people can have it".

My recently Covid-departed friend Kim Veltman, PhD; former director of the McLuhan Institute in Maastricht, and super librarian, was a master in the five uppermost layers of the tower of Babel layering shown above.

III The third transition shown in this paper is that from vertical info/command/control flow in Hierarchical organizations to forms of cooperation and co-creation directly between peers: Peer-to-Peer (P2P). This thinking in terms of hierarchies is so deeply embedded in all human societies that most of us have difficulty to NOT think in terms of a leader below which layers of reporting managers are busy. Even in football teams and demonstrations the public wants to know "who is the leader?". Sure, ships have captains. They are not organized in a democratic way by voting. Most simply put, Napoleon established the 'hierarchy' for his vast army. He could still oversee all that happened and control it very effectively by commands to lower level officers, who just obeyed his orders. And they reported upwards what they did see as the results. Wonderful in a not so complex situation with few sudden surprises. And there was simply no time or communication system to accompany the commands with overviews and explanations why the decisions where taken.

But wait a minute, NOW THERE IS, with the help of ICT tools.

The standard hierarchy has a lot of handicaps. The main ones are: it is slow (notice for instance the reaction time of government in Beijing to things done in the streets of Hong Kong: about four weeks), upward reporting is flawed, filtered and sometimes containing only good news, the central leadership cannot handle too much complexity and uncertainty. This is a consequence of the reality being more and more interconnected and central control being confronted with the boundaries dictated by Ashby's Law (law of requisite variety). A frightening prospect is that the tendency of central leaders may be to seek refuge in simplifying Reality. In other words, they sometimes start arresting and 'educating' and even killing people who do not fit in their simple model for society.

Again, we can now scale up with the help of ICT tools and handle complexity with a **transition** from vertical hierarchical control to horizontal P2P transparency and informing all participants. Is such constructions decisions can be distributed to nearer where the actions are, while still informing all participants and distributing and connecting the models too, so complexity can be handled. The problem with this transition III is not that there are no experiments or examples fort his 90 degrees turning from vertical to horizontal. It is just that most people are accustomed to top-down command and control and they feel kind of safe being told what to do and what to think. This makes people reluctant to make decisions, make errors and take responsibilities. I do not blame them, but I foresee many smaller agile and well-connected teams that have to rely on each other to work and survive in the future. The Seals and other military

teams have found out that there is no better way. In other words: Transition III is from Hierarchies to P2P interconnected cooperative Swarms, see (Corning, P., 2018) and (Moffett, M. W., 2019).

Figure 5. Hierarchies and their shortcomings

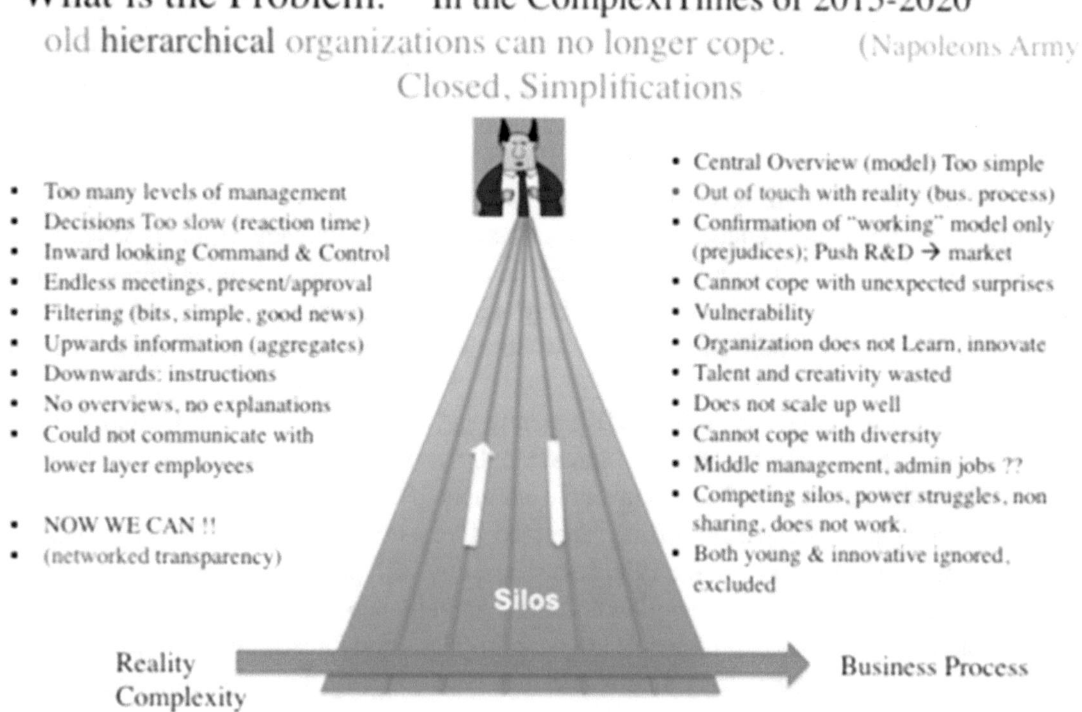

Warnings and Discovery of Unique Persona

Below I will give more examples of this transition III. But first I have to issue some warnings and show a group of people who are not generally known but are vital to our future. Let me be clear about the following. I do not want to present conspiracy theories here. Yes, I observe them and we better look into them, but not here. What is uncontested though is that in large countries the senior officers of the secret services have concluded that they must use mass surveillance, huge big data analysis systems to know what is going on and provide their respective governments with info and tools for executive actions. This is huge ICT and network use, effectively doubling or even tripling all present ICT systems in the world. Now developed nation Governments have the tendency to want to know all telecom and internet transactions from everybody in the world in real time. And store that for present or for later analysis and actions. I will not comment on if that makes sense or not, and if that works or not. Several countries do this. I would however have to warn that, it is very expensive to implement and needs extensive budgets to maintain it. To implement it they have circumvented oversight on the legal and constitutional side of such systems and on checks and balances on the power it will give these executives. So, they invented the method of *outsourcing* the effort to private companies, often with retired generals and admirals in their boards, to make them less visible, relatively immune to legal investigations and constitutional and

Human Rights watchdog scrutiny. They know it is illegal but they are protected by ministries who think they prevent terrorism and chaos. These private companies make a lot of money by **extracting** individual personal, psychological and medical information from billions of people, profiling them with proven computer systems invented for personal targeted advertising. This is a new industry. Even the silliest App asks you to fill in a lot of info about yourself, totally irrelevant for the App. Ask yourself why do this? Because they can sell your data. You are the fruit they want to pick and extract digital juice! For example, just look up what is the business model and mission of Facebook. They do sell these profiles to companies to help them sell you things, tailored to you. Wonderful right? No! There are lots of errors in that data and they go further, forcing you to buy things. And what is illegal, is that they have found that these big data ICT systems can personally manipulate the choices of millions of people not just as consumers but as electors. Democracy is gone in many countries already. If this is widely known, why has it not been stopped? Because in many countries the government hire these retired outsourcing generals to buy elections and stay in power. Yes, maybe in your country to.

Warning 1: The greed of these parasites with wonderful business plans and PR covers is not to be underestimated.

We have to make the transitions I, II and III urgently and many more at the same time, in this ICT penetrated age and I hope under the banner of transition to Synthecracy and cooperation. But my Warning 2 is that there will be many visible and invisible attempts to stop change, stop transitions. And even attempts to return to more stable unsurprising times, the 'Pleasantvilles" of the 1970's are not possible. And while trying we might end up in the 1930 fascist uprising with promises all over again. And trying to control the masses with facial recognition and mass surveillance and mind messing will not work unless the thousands and thousands of people are put into prison and forced education. It will not work.

I have made an interesting discovery, I think. There are two unique groups of people who are *immune* to propaganda and mind-bending.

The first group are those who make or are ordered to broadcast the lies. For instance, the silly but well-paid young smarts who work (office hours!!) in the troll farms in St. Petersburg. They fabricate tweets meant to distract and create diversions outside Russia, often for both sides of activist groups. These trolls know that they are lying, and may even know the truth, but they do not seem to care. A more explicit example is what I was shown on invitation in Lithuania, just leaving the USSR, in 1991. In every major city they had a huge steel construction with an enormous wire grid on top. An antenna with a powerful radio jamming signal to disturb radio reception in the country of foreign propaganda stations. In a little shed at the basis of these towers worked the KGB / FSB team to service the power and the transmitter. But as one of them told me there they had the clearest radio reception in the USSR of foreign stations. How? They had the jamming signal there and could with a simple OpAmp subtract that from the receiver antenna signal of a transistor radio they had there. So somewhere in the Kremlin and somewhere in the White House there are a few people who know the truth. They are immune to their own propaganda. So will be a couple of crooks in the world. The Dictators should be aware of them!

The second immune group is very special. I call them the *#ExtraOrdi*. And they are absolutely vital for the future of societies and humanity worldwide. I guess that the spy services of GCHQ, BND, NSA, GRU, Beijing et. al. has stumbled on these immovable mental rocks too. Despite billion-dollar mind-manipulation tools and mental massages these are immune to propaganda on internet and social media, (see Pomerantsev; 2019, and (Benkler, Faris, Roberts, 2018).

These #extraordi people dance to their own music in their own heads and are masters on the high planes of the above mentioned: action, imagination, wisdom and knowledge levels. For instance: Steve

Jobs, Elon Musk and Stephen Wolfram. Yes, they do make mistakes, they are far from perfect, eccentrics, outliers, edgelings, 'leftfield', and laughed at, until they DO act, innovate with the help of ICT, and inspire us with surprises.

Let me sketch the characteristics that these ExtraOrdis have, not in any order of importance.

a. Several of them have left school at an early age, to educate themselves; Ted Nelson, Allan Kay, Audry Teng see (Till, J. van, 2020).
b. They have a huge appetite for knowledge and are constantly curious and have empathy, want to look through the eyes of others at different angle than their own.
c. They have huge and weird imaginations, daydream while awake, love science fiction and patterns in graphic novels. Hence the title of this chapter.
d. Have crystal clear visions about the future. Eager to Learn constantly.
e. Understand maths, physics, biology and the impact of ICT. *Wolfram* laid a new basis for them (Wolfram, 2020). Do not want to be told what to do or think, see a. *Arthur Dokters van Leeuwen* [NL]
    g. Stubborn, Knowbetters. *De Gaulle. Churchill. Greta Thunberg.*
    h. Unexpected. *Claude Shannon.*
    i. Daring, brave and **fearless**. They do not care what others say or think. Are not in the confirmation mode. *Galilei. Newton, Einstein.*
    j. Creative and innovative.
    k. Decide and have agency to DO things.
    l. Open for constructive critique.
    m. Not all teachers and parents like these characteristics ☺, the extraordi dis-obey.
    n. Most of them are addicted to science fiction, the feast of fantasy and imagination.
    o. They have visions on the future and believe in something they have discovered/ recognized/ imagined/ dreamed.
    p. Many of them do not design or create very logically, but write or draw what a 'little voice' in their head tells them. Especially poets and writers do that. As if it is dictated to them from another realm. Extraordinary indeed. The Greeks called this: "whispered by a Muse".

From the subconscious more likely, but usually it is the right thing at the right time in the right place to do.

q. Often the #extraordi function as important nodes in informal networks that can refer

somebody with a well-expressed problem to somebody who they trust to help them solve it, or refer them further in a few steps to where it can be solved. Such referers are called "weak links" to distinguish them from "strong links" = family or direct circle of friends.

I recommend the brilliant book (Csermely, P, 2006) about this function, which is present all over Nature and in our body and brain (to repair injuries). Weak links between extraordi can increase stability in society.

I do know a large number of these #ExtraOrdi people, often in hiding in clear view, because they have been threatened, because, as explained above, many powerful people do not want change or innovation. Indeed, they want these people to be stopped or silenced. So, we should protect them. The

#extraordi are the valuable anchors or even vital mental leaders of the upcoming **swarm society** in Age (6), phase C and D.

I will explain why. The late famous biologist Dick Helenius in Amsterdam once performed an experiment with a school of fish in a large tank of water. They swirled together in formation through the water, without bumping into each other, by watching 4 to 7 other fish around them. And adapting their own direction of swimming accordingly, if necessary. Such a school as a group has advantages for the safety of all participants because they can avoid coming into the path of predators like sharks, and they can together as a swarm goin the direction of food and water, like bees do together. And all the eyes and brains of the fish interconnected as one brain has advantages over the unsure individuals without a swarm. So usually the participants are afraid to be locked out of the flock, and obey each other. Helenius took out and covered the eyes of one of the fish. And put that fish back in the school of fish. They immediately followed this blind fish, who did not care what other fish did or see anymore, as a leader. This 'not caring about what the neighbors say' is characteristic (i.) above. And yes, they do direct others who are less brave and less stubborn.

Helenius often told this story in front of conference halls of managers, who were not amused. So, the #extraordi have a natural authority because they are NOT uncertain and NOT afraid to think or do things their surrounding people find non-average or even shocking. They are not interested to be leaders or media talking heads, but are interested in others and do useful and valuable things for the common interest. Here is a story by Isaac Asimov that tells you how such a #extraordi can feel. Often, they do not feel as I they 'fit in,', as many very bright and creative kids do. That is why they should be introduced to other kids who have the same "affliction"!

The story (Asimov, 1957) is as follows.

A schoolboy in the 66th century is anxiously awaiting the Education Day on May 1 where all his classmates are selected for their future job and will be brainloaded with the necessary skills from special computers. To his great consternation he is not selected at all to become doctor or carpenter or any other job, but to be sent to a home for the silly. Which he refuses. And feels abandoned. A kind gentleman however leads him out through a hidden door and explains to him that he is selected from hundreds of thousands of boys to be trained and schooled to be one of the extraordi that can design such brainloads for others.

I read this story in an 'Asimov collected stories' book when I was 15 or 16 and it made a huge impression on me.

What Lies Ahead

The focus of this book is on ICT technology and its use and what effect it has on society and the economy. Well, we are in the midst of chaotic transitions, as described above. The reason behind most of the riots, rebellions and revolutions in the world right now is that the unwritten *Hierarchy Pact* is broken between the Establishment in each country (I prefer that word over 'Elite', since that would imply they are better people) and the rest of the population, that they will lead and protect them in return for the privileges of exclusive right to *knowledge* and exclusive right to *broadcast* their views and decisions for action and commands. Not only did the Establishment fail to lead in the economic crash and the pandemic, but the Internet and WWW undermined that Pact. Now everybody in Demos can access all knowledge (transparency) and everybody can express their views and broadcast them to the whole world. This is what

I described above in transition the double shift II and the tilting of the command and control hierarchy described in III. That is why dictators and controlling regimes and large established companies are so nervous about losing and insist on mass surveillance on internet, telecom and social media.

The result will inevitably that the narcissistic leaders, who think their top position is forever, will be toppled. Media magnate Berlusconi was, and so will be Murdoch, in time. And during these times I am certain that that we will be bombarded with "alternative facts" (aka lies) to bury the truth under mountains of nonsense.

My prognosis is that the following things will happen, and maybe are already happening to some degree.

A. With the help of smartphones, etc.pPeople will 'flock' and will physically move fast from nomadic places to other places, under the slogan 'move like water'. This will also apply to migrants. Lots of young people are nomads already. Cities and urban areas will again bloom as meeting places where people gather and combine tasks and cooperate briefly or for longer periods. This 'meeting' has been always the raison d'etre for cities. Remember how Jane Jacobs described the flow of people on the bridge over the river between city halves? But now we can use internet tools to support this meeting. But it is also becoming clear what we missed in human contact during the Covid-lockdowns. Synergy (Corning, 2018) will drive the cooperation and it will Create Value for all participants in such communities. Nationality will be much less relevant for the new class of perpetual expats. I have described in my blog that chains of connected cities will appear. The one I expect is #Corridoria which will be a chain including optic fiber cables and cloud computer centers from Dublin all the way to Shanghai. Much more attractive as a Silk Route than the train infrastructure under construction by China, which will be part of Corridoria.

B. Such flocks of people will grow and WEAVE into Swarms (Moffett, 2019). And such Synthecracy will also be transformed into new types of enterprises with new structures, as described in (Minnaar & Moree, 2020) and (Hamel & Zannini, 2020). They will self-regulate and self-control, bypassing outdated dictates. This is how we can fight back and bypass populists and other authoritarian regimes who want to preserve the status quo and their central power with the help of social media propaganda.

Figure 6. Networks of networks

C. The driver for value creation in this new network **supported group construct**s will be the appearance of:

- consciousness
- awareness
- consensus at the layer of Imagination in the above schematic

How will these appear? As argued above, people will be so well connected to each other that they form what I call a Weavelet. A weavelet is where everybody can see everything everybody else is doing as in a hologram. A kind of energy and information field as Wolfram has introduced in his book (Wolfram, 2020) and as did Haramein. This will be done by implementing Social Super Resolution with people as the connected brain cells and the addition of application of huge amounts of personal computer processing and optic fiber interconnection between them.

What do I mean with this metaphor? Well, it is a common misconception that we see with the lenses of our eyes. Yes, but behind these eyes is a super strong LENS system, called the brain, which is processing images and enhancing them in real time so we can "see" much more clearly with better contrast and dynamic range. Much better than only with the two watery eye balls. In the brain we do 'super resolution', for image improvement of satellite images beyond the resolution of the lenses. If you look around you, you will notice that in your field of vision only a small segment is clear, with high resolution, whilst the rest of your view is blurry around that. If you think that the reason for that is the higher density of eye neuron receptors in the centre of your eye, that is wrong. There is a blind spot for light there, that is not showing up in your sight. That is how the super resolution (lenses) in your brain works: only a part of the view is high resolution. Additionally, for people who are looking at a screen all day (most of us now) it is recommended that you now and then look for some time in the distance, to restart your mental optics (series of lenses and transforms in cascade).

This 'Social Super Resolution' will add a much clearer vision and truth discovery by networks of people sharing their images and different viewing angles.

The Bellingcat volunteers in a number of places connected together can analyse photos on the internet and determine if they are fake or not and where they were shot. This introduced a new kind of journalism and scientific truth-seeking ability in groups. This might grow into Social Super Resolution if they share more powerful ICT tools.

This is the direction in which I expect we will regain use and functionality of the ICT infrastructures. For the benefit of society and respecting and firmly embedded in nature.

We are alive and so will be our Weavelet swarms: a new life form. Part of the future Global Brain.

If ants, dolphins and bacteria can flock and regenerate and co-evolve, why can't we as humans? Even trees in forests are connected underground. Diverse and yet connected, to share food and information. And they emit chemical substances, for instance in the event of giraffes eating their leaves, warning trees downwind to make their leaves there less edible.

My final story in line with all these things is the following. Some scientists have declared that Dinosaurs are extinct, possibly from following the impact of a large meteor hitting the Earth, killing a large number of species. But it is also known that dinosaurs where not very clever and ill adapted in energy and body fluids. It is also known that they evolved into birds and learned to fly. Now was that the next step was flocking into swarms for shared safety. But also shared eyes and brains! Some people therefore suggested that dinosaurs are not extinct but have evolved into a new life form! We humans can with the help of personal computers and connectivity also evolve into swarms, a.k.a # Weavelets. A new form of Life, see (Davies, 2019).

The IAB Directive

Any architecture, including ICT and 'network architecture' is the result of a sequence of conscious steps with choices to achieve many requirements, wishes and constraints of a tribe or organization. And we must now include, what was long a taboo: the social and economic effects once the architecture has been implemented. For instance, banks and stock exchanges work differently in computer networks than they did on papers. It is as if we have handed out Kalashnikovs at a kindergarten school. The kids know how to handle them, not the teachers. But Internet and corporate networks have recently also been criminalized, weaponized and militarized.

The Internet Architecture Board (IAB), the high-level steering team for Internet, has now acknowledged these non-neutral effects (as I have in this chapter) in their directive, the published as RFC 8890, see (IAB, 2020). Here they state "This document explains why the IAB believes that, when there is a conflict between the interests of end users of the Internet and other parties, IETF (The Internet Engineering Task Force)) decisions" should favour end users".

This directive means, in my blunt language, that in the triangle of the Trias Internetica, formulated by me, after Montesqueu's "Trias Politica", – balance of power between law makers, judges and law enforcers-, that the priority should be given to the Demos (= groups of innovative freedom using volunteer-civilians of the Civil Society], instead of profit seeking entrepreneurs or control and power seeking politicians and state governors.

If you want a demonstration of what the Civil Society can do with ICT, take a look what is done, (Applebaum, A, 2020b) in Belarus: unstoppable under the very nose of the government. The social media power tool of Telegram uses blog channels to coordinate what hundreds of thousands are doing in the streets of Belarus, in constant two-way digital democratic dialogue.

Just imagine!

FUTURE RESEARCH DIRECTIONS

As outlined within this chapter, there are a number of trends emerging and starting to gain co-creators. Some segments will collapse and others will boom with exponential growth. The advantage of such growth that it has afixed doubling time, from day one of its start. So they can easily be identified. Uncertain however is their end size, which depends on the target candidate population size. My suggestions for further study are:

- The successors of AI / deep learning: how to implement Social Super Resolution.
- Study "immunity to propaganda" by media and social networks.
- Study and experiment with "Collective Intelligence" in groups of people with diversity of backgrounds, skills, sectors, cultures.
- Study and experiment with "Digital Democracy".
- Micro Cloud server networks

CONCLUSION

ICT penetrates everywhere into society and in our tools. This has a slow but huge effect on how we work and live. Organizations and tasks change in a number of transitions at the same time. This chapter focusses on what is changing and how by ICT and social network use. Above all, living post 2020 means that you have to change your mindset. The way you look at things and what has priority for your life. It is a process of learning together with your family and friends and the parts of Nature we can save and be part of. If we succeed together there is a Renaissance 2.0 in front of us, based on huge computer networks.

REFERENCES

Allende, S. C. (2018). *Be More Pirate*. Penguin Random House.

Applebaum, A. (2020a). *Twilight of Democracy – The Seductive Lure of Authoritarianism*. London: Penguin Random House.

Applebaum, A. (2020b). The 22-Year-Old Blogger Behind Protests in Belarus. *The Atlantic*. https://www.theatlantic.com/ideas/archive/2020/08/22-year-old-blogger-behind-protests-belarus/615526/

Asimov, I. (1957). Profession. In *Astounding Science Fiction*. https://www.abelard.org/asimov.php

Barabási, A. L. (2016). *Network Science*. Cambridge University Press.

Benkler, Y., Faris, R., & Roberts, H. (2018). *Network Propaganda –Manipulation, Disinformation, and Radicalization in American Politics*. Oxford University Press.

Corning, P. (2018). *Synergistic Selection – How Cooperation Has Shaped Evolution and the Rise of Humankind*. World Scientific Publishing.

Csermely, P. (2006). *Weak Links – The Universal key to the Stability of Networks and Complex Systems*. Springer.

Davies, P. (2019). Life's secret ingredient: A radical theory of what makes things alive. *New Scientist*.

Hamel, G., & Zannini, M. (2020). *Humanocracy – Creating Organizations as Amazing as the People inside them*. Harvard Business Review Press.

Internet Architecture Board (IAB). (2020). *RFC 8890 The Internet is for End Users*. https://rfc-editor.org/rfc/rfc8890.pdf

Menczer, F., Fortunato, S., & Davis, C. A. (2020). *A First Course in Network Science*. Cambridge University Press.

Minnaar, J. & de Moree, P. (2020). *Corporate Rebels – make work more fun*. Eindhoven: Corporate Rebels Nederland B.V.

Moffett, M. W. (2019). *The Human Swarm – How Our Societies Arise, Thrive and Fall*. London: Head of Zeus.

Perez, C. (2003). *Technological Revolutions and Financial Capital - The Dynamics of Bubbles and Golden Ages*. Edward Elgar Publishing Ltd.

Perez, C. (2009). After the crisis: creative construction. *Open Democracy News Analysis*. http://www.opendemocracy.net

Pomerantsev, P. (2019). *This Is Not Propaganda – Adventures in the War Against Reality*. Faber & Faber.

Till, J. van. (2015b). *Formal definition of Internet*. https://theconnectivist.wordpress.com/2015/09/01/what-is-internet/

Till, J. van. (2016). *The Financial System is Unstable*. https://theconnectivist.wordpress.com/2016/03/03/the-financial-system-is-unstable/

Till, J. van. (2019). *The Fifth Network Effect*. https://theconnectivist.wordpress.com/2019/08/26/what-can-we-do-8-the-fifth-network-effect-the-law-of-p2p-cooperation-and-scaling-up/

Till, J. van. (2015a). *The Four Network Effects*. https://theconnectivist.wordpress.com/2015/03/25/np9-engines-for-the-new-power-the-four-network-effects/

van Till, J. (2020). *Blog about Audry Tang, interview articles in NRC and FD*. https://theconnectivist.wordpress.com/2020/06/24/digital-democracy-in-taiwan-basic-8-for-synthecracy/

Werbach, K. (Ed.). (2020). *After the Digital Tornado –Networks, Algorithms, Humanity*. Cambridge University Press.

Wolfram, S. (2020). A Project to Find the Fundamental Theory of Physics. Oxfordshire: Wolfram Media.

KEY TERMS AND DEFINITIONS

Effects of Use of Social Media: Impact on tasks and organisation structure.
Extraordi: Extra-ordinary individuals.
ICT: Information and Communication Technologies.
Immune: Immune to propaganda.
Internet: Network of networks, architecture supervised by the IAB (internet architecture board).
Super Resolution: Image enhancement algorithms, developed for satellite photos.
Surveillance: Listening in to nearly all electronic signals emanated or exchanged by persons.
Swarms: Groups of connected and cooperating people, not necessarily co-local.
Transitions: Paradigm shifts.

Chapter 4
The Universal Knowledge Machine

Alan Radley
Kim Veltman Perspective Institute, UK

ABSTRACT

The chapter introduces a technical prescription for a universal knowledge machine (UKM), or World-Brain, a proposed global media system with the capability to encapsulate/organize/index and provide user-friendly access to all human knowledge. The goal is not to develop an artificial brain or any kind of Artificial Intelligence (AI) so-to-speak. Rather, the authors wish to build a collective intelligence repository, a vast 'living' memory bank for everything known and in terms of a totality of knowledge emanating from each of the three worlds of physical, mental, and objective knowledge. Envisaged is a place for humanity to come together collectively and to create, capture, record, link, search, sort, filter, classify, map, granulate, aggregate, chunk, window, overview, catalogue plus communicate a vast number, and great variety, of ideas, facts, claims, variants, data, texts, theories, images, happenings, and opinions. The goal is nothing less than a grand unification of all knowledge such that items are endlessly visible, explorable, linkable, navigable, etc.

INTRODUCTION

Human knowledge – considered as a single entity – is a Leviathan – and consists of aggregates of fragments. The vast majority of recorded knowledge 'atoms '(micro-thoughts/datums) are stored within incompatible/temporary/poorly-indexed and 'lumpy 'media containers – ergo most items lie out of reach. But on a collective World-Brain or Universal Knowledge Machine (UKM) no public item (i.e. open thought/datum) is ever lost, isolated or invisible!

Why propose building a UKM? Are not current Internet/Cloud systems sufficient for our task? No not at all – because (for example) with a World-Wide-Web based search system such as Google you only ever see a small fraction of the myriad of items, associations and pattern(s) present, and can only faintly perceive the countless connections and vast network of relationships of everything to everything else. In reality – items and connections between items – are without limit.

DOI: 10.4018/978-1-7998-7010-4.ch004

A great number of relevant facts/claims/ideas/ causal-paths/histories are known to exist (on all topics); but here you can only scramble about – blindly – amongst a tiny subset. Evidently, the Internet consists mostly of isolated – and ostensibly orphaned – nuggets of information that lie deep inside largely opaque and coarse-grained files and documents, monolithic databases, plus unstructured web-pages etc. Items often become lost, erased or hidden; and useful datums, variants, informative links and contextualizing patterns – are inaccessible.

World Brain

By contrast H.G.Wells, Paul Otlet, Dr Emanuel Goldberg, Dr Douglas Engelbart, Dr Ted Nelson and Dr Kim Veltman, etc; have made a call for the urgent development of a World-Brain – whereby everything is amalgamated into a single properly organized/indexed and fully hyperlinked global media system. Notably, the reasons given for developing a collective World- Brain are not typically equated to the creation of a Utopia; but rather for education, enlightenment and enhanced knowledge plus insight; and for avoidance of outright despotic regimes whereby technologies are used to subjugate man and/ or to block his basic human rights.

In this section we provide technical blue-prints for a UKM – by amalgamating useful World-Brain conceptions and generalized thinking concepts, knowledge systems/theories, World-Library/ Encyclopedia plans and technical solutions from a variety of publication-sources/subject- disciplines and research papers etc. Our goal is to identify top-level features/capabilities of the envisaged UKM, whilst acknowledging that building/populating/cataloguing this system is left to others (and notably by all of humanity).

A World-Brain allows us to know: where we have been, where we are at present, and where we are going – individually and collectively. Urgently desired is all world's knowledge coalesced into a unified whole. Accordingly, it is nothing less than preservation of civilization that is at stake. QED.

Dream of Capturing all Knowledge

The dream of capturing and organizing all knowledge is as old as history.

From ancient Sumeria and the Library of Alexandria to the Library of Congress and the British Library, the World Wide Web and Wikipedia etc; humanity has long wrestled with the problem of harnessing all intellectual output. Despite the various successes afforded by such admirable efforts; the dream of ultimate wisdom remains unfulfilled; and has twin sides. Firstly there is the significant problem of scale. Unfortunately the task of collating together all the world's facts, datums, opinions and ideas etc – within a single system – has proven to be elusive (thus far).

For example the British Library contains some 70 million items – but only holds perhaps 10 percent of all the books ever written. But this is far exceeded by the indexed World Wide Web which in 2016 is said to contain some 5 billion pages! However even the latter is thought to contain less than 0.1 percent of all the world's yearly data output – estimated to be 1.8 zettabytes. We can conclude that the vast majority of potentially useful knowledge and data output world-wide is – at present – lost/hidden/impermanent/ out-of-reach or else goes unrecorded/unsaved.

Information collation is the first crucial aspect of our ambitious task, but even if we could successfully capture everything known; before we can adequately access this enormous data bank; a second problem rears its ugly head. That is the problem of organizing the vast mass of knowledge in such a way that it is visible, indexible, aggregatable, navigable, discoverable, linkable and query-able etc. Unfortunately the twin problems – of scale and organization – often work against each other – and because the larger and more diverse the archive gets – then the harder it is to establish an efficient Universal Data Format (UDF) to hold everything and anything together within a single unified system – or Universal Knowledge Machine.

Establishing a UDF plus efficient access method(s) is difficult – partly because of the huge diversity of content to be encapsulated – and partly because there are so many different ways to arrange, partition, aggregate, link and view information (knowledge is non-linear/multi- dimensional). For example classifying the same under multiple subject headings, numerous topic categories etc; and cross-referencing/grouping/transposing items using different languages, theories, systems, frameworks, representation and viewing schemes etc (knowledge is multi-perspectival).

The aforementioned problems are daunting, to be sure. However today we are being helped tremendously by modern technological advances, which really do – in principle – take care of obstacles like scale of storage, interconnection and obtaining rapid, efficient access to anything from single location. However real-world experimental 'true hyper-media 'systems like Xanadu and SUMS have demonstrated that not all problems are of a technical nature – but that sufficiently powerful information capture/ organizing/navigation schemes are required.

Internet

Some people believe that we have already built a World-Brain; specifically in the form of: the Internet, Cloud(s) and/or the World Wide Web. Whilst these developments have been tentative steps in a useful direction, expert analysis has shown how limited are the resulting systems in terms of the classification (flatness vs hierarchy), synthesis, partition/aggregation, notability and accessibility of all contained/represented thoughts, datums, claims, variants, actions, processes, patterns and relations etc.

Undoubtably, our world is today more connected than ever before, in terms of digital information flows and the rapid communication of (a tiny subset of) ideas/datums. Largely by default, with the Web it does appear that humanity is building a World-Brain. However these valiant – but ultimately suboptimal – efforts do suffer from major limitations, including lack of scale, spread, synthesis, fluidity, and flexibility etc.

Consequently current systems fail to achieve any of the key features that are required to achieve universal accessibility of content (ref. easy way-finding to any item/relation/pattern existing on the microcosm/ macrocosm, performed by anyone who is located anywhere/anytime). In particular knowledge today – for example on the World Wide Web – is lumpy, impermanent, disorganized, largely invisible and unlinked, plus the contained ideas are ephemeral and wholly isolated one from another (they suffer from a lack of context/linkage, adequate partition/aggregation plus query related powers – see below). Missing are contextualizing instruments; and ways to navigate – or point-at/zoom/pan – the different Levels of Metaphysical Existence – truth/facts, belief, phantasy etc.

But it is not all bad news. It is important to note that the concept of a World-Brain is by no means dead; and because a number of modern scholars/ technologists/thinkers have made extensive plans to actually build working examples of the UKM. What is lacking is a unified call for action, and/or an efficient and effective channeling of effort on a world-wide basis. Money may be needed to bring plans into reality; but 'smarts 'or intelligent/correct design is even more important. And we should not underestimate the power of – properly harnessed – collective action.

Cross your fingers that we (humanity) can finally pull our minds together – and build theWorld Encyclopedia. Our approach is not to re-iterate what has been said elsewhere on the World- Brain – and in fact we shall assume much of what has been recommended in the past is available to the reader – and by extension to the designer's of a UKM. Rather we wish to unite all of the sides as together into a single top-level systematic and practical – design/blue-print perspective.

Universal Knowledge Machine

We begin with a critical overview of thinking methods, theories and philosophies; plus knowledge organization practices, systems and techniques etc. Subsequently, we imagine a new approach to knowledge capture/storage/organization/access in terms of a generalized UKM implementation that can work for all possible purposes/tasks – and from all theoretical perspectives.

The top-level goal of the UKM is clear – enabling humankind to think better thoughts (i.e. for all thinking styles: analytical + associationist + analogical); that is to develop: more accurate, relevant, true and comprehensive thoughts.

For example, desired is a knowledge machine that boosts human thinking on the largest and smallest – plus widest and narrowest – knowledge scales (i.e. metered, throttled and windowed item partitions/aggregations/associations etc); and for individual(s) and collective(s), and from the universal and particular viewpoints etc. We wish to develop a practical design for a universal knowledge machine – and our idea is to encompass all human knowledge within this machine in an easily accessible and usefully arranged Universal Data Format (UDF). Pictured is a single knowledge machine that encompasses all thoughts/ideas/facts/claims/variants etc.

As stated, many others have addressed this key goal from H.G.Wells, Paul Otlet, Ted Nelson to Kim Veltman etc. (Otlet, 1935; Wells, 1936; Nelson, 1974; Veltman, 2000; Veltman, 2006). Accordingly we do not think that there is any point in listing all of the many advantages and that would accrue to humanity by developing such a system; or to exhaustively list all of the different ways that current systems such as the World Wide Web fail to deliver on the ultimate promise of a World-Brain. Nevertheless, we shall list top-level societal advantages for the UKM, and in terms of the potential for properly managed, coordinated and coherent solutions for major problem areas – and for humanity as a whole.

Others have established the key goals of the World-Brain (i.e. efficient item organization, full visibility of content, and easy accessibility); and detailed the urgent need for developing the same. Accordingly, we take it as an established fact that establishing a Universal Knowledge Machine is a highly desirable goal – and one that is today no where near even beginning development – or close to existence. Here we shall focus on how to bring the World-Brain about in theoretical terms – or more specifically – to ask what a Universal Knowledge Machine must be in structural/functional terms. Ergo we present top- level blue-prints for the World-Brain.

An attempt is made to encapsulate – or to accommodate – in the proposed system all relevant: thinking-aids, theories, ontologies, knowledge orienting and linkage methods, conceptual schemes, knowledge frameworks, data acquisition techniques and communication approaches; including a wide variety of semantic models, knowledge principles/representation- technique(s) and media aids etc. Accordingly benefitting from the extant and diverse theories/established-methods of language, science, history, art, philosophy, mathematics, library sciences, ICT and media systems etc.

It is our position that the World-Brain must be a mechanism that helps humans to think – that is to gather, process and store data/knowledge, plan for the future, and take the necessary actions to improve the lot of mankind. Such a knowledge machine must help us to think better, more relevant or true thoughts: individually and collectively.

Our proposed collective brain is to be a global thinking machine – only it is not an artificial thinking machine – but rather a human-planned/created/managed – or eminently humanistic – aid for thinking/action processes of all types, scales, magnifications, levels, purposes etc. The UKM is envisaged as a kind of ultimate top-level encapsulating meta-media system – or a single medium that encompasses all the other media types.

In view of these preliminary remarks; building the UKM certainly appears to be a fundamental and difficult task; but before we go on to explore related design issues; first a few words on scope of the UKM.

Definition / Scope of the UKM

The notion of a World-Brain – sometimes named the Global-Brain – is one that has seen wide- ranging usage and application. Hence it is important to properly demarcate the meaning of the term Global/World-Brain or UKM –as employed here in this chapter. Dr Francis Heylighen of the Global-Brain Institute defines the term Global-Brain as follows:

The Global Brain can be defined as the distributed intelligence **emerging** from all human and technological agents as interacting via the Internet. It plays the role of a nervous system for the social super-organism.Accordingly, and in this paper we accept specific aspects of Heylighen's Global-Brain conception - and in particular the idea of a ***distributed intelligence*** - plus his ***nervous system analogy***. But we reject the notion that intelligence can somehow just emerge from ***all possible related systems - irrespective of design form/structure*** - and in an automated manner.

Let me explain. Doubtless we agree with Heylighen's view that ICT technologies – can and do – drastically change the organization and functioning of society. And further we agree that a Global- Brain (potentially) brings us into a new regime named as the ***Information Society*** – which opens up a seemingly infinite variety of new forms of human-to-human and machine-to-machine interaction (including mixture(s) of the same). However we do not accept as ***inevitable*** the notion of a Global- Brain defined as a ***self-organizing, adaptive network*** formed by all the people of the planet working together with the information and communication technologies.

Such a magnificent World-Brain - may lie within the bounds of possibility (here it is our key goal). But we do not assume that the individual actors (i.e. people, machines, knowledge units) are able to 'automatically 'arrange themselves into a single globally cohesive knowledge system. The same self-organizing notion does not have much - if any - supporting theory/overt-mechanism(s) of construction/operation. Rather we have ample contradictory evidence from the last 20 years for a complete lack of coherence in the present system: the Internet / Web. Much needs fixing!

Doubtless interactions between people and machines can sometimes self-organize (to some extent) into efficient sub-systems of finite/locally-useful patterns/processes. But we do not agree that related mechanism(s) taken together (on the biggest of scales) can then optimally (and inevitably) fuse together - to form a fully cohesive system so as to automatically produce a world super-organism. In particular we do not think that any such ad-hoc system (independently of how it is designed/operated) can then become - by itself and without centralized-organization - a global information processing network of super-efficient design.

Desired is a global Memory Palace exhibiting fully clarified/contextualised knowledge unit relation(s) and useful partition(s)/aggregation(s)/associations. However we think that such a system does not just

Figure 1. Popper's Three Worlds of Knowledge: Mental, Physical and Products of the Human Mind

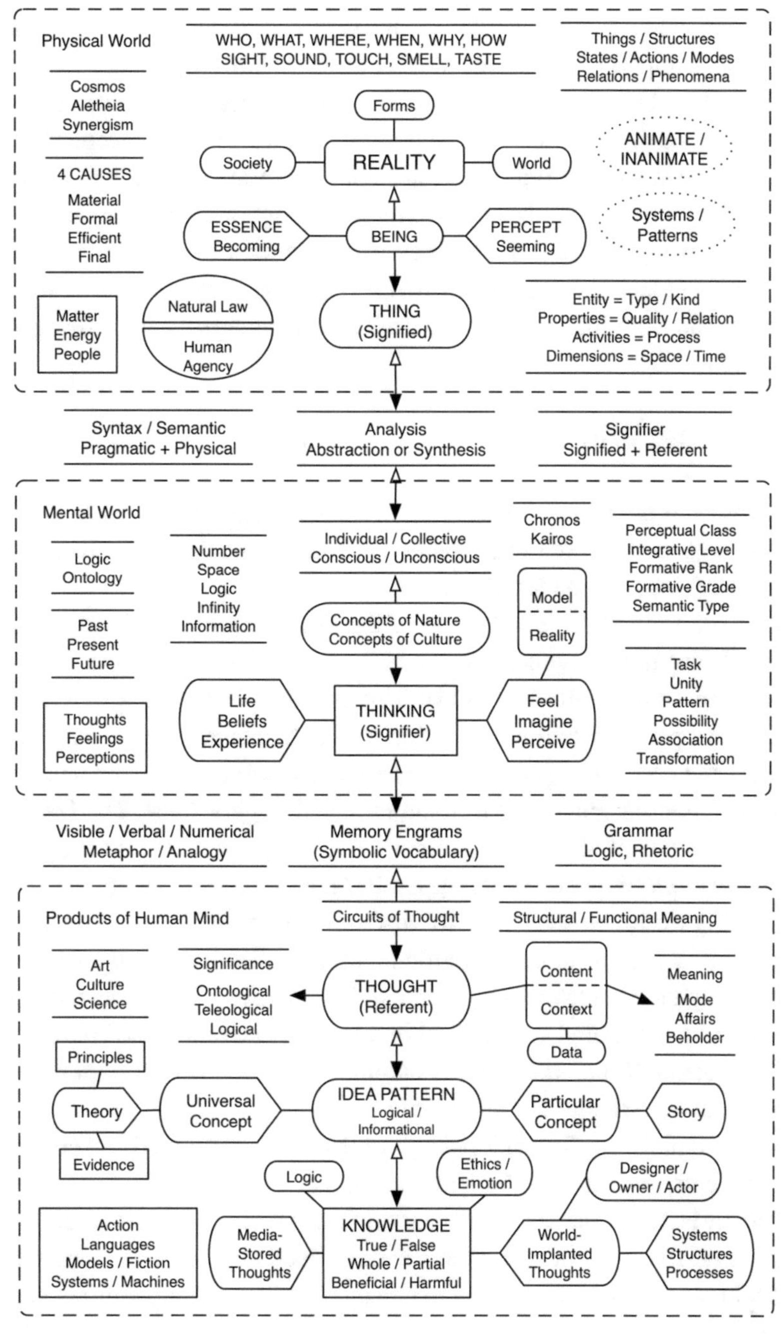

happen. We reject the view that emergent interconnection/feedback mechanism(s) can somehow (automatically) maximize the coordination, efficiency, structure, visibility and usefulness of the various data items/relations present - and within any vision of a ‘self-generating ’World-Brain. Ergo we name this approach the evolutionary Global-Brain project or the ***Emergent-Mind Hypothesis***.

Our view is diametrically opposed to the aforementioned notion of an inexorable World-Brain. We agree with conceptualization of a vast network of social, communication, and economic links between individuals, organizations and machines (plus even living eco-systems etc); that it should be an inter-dependent network of 'competing 'relations, ideas, events, datums, opinions, etc. And we agree that a properly designed/operated UKM can and will partially self-program - only entirely by ***human oversight***. However we do not assume that this network can randomly auto-generate a central nervous- system - or that its capabilities can be independent of UKM structure/operation (ref. A/B/C-Knowledge Machine(s) - see below). Rather the World-Brain must be designed/built/operated as an organized global network of micro-thoughts/datums which are classified/linked-together/organized by the human users themselves.

We call this UKM approach the ***Dependent-Mind Hypothesis***. A properly organized UKM enables humans to collaborate and work together by means of human managed: knowledge gathering / optimized thinking procedures.

Purpose / Aims of the UKM

As stated, our purpose - in proposing the development of a World-Brain - is to allow humans to think better thoughts; and to generate more useful, salient, practical, true, informative and relevant ideas - being ones that (hopefully) lead to a better life for all.

But we do not intend to limit our conception of the World-Brain merely to metaphysical thoughts; but rather desire the UKM to be as much about physical processes, actions and real-world events/data gathering also. Ergo we embrace the Internet of Things (IoT). Our assumption here is that the UKM will be a comprehensive perceptive/thinking/acting tool that enhances the clarity of our views of real-world objects, events and processes; and so it is to be a universal recorder/planner/organizer for datums and real world social actions as much as it is about human thoughts alone. The UKM shall be a faithful reflection of the full contents of all three of Popper's 'worlds'; that of the ***nature/physical, mental*** *and* ***products of the human mind*** (Popper, 1978; Popper, 1972; Nelson, 1974; Veltman, 2000; Veltman, 2001; Veltman, 2013). See Figure 1, and see below for discussion of Kim Veltman's expanded Six 'Worlds'.

It is envisaged to be an aid for improved individual plus collective intelligence – a distributed mind 'amplifier 'that takes inputs from from everywhere and anywhere – but importantly unites the same in order to provide coherent, integrated and re-combinable perspective(s). The UKM is to be a vast agora/ arena of all possible/potential/true: knowledge / datums / theories / events / opinions / processes / happenings - being an accurate reflection of all creation.

The UKM provides rapidly-configurable/vastly-informative, fine-tuned and comprehensive '***Knowledge-Windows*** '- and with respect to all human knowledge.

But how specifically is it possible to improve our thinking processes - individually and/or collectively? Evidently we already do so by use of all previously developed thinking aids, perceptive and communication aids/tools/technologies; which are used to enhance our natural capabilities in this respect; whilst sometimes adding new super-efficient data capture/storage/retrieval/sharing capabilities (e.g. ones that overcome the limitations of space/time). But why do we not see a clarion- call for improved thinking methods? And what is the evidence that such an improvement is even possible to achieve (individually and collectively)? Is the UKM a mere pipe-dream?

Perhaps the 'patternist 'view of thinking processes provides a useful perspective here (Goertzel, 2006). A patternist viewpoint is basically that thinking is solely a process of reflecting 'patterns 'of meaning / relationships that are - for example - present in nature. Ergo once captured pattern images enter into human mind(s) (via direct capture, cognition, intuition, and communication with others and/or media systems) - for recording/analysis and ultimately to provide understanding. An example thinking process is where a particular pattern – for example the idea of a car – is comprised of a series of universal/particular structures of partitioned/aggregated 'ideas '- linked together usefully. Patterns within the mind may more or less accurately – resemble real-world aspect(s) – or the objective pattern(s) that one is trying to map. Accordingly, major thinking/memory tools exist to aid in this 'patterning 'process – and these are diverse and range from:

a) Generalized theoretical symbolic/semantic structuring systems within: language, mathematics, science, logic, culture etc; to:
b) Physical or virtual recoding/output media and communication aids including: books, calculators, telephones, computers, mobile phones etc.

In fact the whole history of mankind can be viewed as the collection and development of a gradually increasing number of tools to aid and augment our mind's ability to capture and manipulate patterns in a variety of different ways. Evidently our minds become systematized, and 'spread-out 'or 'projected 'in/onto the real world in terms of - a great number and variety of - patterns or recorded thoughts/data. Accordingly the clarity, degree of correctness and relevance of human thoughts / actions / choices are dependent on the efficiency and effectiveness of our mind enhancing tools - and hence relevance/truth of human thought-spaces.

Ergo a great variety of cognitive aids plus communication processes for manipulating thought patterns have been developed; and many of these mind augmentation tools would seem to be a natural byproduct of language - being a kind of ultimate pattern - in which all of the other patterns may be represented or contained.

Mind reflects the world - using patterns - and the world 'pattern 'or model in turn makes the mind. Accordingly we end up with a vast range of symbolic and visual/text/image based language(s) and thinking constructs; plus reflective, logical, explanatory and causal systems. Hence the development of science, art, history and logical plus scientific method proceeds; aided by various media such as printed text, photography, film and digital media/computers etc. In a way, computers are a type of ultimate aid for cognition; to the extent that they are memory banks for anything and everything - being 'wired 'or networked thinking tools of particularly diverse application. In fact what we are really talking about when we speak of a World-Brain is a new type of computer - admittedly a massively networked, hugely data populated and well-organized machine that renders information incredibly easy to capture, record, and way-find to items of interest.

Our proposed World-Brain may also be a new type of computer in a separate 'metaphysical ' sense - in terms of employing a new philosophical and etymological approach to the organization of knowledge that has ***universality of relation*** 'baked-in '(ref. hyper-context). Hence the UKM has capabilities that no computer thus far has possessed. However our UKM conception - despite the fact that it is envisaged as a kind of ultimate thinking machine - nevertheless remains that of a computer of one kind or another. Vitally this World-Brain is to be the first example of a new 'micro-thought ' based grouping (partition/aggregation/linkage) of knowledge - or a single system capable of capturing, storing, organizing - and enabling humans to efficiently access - everything known.

Alan Turing first established the basic concept of a computer or ***universal thinking machine***, defined thusly (Turing, 1936; Turing, 1950):

The digital computers... are the machines which move by sudden jumps or clicks from one quite definite state to another. These states are sufficiently different for the possibility of confusion between them to be ignored. Strictly speaking there, are no such machines. Everything really moves continuously. But there are many kinds of machine which can profitably be thought of as being discrete-state machines... This special property of digital computers, that they can mimic any discrete-state machine, is described by saying that they are ***universal machines****. The existence of machines with this property has the important consequence that, considerations of speed apart, it is unnecessary to design various new machines to do various computing processes. They can all be done with one digital computer, suitably programmed for each case... A digital computer can usually be regarded as consisting of three parts: (i) Store. (ii) Executive Unit. (iii) Control. The store is a store of information, and corresponds to the human computer's paper... In so far as the human computer does calculations in his head a part of the store will correspond to his memory. The executive unit is the part which carries out the various individual operations involved in a calculation. What these individual operations are will vary from machine to machine. (Turing, 1950).*

In fact, it is no exaggeration to say that everything we have today in the digital world - from the central processing unit (CPU) to the Internet and the Web etc - all emanate from Alan Turing's idea. Whilst now we have a great variety of different kinds of ***networked electronic digital devices***; from *PC s, mobile-phones to tablets and even smart watches etc*; all of these innovations are simply evolutionary developments patterned after Turing's basic idea.

The so-called 'Turing Machine 'was envisaged by Alan Turing in 1950 - as an ***automatic machine*** - or an **A-MACHINE** (Turing's term) - that merely 'mimicked 'intelligence or intelligent behavior and was not considered by him to be able to think by itself - in any way whatsoever (Turing, 1936; Turing, 1950). However Alan did predict that sometime around the year 2000 computers would be so sophisticated as to be able to converse with humans and be mistaken for intelligent beings (or humans).

In the over 65 years since that seminal paper was published, Artificial Intelligence (AI) has developed considerably as a field - and to such an extent that IBM's Watson computer was able to win the Jeopardy knowledge game show on television against excellent human opponents.

Experiments, judgements and opinions as to whether computers ***can***, ***do*** or ***could*** potentially - ***think*** remain hot topics in related fields. And it is true, that on occasion, and in carefully prescribed circumstances, computing systems have passed Turing's test for 'human 'seeming intelligence (question and answer language type interrogation by humans of the computing system). Putting aside questions related to the ability – actual/potential – of computers to actually 'think 'in human-like ways; we note that here in this paper we are not concerned with like questions or AI. Rather we shall focus solely on thinking as a process taking place in a single human brain – or across a collection of multiple brains – and its perfection and/or optimization; and hence we consider thinking from a purely humanistic-perspective.

In a nutshell, we seek to boost/augment the computing power of the human mind itself - and to provide a facility for ***more focussed and expansive lines of enquiry***. We wish to ***see networks of association on the global data web;*** and to ***perceive previously hidden relations on all knowledge scales/spans***. But we must understand human thinking processes in order to do so (see Figures 2 & 3).

Accordingly, we seek an aetiology of thought - that is to comprehend what the process of thinking is, first of all - because it would seem evident - that one cannot improve something if one does not have at least some understanding of the nature of what one is trying to improve. Aetiology is the science of philosophy or causation; that is, speculation on the causes of phenomena. In the present context aetiology relates to study of: *where thoughts come from, what they mean, how they form, combine and interrelate, and where they go to - plus how they are best used - individually, collectively and socially (or res ponsibly).*

Our ambitious goal (with the UKM) is to render possible a comprehensive map for all the items/ mechanism(s) present in all the territories of human thought/action; being a type of universal Memory Palace - and one aided by standard human capabilities such as perception, cognition, vision, language etc. Only here expanded to include all kinds of thinking aids, data-capture mechanisms, technologies and media types etc (we embrace all current knowledge tools/engines).

Despite the fact that our top-level combined individual/collective 'thinking ' comprehension aim in this respect is a very tall order - we shall nevertheless still attempt the same - and in order to elucidate the types of questions, problems and topics that the developer(s) of a World-Brain would need to address in the first instance.

But lest we forget - an individual thinking act has distinct purposes/goals; and normally is focussed on a specific 'object-of-thought 'or 'object-of-examination '(e.g. an item of perception, imagination or reality). Henceforth focussed cognition helps us to gather relevant information conceptually and/or to form new concepts applicable to specific situational context(s) etc; or simply just to understand, act; and so to predict/control natural objects and events etc. Put simply, goal-oriented thinking gives mankind the necessary power to study the past, control the present, and shape / predict the future.

Embodied / contextualised thinking is how we humans make and understand our realities - whether real-world resident or imagined. Accordingly, desired is a comprehensive theory of thinking processes - or at least a flexible 'container 'for all possible theories/methods; and in order to be able to produce a UKM that can perfect both real-world processes and outcomes in this respect.

The desired thinking theory/procedures/ method(s) will consist of ideas/elements/structure/processes that is/are borrowed/extracted from elsewhere; but it may also contain some new elements. I shall attempt to provide sources for 'borrowed 'ideas wherever possible (or leave room for such links/annotation(s)); but overall I seek here to collect together any and all useful/compatible (but fundamental) techniques related to thinking tools/methods/procedures - and familial concepts - obtained from everywhere and anywhere. Our study of human cognition initially presents itself as list of axioms/definitions or logical 'atoms '(see end-notes).

And we shall attempt to show how these items are supposed to work together on a UKM in order to form a comprehensive, logical, self-consistent and inter-related scheme of perfected human thinking processes. Where a useful thinking-related item/concept cannot be made compatible with the overall scheme - then it shall be listed at the end for possible inclusion later on.

My aim is a comprehensive - but practical - theory of human thought that would take place with the aid of our hypothetical World-Brain, being one that encompasses/condenses down all other theories (where possible), plus can represent any possible thought-structure both flexibly and with great clarity. Where theories-of-cognition cannot be found to be compatible with one another - then we shall leave room in our system to accommodate competing or contradictory theories wherever possible. No scratch that - our UKM must be fully compatible with all theories, thinking systems/tools/representations etc. Ergo we need: ***Centralized Classification Systems; plus organizing,*** consolidating, and uniting schemas/templates/mechanisms - built in to the UKM - and to bind everything together. Perhaps we need to go back to a more Aristotelian '***Tree of Knowledge*** 'approach. Here we can differentiate between the underlying theory of representation, storage and access (the ***A-Machine***)-

Figure 2. The Circuits of Thought

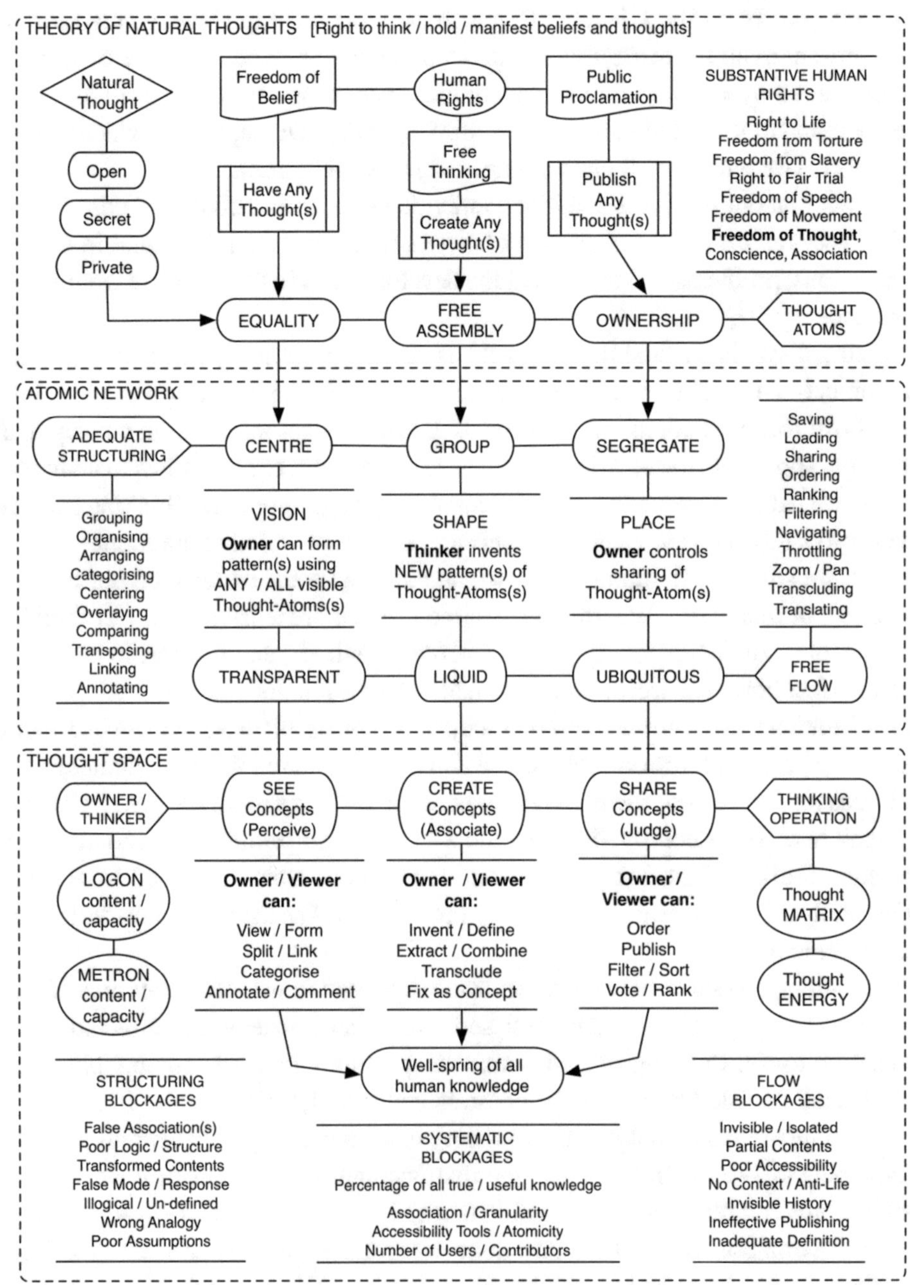

*the physical aspects of the system or brain - from the actual virtual information that is organized/managed centrally (i.e. metaphysical information - **B and C Knowledge Machines** - see later). Our UKM must itself consist of an operational theory that is fully specified in both aspects - physical implementation and logical / working structure. I know that many others have sought the same goal, and had years of*

Figure 3. Representation of a Thought/Thinking Space

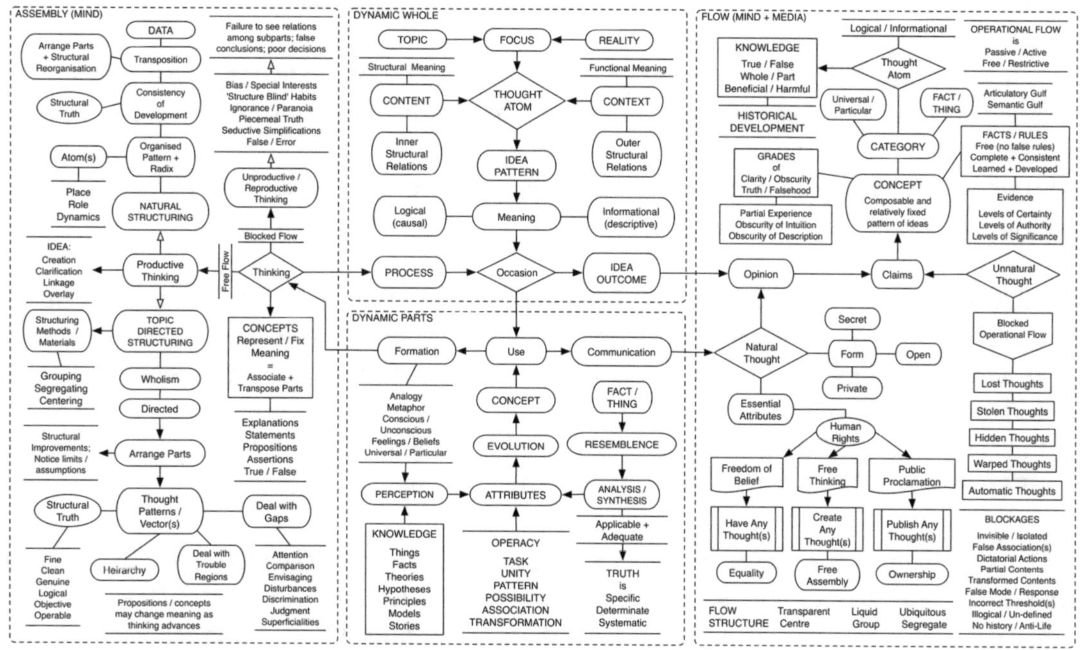

troubles, but that does not put me off because the task is a true one: understanding/modeling/perfecting: how, why, and by what methods: we humans think. QED.

Despite an emphasis on thinking procedures, the present paper also places primary emphasis on human knowledge - its capture, representation and retrieval. Of necessity, we find ourselves dealing with that branch of philosophy known as ***Theory of Knowledge***.

But once again, there is no one universal theory of knowledge - but an immense number of rival theories that deal with same subject matter. Accordingly it is impossible to avoid controversy with respect to related organizational constructs, or to ignore controversial opinions/questions with respect to concepts and ideas present in any specific knowledge classification or representation scheme.

A theory of knowledge must also be a theory about the range, depth and limits of knowing - and it patently must allow the objects of knowledge to be: *known, considered, compared, judged and thought-about.* Ergo the mental operations of perception, belief, memory and judgement are preeminent plus interrelated activities - and ones that impinge on ***knowing***, ***believing, truth/falsehood*** and ***acting***. Accordingly our World-Brain must aid the same processes - and for all facts, variants and claims gathered from everywhere and anywhere - and if it is to be considered a success.

It is tempting to think that building a universal knowledge machine (UKM) would be relatively straightforward procedure - and that one might (for example) just go ahead and build an ordinary networked data-base - but then optimistically make it far larger and more efficient in terms of factors such as speed and remoteness of connection plus ubiquity of access etc. This is really what we got with the system that is Tim Berners-Lee's World Wide Web – which is of course a vast improvement over previous systems in that there is near unlimited storage room for vast amounts of superficially linked documents, images and videos etc. (Berners-Lee, 1999; Berners-Lee, 2014). However experts have noted the limitations and systematic/organizational failure of the 'Web '(ref. ignores PMEST facets, lack of high-level overviews, plus semantic depth/breadth missing).

It is true that the Web makes items more accessible in one way - in that they can be readily stored on a distributed network; but items are easily lost, links break, and items often became 'islands unto themselves'.

In truth, when seeking an item of knowledge on a useful system - one seeks to ask questions or to engage in activities that enable people to:

A) FRAME the Item - Identify / Perceive / Delimit / Partition a Thing (Thought/Datum/Object/Process)
B) FILE the Item - Save / Remember / Store a Thing (Thought/Datum/Object/Process)
C) ORGANIZE / LINK the Item - Contextualize / Form Relations and Aggregations/Partitions to/ with other Thing(s)
D) FIND the Item - Efficiently Locate / View / Extract a Thing (Thought/Datum/Object/Process)
E) EDIT the Item - Effectively Add-to / Delete-from a Thing.

The Items captured can perhaps be superficially classified as: A) Facts/Thoughts; B) Objects/ Processes of Knowledge and C) Records of Sensation or Data or real-world Objects, Events or Processes etc. Note that on most network systems, these tasks would often be performed by separate actors - individuals or collectives (people and/or machines); and at different places/times.

It is salient at this point to ask if the UKM is in any way analogous to a real-world brain?

To begin with, an organism is defined a collection of living cells grouped together, carrying out discrete tasks for the benefit of the whole (i.e. an animal). Ergo our UKM does seem to be quite organic. Whereas a ***brain*** serves as the centre of the nervous system in animals. It is comprised of neurons that communicate with one another to exert centralized control over the other organs of the body. In this respect we can say that our conception of a UKM makes it a brain in the important sense(s) of:

- Centrality of organization
- Interdependence of parts
- Broad distribution of knowledge

It is a whole systems approach to the generation of a collective intelligence; aka the World- Brain. Overall, in the case of a World Brain - all of humanity is involved in building, organizing and using the vast amalgamated system of all human knowledge. The UKM is to be a system that is constantly evolving/ever-growing - and so it must be permanent - and the contained knowledge must 'live 'forever.

So far so good - but how do we proceed to build the UKM? Perhaps we need to develop a little theory - and to help us approach such an ambitious task. But first, it might be informative to delve into the history of the concept of a collective World-Brain.

World Brain Vision

During the early 1920s, the French paleontologist Pierre Teilhard de Chardin (1881-1955) first described the emergence of what he named the ***noosphere***, the network of ideas and communications that eventually envelops the planet (Teilhard-de-Chardin, 1976). In the same time period, Paul Otlet and H.G.Wells

(Otlet, 1935; Wells, 1936) both dreamed of building a ***universal catalogue of all human knowledge*** which would be stored - and accessible - as an enormous cross linked repository (a type of automatic card- indexing system for all the world's ideas/datums).

But ambitions of building a Universal Knowledge Machine and/or Memory Palace - do have a much earlier source - and in fact go right back to Ancient times. The idea of collating or gathering together everything known into a single world encyclopedia or universal knowledge corpus; began with Plato and Aristotle's attempt(s) to group together knowledge of everything in the known universe under consistent laws, frameworks and knowledge classifications. This thrust towards causative description(s) and logical understanding continued with Western attempts during the 17th, 18th and 19th centuries to unify knowledge according to universally applicable laws and principles.

Subsequently, several prominent thinkers took up - and developed/prescribed - the idea of a universal knowledge repository. Scientific and philosophical efforts towards universalism gathered pace during the 19th and 20th centuries, and a number of schemes to build global knowledge catalogues emerged. It is useful for us to briefly review key developments in this respect.

Encyclopedist / Utopian Origins

The quest for ultimate truth is pre-figured by the quest for a universal source/bank of knowledge that occurred during the Enlightenment; whereupon (for example) the French philosopher Denis Diderot (1713-1784) and Jean le Rond d'Alembert (1717-1783) created the Encyclopédie or Systematic Dictionary of the Sciences, Arts, and Crafts; a type of general encyclopedia published between 1751 and 1772; and which was envisaged as a universal storehouse for all human knowledge (Diderot & le-Rond-d'Alembert, 1728). Diderot stated that his Encyclopédie should:

Encompass not only the fields already covered by the academies, but each and every branch of human knowledge... comprehensive knowledge will give 'the power to change men's common way of thinking'.

These are noble and worthy aims indeed; however Diderot's work on his Encyclopédie suffered from many obstacles. The project was mired in controversy from the beginning; and was suspended by the courts in 1752. Just as the second volume was completed; accusations arose, regarding seditious content, and concerning the editor's entries on religion and natural law. Diderot was detained and his house was searched for manuscripts and subsequent articles. Sadly, it would be 12 years, in 1772, before the subscribers received the final 28 folio volumes of the Encyclopédie, ou dictionnaire raisonné des sciences, des arts et des métiers .

Over 170 years later, and shortly after World War 2, Pierre Teilhard de Chardin (1881-1955) wrote:

No one can deny that. a world network of economic and psychic affiliations is being woven at ever increasing speed which envelops and constantly penetrates more deeply within each of us. With every day that passes it becomes a little more impossible for us to act or think otherwise than collectively we are faced with a harmonized collectivity of consciousness, the equivalent of a sort of super- consciousness. The idea is that the earth is becoming enclosed in a single thinking envelope, so as to form, functionally, no more than a single vast grain of thought on the cosmic scale (Teilhard-de-Chardin, 1976).

The alluded to Global-Brain is a metaphor for an emerging, collectively intelligent network that may be formed by all the people of the earth; together with the media, computers, thoughts, knowledge and communication-links that connect them together. It is a vast, complex and (partially) self-organizing knowledge system.

The idea for a Global Brain was first codified in 1935, by Belgian Paul Otlet (1868-1944), who developed a conception of a network that seems eerily prescient of the world-wide web (Otlet, 1935):

Man would no longer need documentation if he were assimilated into a being that has become omniscient, in the manner of God himself. To a less ultimate degree, a machinery would be created that would register [at a distance] everything in the universe, and everything of man, as it was produced. This would establish a moving image of the world, its memory, its true duplicate. From a distance, anyone would be able to read an excerpt, expanded and restricted to the desired subject, which would be projected onto an individual screen (Norman, 1999). In this way, anyone from his armchair will be able to contemplate creation, as a whole or in certain of its parts.

Knowledge is to be coalesced/aggregated/linked; and in accordance with the fundamental definition of a computer -***to arrange items clearly in one's mind***- thus forming a type of universal oracle (OED - 2nd Ed.).

Jumping backwards in time once-more to the late 19th century, William James (1842-1910) said that for thoughts to fuse together (within a mind), there must be some sort of medium; hence he postulated a stream of consciousness where:

Every thought, dies away, and is replaced by another the other knows its predecessor, and finding it warm, greets it saying 'Though art mine, and art the same self with me' (Rheingold, 1985).

Implicit here is that thinking happens within an environment; and the same being one which supports the process, remembering terms and happenings, and also provides access by the thinker to contained knowledge. But what will be the nature of such an environment (or thought-space) for multiple brains? Or how can a new reality be constructed in such a manner that all the correct/true thoughts, choices and actions of mankind are facilitated, and in which any and all thoughts are free to work together for the benefit of man?

H.G.Wells

In the 1930s, futurist Herbert George Wells (1866-1946) wrote a book entitled World B rain; whereby he describes his vision of the World Brain (Wells, 1936); a new, free, synthetic, authoritative, and permanent 'World E ncyclopaedia'; that could help citizens make the best use of universally accessible information resources; and for the benefit of all mankind. According to H.G. Wells, this global entity would provide an improved educational system throughout the whole body of humanity. He said that the World Brain would be a sort of mental clearing house for the mind, a depot where knowledge and ideas are received, sorted, digested, clarified and compared; and it would have the form of a network whereby it is the ***interconnectedness*** that makes it a Brain.

In World Brain, Wells wrote:

My particular line of country has always been generalization of synthesis. I dislike isolated events and disconnected details. I really hate statements, views, prejudices and beliefs that jump at you suddenly out of mid-air. I like my world as coherent and consistent as possible... we do not want dictators, we do not want oligarchic parties or class to rule, we want a widespread world intelligencia conscious of itself... and... without a World Encyclopedia to hold men's minds together in something like a common interpretation of reality, there is no hope whatever of anything but an accidental and transitory alleviation of any of our world troubles (Wiener, 1950).

Wells believed that technological advances such as microfilm could be used towards this end, so that:

Any student, in any part of the world, will be able to sit with his projector in his own study at his or her convenience to examine any book, any document, in an exact replica.

Many people, including Brian R. Gaines, in his book Convergence to the Information Highway, see the World Wide Web as an extension of the World-Brain; allowing individuals to connect and share information remotely (Gaines, 1996).

These concepts surrounding the nature of human thinking, in fact relate to far older ideas; for example in the Indian Upanishads a four part description of the inner instrument of understanding is supplied. Stated is that the function of mind is association and disassociation; synthesis and analysis; whereby internal and external perceptions are evaluated (Radley, 2013a; Radley, 2013b; Radley, 2015).

The World-Encyclopedia envisaged by H.G.Wells likewise proposed the building of a vast machine or mechanism; which would be a university-like global encyclopedia that would collect, organize and make available to everyone a properly contextualised (and approved) knowledge bank of all human knowledge. Many others have contributed to this vision including: Paul Otlet, Wilhelm Ostwald, Emmanuel Goldberg, Dr Vannevar Bush, Dr Douglas Engelbart, Dr Ted Nelson and Dr Kim Veltman (Otlet, 1935; Engelbart, 1962; Nelson, 1974; Veltman, 2000; Veltman, 2001). Such 'mental-visions 'or predictive foresight of a World-Brain, had to wait until the second half of that same century, and to have any chance of becoming physical reality.

Kim Veltman

It is organization that is missing from the world's thought and data atoms. Kim Veltman has written copiously on the related concept of Digital Reference Rooms (DRR). According to Kim, a key problem with the Web is that everyone has their own rules for organising knowledge. On this point, Veltman says that if:

There is no common framework for translating and mapping among these rules, then the whole is only equal to the largest part rather than to the sum of the parts... Hence we need standardized authority lists of names, subjects and places. This may require new kinds of meta-data. Indeed the reference rooms of libraries have served as civilization's cumulative memory concerning search and structure methods through classification systems, dictionaries, encyclopedias, book catalogues, citation indexes, abstracts and reviews. Hence, digital reference rooms offer keys to more comprehensive tools (Wells, 1936; Veltman, 2013). Kim Veltman's requirements (for DRR):

- Standardized names, subjects, places with their variants
- Knowledge in context
- Multicultural approaches through alternative classifications
- Geographic access with adaptive historical maps

- Views of changing terms and categories of knowledge
- Common interfaces for libraries, museums etc
- Adaptive interfaces for different levels of education
- Seamless links with learning tools

Once again we see a vision for a unification of data/thoughts; combined with efficient accessibility tools. According to Kim Veltman, systematic access requires integrating tools for ***searching, structuring, using*** and ***presenting knowledge***; linked with digital reference rooms that provide the aforementioned list of capabilities. Like Nelson, Veltman sees not only the problem, but ambitiously goes ahead and builds a solution; named his System for Universal Media Searching –SUMS (Nelson, 1974; Wells, 1936; Otlet, 1935; Buckland, 2006). His approach includes a few similar ideas to Nelson, but with ***Classifications, Learning Filters and Knowledge Contexts*** identified to help the user cope with ten kinds of materials; namely:

1. Terms (classification systems, subject headings, indexes)
2. Definitions (dictionaries, etymologies)
3. Explanations (encyclopedias)
4. Titles (library catalogues, book catalogues, bibliographies)
5. Partial contents (abstracts, reviews, citation indexes)
6. Full contents which can be divided into another four classes
7. Internal analyses (when the work is being studied in its own right)
8. External analyses (when it is being compared with other works)
9. Restorations (when the work has been been altered and thus has built into it the interpretations of the restorer)
10. Reconstructions (degree of interpretation is larger)

Veltman says that all of these are pointers to the books/items/thoughts in the rest of the digital library. The vision is one of unification and centralized organization - necessary for efficient searching/access.

By use of such schemes the 'reader 'may progress from ***universal categories*** **to** ***particulars*** and using ***ordinal and/or subsumptive relations*** between items/subject categories etc. When querying a knowledge system one may (for example) progress form broader to narrower terms in a quest for specifics.

However as both Nelson and Veltman note; our thoughts and ideas are rarely hierarchically linked or arranged in singular contexts. Thoughts and ideas are related in a myriad of overlapping patterns of unbelievable *complexity, beauty and meaning!*

Possible relations between thought/data atoms and patterns include: ***alternatives, associations, complementaries, duals, identicals, opposites, antonyms, indicators, contextualisers etc***. Strangely, the problem becomes even more obtuse when we consider logical functions; including: ***and/or/not, alternation, conjunction, reciprocal, converse, negative, subsumptive, determinative and ordinal relations etc.*** Veltman says that a possible solution to all of this complexity in terms of organization and classifying of ideas, is the concept of different types of 'knowledge object'; stating:

Such that if one has a term, one can see its synonyms without needing to refer to a thesaurus. All these kinds of relations thus become different hooks or different kinds of net when one is searching for a new term and its connections (Otlet, 1935),

Our abbreviated discussion of Veltman's work highlights the enormity of the challenge facing the developer of a proposed UKM; and in terms of efficiently organizing all the World's ideas/datums. Major problem areas include: finding ways to bring adequate: ***centralization, standard classifications, aggregation/partition and contextualization for knowledge units*** whilst retaining option(s) for ***multi-cultural windowing*** and ***accessing the geographic and historical dimensions of knowledge***, etc.

Google simply blasts lists of stuff at you; in response to keywords, which are entirely unclassified (apart from overly simplistic groupings of images, web-links, videos etc); and in no way lets you see the structural patterns of thought. But it is these patterns that (in fact) underly knowledge at the biggest/smallest senses. Googling is like the game you play as a child whereby one person thinks of something (located in the environment) in his/her head, and the other person attempts to guess the item in question. But this is no way to link-to/access knowledge! (Googling).

With Google you never even approach/begin-to-see the true pattern of knowledge, or what are the diversity of opinions/ideas; but can only scramble about in an ad-hoc manner. This is because data and thought-atoms are grouped into files, isolated and hidden one from another; and so by and large free-assembly of thought-patterns is blocked/impossible.

Veltman again on knowledge organization:

We want to find something particular and yet we use single words, which are universal. The semantic web entails only subsumptive relations: what and who. Needed is a fuller approach that treats who as living entities, separate from what, and includes determinative and ordinal relations which are basic aspects of human life and knowledge: where, when, how, and why.

In his 2016 paper: Means of Certain Knowledge and Interfaces (Veltman, 2016), Veltman outlines his continuing vision of how to obtain efficient access to everything known. He speaks of the random word approach of the search engines; as opposed to the lists of catalogues of authors, titles, and keywords in titles; plus controlled vocabularies in classification schemes and thesauri. Veltman says the 'The goal is to find an item in the collection ranging from a book or article to manuscripts, letters, newspapers, maps, or other media.'

Veltman discusses 3 approaches to efficient knowledge organization/access as follows:

A) One is the potential of searching the complete contents of these materials. This invites new links to sources and implies a need for different levels of searching.
B) In addition, different means of certain knowledge could be identified and used as search criteria.
C) Another entails the possibility of different levels of knowledge relating to a given text.

Kim also states that texts can have ***verbal, numerical and geometrical levels***; which he links to ***matrices of knowledge connections*** - leading to an Internet of Knowledge and Wisdom - as opposed to mere isolated facts/images/videos/numbers/descriptions/definitions etc.

In his copious writings, Veltman carefully opposes current unhelpful trends towards the *internet(s) of opinions, habits, services, things, experiences, plus military, and spying etc.* His is the eminently humanistic perspective; and one that is by no means out of the question for us to develop. But needed are adequate conceptual schemes and effective designs to enable the UKM to work in reality. Kim speaks of the need to separate Concepts into facets - and in this way to fully identify (or fix) the foundations/contexts of anything in particular. A key person in related fields is the Indian scholar Ranganathan, who classified the world in terms of five elements (or facets): ***Personality, Matter, Energy, Space, Time (or PMEST)***. These elements are related to the 5 basic 'W 'questions of Who, Where, Why, What, When (plus also How). Accordingly, Kim Veltman summarizes the desired approach of ***synthesizing information from multiple source***s, combined with the power to obtain ***high-level overviews of knowledge*** as follows (Veltman, 2016):

We need a web of enduring knowledge, understanding and wisdom, that is independent of this social web of habits, changing opinions and fashions. It must be independent of military, secret services and corporate interests. This web of knowledge should give us access not only to sources, but also to hidden layers of knowledge at the level of individual words, letters and numbers. An internet of our experiences, opinions and fears is attractive and legitimate. A cumulative internet of man's achievements through the ages is more important. This entails much more than a reassessment of the past decades. It is a question of understanding how our current methods of understanding the world have evolved.

Centralized classification of a ***universe of micro-thoughts*** plus effective ***command-and-control*** (for knowledge itself); is required to bind information together in such a manner that it is readily available. Webs of data, and networks of association must be organized/visualized. Ted Nelson called this open, transparent approach: 'Promiscuous Linkage and Windowing among all the materials.' Accordingly, we need multiple filtered entry points, global synthesis and cross- references - but it is ***filtering on the way-in with respect to our knowledge queries*** and not on the way-out.

Capabilities of the UKM

Having taken a whistle-stop tour of the concept(s) of World-Brain, World Library and World Encyclopedia; we are now in a position to ask: how is a UKM different? What are its essential features/advantages - what structure/form shall it take - and how can it be built? Upon what technologies/processes/assumptions does it rely?

In simple terms, we wish to build and organize the World-Brain in such a manner that the system is able to cope with immense complexity in terms of the logical, descriptive, prescriptive, ontological and metaphorical variety of all human knowledge - seen in totality; and on a vast range of physical plus metaphysical scales/levels/contexts; and incorporating all known, possible and recorded: ideas, thoughts, facts, categories, objects, subjects, topics, domains and levels -of-being etc. We wish to capture the vast scale of all human knowledge, and record/ visualize the interconnection(s) of everything to everything else.

The UKM is to be a marvelous oracle - or near-endless reflection of the totality of knowledge of the universe - or cosmos; the same being a system that is ever growing - and be inexhaustible in size, scope, context, depth (detail) and breadth of subject areas contained therein. And just like Wikipedia it is the users who will enter all the information. And all this happens in real time - because the new additions and constant edits must be permanently recorded, plus reversible/hideable (for a specific view) and ever changeable/editable. Views must contain an edit history for example - plus offer live annotations and opinions of all flavors - and with respect to each and every 'nugget 'of information.

And all the data will be finely organized and structured into eminently logical categories, complete with 'thickets 'of true relations - and all topic(s) mapped onto classifications/overviews - and with guiding diagrams/orienting-systems/topic-maps/contextualizing-mechanisms available wherever possible. See figures in (Foucault, 1975; Russell, 1963).

On the UKM, we shall have 3 core processes constantly ongoing by millions of simultaneous actors:

- Data Gathering/entry/editing;
- Data Organization: classification/organization/linkage;
- Data Access/viewing/extraction;

Whereby we can have both/either human-processes and/or automatic machine-based processes constantly performing the same tasks.

A primary goal of the UKM, is to store a great variety of ideas, concepts, images, and data - simultaneously gathered and sourced/stored in a distributed sense. All-in-all we can say that the contained information will need to be carefully formatted/organized/curated - and be presented or be accessible within/by-means-of a great variety of different access-methods, display-formats and mappings - at any moment in time. The UKM also partitions and aggregates everything together in a myriad of different ways; at variable/disparate: magnifications/minifications, granularities/chunks, windows and directions of comparison, degrees of difference and linkage, grades of clarity etc. We seek to build a knowledge system whose purpose is nothing less than an all-encompassing and mind-expanding ***Cosmic Unity*** - or top-level synthesis - in which each and every item/relation finds its rightful place(s) within the grand scheme of all human knowledge.

The World-Brain will be a type of ***Disneyland For the Mind*** - in the sense of being an endlessly explorable vista of vast numbers of intellectual worlds/pathways/contexts/panoramas. Revealed will be previously hidden relations, linkages, truths, correspondences etc; in every language and with every possible datum/fact/opinion(claim) on any item saved (source/author 'stamped 'and tied to all other related datums/facts/claims/versions etc) - and all accessible from a single networked location[1]. Kim Veltman put the UKM concept succinctly:

The 20th c. saw a trend whereby "facts" were complemented by facets (e.g. the PMEST of Ranganathan - see below):

i.e. it is not the subject gold per se that is important: it is the facets, how much, where, when, how, why that add up to an important picture. (personal communication to author). We desire to build into the UKM; efficient Memory Theatre's, Memory Tools and Augmented Knowledge Tools, plus Action/Vision/ Contextualizing Tools etc.

Overall we seek to foster properly organized mental, written, logical, visual and action elements such that the sum total of all human knowledge is properly contextualised and topologically mapped, with visible interconnection. Put simply, we wish to enable appropriate and effective '***geometries, topologies and processes of thinking***'. This knowledge web must provide access to not just explicit sources; but also readily guide the user to hidden relationships, invisible links and previously opaque layers of knowledge at the level of words, letters, numbers, geometries etc. Our UKM must release and provide access to, plus facilitate, new: ***Arrangements, Scales, plus Levels and Spans of Knowledge; Classifications, Windows, Linkages, Overviews, Summaries, Partitions, Aggregations, Universals and Particulars etc;*** and all available using PMEST type queries (see below) - Who What, Where, When, How etc.

A capability that needs to be introduced is that we need an historically changing set of "windows" into the universal or global brain of knowledge. i.e. the world accessible to the Greeks, the Romans or the Renaissance Italians were different (Veltman, 2013).

Hence the UKM will be designed from the start to be a place to record - and window - facts, opinions, and matters of human agreement and discord - that is, to faithfully memorize human collective viewpoints, plans, creations and actions. It shall record not only each fact/idea/datam/event and the author/source, but also how that same fact/idea/datam/event is interlinked with related item(s) and also variants (N.B. It may take some considerable period of time and effort to achieve/collate the same into a practical system). Ergo human thoughts and actions shall become collectively visible.

Crucially here, it is the definition of knowledge - used in building the UKM that is important. The Web proceeds as if everything is certain, is true, and exists in isolation[2].

As noted by Kim Veltman, this is where the 10 Indian distinctions between the means of certain knowledge becomes important (see below). Plus Kim notes that the PMEST, giving the missing Who, When and Where must be included; and not only What and How as in the Web. How can this all be achieved you may ask? Is such an all-encompassing system not impossible and/or beyond our imaginations/capabilities to create? Well perhaps the UKM it is not so conceptually difficult to imagine - or at least to begin building. It was Emmanuel Goldberg who first put forward ideas related to the need for an atomisation of knowledge; and so lead to library catalogues becoming properly linked together atomically (using micro-thoughts or thought-atoms as the basic unit of linkable knowledge) and thus with different levels of means of knowledge - not just isolated facts but linked via facetted classifications etc.

Missing on the Web is an explicit consideration of all cogitation seen as an integral part of a universal thinking-space within which all human-activity - mental and physical - takes place and/or derives. Mental relations are saturated with natural, technological and human-made (individual + social _ cultural): laws, events, s tructures, mappings, behaviours and form(s) etc; and the 'rules-of-thought' are (to some extent) pre-existing and pre-determined.

The problem is that we cannot see/touch all of the items plus contexts because they are not very accessible - and because they are not properly linked-together/aggregated in an atomic fashion - but rather they are hidden deep inside opaque files and web pages plus isolated databases. As Ted Nelson has noted the atoms of information might as well be - each and every one - hidden in Canopic Jar(s) - just as the Ancient Egyptians used to do with dead and mummified relatives. In short, data units on the web are too lumpy (files, web pages etc), and items are wholly disconnected, one from another.

An Atomic Network

As a partial solution to some of the issues discussed above, we have developed the idea of an ***atomic network.*** An atomic network is the polar opposite of a centralized or cloud network. It effectively provides a 'save 'and 'load 'function for the Internet, and provides for an indestructible public data type that cannot be controlled/owned and lives forever. Let us examine how such a theoretical network might work.

Let us assume that network members are scattered across the Internet, that is they are located on different IP (Internet Protocol) addresses and some may be behind Network Address Translation devices (NATs). Furthermore, each network member has a special client program on his personal computer or mobile device. Next we provide the following system actions; save and load, based on a unique data unit identifier. When the user chooses an atom (data unit), and saves it to the network, it is automatically given a unique identifier, an owner identifier and a member-specific key and/or password if it is private. Now what the client program does next (upon save) is interesting (and unique), it "atomises" the data unit to the network. The item is split into many thousands of tiny pieces (atoms) which are then disseminated across the network as a whole. There are many, many copies of each piece (data atom) which are saved on many remote computers hard drives, for later retrieval at an unspecified time. Data atoms are encrypted according to the key for the data unit as whole. Next when the owner (or key / password holder) chooses to load (or retrieve) the data unit from the network, then the owner's client knows how to request from the network all of the constituent atoms, re-assemble them and so to reproduce the data unit. Note that network members agree to reserving part of their computer disc for other people's data "atoms".

As an aide, a related idea is to enable construction and use of ***Generic Focussed Pointers [GFS]*** (somewhat related to Nelson's Flinks); which provide ***direct and generic links*** into a specific region (i.e. paragraph) within (for example) a pdf document, or a link to a specific and fully delineated region ***inside*** a web-page, image or movie. Each FS would ideally be immortal (just like - for example - the 'atomized 'data suggested here).

Going back to the atomic network idea; you now have a robust way of backing-up and sharing items using the link identifiers for the data unit. When another network member's client requests such a link, a "torrent" of constituent data "atoms" is sent to that client (from all across the network), until such time as the data unit has been fully reconstructed. Every network member's computer is now a data-atom server! And a sufficient "stock" of identical copies of each data atom (perhaps 100's) is automatically maintained according to continuous network maintenance tasks.

One now asks the question, what has been achieved with such an atom network? Firstly data is effectively immortal and indestructible, and relies on the unbreakable redundancy provided by massive distribution and replication of hundreds of identical atoms across many separate network locations. And the robustness of the network increases with number of network members (computers to store atoms upon). Other key advantages include no longer having central servers; and this is environmentally friendly and brings security advantages. Additionally data save/loading speeds are much faster (i.e. no central server upload times and torrent-like data atom transfers).

We also note that the UKM will be a continually developing (i.e expanding) system; and ways must be found to organize / classify / produce: **Emergent Knowledge** (Veltman, 2016).

UKM - Construction and Growth

Let us recap. We established that Concepts are densely stitched together through relationships of **similarity** and **context**. And also that Concepts exist in a multi-dimensional space - somewhat like separate points in space/time; however around each point there is halo that accounts for the vague, blurry, and flexible quality of the concept.

We stated that all our concepts from the grandest to the humblest, have the same quality of being partially hidden from view but partially unpack-able on request, and the unpacking process is repeatable, several steps up/down. Concepts modify each other - for example the concept of a hub and airplane - and context/relation is how. According to Douglas Hofstadter:

Each concept in our mind owes its existence to a long succession of analogies made unconsciously over many years, initially giving birth to the concept and continuing to enrich it over the course of our lifetime. Furthermore, at every moment of our lives, our concepts are selectively triggered by analogies that our brain makes without letup, in an effort to make sense of the new and unknown on terms of the old and known.

How the human mind combines and uses concepts is at present largely unknown. But we do have some idea of how this might happen by a process of **Conceptual Integration** - sometimes called blending or mental binding. According to this view we develop a network of mental spaces or domains - including contributing spaces and thus forming a blended cognitive space. Metaphors are used to structure preserving mappings (partial homomorphisms) between conceptual domains. It is interesting to ponder how we are able to separate truth from fiction within such a framework.

We do so in terms of the concept of Belief; where we have 5 separate cases as follows:

- Being sure and being right on evidence that is not conclusive
- Being sure being wrong on evidence that is not conclusive
- Being unsure and being right on evidence that is not conclusive
- Being unsure and being wrong on evidence that is not conclusive
- Being sure and being right on evidence that is conclusive

Accordingly it appears that when we are seeking truth by comparing and contrasting several conceptual domains - we can do so by a process of existence and negation within a type of geometrical space that represents true/false polarities across multiple dimensions that are effectively at right angles to each other in the combined conceptual space.

The famous Philosopher Ludwig Wittgenstein said that we humans don't start from certain words, but from certain occasions or activities.

When I think in language, there aren't any 'meanings 'going through my mind in addition to the verbal expressions: the language is itself the vehicle of thought. Many words... then don't have a strict meaning. But this is not a defect. To think it is would be like saying that the light of day of my reading lamp is no real light at all because it has no sharp boundary. - Frege compares a concept to an area and says that an area with vague boundaries cannot be called an area at all. This presumably means that we cannot do anything with it.-But is it senseless to say: 'Stand roughly there'? If a pattern of life is the basis for the use of a word then the word must contain some amount of indefiniteness. The pattern of life, after all, is not one of exact regularity. - Ludwig Wittgenstein

Different linguistic levels tend to interact and merge; including: morpho-lexical, syntactic, semantic (or contextual), and cognitive (or epistemic). And all levels are nested! The former 3 levels belong to the **'linguistic surface levels of communication'**.

A question arises. How can we provide universal thinking methods/aids - that helps us humans to create, view and use these different linguistic levels appropriately and usefully?

Evidently, as suggested in this paper, we can use relational and geometrical constructs to hep us to organize, structure and visualize our conceptual structures and so to manage attendant objects within properly defined **Planes-of-Being/Existence**.

Overall, it appears that Ted Nelson's concepts of Hypertext and Transclusions, plus Emanuel Goldberg's Omni-Links and Micro-Thoughts; can be usefully blended with the concept of a (physical) Atomic Network plus a multitude of (metaphysical) Knowledge-based Organizational methods - such a Kim Veltman's SUMS.

Ergo, a new UKM technology emerges, that supports the recording and viewing of full content/ context(s) by an author, sender, or commentator - plus sharing and re-mixing of content and context by everyone else.

Figure 4. Unified Data Format

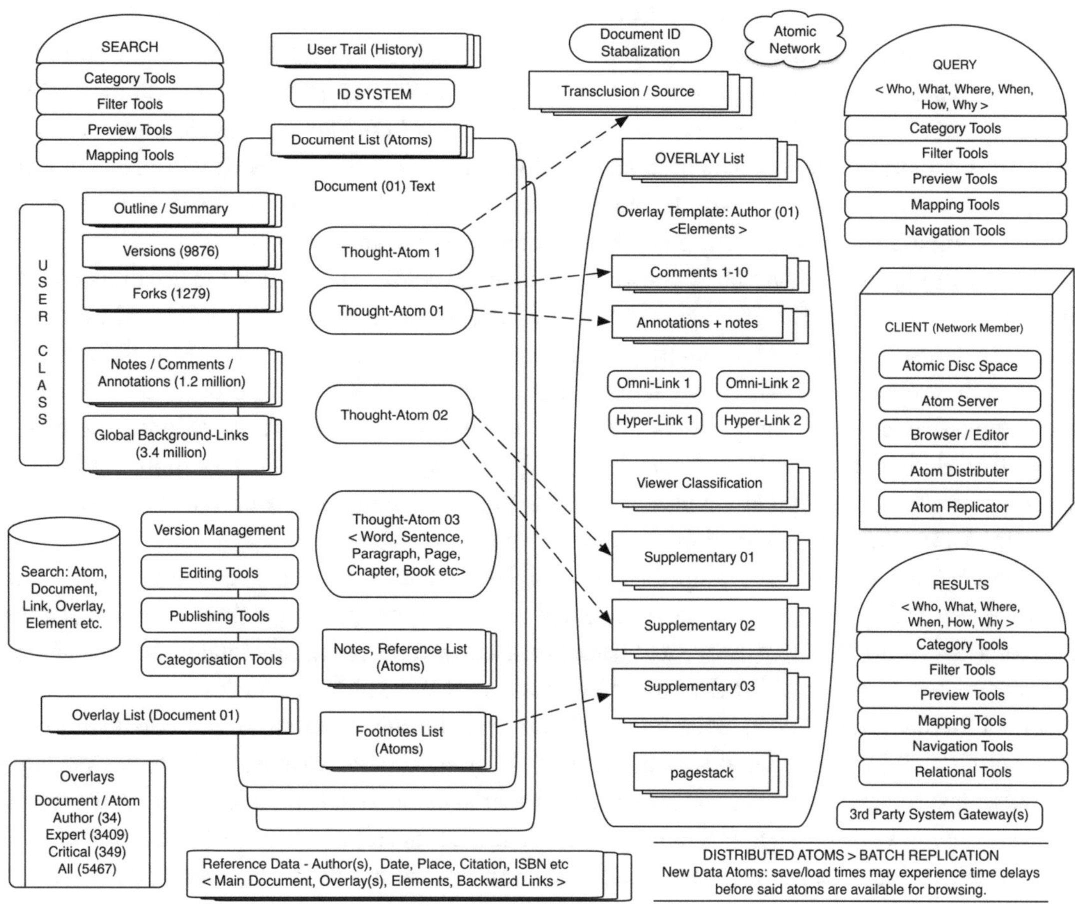

Cognitive / World Media Stacks

As we draw our somewhat speculative, ambitious and partially loosely defined paper to a close, it does seem prudent to ask what it might be like to actually use the proposed UKM. We ask: exactly how would a user go about interacting with a vast World Brain system? What would be the methods of entry, and then the results of query/access/way-finding; which data processing techniques/methods/mechanisms are employed; and how would the information results be input/presented? Obviously in order to provide any kind of meaningful answer for such a vastly unifying, and wholly hypothetical system; then we must ruminate to some degree. It is helpful in this respect to introduce four new concepts as detailed below (ref. Cognitative and World Media Stack(s), Single and Collective Mental Framework(s)).

We wish to introduce the idea of the **Cognitive Media Stack** (CMS); which is a particular set of co-aligned media channel(s), visible/accessible to a single human mind, happening on a particular perceptive/thinking occasion; and which allows ITEMS - or Concepts (universals, class objects), Things (particulars, datums, images etc) and Principles (laws, structural rules) etc; to travel up/down and hence through the various media layers; and thus to transform, mingle, co-exist and inter-relate as ideas/representations within a **Single Mental Framework (SMF) or Thought-Space.**

The role of the **Universal Knowledge Machine** (UKM) shall be (on each usage occasion) to generate a sufficiently detailed, true and useful SMF that supports/enables logical/creative/purposeful thinking processes; and accordingly to 'expand the SEMANTIC APERTURE FOR ITEMS 'on the CMT for a particular human user. In other words, the UKM supports and enables the creation and operation of optimal (or sufficiently broad - that is high-capacity) Cognitative Media Stack(s) within useful thinking context(s); whereby it enables a maximum numberand diversity of ITEMS to be found, gathered together, delineated, compared and contrasted, plus linked etc; and all within his/her mind.

Within a Cognitative Media Stack, constituent media layers through which the co-aligned channels communicate may include for (example): A) The object(s) of attention (i.e. a perceived aspect of the Physical/Mental/Spiritual World (emanating from one of the 'Six Worlds'), B) The Alphabetic/Symbolic Layer (encoding/representation), C) Syntactic/Word/Sentence layer (encoding/processing), D) The Logical/Conceptual/Belief Layer (judgements), and also E) The Mental layer (conclusions). Each layer in the Cognitive Media Stack communicates with its neighbor layer(s) through one or more kinds of media interface(s); and the same typically consisting of one or more meaning transfer/coding/transformation: tools, methods, mechanisms, algorithms, techniques etc.

In summary, the UKM vastly amplifies the number and breadth (i.e. aperture size) of available Cognitative Media Stacks that a user can create and usefully employ on a particular thinking occasion. One might ask - within this new theoretical framework - how multiple minds relate, socialize and intercommunicate. They answer is that they do so by means of a World Media Stack.

A World Media Stack (WMS) is the full spectrum (or cultural panorama) of potentially aligned media channel(s), visible/accessible to a particular social / cultural collective; and which allows Concepts (universals, class objects), Things (particulars, datums, images etc) and Principles (laws, structural rules) etc; to travel up/down and hence through the various media layers; and to transform, mingle, co-exist and inter-relate as ideas/representations within a specific and culturally determined: Collective Mental Framework.

Ergo, we can say that for each thinking occasion or series of such occasions; a number of Cognitative Media Stack(s) (CMSs) for an individual thinker/user are created with the aid of the UKM; and it is these CMSs that fully prescribe all of the ongoing perceptive and thinking processes. However it is important to note that each of these CMSs sit within a far larger World Media Stack that defines scientific and cultural knowledge etc; as a whole.

A World Media Stack is considered to be a major sub-component and/or supporting framework within which a particular culture develops, exists and operates; and consists of the:

A) Sum total (and available channel Semantic Aperture spans(s)) of all the culturally available media layers, communication channels and media interfaces;
B) The mechanism(s) by which meaning is captured by a culture as a whole, recorded and subsequently processed; including: all the encoding, representation and processing tools/mechanisms/methods/machines available to a culture at a particular epoch.

Put simply, and to repeat, the primary role of the UKM is to vastly amplify the number and breadth (i.e. Semantic Aperture size) of all those Cognitative Media Stacks that a user can create and usefully use on a particular thinking occasion. However the degree, efficiency, and effectiveness of how the user is able to do so obviously depends on the size, span and extent of all available World and Cognitative Media Stacks; and these in turn will be determined by the overall size, organization and operational efficiency, plus ease-of-use factors, present in all available Knowledge Machine(s) - that in effect contains and/or allows access to these various Media Stacks.

Six Worlds

According to Kim Veltman we can usefully transform Popper's 3 Worlds, referred to here as the object(s) of attention, into 6 Worlds as follows:

1) Metaphysical (In Brain)
2) Mental (Obviously In Brain)
3) Physical (Nature)
4) Man-Made (Includes Media + Machines etc)
5) Social (Communication Tools / Languages)
6) Natural Built Environment (Life)

These 6 Worlds are what the UKM is designed to enable humans to perceive, understand, organize and manage; in all its variety, mystery and wonder. They are the sum total of everything known, and everything that we can ever know; or all that exists in human terms.

World Trees / Axes

Kim Veltman has identified a number of interesting examples of the so-called Tree-Of-Life and the related World-Trees / Axes; and it is useful to consider / ruminate on the following quote (Veltman, 2014):

Both Plato and Aristotle discussed a ladder of life (scala naturae). It was described in Gnostic texts. But it was the Neoplatonist, Porphyry (246-305 A.D.), who first drew these principles as a tree of life. In the centuries that followed, the tree of life was also called the Great Chain of Being, distinguishing between animal, vegetable and mineral. In the early fourteenth century, Raymond Lull pursued this metaphor, drawing a Ladder of Life or Ladder of Intellect (1304) and a Tree of Nature and Logic (1312). This imagery was adopted by Linnaeus when he developed his system for classifying life into: Kingdom, Phylum, Class, Order, Family, Tribe, Genus, Species. The tree of life metaphor continued into the mid-19th century with Haeckel (1866, 1879). The rise of Phylogenetic Trees of Life, introduced an evolutionary dimension into the imagery. Hereby, the tree image, which had begun with a few minimal branches now reflected all living organisms (Veltman, 2006; Veltman, 2013: Veltman, 2014; Veltman, 2016).

Accordingly, we naturally ask, how can the UKM help is to identify, delineate, visualize and to explore/use the many different kinds of Concept-Trees, Life-Trees and Cosmic-Unity diagrams that can be usefully created? Perhaps a useful starting-point might be to create 2D and 3D visualizations (course-grained) of the Cognitative and World Media Stacks for top-level regions of each of the Six Worlds.

In summary, I think we can say that for any World-Brain questing to become a global media system; top-level overview must be a primary consideration; supporting both panoramic exploration of all plus focussed views; with a concordant ability to drill-down / aggregate through universal-classes, particular datum granularities/aggregations etc;

Figure 5. Cognitive Media Stacks

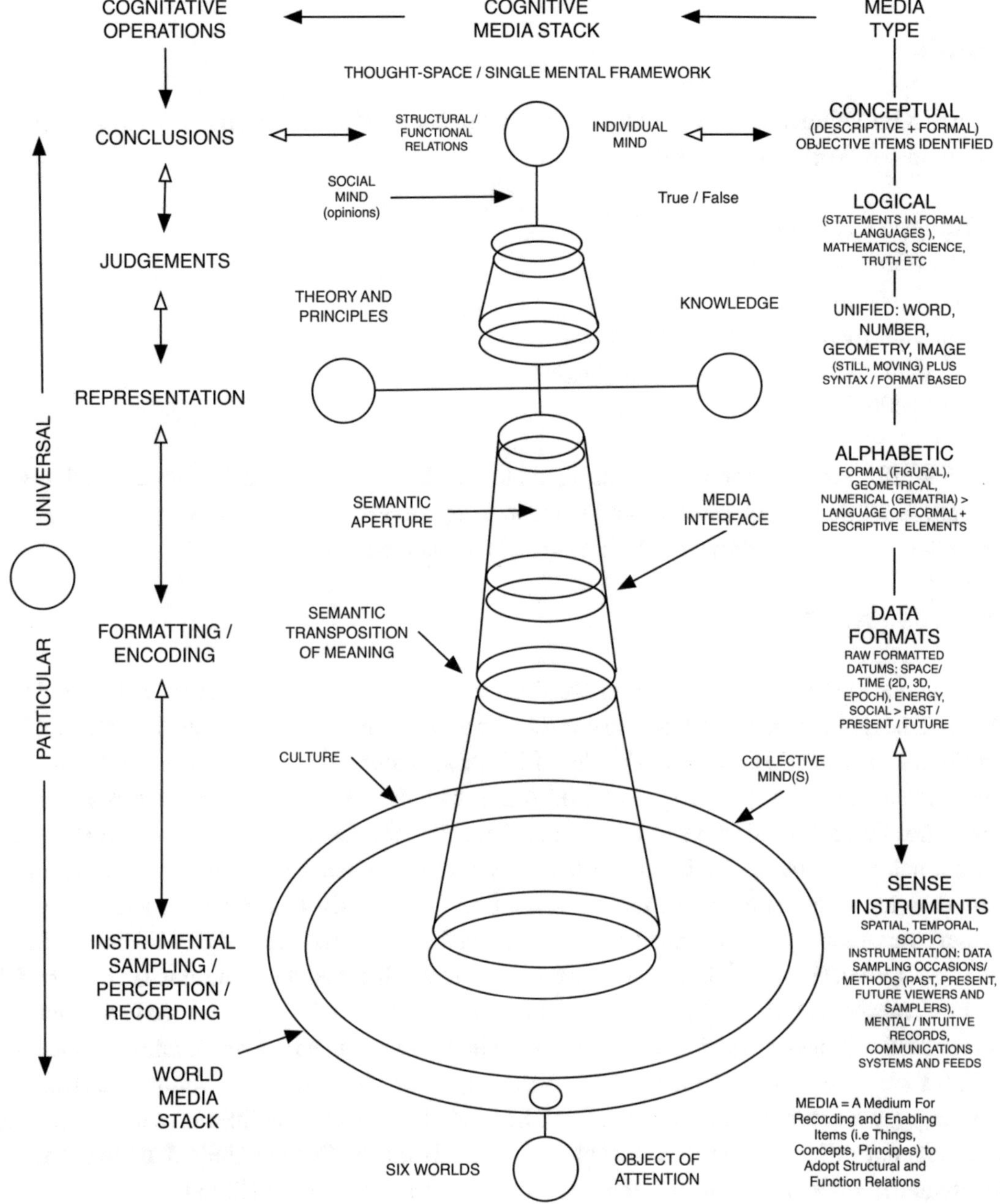

CONCLUSION

The subject of the present chapter has been the design and construction of a universal knowledge-machine - or UKM. This Global-Brain would comprise a universal media system - within which the combined sum of all human/natural: ideas/facts/theories/claims/goals/plans/activities would be faithfully recorded. Building such a system will not be easy - and neither could it happen by accident. Rather much organization (partially centralized) plus distributed planning and effort will be required. But the benefits of so-doing would be epoch-making.

Only in so-doing (building the UKM), could humanity possibly obtain a vastly improved collective intelligence, concordant with the properly unified and fully cohesive integration of all individual and social- forces/understanding/effort worldwide.

Accordingly, we have presented an analysis of individual/collective human thinking processes; in an attempt to learn how we may ***'think better thoughts'***—or develop more useful, relevant, ethical, moral and true: thought-outcomes/ideas. Here we define a ***thinking machine*** as the grouping/representation/usage of certain causally related elements—thoughts and concepts—which accurately reflect things (atoms, physical structures), and processes (mental, physical or metaphysical)—existing in one or more of the three worlds; respectively the ***physical, mental worlds***, plus ***products-of-the-human mind.***

Evidently, despite the fact that the envisaged thinking-machine consists of physical and also metaphysical components, it is still to be embodied as an eminently useful physical/meta-physical machine within human society - or as a (hopefully) properly socially integrated system. It is known that suboptimal or poorly specified systems exhibit a mismatch of actual relationship(s) between—the operational structures—and the planned functional outcomes and/or desired functional outcomes—for a system's design/operation/management (i.e. relations of internal/external structures and functions).

Unfortunately, for the biggest and/or most top-level - and ***poorly specified*** - systems the actual ***relationship(s)*** may be overly complex and/or ungainly, or be unknown/invisible and/or out-of-reach in some way; and hence be poorly understood/represented/modeled and/or be incorrectly mapped. Problems include flawed/incorrect logic, data capture problems, wrong scale/level/plane/granularity for analysis, miss-classification, lack-of-unity, poor-centrality, ignored wrong or unknown items/relationships, unfettered abstraction and/or fragmentary thinking etc.

One example of a poorly specified system is the Internet; which reduces knowledge to questions of Who and What; and ignores the When, Where, How and Why dimensions almost entirely. For example, Kim Veltman has demonstrated that behind every: symbol, letter, word, sentence etc; are a myriad of interrelated: time-lines, places, methods and motivations. Missing from the Web are vast numbers of: common-sources, true connections and interlacing- histories; and parallel/back/omni links are not represented. All human knowledge is mis-represented as a type of monumental palimpsest—a conglomeration of temporary items, loosely held together, being fragile manuscripts (or web-pages) (and events/actions) which are regularly (partially/fully) scraped, re-sued, and overwritten. Knowledge units become isolated/temporary, and ideas/opinions (history) is/are continually rubbed-out/lost.

We suggest building a new mechanism (or World-Brain); to provide detailed (permanent) mapping of, plus evolving and systematic access to: all of humanities thoughts, ideas and knowledge—a vast Memory Palace comprising ALL the universals and particulars—and on multiple scales, timelines and levels/spans/planes-of-analysis. Accordingly, in order to better model/reflect/understand—plus manage—the natural, human and technological worlds; our UKM facilities study of micro-thoughts ***(things of mind)*** and their interrelations in terms of ***flow, structure and combination***. Cross your fingers!

ACKNOWLEDGEMENTS

I am deeply grateful for the support of family and friends, Philip and Ellen Radley, Restie and Rowena Wight, Chris Green, Ruth etc, without whom this chapter would not have been possible. My sincere gratitude and thanks to Prof. Francisco V.C. Ficarra who supported the work financially and also inspired the initial work just over 2 years ago. Thanks also to my mentor Prof. Kim Veltman who has supported and inspired this work over a period of more than a decade.

REFERENCES

Berners-Lee, T. (1999). *Weaving the Web*. HarperCollins.

Berners-Lee, T. (2014). World Wide Web needs bill of rights. *BBC News*. https://www.bbc.co.uk/news/uk-26540635

Buckland, M. (2006). *Emanuel Goldberg and His Knowledge Machine*. Greenwood Publishing Group.

Diderot, D., & le-Rond-d'Alembert, J. (1728). Encyclopedia, or a Systematic Dictionary of the Sciences, Arts, and Crafts. *Wikipedia*. Retrieved April 12, 2020 from https://en.wikipedia.org/wiki/Cyclop%C3%A6dia,_or_an_Universal_Dictionary_of_Arts_and_Sciences

Engelbart, E. (1962). *Augmenting Human Intellect: A Conceptual Framework*. Stanford Research Institute. doi:10.21236/AD0289565

Foucault, M. (1975). *Discipline and Punishment*. Pantheon Books.

Gaines, B. (1996). *Convergence to the Information Highway*. University of Calgary Press.

Goertzel, B. (2006). The Hidden Pattern: A Patternist Theory of Mind. Boca Raton: Brown Walker Press.

Nelson, T. (1974). *Computer Lib / Dream Machines*. Microsoft Press – Pearson Education.

Otlet, P. (1935). *Monde: Essaid'universalisme*. Brussels: Editions Mundaneum. Retrieved April 12, 2020 from https://fr.wikisource.org/wiki/Fichier:Otlet_-_Monde_-_1935.djvu

Popper, K. (1972). *Objective Knowledge: An Evolutionary Approach*. Oxford University Press.

Popper, K. (1978). *The Three Worlds - The Tanner Lectures On Human Values*. University of Michigan Press.

Radley, A. (2013a). Computers as Self. In *Fourth International Workshop on Computer Interaction, Tourism and Cultural Heritage* (pp. 124–135). Bergamo: Blue Herons editions.

Radley, A. (2013b). Lookable User Interfaces and 3D. In *Fourth International Workshop on Computer Interaction, Tourism and Cultural Heritage* (pp. 47–65). Bergamo: Blue Herons editions.

Radley, A. (2015). *Self as Computer*. Radley Press. doi:10.4018/978-1-4666-7377-9.ch011

Rheingold, H. (1985). *Tools for Thought*. MIT Press.

Russell, B. (1963). *Skeptical Essays*. Philosophical Library.

Teilhard-de-Chardin, P. (1976). *The Phenomenon of Man*. HarperCollins.

Turing, A. (1936). On Computable Numbers, with an Application to the Entscheudungsproblem. *Proceedings of the London Mathematical Society*, 2(42), 230–265. Retrieved April 6, 2020, from https://web.archive.org/web/20141222015347/http://draperg.cis.byuh.edu/archive/winter2014/cs320/Turing_Paper_1936.pdf

Turing, A. (1950). Computing Machinery and Intelligence. *Mind*, *49*(236), 433–460. doi:10.1093/mind/LIX.236.433

Veltman, K. (2000). *Frontiers in Conceptual Navigation for Cultural Heritage*. Ontario Library Association.

Veltman, K. (2001). *Syntactic and semantic interoperability: New approaches to knowledge and the semantic web*. The New Review of Information Networking.

Veltman, K. (2006). *Understanding New Media*. University of Calgary Press. doi:10.2307/j.ctv6gqs2k

Veltman, K. (2013). Historical Interfaces for Cultures. In *Fourth International Workshop on Computer Interaction, Tourism and Cultural Heritage* (pp. 1–31). Bergamo: Blue Herons editions.

Veltman, K. (2014). *The Alphabets of Life*. Virtual Maastricht McLuhan Institute.

Veltman, K. (2016). Means of Certain Knowledge, Levels of Knowledge and Interfaces. In *Seventh International Workshop on Computer Interaction, Tourism and Cultural Heritage* (pp. 1-75). Bergamo: Blue Herons editions.

Wells, H. G. (1936). *World Brain*. Methuen.

Wiener, N. (1950). *The Human Use of Human Beings; Cybernetics and Society*. Houghton Mifftin Company.

ADDITIONAL READING

Arthur, C. Google Launches tool to help users plan for digital after life. *The Guardian*. Retrieved August 13, 2013, from http://www.theguardian.com/ technology/2013/apr/12/google-inactive-account-manager-digital-death

Benedek, W., Veronika, B., & Matthias, K. (2008). *Internet Governance and the Information Society*. Eleven International Publishing.

Bradbury, R. (1953). *Fahrenheit 451*. Ballantine Books.

Clark, D., Jacobson, V., Romkey, J., & Salwen, H. (1989). An Analysis of TCP Processing Overhead. *IEEE Communications*, *27*(6), 23–29. doi:10.1109/35.29545

Descartes, R. (1641). *Mediations on First Philosophy*. Retrivied April 12, 2020 from http://www.wright.edu/~charles.taylor/descartes/meditation2.html

Descartes, R. (2008). *Discourse on the Method of Rightly Conducting the Reason, and Seeking Truth in the Sciences*. Wildside Press.

Gibson, W. (1984). *Neuromancer*. ACE Books.

Kurzwel, R. (2005). *The Singularity is Near*. Viking Books.

Lanier, J. (2013). *Who Owns the Future*. Simon & Schuster.

Laurel, B. (1991). *Computers as Theatre*. Addison-Wesley.

Luppicini, R. (2013): The Emerging Field of Technoself Studies. Handbook of Research on Technoself: Identity in a Technological Society, pp. 1–25. Hershey: IGI Global. doi:10.4018/978-1-4666-2211-1.ch001

McLuhan, M. (1964). *Understanding Media: The Extensions of Man*. Signet Books.

McLuhan, M. (1967). *The Mechanical Bride: Folklore of Industrial Man*. RKP.

Norman, D. A. (1999). *The Invisible Computer*. MIT Press.

Orwell, G. (1949). *Nineteen Eight-Four*. Secker & Warburg.

Segal, K. (2012). *Insanely Simple: The Obsession That Drives Apple's Success*. Penguin Books.

UN General Assembly. (1948). *Universal Declaration of Human Rights*. Retrivied April, 10, 2020 from https://www.ohchr.org/en/udhr/documents/udhr_translations/eng.pdf

Wright, A. (2014). *Cataloguing the World, Paul Otlet and the Birth of the Information Age*. Oxford University Press.

ENDNOTES

1 Doubtless machines influence: the settings, accoutrements, passions, strategies, and arrays of forces that shape human lives... and... everything depends upon our ability to focus and direct the will... weave (everything) together into 'circuits 'of both living and inanimate objects... (allowing us to) reorganize the space between mind and world... Mechanical processes seen as instruments of organic teleology. - John Tresch

2 All parts of the cosmos have to be brought together and represented on a single site, in order to focus human activity and remake the world anew! Inert objects have moral and spiritual powers, As a means of humanising science, and unifying society... Devices and machines fused with human actions, intentions and perception.- John Tresch

Chapter 5
Experiences With Computer Architecture Remote Laboratories

Pablo Daniel Godoy
ITIC, Facultad de Ingeniería, FCEN, Universidad Nacional de Cuyo, Argentina

Osvaldo Lucio Marianetti
Facultad de Ingeniería, Universidad Nacional de Cuyo, Argentina

Carlos Gabriel García Garino
ITIC, Facultad de Ingeniería, Universidad Nacional de Cuyo, Argentina

ABSTRACT

This chapter resumes several experiences about using a remote laboratory based on Raspberry Pi computers and Arduino microcontrollers. The remote laboratory has been used to teach computer architecture, parallel programming, and computer networks on computer sciences and telecommunications careers. The laboratory is aimed at students with medium level of programming knowledge, which require flexible access to the computers being able to implement their own solutions. Students can explore the software and hardware of the laboratory computers, deploy, and run their codes, perform input and output operations, and configure the computers. Four different architectures are described, based on cloud computing and remote procedure calls, IoT platforms, VPN, and remote desktop. On the other hand, practical activities performed by students are summarized. Advantages and disadvantages of these architectures, problems that arose during the teaching experiences, and future work are described.

INTRODUCTION

This chapter presents several architectures used to develop and deploy remote laboratories. These remote laboratories have been used to teach topics related to computer sciences in undergraduate, grade and postgraduate courses, and to perform scientific experiments for several years. The chapter does not

DOI: 10.4018/978-1-7998-7010-4.ch005

make an exhaustive analysis about remote laboratories, but rather it presents practical experiences about deployments and usage of remote laboratories for teaching and scientific tasks.

For each remote laboratory presented in this chapter its architecture and variations, advantages and drawbacks, problems that arose during the implementation and usage experiences are described.

The chapter begins with a literature review about remote laboratories. This literature review presents general concepts, applications, common components and requirements of remote laboratories. After, architectures and its variations are described in a different section. Finally, future research directions and conclusions are presented.

The objectives of this chapter are to present a review of the work made about remote laboratories in the last years by the authors, make known architectures and usage experiences about remote laboratories that can be useful to teachers and researchers, and to present future works.

BACKGROUND

Experiments Over Real Equipment and Instruments and Experiments Over Simulators

In order to perform an experiment or practical activity that requires equipment, machines or laboratory instruments there are two alternatives:

- Use real equipment.
- Use simulators.

The use of real equipment and instruments is the best option to both scientific experiments and learning activities. To scientific experiments, the results will not be affected by deficiencies in models used to build simulators. To teaching and learning activities, students can perform real experiences on real equipment. But using real equipment and instruments has some drawbacks regarding simulators:

- The cost can be very high.
- Some researchers and students may not access to real equipment and instrument due to the high cost or the unavailability in some countries or regions.
- Time to carry out real experiments may be very long.
- In learning activities, the concern of students about damaging equipment may lead to limited and little enriching activities.
- The time of use is limited, and equipment have to be shared by several students.

A simulator is a software tool that mimics the behavior of real equipment and instruments. In order to build a simulator, a model of the real equipment is needed. Simulators have several advantages: the cost can be low or without cost, they are easy to install, there is not risk of damaging equipment and instruments, and students can use the equipment without time limitations and without share them. On the other hand, simulators have two important disadvantages:

- It is impossible that a model mimics perfectly a real system, and the experimental results may have errors.
- A teaching or learning activity will not be real. Students may lose the opportunity of learning real details that simulators do not show.

An intermediate option between simulations and experiments over real equipment are emulators. An emulator allows run programs over a virtual platform that is deployed over a real platform. Emulators have two applications:

- Run software applications over a different platform for which they were written.
- Add simulated components to hardware architecture, so that user sees a computer with more resources than the original.

Experimental platforms based on emulators have been found on the literature (Imran, 2010). But they have the same disadvantages of simulators and real experiences. Another intermediate option between simulations and experiments over real equipment are remote laboratories. These have the advantages of simulations and experiments over real equipment, but less drawbacks than both.

Remote Laboratories

A remote laboratory allows users access to real equipment and instruments in a remote way. Users and equipment can be on different or the same locations. Users do not interact directly with the equipment and instruments, but users interact with a user interface. This user interface may be a software, web interface, command line, etc.

The main advantages of remote laboratories are:

- Users can interact with real equipment, so results will not be affected by the simplifications and possible errors of a simulator.
- Learning and teaching experiences through a remote laboratory are closer to the reality than activities through simulators.
- Developers of a remote laboratory can decide which activities and actions are allowed to users.

The main disadvantage of a remote laboratory is that users do not put hands on the equipment and instruments, so there are differences with real experiments and activities. However, these differences depend on the reality of user interface. A good implementation of the user interface is a decisive issue.

Parts of a Remote Laboratory

All architectures of remote laboratories presented in this chapter are formed by two parts:

- The system under test: formed by the laboratory instruments, equipment, machines, auxiliary elements, etc. on which users need to perform their experiments or learning activities. It is comprised by the same equipment that users can use in a classical laboratory. The system under test should be accessible in person or remotely.

- The management system: enables get access to the system under test remotely. The management system transforms a classical laboratory in a remote laboratory. The user interface is part of the management system, runs in the user computer and allows the user to control and monitor the system under test.

The main goal of a remote laboratory is that users do not perceive differences between an in person experience and a remote experience. This objective must be performed by the management system and the web interface.

Physically, these two components could be placed in the same or different locations. In addition, any part could be divided and placed in different locations. For example, the management system usually is a distributed system that runs in different computers.

ARCHITECTURES USED TO DEPLOY THE REMOTE LABORATORIES

This section presents common features of architectures used to deploy the remote laboratories presented in this chapter. These architectures were tested and used to teach different subjects related with computer sciences.

Different Types of Users

The architecture of a remote laboratory is strongly related with the students. Students with low level of knowledge need help and clues in order to resolve an exercise. Remote laboratories aimed to these students usually offer predefined and simple exercises, with part of the exercise already solved. Students have to resolve the unresolved part. For example, in a remote laboratory of programming, part of the code is already written, and students have to write the missing part, and execute the code. In addition, these remote laboratories have protection mechanisms in order to prevent students from performing harmful actions. For example, they could include very restricted access permissions that prevent students from accessing system or configuration files and programs.

On the other hand, remote laboratories for students with high level of knowledge do not have predefined exercises. Students can resolve exercises completely and propose different solutions. In addition, they allow students to get access to system programs and configuration files, to install software, upload, modify and erase files. These remote laboratories should not restrict the actions that students can perform nor impose restricted access permissions, since these are operations that students need to learn. For example, a network computers remote laboratory for students with high level of knowledge must allow students to configure DNS servers, IP addresses, firewall rules, driver interfaces, install software modules, make changes to operating system, etc.

Architectures Deployed Through the Cloud and Without the Cloud

A remote laboratory through the cloud has part of its architecture deployed on a cloud computing platform. This architecture takes advantage of two features of cloud computing: reliability and availability. It is difficult to offer these features through a server deployed on a personal computer or on a university server, but cloud computing providers offer these features to clients. It is suitable that the database, grant permission module and other management modules are hosted on the cloud platform. In this manner, these modules will be always available to users, even if the equipment under test or other modules fail.

Remote laboratories deployed on the cloud have two disadvantages:

- Messages between the equipment under test and user computer are not direct, since they have to pass through the cloud. This could increase the latency.
- Some mechanisms of deploy may not be suitable to the cloud, as it is shown in this chapter.

A PaaS service provides a platform to run user programs, and IaaS provides a computational infrastructure that users can configure, for example, users can configure number of processors and their speeds, memory size, etc. In order to deploy these remote laboratories, it is needed to run on the cloud platform several software modules, no matter the underlying infrastructure. Therefore, the adequate cloud computing services are platform as a service (PaaS) and infrastructure as a service (IaaS).

On the other hand, a remote laboratory without cloud computing does not host any component on the cloud. Thus, all the management modules have to be hosted on a server own by the developers of the remote laboratory. This has a disadvantage: it is difficult to a user and even to a university to offer the level of availability and reliability that a cloud computing provider such as Google Cloud Platform or Amazon Web Service can offer. Figure 1 shows a remote laboratory deployed through the cloud, and figure 2 shows a remote laboratory deployed without components on the cloud.

A REMOTE LABORATORY BASED ON CLOUD COMPUTING AND REMOTE PROCEDURE CALLS

Architecture

A wireless sensor network remote laboratory was deployed with an architecture based on a cloud computing and remote procedure calls. The system under test is a wireless sensor network placed in a laboratory. The management system is formed by several modules with different functions: interaction with the system under test and with the remote users, to create and store activity logs, a reservation system and the web interface. The management system is a distributed system, with some modules deployed in the laboratory, others over a cloud computing platform and the third part on the user computer. Physically, the remote laboratory is deployed on three locations:

- The physical laboratory, in which the system under test is deployed.
- The cloud computing platform.
- The user computer.

Figure 3 shows the physical locations on which the remote laboratory is deployed. The management system is divided in several modules or sub-system. In this architecture, the interconnection system between the web interface and the cloud modules is implemented through remote procedure calls. This mechanism was chosen between the followings:

- Remote procedure calls

Figure 1. remote laboratory deployed through the cloud

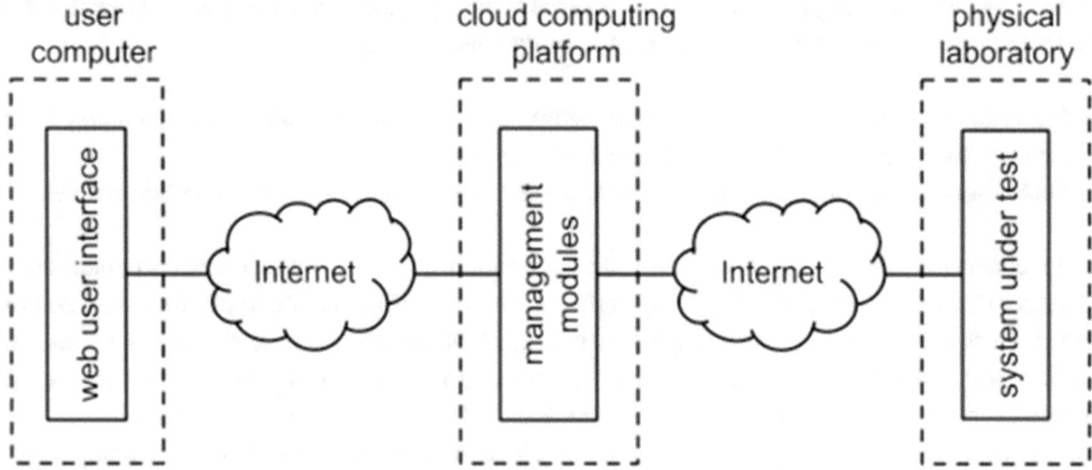

- HTTP requests (POST and GET)
- TCP and UDP sockets
- Synchronization software (like Dropbox or Google Drive).

Remote procedure calls shown two advantages:

Figure 2. remote laboratory deployed without components on the cloud

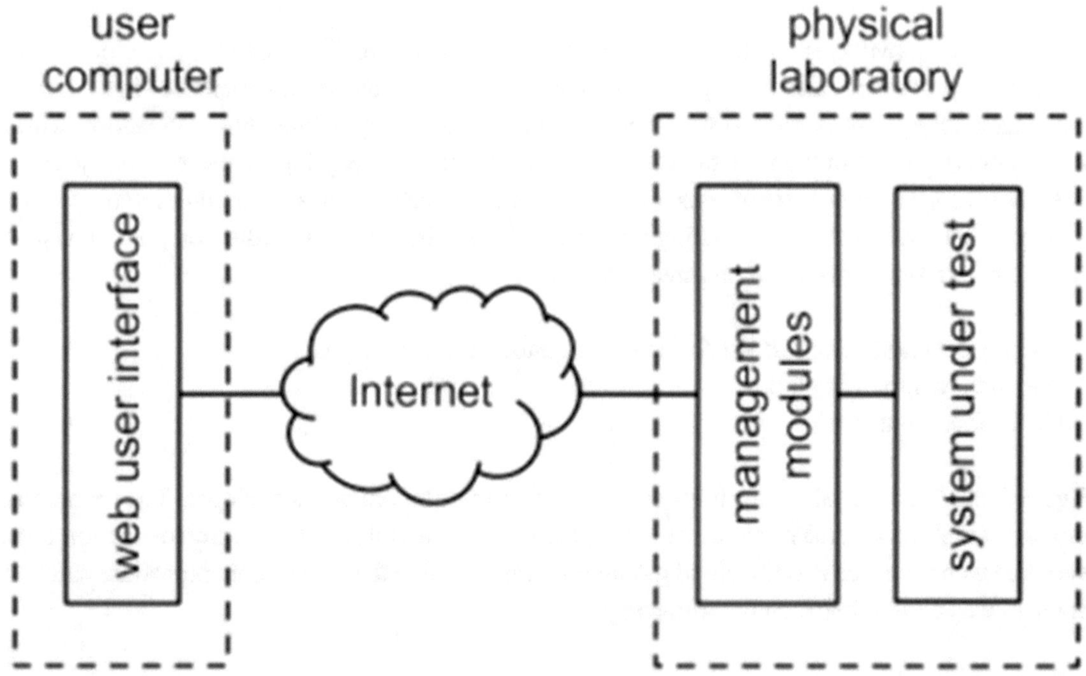

Figure 3. physical locations on which the remote laboratory is deployed

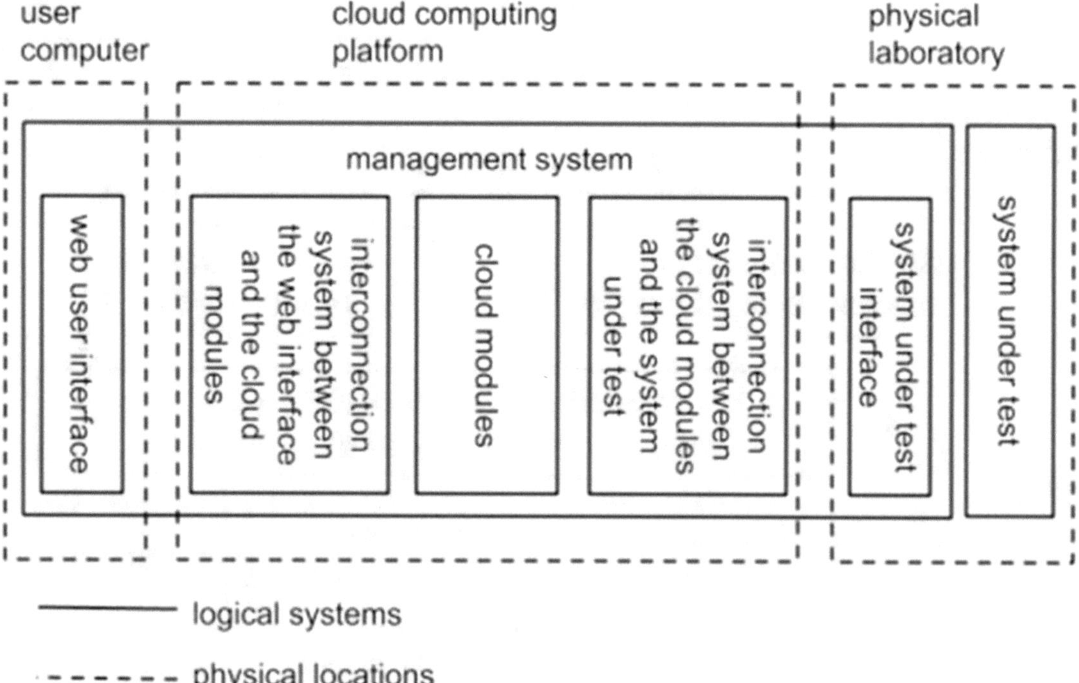

- Performance measurements shown that remote procedure call and TCP socket latencies were shorter than the latencies of the other candidates.
- The cloud computing commercial platforms implement robust and reliable remote procedure calls mechanisms.

In order to perform an action over the system under test, the user has to select the action from the user interface. After, the user interface calls a remote procedure, which is executed on the cloud modules. In order to send the user actions to the equipment under test, the system under test interface requests to the cloud modules actions through a remote procedure call. Then, the cloud modules send the user actions to the system under test. Finally, the system under test interface performs the action over the system under test.

On the other hand, users can view results of the actions that they send to the system under test, and the overall state of the system under test through the web user interface. Several users can view the system under test state at the same time, some with read and write permissions and others with read only permissions. A module called interaction in real time is the intermediary between the system under test and the user interface. This module is part of the cloud modules. To accomplish this objective, the system under test periodically sends to the real time interaction module a state image consisting of the current value of all variables. When the real time interaction module receives this state image, stores it, and waits update requests from the user interfaces. Finally, the user interfaces periodically send update requests to the real time interaction module. When the real time interaction module sends the updated

Figure 4. mechanisms and modules of the remote laboratory

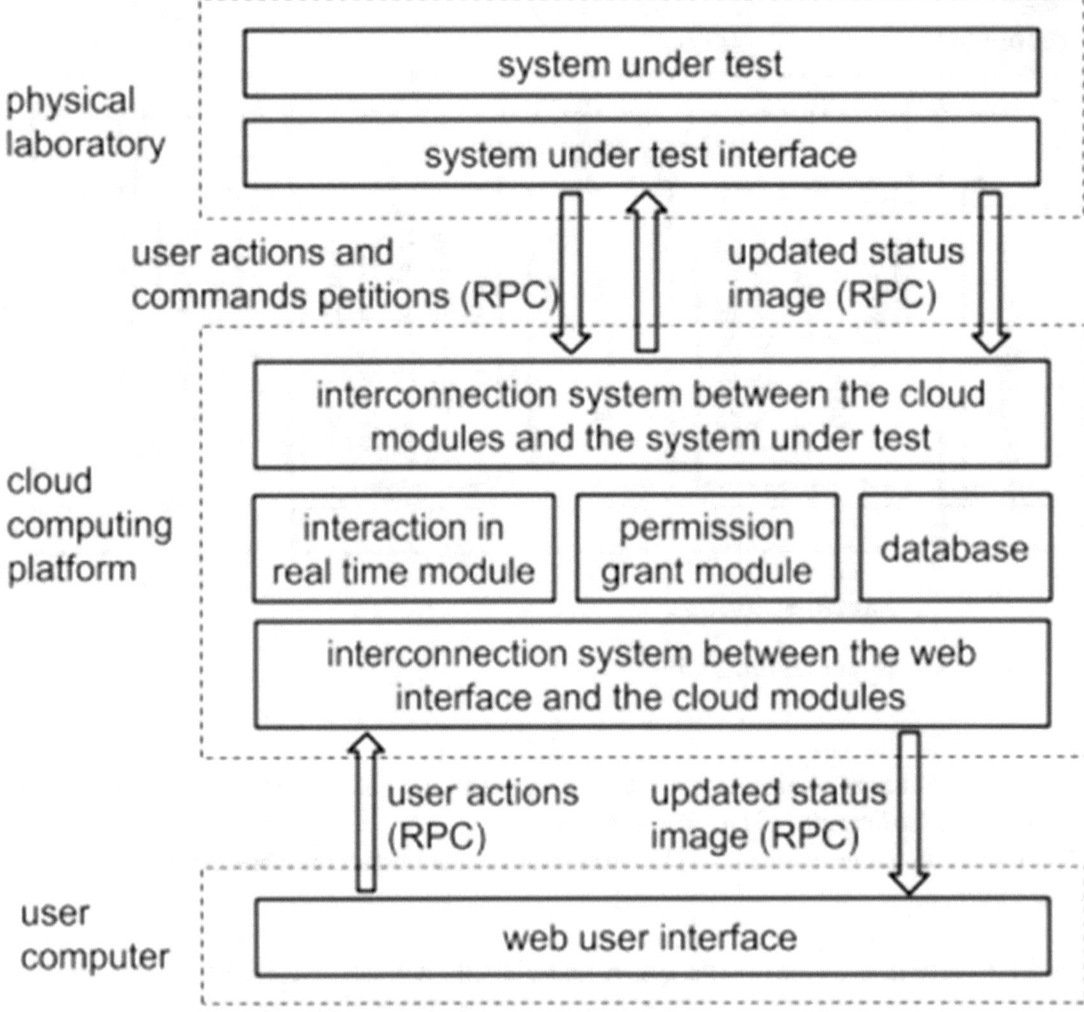

state images, the user interfaces show the new variable values. These mechanism and the modules that comprise the cloud modules are shown in figure 4.

Access control is implemented by a Gmail account, the Google web email service. In order to access the reservation system, and to perform experiments on the remote laboratory, users have to authenticate through their Gmail account with their username and password. Once users have accessed their Gmail account will be redirected to the remote laboratory website and they can schedule a reservation and perform experiments. A user can perform experiments within the time of her/him reservation time. Outside this time, the user can only observe the remote laboratory and the results produced by the experiments of other users. Each reservation is stored as a log in the database. These logs include the username, the start date and time, and the end date and time of the experiments. An application, written in Java language and that runs on the server, keeps these reservation logs in order and it checks availability when a user requests a new reservation. Also, this application indicates to the other modules the authorized username to perform an experiment.

The remote laboratory records actions performed by users. Each log stores the date and time of the action, username and the performed action. The records are stored in the database on the server.

This remote laboratory is aimed to users with low level of knowledge, since it is very easy and intuitive to perform an experiment. But actions that users can perform are predefined and users can not configure some parameters. For example, a user can not change the firmware of the WSN nodes or the network name.

Since all communications between the users and the system under test is through the cloud modules, it is easy to implement a module that stores the user actions and their results. This possibility is an important feature to evaluate students in learning tasks. More details can be found in Godoy et al (2016a).

Usage Experiences

This remote laboratory was used to perform proof of concept experiments and scientific measurements. There are no usage experiences in teaching activities yet. But this remote laboratory will be used in a course about wireless sensor networks that is an elective subject of the Computer Science degree at Universidad Nacional de Cuyo.

Proof of Concept Experiments

These experiments were performed to verify the adequate operation of the remote laboratory, and to measure some performance variables. These experiments show that the latency introduced by the remote laboratory is 505 milliseconds, with a standard deviation of 104 milliseconds. This latency includes the delay since the user sends a command to the system under test, until the user can see the effect of that command on the web interface. This latency does not include the latency introduced by the network and the user computer, since it is not possible to control these latencies. These results, and the results described in the following section, show that this remote laboratory is adequate to teaching activities and research. More details about this work can be found in Godoy et al (2016a).

Scientific Measurements

Experiments and measurements aimed at determining situations that lead to congestion in WSN were performed. Several variables were measured: data packets generation rate, time intervals, transmitter output power and communication channel occupation. In addition, measurements of round trip latency in function of communication channel occupation, time intervals configuration, number of nodes and data packets size for ZigBee wireless sensor networks were performed. Several conclusions were obtained. The most important are cited below:

- Nodes of a WSN are powered by batteries. Also time intervals in active and sleep status can be controlled. It may be wrongly concluded that the ideal choice is to configure the active status time interval to the shortest possible value. The measurements show that this is not the optimal choice, since a shorter time interval than a threshold value leads to collisions and retransmission of packets. This threshold value depends of the communications channel occupation.

- The saturation of the communication channel occupation depends of several parameters, not only of the packet data rate generated by the nodes.
- The round trip latency depends on the number of nodes, the communication channel occupation and the time intervals configuration. The dependencies are not linear, and there are threshold and saturation values.

More details about these results can be found in Godoy et al (2018) and Godoy et al (2016b). These results have been used by other authors to develop several communication protocols and mechanisms to control congestion in wireless sensor networks.

A REMOTE AND NOMADIC LABORATORY BASED ON IOT PLATFORMS

A Computer Architecture remote laboratory based on IoT platforms was deployed. A IoT platform consists of a web service to control IoT devices. This service enables to control IoT devices like Raspberry Pi computers through Internet, without the need of a public IP. There are several providers of these services. In order to implement a prototype of this remote laboratory, the provider Remote-IoT was chosen (RemoteIoT, 2018).

Architecture

There are two ways to get access to this remote laboratory:

- Through a LAN network. Users and the nodes of the remote laboratory are connected to the same LAN network, which can be a wireless network or an Ethernet network.
- Through the Internet, by means of the IoT platform provider.

The system under test is formed by nodes. Each node is comprised by:

- A Raspberry Pi computer and an auxiliary board with buttons and leds. The Raspberry Pi can be connected to Internet through an Ethernet or wireless network.
- An Arduino microcontroller and an auxiliary board with buttons and leds. Arduino microcontroller is connected to the Raspberry computer through a USB cable.

Users can perform experiments on the Raspberry Pi computer, on the Arduino microcontroller, or over both at the same time. The Raspberry Pi computer can be accessed by SSH or VNC protocols, through the LAN network or Internet. In order to access the Arduino computers, users have to access the Raspbery Pi computer, which has the Arduino Integrated Development Environment (IDE) installed.

The system under test is the set of nodes. The management system is formed by a SSH or VNC server installed on the Raspberry computers of the nodes, a SSH or VNC client installed on the user computer, the LAN network or the Internet and the IoT Platform. Figures 5 and 6 show a block diagram of this remote laboratory, including both possibilities.

Figure 5 shows a block diagram of the remote laboratory with a user accessing through a LAN network. Figure 6 shows a block diagram of the remote laboratory with a user accessing through Internet.

Figure 5. Remote and nomadic laboratory accessed by LAN network

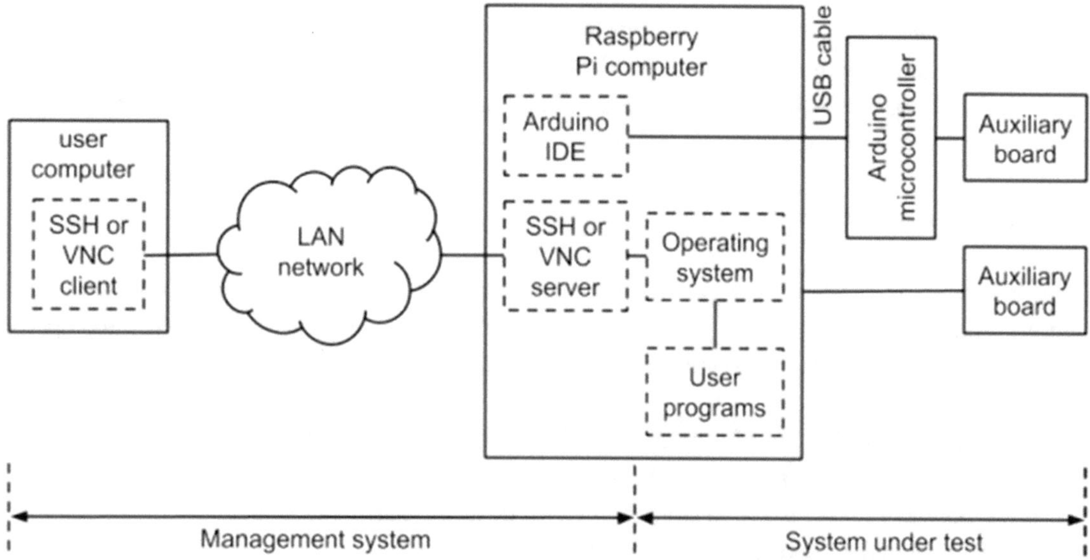

A disadvantage of this architecture is that the permission grant module and the database can not be placed on the cloud. These modules are placed on the Raspberry Pi computers. This has a problem: it is not possible to the university infrastructure to offer high reliability and availability. These features can be offered by cloud computing platforms. Another disadvantage is that the two access methods are different, and it is not transparent to users switch from one access method to the other. In order to overcome these disadvantages, a VPN based remote laboratory was deployed. This architecture is described in the following section.

Figure 6. Remote and nomadic laboratory accessed by Internet and IoT platform

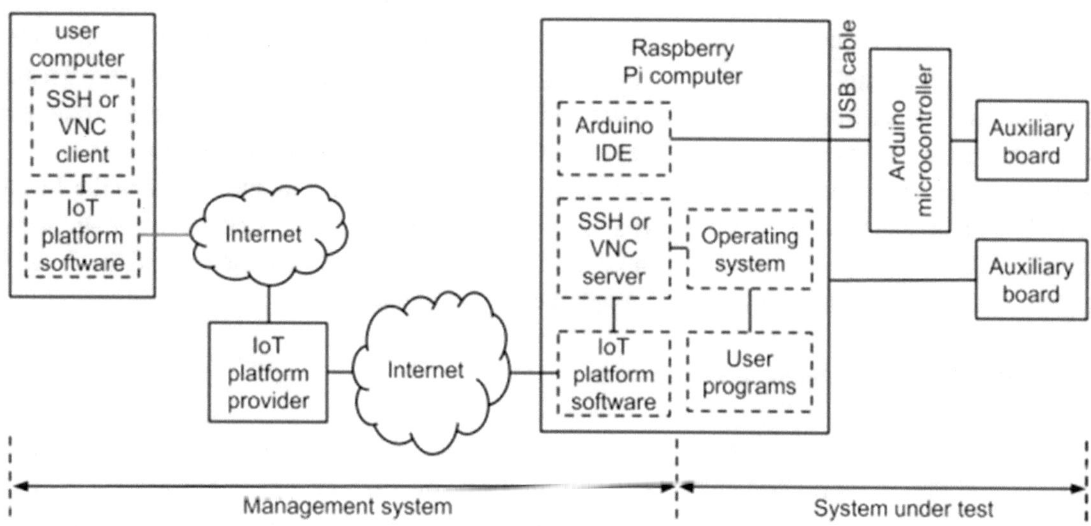

Usage Experiences

The remote laboratory based on IoT platforms and the based on VPN have been used for three years to teach computer architecture, computer networks and distributed architectures in undergraduate, grade and postgraduate courses at Universidad Nacional de Cuyo and Universidad de Mendoza, Argentina. Some of these experiences are resumed below:

Architecture Analysis

In these experiments, students analyze the hardware components and operating system features of a computer through Linux commands. There are several commands to explore the hardware and operating system features of a computer. Students have to use at least the following:

- lshw (HardWare LiSter for Linux): displays information about the hardware and operating system of the computer, including RAM and cache memory information, CPU features and speed, buses, bridges between buses, massive storage devices, different peripherals, etc.
- lspci: displays information about PCI buses and devices.
- free: shows information about used and free memory.
- uname: displays information about the operating system.
- df: displays information about the hard disk.
- ifconfig or ip: displays information about the network interfaces.

Students can use any Linux command, not only the commands shown above. The remote laboratory allows students to access to different computers, and compare different architectures.

Input and Output Operation

The main objective of this activity is that students distinguish the two addressing methods: memory mapped and through special instructions. Students have to write programs that switching off and on leds and to read the state of input pins. These leds and switches have placed on the auxiliary boards. The activity can be performed over the Raspberry Pi computer or the Arduino microcontroller. Students could write their programs with C or C++ languages, but the instruction that write or read the peripherals must be written in assembler language, since a high level language hides details for programmers.

Students can write the program on the Raspberry Pi computer of the node, through the Geany IDE, or on simple text files for input and output operations over the Rasperry Pi computer, or using the Arduino IDE for input and output operations over the Arduino microcontroller. Also, student can download and install other IDE over the nodes, and also can write the programs on their computers and then transferring them to the remote laboratory nodes through the SCP command.

Writing of Interrupt Service Routines

The teaching activities consist of writing service routines to attend interrupts caused by signals detected in input pins of the Arduino UNO microcomputer. Students can analyze concepts as nesting interrupts and priorities. Also students can analyze interrupts over the Raspberry Pi computer. Students can observe statistics about interrupts, number of interrupts in real time, etc. though the system files of the Raspbian operating system running on the Raspberry Pi computers.

Multithreading Programming

Through this activity students can see the speed-up that can be achieved in some tasks using multithreading programming. This activity is carrying out on the Raspberry Pi 3 computers, which have four processor cores. Students can use C++ o Python languages. The activity consists of writing several programs and comparing the execution time between a multithreading execution and one-thread execution. Some of the exercises are:

- Multiplication of matrixes with large number of elements, for example 1000x1000 elements matrixes.
- Patterns search. Students write programs to search patterns consisting of text chains into big files.
- Calculate Taylor series with large number of terms. This exercise is very useful since there are Taylor series highly parallelizable, like the natural logarithm Taylor series, and another with little level of parallelization, like the sine or cosine Taylor series. This allows students to see that the parallelization level depend on the architecture and also of the problem to be solved.

Interference in Wireless Networks

The objective of this activity is to show students the effect of interference on wireless networks (IEEE 802.11). The Raspberries Pi 3 computers are used as wireless access points of IEEE 802.11 wireless networks on infrastructure mode. This election is due to Raspberry Pi 3 computers enable to configure a wider range of parameters than commercial wireless access points, like the inter-frame times. Students measure data rate and latency for a ping command while a large size file is transferred between other nodes on the same wireless channel. Students can modify parameters of the communication protocol, like the inter-frame time intervals and number of interfering nodes, and observe the effect over the data rate and latency. This effect can vary from a no noticeable alteration until the complete blocking of the communication between two nodes.

Client Server Application

The objective of this activity is to understand the client-server model, and to acquire basic skills on PHP and Javascript languages. Students deploy and run a web server and deploy a web site. Students have to install and configure a web server, preferably the Apache HTTP server, on the Raspberry Pi 3 computers of the nodes. Then, students have to write a client server application using PHP and Javascript languages. The advantage of using the remote laboratory is that students can install and configure the nodes, without modify computers in a university laboratory, or the student's personal computers.

A REMOTE AND NOMADIC LABORATORY BASED ON VPN

This remote laboratory has the same nodes that the presented above, but the management system changes. Nodes are also comprised by a Raspberry Pi computer, an Arduino microcontroller, and two auxiliary boards, with switches and leds. Users can perform the same experiments that in the remote laboratory described above.

Architecture

As the remote laboratory described in the previous section, this remote laboratory can be accessed by two ways: through a LAN network and through Internet. The access method through a LAN network is equal to the described for the remote laboratory presented in the previous section, through Ethernet or wireless networks.

The access through Internet is by means of a virtual private network (VPN). The Raspberry Pi computers of the remote laboratory nodes are connected to the VPN. Users have to connect to the VPN in the same way than nodes. The VPN is formed by a virtual LAN network connecting nodes of the system under test and user computers deployed over the Internet. Any user can access to any node or several nodes at the same time. A user can get control of a node through SSH or VNC, and communicate this node with others, transfer files between nodes, run parallel application on several nodes, etc. There are not restrictions to the actions that users can perform over the nodes.

After establishing a connection to the VPN, users can get access to the nodes in the same way than on a LAN network, although they are located in different networks. Thereby, the access through a LAN network or through Internet is identical to the user point of view. Thus, a user can begin an activity connected to the LAN network of the laboratory, and after move to other locations and continue the activities following the same steps through Internet. This is the main advantage of this remote laboratory regarding the previous one.

There are different methods to deploy a VPN. This deployment is direct and simple if the developers own a public IP. In this case, there are several Linux applications for VPN deployments, for example: OpenVPN. If the developers do not own a public IP, it is not possible to deploy a VPN as it is mentioned above, since at least a reachable host through the Internet is needed. There are two possibilities to solve this drawback:

- Use a virtual private server (VPS) as a reachable host into the VPN. Several cloud computing providers offer this service.
- Use a commercial solution to deploy a VPN without public IP.

The remote laboratory presented in this chapter uses the last proposed solution. However, any of the mentioned alternatives for deploying a VPN will work appropriately for this remote laboratory.

Most of the commercial VPNs are oriented to offer tunnels in order to enable to clients access the Internet through a geographically different point of the actual one. This service provides security, hides real location and allows client access services not available in the real geographic location. However, this kind of service is not useful to implement remote laboratories. Few VPN providers offer the needed service to this remote laboratory: the possibility of deploy a virtual LAN over the Internet without a public IP. The selected provider for this remote laboratory is Hamachi LogMeIn (LogMeIn, 2016), which

Figure 7. Remote and nomadic laboratory based on VPN aimed to teaching activities

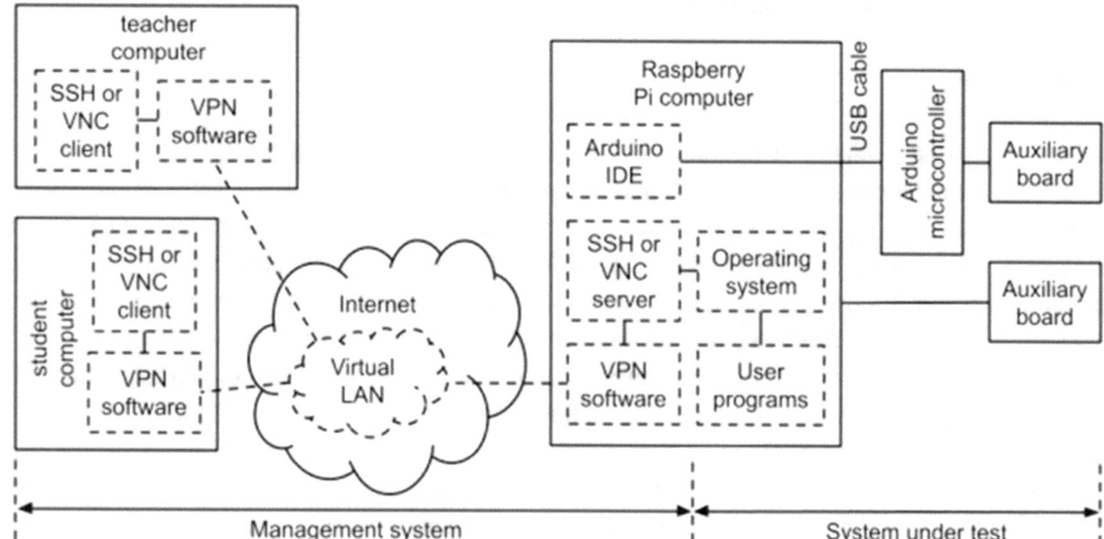

allows to deploy virtual LAN network over the Internet. Figure 7 shows a block diagram of this remote laboratory used to teaching activities.

An advantage of this architecture is the possibility of adding a special computer that hosts the management modules, like a database and a permission grant module. This computer is another computer of the VPN. The current deployed laboratory does not have this computer. Each node has its database, and the permission grant is based on username and password of each node. To add this special computer that hosts these modules is a future work. The mechanism will be based on tokens. Users will send a petition to the permission grant module, and this module will send a token message, which enables the user to get access to a node at a specific time.

Another advantage is that teachers can connect to nodes and monitor in real time students activitie. This capability has been very useful to answer some questions of students, for example, when some code does not work properly. Teacher can login on the node that has the problem, to see the code written by the student, make changes and test the code.

Usage Experiences

This remote and nomadic laboratory was used to perform the same experiments described in the previous section, but in different years.

A REMOTE AND NOMADIC LABORATORY BASED ON REMOTE DESKTOP

Remote desktops and virtual network computing (VNC) are client-server applications that allow the client application to access and take control of the desktop of the computer running the server application.

Even though client and server applications can run on the same computer, the utility of VNC is to run these applications on different computers.

Architecture

It is easy to see the potential of remote desktops to deploy remote laboratories. The problem is that classic VNC applications allow access to another computer on the same LAN network, not over the Internet. Therefore, to deploy a remote laboratory based on remote desktops that run over the Internet, it is necessary to deploy an underlay platform, like IoT platforms or VPN. Remote laboratories described in previous two sections use remote desktops as one of the possibilities to implement the user interface, along with SSH and web interfaces, over an architecture based on IoT platforms or VPN.

However, in the last years, some companies have developed remote desktop platforms that allow to control a computer remotely through Internet, for example: Chrome Remote Desktop developed by Google LLC as an extension of Google Chrome web browser (Google LLC, 2018) and Real VNC Connect developed by RealVNC Ltd. as an additional function of the RealVNC client and RealVNC server applications (RealVNC, 2019). A remote laboratory based on remote desktops has been implemented. This remote laboratory uses the services of RealVNC Connect. This election is due to Chrome Remote Desktop only works on 64 bits Linux, and the Raspberry Pi 3 computers are 32 bits architectures. However, this is a technological issue of this architecture, and Chrome Remote Desktop is alternative that will be evaluated in future works.

A disadvantage of this architecture is that permission grant module and database have to be moved to nodes, because the communication between nodes and users is direct, without an intermediate point into the cloud.

An advantage, similar to the VPN remote laboratory, is that teachers can connect to nodes and monitor in real time activities of students. Teachers can login on the remote desktop of the nodes to see the code written by students, make changes, test the code, etc. Figure 8 shows a block diagram of this remote laboratory.

Usage Experiences

This remote laboratory was used to perform learning tasks about parallel computing through message passing interface (MPI). Students can write their programs in a local computer or over a computer of the remote laboratory. After, students have to configure the host file of MPI, which contain the IP addresses of the computers that will work in parallel. Then students have to execute their programs, and gather usage statistics, like the delay to resolve the problem on several computers and on a single computer, and to calculate the speedup. Some of the experiments performed by students are: pattern search on big text files, calculate if a large number is the product of two prime numbers, Taylor series with large number of terms, etc. all problems that require high processing power.

FUTURE RESEARCH DIRECTIONS

The immediate future work is about the use of remote desktops to implement remote laboratories. Other providers of remote desktops over Internet will be analyzed and compared. In addition, a research issue

Figure 8. Remote and nomadic laboratory based on remote desktops aimed to teaching activities

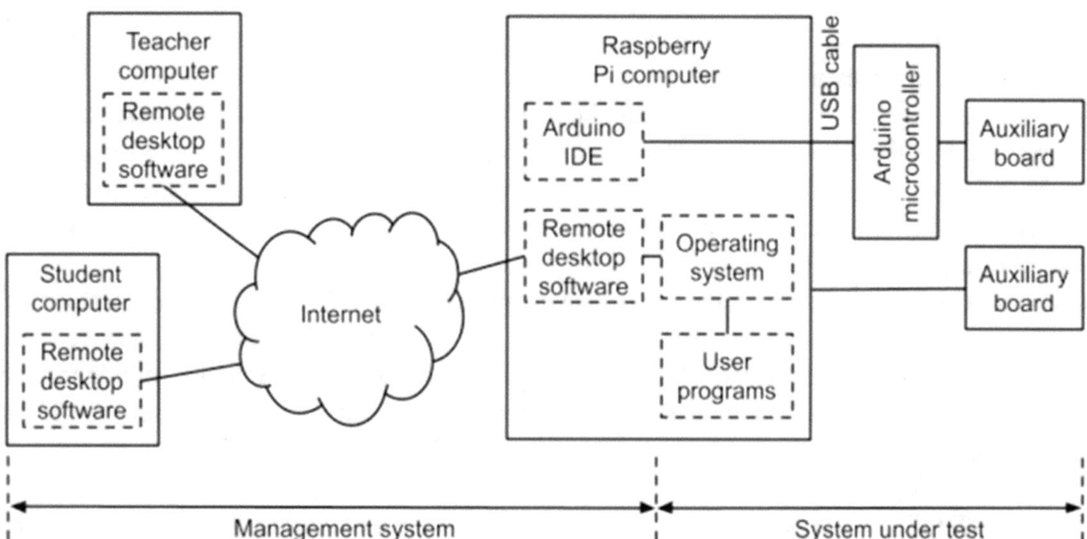

is how to host management modules of remote laboratories based on remote desktops on the cloud, as the permission grant module and database. To deploy these modules on cloud platforms and not over private servers is a premise of these remote laboratories, in order to take advantage of high availability and reliability of current providers of cloud computing services.

Other future work is to test remote laboratories based on VPN and VPS to host management modules on the cloud, and not over private servers.

The remote laboratories presented in this chapter have been used to teach several subjects at two Universities in Argentina. The usage experiences contribute with new needs and improvements. During the 2020 and first half of 2021 they will be used on at least 3 subjects in Universidad Nacional de Cuyo. It is expected that these usage experiences will contribute to new changes and improvements.

The work described in this chapter has been conducted for several years. Several technological advances have taken place over these years. The remote laboratories presented in this chapter have been adapted to these technological advances. It can be noted in this chapter the use of client server models (through remote procedure calls), IoT platforms, VPNs and remote desktops over Internet to implements the remote laboratories presented in this chapter. These changes have followed technologies available in every moment. It is probable that other technological advances emerge in the future, and to analyse possible changes and adaptations to new technological advances of remote laboratories will be a constant future work.

CONCLUSIONS

Several remote and nomadic laboratories have been presented. These remote laboratories were deployed in order to aid in several teaching and research tasks. Usage experiences have been recollected and they have been used to improve the architecture of these remote laboratories. In addition, these architectures have been adapted to technological advances that arose during these years. Some conclusions are exposed bellow.

It is very difficult to build a remote laboratory for all user knowledge levels. Users with low and high knowledge levels require different remote laboratories. Users with low level of knowledge require an intuitive and easy to use user interface, and high level of restrictions to avoid to damage equipment. Users with high level of knowledge require configuring and modifying configuration files, installing software, etc. Then, a realistic user interface and low level of restrictions are needed. Predefined experiments are a good choice for users with low level of knowledge, but they are not wanted for users with high level of knowledge.

Nomadic alternative allows moving the system under test or part of the same to the classroom. This possibility is needed to allow students put hands on the real equipment. Students have answered several surveys about the use of these remote laboratories. These surveys indicate a high level of acceptance, being the remote and nomadic combination the most accepted. Details about these surveys can be found in Godoy et al (2019).

Several technologies are suitable to deploy the management system of a remote laboratory over Internet without a public IP: remote procedure calls, IoT platforms, VPN and remote desktops. Between these, remote procedure calls and VPNs are suitable to deploy a remote laboratory with modules on a cloud computing platform. It is necessary more research about remote laboratories based on remote desktops and compatibility with cloud computing.

ACKNOWLEDGEMENTS

The authors acknowledge the financial support received from the Universidad Nacional de Cuyo through the project B071 "Laboratorio remoto y nómada de arquitectura de computadoras destinado a enseñanza e investigación", and B076 "Dispositivos de lógica programables como alternativa de solución en problemas de seguridad en Internet de las Cosas". Also, authors acknowledge to the professors Lucas Iacono and Osvaldo Marianetti, professors of Introduction to Technology and Computer Architecture respectively, at Universidad Nacional de Cuyo, for allow us to use our platform on their courses.

REFERENCES

Godoy, P. D., Cayssials, R. L., & Garcia Garino, C. (2016). A WSN Testbed for Teaching Purposes. *IEEE Latin America Transactions*, *14*(7), 3351–3357. doi:10.1109/TLA.2016.7587641

Godoy, P. D., Cayssials, R. L., & Garcia Garino, C. (2016). *Zigbee WSN Round Trip Latency in Function of Channel Occupation and Nodes Configuration*. Paper presented at 3rd IEEE Argencon, Buenos Aires, Argentina.

Godoy, P. D., Cayssials, R. L., & García Garino, C. (2018). Communication channel occupation and congestion in wireless sensor networks. *Computers & Electrical Engineering*, *72*, 846–858. doi:10.1016/j.compeleceng.2017.12.049

Godoy, P. D., Cayssials, R. L., & Garcia Garino, C. (2019). *A Nomadic Testbed for Teaching Computer Architecture. In Computer Science – CACIC 2018. Communications in Computer and Information Science*. Springer. doi:10.1007/978-3-030-20787-8_6

Google, L. L. C. (2018). *Google Chrome Remote Desktop*. Retrieved April 2020, from https://remotedesktop.google.com/

LogMeIn, Inc. (2016). *Hamachi, Create virtual private networks on-demand*. Retrieved April 2020, from https://www.vpn.net/

RealVNC Limited. (2019). *RealVNC Connect*. Retrieved April 2020, from https://www.realvnc.com

RemoteIoT Inc. (2018). *Remote Access Raspberry Pi*. Retrieved June 2018, from https://remoteiot.com/

ADDITIONAL READING

Agostinho, L., Farias, A., Faina, L., Guimarães, E., Coelho, P., & Cardozo, E. (2010, September). Netlab web lab: A laboratory of remote experimentation for the education of computer networks based in SOA. *IEEE Latin America Transactions*, *8*(5), 597–604. doi:10.1109/TLA.2010.5623514

Bazzaza, M. W., & Salah, K. (2015). Using the Cloud to Teach Computer Networks. *In: 2015 IEEE/ACM 8th International Conference on Utility and Cloud Computing (UCC)*, 310–314.

Buyya, R., Yeo, C. S., Venugopal, S., Broberg, J., & Brandic, I. (2009). Cloud computing and emerging IT platforms: Vision, hype, and reality for delivering computing as the 5th utility. *Future Generation Computer Systems*, *25*(6), 599–616. doi:10.1016/j.future.2008.12.001

Gerhard, T., Schwerdel, D., & Müller, P. (2014). A networkless data exchange and control mechanism for virtual testbed devices. In: Leung, V.C.M., Chen, M., Wan, J., Zhang, Y. (eds.), TridentCom 2014. LNICST, vol. 137, pp. 14–22. Springer, Cham, from 2 doi:10.1007/978-3-319-13326-3_2

Godoy, P. D. (2016). Plataforma de Desarrollo de Laboratorios Remotos de Redes de Sensores Inalámbricos basados en Cloud Computing. PhD in engineering, Universidad de Mendoza, Facultad de Ingeniería, from http://www.um.edu.ar/es/contenido/fi/Tesis_doctoral_Pablo_Godoy.pdf

Godoy, P. D., Cayssials, R. D., & García Garino, C. G. (2016). Laboratorio remoto para la formación de usuarios basado en el cloud. *Revista Iberoamericana de Educación en Tecnología y Tecnología en Educación*, *18*, 7–18.

Godoy, P. D., Cayssials, R. L., & García Garino, C. G. (2016). A cloud based WSN remote laboratory for user training. Morón, U. (ed.). *In Proceedings of TE&ET (Technology in Education and Education in Technology*.

Iacono, L., García Garino, C., Marianetti, O., & Párraga, C. (2013). Wireless sensor networks: a software as a service approach. In: Prospective and ongoing projects, VI latin American symposium on high performance computing (HPCLatAm). Mendoza, Argentina, 2013, 184–95.

Imran, M., Said, A., & Hasbullah, H. (2010). A survey of simulators, emulators and testbeds for wireless sensor networks. In: Information technology (ITSim), international symposium, Kuala Lumpur, Malaysia, 897–902. doi:10.1109/ITSIM.2010.5561571

Jona, K., & Uttal, D. (Feb 2013). Don't forget the teacher: New tools to support broader adoption of remote labs. *In Remote Engineering and Virtual Instrumentation (REV), 2013 10th International Conference on*, 1–2.

Kabiri, M. N., & Wannous, M. (July 2018). An experimental evaluation of a cloud-based virtual computer laboratory using Openstack. In: 2017 6th IIAI International Congress on Advanced Applied Informatics (IIAI-AAI), pp. 667–672, from https://doi.ieeecomputersociety.org/10.1109/IIAI-AAI.2017.94

Maiti, A., & Tripathy, B. (2013). Remote laboratories: Design of experiments and their web implementation. *Journal of Educational Technology & Society*, *6*(3).

Marianetti, O. (2006). Laboratorios remotos, un aporte para su diseño y gestión. Universidad de Mendoza, Facultad de Ingeniería, Master in Teleinformatics, from http://www.um.edu.ar/es/imagenes-contenido/UM-MTI-MarianettiO.zip

Mostefaoui, H., Benachenhou, A., & Benattia, A. A. (2017). Design of a low cost remote electronic laboratory suitable for low bandwidth connection. *Computer applications in engineering education*, 25(3), 480–488, from https://onlinelibrary.wiley.com/doi/abs/10.1002/cae.21815

Orduña, P., Gómez-Goiri, A., Rodriguez-Gil, L., Diego, J., de Ipiña, D. L., & Garcia Zubia, J. (February 2015). wCloud: automatic generation of WebLab-Deusto deployments in the cloud. In: *Proceedings of 2015 12th International Conference on Remote Engineering and Virtual Instrumentation (REV)*, pp. 223–229. 10.1109/REV.2015.7087296

Orduna, P., Larrakoetxea, X., Bujan, D., Angulo, I., Dziabenko, O., Rodriguez-Gil, L., Lopezde-Ipina, D., & Garcia-Zubia, J. (2013). Weblab-deployer: Exporting remote laboratories as saas through federation protocols. *In Remote Engineering and Virtual Instrumentation (REV), 2013 10th International Conference on*, 1–5.

PlanetLab Consortium. Planetlab research network. Retrieved 2015, from http://www.planet-lab.org/

Raychaudhuri, D., Seskar, I., Ott, M., Ganu, S., Ramachandran, K., Kremo, H., Siracusa, R., Liu, H., & Singh, M. (2005). Overview of the ORBIT radio grid testbed for evaluation of next-generation wireless network protocols. *In Wireless Communications and Networking Conference,* 2005 *IEEE*, 3, 1664–1669. 10.1109/WCNC.2005.1424763

Rutgers University. (2005). ORBIT network testbed website. Retrieved 2015, from https://www.orbit-lab.org/

Salah, K. (2014). Harnessing the Cloud for Teaching cybersecurity. *In: Proceedings of the 45th ACM Technical Symposium on Computer Science Education, SIGCSE '14, ACM, New York, NY, USA*, 529–534. 10.1145/2538862.2538880

Salah, K., Hammoud, M., & Zeadally, S. (2015). Teaching Cybersecurity Using the Cloud. *IEEE Transactions on Learning Technologies*, *8*(4), 383–392. doi:10.1109/TLT.2015.2424692

Tawfik, M., Salzmann, C., Gillet, D., Lowe, D., Saliah-Hassane, H., Sancristobal, E., & Castro, M. (Feb 2014). Laboratory as a service (LaaS): A model for developing and implementing remote laboratories as modular components. *In Remote Engineering and Virtual Instrumentation (REV), 2014 11th International Conference on*, 11–20.

Waldrop, M. (2013). Campus 2.0. *Nature*, *495*(7440), 160–163. doi:10.1038/495160a PMID:23486040

Waldrop, M. (2013). Education online: The virtual lab. *Nature*, *499*(7458), 268–270. doi:10.1038/499268a PMID:23868243

Werner-Allen, G., Swieskowski, P., & Welsh, M. (2005). MoteLab: a wireless sensor network testbed. *In Information Processing in Sensor Networks, Fourth International Symposium on*, 483 – 488.

Yick, J., Mukherjee, B., & Ghosal, D. (2008). Wireless sensor network survey. *Computer Networks*, *52*(12), 2292–2330. doi:10.1016/j.comnet.2008.04.002

KEY TERMS AND DEFINITIONS

Cloud Laboratories: Laboratories that use cloud computing services to store some software modules.

Nomadic Laboratories: Platform to practical and experimental activities that can move.

Online Experiments: Experiments performed remotely through a web interface.

Remote Control: Control a system remotely.

Remote Experiments: Experiments that can be performed over a laboratory located on a different location that the experimenter.

Remote Laboratories: Platform to access laboratory equipment remotely.

Remote Learning: Learning tasks performed by students remotely.

Remote Teaching: Teaching tasks performed remotely.

Web Interface: Interface formed by web pages that allows to access a system.

Chapter 6
The Method and Tools Development for Web-Cameras Color Correction in Binocular Vision Systems

Konstantin Dergachov
https://orcid.org/0000-0002-6939-3100
Kharkiv Aviation Institute, Ukraine

Leonid Krasnov
Kharkiv Aviation Institute, Ukraine

Olexander Cheliadin
Kharkiv Aviation Institute, Ukraine

Olexander Plakhotnyi
https://orcid.org/0000-0002-6406-8501
National Aerospace University KhAI, Ukraine

ABSTRACT

The possibilities of using an adaptation principle in application for organizing the close-loop life circuit of autonomous fly vehicles (FV) are discussed in chapter. The uncertainties arising at each stage of the life cycle of an autonomous fly vehicles (FV) are considered. To solve a problem, the approach using intelligent, rational objects, and using knowledge database tool is proposed. The main theses of rational adaptation control system (CS) are represented. The preliminary designing tools for constructing rational adaptation algorithms for motion control system (CS) are considered. The practical applications of the proposed approach at the stage of preliminary design of control systems for autonomous fly vehicles are presented.

DOI: 10.4018/978-1-7998-7010-4.ch006

BACKGROUND

Currently, the most relevant direction in the development of computer vision is the improvement of stereo-visualization and stereo-matching algorithms in determining distances, 3D-reconstruction of the scene, the formation of three-dimensional images in virtual reality systems (Linda & Stockman, 2001). Therefore, the demand for low-cost but high-quality stereo vision systems is growing (Dergachov et al, 2019). Cheap uncalibrated web-cameras with the ability to connect them to a computer via USB ports are quite suitable for creating accurate stereo systems with easily adjustable parameters. But even minor discrepancies in the parameters of stereoscopic volumes lead to a significant deterioration in the quality of their work, even to the disappearance of the stereo effect.

Discrepancies of the space-time characteristics and color rendition parameters lead to a distortion of the measurement space and a decrease in the accuracy of stereo systems (Shin et al, 2012). Therefore, to form high-quality images of a stereo pair, the following actions need to be performed (Doutre & Nasiopoulos, 2009):

- software synchronization of cameras` work (Zhang, 2004);
- calibration of cameras to determine their parameters (focal length, optical distortion, etc.) and stereo calibration in the general coordinate system (Korotaev et al, 2014);
- image rectification to determine conformity between epipolar lines on a stereo pair in stereo-matching algorithms (Krylovetsky & Protasov, 2010);
- color correction of stereo channels (Bagga, 2013).

There is a common opinion that different brightness and white balance of stereo channels have a small effect on accuracy in solving stereo matching problems, but are detrimental in stereo visualization (Chafonova & Gazeeva, 2014). However, according to the authors, the different intensity of the color components significantly distorts not only visual perception but also substantially affects the quality of the assessment of the spatial position of the fragments of the observed scene.

These issues are relatively easy to solve with fairly traditional methods (Hubel, 1990). For example, calibration of used webcams can be performed using the Matlab-based Camera Calibration Toolbox for Matlab (Shao et al, 2009) or using the resources of the OpenCV library (Park & Kak, 2003). However, there are a number of unsolved problems. So the complexity of the precision adjustment of the stereo system is associated with the lack of a unified approach to the choice of methods for color correction of cameras and their rectification (Mallon & Whelan 2005). This makes the task always relevant and requires new constructive solutions.

The color correction of the stereo pair cameras, as well as their spatial calibration it is advisable to carry out in two stages, according to the authors. First, it is necessary to accurately set the white balance and correct the differences in the intensity of the color components of the images of the video sequences of each camera separately, and then carry out a joint adjustment of these parameters taking into account the results of mutual rectification of the cameras. A more detailed explanation is included below.

The main difficulties in performing color corrections are due to local and global color discrepancies between the cameras as part of a stereo pair (Protasov et al, 2011). A significant factor is also the presence of glare on objects when observing them from different angles. Such discrepancies are due to the differences in the photosensitive arrays and light filters of the stereo pair cameras, and their unequal position relative to the sources of illumination of the scene.

Global color correction methods can be divided into three main classes – histogram matching, global color transfer, and clustering method (Fecker et al, 2008).

When classifying local methods of color correction of images, it is appropriate to distinguish two main methods – block-based method and local color correction for underwater stereo images.

Any of the above color correction methods require the addition of such processing with detection and compensation algorithms for glare.

When using histogram matching methods, the work of color correction algorithms is reduced to the stratification of images in the RGB space into separate components R, G and B, followed by the construction of histograms of pixel brightness distribution for the left and right views of stereo images. Then a conversion function is formed for one of the angles to obtain the minimum difference of each of the color components.

The global color transfer methods are based on the synthesis of a linear transformation function of the RGB color space in order to modify the target image to be in the same color tone as the original image. In this case, the average values of the pixels are calculated for each of the R, G, B channels for the source and target images, and then using the shift, rotation, and scaling matrices, the necessary joint transformation is performed on the three color channels.

The application of the clustering method of correction is based on the selection of keyframes and carrying out probabilistic congregating of pixels, followed by the calculation of the color correction parameters and their interpolation in non-key frames.

Similar principles are applied when constructing local color correction methods and glare elimination algorithms (Dergachov et al, 2019).

Unfortunately, the described methods of color correction of images, which have a number of undoubted advantages, are distinguished by a large number of calculations and are unsuitable for working in real-time. Therefore, it is advisable to explore the possibilities of optimizing the structure of such algorithms for creating software that allows you to quickly and efficiently carry out the color correction of stereo pair cameras.

CONSTRUCTION OF A SEPARATE CAMERA COLOR CORRECTION ALGORITHMS

Color correction of the stereo pair cameras is advisable to carry out in two stages. First, the white balance is precisely set and the differences in intensity of the color components of each camera are eliminated separately, and then a joint adjustment of these parameters is carried out taking into account the results of mutual rectification of the chambers.

Gray World algorithm

The most popular method of automatic color correction of images is the method called "Gray World" since it is assumed that the sum of all the colors in the image of a natural scene gives a gray color. When using this method in space, the original image I_{src} (with $M \times N$ dimension) is decomposed into three components $R_{src}, G_{src}, B_{src}$. Here I_{src} – is a source image and I_{dst} – is a destination image. Then the average brightness values of the pixels for each of these components are calculated:

$$\overline{R} = \frac{1}{MN}\sum_{i=1}^{M}\sum_{j=1}^{N} R_{src}\left(x_i, y_i\right),\ \overline{G} = \frac{1}{MN}\sum_{i=1}^{M}\sum_{j=1}^{N} G_{src}\left(x_i, y_i\right),\ \overline{B} = \frac{1}{MN}\sum_{i=1}^{M}\sum_{j=1}^{N} B_{src}\left(x_i, y_i\right).$$

Here x_i and y_j – are a current row and column number of the original image. Then, a generalized coefficient of average brightness of pixels (Medium Brightness) is determined as

$$MB = \frac{\overline{R} + \overline{G} + \overline{B}}{3}.$$

and then occurs scaling the pixels of the source image of the scene I_{src} with the corresponding coefficients to obtain $(R_{dst}, G_{dst}, B_{dst})$ – components of the output image I_{dst}:

$$R_{dst} = R_{src} \cdot \frac{MB}{\overline{R}},\ G_{dst} = G_{src} \cdot \frac{MB}{\overline{G}},\ B_{dst} = B_{src} \cdot \frac{MB}{\overline{B}}.$$

After adjustment, these components are combined into a color image I_{dst} that can be easily compared with the original image I_{src} visually, and for additional clarity, images of the difference between the destination and source brightness of all pixels are used for the corresponding color components resulting from the conversion:

$$\Delta R = R_{dst} - R_{src},\ \Delta G = G_{dst} - G_{src},\ \Delta B = B_{dst} - B_{src}.$$

«Perfect Reflector» Algorithm

It is based on the assumption that the brightest areas of the image relate to glare on surfaces, the model of reflection of which is such that the color of the glare is equal to the color of the illumination (dichromatic model). For such a model, using the three color components $R_{src}, G_{src}, B_{src}$ of the original image I_{src}, it is necessary to determine the maximum brightness values of the pixels $R_{src\max}, G_{src\max}, B_{src\max}$. After that, the brightness of the image pixels is scaled according to the rule

$$R_{dst} = R_{src} \cdot \frac{255}{R_{src\max}},\ G_{dst} = G_{src} \cdot \frac{255}{G_{src\max}},\ B_{dst} = B_{src} \cdot \frac{255}{B_{src\max}}.$$

Contrast Stretching Algorithm «Auto Levels»

The contrast stretching algorithm "auto levels" is based on the idea of stretching the intensity of the color components $R_{src}, G_{src}, B_{src}$ of the original image over the entire range.

For this, the maxima and minima of the color components $R_{src\max}, G_{src\max}, B_{src\max}$, $R_{src\min}$, $B_{src\min}, G_{src\min}$, $B_{src\min}$ are determined, and then the following transformations are performed

$$R_{dst} = (R_{src} - R_{src\min}) \cdot \frac{(225-0)}{(R_{src\max} - R_{src\min})},\ G_{dst} = (G_{src} - G_{src\min}) \cdot \frac{(225-0)}{(G_{src\max} - G_{src\min})},$$

$$B_{dst} = (B_{src} - B_{src\min}) \cdot \frac{(225-0)}{(B_{src\max} - B_{src\min})}.$$

Algorithm of the Color Images` Contrast Improvement (Equalization)

Algorithm of the color images` contrast improvement (Equalization) with the transition from *RGB* color space into YUV space. This is a color space, in which the color is represented as 3 components - brightness (*Y*) and two-color difference (U и V). An image in YUV space only (*Y*) component can be equalized using the *OpenCV* library function (Minichino & Howse, 2015):

```
img_yuv[:,:,0] = cv2.equalizeHist(img_yuv[:,:,0])
```

Then, the image is inversely transformed from *YUV* format into *RGB* format. At the same time, the color balance remains unchanged, since the color difference components *U* and *V* have not been converted.

For clarity, we give an example of the program code of the algorithm for enhancing the contrast of a color image synthesized in the language Python using OpenCV functions (Joshi, 2015).

```
import cv2
import numpy as np
img = cv2.imread('input.jpg')
img_yuv = cv2.cvtColor(img,cv2.COLOR_BGR2YUV)
# equalize the histogram of the Y channel
img_yuv[:,:,0] = cv2.equalizeHist(img_yuv[:,:,0])
# convert the YUV image back to RGB
img_output = cv2.cvtColor(img_yuv,cv2.COLOR_YUV2BGR)
cv2.imshow('Color input image',img)
cv2.imshow('Histogram equalized',img_output)
cv2.waitKey(0)
```

There are other options present for building such algorithms. However, it should be emphasized that the choice of a specific version of the color correction of the camera (or their combination) is due to the peculiarities of the scene lighting. Therefore, it is advisable when creating software for this task to provide the possibility of an interactive change of the algorithm.

Figure 1. Block diagrams of various color correction algorithms of individual stereo camera pairs

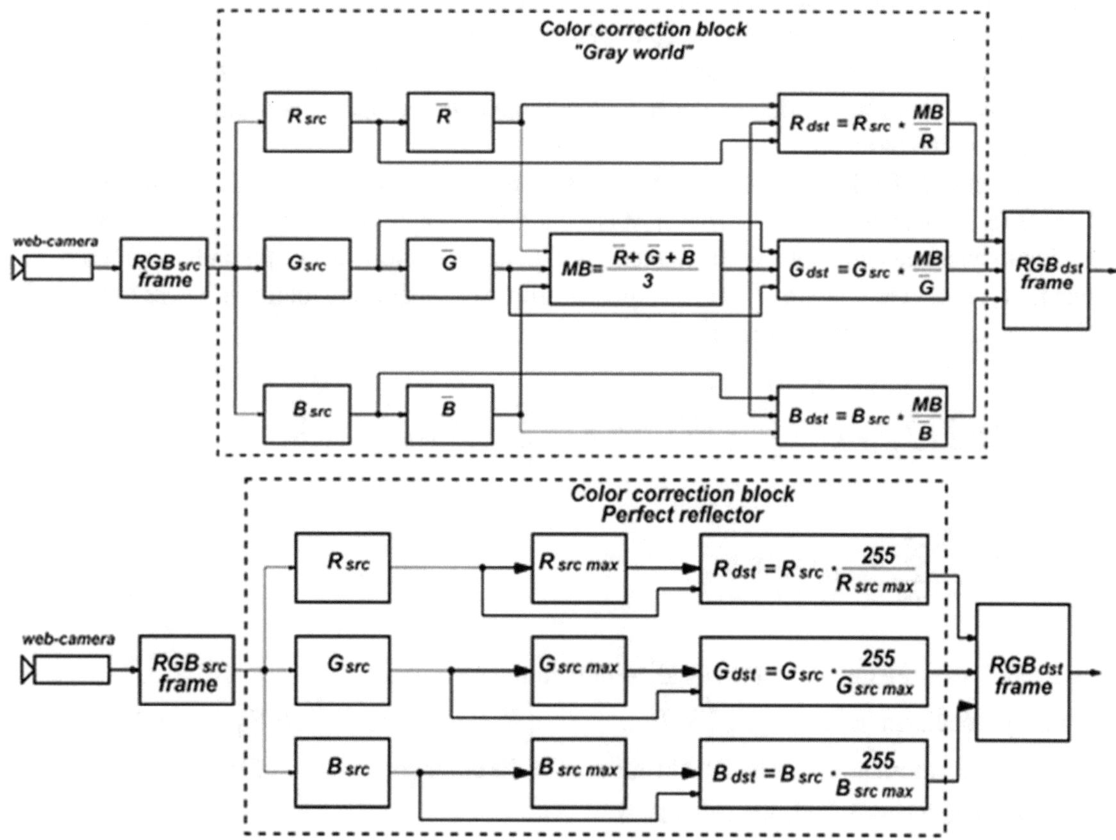

In Figure 1 As an example, the block diagram of two-color correction algorithms for individual stereo pairs of cameras are shown: a - Gray World algorithm and b – «Perfect reflector» algorithm.

Joint Color Correction of Stereo Pair Cameras Algorithm

Consider the operation of the joint color correction algorithm for scene images in the left and right stereo channels (joint color correction).

After the images are rectified by shifting the image of the right channel relative to the left channel by the amount of vertical parallax, areas of interest are selected. (ROI_left and ROI_right). Note that the convergence (exact alignment) of these images is based on the horizontal parallax between the left and right channels of the stereo pair.

It should be remembered that the size of the *ROI* channels should adequately reflect the nature of the scene illumination, and therefore should not be too small. But they cannot be chosen too large since this will lead to an unjustified increase in the computational complexity of the algorithm. In our opinion, the optimal size of *ROI* is the central fragment of the image approximately equal to the central undistorted fragment, selected during the calibration process of the stereo pair. There is no doubt that the user should choose the fragments of *ROI* interactively.

The joint color correction of the stereo pair cameras is performed under the assumption that one of the images is basic. In our case, we take the white balance and image brightness *ROI_left*. The second image *(ROI_right)* will be considered dependent, and the color components of this image will be corrected relative to the basic one.

By comparing *ROI*, it is possible to construct histograms of the distribution of the color components R, G and B for visual comparison. However, it is clear that this approach is ineffective. It is much more productive to evaluate and compare the numerical integral characteristics of the individual color components *ROI_left* and *ROI_right*: Therefore, this algorithm calculates the total brightness indices of the individual color components for the left and right channels:

$$R_{\Sigma}\left(ROI_{left}\right)=\sum_{k=1}^{K}\sum_{l=1}^{L}R_{src\,left}(x_k,y_l),\ G_{\Sigma}\left(ROI_{left}\right)=\sum_{k=1}^{K}\sum_{l=1}^{L}G_{src\,left}(x_k,y_l),$$

$$B_{\Sigma}\left(ROI_{left}\right)=\sum_{k=1}^{K}\sum_{l=1}^{L}B_{src\,left}(x_k,y_l),$$

where x_k and y_l – are the current row and column numbers of the.

Similarly calculated indicators $R_{\Sigma}\left(ROI_{right}\right)$, $G_{\Sigma}\left(ROI_{right}\right)$ and $B_{\Sigma}\left(ROI_{right}\right)$ for the right channel. Based on the information on the total brightness of the color components of the images ROI_{left} and ROI_{right} correction coefficients are calculated

$$k_R=\frac{R_{\Sigma}(ROI_{left})}{R_{\Sigma}(ROI_{right})},\ k_G=\frac{G_{\Sigma}(ROI_{left})}{G_{\Sigma}(ROI_{right})},\ k_B=\frac{B_{\Sigma}(ROI_{left})}{B_{\Sigma}(ROI_{right})}.$$

The resulting coefficients k_R, k_G and k_B are used to adjust the white balance of the dependent image (in our case, the right stereo channel) relative to the base (left stereo channel). The color components *R*, *G* and *B* are multiplied by these coefficients. Note that with sufficiently accurate white balancing, it is usually not necessary to adjust the brightness in the stereo channels.

Nevertheless, consider in more detail the method of compensating for differences in the integral brightness of the left and right channels. For a comfortable perception of images when playing a stereoscopic recording, it is necessary to adjust the total brightness of the base image in the region of interest $I_{\Sigma}\left(ROI_{left}\right)$. It can be calculated using weighting coefficients *p* by the formula:

$$I_{\Sigma}\left(ROI_{left}\right)=p_1R_{\Sigma}(ROI_{left})+p_1G_{\Sigma}(ROI_{left})+p_1B_{\Sigma}(ROI_{left}),$$

The values of the coefficients *p* are determined by the physiological properties of the human eye (Laganière, 2014) and are taken equal to: $p_1=0.2126;\ p_2=0.7152;\ p_3=0.0722$.

Let us give a more detailed record of the formula for calculating the integral brightness of the base (left) channel:

$$I_{\Sigma}(C) = p_1 \sum_{k=1}^{K} \sum_{l=1}^{L} R_{src\ left}(x_k, y_l) + p_2 \sum_{k=1}^{K} \sum_{l=1}^{L} G_{src\ left}(x_k, y_l) + p_3 \sum_{k=1}^{K} \sum_{l=1}^{L} B_{src\ left}(x_k, y_l).$$

Similarly, the coefficient of the total brightness $I_{\Sigma}\left(ROI_{right}\right)$ is calculated for the right (dependent) channel.

$$I_{\Sigma}\left(ROI_{right}\right)^{*} = p_1 \cdot \frac{1}{KL} \sum_{k=1}^{K} \sum_{l=1}^{L} R_{src\ right}(x_k, y_l) + p_2 \cdot \frac{1}{KL} \sum_{k=1}^{K} \sum_{l=1}^{L} G_{src\ right}(x_k, y_l) +$$

$$+ p_3 \cdot \frac{1}{KL} \sum_{k=1}^{K} \sum_{l=1}^{L} B_{src\ right}(x_k, y_l)$$

To achieve a complete balance of the total brightness in stereo channels, it is necessary to adjust the indicators obtained for this channel with the help of correction coefficients K_R, K_G, and K_B, calculated as a ratio

$$K_{R,G,B} = I_{\Sigma}\left(ROI_{left}\right) / I_{\Sigma}\left(ROI_{right}\right)$$

Thus, it is possible to correct the relative deviation of the total brightness of the channels after adjusting the white balance. The block diagram of the algorithm for the joint color correction of the left and right cameras of the stereo pair is shown in Figure 2.

ESSENCE OF THE PROPOSED COLOR CORRECTION METHOD

When formulating the task of creating stereo pair color correction algorithms, it was necessary to solve the main issue - to determine the displacement of images (parallax) of the left and right frames relative to each other. The authors proposed to use a method based on determining the vertical and horizontal parallax of the image of the marker target when combining images of the left and right cameras Δx and Δy. To do this, two fragments of the same dimension are selected on the left and right images of the scene. Let's call them as *ROI* (Region Of Interest). Based on the previously obtained offsets Δx and Δy digital convergence (a combination of pixel precision) of these fragments (*ROI_left* and *ROI_right*) is performed. Then the color characteristics of the right channel are corrected relative to the left one, which is selected as the supporting.

While solving stereo mapping tasks (i.e. distance measuring and building depth map) it is conventional to use marker points (which have specific distinctive features like brightness, color, etc.). Authors consider point with saturated color (in our case — red one) to be the most stable and the least sensitive to scene brightness. It is fixed on a special screen. Therefore selection by color methodology is used for reliable point detection. The recording of a scene with marker point is performed by calibrated cameras stereo

Figure 2. The structure of the stereo pair color balance algorithm

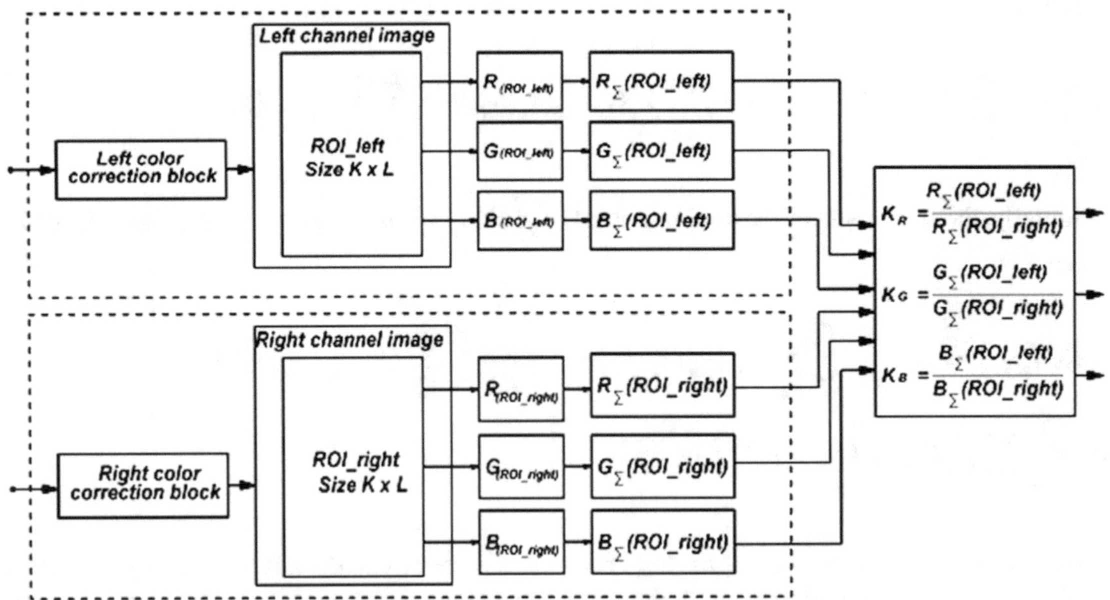

pair. The technique, camera calibration, and rectification algorithms and their program implementation are going to be described in more detail further.marker.

Usually, web-camera signals are a sequence of images in RGB format. It is necessary to apply preliminary color correction and white color balancing for each camera. due to the high variability of the scene brightness. The set of the most effective algorithms was described earlier.

But usage of RGB color space is inefficient because the detection of regions with needed color assumes all three components R, G and B analysis. Therefore it is advisable to switch to another color space. HSV color space (where H - is Hue, S - is saturation and V - for value) is usually used for searching objects by color and brightness in the image. They are normalized as follows: Hue – 0 – 360o; Saturation – (0 – 100) %; Value – (0 – 100) %. Therefore, the most important procedure after the input and color correction of the video data of stereo channels was to convert the RGB color space to the HSV space using the corresponding OpenCV function (Bovyrin, 2013).

```
hsv=cv2.cvtColor(frame,cv2.COLOR_BGR2HSV)
```

Selection accuracy of components, which correspond to the color of the observed object under various conditions of the scene lighting, has a major impact on detection quality. Any point on the H axes determines a two-dimensional area with different S and V values. The target area in the two-dimensional space for the selected H value is reliably determined with the next conditions: V > Vmin and S > Smin, where Vmin, Smin – some constants. Therefore it is common to select target range on the H axes, pointing Hmin and Hmax. Note that the range of values for the HSV parameters for red color highlighting usually lies within the range:

```
lower_range = np.array([0,50,100]), up_range = np.array([10,255,255]).
```

The procedure for selecting the operating range of the *HSV* space parameters for the observed object is best carried out interactively, depending on the current lighting conditions and the color of the object itself. This approach is implemented in the following program with the help of interface settings. To select the range of desired color components (for example, blue) filtering was performed (setting the color mask) using the threshold function:

```
mask_color = cv2.threshold(mask_color,p,255,cv2.THRESH_BINARY)[1].
```

Note the selection of the cutoff threshold for brightness p in this function, it depends on the level of interference. It is desirable to install it interactively

The next important step in the algorithm construction is to determine the coordinates of the marker point in the current frames of the left and right cameras. When working with binary images, the most productive way of this solution is to calculate the moment invariants of such an image, which allows determining the coordinates with a high degree of accuracy. Image moments are calculated using the function

```
moments = cv2.moments(thresh,1).
```

The 'moments' function returns an array of moments up to the third order. However, to calculate the coordinates of the object center, only the first-order moments m01 and m10 are required, as well as the zero-order moment m00. They are determined as follows

```
dM01 = moments['m01'], dM10 = moments['m10'], dArea = moments['m00'].
```

Moment m00 is the number of all single pixels belonging to the selected object, and moments m01 and m10 are the sums of the X and Y coordinates of these pixels. To determine the coordinates of the observed object center, it is necessary to perform the normalization of these moments to the moment of zero order.

When performing this procedure, it is advisable to perform an additional threshold operation that allows you to filter out false objects, the likelihood of which during the color filter operation is not excluded. In this case, if there is a priori information about the observed object size, it is possible by the condition if dArea> N, where N is the number of single pixels of the moment m00, to eliminate false objects. In the following example, the program will only respond to moments containing more than 50 pixels.

```
if dArea > 50:
x = int(dM10 / dArea),
y = int(dM01 / dArea).
```

In this example, random red highlights that have a relatively small area in the frame are eliminated.

After binarizing the images and determining the coordinates of the marker point in the left and right channels, these images are combined using the direct overlay method. Based on the results of combining these images, the values of horizontal and vertical offsets Δx and Δy are calculated, which are used for the digital convergence of the allocated ROI areas. Note that the evaluation of images offsets in stereo-matching tasks is a key information parameter, the definition of which allows solving many applied problems with high accuracy, such as determining the distance to scene objects and triangulation (restoring the three-dimensional coordinates of all points of space present in both stereo-pair images).

It is appropriate to recall that the successful solution of the problem of determining the values of stereo pair horizontal and vertical offsets Δx and Δy is possible only if the preliminary calibration of the webcams calibration and rectification is performed.

CALIBRATION AND RECTIFICATION OF WEB CAMERAS STEREO PAIR

For calibration and rectification of stereo pair cameras, algorithmic and software resources of the OpenCV library were used to eliminate the spatial channel mismatch with an accuracy acceptable for solving the main task (Dawson-Howe, 2014). Calibration is necessary both before starting work and when replacing one of the cameras with a new one or when changing the base distance between them. Exactly in such cases, the quality of the stereo vision system may deteriorate since the restoration of the exact mutual spatial position of the cameras is not guaranteed. The calibration and rectification procedure in these cases is of an auxiliary nature and does not require the processing of video data in real-time. Therefore, it was decided to create a separate software block "Calibration and rectification block" to implement the necessary amendments. The block diagram of this block is shown in Figure 3, and its connection with the main program is clearly visible in Figure 3.

Figure 3. Diagram of a software block for calibration and rectification of stereo pair web-cameras

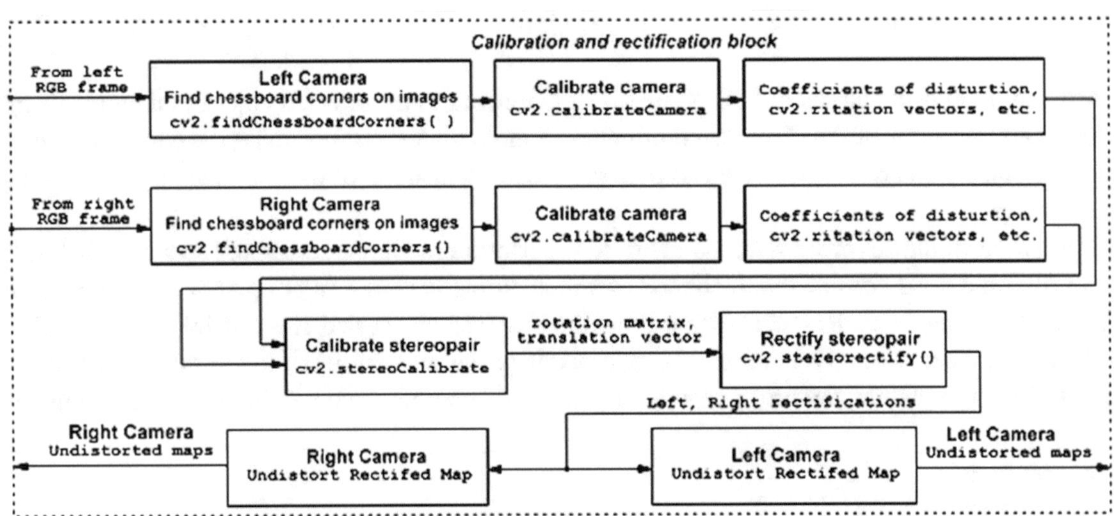

We will not dwell on the theoretical aspects of calibrating and rectifying stereo pairs since these methods are well known (Protasov et al, 2011). We only note that during calibration, the internal parameters of the cameras are estimated (the focal lengths of each of them, the distortion coefficients determining the angle between the x and y axes; the image distortion coefficients are radial and tangential). Evaluation of the external calibration parameters of the stereoscopic camera means determining the spatial position of the frontal plane of the stereo pair cameras relative to the global coordinate system, determined by the displacement vector of the camera relative to the origin of this system, as well as a three-dimensional rotation matrix in orthogonal space. By image rectification, we will mean the reduction of images to a common coordinate system so that the horizontal lines on these images correspond to the same plane.

For calibration, informative signs of discrepancies were used, which are highlighted on the stereo pair images by the test or reference object of the observed scene. A flat pattern with the image of a chess pattern, located in the visibility zone of the stereo-pair cameras, was used as a reference object. In Figure 4 shows a pair of synchronous calibration images of the stereo pair. n more detail the technology of forming a package of stereo pair snapshots for calibration will be given later in the description section of the video data processing program in the stereo system.

Figure 4. Snapshots of a calibration pattern using a stereo pair

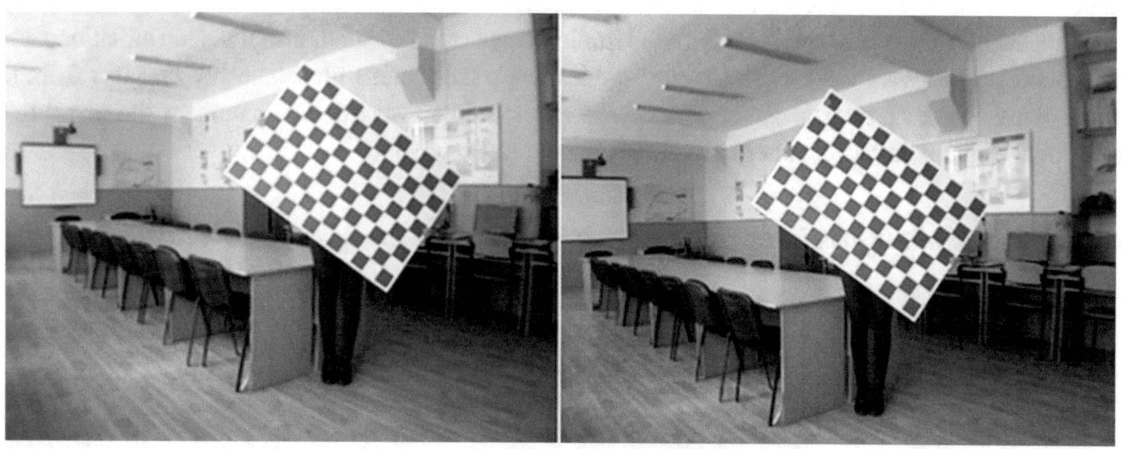

Since the required accuracy is achieved with substantial redundancy of the initial information for calibration, it was decided to record at least 10 images of the calibration pattern from different angles for each of the two channels. It is desirable to make these pictures in such a way, that the template plane is close enough to the frontal plane of the stereo pair to be calibrated.

To create variable rectification of stereo pair images, you must first calibrate each camera separately in order to use its characteristics for further compensating of errors.

A brief look at the main stages of calibration and rectification, features of their implementation using the appropriate functions of the OpenCV library (Baggio et al, 2017).

When forming the input sequence of calibration images, each image from the RGB color space is usually converted to a grayscale color space using the *cv2.COLOR_BGR2GRAY* function. This is done to reduce the dimension of the input sequence. This procedure corresponds to the following fragment of Python code.

```
image = cv2.imread(image_path).
gray = cv2.cvtColor(image, cv2.COLOR_BGR2GRAY).
```

Then, on the gray halftone image it is necessary to find the angles of the chessboard, assuming that the chess pattern is known in advance, using the OpcenCV function (Gupta et al, 2017). In our program, the dimension is *CHESSBOARD_SIZE = (12.8)*. The parameter *SIZE = (12,8)* means that the size of the chess field is 12 × 8 cells. This is done using the function *cv2.findChessboardCorners*. The syntax of this procedure is as follows:

```
has_corners,corners = cv2.findChessboardCorners(gray,CHESSBOARD_SIZE,cv2.
CALIB_CB_FAST_CHECK).
```

According to the results of this operation, it is necessary to assess the status of the has_corners flag, which indicates whether the chess board and all the corners of the internal squares were successfully found. The corners parameter indicates the coordinates of the angles found. In case of unsuccessful search and determination of the corners of the chess pattern in this photo, a message is generated about the need to replace this photo and a command is generated to create a new calibration image instead of the unsuccessful one and the procedure for finding corners is repeated. Usually such situations arise when photographing a checkerboard at such angles when the pattern plane sharply deviates from the frontal plane of the stereo pair cameras. Such errors should be avoided. The results of the marking of the corners of the calibration pattern are clearly shown in Figure 5.

Figure 5. The Results of found chess pattern corners on each camera of stereo pair

Left Right

After that, for images on which the corners of the chessboard were successfully found, it is possible to calibrate each camera separately using the following procedure:

```
leftRet,leftMtx,leftDist,leftRvecs,leftTvecs=cv2.calibrateCamera(left_ob-
ject_points, left_image_points,image_size,None,None,flags=cv2.CALIB_FIX_
INTRINSIC,criteria = TERMINATION_CRITERIA)
```

Based on the obtained calibration data of each camera separately, it is possible to jointly calibrate the cameras in the stereo pair using the library function OpenCV stereo Calibrate (), which calculates the internal parameters of the stereo pair:

```
(_,_,_,_,_,rotationMatrix,translationVector,_,_)= cv2.stereoCalibrate(
object_points,left_image_points,right_image_points,
leftMtx, leftDist,
rightMtx, rightDist,
image_size, None, None, None, None,
flags=cv2.CALIB_FIX_INTRINSIC,criteria=TERMINATION_CRITERIA).
```

As a result, we obtain the rotation matrix and the displacement vector of the stereopair cameras relative to the global coordinates.

Next, it is necessary to calculate the matrices of the rectifications and projections for the stereo pair using the data obtained from the previous calculations. This is done using this code:

```
(leftRectification,rightRectification,leftProjection,rightProjection,
dispartityToDepthMap,leftROI,rightROI)= cv2.stereoRectify(
leftMtx, leftDist,
rightMtx, rightDist,
image_size,rotationMatrix,translationVector,
None, None, None, None, None,
cv2.CALIB_ZERO_DISPARITY,OPTIMIZE_ALPHA).
```

Then you need to get the matrix representing the coordinates of the undistorted pixels for the left and right cameras separately.

```
leftMapX, leftMapY = cv2.initUndistortRectifyMap(
leftMtx, leftDist, leftRectification,
leftProjection, image_size, cv2.CV_32FC1).
```

These matrices are essentially the mask of the imaging area in which the epipolar lines coincide for both cameras. They need to be used subsequently for frames on which the distance to the object of interest will be calculated. To “fix” these images, the remap function is used:

```
img = cv2.remap(img1,leftMapX,leftMapY,cv2.INTER_LINEAR)
```

Figure 6 shows the results of image calibration and rectification with the minimum and maximum distortion areas of the peripheral parts of the scene depending on the values of the OPTIMIZE_ALPHA coefficient.

As a result, we get a corrected image. This procedure should be applied to pictures from each camera.

Figure 6. Corrected image

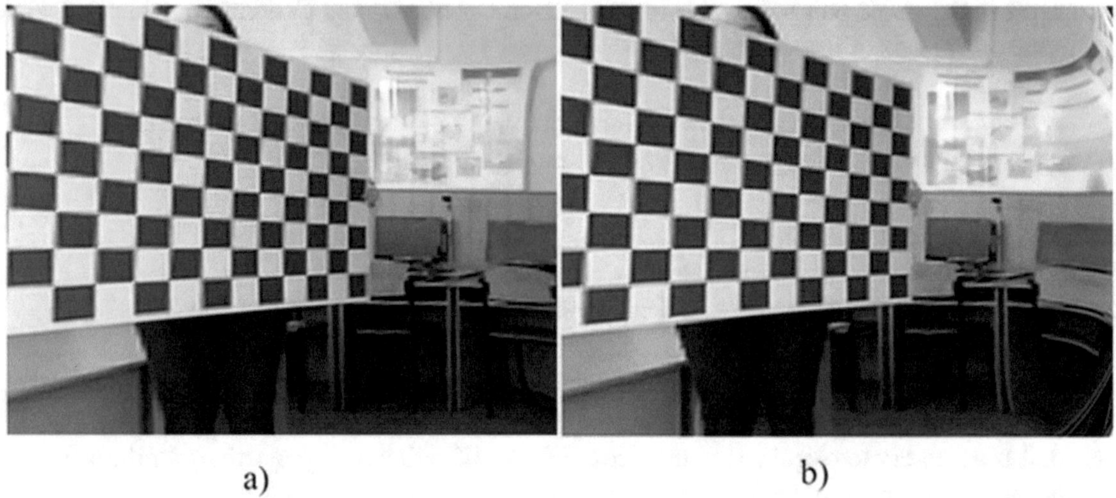

a) b)

A complete calibration and rectification procedure should be carried out for a certain distance between the cameras (stereo base). With various changes in camera positions, it is necessary to repeat the calibration and rectification procedure in order to obtain new matrices that will be correct for the new camera position in the stereo pair.

EFFICIENCY ASSESSMENT OF THE USED COLOR CORRECTION ALGORITHM

To describe the degree of compliance of the original I_{src} and the resulting conversion value I_{dst} of the image it is possible to use different criteria. We believe that in our case it is appropriate to calculate the dispersion indicators for each color component:

$$MSE_R = \frac{1}{MN}\sum_{i=1}^{M}\sum_{j=1}^{N}\left[R_{src}(x_i,y_i) - R_{dst}(x_i,y_i)\right]^2$$

$$MSE_G = \frac{1}{MN}\sum_{i=1}^{M}\sum_{j=1}^{N}\left[G_{src}(x_i,y_i) - G_{dst}(x_i,y_i)\right]^2$$

$$MSE_B = \frac{1}{MN}\sum_{i=1}^{M}\sum_{j=1}^{N}\left[B_{src}(x_i,y_i) - B_{dst}(x_i,y_i)\right]^2$$

The dispersion of information parameters is the most common, but not the only criterion for assessing the degree of difference between two images or their color components. For this purpose, it is possible to successfully use the linear norm of difference (the normalized sum of the modules of the differences in the brightness values of the corresponding pixels of two images). This data is used to evaluate the effectiveness of algorithms.

But the degree of color components` change is most clearly characterized by pairwise presented histograms of pixel brightness distribution. Such visual data successfully complements digital quality indicators.

Let us further consider the method for determining the performance of color correction algorithms for individual channels. It consists of three components.

- visual assessment of the quality of processing the original image I_{src}. Unfortunately, it is often subjective and depends on the quality of the experts' vision. This does not always make it possible to correctly distinguish the differences of the destination image I_{dst} from the source image I_{src} visually.
- the source images I_{src} histograms are displayed as solid curves, and histograms of destination images I_{dst} are dotted. It clearly shows how the ratio of bright and dark pixels changes as a result of the tested algorithm action;
- quantitative indicators of color correction.

As a generalized indicator of the performance of the algorithms used, the authors first proposed a statistical brightness mismatch vector σ_{Σ} of the source image I_{src} and the destination image I_{dst}. Further this vector will be called as Color balance vector. It is presented in the orthogonal three-dimensional RGB color space. The color space in this case is usually represented in the form of an *RGB* color cube, shown in Figure 7. It is known that the diagonal points of this cube, which connects two opposite vertices with coordinates (0,0,0) and (255,255,255), are called Gray scale. They change their shade from black to bright white.

In this coordinate system, the beginning of the vector σ_{Σ} is aligned with the zero (black) point, its module is determined by the set of dispersion indicators for each color component MSE_R, MSE_G and MSE_B which are used to describe the degree of compliance of the source I_{src} and the resulting destination image I_{dst}. The formulas for calculating these dispersions are given above.

The magnitude of the module color balance vector is determined by the formula:

$$\sigma_{\Sigma} = \sqrt{MSE_R + MSE_G + MSE_B}$$

or sum of squared deviations (Standard deviation $\sigma_{R,G,B}$) as following

$$\sigma_{\Sigma} = \sqrt{\left(\sigma_R^2 + \sigma_G^2 + \sigma_B^2\right)}.$$

If necessary, you can analyze the angular position of the color balance vector σ_{Σ} defining these angles $\alpha_R, \alpha_G, \alpha_B$ relative to the magnitude of the vector to its projections on the axes of the cube $(\sigma_R, \sigma_G, \sigma_B)$.

Figure 7. Color balance vector σ_Σ in the orthogonal three-dimensional space RGB

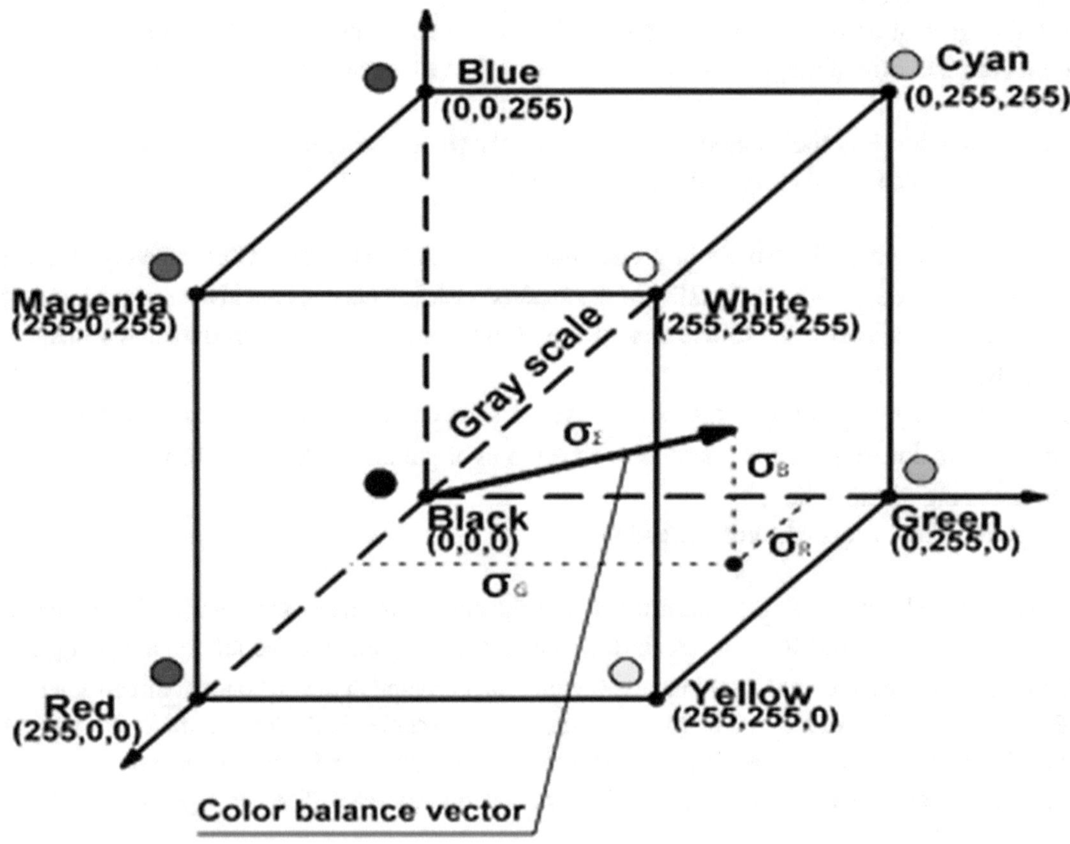

Note that the proposed methodology for evaluating the performance of color correction algorithms are equally applicable for both: color correction algorithms for individual channels and for evaluating the performance of the stereo pair color balance algorithm. The smaller the magnitude of the modulus of the color balance vector σ_Σ, the quality of operation of these algorithms is the higher.

LABORATORY STAND AND STEREO VISION RESEARCH PROGRAM

The Stand`s Design and Composition

For the joint color correction of a stereo pair consisting of two web-cameras, a laboratory stand was used, the general view of which is shown in Figure 8a. It includes a computer with software, a stereo pair based on two identical web-cameras with the ability to connect them to a computer via USB ports, and a rectangular screen on a tripod for mounting a special target mark. Figure 8b shows in more detail the design features of the stereo pair.

When the cameras are rigidly mounted relative to each other, it is possible to change the height of the stereo pair and expand it to 3600 around the vertical axis. In addition, each camera can be rotated at

Figure 8. General view of the laboratory stand - a; stereo pair design –b

a) b)

a small angle in the horizontal and vertical planes. But the main quality is the adjustment of the basic distance between the cameras using a special control ruler. This ensures that the base distance is set to an accuracy of a fraction of a mm. With the help of such a booth, you can successfully solve a wide range of stereo vision tasks — calibrate cameras, stereotype images, color channels, determine the distance to objects to be observed with high accuracy, and create scene depth maps.

When formulating the research problem, the concept of the proposed method, the structure of the algorithms for its implementation were discussed in some detail, and the choice of programming tools and methods was justified. The generalized structure of the software is shown in Figure 9. The program received the conditional name «StereoSensor». Python programming language was chosen using the OpenCV library resources.

In this section we will discuss the possibilities of the software created, the most important element of which is the user interface.

Figure 9. The structure of the software stereo vision

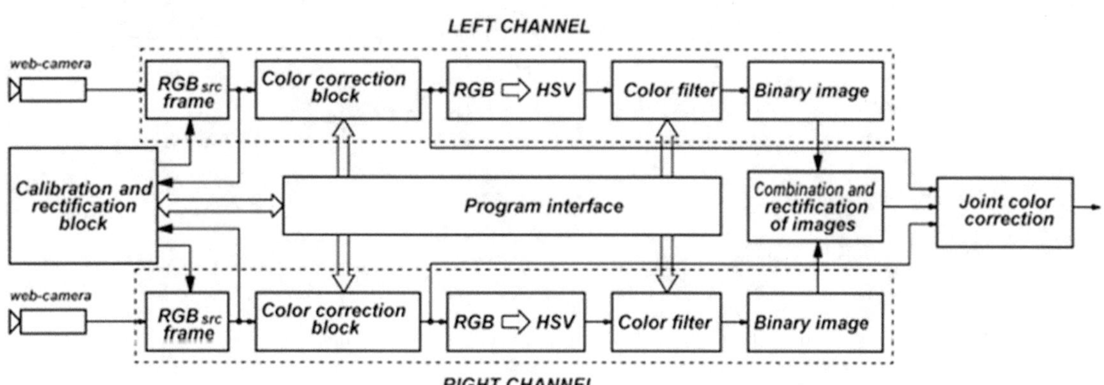

In figure 10 shows the program launch window. The user has the opportunity to choose one of two modes of operation - online mode with recording video data directly from webcams, or using previously saved video files. In the first case, you must specify the Id-numbers used in the program of web-cameras (usually 0 is assigned to the built-in Notebook camera). To search for files with the necessary video data in the second case, you must specify their names and the full path to them. Note that this method of inputting video data provides the possibility of multiple repetition of data processing using various algorithms, which allows us to objectively evaluate and compare the results of work in different ways.

In essence, the program interface is a specialized program desktop. Such an interface construction allows flexible interactive system configuration. Two windows of 640x480 pixels each are symmetrically located on the program's desktop (Figure 11), which corresponds to the avi* format of the left and right channels of the stereo system. In these windows, you can display in the various combinations: the

Figure 10. The launch window of «StereoSensor» program

input frames of the received stereo stream, the results of the video frame transformations and the final processing results. In addition, on the desktop there is a row of buttons and controls that allow you to interactively configure the system to solve the desired task in the shortest possible time. Consider their properties in more detail.

Figure 11. The main window of the program interface

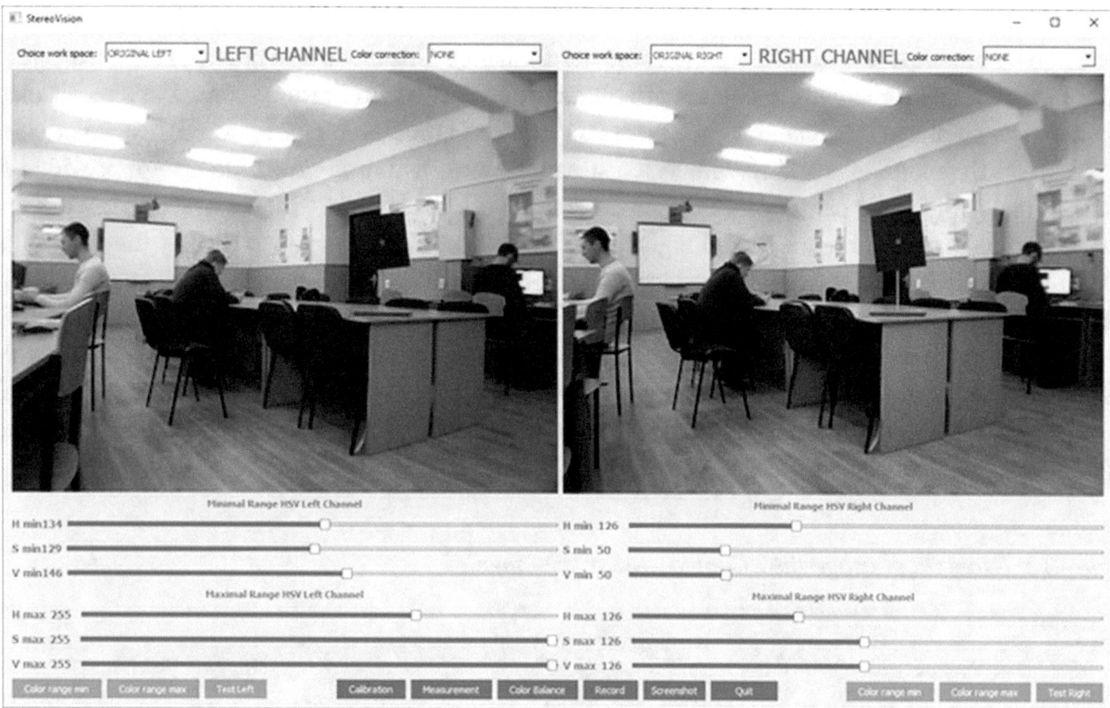

There is a row of buttons at the bottom of the interface. The group located in the center contains buttons «Record», «Screenshot», «Calibration», «Color Balance», «Measurement» and «Quit». Consider the purpose of each of these buttons in more detail.

When registering video data from webcams in the program, it is possible to record a video stream of the desired length by pressing a button «Record». If further replay is necessary in the program, this record should be saved in the system folder Python. This record is saved as two files for left and right cameras in avi* format. The file name shows the system time of synchronous registration (for example, left_cam_19-01-31-12-59, right_cam_19-01-31-12-59, which shows the year, month, date and time of the start of registration with an accuracy of a second). Such records should be used for reprocessing video data and selecting the optimal modes of the program.

Similarly, for analyzing the operation of channel color correction algorithms by pressing the "Screenshot" button, two images of current frames in the png format are saved in the system folder (left_cam_19-01-31-13-10.png and right_cam_19-01-31-13-10. png). The benefits of such an option are evident in the example of creating a series of snapshots for reports on the work done.

The "Calibration" button is designed to proceed to the calibration procedure of the stereo pair. As noted earlier, this is the most important mode of operation, ensuring the elimination of errors caused by inaccuracies in the manufacture and spatial position of web cameras. In this mode of operation, the rectification of the stereopair cameras is also performed. Since calibration is quite a laborious process (a series of 10-15 images of a chessboard from different angles for the left and right channels are required, as well as the description of calibration conditions, etc.), a special interface window was created for these procedures, the construction features and functionality will be described later.

The "Color Balance" button, if necessary, makes it possible to equalize the brightness of the right channel of the stereo pair relative to the left one.

The "Measurement" interface button is used to switch to the measurement mode of the distance from the stereo pair to the reference point of the scene (target mark). This mode also provides for the construction of depth maps for solving problems of volumetric reconstruction of the scene. Let's recall that a depth map is an image in which, for each pixel its distance to the stereo pair is stored, instead of color.

To select the mode of working with video stream frames, two drop-down menus are provided for each channel in the upper part of the interface - "Choice work space" and "Color correction". Work with one of them is shown in Figure 12 and Figure 13. The first menu allows you to display the view of the ORIGINAL LEFT / RIGHT input sequences, BINARY LEFT / RIGHT binary images obtained after color filtering, the BINARY TOGETHER cumulative effect and frame images after RESULT LEFT / RIGHT data processing. The "Color correction" menu contains the names of the algorithms for color correction of the corresponding stereo channel - GRAY WORLD, AUTOLEVELS, PERFECT REFLECTOR and EQUALIZATION. Note that it is possible to use different color correction algorithms in the left and right channels independently of each other.

Figure 12. Example of usage the «Choice workspace» menu

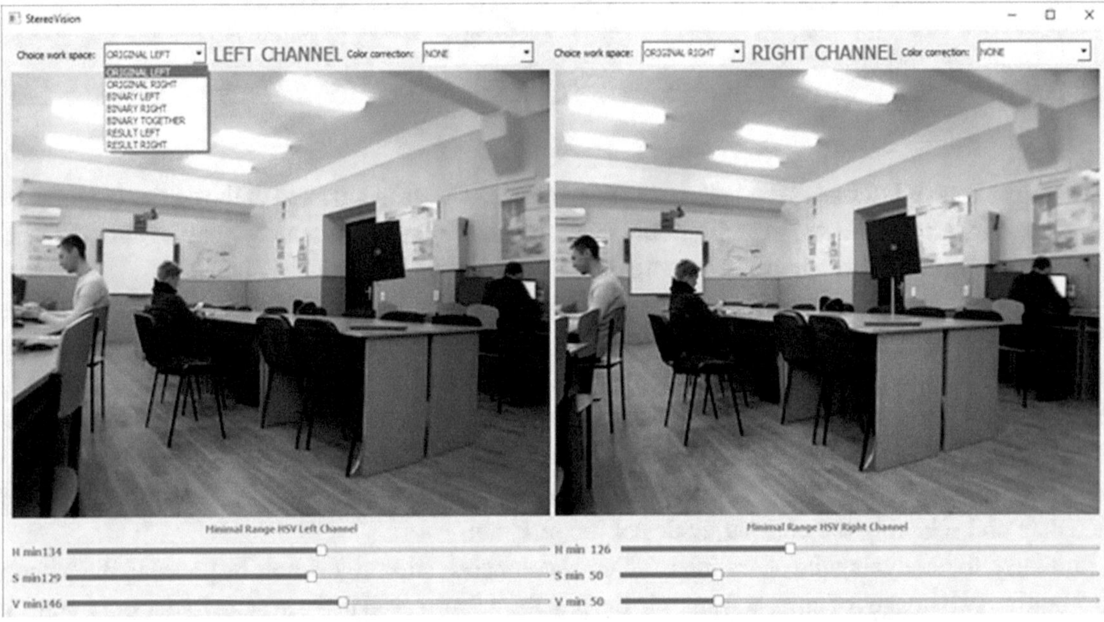

But the most interesting is setting the parameters of color filters to highlight objects of interest to us and assess their position in the frame. In order to do this, it is necessary to use the settings of the color

Figure 13. Color correction channels algorithms selection in the «Color correction» menu

filter, the results of which are displayed in the selected window BINARY LEFT or BINARY RIGHT. Mouse-controlled engines enable interactive selection of the desired range of H, S and V parameters in the HSV color space in the low_range - up_range interval. However, the procedure for selecting the HSV parameters to highlight the object of interest is quite a laborious process, sometimes requiring a long time. Figure 14 visually shows how the result of binarization with clipping off the frames brightness looks like after their color filtering and inaccurate setting the desired HSV parameter range.To eliminate this drawback, the program introduced a pre-setting the HSV color filter parameters range. In the lower row of the interface, for each stereo channel, a pair of "Color range min" and "Color range max" buttons is provided, which allows to open the standard settings window for color characteristics "Select color" (Figure 15). After selecting the desired color characteristics and pressing the "Ok" button the parameters of the HSV interface to the desired position will be automatically adjusted in this window.

After the target mark is detected, current frames of the stereo pair are binarized and the coordinates of the target are determined to the nearest pixel. The results of the calculation can be displayed, as shown in Figure 16, in the BINARY LEFT / RIGHT binary image window. To do this, select the BINARY LEFT or BINARY RIGHT item in the drop-down menu "Choice work space". This window displays the numerical values of the coordinates of the marker target. The first pixel of the upper left corner of the frame is traditionally taken as the frame origin.

After obtaining the results of the marker target coordinates for the left and right frames of the stereo pair, the difference of coordinates is calculated �x and �y. These are the parallax values of the image along the axes x and y, which are used in the task of color correction of a stereo pair for image convergence. But this data can also be used to solve other problems (for example, determining the distance to an object). This data is viewed using the BINARY TOGETHER window, which is also selected in the menu «Choice work space». The view of this window is shown in Figure 17.

Figure 14. The result of binarization with clipping the brightness threshold of the frame

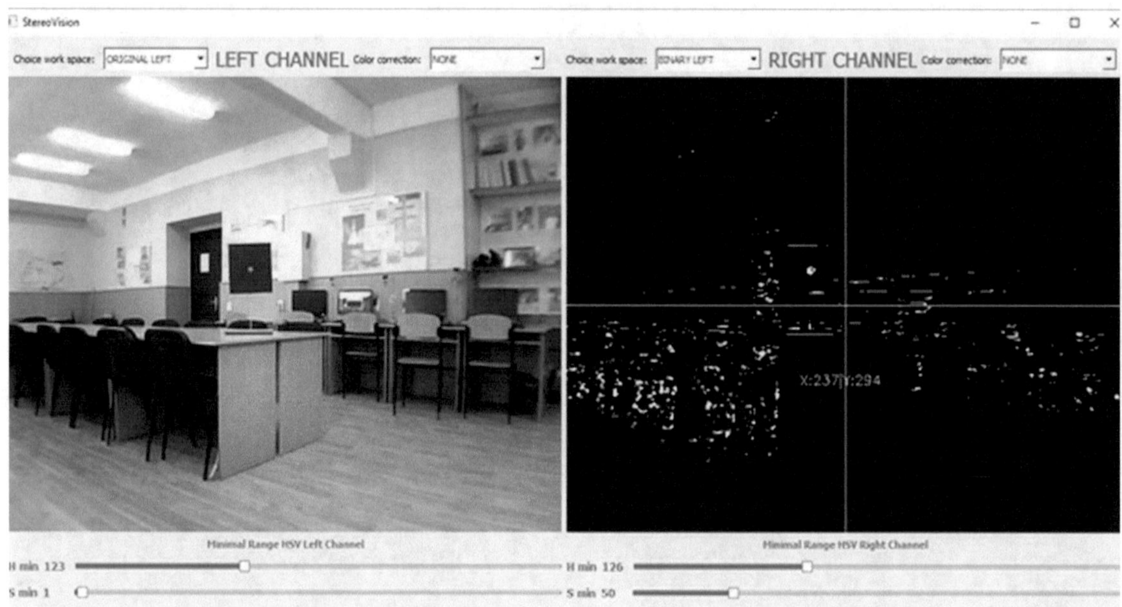

Consider another very important issue. As already noted, due to the large variability in the illumination of the scene, the color characteristics and white balance in each channel may change. Therefore, the

Figure 15. Filter color adjustment window for highlighting the marker target

Figure 16. Binary Image Window - BINARY LEFT / RIGHT

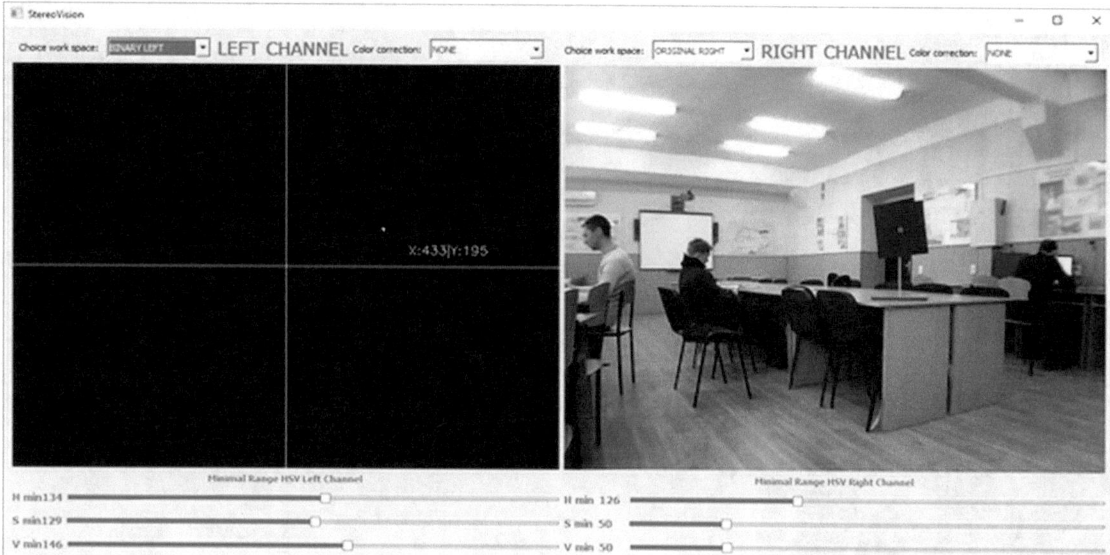

program provides the ability to balance the colors of each camera separately using a set of corrective algorithms. To do this, the user must obtain information about the quality of video transformations using each algorithm built into this program. This can be done in the main interface window by clicking the Test left or Test right button. The program will navigate to the window to the information window "Algorithm Tester Left Channel" or "Algorithm Tester Right Channel", the view of which is shown in Figure 18.

Figure 17. Stereo pair parallax data Δx and Δy in the BINARY TOGETHER window

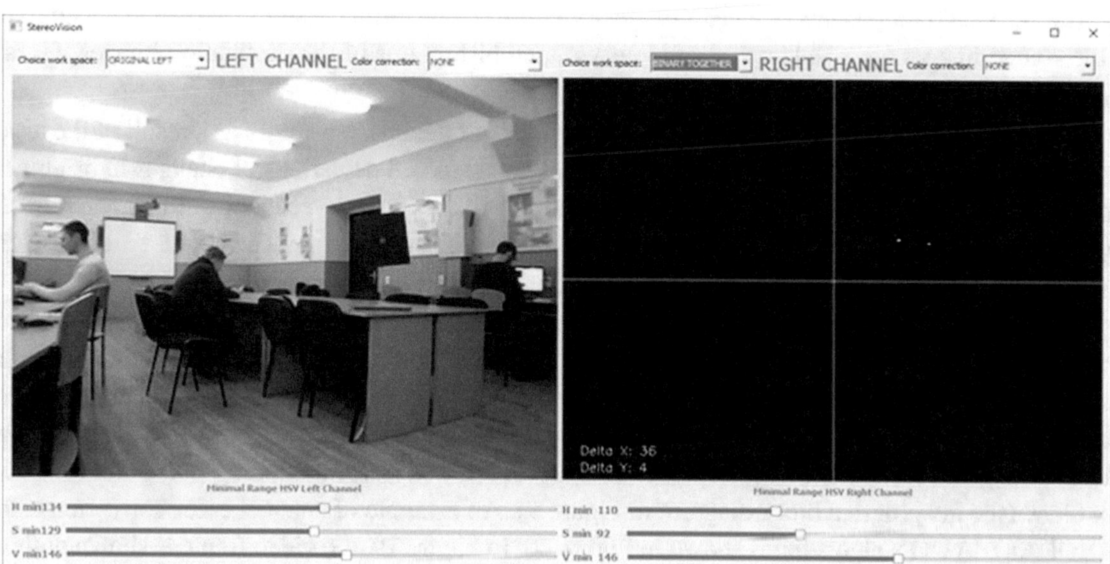

Figure 18. The "Algorithm Tester Left Channel" or "Algorithm Tester Right Channel" windows view

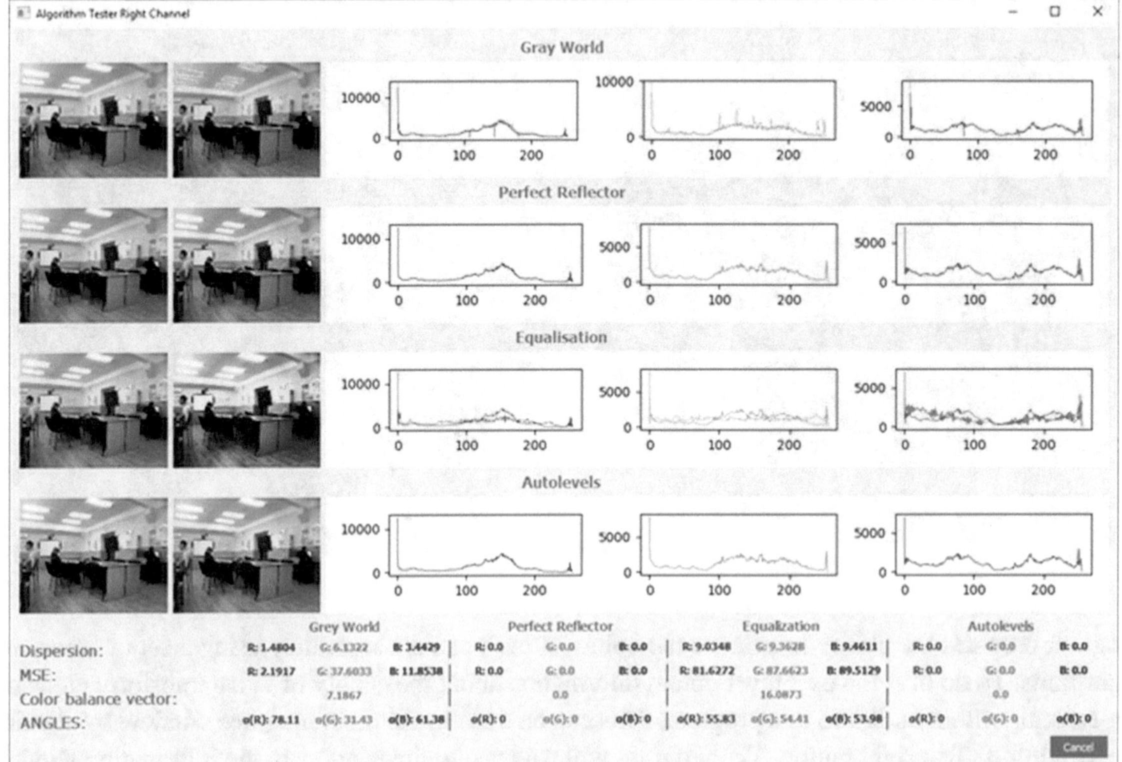

There are visual and digital data characterizing the degree of correction of video data in these windows. For the four color correction algorithms of the corresponding stereo channel (GRAY WORLD, AUTOLEVELS, PERFECT REFLECTOR and EQUALIZATION) the view of the original and transformed frames is shown. In addition, for each algorithm, the histograms of the brightness distribution for the R, G and B components of images of the original and transformed frames are plotted. Histograms of the source images I_{src} displayed as solid curves, and histograms of the destination images I_{dst} are dotted.

It clearly shows how the ratio of bright and dark pixels of the image changes as a result of the tested algorithm action. The statistical indicators (variances and standard deviations of changes in brightness for each color component), as well as the magnitude of the statistical vector of the mismatch of the original image I_{src} brightness and the transformed one, are calculated I_{dst}. The angular indices of the position of this vector in the orthogonal three-dimensional RGB color space are calculated.

Despite the large amount of information received in this window, it is easy for the user to evaluate which of the four proposed algorithms provides the best color correction of the frame in this particular case. Then it is necessary to activate the drop-down menu "Color correction" for the corresponding channel in the main window of the program interface (Figure 19) and select the desired color correction filter for the given scene lighting conditions. This algorithm will start functioning in the Color correction block (see the program block diagram in Figure 9). An example of channel color correction using the EQUALIZATION algorithm is shown in Figure 20. In Figure 19, the video frame is shown without

Figure 19. Using the Color correction menu

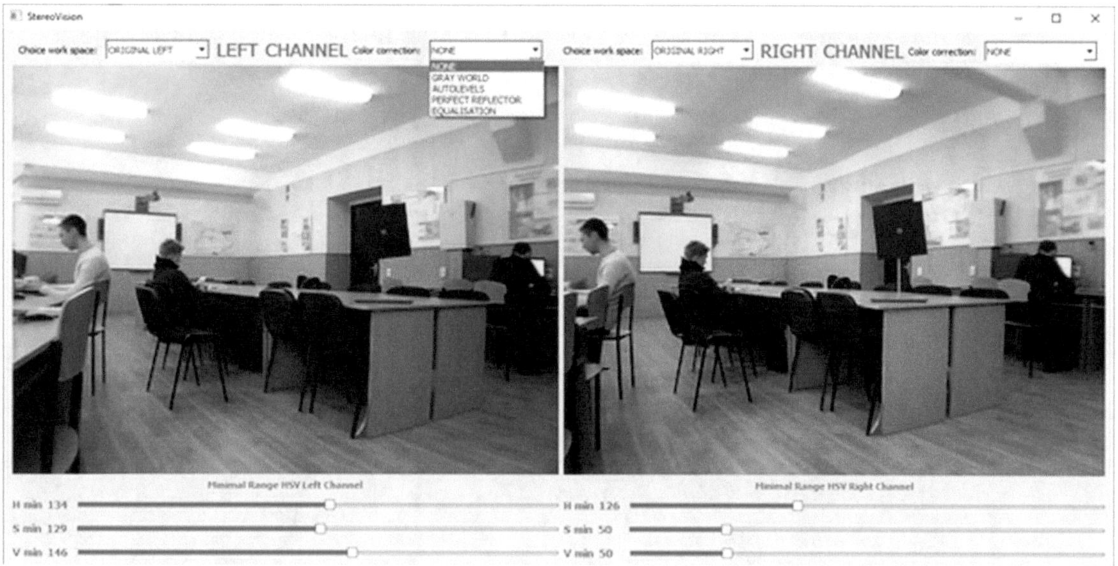

processing (the NONE item in the Color correction menu) and the image of the same video frame after the correction (the EQUALIZATION item is also in the Color correction menu). The difference in contrast of these frames is obvious. The authors believe that such an interactive method of setting the color correction parameters of the channels is most convenient when using the program.

Figure 20. Demonstration of the color correction algorithm of one of the stereo channels

Figure 21. The location of the cameras relative to the object of observation

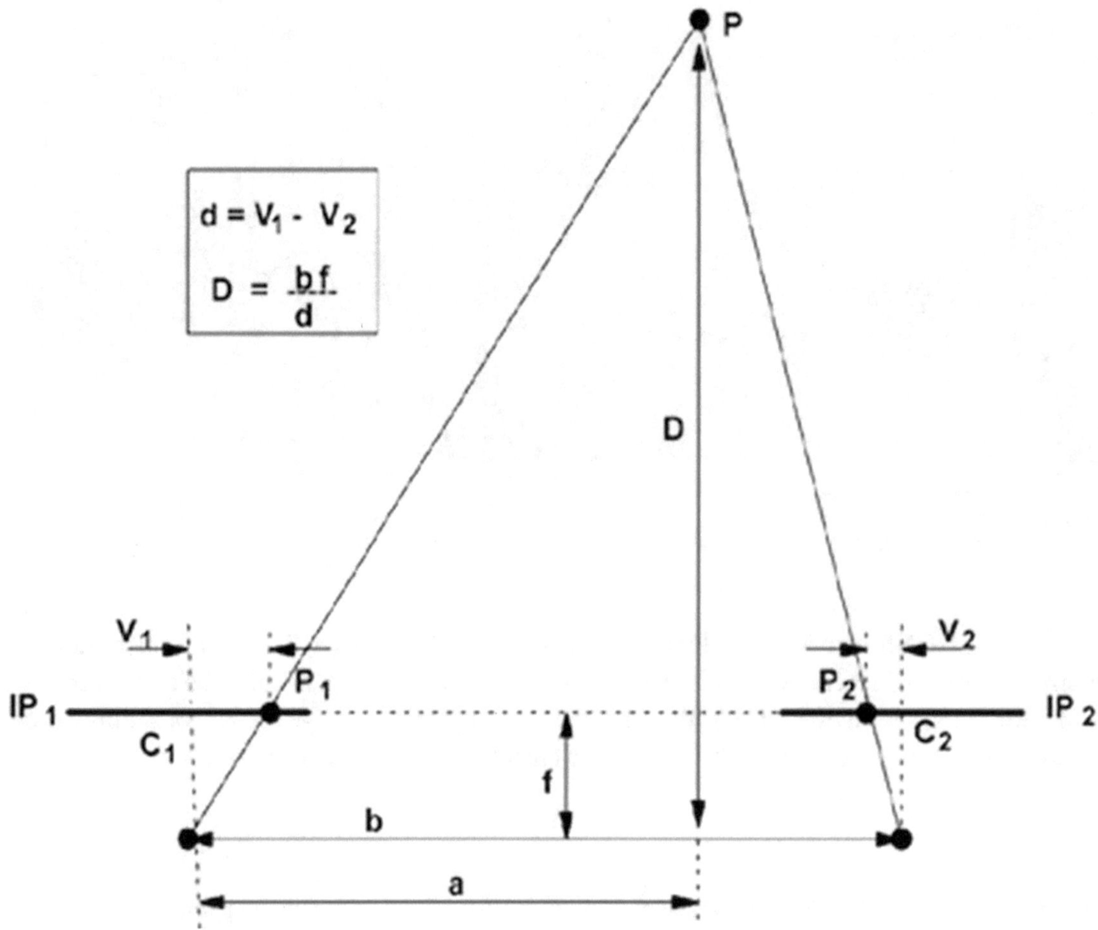

Distance Measurement and Depth Mapping Using Stereo Pair Images

The most important function of the stereo pair is the ability to measure the distance from the plane of the web-cameras of the stereo pair to the color target mark, which can be fixed anywhere in the field of view of the scene (Kulik et al, 2015). This makes it possible to restore the spatial parameters of the position of the observed objects. This procedure does not cause significant difficulties.

Figure 21 shows a structural diagram of the scene, clearly illustrating the essence of the task. Here C_1 and C_2 are the centers of the cameras, IP_1 and IP_2 – image planes (photos), P – target point being observed, p_1 and p_2 – perspective projections on the corresponding image planes, b – base (distance between cameras). The task is to find D distance to the point in the real world. For this purpose, the disparity is calculated $d = V_1 - V_2$ for the point P, where V_1 is a point offset P_1 relative to the center of the first camera C_1, V_2 – point offset P_2 relative to the second camera C_2. Disparity - the discrepancy between the positions of the image of some object for two frames. The process of measuring stereoscopic disparity consists in choosing a certain point in the first image, finding the same point in the second image and measuring the distance between these positions. Recall that the disparity is determined only for rectified images.

Obviously, the distance to the target mark is determined by the simplest formula

$$D = \frac{bf}{d}, \quad d = V_1 - V_2,$$

where f – focal length of stereo cameras, usually expressed in pixels. Focal length f determined when calibrating cameras. Recall that the accuracy of the measurement range increases with increasing size of the stereo base b and improves as the distance to the target decreases as the d parameter increases.

The second most important feature of stereo vision is to build a scene depth map. Depth map or disparity map – this is an image in which for each pixel, instead of color, its distance from the camera is stored. Note that the dimension of the depth map coincides with the dimension of the stereo pair frames in pixels. According to the depth map and the position of the cameras relative to each other, it is easy to determine the distance to objects, the shape and size of objects, restore the 3D model of the room.

Without dwelling in detail on the features of constructing depth maps, consider the great computational complexity of this task. To overcome this difficulty, it is advisable to use the algorithms for building maps from the OpenCV library, which offers two main options - the algorithms StereoBM and StereoSGBM. The first of them provides high speed (up to a real time scale), but does not provide sufficient accuracy. The StereoSGBM algorithm requires much more computational resources, but gives a higher quality of mapping.

In this study, the StereoBM algorithm is used to build depth maps. The StereoBM function analyzes the image of the left channel in rows and sets each point of this line into a similar set of points from the same line of the image of the right channel, and evaluates the displacement of these points relative to each other. Of course, the frames of the left and right channels must be pre-rectified.

Two parameters are predefined for the StereoBM function:

- Ndisparities – disparity search range. For each pixel, the algorithm finds the best mismatch from 0 (minimum mismatch by default) to the differences. The search range can then be shifted by changing the minimum disparity.
- SADWindowSize linear size of blocks compared by the algorithm. Their size must be odd (since the block is centered on the current pixel). A larger block size implies a smoother, but less accurate disparity map. The smaller block size gives a more detailed disparity map, but the probability of finding the wrong match increases.

To display correctly, it is needed to normalize the result - to make the minimum value equal to 0, and the maximum value to 255. Obviously, such a map is an image represented in shades of gray. However, it can be presented in the form of a color image using some standard palette. For example:

```
disparity_color=cv2.applyColorMap(disparity_grayscale,cv2.COLORMAP_JET).
```

This map is built in BGR (Blue-Green-Red) format. To display it in the RGB (Red-Green-Blue) format, it is necessary to perform the following conversion:

```
disparity = cv2.cvtColor (disparity, cv2.COLOR_BGR2RGB).
```

The implementation of depth mapping algorithms in the StereoSensor program will be considered further.

EXPERIMENTAL RESEARCH AND MAIN RESULTS

The results of experimental studies are presented below in the form of Figure 22, Figure 23, Figure 24, Figure 25, Figure 26, each of which contains data on the analysis of the effectiveness of one of the color correction algorithms. The table cells consist of the source image I_{src}, destination image I_{dst}, data of statistical processing and histogram of the brightness distribution of the three color components. The histograms of the input (solid line) and output (dashed line) images are arranged in pairs for each color component. This creates convenience for analysis. Also, according to the results of statistical analysis, the module of the color balance vector σ_{Σ} is calculated and entered into the table.

Analysis of the particular investigated algorithms and comparative analysis of their quality should be carried out on the basis of an objective complex criterion, which should take into account both the nature of the visual perception of image changes and the variability of histograms as a result of transformations. An equally important aspect of the analysis is the accounting of statistical indicators. It is also necessary to evaluate the module and the angular position of the color balance vector σ_{Σ} in the orthogonal *RGB* color space.

A comparative analysis of the four color correction algorithms showed that each of them has both advantages and disadvantages. For example, it should be noted that when processing the image using the "Gray World" algorithm, a significant imbalance of color occurred (Figure 22). This means that such an algorithm is not effective under all conditions of illumination of the scene. The example given in Table 1 shows that under certain conditions it is quite applicable and sufficiently effective.

For convenience of analysis, data on the color balance vector module σ_{Σ} magnitude tabulated.

It is clear that in the absence of noticeable irregularities in the image of the white balance, the discrepancy of the histograms of the original and processed images is reduced, and in the limit becomes zero. Therefore, the reduction factor of the color balance vector is also a positive factor. According to the authors, the use of the "Autolevels" and "Equalization" algorithms is practically most preferable. The latter is most effective at low levels of illumination of the scene, as it allows the image brightness to lead to an average level of illumination. The described method of assessing the effectiveness of color correction is fully applicable for the joint color balancing of stereopair cameras.

FUTURE RESEARCH DIRECTIONS

The proposed methods of cameras color correction allow to successfully solve the problem of setting white balance in each of the stereopair cameras and to balance the integral brightness of the left and right channels images with not only high accuracy, but also taking into account the physiological features of the human eye perception of these images. However, the effectiveness of their application may significantly decrease due to the action of various disturbing factors. The main one is the spontaneously

Figure 22. Quality indicators of the "Grey world" algorithm processing results

Processing method – «Gray World»

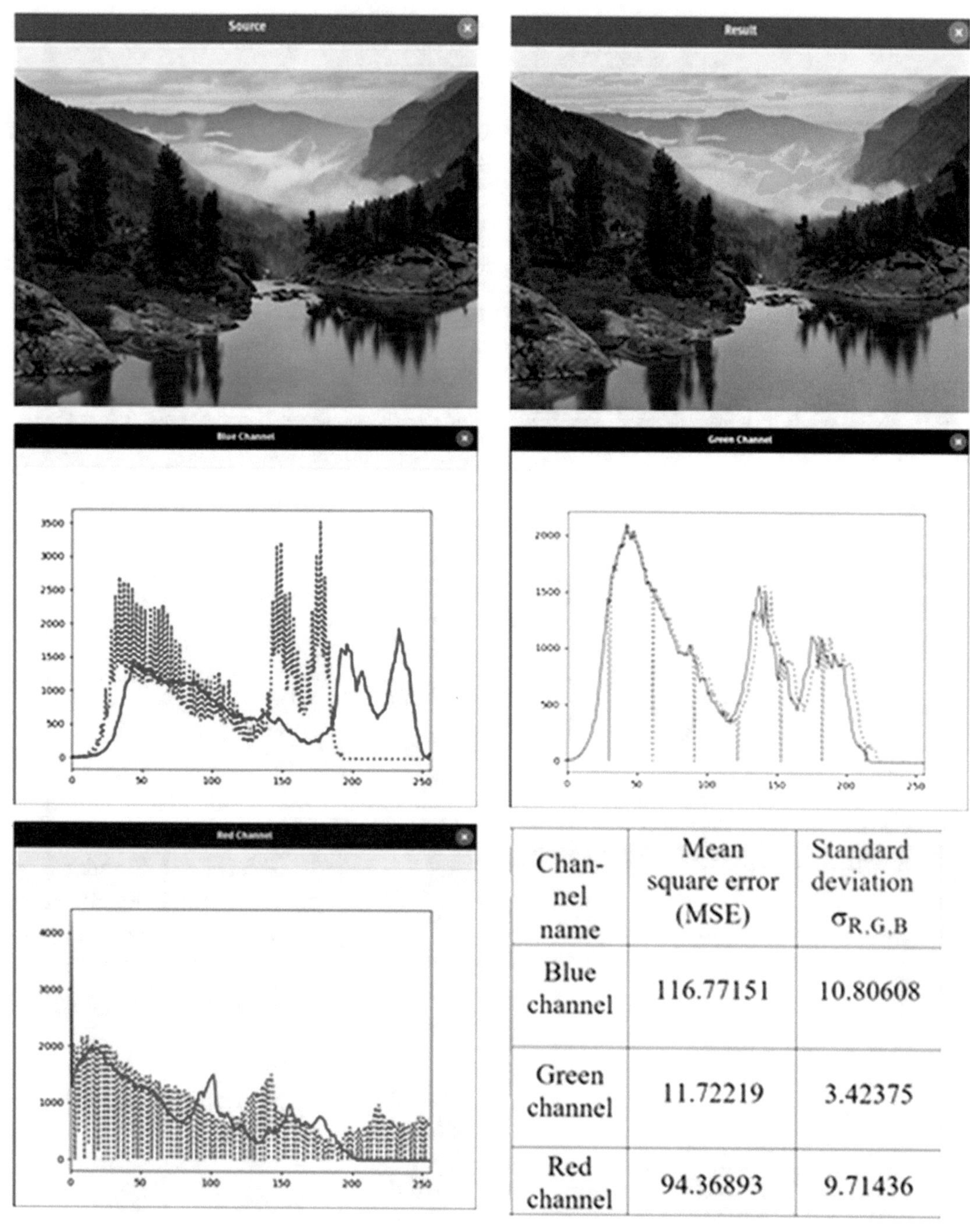

Channel name	Mean square error (MSE)	Standard deviation $\sigma_{R,G,B}$
Blue channel	116.77151	10.80608
Green channel	11.72219	3.42375
Red channel	94.36893	9.71436

Color balance vector = 14.928

Figure 23. Quality indicators of the "Perfect reflector" algorithm processing results

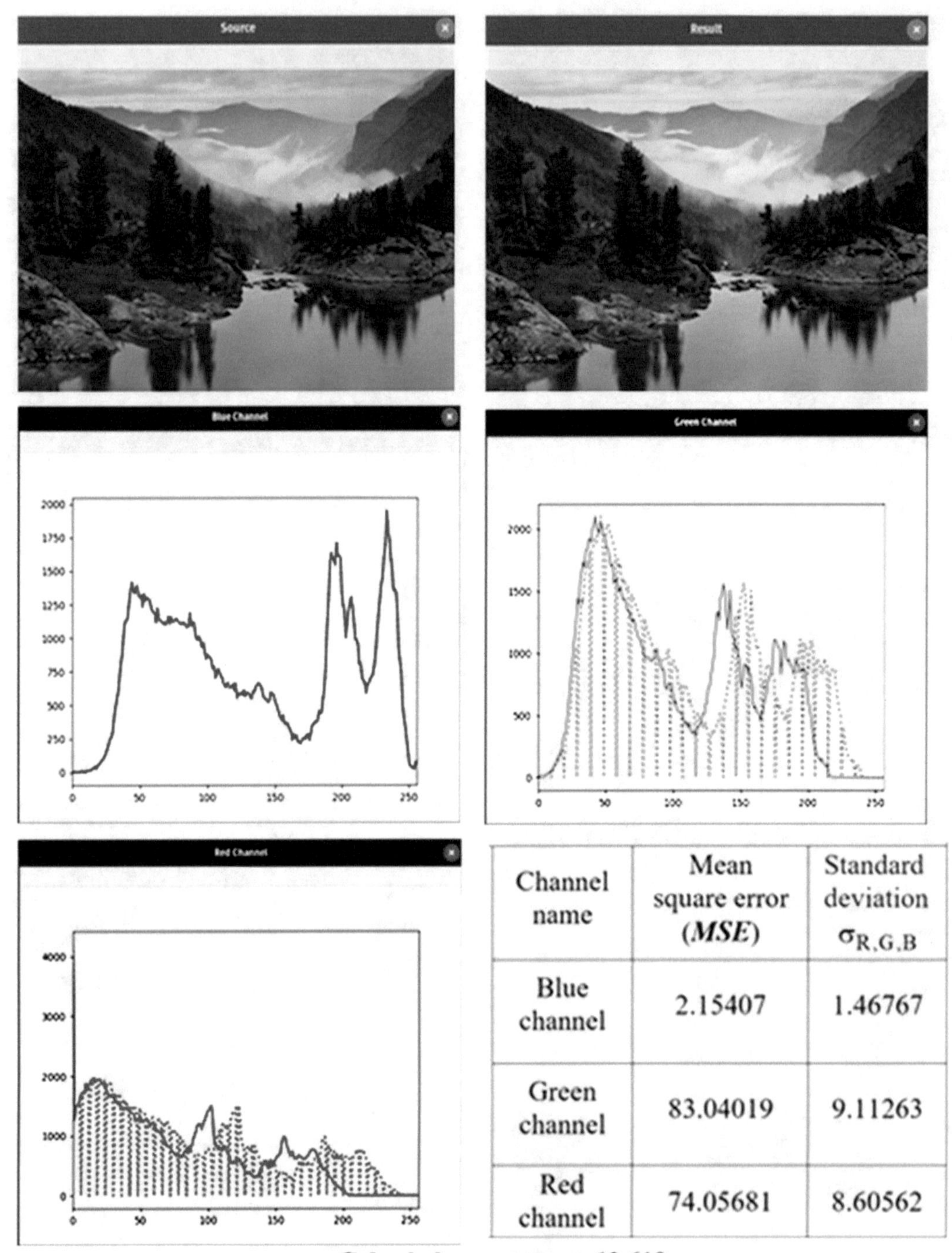

Channel name	Mean square error (*MSE*)	Standard deviation $\sigma_{R,G,B}$
Blue channel	2.15407	1.46767
Green channel	83.04019	9.11263
Red channel	74.05681	8.60562

Figure 24. Quality indicators of the "Auto levels" algorithm processing results

Processing method – «Autolevels»

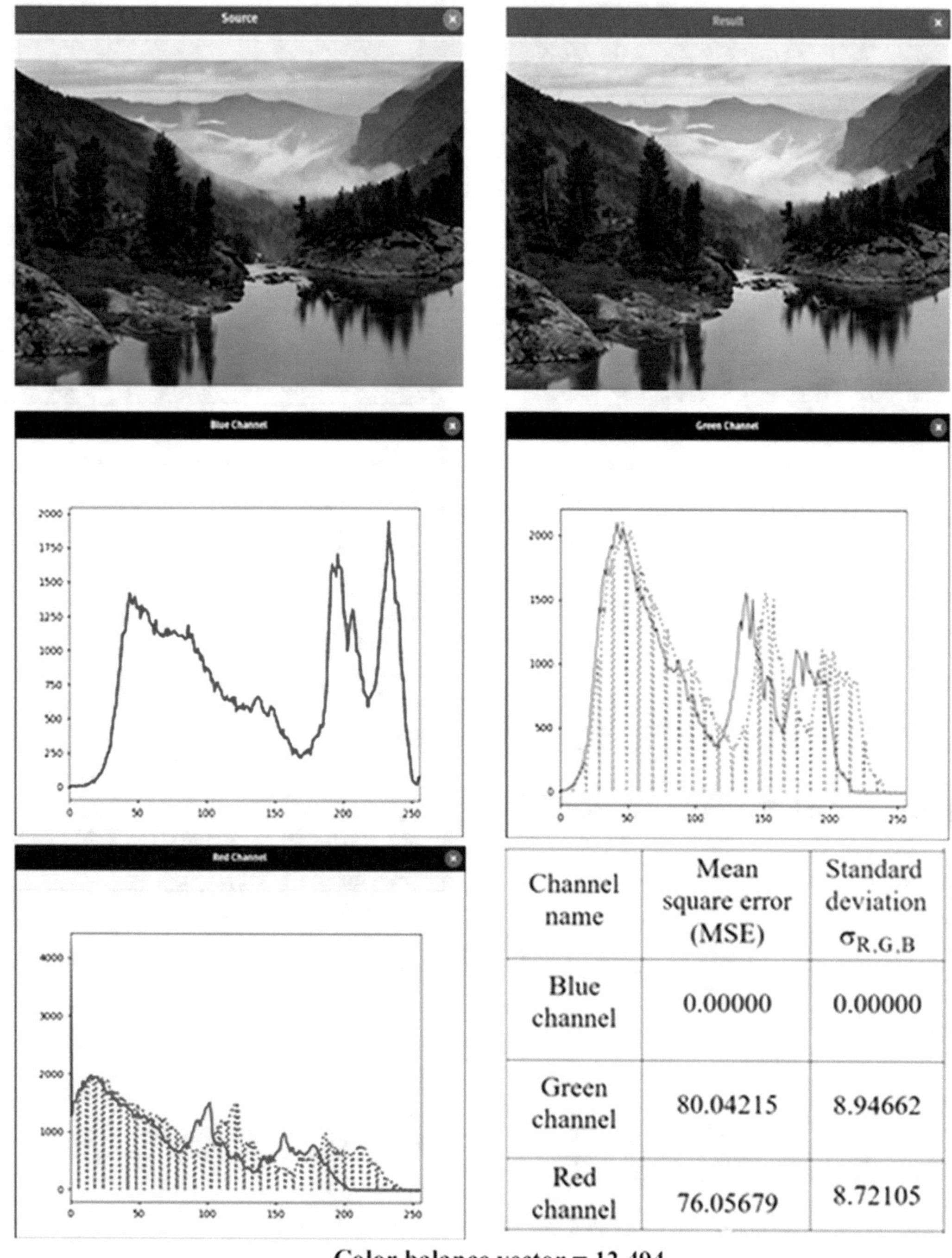

Channel name	Mean square error (MSE)	Standard deviation $\sigma_{R,G,B}$
Blue channel	0.00000	0.00000
Green channel	80.04215	8.94662
Red channel	76.05679	8.72105

Figure 25. Quality indicators of the equalization algorithm processing results

Processing method – «Equalization»

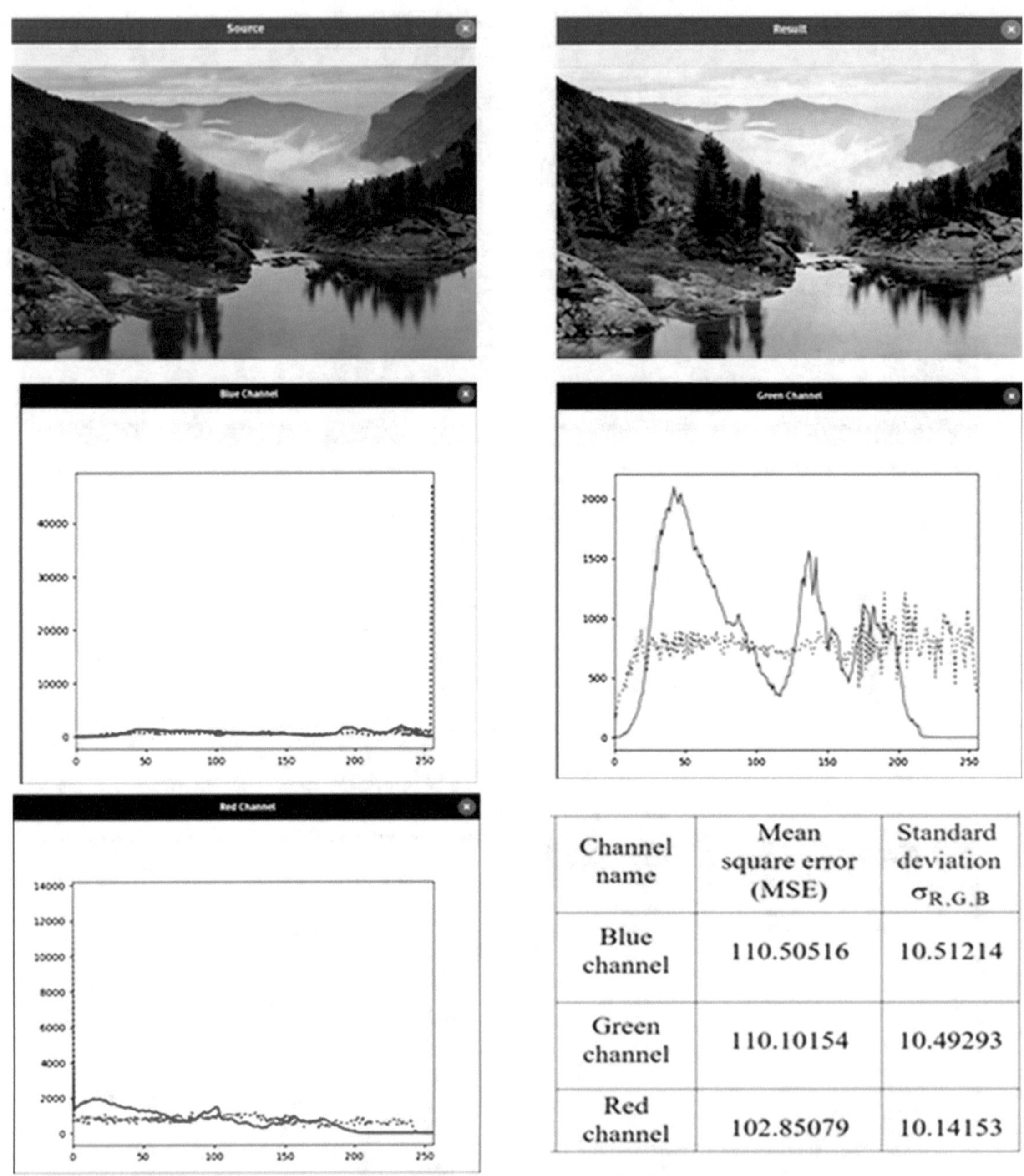

Channel name	Mean square error (MSE)	Standard deviation $\sigma_{R,G,B}$
Blue channel	110.50516	10.51214
Green channel	110.10154	10.49293
Red channel	102.85079	10.14153

Color balance vector = 17.985

Figure 26. Quality indicators of the "Grey world" algorithm processing results

Processing method – « Gray World »

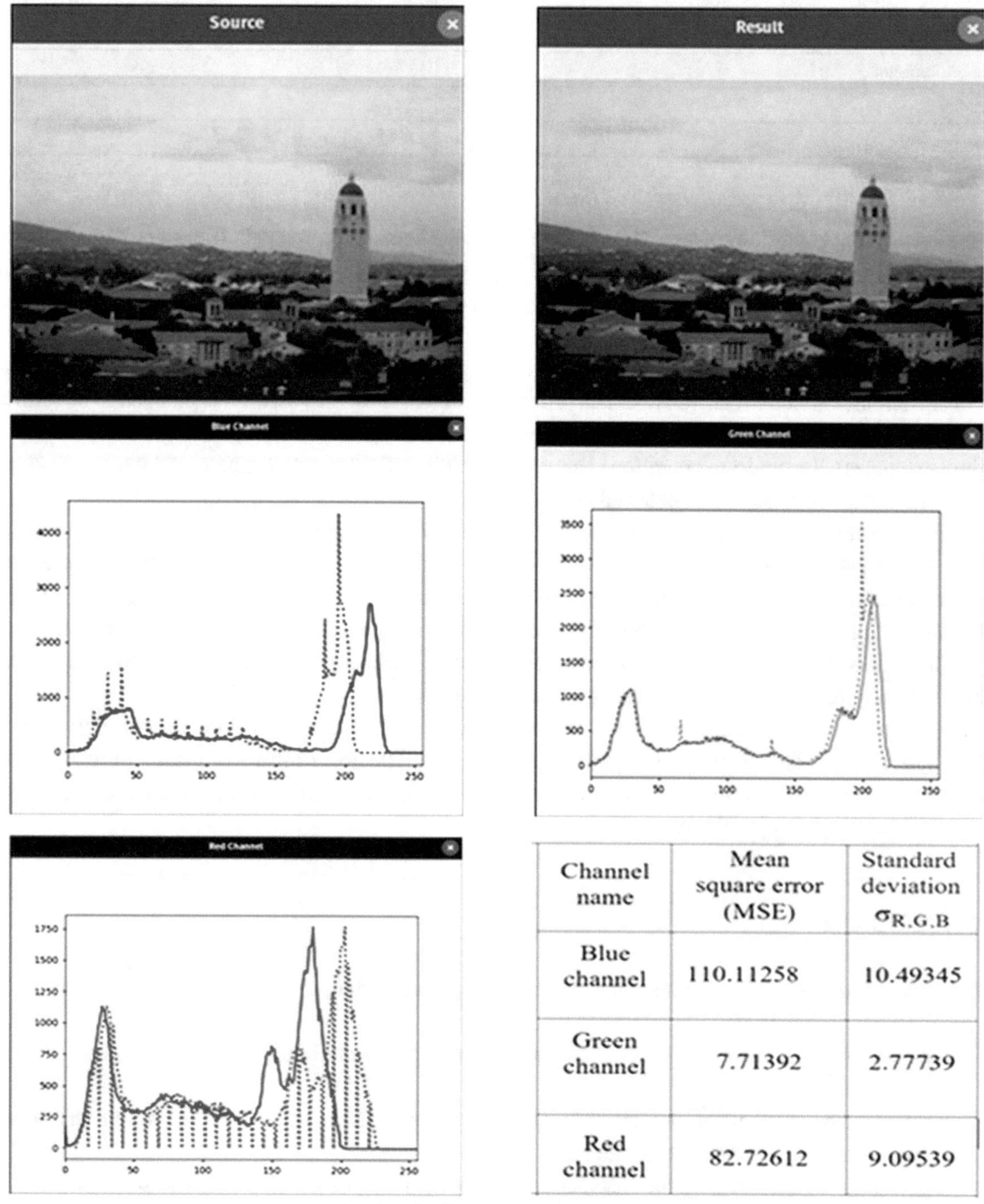

Channel name	Mean square error (MSE)	Standard deviation $\sigma_{R,G,B}$
Blue channel	110.11258	10.49345
Green channel	7.71392	2.77739
Red channel	82.72612	9.09539

Color balance vector = 14.161

Table 1. Data on the colour balance vector

Processing method	Color balance vector, σ_{Σ}
Gray World	14.928
Perfect Reflector	12.619
Autolevels	12.494
Equalization	17.985

changing lighting conditions of the scene observed with the help of a stereo pair. Illumination parameters can change slowly, but they are often characterized by rapid fluctuations in illumination up to spasmodic changes. For example, when a stereo pair is used in a room environment, the inclusion of artificial lighting dramatically changes the illumination of the scene.

These factors have been considered while developing the project. Therefore, in the presence of a large set of sufficiently effective and verified data processing algorithms, the software is planned to be refined in the future so that in the process of working in the external conditions change (in our case, the scene lighting changes), the program operation changes either interactively (with the help of the operator-user) or fully automatically adapted to external conditions.

This approach allows to fully ensure the high efficiency of the integrated method of quality control of the stereo pair. The good quality and convenience of the procedure for calibrating the stereopair cameras and the rectification of channel images provides high accuracy of distance measurement and the construction of maps of the depth of the scene. This creates prerequisites for solving a wide range of applied tasks in the field of mobile robots navigation, 3D scene reconstruction, pattern recognition, taking into account the volumetric characteristics of objects.

In the future, the authors plan to concentrate efforts on conducting experimental research using a vision system based on the created program "StereoSensor". The goal of this work is not only to further improve the software and improve the quality of the stereo vision system, but also to solve a wide range of applied stereo vision problems.

CONCLUSION

A new integrated method for managing the quality of the vision system stereo pair is proposed. It includes

- algorithms and software implementation of procedures for calibration and rectification of web-cameras of a stereo pair;
- a set of stereo channels color correction algorithms for different scene lighting conditions, based on an estimate of the position of the target color label;
- algorithms for determining the distance and building maps of the depth of the scene to solve a wide range of applied problems by stereo vision methods;

The efficiency of using the proposed algorithms was experimentally analyzed using original statistical criteria for evaluating the quality of the transformation. Created new software in the Python language using the resources of the OpenCV library. This made it possible to implement the work of new algorithms in real time. It is possible to adapt the program to various structural changes in the scene and the conditions of its lighting. It is useful to have an interactive correction of the stereopair parameters when the operating conditions of the system change.

The use of the obtained results makes it possible to improve the quality of work of the vision systems when solving various tasks set for both stereo-visualization and stereo-matching.

REFERENCES

Bagga, P. (2013). Real Time Depth Computation Using Stereo Imaging. *JEEE, 1*(2), 51. doi:10.11648/j.jeee.20130102.13

Baggio, D. L., Emami, S., Escriva, D. M., Ievgen, K., Saragih, J., & Shilkrot, R. (2017). [Packt Publishing Ltd.]. *Mastering Open, CV*, 3.

Bellekens, B., Spruyt, V., Berkvens, R., & Weyn, M. (2014). A survey of rigid 3d pointcloud registration algorithms. In *AMBIENT 2014: the Fourth International Conference on Ambient Computing, Applications, Services and Technologies, August 24-28, 2014, Rome, Italy* (pp. 8-13). Academic Press.

Bovyrin, A. V. (2013). *Development of Multimedia Applications Using the OpenCV and IPP Libraries: studies. course*. NGU N.Lobachevsky.

Chafonova, V. G., & Gazeeva, I. V. (2014). Methods of Imaging a Stereo Pair With A Given Parallax Value. *Scientific and Technical Journal of Information Technologies, Mechanics and Optics, 6*(94).

Dawson-Howe, K. (2014). *A Practical Introduction to Computer Vision with OPENCV*. John Wiley & Sons.

Dergachov, K., Krasnov, L., Cheliadin, O., & Plakhotnyi, O. (2019). Development of Methods and Means of Color Correction of Web-Cameras in Binocular Systems. Systems of Control, Navigation and Communication. *Collection of Scientific Works, 2*(54), 87-98.

Dergachov, K., Kulik, A., & Zymovin, A. (2019). Environments Diagnosis by Means of Computer Vision System of Autonomous Flying Robots. In Automated Systems in the Aviation and Aerospace Industries (pp. 115-137). IGI Global. doi:10.4018/978-1-5225-7709-6.ch004

Doutre, C., & Nasiopoulos, P. (2009). Color Correction Preprocessing for Multiview Video Coding. *IEEE Transactions on Circuits and Systems for Video Technology, 19*(9), 1400–1406. doi:10.1109/TCSVT.2009.2022780

Fecker, U., Barkowsky, M., & Kaup, A. (2008). Histogram-Based Prefiltering for Luminance and Chrominance Compensation of Multiview Video. *IEEE Transactions on Circuits and Systems for Video Technology, 18*(9), 1258–1267. doi:10.1109/TCSVT.2008.926997

Gupta, B., Chaube, A., Negi, A., & Goel, U. (2017). Study on Object Detection using Open CV-Python. *International Journal of Computers and Applications, 162*(8), 17–21. doi:10.5120/ijca2017913391

Hubel, D. (1990). *The eye, brain, vision* (Vol. 239). Moscow: Mir.

Joshi, P. (2015). *OpenCV with Python by example*. Packt Publishing Ltd.

Kapur, S. (2017). *Computer Vision with Python 3*. Packt Publishing Ltd.

Korotaev, V.V., Krasnyaschih, A.V., Yaryshev, S.N., & Viet, N.H. (2014). The Method of Automatic Calibration of the Stereoscopic System. *Scientific and Technical Journal of Information Technologies, Mechanics and Optics, 4*(92).

Krylovetsky, A. A., & Protasov, S. I. (2010). Algorithms for Image Analysis in Real-Time Stereo Vision Systems. *Bulletin of the Voronezh State University*, (2), 9-18.

Kulik, A., Dergachov, K., & Radomskyi, O. (2015). Binocular Technical Vision for Wheeled Robot Controlling. *Transport Problems*, *10*(1), 55–62. doi:10.21307/tp-2015-006

Laganière, R. (2014). *OpenCV Computer Vision Application Programming Cookbook* (2nd ed.). Packt Publishing Ltd.

Mallon, J., & Whelan, P. F. (2005). Projective Rectification from the Fundamental Matrix. *Image and Vision Computing*, *23*(7), 643–650. doi:10.1016/j.imavis.2005.03.002

Minichino, J., & Howse, J. (2015). *Computer Vision with Python*. Packt Publishing Ltd.

Park, J. B., & Kak, A. C. (2003, September). A Truncated Least Squares Approach to the Detection of Specular Highlights in Color Images. In *2003 IEEE International Conference on Robotics and Automation (Cat. No. 03CH37422)* (Vol. 1, pp. 1397-1403). IEEE.

Protasov, S.I., Kurgalin, S.D., & Krylovetsky, A.A. (2011). Use of a Web Camera as a Source Steeropar. *Bulletin of the Voronezh State University*, (2), 80-86.

Shao, F., Yu, M., Jiang, G. Y., & Yang, R. E. (2010, May). Color Correction for Multi-View Video Based On Color Variation Curve. In *2010 International Conference on Intelligent Computation Technology and Automation* (Vol. 1, pp. 970-973). IEEE. 10.1109/ICICTA.2010.350

Shapiro, L. G., & Stockman, G. C. (2001). *Computer Vision*. Prentice Hall.

Shin, H., Yang, U., & Sohn, K. (2012). Local Color Correction with Three Dimensional Point Set Registration for Underwater Stereo Images. *Optical Engineering (Redondo Beach, Calif.)*, *51*(4), 047002. doi:10.1117/1.OE.51.4.047002

Sorokin, M. I. (2017). Pattern Recognition Methods on Images. *Alley of Science*, *2*(9), 895–906.

Zhang, Z. (2004). Camera Calibration with One-Dimensional Objects. *IEEE Transactions on Pattern Analysis and Machine Intelligence*, *26*(7), 892–899. doi:10.1109/TPAMI.2004.21 PMID:18579947

ADDITIONAL READING

Bradski, G., & Kaehler, A. (2008). *Learning OpenCV: Computer vision with the OpenCV library*. O'Reilly Media, Inc.

Chen, C. H. (2015). *Handbook of Pattern Recognition And Computer Vision*. World Scientific.

Grundland, M., & Dodgson, N. A. (2005, January). Color Histogram Specification by Histogram Warping. In Color Imaging X: Processing, Hardcopy, and Applications (Vol. 5667, pp. 610-621). International Society for Optics and Photonics. doi:10.1117/12.596953

Hassaballah, M., & Hosny, K. M. (Eds.). (2018). *Recent Advances in Computer Vision: Theories and Applications* (Vol. 804). Springer.

Shmelova, T., Sikirda, Y., Rizun, N., Kucherov, D., & Dergachov, K. (Eds.). (2019). *Automated Systems in the Aviation and Aerospace Industries*. Engineering Science Reference. doi:10.4018/978-1-5225-7709-6

Xiao, X., & Ma, L. (2006, June). Color Transfer in Correlated Color Space. In *Proceedings of the 2006 ACM international conference on Virtual reality continuum and its applications* (pp. 305-309). ACM.

Yang, H., Shao, L., Zheng, F., Wang, L., & Song, Z. (2011). Recent advances and trends in visual tracking: A review. *Neurocomputing*, *74*(18), 3823–3831. doi:10.1016/j.neucom.2011.07.024

KEY TERMS AND DEFINITIONS

Captured by Web-Cameras Stereo-System: Software image capture webcam stereo system.

Color Balance of the Left and Right Chambers: Converting the color components of the RGB image in right channel of the stereo pair so that the brightness of this image exactly matches the brightness of the image in the left channel.

Color Correction: Converting the color components of an RGB image for accurate white balance.

Joint Rectification of the Left and Right Chambers: Joint rectification is the process of aligning the images so that for each point of the image of the left camera the corresponding paired point of the image of the right camera is located on one line.

Stereoscopic Vision Systems: Systems containing two spatially separated video cameras that synchronously record the visible scene. Due to the different spatial position of the cameras, a three-dimensional vision effect is created.

Video Stream Images: Video frame sequence images.

Chapter 7
A Communication Model Based on Fractal Geometry for Internet of Things

Sergio Ariel Salinas
ITIC, Universidad Nacional de Cuyo, Argentina

ABSTRACT

Internet of things (IoT) is a paradigm that involves an increasing number of human activities. IoT fuses heterogeneous electronic devices and processes into cyber physical system (CPS) to improve conventional processes efficiency in terms of performance and resource usage. The Institute of Electrical and Electronics Engineering (IEEE) has polled more than 150 IoT scenarios based on CPSs to be developed in the next years. A CPS is strongly coupled to a communication system for interchanging data among devices that orchestrate actions in certain environments such as a factory. In general, a decentralized communication model is more resilient and efficient in data traffic management than centralized model. A problem with decentralized models is how to keep track of nodes location without a centralized service that keeps updated data of nodes. This work describes a decentralized model where any node is able to be located based on its identification in the system.

INTRODUCTION

Internet of Things (IoT) emerged from integrating electronic devices, wireless communication systems, programming languages, services over the Internet to implement applications that improve the performance of different human activities. IoT applications are becoming part of the human environment raising a new class of services and business, changing the world as we know it (AlFuqaha, & et al. 2015).

In the next few years, Internet will communicate a significant number of heterogeneous devices spread over the world. Different surveys show that by 2025 there will be around 7 billions of IoT devices operating on different application around the world (Vincentelli, 2015). This number will grow with the development of new services and products.

DOI: 10.4018/978-1-7998-7010-4.ch007

A fundamental concept in IoT is the integration of Information and Communication Technology (ICT) and physical systems. From this fusion emerged the term Cyber Physical System (CPS) to denote a mechanism controlled by computer programs where sensors, actuators assist processes or users to achieve determined goal (Vincentelli, 2015).

The main goal of CPS is to optimize the performance of a wide range of processes involved in the most diverse application scenarios. The efficient usage of scarce resources drives the use of CPS in industry, agriculture, logistics, transportation, tourism, recreation, security in public spaces, health care among others. The Institute of Electrical and Electronics Engineering (IEEE) has polled more than 150 IoT scenarios that involve diverse CPS ("IoT scenarios", 2019) domains.

Industry domain includes diverse IoT applications involved in sectors such as agriculture, manufacturing and services. Diverse CPS will be combined in the production of heterogeneous commodity, quality control, stock management, logistics, customer satisfaction control and so on. The use of IoT in these domains drive a new industrial revolution called Industry 4.0 (Zhou,Liu & Zhou, 2015).

The domain of smart cities (Okai, Feng & Sant, 2018) has an impact in the way daily human activities will be performed. IoT application will be part of the efficient management of houses and buildings where heterogeneous devices will control and improve the use of energy, home appliances and security.

In these cities, public transportation systems will be orchestrated by IoT applications as well as vehicle traffic. Additionally, Smart Grids will transport energy from heterogeneous source over the city where customers will be able to generate energy for their own consumption and for the other users (Hashmi, Hänninen & Maki, 2011).

Healthcare is a promising domain that will enable medical equipment to monitor, collect and share data using integrated cloud service to facilitate the assistance to patients at their home (Gandhi, & Ghosal, 2018). IoT-based healthcare services will reduce costs, increase the quality of life and enhance the user experience. Furthermore, they will enable the assistance of elderly people to improve their quality of life.

The IoT scenarios mentioned before will not be feasible to implement without an underlying communication system. Communication services enable devices to exchange data, orchestrate actions and make decisions. Most of these devices provide wireless communication services, are geographically dispersed and continuously generate data to share within the system.

The communication model adopted by most of Internet-based applications is client-server. This centralized model introduces a single point of failure in the system; if the server fails then clients will become inaccessible. Besides, if clients simultaneously request services the server is prune to crush. For these reasons, when decentralized communication models emerged they became an alternative to address these disadvantages.

Peer-to-Peer (P2P) networks implemented decentralized models around 1999 (Wehrle, Steinmetz, 2005). These networks were popularized by file-sharing systems such as Napster (Bengt, 2001). Clients obtained from a central directory a set of peers containing a searched file and then peers communicate with each other independently. The main features studied in these networks are scalability, resiliency and self-organization.

Despite the advantages of decentralized models for IoT applications, the lack of a centralized service affects the searching performance of these systems. When a device must send a message to another the problem of calculating the communication path between them arise.

The purpose of this chapter is to present a decentralized communication model for IoT scenarios based on a fractal schema. The fractal shape introduced in the network topology enables the calculation of the communication path between two devices just using their unique identification. This important property enables a decentralized communication among a scalable number of geographically distributed devices.

The contributions of this work are the following. First, the definition of a decentralized communication model based on fractal geometry. Second, the description of the algorithm for unicast and broadcast services. Finally, the performance assessment of a network based on the proposed model and a super peer network.

The content of this chapter is organized as follows. First, the background required to support the model understanding is provided. Second, the communication model based on fractal geometry is described. Third, a description of the unicast and broadcast services is introduced. Additionally, equations to calculate the performance of these services is presented. Next, a model performance evaluation is presented. Finally, future research directions and conclusions are introduced.

Background

Internet of Things is a disruptive technology that fuses ubiquitous computing, Internet protocols, monitoring systems, embedded systems and heterogeneous communication protocols to implement Cyber Physical Systems (CPS) (Vincentelli, 2015). The main goal of a CPS is to optimize the performance of a wide range set of processes and activities involved in different scenarios of human life.

The IoT scenarios where CPS takes place can be grouped into three broad domains: industry, smart cities and health well-being (Borgia, 2014). The industry domain mainly includes areas of manufacturing and logistics of diverse products. Smart cities promote the development of a sustainable environment by making efficient use of resources and taking care of the environment. Health well-being involves independent living and health care (Paul & Saraswathi, 2017).

In order to deal with the complexity of different IoT domains the integration of heterogeneous communication protocols is needed. In this sense, wireless protocols play a key role to support the interaction among thousands of devices. IoT involve wireless protocols such as WiFi, Bluetooth, IEEE 802.15.4, Z-wave and LTE-Advanced (Al-Sarawi, & et al. 2017). These protocols enable a point-to-point communication to exchange messages among nodes within certain geographic scope.

The communication range of these protocols is variable; WiFi technology (Farris, Militano, Nitti, Atzori & Iera, 2016) uses radio signals to exchange data in a range of 100 meters. The coverage radius of Bluetooth (Dideles, 2003) varies from 10 and 15 meters. The Z-Wave protocol (Yassein, Mardini & Khalil, 2016) has a communication scope between 30 and 40 meters while the IEEE 802.15 standard (Misic, 2008) has a range up to 1000 meters. Finally, LTE technology is utilized to transfer data between smart mobile devices (Ghosh, Ratasuk, Mondal, Mangalvedhe & Thomas, 2010).

There are two main communication services required to implement IoT scenarios. First, the unicast service enable the interchange of messages between two devices placed anywhere in the IoT scenario. Possible use case of this service is sending orders to be performed by a device or request a sensed data. Second, the broadcast service propagates a message to a set of devices for example to request certain data. Both services can be implemented based on a decentralized model using point-to-point communication.

The protocols available for IoT communication enable the development of a decentralized model based on Peer-to-Peer (P2P) model. These networks have three main characteristics: self-organization, symmetric communication and distributed control. Self-organization means the automatic network adaptation when nodes fail, join or leave the network. Communication is symmetric because peers act as both clients and servers without a central point of control. P2P overlay network models introduce a wide variety of communication frameworks classified into structured and unstructured networks (Eng, Crowcroft, et Al., 2005).

Structured P2P networks have a topology tightly controlled to store user content in specific nodes. The network uses a Distributed Hash Table (DHT) to organize the content distribution over the network. This table is distributed over all nodes in the network. When the network stores a user content into a node, it is selected deterministically. The system creates a unique key associated to the content, then it stores the key and content in the node responsible for the management of the identifiers range.

The topology geometry utilized by structured networks are the following:

1. **Mesh topology:** in mesh-based topologies peers form a randomly connected overlay named mesh (Carra, Lo Cigno & Biersack, 2007). Each peer tries to maintain a certain number of parents and serve to a specific number of child peers.
2. **Tree topology:** this topology uses a correlation between a node id and a key to route a message. These topologies are very efficient in multicast protocols. The main application of mesh and tree-based topologies is the live P2P streaming (Magharei, Rejaie & Guo, 2007).
3. **XOR-tree topology:** the topology is organized around XOR operation. The key and value are stored on the nodes whose id are close to the keys in terms of XOR metric.
4. **Rings:** the space in this topology is organized in a circle. The packets are always sent to one direction via the ring until they arrive to the destination node (Wauters, Coppens, De Turck, Dhoedt & Demeester,2006).
5. **Butterfly:** this topology creates a constant degree connection graph with logarithmic diameter approximation. Each peer maintains general ring pointers (predecessor and successor), level ring pointers (next on level and previous on level) and butterflies' pointer (left, right and up). When a peer departs, it normally passes its key pairs to a successor, and notifies other peers to find a replacement peer (Cicerone, Di Stefano & Handke,2005).
6. **De Bruijn graphs:** this overlay is a directed graph representing overlaps between sequences of symbols. An example of a P2P overlay based on de Bruijn graphs is introduced in (Fraigniaud P. & Gauron P. 2006).
7. **Skip graphs:** this overlay topology is based on a skip list. Like in other DHT-based overlays a search operation takes O(log n) hops and have the advantage of supporting range queries. This feature is due to the fact that a skip graph consists of a collection of lists in which peers are lexicographically sorted in their keys (Makikawa, Tsuchiya & Kikuno 2010).
8. **Multi-dimensional Cartesian space topology:** this topology is based on a virtual multidimensional Cartesian coordinate space. Each node is assigned a unique area in the coordinate space. The coordinates of this area identify the node and are used by the routing mechanism (Ratnasam, Francis, Handley, Karp & Shenker, 2001).

The main drawbacks of DHT based systems are their inability to support complex queries and the peer transience. Complex queries involve request object with restriction related to multiple attributes. Peer transience is related to peer arriving and departing to the overlay. Structured overlays are prone to node failure, and unpredictable node departures. These systems have high maintenance cost in the presence of high peer churn.

Unstructured Peer-to-Peer networks are overlay where each peer maintains a constant number of connections to other peers. These networks implement a completely decentralized scheme and do not rely on any central server to locate the content requested by users. Hence, there is no predefined underlying structure and there is no information about node location. As a consequence, unstructured Peer-to-Peer overlays requires sophisticated search techniques to support complex or free-form queries. In general, most of the search algorithms are based on heuristics (Risson & Moors, 2006).

In order to improve the performance of unstructured Peer-to-Peer networks, different hierarchical models emerged. These networks organize nodes into clusters of peers managed by a super peer. This last one is responsible for managing information within the cluster, organizing peer and other network maintenance service. Tree-based or hierarchical clustering is a logical extension of super-peer clustering. These topologies add additional overlays on top of super-peer overlay to increase the scalability of the system. Locality clustering is a technique where nodes are clustered on the basis of the physical proximity in terms of delay or number of hops (Shicong, et al. 2005).

The Arigatoni (Michel Cosnarda, et al. 2007) system introduces a hierarchical model that joins host from the same intranet, and then from intranet to intranet by overlapping an overlay network on top of the actual network. This model organizes resources in colonies governed by a leader named Global Broker. Global computers belong to only one colony. A colony is a simple virtual organization composed by exactly one leader and some set of individuals, which may be global computers or subcolonies. A community is a set of colonies and global computers.

Global Brokers are organized in a dynamic tree structure where nodes represent Global Brokers of the overlay network. This model is suitable for scenarios from classical P2P applications to more sophisticated Grid applications (Raphael Chand, et al. 2007).

A unified P2P database framework (Hoschek, 2002). has been introduced as the first steps towards unifying the fields of database management systems and P2P systems. In this framework, each node is an autonomous database that maintains services and resources information. This framework propagates resource queries recursively over the network to some or all the database nodes. Results are collected and send back to the client.

The lack of centralized control in unstructured P2P models raises the problem of blind search. In general, this implies performing a controlled flooding of message in the systems. A node sends a message to all its neighbors and they repeat this process a limited number of times. The disadvantage of this strategy is redundant messages and only a limited number of nodes are included in the process.

Decentralized communication models are attractive for IoT applications, however unicast and broadcast services based on blind search are not efficiently or even feasible to implement. The proposed model aims to improve these two services by creating a topology based on fractal geometry in order to outperform flooding algorithm in decentralized models.

COMMUNICATION MODEL BASED ON FRACTAL GEOMETRY

This section introduces a communication model to create a network topology based on fractal geometry (Mandelbrot, 1982). This geometry along with unique node identification enables the calculation of paths among nodes in the system. In this way, it is possible to exchange messages between two nodes based on their ids.

The topology creation takes place as nodes join the system and occupy a determined place in network. Every node will have a limited number of neighbors to which they can exchange messages and a unique identification. As the number of nodes grows, connections among them create a fractal geometry.

The model organizes nodes into groups named Federations. A fixed number of self-organized nodes represented by the variable ***maxNodes*** define a Federation. When the value of ***maxNodes*** is reached then a new federation is created under the same rules. As the number of federations grows a new level of federation represented by the variable, ***maxLevels*** is created based on a recursive process.

The parameters ***maxNodes*** and ***maxLevels*** are important in the model because they determine how the topology will grow, behave and scale. These values play a key role to calculate the communication path between two nodes. In addition, it will determine the maximum number of nodes supported by the network based on the following equation:

totalNodes=power(maxNodes,maxLevels) (1)

Nodes that participate in the topology are named stable. This type of nodes can provide communication services to guest nodes that spontaneously use the network to send a message to other stable or guest node.

Although the model states a maximum number of participating nodes in the network, it is feasible to set these parameters values to include the expected number of stable nodes in a system. Since stable nodes can communicate guest nodes, the number of participants is flexible and not limited by the model parameters.

Figure 1 shows an example of a network created based on the proposed model. Circles represent stable nodes, numbers upon circles are the **id** assigned to each node and lines represent a service that communicates nodes. In this example, the value of the parameter ***maxNodes*** is 5 and the value of ***maxLevels*** is 3. According to equation **(1)** the total number of stable nodes is 125.

Figure 1. Network topology with three communication levels and five nodes per federation

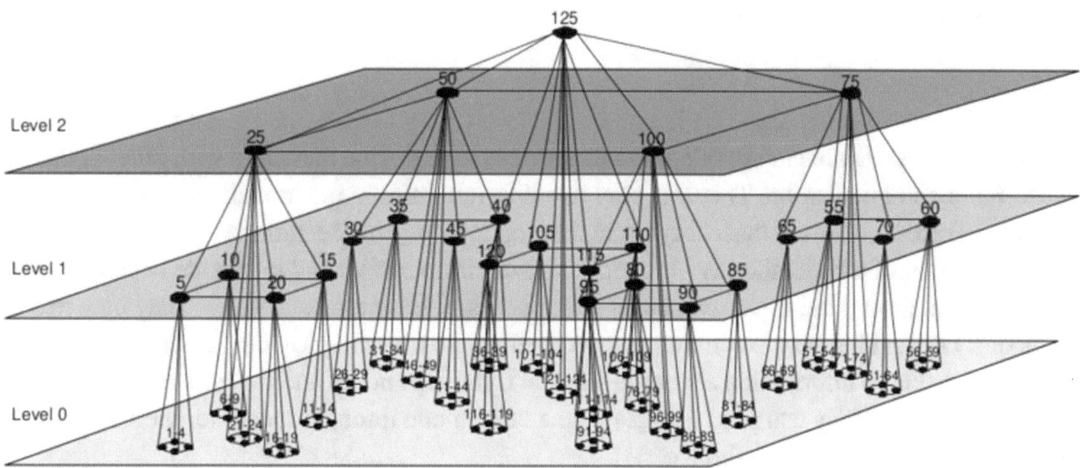

The groups of nodes represent federations distributed at three levels. At level 0 there are twenty five federations, at level 1 there are five and at level 2 there is only one.

Federations

A Federation is a limited set of stable nodes where the maximum number of members is determined by the value of the parameter ***maxNodes.*** A fixed number of nodes in every federation make it feasible to calculate paths among nodes.

Every federation only includes stable nodes classified into edge nodes and broker. Edge nodes participate in message routing and they provide communication services to guest nodes. Every federation has only one broker responsible for edge nodes membership, numbering nodes within a federation and message routing.

The identification of stable nodes in the whole system is unique and every broker in each federation is responsible for this task. A broker has a predefined and unique range of ids distributed among nodes in a federation as they request their membership.

A fusion of a ring and star topology supports communication among nodes as shown in **(2)**. Gray circles represent edge nodes and the black circle in the middle represent a broker. The number on each circle is the node identification and lines identify the capability of exchanging messages among nodes.

Communication based on the proposed topology has the advantages of being fault-tolerance. In case any edge node fails the node's neighbors will automatically reestablish the circle. When a broker fails any edge node will be able to replace it and after that rebuild the federation topology.

The model scales by creating new federations and new levels of communication. When the number of nodes in a federation reaches the maximum number of nodes allowed the system creates a new federation. The system will connect brokers from different federation creating a new communication level.

Figure **(3)** shows nine federations where brokers create a new federation in a new communication level. For the sake of simplicity, nodes representation the figure omits their identifications. It is possible to observe how a fractal geometry emerge as the system expands creating federations of federations at different levels. The system will scale until the system reaches the maximum number of nodes according to equation **(1)**.

Nodes

A node is any device capable to provide wireless services to exchange messages with other nodes using a point-to-point communication. They can play two different roles in the model: edge node or broker.

In figure **(3)** edge nodes are those located in the ring topology of federations at level 0 whilst nodes placed in the center of a Federation is a broker. However, from level 0 and on a node becomes a broker for a federation at level 0 but it also can be an edge node in a federation at level 1. They play two roles simultaneously depending on the communication level where they are providing a service.

An edge node keeps information about the left, the right edge nodes and the broker of the federation where it is associated. They can send a message to a target node through the broker; however, they can receive messages from any of the three nodes.

A broker manages node identification within a federation based on a predefined number interval for nodes, the maximum number of nodes per federation and the maximum number of communication levels allowed in the system.

Figure 2. Example of a node federation

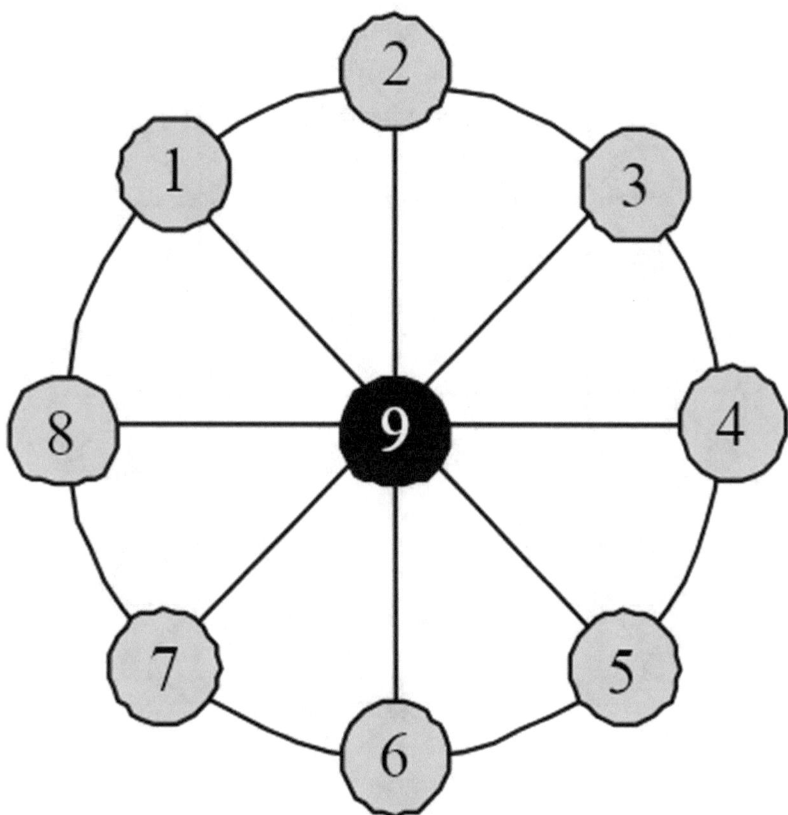

COMMUNICATION SERVICES

The implementation of a network based on the proposed model can take advantage of the topology geometry to provide efficient unicast and broadcast communication services. These services include a sender, intermediary nodes and one or more receivers. A node sent a message through different nodes until reach the receiver.

A network based on the proposed model can implement functions to obtain information about the topology for different purposes.

1. **Paths available between two nodes:** this function may calculate paths between nodes taking into account one or more metrics such as failure rate, availability, geographic distance, battery level among others.
2. **Workload of a given federation:** provide information about the number of guest nodes associated to a federation.
3. **Broker availability:** calculate the number of available brokers at different communication levels.
4. **Topology balance:** estimate the distributions of available nodes over the network at different time intervals.

Figure 3. Example of a federation of federations

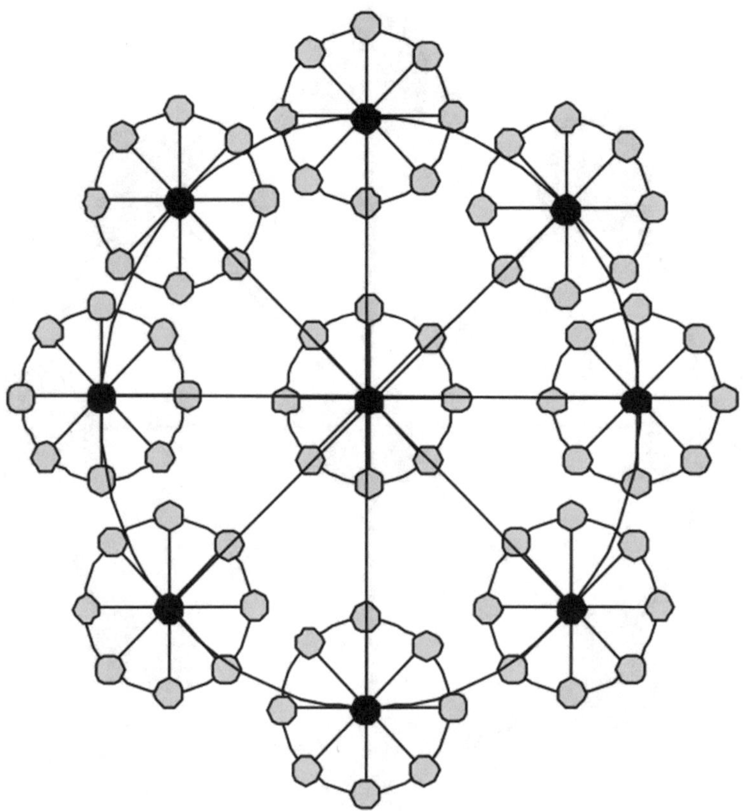

5. **Data traffic distribution:** gather information about average number of messages sent and received by different federations.
6. **Topology health:** it identifies failures rate, duration, availability of federations and nodes.

In order to limit the scope of this work, the chapter includes the algorithms required to calculate the path between two nodes based on their identification.

Path Calculation Between two Nodes

In order to calculate the path between two nodes, we propose two functions named getBrokerId and getPath. The first function returns the broker id associated to a node id and the second one calculates a path using the first function repeatedly.

The function getBrokerId requires three parameters a node id, the maximum number of nodes allowed per federation and the maximum number of communication levels supported. The function uses these parameters within a loop to get the broker id as shown in figure **(4)**. For the parameters values nodeId=37, maxNodes=5 and maxLevels=3 the function will return the value 40 as result. Since the function returns the broker id of any node id, enable the calculation of a path using this function repeatedly.

The function getPath utilizes getBrokerId in a loop as shown in figure **(5)**. The input parameters are the node id, the maximum number of nodes per federation and the maximum number of communication levels. There are three steps to calculate the shortest path between two nodes. The first one calculates the path from the sender node until the maximum broker id in the network. The second one repeats the calculation for the receiver node. Finally, both results are merged and redundant nodes are removed.

Figure 4. Function to get a broker identifier

Algorithm 1 getBrokerId

```
function GETBROKERID(nodeId,maxNodes,maxLevels)
    exp = 1
    while remainder = 0 and exp < maxLevels do
        unit = maxNodes^exp
        quotient = nodeId/unit
        remainder = nodeId mod unit
        if remainder > 0 and quotient > 0 then
            brokerId = nodeId − remainder + unit
        end if
        if remainder > 0 and quotient = 0 then
            brokerId = unit
        end if
        exp = exp + 1
    end while
    if brokerId = 0 then
        brokerId = nodeId
    end if
    return brokerId
end function
```

Unicast Service

The unicast service sends a message to whichever node available in the network. Every message has a head with system information and a body with the message content. Any node can create a message including the receiver node id and the content. Then, it sends the message to the broker of the federation where it belongs.

The broker will calculate the path to reach the receiver node and it will include the path into the head of the message. Next, the message will be resend to the next node in the path and this process repeats until reaching the target node. The answer from the target node will follow the reverse path based on the information available in the message head.

Figure 5. Function to calculate the path between two nodes

Algorithm 2 getPath

```
function GETPATH(targetNodeId,maxNodes,maxLevels)
    nodeId = targetNodeId
    while nodeId = maxNodes^maxLevels do
        nodeId = getBrokerId(nodeId,maxNodes,maxLevels)
        path[] = nodeId
    end while
    return path
end function
```

In case the process fails because of nodes included in the path the last available node will calculate a new path to the target and will restart the communication process. The path and unavailable node id will be updated in the message head for future process. All information about past communication stored in a node will have a predetermined lifetime. After that, the process of calculating path to nodes will restart.

Unicast service performance: is a value calculated taking into account the average time required to send a message from one node to another. The number of nodes included in the path between two nodes is variable, in the best case, the path will include only one node and in the worst case, this value will be twice the number of communication levels.

The performance of unicast service in terms of delivery time is calculated according to the following equation:

perfUnicast = 2 x maxLevels x average(transmissionTime) (2)

The equation takes as input variables the number of communication levels in the system and the average transmission time between nodes.

Broadcast Service

The broadcast service distributes a message from a node to all nodes in the system. Similar to the unicast service, the message has a head with information about the actions nodes must perform. The service involves a set of actions simultaneously executed.

1. A node starts the message propagation over the federation where it belongs.
2. Next, the broker sends the message to a higher level in the communication hierarchy.
3. Once the higher node id in the system receives the message, it will send it to brokers in a lower communication level.
4. Every node starts the message propagation over its federation and sends it to lower levels.
5. The process stops when the message reaches nodes at level zero.

The message propagation within a federation uses the ring topology according to the following steps:

1. A node of the federation sends a message to its left and right neighbor.
2. When a node receives a broadcast message from its right neighbor, it will send it to its left neighbor.
3. When a node receives a broadcast message from its left neighbor, it will send it to its right neighbor.
4. The process stops when all nodes receive the message.

Broadcast service performance: is a value calculated taking into account the average time required to deliver a message to all nodes in the system. This value is the sum of the time required by each federation to distribute a message to all their nodes. A node can send a message to only one node at a determined instant of time $\mathbf{m_i}$. Federations can have odd or even number of nodes and this value will affect the performance value.

Figure **(6)** shows a federation with an even number of nodes enumerated from 1 to 4 where node 4 is the broker. Lines between nodes represent a communication service to exchange messages.

Figure 6. Broadcast service performance in a federation with an even number of nodes

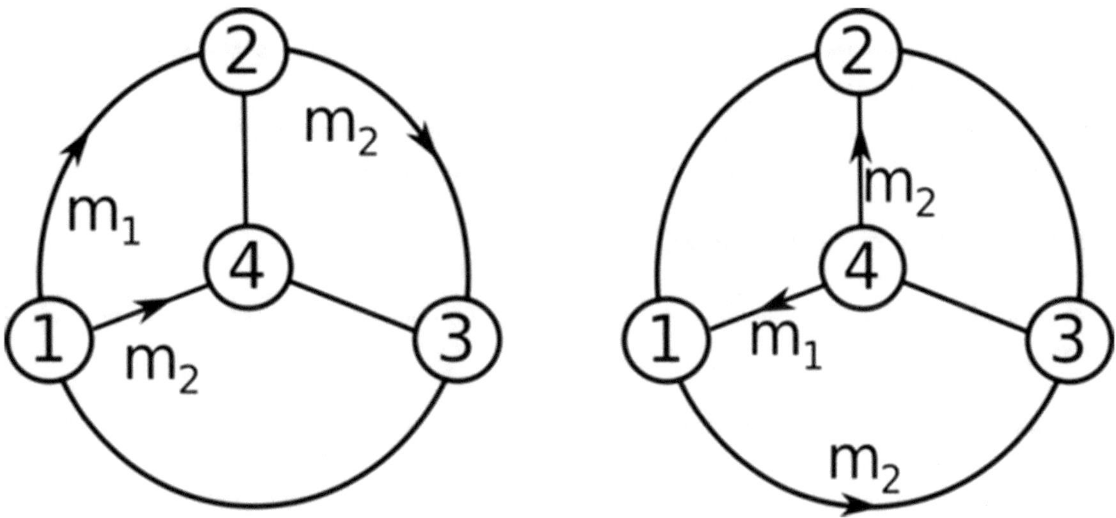

Figure at the left side shows how the node with id equals to 1 start the broadcast service. At the moment $\mathbf{m_1}$ it sends the message to node 2. Then, at the instant $\mathbf{m_2}$ node 2 sends the message to node 3 and simultaneously node 1 sends the message to node 4. The figure at the right shows the same process but in this case, the broker starts the service.

Figure **(7)** shows a federation with an odd number of nodes and two different situations. In the figure at the left, the node 1 generates a message and at the instant $\mathbf{m_1}$ sends it to node 2. Then, at the moment $\mathbf{m_2}$ nodes, 2 and 1 sends simultaneously the message to nodes 3 and 4 respectively. Finally, at the instant $\mathbf{m_3}$ node 4 sends the message to node 5. Figure at the right show the same case but the broker starts the service.

In both cases whether a node or a broker starts the service the number of moments or instants of time needed to deliver the message to all nodes is the same. According to the cases represented by figures **(7)**

Figure 7. Broadcast service performance in a federation with an odd number of nodes

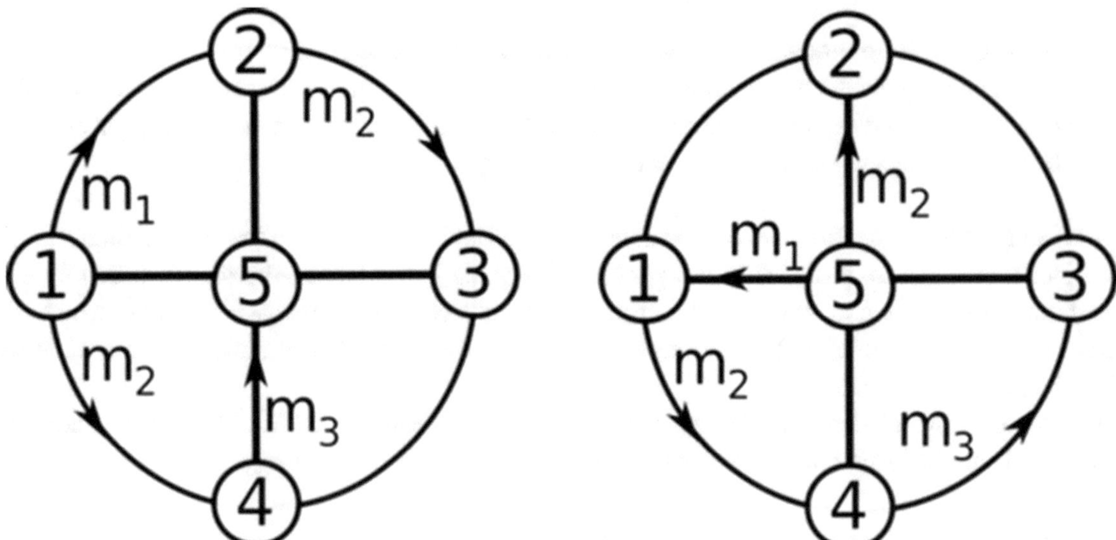

and **(8)**, the number of units of time required to broadcast a message within a federation will depend on the number of nodes and if this value is even or odd.

If the number of nodes is even the performance equals to the maximum number of nodes in the federation divide by 2, otherwise this value adds plus 0.5. Equation **(3)** includes both cases.

perfBroadcast = roundUp(maxNodes/2) (3)

Equation **(4)** shows how to calculate the performance of broadcasting a message to all nodes in the network.

perfBroadcast = maxLevels + maxLevels x perfBroadcast (4)

The equation calculates the average time required to broadcast a message to all nodes in the system. To this end, it is necessary to reach the broker with the highest id in the system. When a broker receives a message, it starts the broadcast service within the federation. Brokers perform this process simultaneously as they receive the message.

PERFORMANCE ASSESSMENT

This section presents the performance comparison of a network based on the super peer model and the proposed model. The assessment includes the unicast and broadcast services taking into account the units of time consumed in each case. Additionally, an analysis of the scalability of the proposed model is presented at the end of this section.

The super peer model organizes nodes into a communication hierarchy where peers are linked to a super peer and then super peers are linked randomly. In general, the number of links among super peers equals three.

Since the super peer model is generated based on random connection, the same number of nodes can be connected in different ways. Therefore, the performance of communication service will vary. In order to clarify the comparison of both models, the analysis considers a super peer model based on a tree topology. This network configuration will perform better than another random topology.

Figure **(8)** shows an example of 85 nodes connected by where the maximum depth of the tree equals three. For the sake of simplicity, the assessment considers that sending a message between two nodes takes one second. In order to communicate the node id 25 and 85 the system needs 14 seconds to deliver the message.

Figure 8. Super peer model organized as a tree topology

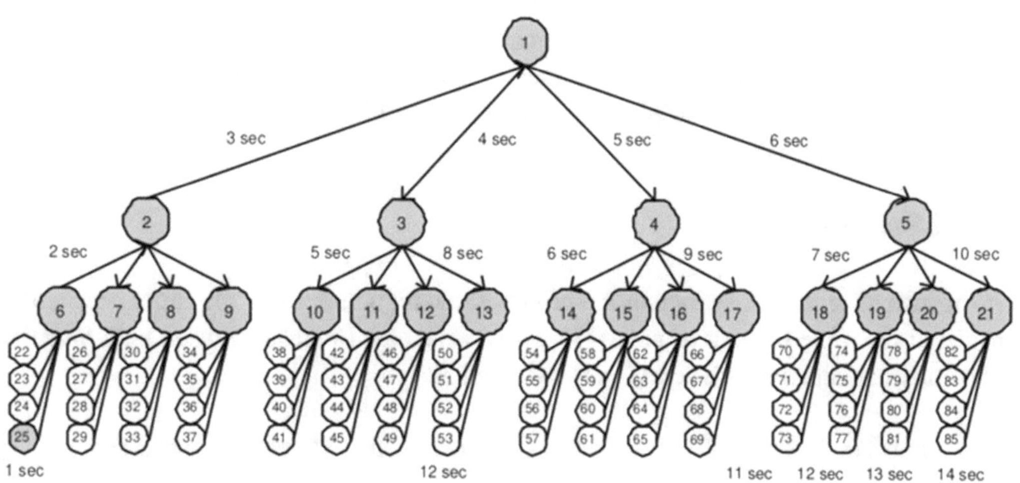

This is the largest path between two nodes and the performance equals the time required to broadcast a message. Equation **(5)** shows how to calculate the performance of unicast and broadcast services in this network configuration.

$$\textbf{\textit{SPperformance}} = (treeDepth - 1 + treeDepth \times maxLeaf) \times average(transmissionTime) \tag{5}$$

The performance takes into account the tree depth, the maximum number of leaf nodes and the average time required to send a message between two nodes. The tree depth is the number of edges from the node to the tree's root node. The same equation is utilized for both services because the same criteria will be applied when calculating the performance of the proposed model.

Unicast Service Analysis

In the previous section, equations **(2)** and **(4)** define the performance of the proposed model for the unicast and broadcast services respectively. To simplify calculations, the value of the transmission time in all cases is the same, for example one second.

The unicast service performance will vary depending on where the nodes are located in the network topology. In both models, the largest communication path between two nodes is calculated. From the comparison of both equations, it is possible to observe that the proposed model outperforms the super peer model as shown in the inequality below.

2 x maxLevels < (treeDepth –1 + treeDepth x maxLeaf)

It is important to remark that the number of nodes in both models must be the same for this inequality to be true. The reason the proposed model improves the unicast service performance is because it is possible to calculate the path between any nodes. The message will be delivered according to a predefined path. Thus, in the worst scenario the largest path will include twice the number of communication levels.

The super peer model creates random connections among nodes and lack of a identifiers schema related to the underlying topology. As a consequence, a unicast service will require a blind search over the network. Even in the best escenario, where random connections create a tree as shown in figure **(8)**, the time required will be higher.

Broadcast Service Analysis

The performance of broadcast service in the proposed model outperforms the super peer model when it is considered the same number of nodes. The performance difference between both models can be analyzed comparing equations **(4)** and **(5)** as shown below.

maxLevels + maxLevels x roundUp(maxNodes/2) < (treeDepth-1+treeDepth x maxLeaf)

Figures **(9)** and **(10)** facilitates the analysis of the broadcast service performance difference stated in the inequation where the communication levels are three and five respectively. The x-axis shows the number of leaves and the number of nodes per federation corresponding to each model. The y-axis represents the units of time required by the service. As mentioned before, this value is constant to simplify the comparison, for example one second.

The performance of the super peer model shows a linear grow with a steeper slope than the curve for the proposed model. Furthermore, the difference between both models increases as the federation size grows.

Scalability Analysis

The model presented in this chapter will scale according to the values of the number of nodes per federation and the communication levels. These parameters will define the limits for the topology to expand. However, as previously shown the performance of unicast and broadcast services is influenced by the communication level.

Figure 9. Broadcast service performance for a topology hierarchy of 3 levels

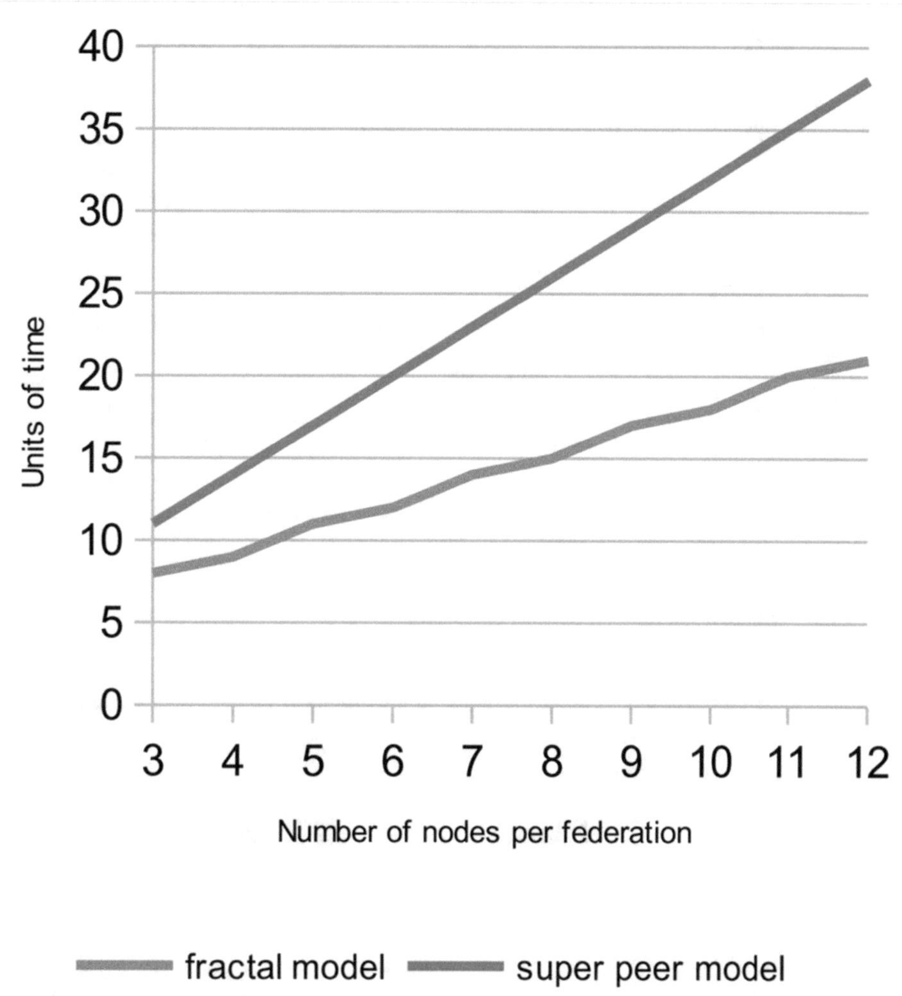

The values of these parameters will depend on the expected numbers of stable nodes in the network. However, they will not limit the system scalability because the network can include new guest nodes without changing its configuration.

Figures **(11)** and **(12)** show how a network will scale when the parameters mentioned before change. The x-axis shows the number of nodes per federation and the y-axis presents the number of nodes in the whole network.

Figure **(11)** compares the scalability of a network with two and three communication levels whilst figure **(12)** shows the same information when the communication levels are four and five. In both cases, it is possible to observe a steep increase in the number of nodes just adding one level. The increase of the cost in the performance of unicast and broadcast services is low taking into account the scalability of the network.

Figure 10. Broadcast service performance for a topology hierarchy of 5 levels

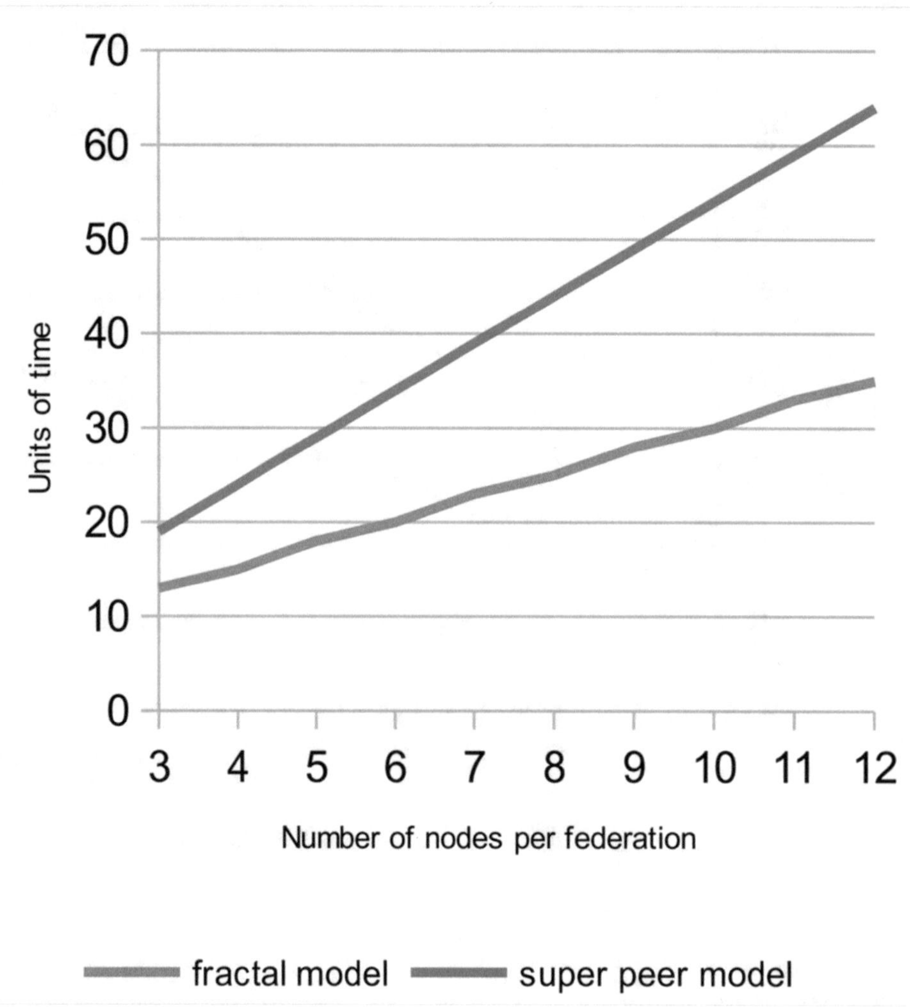

CONCLUSION

This chapter presented a communication model based on fractal geometry for IoT applications. Communication systems will play a fundamental role in the development of IoT scenarios where a large number of devices will constantly exchange information to perform in some cases critical tasks.

IoT scenarios include heterogeneous devices to sense data from different environments and perform action based on predefined parameters. This interaction will increase significantly the data traffic on communication systems. For this reason, the performance of communication models and its scalability becomes important aspects of the IoT paradigm.

The centralized communication model has been for years the standard for Internet-based application. However, they are vulnerable when server fails because the whole system becomes unavailable. Additionally, servers may generate communication bottlenecks when the rate of data traffic grows.

Figure 11. Scalability curve for two and three communication levels

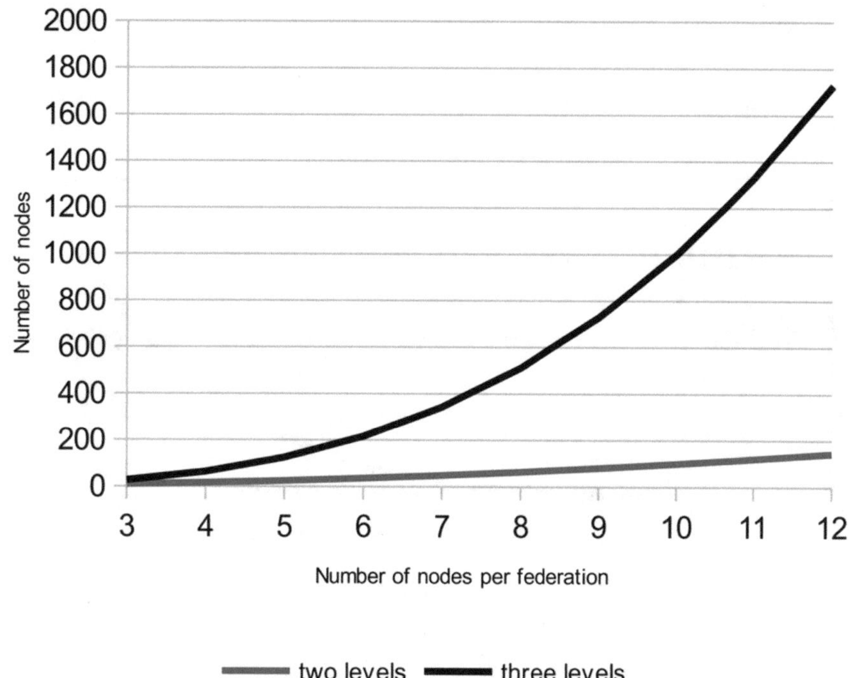

Decentralized models drawn much attention in the research community when P2P networks emerged to support file-sharing among Internet users. The super peer model became popular because of its scalability and simplicity to create a random network of nodes. This model uses flooding of message for unicast and broadcast communication, which has the disadvantages of duplicating messages when searching for a node and it has a limited scope.

The model proposed in this chapter is inspired in the super peer model because of its simplicity create a network topology and scalability. It creates a fractal geometry to improve the disadvantages of flooding mechanism to support communication services. This geometry along with a unique identification schema for nodes enables the delivery of messages efficiently. Since every node has an id that depends on its location within the network topology, it is possible to calculate the communication path between two nodes efficiently.

This chapter describes the model and define the equations to measure the performance of unicast and broadcast services. The performance takes into account the time required to communicate nodes using unicast or broadcast services.

The model introduced was compared with an improved super peer model organized into a balanced tree. The analysis includes the performance of unicast and broadcast services over both models. Results show how the proposed model outperforms its counterpart in both services. Additionally, an analysis of the network scalability is presented to show how adding only one additional communication level to the system increases significantly the number of nodes in the network.

Figure 12. Scalability curve for four and five communication levels

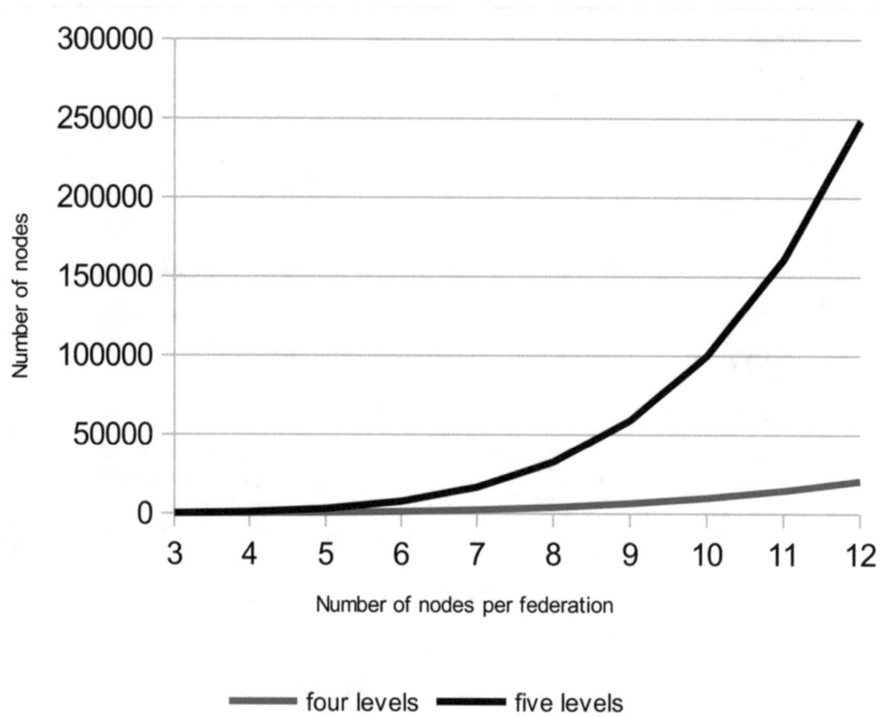

Efficient unicast and broadcast services along with network scalability are important requirements for future IoT applications. These services support the execution of actions on devices, the data request simultaneously to a set of nodes, the gathering of information from different sensors, among others.

REFERENCES

Al-Fuqaha, A., Guizani, M., Mohammadi, M., Aledhari, M., & Ayyash, M. (2015). Internet of things: A survey on enabling technologies, protocols, and applications. *IEEE Communications Surveys and Tutorials*, *17*(4), 2347–2376. doi:10.1109/COMST.2015.2444095

Al-Sarawi, S., Anbar, M., Alieyan, K., & Alzubaidi, M. (2017). Internet of things (iot) communication protocols: Review. *8th International Conference on Information Technology (ICIT)*, 685–690. 10.1109/ICITECH.2017.8079928

Borgia, E. (2014). The internet of things vision: Key features, applications and open issues. *Computer Communications*, *54*, 1–31. doi:10.1016/j.comcom.2014.09.008

Carlsson & Gustavsson. (2001). The rise and fall of napster - an evolutionary approach. In Active Media Technology, volume 2252 of Lecture Notes in Computer Science, (pp. 347–354). Springer.

Carra, D., Lo Cigno, R., & Biersack, E. W. (2007). Graph based analysis of mesh overlay streaming systems. Selected Areas in Communications. *IEEE Journal on*, *25*(9), 1667–1677.

Cicerone, S., Di Stefano, G., & Handke, D. (2005). Self-spanner graphs. *Discrete Applied Mathematics, 150*(1-3), 99–120. doi:10.1016/j.dam.2005.04.004

Dideles, M. (2003). Bluetooth: A technical overview. *XRDS, 9*(4), 11–18. doi:10.1145/904080.904083

Eng Keong Lua, J. (2005). A survey and comparison of peer-to-peer overlay network schemes. *IEEE Communications Surveys and Tutorials, 7*(2), 72–93. doi:10.1109/COMST.2005.1610546

Farris, I., Militano, L., Nitti, M., Atzori, L., & Iera, A. (2016). Mifaas: A mobile IoT federation as a service model for dynamic cooperation of iot cloud providers. *Future Generation Computer Systems*, 126–137.

Fraigniaud, P., & Gauron, P. (2006). D2b: A de bruijn based content-addressable network. *Theoretical Computer Science, 355*(1), 65–79. doi:10.1016/j.tcs.2005.12.006

Gandhi, D. A., & Ghosal, P. M. (2018). Intelligent Healthcare Using IoT: Extensive Survey. *2018 Second International Conference on Inventive Communication and Computational Technologies (ICICCT)*, 800-802.

Ghosh, A., Ratasuk, R., Mondal, B., Mangalvedhe, N., & Thomas, T. (2010). Lte-advanced: Next generation wireless broadband technology. *IEEE Wireless Communications, 17*(3), 10–22. doi:10.1109/MWC.2010.5490974

Hashmi, M., Hänninen, S., & Maki, K. (2011). *Survey of smart grid concepts, architectures, and technological demonstrations worldwide. In 2011 IEEE PES Conference on Innovative Smart Grid Technologies Latin America*. ISGT LA.

Hoschek, W. (2002). A Unified Peer-to-Peer Database Framework for Scalable Service and Resource Discovery (vol. 2536). Springer. doi:10.1007/3-540-36133-2_12

IoT Scenarios. (2019). Retrieved from https://iot.ieee.org/iot-scenarios.html

Magharei, N., Rejaie, R., & Yang, G. (2007). Mesh or multiple-tree: A comparative study of live p2p streaming approaches. In *INFOCOM 2007. 26th IEEE International Conference on Computer Communications*. IEEE.

Makikawa, F., Tsuchiya, T., & Kikuno, T. (2010). Balance and proximity-aware skip graph construction. *Networking and Computing (ICNC), 2010 First International Conference on*, 268 –271. 10.1109/IC-NC.2010.59

Mandelbrot, B. B. (1982). *The Fractal Geometry of Nature. W. H. Freeman and Company.*

Meng, S., Cong Shi, D.H.X.Z., & Yu, Y. (2005). Gnutella 0.6. Volume 3841 of LNCS. Springer.

Michel Cosnarda, L. L., & Chanda, R. (2007). Virtual organizations in arigatoni. *Electronic Notes in Theoretical Computer Science, 171*(3), 55–75. doi:10.1016/j.entcs.2006.11.035

Misic, J. (2008). Analysis of Slave–Slave Bridging in IEEE 802.15.4 Beacon-Enabled Networks. *IEEE Transactions on Vehicular Technology, 57*(3), 1846–1863. doi:10.1109/TVT.2007.909263

Okai, E., Feng, X., & Sant, P. (2018). Smart Cities Survey. *IEEE 20th International Conference on High Performance Computing and Communications; IEEE 16th International Conference on Smart City; IEEE 4th International Conference on Data Science and Systems (HPCC/SmartCity/DSS),* 1726-1730. 10.1109/HPCC/SmartCity/DSS.2018.00282

Paul, P. V., & Saraswathi, R. (2017). The Internet of Things — A comprehensive survey. *2017 International Conference on Computation of Power, Energy Information and Commuincation (ICCPEIC),* 421-426. 10.1109/ICCPEIC.2017.8290405

Raphael Chand, L. L., & Cosnard, M. (2007). Improving resource discovery in the arigatoni overlay network. In Architecture of Computing Systems. Volume 4415 of LNCS. Springer.

Ratnasamy, S., Francis, P., Handley, M., Karp, R., & Shenker, S. (2001). A scalable content-addressable network. *Computer Communication Review, 31*(4), 161–172. doi:10.1145/964723.383072

Risson, J., & Moors, T. (2006). Survey of research towards robust peer-to-peer networks: Search methods. *Computer Networks, 50*(17), 3485–3521. doi:10.1016/j.comnet.2006.02.001

Vincentelli, A. S. (2015). Let's get physical: Adding physical dimensions to cyber systems. *Low Power Electronics and Design (ISLPED), 2015 IEEE/ACM International Symposium on,* 1–2.

Wauters, T., Coppens, J., De Turck, F., Dhoedt, B., & Demeester, P. (2006). Replica placement in ring-based content delivery networks. *Computer Communications, 29*(16), 3313–3326. doi:10.1016/j.comcom.2006.05.008

Wehrle, K., & Steinmetz, R. (2005) What is this Peer-to-Peer about? Volume 3485 of LNCS. Springer-Verlag.

Yassein, M. B., Mardini, W., & Khalil, A. (2016). Smart homes automation using z-wave protocol. *International Conference on Engineering MIS (ICEMIS),* 1–6.

Zhou, K., Liu, T., & Zhou, L. (2015). Industry 4.0: Towards future industrial opportunities and challenges. *12th International Conference on Fuzzy Systems and Knowledge Discovery (FSKD),* 2147-2152. 10.1109/FSKD.2015.7382284

Chapter 8
The Science of Smart Things

Alan Radley
Kim Veltman Perspective Institute, UK

ABSTRACT

An ontological analysis of the application of the key concept of synergy to the internet of things (IoT) is presented. The authors begin by defining synergy as it applies to all types of human-made objects, and in particular to connected things, along the way developing a new theory of synergetic accommodation that provides a detailed aetiology of smart technology. A presentation of the history, routes, plus a complete definition of smart technology is given before looking at how the IoT is developing today and might progress in the future for the benefit of all humankind. Accordingly, the authors develop two new concepts, situated and distributed intelligence, that may be used to develop practically useful smart technology that fully meets the needs of the future in terms of providing efficient, magnified, reliable, safe, automated, and economical services.

INTRODUCTION

We are now entering the 4th Industrial Revolution; whereby technologies combine hardware, software, and biology (cyber-physical systems), placing emphasis on advances in communication and connectivity. It is the fusion of these technologies and their interaction across the **physical**, **digital** and **biological domains** that will make this new age fundamentally different from any other.

Our focus is on the creation of profoundly humanistic—plus environmentally sustainable—technology. Learning from nature's vast library of proven methods—both animate and inanimate—is a key goal; whereby we usefully engage, copy and apply certain universal design/operating principles. Ergo, we wish to embrace total thinking; and create comprehensive systems with truly beneficial outcomes—for the benefit of all humankind.

In particular, the key principle of **Synergy** can help us to address the complex challenges of the new era—and to create technological solutions with real unity of purpose; whereby we embrace total thinking; and create comprehensive systems with truly beneficial outcomes.

DOI: 10.4018/978-1-7998-7010-4.ch008

What is Synergy?

Understood correctly, the Universe is nothing more than—**Energy**—flowing here and there—in a near infinity of matter-shaping processes. Whereby everything happens according to the laws of nature— and the whole procedure is what we call reality—or the **Physical World**. Nonetheless, the Universe would be a very chaotic place without another fundamental law of nature—**Synergy**—which is the direct corollary of Energy.

Energy refers to the ability to make CHANGE happen within a specific region of the physical Universe—typically consisting of unrestricted or free-flowing Energy which impels DISORDERED CHANGE; whereby Energy is naturally chaotic in nature (ref. centrifugal or explosive energy which is energy-loosing).

Synergy—is the ability to CREATE/MAINTAIN ORDER—that is to cause structured Energy patterns to form which persist and are energy-conserving in nature (they tend to guide Energy across space/time and are centripetal).

The upshot is a fundamental truth often overlooked by Physicists, Chemists and Biologists—that Synergy is the **key operating principle of the Universe**; and because it provides evident structure(s) amongst the chaos. Synergy refers to generalised Energy patterns—which are often useful and/or pertinent to a particular outcome. Synergy is **maximisation of order** within a region of the Universe—and is recognised when energy forms/flows in a particular kind of idealised pattern that might not otherwise occur (in any other way).

Synergetic Design

The Universe is a constant battle between chaotic and Synergetic energy structures; whereby energy patterns form, then stabilise and later dissolve over time. Evidently, the Universe has certain general Energy patterning tendencies—including small-scaled examples such as sub-atomic, atomic, and molecular energy/matter structures—plus large-scale ones such as gravity. However, in between these extremes—exists a vast number of other general-purpose—or universally applicable—Synergetic patterns (***many of which have yet to be discovered***).

Synergy refers to the surprising effects of combining Things in a certain way; whereby what happens—is wholly determined by ***changes in Energy patterns across particular elements of the whole***. Whereby new behaviours and possibilities are enabled due to the nature of the pattern itself. Synergetic patterns—as fundamental laws of the Universe—are discovered and not invented. Synergetic design is the application of general Synergetic patterns to a specific application area; and multiple patterns may be combined to affect complex results.

It is important to realise that we humans make constant use of Synergy (ref. organised technology designs)—existing in modular assemblies/hierarchies of Things/Energies—to build/operate various tools, computers and machines (Radley, 2015). However, it does not follow that we are always able to successfully apply Synergetic principles in optimal way(s)—primarily because we often lack sufficient knowledge of how to efficiently locate the most opportune solutions (highest ordered Synergetic designs).

Put simply, we need full knowledge of what Synergy actually is—and the different forms/classes of Synergy patterns that are possible—to solve problems in the most advantageous ways. QED.

Flow of Energy and Information

The universe is comprised of vast numbers of overlaid, interlacing and coordinated systems, whereby structures of things and processes exist and inter-accommodate at every scale from the quantum level to the cosmic. Humanity articulates the behaviour of systems—using natural and human-made technologies—to solve problems; and by directing resources towards particular aims.

A refined way of viewing a system is as a set of structures and processes for efficiently organising specific flows of **Energy** and **Information**. The job of the system is to apply **Intelligence**—or useful problem solving capability—to purposefully manage these same assets. Whereby all three elements are the **Synergetic Facets** of a system.

A basic question is: are there general principles of design and self-organisation irrespective of the nature of the individual parts of a system? Often, we find that the answer is yes; because **Synergetic Systems**, just like living organisms, have coordinated parts that operate in close harmony with all environmental requirements. A Synergetic system is self-regulating and intelligently applies resources precisely where, when and how they are needed—without wasting any energy/information—a procedure known as **Synergetic Inter-Accommodation**.

Synergetics aligns the natural with the artificial—in auspicious ways; and usefully merges the humanistic outlook with automated/computerised elements.

Synergetic Systems

Synergetics is the study of systems in transformation, with an emphasis on total system behaviour unpredicted by the behaviour of any isolated components, including humanity's role as user, participant and observer of universal operating principles. Synergetics adopts the most advantageous **Macro-Micro viewpoint**, seeking to co-opt **natural principles** favourably, plus apply **human** and **machine intelligence** comprehensively—using holistic design principles—to create technologies that fully meet the needs of the environment (in the broadest possible sense(s)).

Synergetics eschews the role of specialists who deal only in parts—championing the approach of the generalist who applies a wide array of knowledge from a wide variety of subjects. A key question follows: ***how do we—avoid the dangers of analytical fragmentation—and Think in Terms of Wholes***?

Classical and Smart Synergetics

Buckminster Fuller (1895–1983) first coined the term Synergetic (Fuller, 1969); and attempted to define its scope in his two-volume work *Synergetics*. Fuller suggested that when looked at from the synergetic point of view, all problems and their solutions are seen from a single unifying perspective (Fuller, 1972a; Fuller, 1972b); whereby both macroscopic and microscopic points of view must be taken fully into account—for the benefit of all.

Classical Synergetics is a very broad discipline, and embraces a range of scientific studies including tetrahedral and close-packed-sphere geometries, and various 'system operating' concepts in thermodynamics, physics, engineering, chemistry, psychology, biochemistry, economics, and philosophy etc.

But there is also another type of synergy—named here as **Smart Synergetics**; whereby technologies (Things/Systems) and People exist in ideal synthesises, often remotely arranged, but always within streamlined intelligence/action/information sharing networks. Here one technology is comprised of many

Figure 1. Aetiology of a Smart Technology

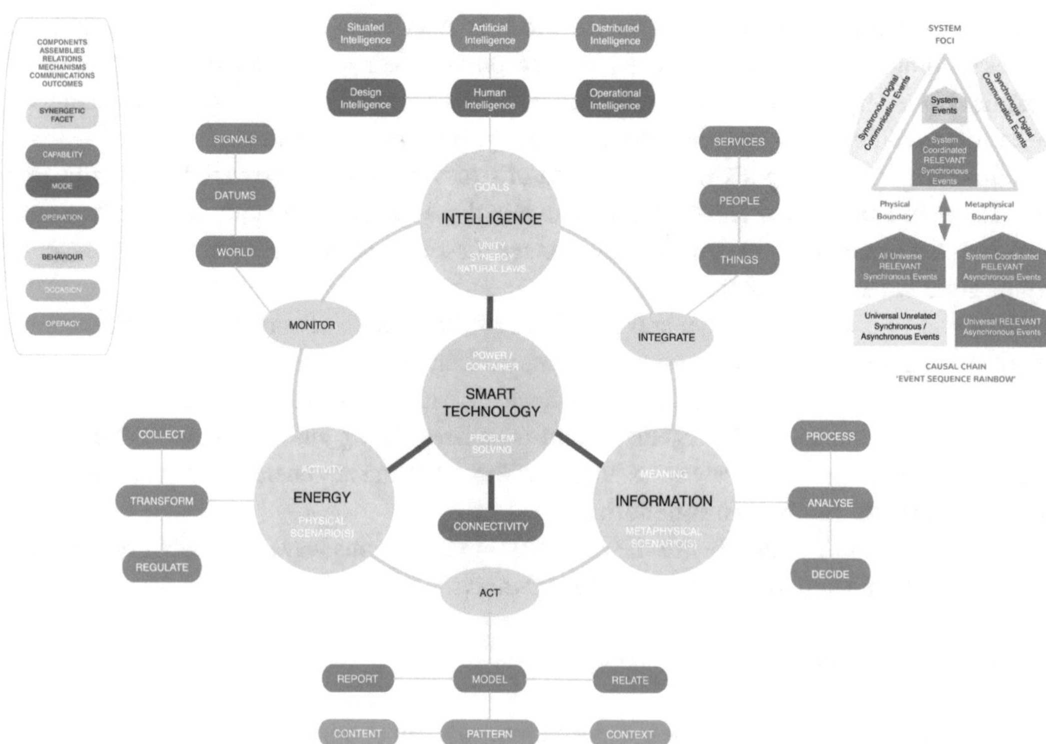

sub-technologies which are bundled together in collections and/or groups—but notably these parts are then able to collaborate purposefully by means of a digital network.

Smart Synergetics is largely concerned with systems that provide enhanced **Human Intelligence** (Virtual/Augmented-Reality, Knowledge Machines) and/or **Artificial Intelligence** (AI, Robotics, IoT). Typically an AI system will employ **Situated Intelligence** and/or **Distributed Intelligence**.

In summary, a Synergetic System consists of certain natural phenomena programmed and orchestrated in an optimal fashion for some carefully considered purpose(s). QED.

Key Technology Topics

A key goal is to establish the founding principles for seven key areas of the **Synergetic Technology** landscape; named as:

- **Data Protection, Privacy and Cybersecurity**
- **Augmented Human Intelligence and Artificial Intelligence (AI)**
- **Automata: Robots, Computers, and Smart Tools**
- **Communication Networks (M2M, H2M, M2H)**
- **Virtual and Augmented Reality (VR)**

Figure 2. Operacy of a Synergetic Technology

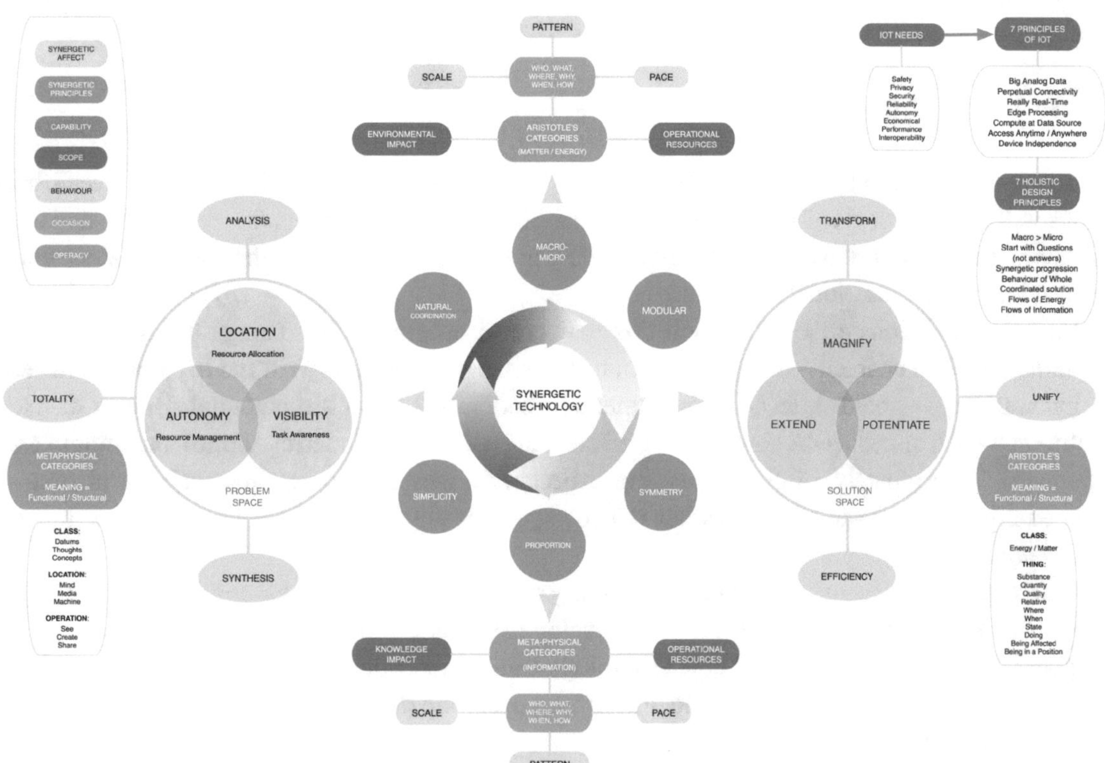

- **Knowledge Machines, New Media and the World Brain (H2H)**
- **Internet Of Things (IoT) and Smart Products/Services**

Human knowledge and capability must advance to the stage where collectively we become an authoritative source of knowledge for each of these seven industry defining topics—and to probe related matters in great depth. Obviously, we cannot achieve such an objective alone and/or right away; but we do aim to take significant steps towards the same goal by means of logical, integrated and holistic perspective(s)—combined with use of the scientific method.

Already significant progress in the Cybersecurity field along these same lines—and by supplying a scientific framework that allows theoreticians and practitioners alike to develop, share and apply state-of-the-art Cybersecurity principles and practical knowledge.

Our hope is that the principles and theoretical models developed herein—can be used used to create eminently practical technological solutions that are in close harmony with humanistic principles. Nevertheless, and despite remaining optimistic, we must admit that the **Age of Intelligent Machines** has many potential dangers; and not the least of which are the increased likelihood of data breaches, hacks and system exploits.

Space precludes a full examination in this paper of each of the seven key areas detailed above; however we shall make a start on this quest by examining the Internet of Things or IoT and the synergetic principles upon which is should be built.

Internet of Things (IOT)

The IoT would seem to be a very big deal. Indeed, it is claimed that within 20-30 years, over 1 billion Things will be connected to the Internet. Doubtless the technology soothsayers are correct—and the IoT will revolutionise almost every area of human life—in the process changing the way(s) that we humans perform business, educational and leisure activities.

But many questions arise. What will this new era of programmable Things be like? Which new capabilities will be enabled—and how will our lives change as a result? Will the IoT limit us in certain detrimental ways—and/or affect our fundamental freedom(s)? What are potential dangers of the IoT revolution—such as reduced/compromised privacy and security – rendering the IoT dream into an IoT nightmare? Unfortunately, often the negative aspects of a new technology are not clear at first—but rather emerge later on—and perhaps when it is too late to do anything to correct or reduce the impact(s) of the same.

Ergo, vigilance and carefully monitored design goals—plus managed technology trajectories—would seem to be the best way to proceed. We must develop IoT solutions that avoid the big dangers and negative potentials that such a powerful new technology could foreshadow. Rather we wish to provide truly humanistic benefits for all of human kind. Put simply, everyone must have the opportunity to profit from the IoT revolution.

Herein, whilst we do acknowledge the existence of significant dangers within the boundaries of the emerging and highly technical field of IoT; it is our belief that application of the scientific method—consisting of a combination of empirical observation and logical reasoning—must always play a significant and foundational role in any IoT scenario whatsoever. QED.

Accordingly, we seek to establish a foundational framework for the entire field of: the Internet of Things; and by means of logical, integrated and holistic perspective(s)—combined with use of the scientific method.

IoT History

How can we define the Internet of Things, or IoT? A commonly employed definition states that—the IoT—is a system of interrelated computing devices, mechanical and digital machines, objects, systems, animals or people that are provided with unique identifiers (UIDs) and the ability to transfer data over a network without requiring human intervention.

But the IoT has come to mean more than just connected Things—but rather relates to Things that are imbued—at the same time—with useful abilities surrounding the concept of '**Smartness**' and/or with what we name here as '**Situated Intelligence**'.

Situated Intelligence refers to an IoT Thing or IoT System that has a unique ability to Monitor, Act and Integrate within its environment in useful ways; and in particular to how objects that are 'awake' to the environment can/will usefully **automate** and **enhance** human problem solving capabilities. Doubtless the IoT is a very exciting part of our collective future; henceforth in this paper we examine how Situated Intelligence is/can/could be applied to a range of different problem application area(s). But first in this section it is salient to briefly examine the history of the IoT, and thus to learn where these ideas came from—specifically for Connected and Intelligent Things.

We begin with a brief definition of the IoT as it exists today.

IoT Defined

The definition of the Internet of Things has evolved due to the convergence of multiple technologies; including real-time analytics, machine learning, commodity sensors and embedded systems etc. A number of related technologies are typically employed to enable the Internet of Things; including combinations of embedded systems, wireless sensor networks, plus control systems and automation etc.

In the consumer market, IoT technology is most synonymous with products pertaining to the concept of the "smart home", covering a variety of appliances such as as lighting fixtures, thermostats, home security systems and cameras. Said devices are typically designed to support one or more common ecosystems, and can be controlled via devices associated with each ecosystem, such as smartphones and smart speakers.

But how did we arrive at the modern conception of the IOT? In order to find the answer we must turn to the many and varied worlds of science-fiction.

Science Fiction and the IoT

Science fiction (SciFi) is a good place to begin our study of the history of the IoT—and associated language—and so to discover where and how these ideas first came to be employed within the public agora. Indeed some people even think that the IoT was first conceptualised within the minds of a variety of SciFi writers. This may be so—or it may not be so—but certainly we can say that SciFi has played a big part in popularising related concepts.

For example, the concept of connected devices has been around since at least the 1930s and seems to have first emerged in SciFi stories of the 1930s, 1940s and 1950s. In early SciFi magazines such as Amazing Stories and Astounding Stories of Super-Science many aspects of the IOT were foreseen and/or foreshadowed.

IoT-like technologies depicted in early SciFi stores include:

- Radio controlled devices
- Mechanical / electronic brains
- Human-brain interfaces (usually wired implants)
- Voice controlled robots and remote devices
- Computer terminals (TV-like)
- Speaking / thinking robots
- Automated lights/doors/windows/escalators etc

Later more sophisticated IoT-like devices were depicted in science fiction movies such as 2001 (1968), Colossus: The Forbin Project (1970), WestWorld (1973), Logan's Run (1976), Blade Runner (1982), Back to the Future (1989) and Minority Report (2002), etc. Foreseen in these films were voice-operated computers, automated doors, robot helpers, video conferencing, video surveillance 3D displays, voice / gesture User Interfaces and 3D scanners/sensors etc.

And similar IoT-like devices were seen on television Sci-Fi programmes such as The Jetsons (1962), Star Trek (1967) and Space 1999 (1975)—where notable examples include mobile-phone like communicators, connected tablets, robot helpers, 3D printers, human to machine communication (and vice-versa), machine-to-machine communication (M2M), driverless cars, automated sensors, wearables, real-time and remote data gathering, data-rich screens and multi-touch displays (big and small), remote screens to summarise real-time information and also to control objects from distant locations etc. In actual fact, all of these ideas relate to a merging of the real world of Things with embodied intelligence and connectivity.

Perhaps the SciFi movie that most predicts the future in this respect is the Matrix (1999)—which is about a hacker named Neo who is recruited by a group of humans who've broken free of the digital matrix controlling humans in the future. Perhaps the IoT will place us in a matrix and it may very well be nigh impossible to escape.

Doubtless the exciting theme—within SciFi stories—of an epic struggle between human beings and AI plus IoT-like technology has been an excellent plot vehicle. However the the fact that technologies can have (intentionally or not) both positive and negative effects is a truism proven by past events including not least the industrial revolution which left countless millions unemployed as a result of the efficiencies of mass production.

Sci-Fi has always been a good way to examine—or predict—what may be the future benefits and dangers of any new and/or envisaged technology—indeed perhaps that may be part its true purpose—as an imaginary testing ground to explore possible future world(s). The issue of human control seems to be a key part of that process. The question of how can/do we control our inventions—and thus to manage the purposes that they are put to – remains evident today.

With the emergence of AI in the real world—capable thinking machines—the dangers seem only to multiply—and making accurate predictions in relation to what may happen as a result of AI becomes very difficult or nigh impossible. As a result, thinkers like Elon Musk and Steven Hawking have warned that we must place humanistic controls on AI to prevent a catastrophe in this respect.

The emergence of an AI that is somehow out of control remains a real danger—no matter if it is an AI that somehow misunderstands its true purpose (helping humans), or rather more likely—where AI is the result of powerful humans wielding technology towards their own personal gain and/or at the expense of the masses.

The upshot is that it is up to—us all as a collective—to work out how to build humanity into our IoT future; and in this respect it is salient to remember the past.

Real World Origins

It is important to realise that the IoT as it exists today is a technology that has a far longer history than one might think—because the IoT sits atop of a vast number of constituent technological inventions, scientific breakthroughs and supporting plus encapsulated products and communication systems/protocols etc.

Early breakthroughs that were necessary to make the IoT possible go right back to 1832 with the invention of the telegraph. Other important developments in this respect include: binary mathematics, morse-code, radio communications, ASCII coding, transistors, integrated circuits, the Arpnet, microprocessors, satellite communications, mobile technologies including GSM, CDMA 1G-4G, 5G, TCP/IP, domain names, the World Wide Web and the Cloud etc.

At various times throughout the 20th century, several visionaries have made prescient comments that appear to foresee the IoT:

- **1926**: **Nikola Tesla** said: "When wireless is perfectly applied the whole earth will be converted into a huge brain, which in fact it is, all things being particles of a real and rhythmic whole… and the instruments through which we shall be able to do this will be amazingly simple compared with our present telephone. A man will be able to carry one in his vest pocket."
- **1950**: **Alan Turing** commented: "It can also be maintained that it is best to provide the machine with the best sense organs that money can buy, and then teach it to understand and speak English."
- **1964: Marshall McLuhan** in Understanding Media stated: "by means of electric media, we set up a dynamic by which all previous technologies—including cities—will be translated into information systems."
- **1966: Karl Steinbuch** a German computer scientist said: "In a few decades time, computers will be interwoven into almost every industrial product."
- **1999: Neil Gross** in Business Week commented: "In the next century, planet earth will don an electronic skin. It will use the Internet as a scaffold to support and transmit its sensations. This skin is already being stitched together. It consists of millions of embedded electronic measuring devices: thermostats, pressure gauges, pollution detectors, cameras, microphones, glucose sensors, EKGs, electroencephalographs. These will probe and monitor cities and endangered species, the atmosphere, our ships, highways and fleets of trucks, our conversations, our bodies–even our dreams."

These interesting comments indicate that the origins of the IoT has a far longer history than most people realise. Seen in its proper light, the IoT can be seen as nothing more than an extrapolation from, and combination of, many previous ideas related to mechanisation and systemisation, long-distance communication, automation, AI, plus media making efforts etc.

The Merging of Bits and Atoms

The IoT is set to become a revolution as great as any previous one. The IoT is a new phenomenon that potentially swallows-up and/or radically changes many traditional industries—including many manual jobs and manual processes plus industrial manufacturing and in many cases the building and operation of systems and machines. Everything in the real-world becomes merged with integrated circuits, digital communications, software and computers etc. (Radley, 2015).

Put simply the world will soon be resplendent with countless millions of 'intelligent and connected' Things that are able to sense, act and integrate—just as we do—relative to the real world, and in combination with the animate and inanimate world(s), and also each-other.

Soon all around us objects will wake-up—and be actively engaged in going about their daily business as a result of hidden programming logic—seemingly self-powered, self-actuated, self-controlled and self-motivated. Sometimes they will do so with our help/approval and so be under overt human command (localised and/or remote control); but more often these smart Things will just be following their own inner programming—based on programmed decision making processes—alone and/or in combination with other remote Things and/or networked controlling logic.

The IoT merges the old world of Atoms with the new World of Bits. Henceforth each smart Thing in the real-world is to be imbued with what we used to call an electronic brain. And the big picture is that these smart Things will together form a new super-intelligent environment that hopefully can provide a better world for us humans to live inside.

Dangers do exist for such an IoT dominated world. Privacy and security dangers could be magnified and many new dangers may emerge for example. And as with any technology, the IoT can be used to promulgate good or evil; either deliberately or by accident. The IoT may have inadvertently bad consequences for ordinary humans in certain circumstances—such as reduced opportunities for Jobs and/or less say in how society operates. As a result—we must find ways to humanise this new IoT revolution (see the author's book: Self As Computer—for related issues/arguments).

In any case, the instrumenting of the entire world has begun. Let is now examine some key issues—and in order to discover what may be the choices, and/or advantages and disadvantages, in terms of the design and operation of our newly intelligent and super-connected habitat.

IoT Today

The actual term "Internet of Things" was first coined by Kevin Ashton in 1999 during his work at Procter&Gamble. Ashton worked on supply chain optimisation, and he wanted to attract senior management's attention to a new exciting technology called RFID. Partly because the Internet was the hottest new trend in 1999 and partly because it somehow made sense, he called his presentation "Internet of Things" or IoT.

Despite the fact that Kevin indeed grabbed the interest of some P&G executives, the term Internet of Things did not get widespread attention for around the next 10 years. Whereby the concept of IoT began to gain popularity in the summer of 2010. In that year Google's StreetView service made 360 degree pictures available for exploration from everybody's computer, smart phone or tablet. Google's strategy seemed to be the indexing of the physical world.

The term Internet of Things reached mass market awareness when in January 2014 Google announced that it would buy the Nest connected home system for $3.2bn. At the same time the Consumer Electronics Show (CES) in Las Vegas was held under the theme of IoT.

But before we can go on discussing the IoT, we must ask ourselves what exactly is the IoT? What kinds of technologies does the term encompass? And how can we define the IoT? Well as a partial answer, Gartner has defined the The Internet of Things as: "a concept that describes how the Internet will expand as sensors and intelligence are added to physical items such as consumer devices or physical assets and these objects are connected to the Internet."

Gartner identifies IoT related technologies as:

1. Media Tablets and Beyond
2. Mobile-Centric Applications and Interfaces
3. Contextual and Social User Experience
4. App Stores and Marketplaces
5. Next-Generation Analytics
6. Big Data
7. In-Memory Computing
8. Extreme Low-Energy Servers
9. Cloud Computing

A number of terms have been applied to IoT-like systems. For example, Cisco has been driving the term **Internet of Everything (IoE**). Intel called it the "**embedded internet**". Whilst others have spoken of **Edge Computing** and **Mobile IoT** etc.

A sampling of other terms that have been proposed but don't mean exactly all the same are (see our IOT Lexicon for a more complete list):

- IOT Cloud Platform
- IOT Protocol
- Global Navigation Satellite System
- Bluetooth Low Energy / Narrowband IOT
- M2M (Machine to machine) communication
- Web of Things
- Industry 4.0
- Mesh Network
- Connected Human / Smart Wearables
- Near-Field Communication
- Telematics / Big Data
- Industrial internet (of Things)
- Smart Systems / Smart Meter
- Smart City; Smart Buildings;
- Pervasive computing
- Intelligent systems
- Embedded Software
- Sensor Network
- System on a Chip

Whilst these varied definitions are somewhat broad, vague and/or ill-defined, the same allegation can be applied to the Internet of Things. Indeed there seems hardly to be an envisaged future technology that does not relate to one or more of these terms in one way or another.

So how can we clarify the vision for the IoT? How do we grasp what this term is all about in the most fundamental way? Perhaps a good starting point is to go back to the beginning, and look at where these ideas came from in the first place—irrespective of the actual term(s) employed to encapsulate the area as a whole.

A good starting place is to examine the work of scientist Dr Mark Weiser.

Ubiquitous Computing

Back in the early 1990s Dr Mark Weiser from Xerox Parc wrote several papers on the future of computing; whereupon he summed up his ideas by means of the concept of '**Ubiquitous Computing**'—which is the idea of integrating computers seamlessly into the world to invisibly enhance pre-existing objects / things / machines (Weiser, 1991) . Dr Weiser was also the first to define invisible computing; also referring to as **embodied virtuality**, whereby the key goal is to help users to activate the world in helpful ways!

At their core, all models of ubiquitous computing and hence the IoT—share a vision of small, inexpensive, networked and processing devices, distributed at all scales throughout everyday life.

In a 1991 article for Scientific American entitled 'The Computer for the 21st Century', Dr Weiser first introduced the related concept of **Pervasive Computing** whereby he stated that: 'the most profound technologies are those that disappear. They weave themselves into the fabric of everyday life until they are indistinguishable from it… In the 21st century… specialised elements of hardware and software, connected by wires, radio waves and infrared, will be so ubiquitous that no one will notice their presence.'

In summary, with these ideas, Dr Weiser conceived of a new way of thinking about computers, the same being a vision that takes into account the human world and allows the computers themselves to vanish into the background. Along these lines Dr Weiser makes a rather salient point as follows: 'in essence, the only way things disappear is when we are freed to use them without thinking and so to focus beyond them on new— and often inherently better—goals.

Embodied Virtuality

In a 1993 paper named 'Ubiquitous Computing', Dr Weiser further explored his concept of what it might be like to live in a world of invisible and intelligent widgets—something he named **embodied virtuality.** Therein Dr Weiser remarked 'computing access will be everywhere': in walls, on wrists, and in 'scrap' computers; (like paper, lying about). This is called 'ubiquitous computing'.

Dr Weiser noted that: "Ubiquitous computing has as its goal enhancing computer use by making many computers available throughout the physical environment, but making them effectively invisible to the user. You need not carry anything with you, since information will be accessible everywhere. Unlike the intimate agent computer that responds to one's voice and is a personal friend and assistant, **ubiquitous computing envisions computation primarily in the background where it may not even be noticed**. Whereas the intimate computer does your bidding, the ubiquitous computer leaves you feeling as though you did it yourself." Dr Weiser continued: "A good tool is an **invisible tool**. By invisible, I mean that the tool does not intrude on your consciousness; you focus on the task, not the tool. Eyeglasses are a good tool—you look at the world, not the eyeglasses."

Of course, such tools are not (always) invisible in themselves, but as part of a context of use. Good tools enhance invisibility—but it is often an invisibility that relates only to those specific aspects of the environment that the human user does not need to see at any particular moment.

Calm Technology

Another way of thinking about invisible computers is in terms of the affect a technology has on our level of arousal or simulation (when using a particular tool).

In 1995 Dr Weiser in collaboration with John Seely Brown wrote a paper on this topic entitled: Designing Clam Technology; in which they said: 'Our computers should be like our childhood: an invisible foundation that is quickly forgotten but always with us, and effortlessly used throughout our lives. We should be creating technologies that encalm and inform. Calm technology engages both the ***center*** and the ***periphery*** of our attention, and in fact moves back and forth between the two.'

The term "periphery" refers to a situation we are attuned to without attending to it explicitly. Ordinarily when driving our attention is centred on the road, the radio, our passenger, but not the noise of the engine. But an unusual noise is noticed immediately, showing that we were attuned to the noise in the periphery, and could come quickly to attend to it. A calm technology will move easily from the periphery of our attention, to the center, and back.

This is fundamentally encalming, for two reasons. First, by placing things in the periphery we are able to attune to many more things than we could if everything had to be at the center. Things in the periphery are attuned to by the large portion of our brains devoted to peripheral (sensory) processing. Thus the periphery is informing without overburdening. Second, by recentering something formerly in the periphery we take control of it.

Smart Things

A **Smart Thing** is an object that can **solve problems** with respect to its environment (consisting of other People, Things/Systems [smart or stand-alone] and Services etc).

In order to solve problems with respect to its environment – a Smart Thing must adequately **Interpret, securely Process and appropriately Act** on the information it collects, whilst protecting itself from from threats and intrusions, plus communicating the results to other smart objects, people and systems (while at the same time managing power consumption).

Importantly, connectivity also enables capabilities of the product to exist outside of the physical device itself, in what is (sometimes) known as the **product cloud**. The data collected from these products can be then analysed to inform decision-making (human and/or machine), enable operational efficiencies and so to continuously improve the level of performance of the product and related classes of products. Henceforth Smart Object interaction not only refers to interaction with physical world objects but also to interaction with virtual computing environments—and in this way the real world becomes part of the digital world.

It is important to realise that the smartness capability of a thing/system typically will relate to several problem-solving facets. The job of the Smart Thing is to help humans achieve certain Goals (relating to the specific purpose(es) for which it has been specifically designed to meet). Now regardless of whether or not a particular Goal is met – by the Smart Thing – by means of automatic, semi-automatic and/or entirely human-controlled decisions, actions and procedures—it is a fact that all Goals tend to share certain common features.

A famous design guru in relation to Smart Things is Dr Donald Norman – who in his book 'The Design Of Everyday Things' – has made an exhaustive study of the nature of Goals and how Things may be designed for efficient purposes (Norman, 1988) . For an explanation of Dr Norman's work as applied to the IoT, take a look at **Situated Intelligence** as explained here.

The Future of the IoT

The internet of things and devices such as machines and sensors are expected to generate approximately 80 Zettabytes of data in 2025—as predicted by IDC (International Data Corporation). Also, IoT will grow at a compound annual growth rate of 28% over 2020 to 2025. According to the projection of the statista Research Department, 75 billion devices will be connected with the IoT worldwide by 2025.

The IoT will generate almost unimaginable amounts of data—(the so-called Big-Data problem) and the question of how to manage this amount of data remains unsolved. Also, organizations must work to protect all of this this data wherever it relates to customers and their personal information.

Machine Learning is a type of AI (Artificial Intelligence) that helps computers to learn—and it is likely that the solution to the Big-Data problem will be found in this subject area. Ergo, AI is considered a key propellant to the growth of the IoT revolution. 5G is another technology that is central to the IoT—both for fundamental connectivity speed—and also to enable a single network for billions of applications (the so-called IoT of Everything/Things).

In a span of ten years, from 2020 to 2030, IoT devices will grow from 75 billion to more than 100 billion, and the improvement—of data flow speeds—from 4G to 5G is set to be a major factor in this revolution. Today's 4G network can support up to 5500 to 6000 IoT devices on a single cell (geographical region). With a 5G network, up to one million devices can be handled by a single cell—henceforth there should be no limits to the number of objects and Things that can be placed onto the global network and/or countless smaller sub-networks.

The upshot of all these breakthroughs and advancements is that the future of the IoT is not likely to be limited by technological advancements—and that anything we can imagine—or put resources into—can be achieved or made into a reality. Henceforth when it comes to the exciting future of the IoT—we are—truly—limited only by our individual and collective imagination(s)!

IoT History - Conclusions

At the present date—in the year 2020—the internet of things and devices is no longer a dream, prediction or some kind of vapour-tech; but rather it is already here—and developing/evolving rapidly. Whereby everything we do—all of our activities (or most daily interactions with objects, systems and machines)—is/are about to be transformed— and in a huge variety of different ways.

Predicting exactly what these changes will be—that are enabled by the IoT—and how they will affect us in 5-10 years time would seem to be an impossible task. All most of us can do is—to sit back—and keep a close eye on developments!

Increasingly, we see connectivity being built into ordinary smart-home devices such as lights, heating appliances, speakers, TVs, speakers, kitchen appliances etc. Plus the industrial internet is taking off with smart-buildings, smart-factories, smart supply-chain etc; indeed there seems to be nowhere that the IoT—is not present—and almost no area of human activity that the IoT is not set to revolutionise or dramatically improve. And all of this will happen sooner than you might believe.

The future for us humans is one of **Situated Intelligence** embedded into almost every action, trip, task and need—no matter if we are talking about leisure and/or working activity. And these multiple intelligences will be alive to our specific and local needs and requirements, whereby they will provide fully tailored—and real-time—solutions that both see and adapt themselves carefully to the intricacies of a particular situation and henceforth to the diversity and uniqueness of human activity.

IoT Goals

One way to classify an IoT System is by where you find them. We can have IoT in the Home, Shops, Workplaces, Hospitals, Factories, Cities, Hotels, Amusement Parks, Roads, Airports, Schools, Universities and even in Outer Space! Accordingly we have the so-called Smart: Home, City, Utilities, Retail, Grids, Buildings, Offices, Supply Chain, Farming; plus a host of other industrial application areas including Industrial Internet, and in the consumer marketplace Wearables; plus Connected: Health, Car etc.

Another way is to distinguish IoT systems is in terms of technology employed. In this respect, it is clear is that many new technologies are emerging—the same being ones that could potentially be applied to many of these application areas. Indeed, technology is evolving at such a rapid rate that it is valid to speak of a new era in which everything is being instrumented and connected for control, data-logging and real-time collaborative purposes.

In summary, the changing nature of the technological landscape will create a number of seismic changes to the ways in which we will live, work and play in the future—and it is possible to identify key formative and shaping factors in this new era as listed below.

Major changes and forces impacting the IoT technological landscape are as follows:

- Instrumenting the entire world (systems/machines are everywhere).
- Machines are becoming smaller and more powerful.
- Machines are receding into the background and becoming invisible!
- Machines collaborate with each other.
- Machines manage everything—every transaction / process.
- Everything comes with a chip inside—everything has intelligence.
- Every device is connected—for control, data logging, collaboration.
- Perpetual connectivity—everything is connected to a network.
- The Internet is becoming a data-source and less of a destination!
- The world is turning into data—and the machines know the data.
- Stuff just works or gets work done.
- Screens are not required for most tasks.
- What was human initiated is now machine dominated!
- Apps are becoming verbs—computer managed tasks just happen.
- Devices automatically discern human intent!
- Products self-work —they manage and switch themselves on/off alone.

Over and above this list of technological aspects of the IoT landscape are 7 basic principles that encompass general IoT design principles:

IoT needs (general systems):

- **Reliability**—stable services
- **Safety**—not harmful to humans / ecosystems
- **Security**— no hacking / system exploits
- **Privacy**—personal / private data is secure
- **Interoperability**—works across brands
- **Autonomy**—no Internet and the system still works (within limits)
- **Speed**—fast and real-time response times, timely data-aggregation

Doubtless it is relatively easy to list all of the general requirements that our new wonder technology must be able to meet—but it is rather more difficult to design, build and operate these seemingly magical solutions with any degree of success.

IoT Design Principles

In fact, optimally managing and/or shaping the IoT design process (in general terms)—so far as this is possible—is the key goal of the present paper. Towards this aim we have formulated an actual science of the Internet of Things; and our new science is grounded upon a single concept: that of **Situated Intelligence.**

Interestingly our concept of **Situated Intelligence** (see later article) is in close alignment with the Dr. Tom Bradicich, VP of Server Engineering at HP—who has generated a related analysis "The 7 Principles of the IoT"; named as:

1. **Big Analog Data** (ref. MONITOR, INTEGRATE, ACT appropriately within the IoT Environment)—whereby the natural and physical world is/are fully/densely instrumented plus appropriately connected for DISTRIBUTED INTELLIGENCE;
2. **Perpetual Connectivity** (ref. MONITOR, INTEGRATE, ACT)—IoT is always connected, system is always on and working. Likewise problems are self-reported, and fixes are pushed automatically, maintenance is semi-automatic—upgrades, fixes pushed instantly as needed, plus keep/motivate everyone informed—that is keep people/employees/users in the design/build/operation loop(s)—and thus create IoT devices with solution space(s) that are closely matched to problem space(s);
3. **Really Real-Time** (ref. MONITOR, INTEGRATE, ACT)—for IoT real-time actually begins back at the IoT Thing itself—at the sensor or the moment the data is acquired—ergo we blend the world of operational technology (OT), sensors, and data measurement with the world of IT;
4. **Immediacy Versus Depth** (ref. MONITOR, INTEGRATE, ACT)—there is always a trade-off between speed and depth; but it is better (in general) to compute everything at the first instant that it can be—and so to push data processing to the edge (see point 5);
5. **Compute shift to Data Source** (ref. MONITOR, INTEGRATE, ACT)—compute moves ***closer to the source of data***; we wish to avoid transferring large amounts of unnecessary data around the IOT system – but rather to send small, narrowly focussed data sets on a just-in-time basis (see point 6 below);
6. **The Next 'V'** (ref. MONITOR, INTEGRATE, ACT)—Big data is commonly characterised by the infamous "V's"— Volume, Velocity, Variety, and Value. With IOT there is a fifth "V"—**Visibility**. (Visibility refers to the benefit afforded by not having to transfer large amounts of data to remote people or locations). Ergo we have the concept of access to data and applications "***independent of time and place***". Mark Templeton, CEO of Citrix, adds a third independence: "***independence of device***".

The upshot of Tom's analysis of the rapidly evolving IoT field is that the IoT is driving a new set of five key design requirements:

- **Big Analog Data**—capture/process/act-on/report as much relevant data as possible—in relation to relevant problem/solution spaces;
- **Perpetual Connectivity**—core activities / services are never interrupted;
- **Real time reporting/control/action**—appropriate data-processing / data-aggregation, leading to optimal problem resolution as required;
- **Visibility of Services**—instrumented objects have real-time visibility system-wide; henceforth distributed computing is enabled;
- **Objects self-manage/self-analyse/self-report**—autonomous operations with escalation (to central/distributed control node(s)).

Ergo, the Internet of Things (IOT) is a nexus of devices and services that allow for data exchange and appropriate data-analysis/data-processing no matter where the end-user (human and/or machine) may be located. The author calls this '**Situated Intelligence**'—whereby a smart device knows WHO/ WHAT needs WHICH capability WHERE, WHEN and HOW. Note that the Who/What (the requesting actor), Which (requested data/capability), When (normally ASAP) are normally known—and all that remains is WHERE AND HOW.

Henceforth, by means of a detailed ontological analysis—we have defined in general terms what the IoT subject area is all about. In other words we have specified all of the key features (that is goal-specific aims) that comprise this unique and complex domain of computing/instrumented technology. It only remains for us to delve into the identified areas in greater detail—and in order to see how these elements are built into real-world IoT systems and instrumented environments etc.

Why not join us now—as we embark on a fascinating journey into these topics in the hope of discovering in detail what the future world of IoT will be like.

Situated Intelligence

IF WE ARE to establish a new Science Of IoT, then it is vitally important to be certain that we are founding—or building—upon a firm substructure. In normal scientific language, the foundation, or basis of any argument is named as the hypothesis, and is often a subject's supposition, or primary subject-matter.

In this respect, and in order to provide a focus for detailed analysis of IoT subject matter; we hereby provide a comprehensive definition for: **Situated Intelligence**. This new concept of Situated Intelligence is closely associated with the concept of Distributed Intelligence; and both should be considered twin sides of the same coin; namely constructive application of AI to the IoT problem space.

Situated Intelligence is when we have embedded Intelligence and Connectivity **into the environment in useful ways**. The result is a real-world object/system that gains the ability to sense, calculate, process and decide in relation to a specific class of problem-space; whereby aspects of the world (aka Things) suddenly 'wakeup' and begin engaging and interacting with people—and the environment—in a highly useful manner.

Situated Intelligence is what the IOT is all about—namely providing enhanced problem solving capabilities: including solution **AUTONOMY** (task replacement/management) and solution **VISIBILITY** (task awareness) with respect to **Smart Things**—or instrumented Devices, Systems and People—located at **singular geographic LOCATIONS** (specific IoT environments).

However, before we can attempt to discuss Situated Intelligence and what an IoT Science is, could or should be; we must first establish a clear concept of our primary subject matter. Henceforth we ask—what is the nature—and purpose—of the **Smart Things** that are spoken of specifically in relation to the IoT?

In order to find the answer, we must first consider the nature of technology—asking what it is—and where does it come from?

Nature of Technology

Noted technology experts and historians of science have given many and varied explanations of what technology actually is—and in terms of its most essential components/attributes – whereby they have attempted to define its most fundamental purpose or nature. Many have asked related questions—such as—why and how does a technology come to be?

In this respect, some people ascribe to an evolutionary theory—whereby new technologies are said to gradually evolve (semi-automatically?) from past developments, bolstered by improving human knowledge and manufacturing capabilities etc. Other commentators have stressed the key role that an inventor has to play in such a process.

Patently new technologies evolve or develop and they do become more sophisticated over time—and thus are rendered capable of—that is they enable—more complex capabilities as civilisation moves ahead. Typically newer technologies are comprised of combinations and assemblies of other (often older) technologies.

Technologies tend to appear as 'bundles' of other technologies—whereby one technology —over time—tends to becomes an atomic element—or component—inside another larger and more complex technology (in terms of both constructive elements and solution capabilities). In this way newer technologies 'consume' and are comprised of older ones.

This 'bundling' and evolution of technologies is not always the case (for example the hammer has remained relatively constant throughout time—a wooden handle attached to a heavy stone or metal head). But often it is true that before a new technology emerges—that one or more older technologies which must have previously come onto the scene. For example, in order to develop the computer, human kind had to develop countless thousands of other technologies such as binary mathematics, manufacturing techniques for exotic materials such as silicon, transistors, microchips and microprocessors, plus memory chips etc.

Patently when we speak of the Internet of Things (IoT)—we are dealing with a vast number and range of different technology types, components and complex assemblies of sub-technologies; which are brought together for a huge variety of different reasons. But if this is so—what if anything—do all of these IoT technologies have in common?

It is salient to examine what are reasons behind the development of the IoT as a topic in the first place—and so to ask—what is the purpose of the IoT?

IoT Purposes

We shall not examine—or argue—about how technologies come into being; but rather our focus shall be on the underlying goals/purposes of technology and how they can be achieved. What we are considering here, are the psychic, mental and sociological consequences of technology as it pertains to our individual and collective problem solving capabilities.

In other words, how does a technology **amplify** and/or **accelerate** existing human-managed processes (mental and physical); plus **enable** and/or **extend** new examples of the same.

Henceforth, the purposes of technology are to:

1. **Amplify / accelerate** a state-of-affairs.
2. **Enable** a state-of-affairs.
3. **Extend** a state-of-affairs.

Whereby we define the meaning of a state-of-affairs to be a mental and/or physical state/process and/or product outcomes. One could say that the improved state-of-affairs relates to enhanced problem solving ability as detailed in the list of service aspects below.

Problem solving ability enhancement (service provision):

1. **Efficient service** = faster workflows—timescale of task completion (pace).
2. **Magnified service** = effective workflows—greater impact of task (scale).
3. **Reliable service** = measurable workflows (reduced task uncertainty).
4. **Safe service** = secure workflows—no negative consequences of task (safety).
5. **Automated service** = automatic workflows (reduced human supervision).
6. **Economical service** = cost-effective workflows (energy, environmental impact).

Henceforth, and put simply, the key attribute that a good or useful technology has—is that it produces a **change of scale** or **pace**, and/or **enables a new pattern** that is introduced into human affairs such as improved processes and/or enhanced knowledge (ref. mental and/or physical procedures etc). Technology accelerates and enlarges the scale of previous human functions, creating totally new kinds of cities and new kinds of work and leisure.

Put simply, here we shall define an IoT technology as something which enhances the efficiency and/or effectiveness of human problem solving capabilities.

All in all, and to be practically useful, the application of any useful technology must surpass the alternative(s) in one or more of the aforementioned respects; wherein the technology itself affords the solution of one or problems according to a set of task-specific efficiency factors.

Ergo, problems that may be solved by a properly applied IoT technology are:

1. **Pace:** Results achieved in a shorter timespan (pace);
2. **Scale:** Results achieved on new scales (physical/geographic);
3. **Pattern:** New patterns are imbued into human affairs (mental/spatial/procedural);
4. **Energy:** One or more of above are achieved with less effort/energy.

Goals, Intentions and Actions

A human-made Thing (Object/Tool/System/Machine)—constitutes a kind of extension of the human being, a manifestation of his physical, mental and psychical constitution.

In relation to the Internet Of Things or IoT we are normally speaking of a Thing that has been designed to provide a practical problem solving capability to one or more human beings—that is to get something done or else to perform useful Actions in the real-world. In other words we are talking of a technology that is created with a specific goal in mind; that is; the technology or Thing has a design purpose.

Often we can speak of the human as a tool-user who works in combination with the Thing or technology to achieve a specific goal or real-world state-of-affairs. This is achieved by means of an appropriate problem-solution model. Whereby we must start with some notion of what is wanted—and thus adequately define the Goal to be achieved. Next in order to meet a particular Goal any 'helper' Thing/Actor must interact with the world in such a manner as to foster its attainment (either autonomously or with human supervision).

We can speak of 4 different aspects of goal-achievement to consider:

1. **Goal:** The Goal (what we want to happen in the real world);
2. **Action:** What is done in the World (the Action);
3. **World:** How it affects the outcome—possibly external to model;
4. **Evaluate**: Check of the World.

Luckily famous design guru Dr Donald Norman has made an exhaustive study of the nature of Goals and how Things may be designed for efficient purposes (see his book 'The Design Of Everyday Things').

Donald has discovered that the Action has two aspects:

- **Execution**: What we do to the World.
- **Evaluation**: Comparing what happened with what we wanted to happen.

But real tasks are not so simple, because the original goal may be imprecisely specified, perhaps just 'clean up the front-room' is the top level goal—whereupon the Actor (a human or robot Hoover) must navigate a complex and changing world that is full of many obstacles and (potentially) blocking processes etc.

Goals do not expressly state what to do—or how to do it. In order to lead to appropriate action a goal must be transformed into specific statements of what is to be done—and Donald calls these **intentions.** An intention is a specific action taken to get to the goal.

Seven Stages of Action

Yet even intentions are not specific enough to control actions in such a manner as to successfully meet a goal. In fact there are seven stages of action that must be performed to achieve a Goal as follows:

- Forming the Goal
- Forming the Intention
- Specifying the Action
- Executing the Action
- Perceiving the State of the World
- Interpreting the State of the World
- Evaluating the Outcome

These 7 stages form a problem-solution model of how to act to achieve a solution to a particular problem that needs to be solved; however the stages are almost certainly not discrete entities; and most behaviour does not require going through all stages in sequence (on every occasion).

Most activities will not be satisfied by a single action (for example). There must be numerous sequences, and the top-level activities could last hours or even days (for example). There is a continual feedback loop—in which the results of one activity are used to direct further ones; in which goals lead to subgoals, intentions and sub-intentions etc. Likewise there are activities in which goals are forgotten, discarded or super-seeded.

In conclusion, Norman's analysis is highly illuminating—and because it draws our attention to key aspects of problem solving as a process which is fraught with difficulty that arises from basically 2 sources. Once a Goal is identified—firstly we have the problem of specifying and **executing** the supposed intentions and actions that may lead to problem solution; but secondly we have the problem of **evaluating** the results of actions. In any case, everything is dependant upon adequate specification of the problem context.

Problem Context

As stated the IoT is concerned with solving real-world problems—or (typically) with physical action aimed at the achievement of practical goals. Now with respect to the kinds of problems that arise in the physical world—a **problem context** has three aspects:

- **VISIBILITY—task awareness (problem/goal/solution specification)**—create a visible mapping between the problem and solution space(s); form goal/intention/action facets accurately and precisely;
- **LOCATION—task enhancement (resource allocation)**—deal with constraints of location: perform key functions at a single or distributed location(s) and at the correct magnitude/scale and/or at specific multiple(s) of the same;
- **AUTONOMY—task replacement (resource management)**—deal with system control/management/power overheads: autonomously or with an element of external support.

Now all three aspects of the problem context will involve specific challenges in terms of solution design and execution, and once again Donald Norman has indicated key aspects of a useful model.

Gulf of Evaluation and Gulf of Execution

In actual fact the world is a vast living process; and to be successful any Actor must constantly asses and re-sasses changing requirements—of essentially a constantly new situation.

One way of accurately modelling the world including all of this complexity/uncertainty is to admit, right away, that the difficulty arises in deriving the relationships between desired intentions and interpretations of the physical actions and states. There are several **gulfs** that separate modelling (or mental) states from physical ones —and these are to be avoided in the design of Things that are to be used by humans and/or that operate automatically on behalf of humans.

Firstly we have the **Gulf of Execution—**which asks—does the system provide actions that correspond to the Goal? The difference between intentions and the allowable actions is the Gulf of Execution. One measure of this gulf is how well the system allows the Actor to do the intended actions directly, without extra effort.

Secondly we have the **Gulf of Evaluation—**which asks—does the system provide a physical representation that can be directly perceived and that is directly interpretable in terms of the intentions and expectations of the Actor. The Gulf of Evaluation reflects the amount of effort that the Actor must exert to interpret the physical state of the system and to determine how well intentions have been met.

Now the Actor in question may be a human being operating a Thing—or the Actor (or Human) may be an automated Thing acting alone—or a combination of the two. Henceforth, these Gulfs of—Execution and Evaluation—will vary according to the **problem context—**and also with respect to the **solution design** (the problem solving Actor's status and capability etc).

Solution Design: Classes of Action

Patently once we have specified the problem context sufficiently, we must turn our attention to solution design.

Now when considering the 7 stages of goal achievement; one would expect that the human designer of a Thing would normally play a large part in specifying the Goal, Intention(s) and appropriate Action(s) to attain the same. However when speaking of an IoT system we are typically concerned with imbuing the Thing (essentially a man-made Actor) with a certain degree of intelligence and hence decision making plus self-automation with respect to the problem-solution process. Essentially this is a procedure that necessarily involves embedding a computer chip into the object to foster the same.

Perhaps the key attribute of a computer is that it can be programmed to perform a wide range of complex and highly specific tasks—and so to solve problems with a high degree of precision and accuracy.

It is salient therefore to examine human-made Things in terms of the key concept of programability; whereby the OED defines program as: "A definite plan or scheme of any intended proceedings; an outline or plan of something to be done… and as.. a sequence of objects, scenes, or events intended… a finally—a sequence of operations that a machine can be set to perform automatically."

Henceforth, IoT objects/systems can be split into four kinds – according to the particular type of programmability enabled (or active capability), as follows:

- **INERT THING—Controlled Action:** provides particular functional abilities with respect to a specific context of use; an Inert Thing has no self-generated power of action, motion, or resistance; must be operated under external power and/or control; whereby such a device has no decision making ability whatsoever;
- **AUTOMATED THING—Automated Action = sensing/action/feedback loop (fixed problem-solution model):** always responds to the environment in terms of a fixed pattern of predetermined behaviours according to specific pattern of events; reactive in nature and has purely ***reflexive decision making*** (may be internally powered by some means);
- **PROGRAMMABLE THING—Programmable Action = sensing/action/feedback loop (programmable problem-solution model):** responds to the environment in an appropriate way given a particular scenario; has ***pre-programmed decision making***;
- **INTELLIGENT THING—Intelligent Action = sensing/action/feedback loop (adaptive problem-solution model):** responds to the environment in an intelligent manner; has an ability to consider a range of options and/or allows for a scope of future 'possibilities' to be taken into account; can to adapt its own programming to new situations via learning behaviours; whereby said device has has ***pro-active decision making***.

Now an IoT object will be not merely intelligent in terms of Actions provided; but will be capable of remote operation, environmental sensing, environmental integration and henceforth remote communication over a communication network etc: thus often connectivity will be provided to support associated functionality (e.g. Internet, WAN, LAN, WiFi, Bluetooth, Radio connectivity etc);

IoT Thing/Object – connectivity types are as follows:

- **CONTROL CONNECTIVITY** (Remote access/control/programming capability)
- **MONITORING CONNECTIVITY** (Environmental sensing data)
- **INTEGRATION CONNECTIVITY** (Collaborative operation data)
- **HOUSEKEEPING CONNECTIVITY** (System status reporting data)

Plus the IoT object may be connected to environmental sensors (cameras, movement sensors etc) which may be provided and integrated into the overall IoT object/system (locally and/or remotely).

Now the IoT is concerned largely with **Automated**, **Programmable** and **Intelligent Actions**—and henceforth with respect to the aforementioned types of Things; each of which effectively prolong human problem solving abilities in the described ways. However when considering a solution space—programmability of Action is not the only dimension of interest; because as previously stated we are concerned also with the specific **problem context** in which said Action takes place (and associated intelligent responses).

Situated Intelligence

As stated, the problem context has 3 aspects: **Visibility**, **Location** and **Autonomy**; whereby we can define a solution in terms of **Situational Intelligence—**which encapsulates a Thing's combined ability to provide a solution within a specific context; or in other words to: sense, cooperate, process/model, calculate, decide, plus act upon environmental data etc;

- SITUATIONAL INTELLIGENCE is defined as the ability of an IoT Thing/System to provide the following functional qualities (problem solving facets):
- **MONITOR** (ENVIRONMENTAL SENSING): degree to which an IoT object/system usefully *SENSES* data in relation to the environment;
- **INTEGRATE** (PEOPLE, THINGS, SERVICES): degree to which an IoT object/system *COOPERATES* usefully with the environment;
- **ACT** (MODEL, REPORT, CONTROL): degree to which an IoT object/system *INTERACTS* usefully with the environment.

Our new theory of IoT is grounded on a set of core principles, including for example the IoT Situated Intelligence (IOTSI) diagram (see below).

The IOTSI diagram teaches that in order for an IoT THING (or IoT Element)—existing within an IOT Environment—to provide a problem-solving capability in relation to a particular GOAL —then that same IoT THING must possess SITUATED INTELLIGENCE comprising a means of MONITORING, INTEGRATING and ACTING appropriately within said IoT Environment.

The IoT Environment Consists of People, Things and Services

The GOAL of an IoT SYSTEM (often comprising multiple connected IoT Elements) is to sense/know: Who/What needs Which capability, When, Where and How within this IoT Environment—and hence to provide the same. Whereby the IoT SYSTEM affords problem solving capabilities as follows: AUTONOMY (task replacement) plus VISIBILITY (task awareness) at a particular LOCATION (task enhancement). The IOTSA diagram indicates how a set of external GOALS (ref. MONITOR, INTEGRATE, ACT) are met using resources available to the IoT SYSTEM.

Patently an IoT System typically consists of a network of communicating IoT THING(S), the same 'intelligent' items connected together on a computer network; and each being capable of independently programmable yet coordinated behaviours, whereby SITUATED INTELLIGENCE is applied to meet the overall GOAL(s) of said IoT SYSTEM. Henceforth, SITUATED INTELLIGENCE refers to an IoT

Figure 3. Situated Intelligence

THING and/or group of IoT THINGS (an IoT SYSTEM) providing—and/or contributing to—an appropriate problem solving capability – aligned with one or more GOAL(S) (plus associated Tasks) – at a required geographical location and/or across a distributed set of geographical location(s).

The IOTSA diagram indicates how a set of system-wide Goals (ref. MONITOR, INTEGRATE, ACT) are met using resources available to the IoT System. Patently an IoT System typically consists of a network of communicating IoT Things, the same 'intelligent' items being connected together on a computer network; and each one is capable of independently programmable yet coordinated behaviours, whereby Situated Intelligence is applied to meet the goal(s) of said IoT System.

Situated Intelligence is what the IOT is all about—namely providing enhanced problem solving capabilities: including solution AUTONOMY (task replacement) and solution VISIBILITY (task awareness) with respect to Things—instrumented Devices, Systems and People—located at disparate geographic LOCATIONS.

Ergo, the Internet of Things (IOT) is a nexus of devices and services that allow for data exchange no matter where the end-user (human and/or machine) may be located. The author calls this 'Situated Intelligence"—whereby a smart device knows WHO/WHAT needs WHICH capability WHERE, WHEN and HOW. Note that the Who/What (the requesting actor), Which (requested data/capability), When (normally ASAP) are normally known—and all that remains is WHERE AND HOW.

Problem Solving Ability

Notice that the concept of **Situational Intelligence** (aka Smartness) strongly relates to the concept of usefulness—here defined as the ability or quality to bring about good, advantage or benefit in a particular situational context; whereby a Thing possesses appropriate functional qualities that relate to a specific purpose; whereby said object is serviceable to achieve a particular Goal.

Importantly Situational Intelligence (SI) relates to the purpose or Goal for which an IoT system has been designed or is being applied/used for a specific practical function. Whereby the Thing normally also presents itself as a summing-up, of said functionality; and has external (operative) aspects plus internal operational aspects.

An object imbued with Situated Intelligence possesses an ACTIVE aspect—which:

- **POTENTIATES** (enables new capabilities—automation): Extends Operative Faculty of Human(s)
- **PROLONGS** (current capabilities—available at new locations): Enhances Operative Faculty of Human(s)
- **MAGNIFIES** (human powers—at new scale(s) etc): Amplifies Operative Faculty of Human(s)

Situated Intelligence is when we have embedded **Intelligence** and **Connectivity** into the environment in useful ways. The result is a real-world object/system that gains the ability to calculate, process and decide in relation to a specific class of problem-space; whereby aspects of the world suddenly 'wakeup' and begin looking-at and interacting with the environment in a highly useful manner.

The upshot is that each IOT Thing is imbued with **situated intelligence** for a distinct context-of-use. The result being—a sophisticated problem solving capability— that inherently includes both **geographical and/or contextual knowledge** plus an ability to perform targeted **context-relevant actions** etc.

A **Smart Thing** is an object can **sense** (Monitor) and **actuate/react** (Act) plus **engage** with objects/states/processes (Integrate) with respect to its environment (consisting of other People, Things/Systems [smart or stand-alone], and Services etc). In order to **interact** with its environment—in a useful/helpful manner—a Smart Thing must adequately **interpret** and **securely process** the information it collects, whilst protecting itself (and humans) from from threats and intrusions, plus communicating the results to other smart objects, people and systems while at the same time managing its own power consumption.

And it may be that the instrumented—or computerised/networked—elements of an IoT System and/or IoT Thing recede into the background of life. Whereupon we will have IoT Things scattered about – and these intelligent Things just know what they should be doing at any moment in time—and they just solve problems that arise of their own volition.

In other words, and as we stated earlier, IoT Things and Systems: Amplify, Enable and Extend human problem solving abilities. But the question remains as to how we should design an IoT System to adequately recognise and analyse problems, and to calculate, network and create/change a situation towards positive ends.

In other words, how do we design quality of service into the IoT?

Quality of Service

An IoT Thing (or IoT System) is designed to provide a real-world problem solving capability – a goal which often relates directly to an embodied place—or **situational context—**in the physical world. **Location** (X,Y,Z position), **scale** (physical dimensions—size) and **responsiveness (temporal scale)** are three key attributes in this respect.

Firstly in terms of **location**, individual IOT devices would typically be geographically located very close to the point at which the problem manifests—in situ—so-to-speak (or at least the IoT device would be able to remotely sense desired remote and/or extensive/pinpointed regions of the environment). In other words both problem solving **recognition** (monitoring facets) and problem solving **means** (solution facets) are tied closely together (i.e are either adjacent geographically, contextually coupled, and/or linked together by means of a network system).

Secondly, the issue of **scale** is crucial to the modern IoT vision—whereby the **situated intelligence—**or problem solving capability—is applied at the correct spatial size, and/or temporal timespan, plus at the correct magnitude (e.g. number of locations).

In terms of magnitude, we may have large numbers of connected objects scattered about the environment on tiny or large scales (for example). Some examples in this respect are street lighting control systems, wind farm turbines with individual adjustments, cellular pressure sensors, multiple heating elements, groups of sensors etc. Thirdly, the issue of temporal scale (typically including system responsiveness) is a vital aspect; whereby the problem solution should normally be provided within an adequate—or minimum— timescale.

Henceforth, as stated earlier, the key attribute that a good or useful IoT system has—is that it produces a **change of scale** or **pace**, and/or **enables a new pattern** that is introduced into human affairs such as improved processes/knowledge (mental and/or physical procedures etc).

Ergo, the IoT service would allow task-specific problem solution benefits as follows:

1. **Pace:** Results achieved in a shorter timespan (pace);
2. **Scale:** Results achieved on new scales (physical/geographic);
3. **Pattern:** New patterns are imbued into human affairs (mental/spatial/procedural);
4. **Energy**: One or more of above are achieved with less effort/energy.

In summary, we can measure the quality of service provision—for an IoT Service/Thing—by examination of how well the system provides and/or enables specific task-completion benefits—which carry over productively to the wider system Goal(s).

Henceforth, the productivity of an IoT System can be established and measured using generalised **Quality of Service** factors for an IoT System follows:

1. **Efficient service** = faster workflows—reduced timescale of task (pace).
2. **Magnified service** = effective workflows—greater impact of task (scale).
3. **Reliable service** = accurate and reliable service (predictable results).
4. **Safe Service** = secure workflows—free from negative consequences (safety).
5. **Automated service** = efficient workflows (reduced supervision of task).
6. **Economical service** = cost-effective workflows (energy, environment impact).

Situated Intelligence: Key Factors to Consider

A new world of Programmable Things is on the horizon; whereby objects/systems are designed to possess embedded intelligence and connectivity—and henceforth an ability to calculate, process and analyse sensed information—whereby they can decide what form to adopt, plus functions and actions to exhibit or act; and in order to achieve a specified Goal.

In this section we have examined salient features of a generalised IoT system; whereby we have demonstrated how a particular IoT problem context is matched to its specific IoT solution space using the new concept of **Situated Intelligence**.

Along the way we have identified 3 key aspects that all problem context(s) have in common; namely: **Visibility**, **Location** and **Autonomy** of problem context. Plus we have described 4 classes of IoT Things (**Inert**, **Automated**, **Programable** and **Intelligent**) that may be employed to address said problem contextual aspects. Finally we have delineated 3 functional problem solving capabilities; namely the ability to: **Monitor**, **Integrate** and **Act** appropriately within the IoT environment.

In sum, it is hoped that this new analytical framework can enable a close mapping between problem and solution spaces—leading to IoT System designs that perform optimally and in predictable ways. All in all, we have demonstrated how a set of generalised **Quality Of Service** factors can be used to ensure that the IoT System is designed and built to meet operational requirements in full.

Distributed Intelligence

IN ORDER TO provide a focus for detailed analysis of IoT subject matter; we hereby provide a comprehensive definition for: **Distributed Intelligence**. This new concept of Distributed Intelligence is closely associated with the related concept of **Situated Intelligence;** and both should be considered twin sides of the same coin; namely constructive application of AI to the IoT problem space.

Distributed Intelligence is when we have embedded **Intelligence** and **Connectivity across the environment in useful ways**. In other words it is recognised by a spatial distribution of computing resources/elements. Whereby the problem-solving capability is supplied by several networked IoT objects/systems; and so benefits from expansive knowledge of the same problem-space, whilst typically engaging multiple computing elements (sensing/processing/active capacities) towards an extended geographical region.

Distributed Intelligence (plus Situated Intelligence) is what the IOT is all about—namely providing enhanced problem solving capabilities: including solution **AUTONOMY** (task replacement/management) and solution **VISIBILITY** (task awareness) with respect to **Smart Things**—or instrumented Devices, Systems and People—located at disparate geographic **LOCATIONS** (within and across IoT environments).

Here in this section, we explain those particular advantages that may be supplied by a Distributed Intelligence: specifically in relation to the provision of an enhanced problem solving capability.

Problem Context

Distributed Intelligence is defined as the ability of an IoT Thing/System to provide the following functional qualities (problem solving facets):

- **MONITOR** (ENVIRONMENTAL SENSING): degree to which an IoT object/system usefully *SENSES* data within and/or across the ***IoT environment*;**
- **INTEGRATE** (PEOPLE, THINGS, SERVICES): degree to which an IoT object/system *COOPERATES* usefully within and/or across the ***IOT environment*;**
- **ACT** (MODEL, REPORT, CONTROL): degree to which an IoT object/system
- *INTERACTS* usefully within and/or across the ***IOT environment***.

Note the important definition change for Distributed Intelligence, as opposed to the related concept of Situated Intelligence; whereby we have replaced the term: "within the Environment"; with the term: "within and/or across the Environment".

As stated, Distributed Intelligence is when we have embedded **Intelligence** and **Connectivity** across the the environment in useful ways. The result is a real-world object/system that gains the ability to **calculate**, **process** and **decide** in relation to a specific class of problem-space; whereby aspects of the world suddenly 'wakeup' and begin looking-at and interacting with "extended and/or geographically remote" aspects of the environment in a highly useful manner.

Distributed Logic

Distributed Intelligence (Distributed Artificial Intelligence)—or Multi-Agent systems—refers to systems which employ "distributed logic"; whereby we separate the processing from a large problem space into multiple subsystems or extract certain processing functions from the main system and place them into separate machines and/or at geographically separated computing 'nodes'.

Systems built to exploit and/or employ Distributed Intelligence consist of **autonomous learning** plus **autonomous processing nodes** (or agents). Said nodes are distributed widely across the environment, often at a very large scale (i.e. large numbers of nodes are deployed and/or we have these nodes separated by large distances). Whereby these nodes can act independently and partial solutions are provided and integrated by communication between nodes, often asynchronously.

By virtue of their scale, systems using Distributed Intelligence are **robust** and **elastic**, and by design, **loosely coupled**. Furthermore, DAI systems are built to be adaptive to changes in the problem definition (problem space) and/or built to be adaptive to changes (possibly structural) within underlying data sets (often due to the scale of deployment and/or difficulty in redeployment etc).

In summary, Distributed Intelligence provides:

- Autonomous processing / learning
- Enhanced coordination of problem / solution space(s)
- Reduced central dependancies (no data bottlenecks)
- Adaptive problem solving / flexible to problem re-definition
- Independent and locally optimised actions
- Robust / independent: data processing pipelines
- Elastic / non-brittle: logic dependancies
- Faster and localised responses to the environment
- Live command and control sequences (updates)
- Loosely coupled nodes / asynchronous computing

A key advantage of distributed systems is that they do not require all the relevant data to be aggregated to a single location (aka the Cloud / central server), in contrast to monolithic or centralised Artificial Intelligence systems which have tightly coupled and geographically close processing nodes.

In summary, distributed systems often operate (beneficially) on sub-samples or hashed impressions of very large datasets. Faster, more robust and elastic computing solutions are the case; whereby logical conundrums do not cause the whole system logic to halt. In addition, the source dataset may change and/or be updated during the course of the execution of the overall (distributed) data processing system.

Goals

A key objective of Distributed Intelligence is to solve the **reasoning**, **planning**, **learning** and **perception problems** of artificial intelligence. Whereby a distributed approach is especially useful when dealing with large data sets and/or big analogue data, and because the data-processing problem can be tackled efficiently by distributing the problem to autonomous processing nodes (agents).

Advantages of a Distributed System may include:

- **Robust and elastic computation**: Data processing (system-wide) continues regardless of unreliable and failing resources due to loose coupling of nodes;
- **Enhanced coordination:** Coordination of the actions and communication of the nodes—leading to optimal problem solutions that can solve the big-picture problem with utmost efficiency;
- **Multi-tasking**: processing of many subsamples continue simultaneously on large data sets, leading to faster processing overall; plus on-line machine learning provides for sharing of intelligence amongst nodes.

In terms of any particular usage scenario; there can be many reasons for wanting to distribute intelligence; whereby the following may apply:

- **Parallel problem solving**: deals with how classic artificial intelligence concepts can be modified, so that multi-processor systems and clusters of computers can be used to speed-up analysis / calculation and/or to render more effective (impactful) machine logic.
- **Distributed problem solving**: refers to multi-agent systems that work together to solve a large-scale problem like collaborating insects, and/or to autonomous entities that can communicate to foster a coordinated approach to problem solution. This approach lends itself to problem abstraction whereby a central commanding node can rely on multiple sub-nodes to solve localised problems optimally in terms of the overall problem space.
- **Multi-agent simulation**: a branch of computing that builds the foundation for simulations that need to analyze not only phenomena at **macro-level** but also at **micro-level**, as is the case in many social simulation scenarios.

Two classic approaches to distributed computing are as follows:

- **Multi-Agent Systems**: coordinate their knowledge and activities and reason about the processes and results of coordination. Whereby agents are physical or virtual entities that can act, perceive and communicate with other agents. Each agent is semi-autonomous and has skills/knowledge to achieve certain goals (the overall focus here may be on solution of either local and/or global tasks—or both). Whereby each agent can adjust its programming and/or goals and/or implemented logic—as a result of information received from the other nodes present in the network (solution coordination).

- **Distributed Problem Solving**: In a distributed problem solving computing system, the tasks are divided among nodes and the knowledge is shared (typically each node is concerned with only with a specific set of local tasks—whereby said local tasks are coordinated or set externally to the network of nodes by macro-level problem division). The main issues here relate to task decomposition and synthesis of the data-gathering, knowledge and solutions.

The upshot of both approaches is that we can apply a **bottom-up approach** to AI and problem solution, whereby a subsumption architecture can be applied to the problem space; as well as the traditional **top-down approach** of AI.

In addition, both methods can become a vehicle for **emergence behaviours** in which the problem space is tackled using an emergent type algorithm. In essence an emergent algorithm provides a set of simple *building block* behaviours that when combined exhibit more complex behaviours. One example of this is the implementation of fuzzy-logic motion controllers which are used to (for example) adapt robot movement in response to environmental obstacles and/or otherwise be applied to solve issues related to massive environmental complexity and/or constantly varying 3D problems and/or varied environments.

Coordination Age

The world is entering a new age of programmable and connected Things. Some experts have called this the **Coordination Age**, which is being driven by a growing need for resource efficiency—irrespective of service user/delivery location(s)—and enabled by next generation 5G networks, AI, SDNs and the IoT.

To release the benefits of the Coordination Age, all manner of intelligent "things" will need to be able to discover each other, communicate autonomously, collaborate, and then self-decide plus self-act to solve problems with new vigour. Accordingly, Industry 4.0 must dramatically improve the efficiency of resource utilisation, arising from a combination of developments in the demand and supply of services.

Evidently – problem and solution space – *coordination* is the key job that needs to be done across many market areas. People, Things and Services need to be brought together at the right time and in the right place to deliver the desired outcome.

Forces driving coordination include:

- **SMART HOME**: devices, sensors, appliances and applications created by many different companies need to be coordinated into an easy-to-manage solution for consumers (key requirements: enhanced **solution INTEROPERABILITY** and **high SYSTEM RESPONSIVENESS** enabled by the plug-and-play IoT plus situated intelligence capabilities);
- **SMART ENERGY**: to manage the generation, storage and delivery of power (e.g solar/wind energy) across highly complex, disparate and sometimes international supply chains (key requirements: **optimised solution OPERATIONAL FACETS** provided by the efficient real-time optimisation of network operational and maintenance tasks: requires tailored and aggregated generation/storage/delivery facets and efficient use of communication and power transportation/delivery networks [M2M, M2H and H2M systems] – and all provided by distributed / situated intelligence);

- **SMART HEALTHCARE**: clinicians, patients, treatments, resources and information need to be coordinated for successful healthcare outcomes (key requirements: **highest service RELIABILITY/RESPONSIVENESS** plus **comprehensive SECURITY FRAMEWORK** delivered with full **solution INTEGRATION** (distributed intelligence) and **real-time sharing of resources** [i.e. intelligence + command/control aspects are plug-and-play also]);
- **SMART TRANSPORT**: manage transport flows for both public and private transportation, to ensure the best use of available resources and where to direct investment most effectively (key requirements: **DISTRIBUTED LOGIC SOLUTION** providing **comprehensive transportation management capability** provided by macro-level understanding of micro-level happenings (distributed intelligence): large scale sensor networks adapt themselves to local problem-spaces and report using real-time service data aggregation at the correct granularity);
- **SMART LOGISTICS**: to manage the distribution and delivery of stock and produced goods across highly complex, international supply chains (key requirements: **optimised solution OPERATIONAL FACETS** provided by the efficient real-time tracking of consignments and tailored packaging/transportation and just-in-time networks [M2M, M2H and H2M navigation systems] – and all provided by distributed / situated intelligence);
- **SMART INDUSTRY**: to ensure that manufacturing and supply-chain processes deliver, assemble and process goods and materials efficiently (key requirements: **optimised solution AUTOMATION** by enabling accurate, precise and cost-effective matching of problem and solution spaces – at the correct scale and place/time – whereby macro and micro problem-solution space views are closely matched, henceforth the solution employs a combination of situated and distributed intelligence).

The upshot is that we need new kinds of advanced plug-and-play IoT systems – and each one carefully designed and hence tailored specifically to its own specific purpose(s) and/or usage-scenario(s). Whereby we apply advanced Artificial Intelligence (situated and/or distributed intelligence) to automate, manage and accelerate solution delivery. Put simply, the Coordination Age is about improving what people and companies get for their time, money, effort and attention.

But there is a problem (or open secret) that limits the development of the Coordination Age; whereby there is something inherently wrong with the very idea of the IoT.

What is Wrong With the Internet of Things?

There's a problem with the current concept of the 'Internet of Things'; put simply: it isn't an internet. The IoT isn't even a continuous network, whereby it is severely limited in its capacity to operate efficiently, grow, evolve in intelligence and capability, and deliver the benefits that have been envisaged for it. Most current applications are in reality closed – and private – command and control solutions using standalone technology that is applied to limited application areas.

Oftentimes, a private network of IoT Things is the right solution – and especially to protect data privacy, security and to provide speed, low latency, and service reliability etc. However in order to make some of the most complex and dynamic applications work, specific sets of "things" (present within the problem/solution space), including not just sensors but also IT systems, will need to be able to find and communicate with each other autonomously (rapidly, efficiently and without low-level design work etc).

The upshot is that the world has an urgent requirement for a true Internet of Things (IoT) platform; which would provide: a combined SITUATIONAL INTELLIGENCE and DISTRIBUTED INTELLIGENCE that is defined as the ability of an IoT Thing/System to provide the following functional qualities (problem solving facets) – whereby these are supplied in a plug-and-play fashion (often on a private and/or secured network):

- **MONITOR** (ENVIRONMENTAL SENSING): degree to which an IoT object/system usefully *SENSES* data within/across the environment;
- **INTEGRATE** (PEOPLE, THINGS, SERVICES): degree to which an IoT object/system *COOPERATES* usefully within/across the environment;
- **ACT** (MODEL, REPORT, CONTROL): degree to which an IoT object/system *INTERACTS* usefully within/across the environment.

Advantages of an Internet FOR Things (I4T)

Another way of stating the problem is to say that we need an **Internet For Things (I4T)**; or in other words a broadly-applicable connectivity solution that is designed to allow Things to be connected and to interoperate with Plug-And-Play functionality. An Internet for Things would be a digital enabling fabric for wholly new levels of functionality, the same being of potentially great benefit to individuals, enterprises and our environment.

Potential advantages of I4T (sample):

- **COMBINATIONAL INTELLIGENCE**: An Internet for Things would allow data to be combined and enriched in previously inconceivable ways; by means of enhanced collaboration between seemingly unrelated IoT Systems – mashing up intelligence from different and seemingly unconnected sources for informational, security and commercial purposes.
- **CONTEXTUALISED INTELLIGENCE:** It would enable more meaningful machine to machine conversations. One device might offer enhanced functionality by deriving important contextual information from other communicable entities and/or devices in its environment.
- **SITUATED INTELLIGENCE:** A truly intelligent objects integrates with its whole environment – or its purpose – in a seamless manner (including all factors of relevance). For example, an in-building climate controller could offer more accurate control based on combined data from sources within its network, such as security devices and thermostats, plus external sources such as personal smartphones and smart watches, plus weather channels etc.
- **AUGMENTED INTELLIGENCE:** Intelligence should be (potentially at least) gathered and combined from everywhere and anywhere. It would trigger a quantum leap in the volume and quality of intelligence available to IoT Systems, Things, individuals and organisations. All kinds of "things" – buildings, vehicles, infrastructure elements, people – become **data points** and **data sources**, some static, some mobile, all contributing to a vast, accessible pool of crowd-sourced information (data sets may be public or private to a specific system/user).
- **DISTRIBUTED INTELLIGENCE:** It is the potential for the automatic collaboration via distributed intelligence capabilities – between Things when solving problems that makes the I4T a real game-changer. The potential of the Internet for Things – and related intelligence related

coordination factors – are emerging just as the world is facing massive challenges in terms of the use of its resources.

- **COLLECTIVE INTELLIGENCE**: is shared or group intelligence that emerges from the collaboration, collective efforts, and competition of many individuals and appears in consensus decision making. The related concept of **Cognitive City** is a term which expands the concept of the **Smart City** with the aspect of cognition or refers to a virtual environment where goal-driven communities gather to share knowledge. A physical cognitive city differs from conventional cities and smart cities in the fact that it is steadily learning through constant interaction with its citizens through advanced information and communication technologies –see work of E. Portmann (Portman, 2016).

Distributed Intelligence: Conclusions

In this paper we have examined salient features of IoT system design. Whereby we have demonstrated how a particular set of IoT problem space(s) can be optimally addressed – or closely matched (each one) – to its specific IoT solution space using the new concept(s) of **Combinational**, **Contextualised**, **Situated**, and **Augmented Intelligence(s);** plus **Distributed** and **Collective Intelligence**.

In sum, it is hoped that this new analytical framework can be a game-changer; in terms of the development of IoT systems that engender far more detailed, effective and tailored relations between IoT problem and solution space(s). The inevitable result will be IoT Systems that perform optimally and in predictable ways. All in all, we have demonstrated how a set of generalised **intelligence provision factors** can be used to ensure that IoT Systems are designed and built to meet operational requirements in full.

Synergetic Design and the IoT: Conclusions

In summary, a Synergetic System consists of certain natural phenomena programmed and orchestrated in an optimal fashion for some carefully considered purpose(s). We have explored how to apply the fundamental principles of Synergetic systems to a practical application: The Internet of Things (IoT). Put simply, we wished to learn how to blend the **physical**, **digital** and **biological spheres** in beneficial and optimal ways. Really what we have been talking about is how to build all of the capabilities of the computer into Things - rendering them with new abilities and so making them into Smart Things.

At first sight the computer, based as it is on logic and digital electronic circuits; appears to be a benevolent force in human society. This might reasonably be so for several reasons; and notably because they all contain identical components, implement similar plans, plus they are (in any case) designed by humans. However after delving a little deeper into the matter, one wishes that it were only so. Unfortunately computers everywhere are following dark and hidden agendas; for example spying on us, limiting and controlling actions, plus collecting/hoarding our personal data for nefarious/unknown purposes. And in the author's view, rather than making all forms of communication easier to achieve, computers routinely block the open and free exchange of ideas.

Therefore despite apparent advantages, computers are today— all too often—about restrictions, limitations and control. And so unlike the great thinker Dr Gottfried Leibniz (1646-1716), I cannot agree that we are living in the *best of all possible worlds. Au contraire*; because when it comes to modern computers, there is enormous room for improvement—and in terms of the capabilities, helpfulness, and ultimate purposes of information systems, and their corresponding influence(s) on humanity.

Goodfluence(s) / Badfluence(s) of Computers

Patently and obviously, computers (taken *en masse*) are too often—and in many ways—operating to the detriment of mankind. Despite undoubted effectiveness in specific areas, and convenience-of-use (sometimes) for tasks such as data processing, information retrieval and rapid communication; computers operate as a net ***badfluence*** with respect to the true needs, wishes and basic requirements of the vast majority of people in the world (evidence coming soon).

You may now be wondering; to which limitations do I refer? But instead of making a long list of the same here, I ask the reader to (briefly) accept that these same computer-related negative tendencies do, in fact, exist; and in anticipation of full explanation(s) to be given later-on. In this section, we put aside all consideration of machines as real-world entities, and skip-over issues related to the design, operation, and practical function(s) of computers.

Prior to discussing these applied aspects of computer systems; it is necessary to first understand what these machines actually are, in and of themselves. Accordingly, we ask: what are computers fundamentally? Do they posses an inherent nature? Can computers—in any sense—think? Do they self-evolve? Do they possess self-determination? Or are computers merely implementers of human desires/instructions?

Computers as Self

Philosophical questions of this kind may engender lack of focus. Therefore lest we forget our ultimate purpose, a brief reminder is useful. Desired here is clarity of vision with respect to the end-results of the computerisation of everything. In this regard, what seems most perplexing in the present year of 2020, is not only *how* computers have came to have negative effects for humanity as whole; but *why* human beings have allowed profoundly anti-humanistic policies and outcomes to occur in relation to computers (examples coming soon).

Are computers somehow evil—following dark and self- determined purposes? Or is there always a human designer—A WIZARD OF OZ—for example Steve Jobs (1955-2011) or Mark Zuckerberg (1984-)—behind all computer systems.

Do we blame the *megalomaniacs* or the *demonic machines*? As a foretaste of my thesis; it shall be my position that all the negative effects of computer systems stem from a poor understanding of what computers actually are; because they are not tools or independent entities, but, as I shall argue and demonstrate, an intimate and inseparable part of self.

Negative Aspects of Computers

Most of us prefer logical explanations, and so we begin by exploring the machine world. Once we fully understand the nature of computers, we can then consider the potential form(s) of those relationships that human beings can and do have vis-a- vi computers. In this respect, one assumes that computers could in no way surpass human understanding, and because they are human creations. But if computers are truly following negative agendas—what on earth is happening—and how? In coming chapters, we also ask: can/do computers—in any sense—make slaves of humans? If so, how can we prevent such outrages?

Firstly, my apologies to Artificial Intelligence (AI) fans, but I do not believe in machine: *intelligence, thought, free- will, motivations, self-determination, sentience or life!* I agree with Jaron Lanier (1960-) and class computers as: a mere artefact of human thought. It is not that I do not believe *per-se* in the possibility of any of type of machine based life/ consciousness; only that I do not believe it has happened yet —on earth—or else will happen here any time soon.

But others *do believe* in AI, and even in machine self- determination. Therefore we must consider such views carefully—because if these ideas do turn out to be true—then there will be profound implications for humanity.

A first approach is to consider computers as 'patterned' actionable machine-processes (without self-determination); that ultimately follow human instructed agendas. It logically follows that computers must necessarily, on the whole, have outcomes that turn out to be for the benefit of man—or at least the computer owners/programmers. One assumes that only a defective technology would fail to meet its original purpose; or else, when in error, its creators would simply shut it down.

As an aside, we do acknowledge the fact that technologies sometimes have unintended consequences. However we put aside any consideration of accidental negative outcomes (initially). Later on we do list examples of unexpected outcomes

Machine Autonomy

My purpose in this section is to introduce the reader to the interesting topics of machine autonomy/ thought/free-will. Human-designed artefacts are created for specific purposes, and one might expect any created semi-intelligent things to likewise respect or follow their designed purpose; and hence to do everything they can—within the design framework—to ensure that said purpose is achieved. Such simplistic (but infallible?) logic would appear to be self-evident.

But the corollary must be also true, that computers, if operating to the detriment of mankind (as a whole) must have been deliberately designed to harm. That is so unless we accept the other (opposite) viewpoint—that computers are somehow self- determining, and can follow anti-humanistic agendas by themselves, or else are capable of fulfilling their own specific purposes in some way (deliberately and/ or accidentally).

Questions of machine: *self-determination, evolution and independent decision-making*—are the focus of this chapter. In particular… Do computers control the functions/purposes of computers? OR—Do humans control the functions/purposes of computers? and… on which factors does the future of mankind depend?

The answer(s) will have major import for human destiny. Put in another way, we seek to identify:

- Evidence of self-determination for computers
- A process of intelligent self-design for computers

Computer Defined

Originally the term 'computer' referred to a human being who performed mathematical calculations, but such a meaning is no longer used. From our perspective, it is useful to begin with a modern definition of the term computer. A computer is a general purpose device that can be programmed to carry out a set of arithmetic or logical operations. Since a sequence of operations can be readily changed, the computer can solve more than one kind of problem. Conventionally, a computer consists of at least one processing element, typically a central processing unit (CPU) and some form of memory.

The processing element carries out arithmetic and logic operations, and contains a sequencing and control unit that can change the order of operations based on stored information. Peripheral devices allow information to be retrieved from an external source, and the results of operations to be saved and retrieved.

Etymology of computer: Combination of COM: to come together; and PUTER: to clean, arrange, value, judge, suppose, ponder, consider, think, settle, adjust. The primary notion of putare was to make clean, then to bring cleanliness, to make clear, to reckon, to think, to purify. Hence to compute; is to: arrange items clearly in one's mind.

Computers are logic machines; following sets or sequences of instructions (without deviance). At once here we put aside such an 'ordinary' definition—and the normal functions of the computer—and skip forward to consider a bigger question.

Machine Creativity

Can a computer think creatively; does it have any intuition—can it make an educated guess about unforeseen events and/or likely future outcomes? The field of Artificial Intelligence (AI) attempts to create such true 'thinking' computers.

The OED defines ***intuition*** as:The action of looking upon or into; contemplation, inspection, a sight or view. The action of mentally looking at; perception, recognition, mental view. According to such a definition – we can categorically state that machines do not posses intuition; and henceforth they can only follow instructions one-step-at-a-time (and without any deviation from these steps); whereby in a human sense they do not think in anyway whatsoever.

The conclusion must be that Machines do not possess freedom-of-thought and they have no free-will. Ergo, we are forced to disbelieve in machine-thought (at least for the machines of the present day). Despite the fact that computers can (in a sense) perceive and process certain pre-programmed facts and situations, they do not—and cannot—think, form an opinion, or relate data and events to a private world-view; and they cannot have empathy—or care about what happens to other living beings.

Computers do not 'see' the world – or know that they are embedded inside the world. They are, patently, blind and stupid; and devoid of any reflective capability. Today's computers do not 'wish' to remain existent—in fact they do not have wishes of any kind; or even realise that they exist in any sense whatsoever. Can arguments over computer intuition be so easily cast aside? Perhaps not, and so it is worth delving a little more deeply into issues surrounding the nature of 'thinking' machines; because these topics relate to computer self-determination and even questions of the nature—and possibility—of machine life. But above everything it is humans that create Computers - and we are as Gods to them!

Purpose Drives Technology

The term technology comes from the Greek word techne, meaning art and craft, and the word logos, meaning word and speech. It was first used to describe applied arts, but it is now used to describe advancements and changes which affect the environment in which we humans operate. Ergo technology refers to capability magnification/extension tools of one kind or another.

All technologies are born out of **purpose**. One example is that search engines were created to sort through the massive amounts of data online. With each upgrade – a new technology compounds existing technologies to create something better than what was previously used before. Technologies feed – or are built – one on top of another ad-infinitum.

We end up with a mind-blowing technology such as an iPhone that represents perhaps millions of technologies bundled together in the most sophisticated manner imaginable – forming a technology that can be used for literally millions of different purposes.

But we are immersed in a vast number (and range) of other technologies which shape all of our lives profoundly (ie. overtly and visibly, and/or invisibly) such as: news sites, banking systems, shopping sites, social media platforms etc. Add each technology assembly may – and often will – have quite dramatic implications for potentially millions of humans. Accordingly, we must ask ourselves – if each new technology is affecting each individual human beneficially. Are new technologies optimal/humane? And if not – how can we make them so – or prevent their development and deployment?

It is salient to consider this key question – related to the social impact of technology – as we attempt to build 'smartness' into our world of physical and biological Things.

The Science of Smart Things: Conclusions

Technology runs our lives these days. Smartphones, tablets and computers – we really can't seem to function without them. Technology has exploded in the market and now, many people cannot imagine a life without it.

But what exactly is technology? Well, we have given related definitions of technology here; and in fact one could say that answering this question is the primary goal of all the work presented here. Technology refers to tools and techniques that are used for solving problems. Technology can refer to methods ranging from as simple as stone tools to the complex genetic engineering and information technology that has emerged since the 1980s.

Here in this paper we have placed focus on those particular classes of technology that involve computers and machines. Basically we are concerned with the application and embedding of information technology into the real world (i.e. problem solving using a data processing and data networking capacity). Put simply, we wish to place chips and connectivity into everything; that is, we wish to beneficially apply: knowledge machines, AI, IoT, Virtual Reality, Robotics etc. to all human activities (mental and physical). It is surprising how far, in just over 200 years of history, the field of computing has progressed. Indeed, there is no area of human activity, or thought, that this IT revolution has not transformed. Doubtless the next 200 years will see even more incredible progress – and one could ask where, precisely, is it all headed. What will be the end result for humanity as a whole – and for ordinary humans in particular?

The answer is almost impossible to predict; but what we can say is that barring a large-scale catastrophe of some kind (i.e. the coming of a world war, environmental disaster etc); progress will continue unabated. The premise of the present paper is that we cannot just let technology develop as it may; but rather that we must carefully manage (or guide) developments in a direction that provides real benefits (and opportunities) for all.

ACKNOWLEDGMENT

I am deeply grateful for the support of family and friends, Philip and Ellen Radley, Restie and Rowena Wight, Chris Green, Ruth etc, without whom this chapter would not have been possible. My sincere gratitude and thanks to Prof. Francisco V.C. Ficarra who supported the work financially and also inspired the initial work just over 2 years ago. Thanks also to my mentor Prof. Kim Veltman who has supported and inspired this work over a period of more than a decade.

REFERENCES

Fuller, R. B. (1969). *Operating Manual for Spaceship Earth*. Lasr Muller Publishers.

Fuller, R. B. (1972a). *Synergetics, Explorations in the Geometry of Thinking*. Macmillan.

Fuller, R. B. (1972b). *Utopia or Oblivion: The Prospects for Humanity*. Macmillan.

Norman, D. (1988). *The Design of Everyday Things*. Basic Books.

Portman, E. (2016). *Towards Cognitive Cities: Advances in Cognitive Computing and its Application to the Governance of Large Urban Systems*. Springer. doi:10.1007/978-3-319-33798-2

Radley, A. (2015). *Computers as Self, BluePrints Visions and Dreams of Technopia*. Radley Books.

Weiser, M. (1991). The Computer for the 21st Century, Scientific American Special Issue on Communications, Computers and Networks. *YouTube*. Retrieved 5 August 2020, from https://www.youtube.com/watch?v=7jwLWosmmjE

KEY TERMS AND DEFINITIONS

Automated Thing-Automated Action: Sensing/action/feedback loop (fixed problem-solution model): always responds to the environment in terms of a fixed pattern of predetermined behaviours according to specific pattern of events; reactive in nature and has purely reflexive decision making (may be internally powered by some means).

Distributed Intelligence: Distributed Intelligence is when we have embedded Intelligence and Connectivity across the environment in useful ways.

Embodied Virtuality: Situation whereby humans are living in a world of invisible and intelligent widgets that surround us completely, or at least are numerous and common.

Inert Thing-Controlled Action: Provides particular functional abilities with respect to a specific context of use; an Inert Thing has no self-generated power of action, motion, or resistance; must be operated under external power and/or control; whereby such a device has no decision making ability whatsoever;

Intelligent Thing-Intelligent Action: Sensing/action/feedback loop (adaptive problem-solution model): responds to the environment in an intelligent manner; has an ability to consider a range of options and/or allows for a scope of future 'possibilities' to be taken into account; can to adapt its own programming to new situations via learning behaviours; whereby said device has pro-active decision making.

Programmable Thing-Programmable Action: Sensing/action/feedback loop (programmable problem-solution model): responds to the environment in an appropriate way given a particular scenario; has pre-programmed decision making.

Situated Intelligence: Situated intelligence refers to an IoT thing or IoT system that has a unique ability to Monitor, Act and Integrate within its environment in useful ways; and in particular to how objects that are 'awake' to the environment can/will usefully automate and enhance human problem solving capabilities.

Synergetic Inter-Accommodation: A synergetic system that is self-regulating and intelligently applies resources precisely where, when, and how they are needed—without wasting any energy/information.

Synergy: Synergy is the ability to create/maintain order—that is to cause structured Energy patterns to form which persist and are energy-conserving in nature (they tend to guide energy across space/time and are centripetal).

Chapter 9
Autonomous Communication Model for Internet of Things

Sergio Ariel Salinas
Universidad Nacional de Cuyo, Argentina

ABSTRACT

The internet has changed the way human activities are performed. In a few years, this communication infrastructure evolved to leverage a new technological paradigm named internet of things (IoT). This technology fuses processes and devices to create multipurpose cyber-physical systems (CFS) that improve human quality of life. These systems rely on internet availability, which can be affected by natural phenomena such as earthquakes carrying out economic and social consequences. In this work, an autonomous communication model for IoT domains is proposed. The main goal of this model is to set the basis for the development of a communication system capable of operating independently of the internet. This communication autonomy is critical in catastrophe scenarios where information broadcasts can support disaster management. According to simulation results, the proposed model can be implemented in different IoT scenarios including cities developed under this technology.

INTRODUCTION

The Internet has become an important communication infrastructure that involves an increasing number of human activities. This complex communication system doubles its size every five years including a wide variety of devices. Different surveys show that by 2025 there will be around 7 billion IoT devices operating on different applications around the world (Vincentelli, 2015). This number will grow with the development of new services and products.

The development of the Internet over the years enabled the communication of a large number of heterogeneous devices, which are utilized to automate diverse human activities. In this context, a new technological paradigm evolved and it was named Internet of Things (IoT) (Atzori, Iera & Morabito, 2010). This technology involves several scenarios that can be grouped into three broad domains: industry, smart cities, and health well-being (Borgia, 2014).

DOI: 10.4018/978-1-7998-7010-4.ch009

The industry domain includes areas such as logistics, manufacturing, process control, customer services, bank, and financial management, government controls, among others. Smart cities promote the development of a sustainable environment by making efficient use of resources and taking care of the environment. Health well-being involves independent living and health care. IoT technology for independent living assists people with a physical disability to improve their quality of life. Nowadays, for example, there are health care centers that provide services based on IoT to remotely take care of patients at their homes.

In these scenarios, it is possible to observe how IoT is a pervasive technology that encompasses a growing range of human activities. This phenomenon is integrating and fusing processes and devices to create cyber-physical systems (CPS) (Vincentelli, 2015). The Institute of Electrical and Electronics Engineering (IEEE) has polled more than 150 IoT scenarios that involve diverse CPS ("IoT scenarios", 2019) domains. In the near future, governments, industries, and societies will depend on these systems to perform daily activities.

A CPS fuses physical processes and information technology to optimize the use of resources needed to accomplish certain goals. These systems gather heterogeneous electronic devices that interact to perform actions on the environment where they operate based on sensed data or preset settings. The interaction among devices is supported by a communication infrastructure such as the Internet.

The deployment and interaction of CPSs involve a large number of devices sending and receiving messages over the Internet. In this scenario, the communication infrastructure must deal with requirements such as scalability, interoperability, and integration of diverse protocols.

IoT emerged from the evolution of the Internet, as a consequence it has developed an important dependency between IoT technology and the underlying communication systems. Although it is unlikely that the Internet infrastructure collapses at a global scale, it is feasible that failures of lower scale occur. For example, smart cities built on seismic zones are prone to failures after an earthquake. In such a case, there might be an important social and economic impact on the citizen's lives.

In this work, the dependency between IoT applications and the communication systems is stated as a problem. In order to address this problem, an autonomous communication model is proposed. The main goal of this model is to set the basis to build an autonomous communication system capable of operating in IoT domains such as a smart city. An autonomous system could provide basic messages exchange services that can be crucial, for example in catastrophe scenarios.

The contributions of this work are the following. First, the definition of an autonomous communication model that can be applied in IoT domains. Second, the estimation of the number of devices required to communicate certain areas autonomously. Finally, the analysis of how the number of devices within an area affects the communication routes between two random devices.

The content of this chapter is organized as follows. First, the background that supports the model is presented. Second, the proposed model is introduced. Third, results about the number of devices required to communicate autonomously in an area are discussed. Fourth, an analysis of how the number of devices within an area alters the communication route between nodes is analyzed. Finally, future research directions and conclusions are presented.

Background

The Internet of Things requires a global communication infrastructure to connect efficiently geographically dispersed devices. These devices are the building blocks of this new evolution of the Internet and they need six main elements to provide the services required by a CPS (Fuqaha, Guizani, Mohammadi, Aledhari & Ayyash, 2015).

The first element is the identification of objects involved in IoT scenarios that involve a unique id and a network address. There are different identification methods for creating ids for objects such as ubiquitous codes (uCode) and electronic product code (EPC) (Koshizuka & Sakamura, 2010). The network addressing methods include IPv6 and IPv4.

The second element is the capability of devices for sensing variables from the environment and sending these data through the network to a data storage. The collected data is used to take certain actions based on predefined settings and services. For example, a growing number of services enable users to control remotely a set of appliances located in houses and offices.

Computation is the third element needed for the IoT functionality delivery and it involves processing units and software applications. Different hardware has been developed for IoT applications namely Arduino, UDOO, FriendlyARM, Intel Galileo, Raspberry PI, Gadgeteer, BeagleBone, Cubieboard, Z1, WiSense, Mulle, and T-Mote Sky. This hardware fosters the development of software for IoT such as Real-Time Operating Systems (RTOS), TinyOS, LiteOS, and Riot OS (Ray, P., 2018).

The fourth element is named services and they can be classified into four categories: identity-related, information aggregation, collaborative-aware, and ubiquitous services. Identity-related services are required to link physical and virtual objects. Aggregation services summarize data sensed by different devices. Collaborative-aware services use summarized information to make decisions about actions to be performed in a certain environment. Ubiquitous services deal with mechanisms required to make services available anytime and anywhere they are needed.

Semantics is the fifth element and it refers to the logic to extract knowledge that enables the identification of required services. In this context, modeling information, data recognition, and data analysis play a key role and they are supported by Semantic Web technologies such as the Resource Description Framework (RDF) and the Web Ontology Language (OWL).

Finally, the sixth element is the communication technology required to connect heterogeneous devices to support IoT services. There are different efforts to improve the scalability, integration, interoperability, and standardization of existing communication protocols (Gubbi, Buyya, Marusic & Palaniswami, 2013; Botta, de Donato, Persico, Pescapé, 2016; Miorandi, Sicari, Pellegrini & Chlamtac, 2012). These features are needed to make it feasible to implement any of the 150 proposed IoT domains in the next few years ("IoT scenarios", 2018).

The communication protocols for IoT are expected to enable not only communication among objects but also people and objects to control different environments anytime and anywhere. Devices used in IoT are limited in processing and storage volume capabilities as well as power life and radio range. These constraints have influenced IoT communication protocols adoption, which can be classified into two categories: i) low power wide area network (LPWAN) and ii) short-range networks.

The first category of protocols allows long-range communications at a low bit rate among things and it includes technologies such as SigFox and Cellular. The second one enables the communication within a limited area such as buildings, factories, or houses. The main technology and protocols involved in this group are 6LoWPAN, ZigBee, Z-Wave, Bluetooth, RFID, and NFC.

SigFox is a low power technology that enables the transmission of small amounts of data within areas up to 50 kilometers (Samie, Bauer & Henkel, 2016). It enables the communication of low power objects such as electricity meters and wearable devices. Cellular technology provides reliable high-speed connectivity to the Internet through GSM/3G/4G cellular communication networks (Frantz & Carley, 2005). It is suitable for applications that involve mobile devices where it is required high data throughput.

6LoWPAN (Lu, Li & Wu, 2011) was one of the first standard protocols for IoT communication created by the Internet Engineering Task Force (IETF). It was designed based on IEEE802.15.4 standard to implement low power wireless personal area networks utilizing IPv6. Communication within a 6LoWPAN network is low cost and consumes low bandwidth power. Devices can use this protocol to communicate directly with another IP network without intermediate gateways or proxies.

ZigBee is a protocol based on low-power wireless IEEE802.15.4 networks standard created by the ZigBee Alliance (Kinney, 2003). This protocol uses the 2.4GHz band to transmit data over long distances based on a low data rate that makes it possible to extend the battery life. It supports two-way communication between a sensor and a control system that enables the deployment of personal network areas.

Z-Wave is a low power protocol developed by Zensys to implement applications for home automation (Yassein, Mardini & Khalil, 2016). It uses low-energy radio waves to provide a device to device communication to control security systems, windows, swimming pools, door openers, lights, locks, among others. Devices can be controlled via the Internet using a smartphone, tablet, or computer by sending small messages. In this sense, this protocol has been designed for a small data packet to be transmitted at low speeds up to 100 kbps within an area of approximately 30 meters.

Bluetooth is a wireless protocol designed to exchange data between devices over short distances within radio bands from 2.402 GHz to 2.480 GHz (Bhagwat, 2001). It is a low power consumption protocol that uses low-cost transceiver microchips in devices that enable the department of personal network areas.

Radio-Frequency Identification (RFID) is a technology that uses electromagnetic fields to automatically identify and track tags attached to objects (Want, 2006). Tags implement a tiny radio transponder; a radio receiver and transmitter. These electronic components can be triggered by an electromagnetic interrogation pulse from a nearby RFID reader device to access data stored in the tag, usually an identifying inventory number.

Near-Field-Communication (NFC) is a very short-range wireless communication technology designed for data transmission among devices by touching or bringing them together no more than a few inches (Coskun, Ozdenizci & Ok, 2013). The technology principles used by NFC are similar to RFID but it can be used for identification as well as for more elaborate two-way communication. This technology can be used for example in industrial processes and contactless payment systems.

The autonomous communication model is based on three premises: i) heterogeneous devices provide wireless communication services, ii) devices are capable to store their global positioning information, and iii) messages exchange can be performed based on a decentralized routing algorithm.

IoT devices are heterogeneous and their interoperability is needed to implement any scenario (Borgia, 2014). The proposed model could use any of several IoT wireless communication protocols such as WiFi, Zigbee, Bluetooth, 6LoWPAN, Z-wave, or Cellular technology.

The communication range of these protocols is variable; WiFi technology (Farris, Militano, Nitti, Atzori & Iera, 2016) uses radio signals to exchange data in a range of 100 meters. The coverage radius of Bluetooth (Dideles, 2003) varies from 10 and 15 meters. The Z-Wave protocol (Yassein, Mardini & Khalil, 2016) has a communication scope between 30 and 40 meters while the IEEE 802.15 standard (Misic, 2008) has a range of up to 1000 meters. Finally, Cellular technology can be used to transfer data between smart mobile devices (Ghosh, Ratasuk, Mondal, Mangalvedhe & Thomas, 2010).

Nowadays, several devices can store data about their geographical position and use this data to route messages (Perkins & Royer, 1999; Baronti, Pillai, Chook, Chessa, Gotta & Hu, 2007). This strategy is used by the following protocols:

- Minimum Energy Communication Network (MECN): this technology uses low power GPS. For each node, a region is established in which it is cheaper, from the energy point of view, to send data through intermediate nodes instead of sending it directly. It also uses complex algorithms to select a path between two nodes.
- Geographic Adaptive Fidelity (GAF): it is based on turning off nodes that are not strictly necessary to route data, but ensuring that no connectivity between nodes is lost. The nodes change their status (off or on) periodically to guarantee load balance.
- Ad hoc On-Demand Distance Vector (AODV): It is a reactive protocol based on a distance-vector, which selects a path based on the least number of jumps. When a node needs to know the route to another node, it sends a route request that floods the network. If one of the route request messages reaches the destination or reaches an intermediate node that knows the route to the destination, that node responds with the requested route. All the intermediate nodes that listen and route the message that contains information of the requested route, store this information. This protocol emerges as evolution and improvement of several similar prior protocols. It is the protocol selected by the ZigBee network layer protocol.

There are several routing protocols (Akkaya & Younis, 2005) utilized in wireless communication devices classified into four categories.

- Data-centric protocols: instead of addressing nodes, data with certain characteristics is routed. Nodes collaborate with each other to provide certain data. These protocols are suitable to summarize information. For example, a node could make a request for temperatures above a certain value or the average temperature in a region.
- Hierarchical protocols: nodes are grouped into clusters and the data is sent from a source node through different clusters until reaching the target node. In each cluster, it is possible to calculate the average, minimum and maximum values of certain features from available data in the network.
- Location-based protocols: these protocols are based on geographical data of nodes in the network. They require the use of low-consumption geo-positioning systems (such as GPS) or location techniques.
- Protocols based on the quality of service: the main goal of these protocols is to guarantee the quality of a service or characteristic necessary according to the application. In the field of WSN, some necessary features may be to guarantee data coverage for as long as possible or to decrease the response latency to a certain data request.

Many of the communication systems presented before were designed to operate under specific constraints. In some situations, devices must save energy, deliver messages as fast as possible, use a minimum number of resources, or accomplish a simple task as temperature measuring. Since IoT integrates existing technologies, it will be necessary for the interoperability and integration of current and new devices to make it feasible for the development of IoT domains (Borgia, 2014). For these reasons, there will be available resources to make it feasible for the definition of an autonomous communication model that operates independently from the Internet.

AUTONOMOUS COMMUNICATION MODEL

An autonomous communication model is proposed for the exchange of messages between devices independently of the Internet. As mentioned before the model is based on three premises: i) heterogeneous devices provide wireless communication services, ii) devices can keep their geographical position information, and iii) message exchange can be performed based on a decentralized routing algorithm.

IoT domains will encompass mobile and fixed devices such as routers, switches, access points, and wireless devices located on public roads, traffic lights, advertising, and information posters. In smart cities (Zanella, Bui, Castellani, Vangelista & Zorzi, 2014) a set of geographically fixed devices is necessary for IoT domains to allow access to different intelligent environments such as houses, buildings, industries, hospitals, and public spaces. These communication devices have global positioning information (GPS) (Misra & Enge, 2006) that can be obtained automatically or can be set externally.

The number of devices utilized by IoT domains is estimated to rise up to 7 billion globally by the year 2025 and its growth will continue over time. Smart cities will demand a large number of devices to implement a wide range of scenarios. In this sense, it is expected a large number of devices per square meter which facilitates the definition of autonomous communication areas.

The distribution of IoT devices over cities will depend on buildings and houses allocation. Usually, city development follows urban planning where buildings are organized in blocks of determined dimension. In Argentina, the size can vary between 80 and 100 meters on each side of the block.

The distribution of blocks in a city is similar to a grid that can be represented by a Cartesian plane. From this observation and considering the premises presented above, it is proposed a decentralized and autonomous communication model based on geographically mobile and fixed nodes distributed over an autonomous communication area.

Nodes are devices capable of communicating with other nodes independently of the network protocol they implement according to the premise of interoperability. In the proposed model, there are two types of nodes: static and dynamic. A static node has a fixed geographical location while a dynamic node changes its geographical position over time.

Communication between a source and a target node can involve intermediary nodes, which exchange messages through a selective routing algorithm. The algorithm dynamically creates a route between two nodes. The selection criteria for the nodes is based on a numerical mark that aims to identify which nodes are suitable to be included in a communication route. The mark assigned to a node is defined by its behavior in the past in the communication process and its distance to the target node.

In case the target node is not within the communication area, the node that identifies this situation will report the result to the source node. In this sense, the communication service does not guarantee the delivery of messages if the node is not available in the area. The concepts mentioned before are described in detail next.

Autonomous Communication Area

An autonomous communication area is a geographical region represented by a Cartesian plane. The limits of an area and nodes position within it are calculated using the global positioning system (GPS). This system defines coordinates expressed in degrees, minutes, and seconds where one degree equals approximately 111,325 km, one minute equals 1,855 meters and one second equals 30.91 meters [19].

A Cartesian plane is defined by two points **p(x1,y1)**, **p(x2,y2)** that identifies where an area starts and ends according to GPS information. This information is transformed into an integer value that represents a point in the plane using the following expression **value = seconds + minutes*60 + grades*3.600**.

This particular Cartesian plane starts at the point **p(0,0)** and ends at the point **p(x2-x1,y2-y1)** where the difference between the values of $\mathbf{x_i}$ and $\mathbf{y_i}$ represents the length of an area. The variation of one unit in any axis equals one second in GPS information format i.e. 30.91 meters. This value is suitable considering that most IoT devices have a wireless communication range greater or equal to 30 meters.

A point in the Cartesian plane represents nodes by their x and y coordinates. Two contiguous nodes represent two devices that are able to communicate with each other. These devices exchange messages using wireless connection independent from the Internet.

Since a Cartesian plane represents a geographical region it is possible to estimate the number of nodes required to cover the whole area by the following equation **(1)**. The values of **b** and **h** represent the max values of the **x** and **y** axes in the Cartesian plane. For example, in order to cover an area where the values of **b** and **h** are 216 meters, it is required approximately 49 nodes.

Nodes within an area can exchange messages using their coordinates. Every node keeps a list of neighbors within its wireless communication range to which it can exchange messages. In order to send a message, the source node must have information about the coordinates of the target node. The source node will select a node from its list of neighbors and send the message. The neighbor node is named broker and it will repeat the process of selecting a neighbor and passing the message until the target is reached.

In this communication process, every node must select a neighbor to which send the message. Since every node has scarce information about other nodes in the region, a broker selection criterion must be defined. The selected brokers between the source and target nodes will define a communication route that can vary based on the decisions made by broker nodes. This strategy defines a dynamic routing algorithm introduced next.

Dynamic Routing Algorithm

The main goal of the dynamic routing algorithm is to distribute messages between two nodes within an autonomous communication area in a decentralized way and independently from the Internet service.

The algorithm creates a route between the source and target nodes compound of a set of broker nodes. These nodes do not include the source and target. If the message is sent over a predefined path, the routing is named predetermined routing. In contrast, if the route must be discovered at the moment of sending a message the routing is indeterminate.

To build a communication path, each node uses a routing table that contains a list of neighboring nodes. This list keeps data about four metrics about each node: i) availability over time, ii) efficiency sending messages, and iii) visibility that is the number of neighbors known by the node.

The routing process of a message starts when a source node sends a message to a target node. The message contains the identification of the source and target node. Based on this data, a broker node that receives a message creates a ranking of neighboring nodes and selects a subset of nodes with the highest score. The number of elements into the subset is a parameter setting that enables the definition of redundant and parallel routes.

Every time a message is sent between nodes data about, the last visited node is added to the message. If the message is delivered successfully, a route between the source and target node is created. In contrast, if there is a failure trying to reach the target node an error message will be sent back to the source node.

Ranking of Neighboring Nodes

The routing algorithm uses a subset of brokers selected from a ranking created and updated by each node. Every neighbor node has a position in the ranking according to a value calculated considering a set of metrics. Periodically, a node requests their neighbors for these metrics to keep updated information about their neighbor's performance.

The metrics used to calculate the mark assigned to each broker are the following:

1. **Distance:** this value is represented by the variable **d** and is defined by the distance between a broker and the target node to which a message is addressed, it is calculated using the following equation **(2)**.
2. **Efficiency:** it is represented by the variable **e** and it is a ratio calculated from the number of messages successfully sent to other nodes and the total of messages received from other nodes in a certain time interval, which is a configuration parameter.
3. **Availability:** this ratio is represented by the variable **a** and it is computed taking into account the time a node is operational over the total time in which the node is being evaluated. The time window that is considered to calculate this metric it is also a configuration parameter.
4. **Visibility in the network:** it is a value represented by the variable **v** that is calculated using the Sigmoid function **(3)** where **x** is the number of neighbors to which a node can send a message. The variable **k** can be utilized to adjust the growth rate of the function when the number of neighbors is increased. The value of the function tends to one when the number of neighbors is very high.

To compute the mark for a node the following three steps are accomplished:

First, an array named performance vector is computed with values of the aforementioned metrics $p=(w_1*d, w_2*e, w_3*a, w_4*v(x))$ where the variables w_1, w_2, $w_{3,}$ and w_4 are real numbers between 0 and 1. These coefficients make it possible to weigh the importance of each metric in a given communication scenario.

Second, an array called optimal vector $u=(w_1*1, w_2*1, w_3*1, w_4*1)$ is defined with the highest possible values for each metric. For the metric distance, the value one means that the target node is one hop away from the broker. The efficient value will be one when all messages received were sent successfully to another node. The highest value for availability is one meaning the node was 100% of the time accessible and the value one represents the maximum number of neighbors known by a node.

Third, the mark for each neighboring node is calculated by measuring the Euclidean distance between the performance vector of each node and the optimal vector. In this way, it is feasible to obtain a single numerical value that represents how similar is a node to its ideal values. The Euclidean distance is computed according to the following equation: **(4)**.

The calculation of the mark of each node is performed when a node receives a message that must be sent to a broker or target node. Since the mark is computed based on metrics from other neighbors these values must be updated. For this reason, after a time interval, every node broadcasts information about its metrics. This information is used to update a routing table that includes the coordinates of the node, a timestamp as well as the values of the metrics efficiency, availability, number of neighbors, and visibility.

Table 1 shows an example of a ranking calculated by a node at the moment of selecting a broker to send a message to a target node placed at the coordinates **p (7,9)**. In this case, the values for the w_i variables are one and the values for the optimal vector are one.

Table 1. Example of neighbors ranking

Node	Coord	Distance	Efficiency	Availability	#Neighbors	Visibility	Mark
1	(2,2)	8.60	1.00	1.00	8	0.98	7.60
2	(3,4)	6.40	0.66	1.00	7	0.97	5.41
3	(2,5)	7.81	0.66	0.91	5	0.92	6.81
4	(3,5)	6.65	0.33	0.41	1	0.62	4.75

In the example, it is possible to observe that node 4 is closest to the target than node 1. However, node 4 has low efficiency and availability in comparison to node 1. Additionally, node 4 knows only one neighbor, which may be risky because if that neighbor node fails there are no additional nodes. Although the distance between node 1 and the target node is the highest, it has the highest mark because of the values of the other metrics. For this reason, it is the first broker candidate to be part of the route and send the message.

The proposed method to rate neighbors is flexible, adaptive, and easy to compute. The performance and optimal vectors can be tuned according to different scenarios. The weights utilized in vectors make it possible to set the relevance of each metric. For example, in scenarios where it is required a fast delivery of message the metric distance could be more important than the visibility. In contrast, if the number of devices is low in certain areas then the visibility could be more relevant than other metrics.

ANALYSIS OF OPERATIONAL FEASIBILITY

To analyze the operational feasibility of the model, a simulation software was developed to evaluate geographical areas of different dimensions. To simplify the analysis, square-shaped areas with values of 5, 15, 40 and 60 square kilometers were considered. These dimensions were estimated taking into account possible IoT scenarios such as a smart city or industrial zone.

The simulation process computes the optimal number of nodes required to cover a whole area using the equation **(1)**. The calculation assumes that devices are placed equidistant from each other. For example, an area of 5 km^2 that has two sides of 2,230 meters each one will require 5,205 devices that have a communication range greater than 30.91 meters.

The optimal number of nodes is a value of reference, since in real scenarios nodes are not located equidistant from each other. However, this value is taken into account as the initial number of devices in the area under analysis. The simulator places that number of devices within the area according to coordinates generated randomly based on a uniform statistical distribution.

After allocating nodes in the area under analysis, the percentage of coverage achieved with those nodes is calculated. Then, the optimal number is increased by one unit, the nodes are randomly distributed again from scratch in an empty area and the percentage of coverage is computed again. The optimal number is increased until the covered area is closed to 100% and this process is repeated 30 times to obtain statistically representative values.

Figure 1. Coverage areas of 5, 15, 40 and 60 square km, a) Coverage area of 5 km, b) Coverage area of 15 km, c) Coverage area of 40 km, d) Coverage area of 60 km

$$n = \frac{b}{30.91} \times \frac{h}{30.91}$$

Figure 1 shows the results presented above. On the one hand, similar behavior is observed in the different evaluated areas where the growth of the number of nodes is not linear with respect to the coverage percentage. In general, if the number of nodes is doubled, approximately 90% coverage in the area is reached. It is possible to observe that in general the initial value of nodes covers approximately 63% of the analyzed areas. In addition, it is observed that the standard deviation is low in almost all of the evaluated scenarios.

It is possible to estimate the number of devices in a city taking into account its dimensions. For instance, Mendoza is a city located on the west side of Argentina where the downtown has a size of approximately 900 meters by 1,300 meters. According to this dimension and using equation (1) the optimal number of devices is equal to 1,224.

Mendoza downtown is distributed in approximately 9 by 13 blocks where the dimension of each block is approximately 100 square meters. Usually, a block has 40 buildings where there are several devices with wireless communication services. However, let us take into account only one device per building that results in 40*9*13=4,680 nodes in the downtown. This value is significantly higher than the optimal value even when it is considered only one device per building.

Results show that if the optimal number of devices randomly distributed in a city is doubled then it is feasible to cover 90% of the area. This value is under the estimation made for a real city in a pessimistic scenario of only one device per building. For these reasons, it is feasible to create an autonomous communication area using IoT devices.

ANALYSIS OF COMMUNICATION ROUTES

The number of devices available within an autonomous communication area affects the length of communication routes between any two nodes. The route length depends on the number of available brokers between the source and target nodes. In areas where the density of nodes is high routes will tend to be shorter than routes in areas with a low density of nodes. To assess the relationship between route lengths between nodes and the percentage of coverage in a communication area a second simulation software was developed, which performed the following tasks.

First, an autonomous communication area with a certain percentage of coverage is created, as explained in the previous section. Second, a statistical sample of nodes is calculated according to the following parameters: i) population size equal to the total number of nodes in the area, ii) 95% confidence level, and iii) estimated error of 1% and iv) expected proportion 0.5. Third, two nodes are randomly selected based on the uniform probability distribution. Fourth, the shortest possible route between the two nodes is searched, the length of the route and the geographical distance between the nodes are calculated. These steps are performed until the sample population of nodes is evaluated. The process is repeated 30 times in order to obtain statistically significant results wherein each iteration random communication areas of equal coverage percentage are generated.

Table (2) presents a summary of the results obtained for a coverage percentage that varies between 50% and 100%. For each case, it is shown the following data: number of pairs of nodes evaluated, percentage of outliers, the average geographical distance, length of the average route, average number of nodes that are part of the route, and their corresponding standard deviation.

Table 2. Summary of communication route analysis

% coverage	nodes	% outliers	$\bar{x}$ geo distance	*A* geo distance	$\bar{x}$ route length	*A* route length	$\bar{x}$ nodes	σ nodes
0.50	67,386	35.65	37.77	17.58	101.37	97.85	80.63	79.87
0.60	70,500	7.53	37.97	17.75	57.53	39.75	44.90	32.22
0.70	84,288	0.88	37.99	17.75	47.06	23.55	36.59	18.79
0.80	86,125	0.49	38.00	17.71	45.15	22.79	35.28	18.28
0.90	94,230	0.01	37.92	17.69	41.55	19.29	33.19	15.82
1.00	101,010	0,00	37.86	17.76	39.95	18.69	32.84	15.82

In the table, it is possible to observe that the average geographical distance and its standard deviation is similar in all cases because the size of the area is the same in each analysis. In the case where there is 100% coverage, the maximum length of the communication routes is approximately 98 units. This value was considered to calculate the number of outliers in each scenario where a significant increase is observed when the coverage area varies from 60 to 50%.

Figure (2) shows the results for an area of 5 km^2, the average size of a city in Argentina. In each case, the y-axis shows the distance of the communication path and the x-axis shows the geographical distance. It is possible to observe that in the case where the coverage area is 100% there is a linear relationship between both distances. In this case, it is expected that the length of the communication path is very

Figure 2. Coverage percentages of 50, 60, 80 and 100%, a) Coverage percentage of 100%, b) Coverage percentage of 80%, c) Coverage percentage of 60%, d) Coverage percentage of 50%

$$d = \sqrt[2]{(x_2 - x_1)^2 + (y_2 - y_1)^2}$$

close to the geographical distance between the nodes. However, as the percentage of coverage decreases, the length of the communication route increases with respect to the geographical distance.

In the case where the percentage of coverage is 50%, the communication between nodes shows an unstable behavior in terms of the length of the communication route. It is possible to observe that data is very scattered in comparison to cases where the coverage percentage is higher. In contrast, an autonomous communication area with up to 80% of coverage can provide a service with the length of communication routes close to the case of 100% coverage.

CONCLUSION

In this work, a communication model was presented to create an autonomous communication area that can be implemented in different domains of IoT as a smart city or industrial zone. In this way, it is feasible to implement a message exchange service in a geographical area even if the Internet does not work as it might be in a catastrophe scenario.

The model enables access to a message exchange service between two nodes. To do this, a Cartesian plane is defined where the nodes' position depends on their geographical positioning information. The positioning data in the plane makes it possible to create a communication path between two nodes. The exchange of messages is done through a selective routing algorithm that uses a mark value to select the nodes that define a communication route.

The rate of a node depends on its distance to the target node, the number of neighboring nodes in its coverage area, the quality of service, and the availability in a given period of time.

The proposed model was evaluated using two simulators that considered two aspects of analysis. On the one hand, the feasibility of implementing the model in a real scenario such as a smart city. On the other hand, the behavior of the communication routes according to the percentage of coverage in the autonomous communication area.

In the first analysis, areas of sizes of 5, 15, 40, and 60 were evaluated, where in each case it was taking into account what percentage of the area could be communicated with a determined number of nodes. For each area, an iterative process was started and in each iteration, the number of nodes was located randomly based on a uniform statistical distribution.

From the simulation result, it is observed that if the number of nodes is obtained by dividing the total area by the coverage area of each node and then these nodes are randomly distributed, approximately 60% coverage is obtained and if this number is double more than 80% coverage is achieved.

The results obtained in the simulation process were compared with an estimate of nodes in the city of Mendoza, where it was observed that there would be three times as many devices as the estimated number in the simulation process. In this way, it is concluded that it is feasible to create an autonomous communication area for IoT application domains that would allow operating in case of catastrophe scenarios.

The second analysis considered the behavior of the communication routes when the coverage percentage varies between 50 and 100%. As a result, unstable average values are observed for the route length in the case where the coverage percentage is 50%. In the event that the percentage is greater than 80%, it is possible to observe a route length similar to the case of 100% coverage.

From both analyzes, it is possible to conclude that according to the results obtained by simulation it is possible to obtain 80% coverage with a number of devices below that obtained by observing the distribution of a city like Mendoza. In addition, for this percentage of coverage, it is possible to obtain communication routes close to the geographical distance between nodes. Although the results obtained are preliminary, they provide evidence on the feasibility of creating a communication system independent of the Internet that can operate in certain cities in emergency scenarios.

REFERENCES

Akkaya, K., & Younis, M. (2005). A survey on routing protocols for wireless sensor networks. *Ad Hoc Networks*, *3*(3), 325–349. doi:10.1016/j.adhoc.2003.09.010

Al-Fuqaha, A., Guizani, M., Mohammadi, M., Aledhari, M., & Ayyash, M. (2015). Internet of things: A survey on enabling technologies, protocols, and applications. *IEEE Communications Surveys and Tutorials*, *17*(4), 2347–2376. doi:10.1109/COMST.2015.2444095

Al-Sarawi, S., Anbar, M., Alieyan, K., & Alzubaidi, M. (2017). Internet of things (iot) communication protocols: Review. *8th International Conference on Information Technology (ICIT)*, 685–690. 10.1109/ICITECH.2017.8079928

Atzori, L., Iera, A., & Morabito, G. (2010). The internet of things: A survey. *Computer Networks*, *54*(15), 2787–2805. doi:10.1016/j.comnet.2010.05.010

Baronti, P., Pillai, P., Chook, V. W., Chessa, S., Gotta, A., & Hu, Y. F. (2007). Wireless sensor networks: A survey on the state of the art and the 802.15.4 and zigbee standards. *Computer Communications*, *30*(7), 1655–1695. doi:10.1016/j.comcom.2006.12.020

Bhagwat, P. (2001). Bluetooth: Technology for short-range wireless apps. *IEEE Internet Computing*, *5*(3), 96–103. doi:10.1109/4236.935183

Borgia, E. (2014). The internet of things vision: Key features, applications and open issues. *Computer Communications*, *54*, 1–31. doi:10.1016/j.comcom.2014.09.008

Botta, A., de Donato, W., Persico, V., & Pescapé, A. (2016). Integration of cloud computing and internet of things: A survey. *Future Generation Computer Systems*, *56*, 684–700. doi:10.1016/j.future.2015.09.021

Coskun, V., Ozdenizci, B., & Ok, K. (2013). A survey on near field communication (NFC) technology. *Wireless Personal Communications*, *71*(3), 2259–2294. doi:10.100711277-012-0935-5

Dideles, M. (2003). Bluetooth: A technical overview. *XRDS*, *9*(4), 11–18. doi:10.1145/904080.904083

Farris, I., Militano, L., Nitti, M., Atzori, L., & Iera, A. (2016). Mifaas: A mobile-iot-federation-as-a-service model for dynamic cooperation of iot cloud providers. *Future Generation Computer Systems*, 126–137.

Frantz, T. L., & Carley, K. M. (2005). *A formal characterization of cellular networks*. Available at SSRN 2726808.

Ghosh, A., Ratasuk, R., Mondal, B., Mangalvedhe, N., & Thomas, T. (2010). Lte-advanced: Next-generation wireless broadband technology. *IEEE Wireless Communications*, *17*(3), 10–22. doi:10.1109/MWC.2010.5490974

Gubbi, J., Buyya, R., Marusic, S., & Palaniswami, M. (2013). Internet of things (iot): A vision, architectural elements, and future directions. *Future Generation Computer Systems*, *29*(7), 1645–1660. doi:10.1016/j.future.2013.01.010

IoT Scenarios. (2020). Retrieved from https://iot.ieee.org/iot-scenarios.html

Kinney, P. (2003). Zigbee technology: Wireless control that simply works. In Communications design conference (Vol. 2, pp. 1-7). Academic Press.

Koshizuka, N., & Sakamura, K. (2010). Ubiquitous ID: Standards for Ubiquitous Computing and the Internet of Things. *Pervasive Computing, IEEE*, *9*(4), 98–101. doi:10.1109/MPRV.2010.87

Lu, C. W., Li, S. C., & Wu, Q. (2011). Interconnecting ZigBee and 6LoWPAN wireless sensor networks for smart grid applications. In *2011 Fifth International Conference on Sensing Technology* (pp. 267-272). IEEE.

Miorandi, D., Sicari, S., Pellegrini, F. D., & Chlamtac, I. (2012). Internet of things: Vision, applications and research challenges. *Ad Hoc Networks*, *10*(7), 1497–1516. doi:10.1016/j.adhoc.2012.02.016

Misic, J. (2008). Analysis of Slave–Slave Bridging in IEEE 802.15.4 Beacon-Enabled Networks. *IEEE Transactions on Vehicular Technology*, *57*(3), 1846–1863. doi:10.1109/TVT.2007.909263

Misra, P., & Enge, P. (2006). Global Positioning System: Signals, Measurements, and Performance (2nd ed.). Ganga-Jamuna Press.

Perkins, C. E., & Royer, E. M. (1999). Ad-hoc on-demand distance vector routing. *Proceedings WMCSA'99. Second IEEE Workshop on Mobile Computing Systems and Applications*, 90–100. 10.1109/MCSA.1999.749281

Ray, P. (2018). A survey on Internet of Things architectures. *Journal of King Saud University - Computer and Information Sciences, 30*(3), 291-319.

Samie, F., Bauer, L., & Henkel, J. (2016). IoT technologies for embedded computing: A survey. *Hardware/Software Codesign and System Synthesis (CODES+ ISSS), 2016 International Conference on*, 1–10. 10.1145/2968456.2974004

Vincentelli, A. S. (2015). Let's get physical: Adding physical dimensions to cyber systems. *Low Power Electronics and Design (ISLPED), 2015 IEEE/ACM International Symposium on*, 1–2.

Want, R. (2006). An introduction to RFID technology. *IEEE Pervasive Computing*, *5*(1), 25–33. doi:10.1109/MPRV.2006.2

Yassein, M. B., Mardini, W., & Khalil, A. (2016). Smart homes automation using z-wave protocol. *International Conference on Engineering MIS (ICEMIS)*, 1–6.

Zanella, A., Bui, N., Castellani, A., Vangelista, L., & Zorzi, M. (2014). Internet of things for smart cities. *IEEE Internet of Things Journal*, *1*(1), 22–32. doi:10.1109/JIOT.2014.2306328

KEY TERMS & DEFINITIONS

Internet of Things: a communication infrastructure based on the Internet to connect heterogeneous devices utilized by Cyber Physical Systems to assist diverse human activities.

Cyber-physical System: is an adaptable mechanism where algorithms, devices and processes operate together to achieve a predefined set of objectives based on environmental conditions.

Autonomous: Communication Model: is a representation of a communication structure where nodes can exchange messages autonomously independently of the Internet infrastructure.

Smart City: is an urban area where different cyber-physical systems interact to provide services to citizens based on the Internet of Thing infrastructure.

Broadcast Service: is an algorithm to send a message from one node to all other nodes in a communication network.

Unicast Service: is an algorithm to send a message from one node to another node in a communication network.

Chapter 10
The Analytic Hierarchy Process as a Method for the Selection of Resources in the Cloud

Hugo Rolando Haurech
Department of Management Technologies, Misiones National University, Argentina

David Luis la Red Martinez
Northeast National University, Argentina

ABSTRACT

Due to technological advances, organizations have to face many challenges in providing support through the use of information technologies (IT) to carry out tasks that require computing skills. It is important to adopt adequate resources with the aim of developing processing skills that meet actual needs. Cloud computing (CC) represents an alternative that offers many opportunities to be exploited. This chapter introduces characteristics of CC, the technologies that enable its deployment, and a model of selection based on qualifications and mathematical development.

INTRODUCTION

The progress in the fields of computing and communications are changing the way organizations have access to IT resources. CC represents a new technological model through which an institution enters a platform with technical and functional characteristics such as scalability, elasticity and efficiency. According to this, it is possible to define CC as a model that enables "an omnipresent, convenient in demand web access" (Habbal A., Abdullah S. A., Mkpojiogu E. O. C., Hassan S. & Benamar N., 2017) to computing resources, that allows fast and easy scalability.

The possibility of access to computing resources makes the use of CC attractive for organizations because they can reach a number of applications, services and capacities by means of a data network or the Internet. Similarly, the National Institute of Standards and Technology (NIST) defines it as, "a technological model that enables on ubiquitous, adapted, network attached on demand access to a shared

DOI: 10.4018/978-1-7998-7010-4.ch010

group of configurable computing resources - networks, servers, storing equipment, apps and services - that can be quickly stocked and freed with a low management effort or a minimal interaction with the service provider" (Mell P. & Grance T., 2011).

Other authors express that "CC is aimed to provide cloud services via the Internet. Instead of configuring and maintaining costly local hardware and software, cloud services consumers can get the abstract resources as computing, hardware, software and storage according to what they need" (Lei Q., Jiang Y. & Yang M., 2014).

Say them that the delivery of computational abilities by means of visualized resources through a data network is one of the characteristics of CC. Consequently, using CC is convenient for organizations whose infrastructure does not meet the processing needs for making complex calculations, particularly in a parallel way. The virtualized infrastructure for the development of tasks can be used anytime anywhere. The possibility of using a variety of devices such as personal laptops, smartphones and tablets, without installing particular software gives a feeling of Independence.

As regards the support IT team, CC implies a change in the way of working, specially the one referred to the installation of tools and apps in the users, terminals, allowing the team to focus on other tasks such as the correct data network functioning and the Internet connectivity, with the purpose of having an adequate access to resources.

It is right to say that this paradigm has become a technological trend that has changed the way technological resources being offered, thus influencing the IT market motivated by the elimination of complex restrictions on space, time, energy and cost of equipment's of the traditional IT field.

Consequently, it is necessary to know the characteristics of CC, its models, parts, which are the technologies that it involves and how they be selected in the right way.

This section the divided into three parts, which are of interest for the selection of resources in the cloud: (1) it is presented to cloud computing and its characteristics, (2) the hierarchical analytical process is described, (3) the method is applied in the case of selection of computing resources and (4) the conclusions obtained from the study.

Cloud Computing

CC is a paradigm that completely changes the way of accessing services and apps because it is they done through a data network or the Internet. According to (Joyanes Aguilar L., 2012) CC is "the evolution of a group of technologies that affects the approach of the organization in which a group of hardware and software, storing, services and interfaces enable information input as a service". From these definitions it is possible to obtain the word service codes which are offered / acquired through a data network such as the Internet, this being a choice of the CC concept.

Thus, the cloud is not a place but a method of managing IT resources that replaces local machinery and private data centers with virtual infrastructure. As a result, users have access to virtual computing, network and storing resources that are available online through a remote provider. These resources can be they reached instantly. This is very useful for organizations that need to scale its infrastructure or reduce it quickly according to a fluctuating demand.

It is necessary to focus on the word service here. These must be divided in categories to determine which services can be offered and how. Moreover, there are characteristics recognized as essentials by the NIST (Badger L. et al., 2014) that must be bore in mind now of using the cloud.

Essential Characteristics

The CC model of the NIST has five essential characteristics that distinguish it from traditional computing, thus providing the foundations to compare services in the cloud and their implementation strategies. According to the definition provided by the NIST, the five characteristics that an implementation must have to be considered a CC (Badger L. et al., 2014) are:

On-demand self-service: a consumer can store information capacities unilaterally and automatically without interacting with each service provider. In this way, he gets a certain degree of independence in managing resources.

Broad network access: capacities are available on the web and someone can access them through standard mechanisms that promote the use of heterogeneous platforms (mobile phones, tablets, laptops and workstations). This guarantees that any user with any operating system or device have access to services.

Resource pooling: computing resources are grouped to meet the needs of multiple consumers using a model of multiple users, with different physical and virtual resources dynamically assigned and reassigned according to the consumer's demands. This allows the providers to share their resources with the users, reducing costs and maximizing the availability of resources.

Rapid elasticity: capacities can be stored and freed elastically, and in some cases automatically according to users´ demands. In other words, resources must be available according to the client´s needs whenever he requires them. Resources storage can be in two ways: horizontally (adding more physical resources) or vertically (changing actual resources for others with more capacity).

Measured Service: systems on the cloud automatically control and improve the use of resources by using a measuring capacity for the type of service which is offered, for example: storage, processing, bandwidth, active user´s account. The use of resources can be monitored, controlled and informed offering the supplies and consumers transparency of the service. This means that the use of any resource must be measured, audited and reported to the client based measuring system which has been agreed by the provider and the user. Thus, the user is charged with a fee based on the capacity or characteristic of the hired service.

Service Models

These are "specific services to which someone can have access on a CC platform" (Joyanes Aguilar L., 2012), also known as XaaS (as service). The NIST (Badger L. et al., 2014) defines three standardized models: SaaS (software as service), PaaS (platform as service) and IaaS (infrastructure as service) which present the following functionalities: Application development and other services; Data analysis and create statistical models; Software development and administration; Storage, backup and data recovery; Share videos, photos and audios; Website hosting services, Processability.

SaaS: This service gives the consumer the capacity of using a provider's app that runs in a cloud infrastructure. They can be accessed with different devices through a client's interface, as web browser. The consumer cannot manage or control lower level infrastructure in the cloud as they: the web, servers, operating systems, the storage or even individual application´s capacities. However, it is possible, in an exceptional way, accessibility to limited configurations related with user´s specific applications.

PaaS: Consumers have the capacity of implementing new applications in the cloud infrastructure using programming language and tools compatible with the provider. They cannot manage or control lower level infrastructure in the cloud as they: the network, servers, operating systems or the storage.

However, they do have control over the implemented applications and possibly, the configurations of the hosting environment.

IaaS: Consumers can have access to processing, storage, networks and other IT resources where they can implement and run software randomly, that may include operating systems and applications. They do not manage or control low-level infrastructure but they can control operating systems, storage, applications and eventually, selected network components.

Deployment Models

According to NIST, the deployment model distinguishes and defines the aim of the cloud and where it is placed. This classification refers to the level and way hired resources in the cloud are shared with other institutions. There are four categories of managing IT resources in the cloud as follows:

Private cloud: Here, the cloud infrastructure is run for an organization only. This organization or a third party can manage it, and it can exist inside or outside the premise.

It characterizes by (Carlos S., Guzmán B. & Rodríguez M. S., 2007): Requiring capital investment for its implementation; Having full control of the infrastructure, the systems and the information; Having a short time response and a high flexibility in offering resources; Offering the possibility of taking advantage of the existing personnel and the investments done previously.

Public cloud: The cloud infrastructure is available to the public or a big industrial group, and it is owned by an organization that sells services in the cloud.

It characterizes by (Carlos S., Guzmán B. & Rodríguez M. S., 2007): A small number of users compared to those of the public cloud; cost of services adapted to the way they are used; storing the corporate information in the cloud together with information that belongs to other clients.

Community cloud: The cloud infrastructure is shared by many organizations which share common functions and services, allowing collaboration among similar groups of interest. Organizations or a third party can manage it, and it can exist inside or outside premises.

It characterizes by (Carlos S., Guzmán B. & Rodríguez M. S., 2007): A small number of users, compared to those of the public cloud, raising the amount of security services and services related to privacy matters; more available resources than in a private cloud, and with more advantages in terms of elasticity; less available resources than in a public cloud, limiting the elasticity of that cloud.

Hybrid cloud: The cloud infrastructure has two or more clouds (private, community and public) that stand separately but are related by standardized technology that enables data and applications portability.

It characterizes by (Carlos S., Guzmán B. & Rodríguez M. S., 2007): Fast initiation process; high complexity in the integration of services due to the differences in the types of implementations; integrating the best characteristics of the different models; offering a greater flexibility in the services.

According to the models described by the NIST, it is possible to have a cloud structure that complies with all the aims of an organization as regards the services that it wants to offer or use and how it can interact with other organization.

In addition to the position and interaction with other clouds that are looked for with this technology, it is necessary to have providers capable of giving communication and computing resources as the basis for the distribution of services. This is shown in Figure 1, where the pile of program services, platforms and infrastructure is based on the physical resources of the providers. The coexistence of the service models starts in the infrastructure making it possible to reach the resources for software development for PaaS that will be the support of the SaaS applications.

Figure 1. Relationships between service and resource models

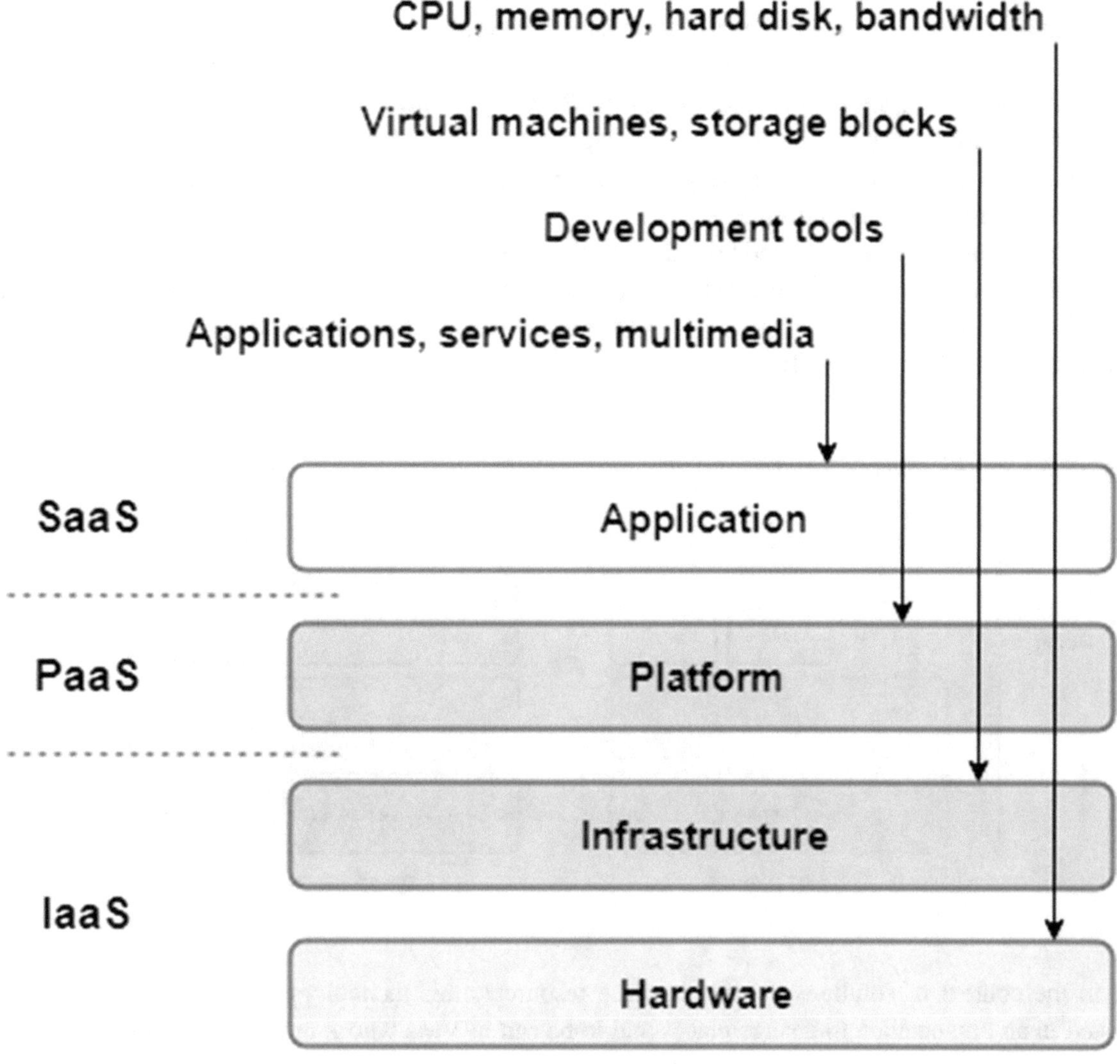

Technologies Associated to Cloud Computing

Given the above, CC can be considered as a distributed system that consists of a group of interconnected and virtualized computers (Chihi H., Chainbi W. & Ghdira K., 2016). At this point, it is important to say that a technological tool like virtualization is considered a key element of CC because it enables elasticity and scalability. It is observed that an infrastructure with this technology lays the basis for high performance clouds. Consequently, it is a successful strategy for the consolidation of data centers as it improves physical resources as well as it provides the basic elements for a fast and flexible delivery of services in a cloud system.

In terms of (Habbal A., Abdullah S. A., Mkpojiogu E. O. C., Hassan S. & Benamar N., 2017), "virtualization is the process of creating a virtual version of something". In the context of IT, it is the ability to create and run multiple different operating systems, applications and other resources in the server. In a model of CC architecture, the infrastructure provides a number of storage capacities and IT resources when dividing physical resources by using virtualization technologies.

This technology conceals the physical characteristics of a computer platform to users, by an abstract emulated computer platform (Marston S., Li Z., Bandyopadhyay S., Zhang J. & Ghalsasi A., 2011), which for practical purposes behaves as an independent system, but unlike a physical system, can be configured on demand and can be maintained and replicated very easily, thus achieving efficient and complete use in the use of hardware.

They are classified in native and hosted, and they are distinguished by the operating system required to manage the hypervisor as Figure 2 shows. About this, using Type 1 (native) virtualization techniques requires a complex management compare to Type 2. However, it has the advantage of direct interaction between virtual machines (VM) and the basic hardware.

Figure 2. Classification of hypervisors

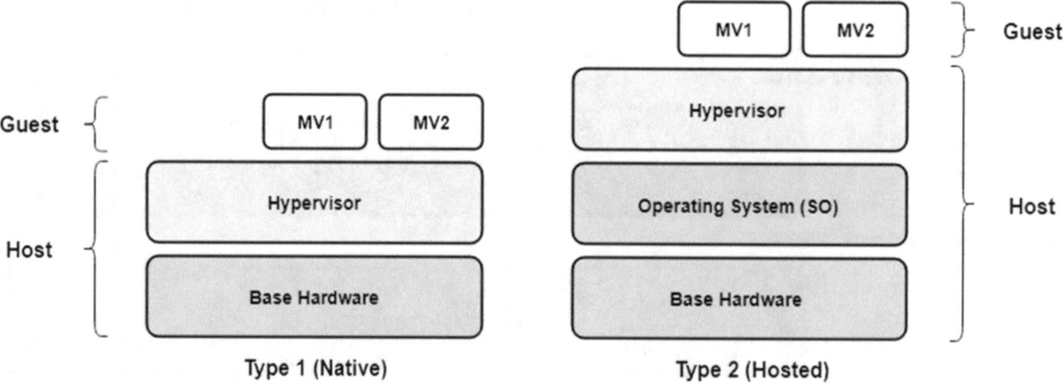

In the context of solutions to infrastructure resources, this technology enables that the services hosted in an organization to change places and to be run in VMs whose processing capacity, memory and storage are adjusted to the needs and to a service agreement. Because of this, it is necessary to know the resources and providers that are able to provide a correct infrastructure service. As there is a wide variety of options, there is a need of a method that enables the selection of providers according to the IaaS capacities they could offer.

Analytic Hierarchy Process

This model was defined by Saaty (Thomas L. Saaty: July 18, 1926 – August 14, 2017, distinguished university professor at the University of Pittsburgh, he is the inventor, architect and principal theorist of the analytical hierarchy process) who was looking for a model that would help with the problem of complex decision-making (Saaty T., 1980). Articles on the subject suggest adopting resolution analysis techniques such as the Analytic Hierarchy Process (AHP), based on a quantitative method with criteria an alternative that must be included. This method outstands among others because of its strong results based on the mathematical development present in its structure.

Thus, (Berumen S. & Redondo F., 2007) defines AHP as a logic and structured method that fosters complex decision making when there are many criteria and characteristics, by dividing the problem in a hierarchical structure, (Medina P., Cruz E. & Gomez R., 2012) believes AHP is a quantitative method with criteria and features to support decision making that contribute to the aims of an organization. Similarly, (Guerrero-Liquet G. C. & Faxas-Guzmán J., 2015) states AHP is a proposal to order analytical thinking which is distinguished by three principles: the principle of hierarchical construction, the principle of priority settings and the principle of logical consistency.

Following that criteria, a complex feature can be divided in a group of simpler features and to determine how what is their influence on the aim of the decision. For this reason, this influence is represented by the values given to each feature or criterion. In other words, this facilitates the objectivity of the process and prevents and institution from making decisions.

Hence, it is possible to state that AHP is a multi-criteria tool for associating the reality that an individual person perceives with a reasonable value scale that shows the relative priorities of the considered elements (Berumen S. & Redondo F., 2007).

Therefore, a problem can be structured visually through a hierarchy of attributes that has at least three levels:

- The overall purpose or goal of the problem at the top.
- The attributes or criteria that define alternatives in the middle.
- The alternatives at bottom.

Once the hierarchy model is ready, comparisons between pairs of elements must be done and numeric values must be assigned to the preferences indicated. Following the proposal of (Bermubez Irreño C. A. & Quiñonez Aguilar E. D., 2018), it is possible to establish a working order using the AHP model as follows:

- Structuring of the hierarchical model (goals, criteria, alternatives).
- Prioritization of the hierarchical model.
- Pairwise comparisons between elements.
- Evaluation of the elements through weight assignment (weighing).
- Measurement of alternatives subject to their weighed values.

Assigning a weighed value to each criterion can be done using a table proposed by (Bermubez Irreño C. A. & Quiñonez Aguilar E. D., 2018) based on Saaty's definitions, as seen on Table 1. It is important to point here that, although weighing is done using a definite table, it is the decision maker who assigns a value to each pair of alternatives. This might imply a certain degree of subjectivity in the selection of preferences towards any particular alternative.

Selection of IaaS Providers

As mentioned before, the offer of cloud services leads to the proposal of a method of selection of cloud resources, particularly those that have the infrastructure for the deployment of services.

In the previous section, the AHP method was presented, which due to its solidity based on mathematical development suggests being an appropriate model to address the selection of providers for infrastructure

Table 1. Pair-wise comparison scale for AHP preferences

Numerical rating	Verbal judgments of preferences
9	Extremely preferred
8	Very strongly to extremely
7	Very strongly preferred
6	Strongly to very strongly
5	Strongly preferred
4	Moderately to strongly
3	Moderately preferred
2	Equally to moderately
1	Equally preferred

service, among others. According to this, the following topics to be discussed will: introduction of providers, characteristics of the services they offer and the development of the suggested method.

IaaS Providers

Nowadays, online search services for infrastructure services providers currently respond to a specific number of those considered as main providers. A list with a description of these providers and their main characteristic services is introduced below.

IBM: It has two services; the first is Bare Metal, a physical server with a hardware that fits the business model. The second is Virtual Servers with a shared physical hardware. The main difference between both types of services is that the second one has many virtualized instances of servers. The services have the following characteristics (values obtained from https://www.ibm.com/cloud/infrastructure):

- Tenancy: simple or Bare Metal (BM), multiple or Virtual Server (VS).
- Billing: per hour or monthly.
- Options of configuration: all the hardware in BM or CPU, RAM and storage in VS.
- Computing power: one CPU with 4 cores to 4 CPUs with 12 cores in BM or more than 56 cores with VS.
- Storage: up to 36 controllers for SSD 800 GB to 1.2 TB in BM or 25GB to 400GB provisioned by SSD in VS.
- RAM: 3 TB in BM or more than 242 GB in VS.
- Output bandwidth: free 500 GB, the exceeded are monthly charged, or free 250 GB and the exceeded also monthly charged.
- Input bandwidth: free.
- Type of service: BM in ideal for data-intensive workloads that prioritized performance and reliability while VS is for highly varying workloads that prioritize flexibility and scalability.

AWS: It has two types of service, the first operates through the host infrastructure whose capacities correspond to instance of services and the second through VS. In general, terms, the foundations of the services are differentiated by instances grouped by categories that: of general purpose, optimized for informatics, optimized for memory, accelerated informatics and optimized for storage. The services offered by the AWS provider have the following characteristics (values obtained from https://aws.amazon.com/es/ec2/):

- Tenancy: physical dedicated hosts or VM.
- Billing: monthly or per hour with the exception of those special contractual terms, that allows establishing a fee per second (60 seconds minimum).
- Options of configuration: fixed for instances in dedicated hosts and in VM.
- Computing power: from 20 to 224 physical cores and from 1 to 128 cores in VM.
- Storage: from 475GB to 60.000 GB in SSD NVMe (NVMe: new generation SSD with PCI or M.2 connector).
- RAM: from 166 GB to 12 TB.
- Bandwidth: from 10 to 25 Gbps with 14.000 Mbps (EBS: Excess Burst Size).
- Type of service: service instances grouped by features or capacities.

RACKSPACE: It has two types of service; the first is through the BM infrastructure (named OnMetal) that corresponds to a physical dedicated server divided in four models. The second is through a Virtual Servers where the physical hardware is shared. It has many virtualized instances, four groups of options (for general purpose, optimized for computing, optimized for I/O and optimized for memory) with four presentations each. The services have the following characteristics (values obtained from https://www.rackspace.com/es-ar/library/what-is-iaas):

- Tenancy: simple for BM or multiple for VS.
- Billing: monthly or per hour.
- Options of configuration: fixed for instances in dedicated hosts and in VS.
- Computing power: one CPU with 6 cores to two CPUs with 6 cores in BM, from two to 32 vCPUs for VS.
- Storage: 2x 240 GB (raid1 - mirror) SSD to 2x 1.6 TB PCIe storage devices in BM or 20 GB o 1.2 TB provisioned by SSD in VS.
- RAM: from 32 GB to 128 GB in BM, or from 1GB to 240 GB in VS.
- Bandwidth: 10 Gbps in BM or from 320 Mbps to 10 Gbps for VS.
- Type of service: service instances grouped by features or capacities.

It is necessary to say that **WMWARE** was not taken into account as an IaaS provider because the service it offers is the software for the implementation and cloud managing.

Structuring and Prioritization of the Hierarchical Model

According to the different steps of the model, it is necessary to establish the goals that represent the solutions to the case study, the criteria for the pairwise comparisons and the alternatives that will be object of evaluation which are:

- **Goal**: IaaS provider whose resources will be used a deployment oriented to high performance computing with workloads that are not uniform.
- **Criteria**: The characteristics of Tenancy (T), Billing (B), Configuration options (O), computing power (P) and RAM (M) will be considered.
- **Alternatives**: IBM, AWS and RACKSPACE.

Binary Comparisons and Weighing

After defining the criteria and alternatives, the tables for comparisons must be done. They will contain number value of the selected preference from Table 1 and the standardization for each element defined as a criterion.

A) Pairwise comparisons and the standardization of the Tenancy criterion

According to the characteristics each provider establishes for the tenancy criterion, the comparative table is constructed. Providers offer similar capacities. Thus, the value that results from the comparisons alternatives has the numeric value "1" in all the cells.

Table 2. Pairwise comparison of the Tenancy criterion

Tenancy	IBM	AWS	RACKSPACE
IBM	1	1	1
AWS	1	1	1
RACKSPACE	1	1	1
Total	**3**	**3**	**3**

From the values obtained above, you should form the normalization table of the elements of the cells and then get the arithmetical average from each line. Thus obtaining the value of the priority assigned to each alternative (provider) related to the analyzed criterion. One can see that, in the particular case of raising equal weight allocations, analogue priority values are obtained.

Based on what is expressed in (Bermubez Irreño C. A. & Quiñonez Aguilar E. D., 2018), the development of the method to be considered to evaluate the congruence of the judgments that resulted in the valuation of the options. For this, it is necessary to resort to the analysis of consistency, from the normal-

Table 3. Definitions of the priorities for the Tenancy criterion

Tenancy	IBM	AWS	RACKSPACE	Priority
IBM	0,333	0,333	0,333	**0,333**
AWS	0,333	0,333	0,333	**0,333**
RACKSPACE	0,333	0,333	0,333	**0,333**

ized matrix and from which it will be considered consistent if the values of the cells of each column are equal. If the rule is not complied with, the degree of inconsistency must be determined.

In the case of the Tenancy criterion, the columns of values of IBM, AWS and RACKSPACE have in each of their rows equal values, with it the consistency and therefore the congruence has been achieved.

B) Pairwise Comparisons and Normalization of the Billing Criterion

Both IBM and RACKSPACE offer an hourly or monthly bill. AWS, on the contrary, offers a measurement per second; this qualifies it as "Very strong to extremely" preferable compared with the other providers. IBM and RACKSPACE are equally preferable.

Table 4. Pairwise comparison of the Billing criterion

Billing	**IBM**	**AWS**	**RACKSPACE**
IBM	1	1/8 = 0,125	1
AWS	8	1	8
RACKSPACE	1	1/8 = 0,125	1
Total	**10**	**1,250**	**10**

When normalizing the values Table 4 is obtained as conclusion, where the priority found over AWS

Table 5. Definitions of the priorities for the Billing criterion

Billing	**IBM**	**AWS**	**RACKSPACE**	**Priority**
IBM	0,1	0,1	0,1	**0,1**
AWS	0,8	0,8	0,8	**0,8**
RACKSPACE	0,1	0,1	0,1	**0,1**

as regards its billing method is higher than the others.

Regarding the Billing criteria, the values obtained from normalization have equal values in each row, which indicates congruence in the valuation decision of the elements.

Table 6. Pairwise comparison of the Configuration Options criterion

Configuration Options	**IBM**	**AWS**	**RACKSPACE**
IBM	1	5	7
AWS	1/5 = 0,2	1	1
RACKSPACE	1/7 = 0,142	1	1
Total	**1,342**	**7**	**9**

Table 7. Definitions of the priorities for the Configuration Options criterion

Configuration Options	IBM	AWS	RACKSPACE	Priority
IBM	0,745	0,714	0,777	**0,745**
AWS	0,149	0,142	0,111	**0,134**
RACKSPACE	0,105	0,142	0,111	**0,119**

C) Pairwise Comparison and Normalization for the Configuration Options Criterion

According to the characteristics of configuration required, the weight value assigned to providers in Table 6 makes IBM more preferable than the others.

The weight value of the preferences found results in IBM being far more preferable than the others, as shown in Table 7.

The values obtained from the standardization of the Configuration Options criterion determine the existence of inconsistency, this results in the need to know what the degree of it is. According to (Bermubez Irreño C. A. & Quiñonez Aguilar E. D., 2018) the above is determined from the Consistency Ratio (CR), if it is less than 0,1 it can be considered "Acceptable" otherwise it should be considered other values for the comparison of peers meet the aforementioned relationship . In this way:

$$RC = I_C / I_A < 0,1$$

Equation 1. Definition of the consistency relationship.Where

I_C = consistency index = $(n_{max} - n) / (n - 1)$

I_A = random consistency index = $(1,98 * (n – 2)) / n$

n_{max} = å comparison matrix * priority matrix

n = grade matrix

Applying the above equations it is obtained that **RC = 0,006 < 0,1** therefore the degree of inconsistency is acceptable and it is not necessary to modify the values of the comparison matrix.

Table 8. Pairwise comparison of the Computing Power criterion

Computing Power	IBM	AWS	RACKSPACE
IBM	1	1/8 = 0,125	4
AWS	8	1	9
RACKSPACE	1/4 = 0,25	1/9 = 0,111	1
Total	**9,25**	**1,236**	**14**

D) Pairwise comparison and normalization for the Computing Power criterion

As in the previous case, the values of preferences over providers results from the definitions of the goals. Table 8 shows that AWS is preferred over the other two providers and that IBM computing capacities compared to those of RACKSPACE are not that better. Therefore, it is considered "Moderately to strongly preferable".

Priorities seen on Table 9 show that AWS is the preferred provider.

Table 9. Definitions of the priorities for the Computing Power criterion

Computing Power	IBM	AWS	RACKSPACE	Priority
IBM	0,108	0,101	0,285	**0,164**
AWS	0,864	0,809	0,642	**0,771**
RACKSPACE	0,027	0,089	0,071	**0,062**

As can be seen in the values in Table 9, there is inconsistency and its degree can be analyzed. Applying the equations mentioned in the previous section, it is obtained that **RC = 0,255 > 0,1** and with this it is determined that "it is not acceptable", which leads to modify the preference values for the pairwise comparisons. Two changes were made, the first corresponds to IBM's relationship with RACKSPACE granting the "Moderately preferred" judgment, the second change occurs in the AWS relationship with IBM granting the "Very strongly preferred" judgment. The comparison of pairs and normalization are shown in Table 10 and Table 11.

Table 10. Pairwise comparison of the Computing Power criterion

Computing Power	IBM	AWS	RACKSPACE
IBM	1	**1/7 = 0,142**	**3**
AWS	**7**	1	9
RACKSPACE	**1/3 = 0,333**	1/9 = 0,111	1
Total	**8,333**	**1,253**	**13**

The consistency ratio is calculated again from the new preference values, the value obtained for **RC = 0,066 < 0,1**, so the consistency is "acceptable".

Table 11. Definitions of the priorities for the Computing Power criterion

Computing Power	IBM	AWS	RACKSPACE	Priority
IBM	0,12	0,113	0,23	**0,153**
AWS	0,84	0,798	0,692	**0,744**
RACKSPACE	0,039	0,088	0,076	**0,0676**

E) Pairwise Comparison and Normalization for the RAM Criterion

After analyzing what providers offer to customers, it is concluded that: AWS stands first on preferences, there is a minimum difference the memory capacity that IBM and RACKSPACE offer.

Table 12. Pairwise comparison of the RAM criterion

RAM	IBM	AWS	RACKSPACE
IBM	1	1/8 = 0,125	2
AWS	8	1	9
RACKSPACE	1/2 = 0,5	1/9 = 0,111	1
Total	**8,5**	**1,236**	**12**

In Table 13 AWS superiority stands out due to the big priority difference compared to the other two providers.

Table 13. Definitions of the priorities for the RAM criterion

RAM	IBM	AWS	RACKSPACE	Priority
IBM	0,105	0,111	0,166	**0,124**
AWS	0,842	0,809	0,75	**0,8**
RACKSPACE	0,052	0,089	0,083	**0,074**

Regarding this criterion, analyzing the values of the pairwise comparison matrix and the priorities, it is obtained that **RC = 0,013 < 0,1** with which the degree of inconsistency is acceptable.

Table 14. Pairwise comparison of the goal against the criteria

Goal	T	F	O	P	M
T	1	1	0,25	0,125	0,125
F	1	1	1	0,25	0,333
O	4	1	1	0,25	0,25
P	8	4	4	1	1
M	8	3	4	1	1
Total	**22**	**10**	**10,25**	**2,625**	**2,708**

F) Pairwise Comparison and Target Normalization Against the Criteria

Here, the pairwise comparison and weighing is based on the preferences over each criterion. Table 14 shows that computing power; memory and configuration possibilities dominate over the other criteria set out in the objectives.

Taking into account the information on the previous table, normalization of values is done, obtaining Table 15.

Table 15. Priorities definitions of the goal

Goal	T	F	O	P	M	Priority
T	1/22	1/10	0,25/10,25	0,125/2,625	0,125/2,708	0,0524
F	1/22	1/10	1/10,25	0,25/2,625	0,333/2,708	0,0918
O	4/22	1/10	1/10,25	0,25/2,625	0,25/2,708	0,113
P	8/22	4/10	4/10,25	1/2,625	1/2,708	0,3804
M	8/22	3/10	4/10,25	1/2,625	1/2,708	0,3604

Outcomes Analysis

Once the assignments phase is over, an analysis of the priorities must be done. Thus, it is necessary to select priorities one by one and do a sum of the outcomes between the priorities of the criteria and the objectives. Equation 2 represents this.

$$ALT(x) = å\ å\ \text{Prioriy (alternative)}_i * \text{Priority (goal)}_j$$

Equation 2. Definition of the alternative.

From the analysis, the following hierarchy of the proposed alternatives is obtained.

IBM = 0,333 . 0,0524 + 0,1 . 0,0918 + 0,745 . 0,113 + 0,153 . 0,3804 + 0,124 . 0,3604 = **0,213**

AWS = 0,333 . 0,0524 + 0,8 . 0,0918 + 0,134 . 0,113 + 0,744 . 0,3804 + 0,8 . 0,3604 = **0,677**

RACKSPACE = 0,333 . 0,0524 + 0,1 . 0,0918 + 0,119 . 0,113 + 0,067 . 0,3804 + 0,074 . 0,3604 = **0,0922**

Performing hierarchy order:

AWS = 0,677

IBM = 0,213

RACKSPACE = 0,0922

CONCLUSIONS

Cloud Computing is a technological model whose resource offers makes it attractive for organizations that want to evolve from traditional computing to that in which resource capacities can be reached by configurations without adding equipment to its infrastructure. Providers of this technology offer a variety of resources for the SaaS, PaaS and IaaS models that can be free paid according to a service contract.

As regards the resources available for IaaS, server virtualization, memory and processing capacities might be a key requisite for the deployment of services with CC technology. In other words, by means of this technology it is possible to overcome the computing capacity limitations as it has an infrastructure with self-service according to customer´s demand, with fast elasticity through virtualization technologies.

Therefore, ITC professionals have to face the challenge of choosing resource providers in the cloud that are adequate for activities that require IaaS computing capacities. There are alternatives for making decisions, such as the Analytic Hierarchy Process. Through the offers of IBM, AWS and RACKSPACE, it is possible to apply techniques of the AHP model and obtain outcomes based on mathematical estimations and development. According to the objective set, the hierarchy establishes that AWS has better service characteristics compared to the other two providers, followed by IBM and RACKSPACE.

Although the methodology has applied in a particular case of the IaaS resource provider, and can be used taking into account other objectives, criteria and alternatives, as well as with other CC models and different providers. This is evidence of how versatile it is.

It can be affirmed that by using a selection method where the development is based on a resolution structure using numerical values, it allows obtain accurate and ambiguity-free results.

Given that there are other models for decision-making, there is a need to propose future research where the results obtained can be compared with other methods, for example aggregation operators. So that the contrast of their results allow determine which of them is better for the selection of resources.

REFERENCES

Badger L. et al. (2014). US Government Cloud Computing Technology Roadmap. *NIST Special Publication, 1*(2), 85.

Bermubez Irreño, C. A., & Quiñonez Aguilar, E. D. (2018). Aplicación Práctica Del Proceso De Análisis Jerárquico (AHP), para la Toma de decisiones. *Revista de Ingeniería. Matemáticas y Ciencias de la Informática, 5*(9), 91–100.

Berumen, S., & Redondo, F. (2007). La utilidad de lis métodos de decisión multicriterio (como el AHP) en un entorno de competitividad creciente. *Cuadernos Americanos, 20*(34), 65–87.

Carlos S., Guzmán B. & Rodríguez M. S. (2007). Computación en la nube, una tecnología emergente en la educación y en el sector empresarial: beneficios y desventajas desde el punto de vista operativo y ambiental. *Revista Iberoamericana para la Investigación y el Desarrollo Educativo*, 1-42.

Chihi, H., Chainbi, W., & Ghdira, K. (2016). Cloud computing architecture and migration strategy for universities and higher education. *2015 IEEE/ACS 12th International Conference of Computer Systems and Applications (AICCSA)*, 1-8.

Guerrero-Liquet, G. C., & Faxas-Guzmán, J. (2015). Análisis de toma de decisión con AHP / ANP de energías renovables en República Dominicana República Dominicana. *Anuario de Jóvenes Investigadores*, *8*, 27–29.

Habbal, A., Abdullah, S. A., Mkpojiogu, E. O. C., Hassan, S., & Benamar, N. (2017). Assessing Experimental Private Cloud Using Web of System Performance Model. *International Journal of Grid and High Performance Computing*, *9*(2), 21–35. doi:10.4018/IJGHPC.2017040102

Joyanes Aguilar L. (2012). Computación en la Nube. Notas para una estrategia española en cloud computing. *Revista del Instituto Español Estudios Estratégicos,* 89–112.

Lei, Q., Jiang, Y., & Yang, M. (2014). Evaluating open IaaS cloud platforms based upon NIST Cloud Computing Reference Model. *17th IEEE International Conference on Computational Science and Engineering CSE 2014, Jointly with 13th IEEE International Conference on Ubiquitous Communications IUCC 2014, 13th International Symposium on Pervasive Systems*, 1909-1914. 10.1109/CSE.2014.350

Marston, S., Li, Z., Bandyopadhyay, S., Zhang, J., & Ghalsasi, A. (2011). Cloud computing - The business perspective. *Decision Support Systems*, *51*(1), 176–189. doi:10.1016/j.dss.2010.12.006

Medina, P., Cruz, E., & Gomez, R. (2012). Selección de proveedor de WMS utilizando método AHP. *Sciences et Techniques (Paris)*, *17*(52), 65–72.

Mell, P., & Grance, T. (2011). The NIST Definition of Cloud Computing Recommendations of the National Institute of Standards and Technology. *Nist Special Publication.*, *145*, 7.

Saaty, T. (1980). *The Analytical Hierarchical Process* (Vol. J). Wiley.

KEY TERMS & DEFINITIONS

Omnipresent: Present in all places at all times. Synonym: ubiquitous.

Ubiquitous: Is something that seems to be present at the same time, everywhere.

Computing resources: In computing, a system resource, or simply resource, is any physical or virtual component of limited availability within a computer system.

Virtualization: In computing, virtualization means creating a virtual version of a device or resource, such as a server, storage device, network or even an operating system where the resource is divided into one or more runtime environments.

Hypervisor: Is a hardware virtualization technique that allows multiple guest operating systems (OS) to run on a single host system at the same time.

Weight: In the context of the application of the AHP methodology, it refers to the assignment of a numerical value that represents the degree of preference.

Bare Metal: Bare-metal servers have a single 'tenant'. They are not shared between customers. Each server may run any amount of work for the customer, or may have multiple simultaneous users, but they are dedicated entirely to the customer who is renting them.

Virtual Server: A virtual server is a server that shares hardware and software resources with other operating systems (OS), versus dedicated servers.

Chapter 11
Exploring Antecedents to Adopt Mobile Augmented Reality Applications:
A Uses and Gratifications Approach

İrem Eren Erdoğmuş
Faculty of Business Administration, Marmara University, Turkey

Pelin Şerefhan Doğanay
Korkmaz Kitchen and Small Home Appliances, Turkey

Görkem Vural
Marmara University, Turkey

ABSTRACT

The concept of augmented reality (AR) is a topic of increasing importance for the future of marketing. Research, especially on AR in mobile devices, is still in its infancy; therefore, this study explored the user motivations to employ mobile augmented reality applications against the hindrance of perceived risks and tried to understand user acceptance and willingness to use this technology and possible marketing-related outcomes. In-depth interviews were carried on with 16 participants as well as three mini focus group interviews with 12 participants. The underlying theories utilized were the technology acceptance model (TAM) and the uses and gratifications (U&G). The results showed that entertainment, obtaining information, experiential qualities, socialization, and personal motivations acted as gratifications in the adoption of AR applications, which exerted positive influence on brand interest, image, and purchase intention of the users.

DOI: 10.4018/978-1-7998-7010-4.ch011

INTRODUCTION

The concept of Augmented reality (AR), which is the visual alignment of virtual content with real-world context (Scholz & Smith, 2016), in real-time interaction (Azuma, 1997), is a topic of increasing importance in marketing (Reese et al., 2016). The upsurge in the AR industry can be tied to the breakout success of Pokemon Go in 2016, and the introduction of Apple's ARKit and Google's ARCore software development kits (SDKs) in 2017. These factors have accelerated the growth of AR, proved the confidence of the technology industry in AR experiences, and led to the creation of AR mobile applications (Petrock, 2019). Javornik (2016) described AR as the new groundbreaking technology of the Century and the Goldman Sachs (2016) reported that AR has the potential to become the next big platform as was the PC and smartphone and that it is expected that new markets were to be created and existing markets were to be disrupted with the AR technologies (www.goldmansachs.com, 2016). By 2020, it is expected that there will be one billion augmented reality users worldwide. Research shows that 70% of the consumers believe that AR technologies can provide them benefits, while 67% of the media planners and buyers want to integrate AR in their future promotion strategies (Moss, 2019). Already, many brands such as IKEA, Sephora, Lego implement AR applications as part of their marketing mix (Scholz & Smith, 2016). Several uses of the AR technology in marketing can be listed as aiding customers in product trial and education, entertaining them with digital gamification features (Rese et al., 2017), increasing brand awareness and influencing the purchase decisions (Pantano & Naccarato, 2010).

The research on AR so far focused on consumer motivations to use it, consumer reactions to, consumers' acceptance of this technology, and creation of consumer-oriented designs (e.g.; Rese et al., 2017; Kim & Forsythe, 2008; Domina et al., 2012; Javornik et al., 2016; Olson et al., 2013). Even though there is an increasing amount of research on the topic in the last decade, research especially on AR in mobile devices is still in its infancy (Rese et al., 2017); therefore an exploratory approach to provide a thorough understanding of the concept is timely and important. The aim of this research is to explore (1) the user motivations to employ mobile augmented reality applications against (2) the hindrance of perceived risks; (3) understand user acceptance and willingness to use this technology based on perceived usefulness and ease of use; and (4) possible marketing-related outcomes. The underlying theories utilized are the Technology Acceptance Model (TAM), which is commonly used in marketing to research consumer acceptance of technological developments and the Uses and Gratifications Theory (U&G), which is another commonly applied theory to explore consumer motivations in using new media technologies.

Providing answers to the questions above contributes to the literature in several ways. First, by understanding the uses and gratifications associated with AR applications, the research attempts to shed light on the theoretical mechanisms related to the intended use of AR. Currently, studies, especially by Rauschnabel et al. (2015, 2017, 2018), have identified the uses and gratifications associated with smart AR glasses. However, our study focuses on a variety of AR applications and tries to form a general framework of motivations to adopt AR applications with the addition of risks associated with AR that impede the adoption process. Second, the framework tests the applicability of the TAM model in AR application adoption from a qualitative point of view. Third, the study will add to the literature on the impact of AR on consumer behavior, which is said to be scant in its current position (Javornik, 2016). Considering that AR applications will be one of the infusing technologies in the future, this study is relevant for future research directions and practice. The insights will also help practitioners in designing their applications, by taking into consideration the dominant consumer motivations while resolving the associated risks.

BACKGROUND

Augmented Reality

One of the most common definitions of augmented reality is by Azuma (1997); who defines AR as a system "in which 3D virtual objects are integrated into a 3D real environment in real time (p.355)". The technology is similar to virtual reality, but it does not replace the real environment, but builds on it as background, and enriches the experiences of the viewers in reality (Daponte et al., 2014). In recent years, with the advent of mobile technologies, various AR applications are introduced in different fields such as entertainment, retailing, furniture, beauty, eyewear, watch, gaming, culture and heritage (Gervautz & Schmalstieg, 2012; Scholz & Duffy, 2018). The ability of AR to overlay physical environment with virtual elements such as images, videos, pictures or information provides possibilities for content delivery to consumers, enhancing or altering a number of consumer activities. The high penetration of smart devices in the society led the AR applications to move from the laboratory to the consumer market rapidly (Daponte et al., 2014). The initial uses of AR were in retailing settings such as virtual dressing rooms and virtual mirrors as AR heads (Demirkan & Spohrer, 2014; Pantano & Naccarato, 2010). Then the AR transformed into mobile applications, which let the customers use it in their private settings as well as retail environments (Rese et al., 2017; Daponte et al., 2014). The AR applications on smart mobile devices allow a consumer to see a virtual product or access digital content, and augment the physical reality with virtual elements, what is AR's defining characteristics compared to other interactive technologies (Javornik, 2016; Scholz & Smith, 2016).

AR is particularly helpful in aiding consumers in product trial, educating them in product use (Baier et al., 2015), help them make decisions with more certainty (Oh et al., 2008) and entertain them in their initial product experience (Gervautz & Schmalstieg, 2012). The greatest opportunity of AR applications lies within marketing, advertising, and sales (Gervautz & Schmalstieg, 2012; Reese et al., 2016; Scholz & Smith, 2016). The marketing outcomes of AR applications can be listed as user experience satisfaction (Poushneh & Vasquez-Parraga, 2017), satisfaction before purchasing (Bulearca & Tamarjan, 2010), maximizing consumer engagement with the brand (Scholz and Smith, 2016), meaningful consumer-brand relationships (Scholz & Duffy, 2018; Shankar et al., 2016), willingness to buy (Poushneh & Vasquez-Parraga, 2017; Huang & Hsu-Liu, 2014; Kim & Forsythe, 2008), brand attitude (Rauschnabel & Ro, 2016) and positive consumer-brand relationships (Poushneh & Vasquez-Parraga, 2017; Scholz & Duffy, 2018).

Usage of Technology Acceptance Model in Augmented Reality

One of the frequently used theories in studying AR is the TAM model (e.g.; Rese et al., 2017; Kim & Forsythe, 2008; Domina et al., 2012). The TAM (Davis, 1989) is the most widely applied theory of information systems in explaining the usage and adoption of technologies by consumers (Lee et al., 2003). The model, drawing from the Theory of Reasoned Action, assumes that the intention of a user to use the system is best explained by the attitude of the user towards using the technology (AT); while AT is best explained by perceived usefulness (PU) and perceived ease of use (PEOU) of the technology; with PEOU directly influencing PU. PU refers to the extent that a user believes that using a particular system would enhance his/her performance; whereas PEOU refers to the degree that a person sees using a particular system is free of effort (Davis, 1989). In short, TAM foresees that new technology will be internalized if it is perceived as easy to use and useful (Davis, 1989).

The TAM2 model (Venkatesh & Davis, 2000) adds antecedents to PU, whereas the TAM3 model adds antecedents to PEOU (Venkatesh & Bala, 2008). Thus, it is accepted that external variables such as personal factors, social norms, system characteristics, or other facilitating conditions as antecedents may act on the TAM model (Venkatesh & Bala, 2008; Rauschnabel & Ro, 2016). A meta-analysis carried out by King and He (2006) incorporated 88 research papers and showed "TAM to be a valid and robust model" (p.740) in the extant literature. Venkatesh et al. (2003) then developed the Unified Theory of Acceptance and Use of Technology (UTAUT) model to combine together previous TAM related studies and incorporated the moderating influences of personal factors such as age, gender on dimensions of UTAUT. In UTAUT, performance expectancy and effort expectancy were used to incorporate PU and PEOU consecutively in the original TAM model. The model posits that effort expectancy may become non-significant over extended usage of technology; hence, PEOU may be more salient in the early stages of using new technology, exerting a positive influence on PU.

The research on AR based on TAM also consistently showed the general appropriateness of TAM for studying AR applications. TAM model was utilized for wearable textiles (Spagnolli et al., 2014), virtual try-on technologies (Kim & Forsythe, 2008), smart watches (Kim & Shin, 2015), reality smart glasses (Rauschnabel et al., 2015; Rauschnabel & Ro, 2016), and mobile AR games (Rauschnabel et al., 2017) to name a few. In general, the studies supported that PEOU and PU positively influenced attitude and intention to use AR and that PEOU also had a positive impact on PU (e.g.; Rese et al.; 2017; Haugstvedt, 2012). A study by Balog & Pribeanu (2010) showed that PU and perceived enjoyment positively affected students' acceptance of augmented reality in education, whereas PEOU had a smaller impact. The study by Lin & Chen (2017), on the other hand, showed that in their study that PEOU and PU influenced attitude and intention to use AR on tour-sharing through their effect on satisfaction with AR application.

Uses and Gratifications in Using Augmented Reality Applications

U&G is a theoretical framework that is used to study how media, including social media, are utilized to fulfill the needs and individual users with different goals (Smock et al., 2011). U&G was first proposed by Katz in 1959, and consecutive relevant studies were conducted by Katz, Blumler, and Gurevitch in 1974. U&G states that the audience selects media based on personal needs and knows which media can satisfy their needs. The theory assumes that as new media and content genres continue to emerge, U&G studies yield their own schemes and terms for classifying motivations (Katz et al. 1974). The extant literature recognizes Mc Quail's (1984) categorization of four U&G (entertainment, integration and social interaction, personal identity, and information) as applicable to modern day media usage with remuneration and empowerment as additions of the social media (Muntinga et al., 2011).

There have been several studies that tried to identify the uses and gratifications in AR usage and adoption. The literature recognizes that utilitarian perspective in using AR applications can be captured by perceived usefulness or performance expectancies dimension of the TAM model (Davis et al., 1989; Venkatesh & Bala, 2008; Rauschnabel et al., 2018); and PU was identified as an important driver of AR satisfaction (Lin & Chen, 2017), attitude and adoption to use AR (Rauschnabel & Ro, 2016; Rese et al., 2017). The underlying assumption is that consumers use technology to improve their performance (Venkatesh et al., 2003); and in a similar understanding, AR technologies provides relevant information in real time and, by doing so, help consumers make decisions; and satisfy their cognitive, utilitarian needs. Among other uses and gratifications defined in the literature for AR, hedonic, social, and sensual gratifications can be counted (Rauschnabel, 2018). Rese et al. (2017) hypothesized that perceived enjoyment and perceived informativeness had an effect on PU of AR applications, and proved that their importance varies for different kinds of AR applications (marker-based versus markerless AR applications). Olsson et al. (2013) discussed in their study that AR applications are a source of hedonic experiences, self-expression, enjoyment, and stimulation as well as a source of digital information. Informativeness of AR applications was said to reduce user anxiety (Tseng-Lung & Feng, 2014) and help consumers in decision-making (Kim & Forsythe, 2008). Javornik (2016), on the other hand, proposed that consumer's experiences with AR applications are more hedonic than utilitarian, and that affective component plays a stronger role in leading to consumer responses than the cognitive. Furthermore, Tseng-Lung & Feng (2014) talked about experiential values associated with AR such as playfulness, aesthetics, service excellence and consumer's return on investment such as the efficiency of the AR.

Studies by Rauschnabel et al. (2015, 2017, 2018) also showed that AR applications such as Google Glass can be adopted for functional benefits, hedonic benefits, and for social benefits such as signaling social inclusion, uniqueness (Rauschnabel et al., 2015, 2017), self-presentation, connecting/socializing with others, and sensual gratifications of enhanced reality or wearable comfort (Rauschnabel et al., 2018; Rauschnabel, 2018). AR games such as Pokemon Go, on the other hand, can be adopted for enjoyment, nostalgia, and to a lesser extent for socialization reasons (Rauschnabel et al., 2017). Extant literature showed that people tend to feel gratification when immersing themselves into artificial, virtual worlds (Rauschnabel, 2018). They feel like they can do things that they cannot do in real life, and escape from realities of life (Lucas & Sherry, 2004) such as placing objects in physical realities, testing different ideas, and achieving their ideal realities through augmentation. This gratification is called "desired enhancement of reality," which allows users to realize dreams, such as buying objects (e.g., cars, art) they cannot afford or owning fictitious pets or phantasy-like creatures that appear realistic from subjective perceptions of their reality (Rauschnabel, 2018, p. 6). As another sensual gratification, Rauschnabel (2018) talks about wearable comfort, defined as consumers' evaluation of the physical comfortability (e.g., pressure, weight, bulkiness) of wearing ARSGs, determine usage intention. Rauschnabel (2018) also talks about life efficiency related to people's belief that AR can help them do certain daily tasks more efficiently, and describes it as a utilitarian gratification of AR smart glasses. Moreover, a study by Lin & Chen (2017) showed that perceived entertainment had a positive effect on PEOU and PU; whereas information sharing influenced PU. Self-presentation, on the other hand, affected the satisfaction of the user with AR application on tourism (Lin & Chen, 2017).

Risks Associated With AR

Risks are an undermined subject in AR studies; the factors that decrease the intensity of use, the risk factors, are omitted in most AR research (Rauschnabel et al., 2017). It is Sharma and Vassiliou (2016) that studied Pokemon Go and revealed that serious road traffic accidents happened due to Pokemon Go, exposing a threat to the user's physical health. Similarly, Rauschnabel et al. (2017) also reported that Pokemon Go induced both physical and also data privacy risks. Privacy risks are defined as a risk factor that reflects intrinsic psychological fear of a possible loss of personal information during a particular technology or media usage (Malhotra et. al., 2004). Physical risks, on the other hand, involve a threat to an individual's safety, physical health, and well-being (Lu et al., 2005). Similar to Rauschnabel et al. (2017), Olsson et al. (2013)'s study showed that users mention their sensitivity for privacy and expect to access to AR applications, that do not require sharing sensitive personal information.

METHODOLOGY

An exploratory research methodology was deemed appropriate to study U&G and TAM in AR applications since mobile AR application studies were novel in marketing literature and lacked sufficient exploratory research. Two complementary exploratory research techniques, in-depth and focus group interviews were carried on to provide rich data and triangulation of the results (Malhotra, 2010), using diverse available techniques/methods for the common interest. It was thought that there might be differences between the responses given by participants according to the experiences they remember and responses given immediately after experiencing the AR. Therefore, the in-depth study took into consideration the past experiences of the respondents with AR applications, whereas the focus groups were designed to let the participants experience the AR application before sharing their ideas about it in focus group interviews.

First of all, an in-depth interview technique was utilized to understand the underlying consumer motivations to accept this technology, perceptions on PEOU and PU, and the resulting consumer-brand related outcomes. This research method is preferred as it enables more privacy and provides comfort for the respondent by one-to-one meetings, and thus easier to retrieve real thoughts (Daymon and Holloway, 2002). The sample included 16 consumers who had prior knowledge and experience in AR applications, and the interviews lasted about an hour and were transcribed separately by the authors. The AR applications that were discussed by the respondents included different markets such as wall paint, home furniture, transportation, and museum. Information about the applicants and related augmented reality applications are presented in Table 1. Four of the respondents had used Snapchat, two of them had used Ikea Place, another two had experienced GPS based navigation AR application. The remaining applications were all used once.

On the other hand, three mini focus group interviews were also conducted with university students to obtain real-time thoughts and reactions to mobile AR applications, searching answers for the same questions. Two AR applications were the emphasis of focus group interviews, Marshall ''See and Paint'' AR application and Lego Playgrounds application. The applications were determined based on brand awareness, brand availability in retail, and presence in both Appstore and Google Play platforms in Turkey. There were four respondents in each focus group, aged between 21-24. At the beginning of the focus group interviews, they were given information about the mobile AR applications, allowed a few minutes to download the application and additional ten minutes to experience the application before the discussions started. All the interviews were recorded and transcribed separately by the authors. Information about the participants is given in Table 2.

Data analysis was carried out with the examination of all responses and discussions, which the subjects expressed (after the transcription). The obtained data were analyzed through content analysis (Belk, 2013) by using Atlas.ti, which is a qualitative data analysis tool. All the text was read and coded carefully with the help of a coding framework; descriptive labels were utilized to help with the organization of the information obtained. To assess the reliability of the coding, a test-retest method was used where three authors coded the data individually and compared the results. Quotes were extracted from the transcripts to enrich the findings to be presented.

Table 1. Sample Profile and Applications Used in In-Depth Interviews

Application Used	Explanation	Respondent Information (name initials, age, gender)
Snapchat	Snapchat is a social messaging platform, which detects objects in the real world and applies filters on them with the help of AR technology. Users can view and take photos, add notes on them and share all of this with the filter (if they prefer) for a certain period of time.	D.G., 22, F Y.K., 21, M S.D., 26, F B.A., 24, F
Ikea Place	This application allows users to experiment with the interior design in their homes by selecting a product from the IKEA catalog and placing it in a real specified location with the help of AR technology.	B.A., 24, F N.P., 28, F
GPS Based Navigation AR Application	Augmented reality navigation displays a map through the use of the device's camera on 3D virtual reality, and lets the user experience real-time driving through their device.	B.G., 35, F E.T., 28, M
SS Museum AR Application	This application lets the users see and experience the historical objects with augmented reality enrichments	G.İ, 18, F
IETT AR Application	If they scan the signs and codes found in IETT stops with the smartphone AR application, users can read the history of the bus stops, some of which dates back to the period of horses or electric trolleys,	G.S., 26, M K.A., 24, F
IOS AR Measurement Application	This application measures the dimensions of the desired object by moving the phone with AR technology.	N.G., 36, F
Dyoscope AR Application	Through the Dyoscope application, users can match any color they see in the outside world with the closest colors on the Dyo paint color boards.	H.Ş., 29, M
Marshall AR Application	With the practical color picker technology, after finding a color on the paint palette, you can capture this color with the application and see an instant mapping on the walls or desired objects.	S.D., 26, F
Pokemon Go	Pokemon GO is a game that is using AR technology. In the game, 722 Pokemon characters are trying to be captured by the cameras of the phones.	E.A., 29, F

FINDINGS

Investigation and codification of data brought categorization of the findings into four main headings as (1) U&G of Using AR Applications; (2) Risks Associated with AR and Other Emergent Themes; (3) PEOU and PU of AR Applications; (4) Brand-Related Outcomes of AR Applications.

Table 2. Sample Profile

Focus Group No	Respondent	Profile	Application Used
G1	E1	M, 22	Marshall AR Application, Lego 3D Catalog
G1	E2	M, 22	Marshall AR Application, Lego 3D Catalog
G1	E3	M, 23	Marshall AR Application, Lego 3D Catalog
G1	E4	M, 23	Marshall AR Application, Lego 3D Catalog
G2	K1	F, 21	Marshall AR Application, Lego 3D Catalog
G2	K1	F, 22	Marshall AR Application, Lego 3D Catalog
G2	K3	F, 21	Marshall AR Application, Lego 3D Catalog
G2	K4	F, 21	Marshall AR Application, Lego 3D Catalog
G3	E5	M, 22	Marshall AR Application, Lego 3D Catalog
G3	E6	M, 24	Marshall AR Application, Lego 3D Catalog
G3	E7	M, 23	Marshall AR Application, Lego 3D Catalog
G3	E8	M, 23	Marshall AR Application, Lego 3D Catalog

U&G of Using AR Applications

In-depth interview results indicated that the major reasons for using all types of AR applications centered on entertainment, sensual, and information seeking gratifications. AR applications were considered as fun to use and entertained the respondents during usage with sensory visual experiences. The applications also provided an experience of the enhanced reality at the convenience of the respondents and provided them good service in return for their time. The applications also provided the users with the information they were interested in. Finally, a common theme in all applications was coolness and prestige. The respondents thought that the AR applications conveyed themselves cool to others, and won their appreciation since it was trendy and novel to use these applications. They liked the idea of other people watching them or asking them questions about their experiences.

I had the opportunity to observe and experience how the products looked in my house before I consider buying it (IKEA Place, B.A., 24, F)

I had the opportunity to choose from different colors on the company palette, and experience how it would look like on my walls (Marshall AR, S.D., 26, F)

I had an enriched experience with animated figures explaining the history (SS Museum AR, G.İ, 18, F)

I was fascinated with how the real world merged with the virtual one (Dyoscope AR Application, H.Ş., 29, M)

No need to measure with meter, the IOS AR gave practicality (IOS AR Measurement Application, N.G., 36, F)

I am interested in history, and the app provides me an interesting history of the bus stops, I use in the city (IETT Transportation Application, K.A., 24, F)

Everyone looks at me with wondering eyes when I use this application (IETT Transportation Application, K.A., 24, F)

Other themes that arose not in all, but in some of the AR applications included self-presentation, self-actualization, and social interaction. Self-presentation was evident in Snapchat. People believed that they felt more beautiful when they used the filters of the application, and loved to share it with others. Moreover, the respondents reported that they felt more creative, improved their abilities when they used Pokemon Go and Dyoscope. They also liked the idea of attracting the attention of others when they use the applications in public and interacting with them over the applications.

I love using this application; it makes me feel like an artist to work with colors and see how colors of nature are reflected in the company paint palette; I feel fulfilled with myself (Dyoscope AR Application, H.Ş., 29, M)

When I play PokemonGo, I push my boundaries to be creative and imagine more (PokemonGo, E.A., 29, F)

I love playing with the filters of Snapchat and make myself interesting or attractive; share it with others and wait for their responses (PokemonGo, E.A., 29, F)

When I use this application, people come up and ask me what is going on, and then a natural dialogue starts. I love it (IETT Transportation Application, G.S., 26, M)

The focus group interview results corresponded on some points with the in-depth interview results. The entertainment and experiential gratifications, and information obtained were prevalent in the responses of focus group interviews. Participants liked the idea of trying out the product before actually buying it in Marshall application. They also liked the idea of seeing how the product is assembled in a three-dimensional format in Lego application. They said that the original print catalog was more confusing; and that they had a better understanding of how to put the Lego parts together by using the application. Furthermore, they talked about the time/productivity ratio as an important driver of using both applications.

I am very indecisive, this application helps me make a choice that I will not regret afterward since I can try alternatives and see the results before I buy (Marshall AR, K4, 21, F)

I cannot imagine how the paint would look like on my walls by looking at the print catalog, but with the application, I can try whatever I like, no need to imagine (Marshall AR, E7, 23, M)

My five-year-old niece gets bored when I place the Lego parts in front of her, but I believe she will have fun when she uses the application while doing the Lego. The application will set a target for her, and make sure that her attention is not lost (Lego Playgrounds AR, E3, 23, M)

It is not easy to assemble the products by looking at the catalog. The application shows you some practical methods that you cannot fully get from the print catalog (Marshall AR, E4., 23, M)

Different from the in-depth interviews, the participants in focus group interviews also mentioned empowerment as a gratification, they obtained or might obtain by using the application.

I like the idea of being in control; I can paint half of the wall in one color and the other half in another color. The feeling that I can decide on the alternative makes me engage more with the application (Marshall AR, E3, 23, M)

I wish that I can intervene the animations more; I want to control more (Lego Playgrounds AR, K4, 21, F)

Risks Associated With AR

The respondents reported different types of risks for different types of applications. Some of the applications such as IKEA Place and SS Museum did not have any risk associated with them. However, for applications related to actual product experience (e.g.; Marshall, Dyoscope and IOS AR Measurement), the risks of misrepresentation were frequently mentioned in both in-depth and also focus group interviews.

The application is very convenient; yet, I have doubts about trusting it completely. What if there is a slight deviation in measurement? This always worries my mind (IOS AR Measurement Application, N.G., 36, F)

What if the color deviates from what I see on the application when I buy it? It is a digital format after all (Marshall AR Application, S.D., 26, F)

Another frequently mentioned risk was related to privacy and security. The respondents feared that third parties would reach and use their information for other purposes without permission. There was this general tendency to not to trust mobile applications with their personal information. Psychological risks were also another area that was mentioned frequently with especially Snapchat since the application can put one in the flow easily and take more time than expected; finally tiring the physique, and brain of the user. The participants of the focus group also mentioned that they had fun, but did not like the idea that they might get carried away and lose the sense of time and reality while using the applications. Mental fatigue was also the case if the application required careful attention to complete its steps and obtain the right results. The digital features of the application also added to this feeling.

Snapchat abstracts one from real life; you may spend a lot of time in the application because of its flow; what might cut you off from social life (Snapchat, D.G., 22, F)

I am pushing my limits to do everything correctly so that the measurement is accurate. It is sometimes mentally tiring (IOS AR Measurement Application, N.G., 36, F)

Even though I enjoy it, I also grow tired of mixing digital with the real world. I sometimes feel mentally tired (Dyoscope AR Application, H.Ş., 29, M)

It was very fun, but I just wondered how much time I would lose if I get carried away painting the walls with different colors. I do not like the idea of losing time and space when using applications (Marshall AR, K1, 21, F)

Physical risks were also mentioned for the Pokemon Go application. One respondent reported that she feared of acting clumsy, and harming herself when in the flow of the game and virtual reality.

PEOU and PU of AR Applications

PEOU and PU dimensions of the TAM Model applied to all the AR applications investigated in this study and were considered as important reasons to adopt the technology. In order to find the app easy to use, respondents mentioned the importance of simplicity, user-friendliness, system efficiency, and personalization. Respondents mentioned *''applications should be easy to understand and use (IOS AR Measurement Application, N.G., 36, F)''*, ''simple interface and easy-to-detect features *(Marshall AR, S.D., 26, F)* '' and *''tabs / steps should be easy (IKEA Place, B.A., 24, F)''* for simplicity, *''a small orientation may be sufficient to learn to use (Snapchat, Y.K., 21, M)''* for user-friendliness, *''applications must be running without being stuck (Dyoscope AR Application, H.Ş., 29, M)''* for system efficiency. They also mentioned that *''the user should be able to direct the applications according to his/her wishes and expectations (Snapchat, D.G., 22, F)''* for personalization. The respondents also mentioned the importance of previous experience with mobile devices or apps. They said that *''you need to know how to use mobile devices (Marshall AR, S.D., 26, F) ''* and *''you need to know how to use the applications well (PokemonGo, E.A., 29, F)''* about this issue.

The respondents were asked about their ideas of the perceived usefulness of the AR applications they used. In order to find the application useful, they indicated the importance of saving time, economic benefits, and adding value in other ways such as convenience, social sharing, excitement, or informativeness.

It should save time, physical fatigue and financial savings (Marshall AR, S.D., 26, F)

It should make life easier (IKEA Place, B.A., 24, F)

It should help to share information (Snapchat, Y.K., 21, M)

It should increase social communication (Snapchat, D.G., 22, F)

It should help you to do things that cannot be done in everyday life (PokemonGo, E.A., 29, F)

It should add value to people (information, learning, ease of perception) (IKEA Place, B.A., 24, F)

It should add to the user's predictive ability for future purchases (Marshall AR, S.D., 26, F)

Brand-Related Outcomes of AR Applications

The respondents were asked about how AR applications had an effect on their attitude and behavior towards the brands in these applications. Their answers centered around a positive brand image aroused interest in the products of the brand, purchase intention.

You wonder and want to take a look at the brand's products after you experience the brand in AR (Dyoscope AR Application, H.Ş., 29, M)

If I believe the application provides one-to-one reality, it can excite me and push me to buy during use if there is a BuyNow button available (Marshall AR, S.D., 26, F)

If you are satisfied with AR application, then the product/service can be purchased (IKEA Place, B.A., 24, F)

Respect for the brand increases (IETT Transportation Application, K.A., 24, F)

If it makes things easier, that brand immediately becomes more attractive (IOS AR Measurement Application, N.G., 36, F)

The idea that the brand that thinks about its customers cares about them, and works in their favor makes me see the brand more attractive (SS Museum AR Application, G.İ, 18, F)

The responses of the participants of the focus group interviews also paralleled the responses of the in-depth interviews. Respect towards the brand was frequently mentioned since it made an effort, followed the latest technological innovations, and applied them to their brand. However, the respondents also said that they needed to check whether the competition was doing the same before they made their final decision on how much they appreciated the brand for the application. Purchase intention was observed in some of the participants. Their remarks centered around the idea that the applications should provide direct links to buying the product in real time. Their interest in and intention to buy the product was heightened after using the application.

If the application had a link to buy, I would buy the product because I really enjoyed the 3D catalog experience and am drawn to the product (Lego Playgrounds AR, E8, 23, M)

It could have been better if they had BuyNow button so that we can order whatever we liked immediately (Marshall AR, K1, 21, F)

DISCUSSION

The results of this study shed a light on one of the future technology and marketing tools (www.goldmansachs.com, 2016); and revealed the motivational antecedents of consumer acceptance to use AR applications, and behavioral outcomes. Based on the findings, a testable model is drawn in Figure 1 and proposed for further examination with quantitative approaches. This is the contribution of this study to extant literature. The model extended Rauschnabel (2018)'s study on U& G involved in using smart glasses, by exploring the risks, the applicability of the TAM model, and related outcomes in one model. The proposed model confirmed that Mc Quail's (1984) commonly accepted the categorization of four U&G (entertainment, integration and social interaction, personal identity, and information) applied to AR applications.

Consumers preferred AR applications for entertainment and informative features, as well as for portraying their self-image to others, feelings of self-actualization, and social interaction. An important motivation that appeared in this study, and not evident in Mc Quail's classification was the experiential value that AR provided to the consumers. The experiential value occurred in terms of consumer return on investment, service excellence, aesthetic appeal, and playfulness as described in Mathwick et al. (2001)'s typology of experiential value. Consumer return on investment was the most evident form of experiential value that consumers gratified by using the applications. They expected and experienced efficiency and economic value when they used the applications. The service excellence that they obtained from the application also created an appreciation of the brand to deliver its promises in real time and raised the brand's image in their eyes. The sensory visual appeal and aesthetics of the application were another reason that was mentioned for using the applications. The essence of AR applications was built on experience and reality enrichment with virtual content (Rauschnabel, 2018). Thus, consumers liked and were fascinated with the idea of enhanced reality and were drawn more into the application since it was visually pleasing and enriching. Finally, the playfulness, which is defined as the intrinsic enjoyment of engaging in activities that are absorbing, to the point of offering an escape from the daily life (Mathwick et al., 2001), was also evident in the consumers. They felt away from real life, moved to the flow of the application even though they also feared the risk of losing the sense of time and space. Another theme that was only mentioned in focus group interviews was empowerment. Empowerment can also be thought of as part of the experiential value that is offered by the applications. Consumers liked the idea of being in control of the activities within the application and using their own discretion in the flow of events.

Remuneration, a common theme in new and social media U&G research (Muntinga et al., 2011), did not find a place in the motivations counted by the respondents in this study. Prizes, contests were not the reasons that consumers tried AR applications. The applications under the scrutiny of this research did not employ any prizes or contests. That might be the reason why they did not emerge as gratification in this research.

Risks had an hindrance effect on PU of AR applications since consumers feared of data privacy, physical risks, and psychological risks when in the flow of virtual reality. PEOU and PU appeared as important themes to adopt AR applications, finding support in the extant literature (e.g.; Rese et al.; 2017; Haugstvedt, 2012). Finally, the study scrutinized brand-related outcomes and found out that AR applications exerted a positive influence on brand interest, brand image, and purchase intention, confirming previous studies.

The results of the study imply some marketing tactics for practitioners. First of all, the outcomes pointed out the AR applications' value in terms of increasing interest in the brand/product, improving brand image and triggering purchase intention. Therefore, designing AR applications based on consumer expectations is important. Experiential values are one of the most evident motivations in adopting AR applications. The AR application should involve some playfulness, keep the consumer entertained while providing some practicality in terms of returns on time and energy devoted to using the application. Simple

Figure 1.

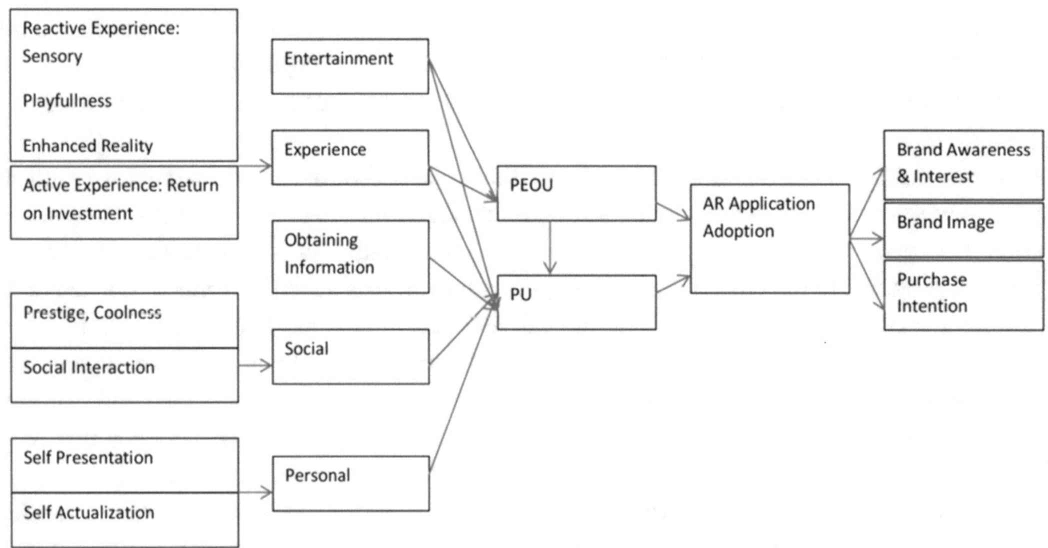

entertainment alone is not enough for an AR application to attract consumer attention; some functional value in use is expected; consumers expect the application to make their lives easier in terms of reaching product information, trying the products, and even making the purchase. The application should also be designed neither too complicated nor too simple. A level of sophistication is expected since the users seek self-actualization. However, user-friendliness and simplicity in usage are also expected. A delicate balance is needed in that sense not to cause mental fatigue risk as well. Users like and want to be in charge of the application, and try things in their own control. Empowerment should be integrated as an essential part of the application, making users active participants in the process, and possibly helping them with their self-actualization.

The duration of the application should also be arranged in a manner that does not cause the user to feel lost in time and virtual reality, and feel irritated. Additionally, the users should be reassured that their data is kept secure since data privacy is a sensitive issue. A method of handling data privacy might be to design an application that does not require sensitive information from the consumers as much as possible. The results of the study also show that consumers like to present themselves using AR application to their social circle, and trigger social conversation over the application. AR applications are new to marketing and consumer practice; therefore consumers may like the idea of being a pioneer in adopting AR applications and earning the appreciation of their peers by showing off. Hence, an omnichannel approach can be pursued in the design of the application, letting integration across channels and omitting the boundaries between them (Verhoef et al., 2015). This way, applications can let consumers share their experience (i.e.; decoration ideas, walls painted, history of the bus stop close to their home) with their friends through social media platforms such as Instagram or Pinterest, stream into a conversation, and gain feedback.

CONCLUSION

This research highlighted the importance of AR applications for the future of consumer-brand relationships. Mobile AR applications create a convenient way for the consumers to get acquainted with the brand, experience its features without an actual purchase. In that way, they can decide to buy or not to buy the brand based on their own simulated experience, what is more convincing compared to other firm promotion tactics. Overall, mobile AR is a modern, enjoyable short cut for the consumer to get to know and evaluate a brand. Given it is a novel and attractive technology; the mobile AR applications will find a permanent position in the promotion mix of the firms in the future. In a world, where time is a precious resource for everyone, mobile AR applications promise to be an important tool of marketing. Furthermore, the results point out that if people are given the chance, there is a strong likelihood that they might also eventually make purchases on the AR applications. Thus, mobile AR applications may also become another channel of both interaction and also purchase for the firms. It is important to create the right design to draw consumer interest to the applications in the future, when there will be a stiff competition among the firms' mobile AR applications. The current research showed that information-providing, practical and enjoyable experience should be blended together to provide a usefull AR application, that will create a difference for the brands, and lead to positive consumer reactions. The risks should also be considered to create the best AR experience for consumers. Data privacy and people's fear of losing track of time and place are important risks stressed in this research and be remedied for. Firms should take into consideration the results of this study to come up with the appropriate mobile AR application that would meet consumer needs.

From a research perspective, it can be said that the research on mobile AR applications are still in the infancy, at the introductory stage. As the market availability and value of mobile AR applications increase in the future, there will be more sophisticated and directed research on the topic. This research is a preliminary step into understanding the concept better and forms a research direction for the future. An interesting array of research would be to explore and test the proposed model in different markets both qualitatively and quantitatively to understand its applicability, and see which motivations are underlined in which contexts. Further research, especially longitudinal research to understand the differences among the introduction, growth, and maturity stages of these applications would also be interesting and strongly recommended. It is possible that in the future, as people get used to mobile AR applications, they will no longer worry about how to use it, and the effect of PEOU will diminish. On the other hand, new motivations may come into play to increase the usefulness of the application in consumer eye. One such motivation, for example, might be remunerative motivations. Further investigation might be conducted to see how consumers may response to rewarding tactics in mobile AR applications since remuneration may create a differentiation point among the competition.

REFERENCES

Azuma, A. T. (1997). A survey on augmented reality. *Presence (Cambridge, Mass.)*, *6*(4), 355–385.

Baier, D., Rese, A., & Schreiber, S. (2015). Analyzing online reviews to measure technology acceptance at the point of scale — the case of IKEA. In E. Pantano (Ed.), *Successful Technological Integration for Competitive Advantage in Retail Settings* (pp. 168–189). IGI Global.

Balog, A., & Pribeanu, C. (2010). The role of perceived enjoyment in the students' acceptance of an augmented reality teaching platform: A structural equation modeling approach. *Studies in Informatics and Control*, *19*(3), 319–330.

Belk, R. (2013). Visual and projective methods in Asian research. *Qualitative Market Research*, *16*(1), 94–107.

Bulearca, M., & Tamarjan, D. (2010). Augmented reality: A sustainable marketing tool? *Global Business and Management Research*, *2*(2–3), 237–252.

Daponte, P., De Vito, L., Picariello, F., & Riccio, M. (2014). State of the art and future developments of the augmented reality for measurement applications. *Measurement*, *57*, 53–70.

Davis, F. D. (1989). Perceived usefulness, perceived ease of use, and user acceptance of information technology. *Management Information Systems Quarterly*, *13*(3), 319–340.

Daymon, C., & Holloway, I. (2002). *Qualitative Research Methods in Public Relations and Marketing Communications*. Routledge.

Demirkan, H., & Spohrer, J. (2014). Developing a framework to improve virtual shopping in digital malls with intelligent self-service systems. *Journal of Retailing and Consumer Services*, *21*(5), 860–868.

Domina, T., Lee, S. E., & MacGillivray, M. (2012). Understanding factors affecting consumer intention to shop in a virtual world. *Journal of Retailing and Consumer Services*, *19*(6), 613–620.

Gervautz, M., & Schmalstieg, D. (2012). Anywhere interfaces using handheld augmented reality. *IEEE Computer*, *45*(7), 26–31.

Huang, T. L., & Hsu Liu, F. (2014). Formation of augmented-reality interactive technology's persuasive effects from the perspective of experiential value. *Internet Research*, *24*(1), 82–109.

Javornik, A. (2016). Augmented reality: Research agenda for studying the impact of its media characteristics on consumer behavior. *Journal of Retailing and Consumer Services*, *30*, 252–261. doi:10.1016/j.jretconser.2016.02.004

Katz, E., Blumler, J. G., & Gurevitch, M. (1974). Utilization of mass communication by the individual. In J. G. Blumler & E. Katz (Eds.), *The uses of mass communications: Current perspectives on gratifications research* (pp. 19–32). Sage.

Kim, J., & Forsythe, S. (2008). Adoption of virtual try-on technology for online apparel shopping. *Journal of International Marketing*, *22*(2), 45–59.

Kim, K. J., & Shin, D.-H. (2015). An acceptance model for smartwatches: Implications for the adoption of future wearable technology. *Internet Research*, *25*(4), 527–541. doi:10.1108/IntR-05-2014-0126

King, W. R., & He, J. (2006). A meta-analysis of the technology acceptance model. *Information & Management*, *43*(6), 740–755. doi:10.1016/j.im.2006.05.003

Lee, Y., Kozar, K. A., & Larsen, K. R. (2003). The technology acceptance model: Past, present, and future. *Communications of the Association for Information Systems*, *12*(1), 50. doi:10.17705/1CAIS.01250

Lin, H. F., & Chen, C. H. (2017). Combining the Technology Acceptance Model and Uses and Gratifications Theory to examine the usage behavior of an Augmented Reality Tour-sharing Application. *Symmetry*, *9*(7), 113. doi:10.3390ym9070113

Lucas, K., & Sherry, J. L. (2004). Sex differences in video game play: A communication-based explanation. *Communication Research*, *31*(5), 499–523. doi:10.1177/0093650204267930

Malhotra, N. K. (2010). *Marketing Research: An Applied Orientation, 6/E*. Pearson Education.

Mathwick, C., Malhotra, N. K., & Rigdon, E. (2001). Experiential value: Conceptualization, measurement, and application in the catalog and Internet shopping environment. *Journal of Retailing*, *77*(1), 39–56. doi:10.1016/S0022-4359(00)00045-2

McQuail, D. (1984). With the benefit of hindsight: Reflections on uses and gratifications research. *Critical Studies in Media Communication*, *1*(2), 177–193.

Moss, A. (2019). *20 Augmented Reality Stats to Keep You Sharp in 2019*. Retrieved from https://techjury.net/stats-about/augmented-reality/

Muntinga, D. G., Moorman, M., & Smit, E. G. (2011). Introducing COBRAs: Exploring motivations for brand-related social media use. *International Journal of Advertising*, *30*(1), 13–46. doi:10.2501/IJA-30-1-013-046

Olsson, T., Lagerstam, E., Kärkkäinen, T., & Väänänen-Vainio-Mattila, K. (2013). Expected user experience of mobile augmented reality services: A user study in the context of shopping centres. *Personal and Ubiquitous Computing*, *17*(2), 287–304. doi:10.100700779-011-0494-x

Pantano, E., & Naccarato, G. (2010). Entertainment in retailing: The influences of advanced technologies. J. Retail. *Consumer Services*, *17*(3), 200–204. doi:10.1016/j.jretconser.2010.03.010

Poushneh, A., & Vasquez-Parraga, A. Z. (2017). Discernible impact of augmented reality on retail customer's experience, satisfaction and willingness to buy. *Journal of Retailing and Consumer Services*, *34*, 229–234. doi:10.1016/j.jretconser.2016.10.005

Rauschnabel, P. A. (2018). Virtually enhancing the real world with holograms: An exploration of expected gratifications of using augmented reality smart glasses. *Psychology and Marketing*, *35*(8), 557–572. doi:10.1002/mar.21106

Rauschnabel, P. A., He, J., & Ro, Y. K. (2018). Antecedents to the adoption of augmented reality smart glasses: A closer look at privacy risks. *Journal of Business Research*, *92*, 374–384. doi:10.1016/j.jbusres.2018.08.008

Rauschnabel, P. A., & Ro, Y. K. (2016). Augmented reality smart glasses: An investigation of technology acceptance drivers. *International Journal of Technology Marketing*, *11*(2), 123–148. doi:10.1504/IJTMKT.2016.075690

Rauschnabel, P. A., Brem, A., & Ivens, B. S. (2015). Who will buy smart glasses? Empirical results of two pre-market-entry studies on the role of personality in individual awareness and intended adoption of Google Glass wearables. *Computers in Human Behavior*, *49*(8), 635–647. doi:10.1016/j.chb.2015.03.003

Rauschnabel, P. A., Rossmann, A., & Tom Dieck, M. C. (2017). An adoption framework for mobile augmented reality games: The case of Pokémon Go. *Computers in Human Behavior*, *76*(6), 276–286. doi:10.1016/j.chb.2017.07.030

Rese, A., Baier, D., Geyer-Schulz, A., & Schreiber, S. (2017). How augmented reality apps are accepted by consumers: A comparative analysis using scales and opinions. *Technological Forecasting and Social Change*, *124*, 306–319. doi:10.1016/j.techfore.2016.10.010

Scholz, J., & Smith, A. N. (2016). Augmented reality: Designing immersive experiences that maximize consumer engagement. *Business Horizons*, *59*(2), 149–161. doi:10.1016/j.bushor.2015.10.003

Shankar, V., Kleijnen, M., Ramanathan, S., Rizley, R., Holland, S., & Morrissey, S. (2016). Mobile shopper marketing: Key issues, current insights, and future research avenues. *Journal of Interactive Marketing*, *34*, 37–48. doi:10.1016/j.intmar.2016.03.002

Smock, A. D., Ellison, N. B., Lampe, C., & Wohn, D. Y. (2011). Facebook as a toolkit: A uses and gratification approach to unbundling feature use. *Computers in Human Behavior*, *27*(6), 2322–2329. doi:10.1016/j.chb.2011.07.011

Spagnolli, A., Guardigli, E., Orso, V., Varotto, A., & Gamberini, L. (2014). *Measuring user acceptance of wearable symbiotic devices: validation study across application scenarios. In Symbiotic Interaction*. Springer International Publishing.

Venkatesh, V., & Bala, H. (2008). Technology acceptance model 3 and a research agenda on interventions. *Decision Sciences*, *39*(2), 273–315. doi:10.1111/j.1540-5915.2008.00192.x

Venkatesh, V., & Davis, F. D. (2000). A theoretical extension of the technology acceptance model: Four longitudinal field studies. *Management Science*, *46*(2), 186–204. doi:10.1287/mnsc.46.2.186.11926

Venkatesh, V., Morris, M. G., Davis, G. B., & Davis, F. D. (2003). User acceptance of information technology: Toward a unified view. *Management Information Systems Quarterly*, *27*(3), 425–478. doi:10.2307/30036540

Verhoef, P. C., Kannan, P. K., & Inman, J. J. (2015). From multi-channel retailing to omni-channel retailing: Introduction to the special issue on multi-channel retailing. *Journal of Retailing*, *91*(2), 174–181. doi:10.1016/j.jretai.2015.02.005

Petrock, V. (2019). *Virtual and Augmented Reality Users 2019*. Retrieved from https://www.emarketer.com/content/virtual-and-augmented-reality-users-2019

Report, G. S. (2016). *Virtual and Augmented Reality: Understanding the race for next computing platform*. https://www.goldmansachs.com/insights/pages/technology-driving-innovation-folder/virtual-and-augmented-reality/report.pdf

KEY TERMS AND DEFINITIONS

Augmented Reality: Enhancing reality with digital objects or information in real time, creating an enriched reality experience for the user.

Brand Loyalty: Extent of attachment of consumers towards a brand expressed through their affection and repeat purchase of that brand.

Focus Group Interview: Qualitative research technique where a group of respondents gather together and discuss a subject under the moderation of the researcher.

In-Depth Interview: Qualitative research technique where the researcher conducts individual interviews to explore an issue in-depth with rich qualitative data.

Perceived Ease of Use: Ease with which consumers can use technology.

Perceived Usefullness: How usefullness consumers find a technology to be.

Technology Acceptance Model: Well-known model used to understand how consumers adopt new technologies.

Uses and Gratifications: Well-known theory used to understand consumer motivations to use media.

Virtual Reality: Computer-generated three-dimensional reality, with which consumers interact with.

Chapter 12
Students in Socially Vulnerable Contexts:
Discovering Their Entrepreneurial Potential

Silvia Victoria Poncio
Facultad de Tecnología Informática, Universidad Abierta Interamericana, Argentina

Daniel Tedini
Facultad de Tecnología Informática, Universidad Abierta Interamericana, Argentina

Veronica Castañeira
Facultad de Tecnología Informática, Universidad Abierta Interamericana, Argentina

Diego E. Marzorati
Facultad de Tecnología Informática, Universidad Abierta Interamericana, Argentina

Eric Hermán Roth
Facultad de Tecnología Informática, Universidad Abierta Interamericana, Argentina

ABSTRACT

A survey was developed based on an adaptation of the resource used by the Association for Training, Research and Development of Entrepreneurship (AFIDE: Asociación para la Formación, Investigación y Desarrollo del Emprendimiento, in Spanish) in the project for the Entrepreneurial Potential of Latin American Undergraduates (PEUL: Potencial Emprendedor de los Universitarios de Latinoamérica, in Spanish). The results showed that more than three-quarters of the students acknowledged having initiative, being creative and innovative, and obtaining and managing information in order to make their own decisions. They also identified that they value flexibility and time management, and they feel confident and motivated by making uncertainty a tool that allows them to recognize mistakes and continue to pursue their projects.

DOI: 10.4018/978-1-7998-7010-4.ch012

INTRODUCTION

The spread of the Internet among the members of societies generated a series of hypotheses that have not been verified over time. For example, new opportunities would be opened in the international and local labor market for the less favored segments of the population, the digital gap between different social classes would be reduced, humanity would march towards a sustained development and safeguarding nature, new technologies would help a transparent and equitable financial management among citizens, etc. (Burton, A. et al., 2020; Yingsaeree, Treleaven & Nuti, 2010; Andriole, 2010) This has not been the case since the end of the 20th century until today.

Although human beings, due to their intrinsic nature, continue to be interested in these technological changes that favor human communications (Schneiderman, 2002), because they continue to relate them to the future, personal and community progress, environmental protection, etc, however, a large part of the world's population has found that there is only a flood of information online (Cerf, 2007) and that contemporary banking financial actions (Yingsaeree, Treleaven & Nuti, 2010), do not provide any solution to the relationship of trust between customers and banking institutions (Cipolla-Ficarra & Alma, 2015), or the promotion of youth employment, to name a few cases. The labor market continues to bet on lowering labor costs, using the panacea derived from ICTs, through the web, such as offshoring (Schaffer, 2006; Tambe & Hitt, 2010), business and market intelligence (Chen, 2010a; Chen, 2010b; Vixie, 2011), cloud computing (Kshetri, 2010), among many others. However, many places in the Americas remain at the crossroads of telecommunications and its derivations, already perfectly described, in the 1980s by Armand Mattelart and Héctor Schmucler (Mattelart & Schmucler, 1983). From the technological, sociological, educational and economic point of view, etc, there is an endless number of works related to this situation (Duening, Hisrich & Lechter, 2014; Bessant & Tidd, 2015), in addition to the classic problem of the transformation of the real economy into a digital economy (Pinker, Seidmann & Foster, 2002), but they are studies, carried out by teams of people who are exogenous to the local reality, and which do not exactly analyze the human being in his or her real context and interact daily with a diverse set of variables, as has been done in this research. In other words, study the local changes with a global projection, and not in the opposite sense.

Nowadays, profound changes are taking place that affect people's ways of being in the world. Vázquez & Mouján-Fernández (2016) state that among the founding factors of these changes are the decline of institutions, immediacy, image, and communications, which are determining factors in personal achievement. In addition, the market introduced a new alteration in the modes of existence given its logic where temporality is speed, bringing with it new ways of linking and being connected to the network.

No one can now doubt that the Internet has brought about one of the most profound changes that human beings have ever experienced, which is that the two axes that by definition have operated as the framework of the subject in its history, have become uncertain, such as space and time. As far as space is concerned, a new space has emerged, which is neither inside nor outside, it is not a specific place, but it is many places at the same time, which is far and which is near? that which is 200 meters away and offline or 20,000 kilometers away and online?. As for time, there is a new time that is characterized by speed and immediacy. It is the "no time". All actions nowadays take very little time (communicating, booking a ticket, a hotel, obtaining a document, etc.) and where the concept of time "little by little" is replaced by that of "instantaneousness", nothing more and nothing less than by the suppression of time. The scope of this conception is so significant that today in society, especially for young people, everything that cannot be resolved with a click, for many people becomes "impossible" (Vázquez & Mouján-Fernández, 2016).

Today's young people, also called "digital natives", were born with technological devices at their fingertips which constituted their way of connecting with each other. They grew up with new conceptions of time and space. They do not need to adapt to immediacy or to chaotic occurrences because this is "their world". Those are generations that can be called "global" (Vázquez & Mouján-Fernández, 2016).

The Spanish Royal Academy of Language –by its acronym in Spanish RAE: Real Academia Española (RAE, n.d, definition 5) defines "Generation" as "a group of people who, because they were born at an early date and have received similar education and cultural and social influences, behave in a similar or comparable manner in some respects" (Real Academia Española, 2019b).

GENERATIONS, NEW TECHNOLOGIES AND EMPLOYMENTS

There are different types of generations divided by intervals, beginning with the so-called "Silent Generation" who were born from 1925 to 1945. Then, the "Baby Boomers Generation" are the ones born from 1946 to 1964, followed by "Generation X" born between 1965 and 1982. This last one was followed by "Generation Y" or millennials, from 1983 to 1994, and finally by "Generation Z" also called Centennials, from 1995 to the last half of the 2000's (Batista, Cabrera & Villanueva, 2014).

The "millennials" are the first generation that can be considered global. Unlike previous generations, for them there are no differences between countries and they can all relate to the same values. They have grown up with the beginnings of digitalization and their access to the labor market is marked by the economic crisis. Also known as 'ni ni' (neither study nor work), it is a stigmatized generation that has been described as lazy, individualistic and bourgeois (Ortega, 2017).

Regarding the employment aspect, these young people of the generation Y or millennials tend to prioritize that which is immediate over the construction of long term projects. That is why the accumulation or saving of money, a characteristic that has crossed several previous generations, is no longer relevant to those who are part of these generations. In fact, it is more important for them to enjoy what they do, a good quality of life, searching for new challenges or horizons, and sustaining an independent mindset outside of established patterns (Rossi-Casé, Doná, Biganzoli & Garzaniti, 2019).

The "Z" generation (Z gen) is the generation after the millennials who are at most 25 years old and outnumber their predecessors. They are more entrepreneurial, quicker to learn and self-taught, which makes them much more irreverent than their fellow millennials who were educated with much more rigid systems (Vilanova & Ortega, 2017).

Vilanova & Ortega (2017) state that this generation of young people is experiencing the democratization of access to employment opportunities, where it no longer matters who your father is or where you were born, only your talent counts.

Since they are digital natives and very creative young people with a high degree of adaptability to new environments, they take advantage of this to seek new opportunities in an increasingly changing job market. They know that they will have to adapt to new working realities many times and have a lot of geographical mobility in an increasingly global world.

Between these last two generations it is possible to identify the following differences:

The millennial generation enjoys being in control of a given situation, while the centennial generation advocates listening to all the voices of the world, rejecting the principle of authority (Solís-Rodríguez, 2020).

For the millennial generation, it is not a priority to help society and/or the environment, since they tend to focus on the acquisition of material and financial resources and their own enrichment. The centennials, on the other hand, seek to drive social change through the search for solutions from a collective perspective, which is why they tend to be socially entrepreneurial (Solís-Rodríguez, 2020).

For both generations, however, the creation of new jobs is important, which shows that they are aware of the economic and employment context of the country in which they are immersed. Both also present a neutral position when it comes to carrying out actions in favor of the environment, demonstrating the difficulty they have in implementing specific proposals in this area, although it is the Centennials who are more inclined to help the environment and/or society (Solís-Rodríguez, 2020).

The millennials find the fact of being their own boss a motivating and important factor for the creation of companies, so they tend to be more independent and autonomous (Solís-Rodríguez, 2020).

In both generations, the economic factor plays an important role in entrepreneurial activity; however, it is more predominant in the centennial generation, since this generation gives greater importance to the social image and its influence on the people around them, which can be considered a motivating factor for entrepreneurship (Solís-Rodríguez, 2020).

In the case of the centennials, the family factor in decision making has greater influence in comparison with the millennial generation, which is more neutral, since the first ones find it a priority to be able to help their family environment economically (Solís-Rodríguez, 2020).

As for the entry into the labor market, if the situation of the millennials was not very promising, generation "Z" suffers even higher unemployment rates (Vilanova & Ortega, 2017).

The International Labor Organization (by its acronym in Spanish OIT: Organización Internacional del Trabajo) warns of a generation marked by an increasingly serious global crisis in youth employment (Organización Internacional del Trabajo, 2017). The exclusion of young people from the path to work translates into current and future welfare losses for society as a whole.

Unemployment impacts people, especially the youth group, not only from the economic point of view, but also from the psychological and social point of view, putting them in vulnerable situations. It affects self-esteem, generates feelings of impotence, diminished social relations, frustration, self-blame, insecurity, feelings of helplessness, anger and resentment, isolation and poor health.

Vulnerability and Entrepreneurship

Vulnerability is a broad multidimensional concept that can refer to the person, the family or the population group in which the vulnerability arises.

According to Spanish Royal Academy of Language (RAE, n.d., definition 1), the term vulnerability refers to the "quality of being vulnerable," (Real Academia Española, 2020a) being referred to as "being able to be hurt or receive injury, physically or morally" (Real Academia Española, 2020b). However, the causes and its manifestations have changed in the last decade, resulting in an exponential increase in its use, both in sociopolitical contexts and at the institutional level, as well as in the media and, therefore, in society itself. Even so, this term has been used with little precision (Batalla, Monsalvo, González Aguña & Santamaría García, 2018).

The United Nations, within the framework of vulnerability reduction for the achievement of the Millennium Development Goals, defines vulnerability as "a state of high exposure to certain risks and uncertainties, combined with a diminished capacity to protect or defend against them and to cope with their negative consequences."

Some authors postulate that the cause of vulnerability is intimately related to daily life and is dynamic, because when there is a sustained increase in it, fragility appears (Batalla, Monsalvo, González Aguña & Santamaría García, 2018).

In this context of vulnerability caused by unemployment, constant change and economic uncertainty, job training proposals for young people are becoming increasingly important, where personal and social entrepreneurial capacities are reinforced so as to facilitate an improvement in their quality of life, reduce the possibility of economic and social vulnerability, and develop tools and attitudes to face the demands of the new society.

The Cuatro Vientos Educational Center (Instituto de Capacitación Laboral del Centro Educativo Cuatro Vientos, in Spanish) is an institution in the city of Rosario (Argentina) belonging to the non-governmental, non-profit organization known as Association Rosarina of Assistance AID (by its acronym in Spanish A.R.A.S. – Asociación Rosarina de Ayuda Solidaria) whose aim is to pitch in people's human and social promotion, aimed at the common good (Asociación Rosarina de Ayuda Solidaria, n.d).

It is located on the border between the towns of Rosario (Godoy neighborhood, Santa Lucía) and Pérez (Cabín 9 neighborhood), surrounded by neighborhoods with high levels of vulnerability, with a marked lack of public services and deficiencies in the existing ones (TECHO, 2016), with high rates of unemployment among its inhabitants, and with violence wanting to take over the streets.

Precisely because of the context in which Cuatro Vientos is immersed, this institution provides integral training to the young people who attend, many of whom are generation "Z" and millennials from low social strata, exposed to material and educational deficiencies and with few opportunities to join an increasingly demanding world of work.

This Center provides a protected environment where young people can establish intra-generational relationships and inter-generational dialogue with teachers and tutors, with a view to training them to discover new horizons through the exchange of experiences and personalized work in tutorials and workshops that motivate them to create, adapt to new environments, to give their best, to discover talent, develop skills and acquire knowledge, to build future opportunities (Armas, 2018).

In the field of job training, Cuatro Vientos prepares those who participate in its activities for a rapid insertion into the world of work, so that they can obtain a job that provides them with the material means necessary to lead a dignified life, leaving behind the current conditions of poverty or indigence. They also promote the relationship between industry and school, through the implementation of agreements with companies in the area. The development of the culture of work is the foundation of their action in this area since currently young people do not have adequate professional training institutions in the area.

They carry out courses with job prospects in computer science and courses of masonry and installation of ceramics, electricity, mechanics, welding and industrial operator. The same courses are given in two workshops: work and the computer office and, when they find it necessary, they also use other industry workshops in the area.

Through the training they provide, Cuatro Vientos seeks to recover the importance of the culture of work as a truly effective and irreplaceable means of growth for the individual and also for the society in which he lives and carries out his activities, helping him to produce a real improvement in his life conditions and those of his family group (Asociación Rosarina de Ayuda Solidaria, 2019).

Young people (and not so young) who attend training courses at the Job Training Institute from Cuatro Vientos Educational Center, like so many other young people of generation Z, are betting on entrepreneurship not only as the ideal job aiming at balancing work and personal life, but also as a possible tool to deal with vulnerability.

According to Peter Drucker, entrepreneurship "is a mixture of opportunity, creativity and determination to create something of value" (López de Toro-Rivera, 2014) and therefore has a very important role for economic development since it is fundamental in promoting innovation, creating employment opportunities and generating well-being and social development. The term has been related especially to innovation, but also to enterprise, change, employment, value and growth. The role of the entrepreneur is to exploit an invention or a technological possibility that generates new products or services, new forms of production, sources of supply of raw materials, forms of organization that revolutionize the established pattern of production.

An entrepreneur is someone who identifies a need in the marketplace, makes decisions about human and financial resources, materials, takes risks, invests time and effort to obtain a monetary reward and personal satisfaction (Rodríguez-Moreno, Diana & Gómez-Murillo, 2014).

There are six schools of thought that define entrepreneurship: the school of entrepreneurship of "the great person" and the school of "psychological characteristics" that define the entrepreneur according to personal qualities; the classical school, which defines the entrepreneur as one who has the ability to recognize opportunities; the school of management and leadership, which focus on the management skills of entrepreneurs; and the sixth school, which defines entrepreneurship in the organization or within the organization (intrapreneurs) as the ability to adapt.

The term "skill" according to the dictionary of the Spanish Royal Academy of Language (RAE, n.d, definition 2.2) refers to having the expertise, aptitude, or suitability to do something or intervene in a given matter (Real Academia Española, 2019a). Therefore, it includes knowledge, know-how, and skills which are materialized into behaviors that are carried out when the knowledge, aptitude, and personality traits are put into practice. According to Sobrado-Fernández & Fernández-Rey (2010), an essential characteristic of skill is action, where motivation, knowledge, values, attitudes, and emotions are integrated.

There are individual characteristics, procedures or knowledge that are definable in action and therefore possess a dynamic character that is a product of experience, that can be used in a given context and that can also be educated, developed, acquired throughout life, these are called skills.

In particular, personal and social skills constitute capacities or abilities that people have to relate to others and to the environment. They are formed by ideas, feelings, beliefs and values that are the result of learning and experience of each one, so they are acquired throughout life. Their importance in daily life is fundamental and allows one to be socially competent and active with the world around us.

Tobón (2010) considers someone to be competent when he can integrate himself into a task with others. To learn to be competent is to train oneself in the personal, cultural and socio-labor conception, but it is not a competitiveness of those who are only trained to have more power or dominate over others, but they are trained to do good in a cooperative way.

Different authors consider it fundamental to foster social skills that promote creativity, imagination, critical thinking, collaboration, pro-activity and teamwork. In this way, a strong sense of self-esteem and confidence is promoted, and where the skills seek to reinforce that people are entrepreneurs, first, as a social subject and then in the work place, to try to change their reality (Sánchez, 2013) (Villanueva, 2013).

Within the field of skills are those called "entrepreneurial skills" which would be those "that allow subjects to develop an entrepreneurial project with which to generate economic growth and social cohesion, thus configuring itself as an integrated social project" (Martínez-Rodriguez, 2011).

Entrepreneurial skills are then a critical success factor for personal development. Although innate abilities exist, others can be stimulated through a process of association between learning and experience. In this sense, the activity of non-governmental associations that promote and provide a framework for the development of entrepreneurship in members of society, especially those who are most disadvantaged, is of vital importance.

In general, there is a certain consensus that the psychological characteristics associated with entrepreneurship are, among others: personal control, propensity for risk, self-efficacy, need for achievement, tolerance for ambiguity, and innovation (García & Sánchez, 2016).

Since 2016, the Association for Training, Research and Development of Entrepreneurship (by its acronym in Spanish AFIDE: Asociación para la Formación, Investigación y Desarrollo del Emprendimiento) through its research project for the Entrepreneurial Potential of Latin American Undergraduates (by its acronym in Spanish PEUL: Potencial Emprendedor de los Universitarios de Latinoamérica) has been working on the analysis of business intention (entrepreneurial potential) and the factors that determine it, in university students from Latin America and Europe.

In this research, a survey was developed to assess the entrepreneurial potential of students who attend the Job Training Institute from Cuatro Vientos Educational Center, based on an adaptation of the resource used in the research project for the Entrepreneurial Potential of Latin American Undergraduates (by its acronym in Spanish PEUL)

For this reason, skills were chosen that reveal an entrepreneurial attitude and that, when the students expressed their agreement, were recognized as having "entrepreneurial potential".

These skills are:

- Initiative, innovation and creativity: Active influence on events instead of passive acceptance of them, vision of opportunities in them. Leads to action by generating innovative responses to complex situations that arise, so as to produce original or unusual solutions. It is not only to have a creative idea but to put it into practice and be valued by some interest group. The creation, united to innovation, generates productivity to the different organizations.
- Self-confidence: It constitutes a judgment or self-perception about one's own capacity. On the other hand, it is a general judgment that is not limited to any particular activity or task for which one's capacities are required.
- Time management and task organization: planning and organization, ability to organize and establish the necessary action plans to achieve the objectives set with the available resources (technical, economic and human).
- Commitment to results: willingness to act with a clear interest in achieving the objectives set, setting challenging goals above standards, improving and maintaining high levels of performance.
- Leadership: ability to set goals, follow through and guide and motivate others to achieve them, creating an environment based on mutual trust and personal/professional development.
- Gathering and management of information for decision making: obtain and process information related to a certain work process, taking as a reference the job position, level of responsibility and requirements of the organization.

- Objective-driven work: Ability to focus efforts in pursuit of an objective, taking into account cost-benefit. Capacity to direct the acts to the expected achievement.

The guiding questions of this research were:

What is the socio-demographic profile of the young people, in terms of gender and age?
What are their expectations in relation to work?
What is the entrepreneurial potential they possess?

Methodology

Universe: Students attending the Job Training Institute from Cuatro Vientos Educational Center, year 2019. Neighborhood Cabín 9, El Chajá Street (border road) Nº 8790, Rosario, Route 33, Southwest Zone, Province of Santa Fe, Argentina.

Population and sample: Students (48) from the Job Training courses, attending during 2019.

Methodological design: This is a descriptive exploratory study of primary sources.

Instruments used: A survey was developed to assess the entrepreneurial potential of students who attend the Job Training Institute from Cuatro Vientos Educational Center, based on an adaptation of the resource used in the research project for the Entrepreneurial Potential of Latin American Undergraduates (by its acronym in Spanish PEUL), consisting of 37 questions, in order to evaluate their entrepreneurial capacity. They were handed out in printed format and self-administered.

Data Analysis and Presentation: Seven skills were selected to evaluate the entrepreneurial potential of the students. These were:

1. Initiative, innovation and creativity.
2. Self-confidence.
3. Time management and task organization.
4. Commitment to results.
5. Leadership
6. Gathering and managing information for decision making
7. Objective-driven work.

To each one of these skills, a set of between 4 and 5 questions were associated, which were placed into a questionnaire and the students were asked to answer with one of the following options according to the Likert scale:

1: Totally disagree
2: Disagreeing
3: Neither agree nor disagree
4: Agree
5: I totally agree

The collected data was imported into an Excel spreadsheet and analyzed, grouping the questions corresponding to each competence.

Results

More than half of the students surveyed (58%) were identified as women.

Figure 1. Demographic characterization of the population (n=48) according to gender. Rosario, Argentina, 2019

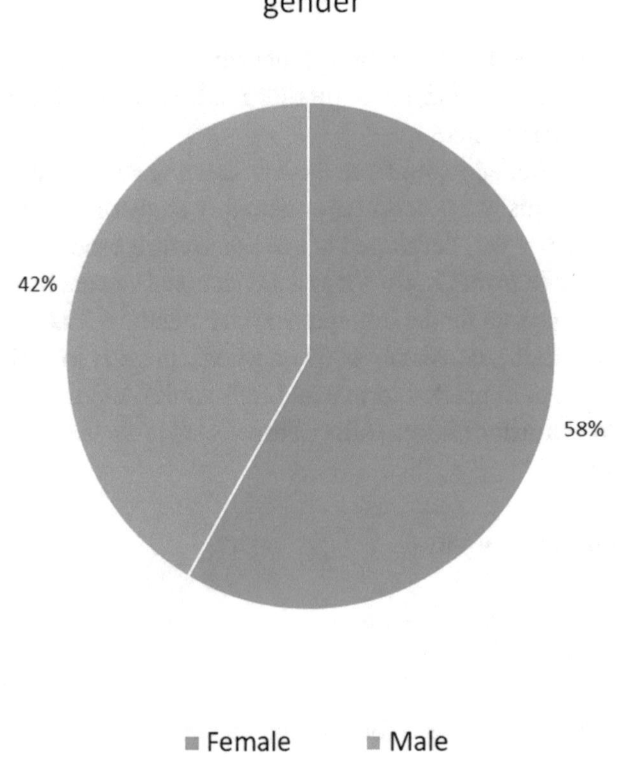

The group of 18-25 years old (generation Z) reached the highest percentage (45.8%); then (39.6%) the group of 25-36 years old (generation millennials) and finally (14.6%) the group of 36-50 years old (generation X).

Half of these young participants (55%) expressed that they prefer to work as employees because they find this option safer and less risky than starting their own business.

Professional Development Expectations of Students

As for the expectation of professional development, (89%) of the students surveyed said they would like to have their own business, (80%) also expressed that they see the creation of a business as a way out

Figure 2. Demographic characterization according to population age (n=48). Rosario, Argentina, 2019

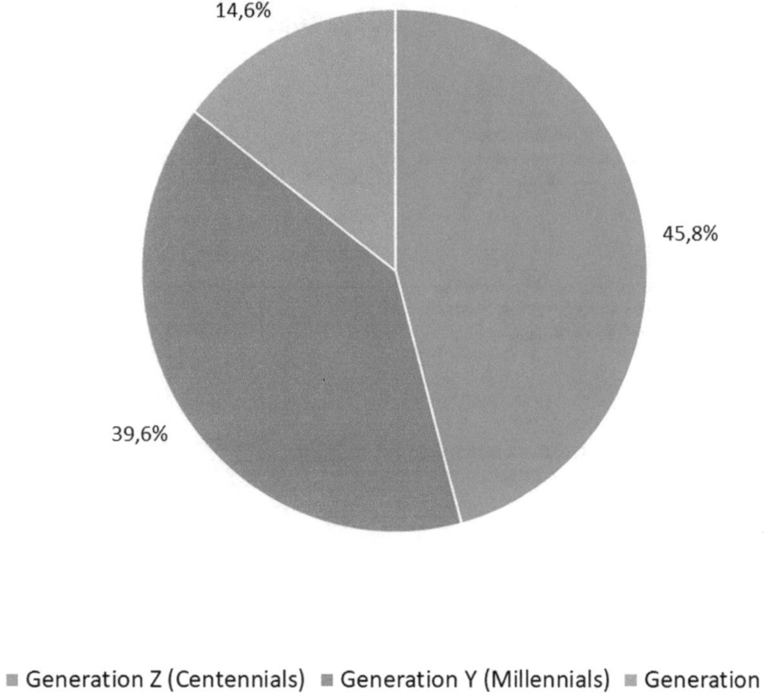

in the future, although (80%) of them are aware that they will have to overcome many difficulties, but still choose to create it.

Entrepreneurial Potential Shown by Students

Within the entrepreneurial skills the young people selected in greater percentage and in decreasing order:

✓ Gathering and managing information for decision making: 75%

They said they knew who to ask about a problem they were facing and where to corroborate information. In addition, they said they would get as much information as possible on a topic and corroborate it even with several sources.

Figure 3. Professional development expectation of students (n=48). Rosario, Argentina, 2019

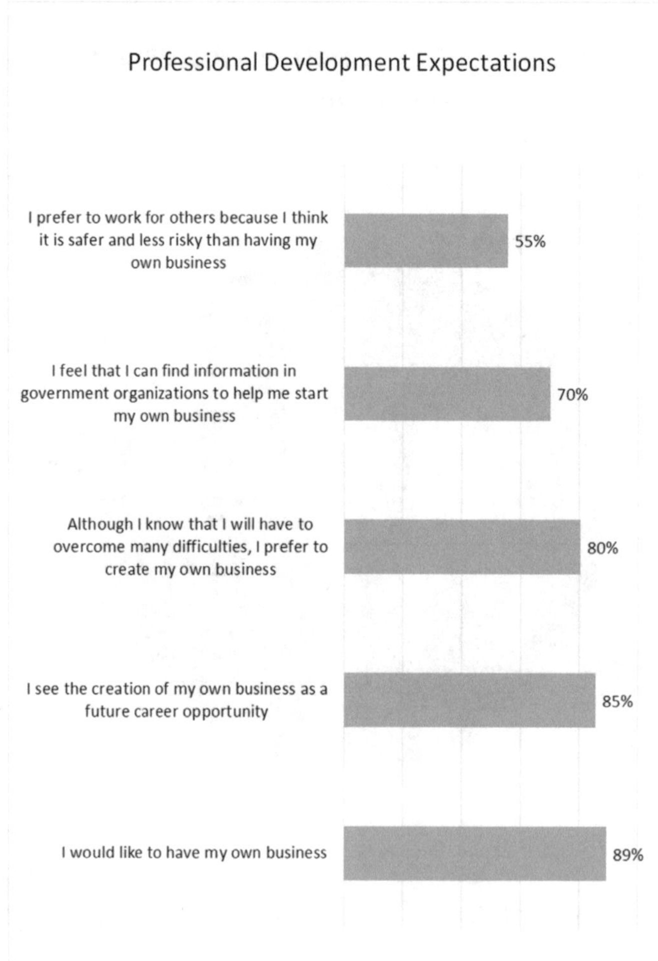

✓ Initiative, innovation and creativity: 75%

They expressed a proactive attitude and were able to create opportunities to demonstrate their skills

✓ Objective-driven work: 74%

They admitted that, although they have failed several times to reach an objective, this time they consider that they have the definitive idea and they assure that they know that it is the way to follow, in spite of not seeing quickly the fruits of the work.

✓ Commitment to results: 71%

They expressed to have the ability to learn from mistakes and successes made and to improve on them. In addition, they stated that the results they obtain are according to the knowledge they have.

Figure 4. Entrepreneurial potential of students (n=48). Rosario, Argentina, 2019

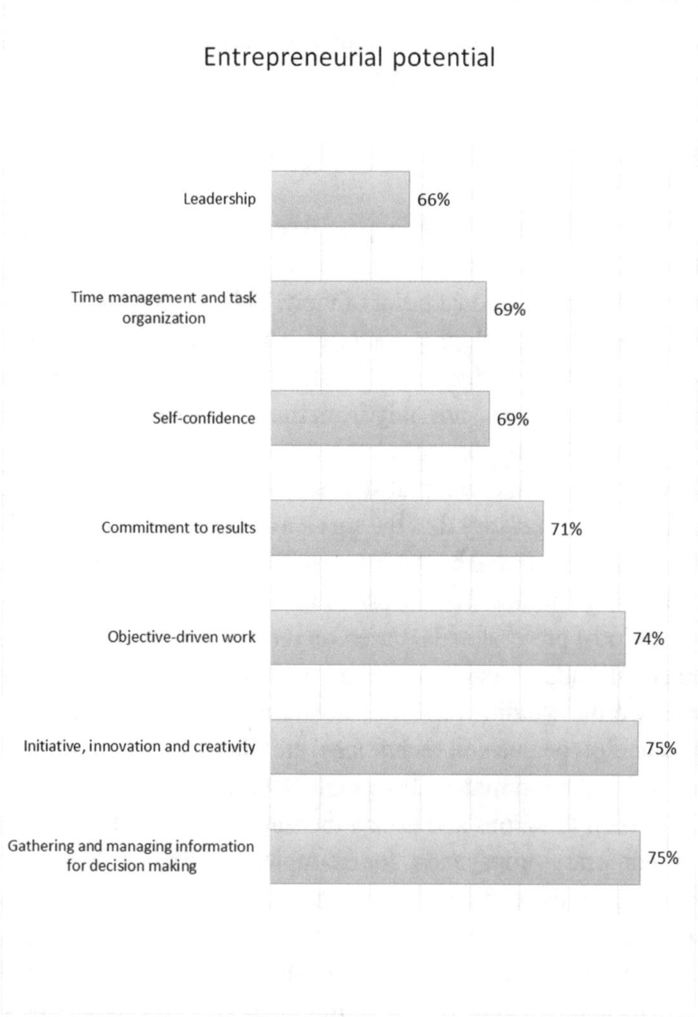

Entrepreneurial potential

Leadership 66%

Time management and task organization 69%

Self-confidence 69%

Commitment to results 71%

Objective-driven work 74%

Initiative, innovation and creativity 75%

Gathering and managing information for decision making 75%

✓ Self-confidence: 69%

They admitted that they consider themselves to be very valuable people in the environment in which they move and that they believe and defend certain values trusting in their own judgment.

✓ Time management and task organization: 69%

They claimed to have the ability to control the unexpected and plenty of time to devote to hobbies and their personal lives.

✓ Leadership: 66%

They said that, in case they have the choice, they prefer to work in a team and lead it. In addition, they commented that they are frequently chosen to fulfill this role.

Lessons Learned

This research shows the increase of the digital gap between the different generations derived from the new global economic and financial models and imposed through the different agents that constitute societies, from the national and international point of view. This is a common denominator, in economically and/or culturally developed or developing societies. Therefore, it is necessary that these studies are carried out entirely by teams of local professionals, since they know in detail the needs and situations of people excluded from the social network, not only from the labor market, but also from the community, considering it as an entity that offers opportunities to each of its members. Although mobile multimedia technology is a resource to which this sector of the population can have access, even though not the latest technological models, it is necessary that the service of being communicated online is free for all, facilitating access to the resources offered by the Internet such as radio, television and educational press.

However, it is not only to guarantee free access to the network, but mainly to educational content, custom-made by a team of local professionals, based on the results obtained, such as the state of the art of certain groups of potential students and that can serve the data collected to implement training development projects. In other words, avoiding the implementation of foreign models of content, educational methodologies, communication persuasion techniques, etc. that lead to the disarticulation of potential groups of entrepreneurs within the community. Potential entrepreneurs that in an isolated way or in groups, are guided by the merit of their functions and not by the transitory favoritism of entities and/or entities, destined to publicity or temporary propaganda, for example, building a false or hypothetical smart city (Gascó-Hernandez, 2019). Training continues to be one of the main pillars that make up the harmonious development of societies in the new millennium, where the web has an important role but is not the center of the universe. The human being continues to be "the driving force" of society, especially the new generations, interested in technological progress, entrepreneurship and social innovation, but who must respect the common good of the rest of the community, that is, reducing the gaps between social classes.

CONCLUSIONS

In relation to the socio-demographic profile of the students who receive job training at the Cuatro Vientos Educational Center, it was found that the majority are women.

The insertion of women in the labor market worldwide has grown notably in the last 20 years. However, recent studies in Latin America have shown a different trend, as there has been a slowdown in the entry of women into the labor market, especially those who come from the most vulnerable homes (Ministerio de Trabajo, Empleo y Seguridad Social, 2017).

The International Labor Organization (ILO) reports that in the last few years, the notable progress in the field of education made by women has not meant an improvement in their position in the labor market (Organización Internacional del Trabajo, 2016). In many regions of the world, women are more likely than men to remain unemployed, have fewer opportunities to enter the workforce, and when they do, must accept lower quality jobs and lower hourly workloads. In addition, the wage gap between men and women in the world is about 23%, where this difference does not depend on skills or abilities, but factors such as gender are determinants.

The responsibility of domestic work, which acts as a social mandate, conditions the type of employment to which they can and want to have access, bound by the social and cultural models in which they are socialized. This responsibility not only has a direct effect on the vulnerability and precariousness of the type of employment, even in the same sectors and professions as men, but also determines fewer possibilities of promotion and a greater probability of being fired, which makes it very easy to cross the boundaries between "inactivity", formal employment and especially informal employment (Gálvez-Muñoz & Rodríguez-Madroño, 2011).

In addition, working women are over-represented in jobs that are considered " womanized ", such as health and social services, education, and family homes, and since 1995 women's employment in the service sector has increased from 41.1% to 65.5%.On the other hand, women dedicate more time to reproductive work (childcare) than men, regardless of their participation in the labor market, which reflects the roles historically attributed to men and women and their impact on the world of work (Organización Internacional del Trabajo, 2016).

Most of these aspects that constitute gender gaps are conditioned by the gender-based division of labor, the division of the public and private spheres, paid and unpaid domestic work, and the roles that men and women are socially expected to play. As a relevant fact, both in terms of participation and intensity of domestic work, women spend three (3) hours more than men. This inequality by gender reflects the persistence of cultural models and gender stereotypes, regardless of age, social class, and educational level (Organización Internacional del Trabajo, 2016).

From the point of view of workforce supply, women are increasing their participation in the labor market as a strategy for homes in the face of temporary drops in family income, caused, for example, by the unemployment of the main contributor, giving rise to the so-called "additional worker" effect (Gálvez-Muñoz & Rodríguez-Madroño, 2011).

In Argentina, there are many homes where women are the main economic source of income, either because they are single-parent homes, or because women are the main income earners, whether they are employed or underemployed, or in homes where both incomes are needed to survive (Organización Internacional del Trabajo, 2016).

In vocational and technical education and training for young people there is an incidence of gender stereotypes both in the constitution of educational offers, training programs, enrollments, jobs, etc.

Hence the importance of spaces such as The Cuatro Vientos Educational Center, which allows female students to train and develop the entrepreneurial skills that are likely to allow them to insert themselves in the world of work, knowing that they are open to change and the search for opportunities.

According to age group, almost half of the young people surveyed are between 18 and 25 years old. If we also consider those between 25 and 36 years of age, we find that almost all of the students who attend the Job Training Institute from Cuatro Vientos Educational Center are part of the two generations that are recognized today as young entrepreneurs: the millennial and centennial generation (Solís-Rodríguez, 2020).

This could be a consequence of the fact that those who belong to the millennial generation have a tendency not to have bosses and to consider themselves as agents of change and innovation contributing to society, which makes them very demanding employees. In 2016, more than half of the young people belonging to the millennial generation expressed their intention to leave their organization by 2020 in search of spaces where they would be taken into account in important decisions. Those who belong to this generation want to work on something they are really passionate about, and their main dream is to be their own boss and start projects that will generate profits for them to pay for their expenses at an early age (Solís-Rodríguez, 2020).

In addition, young people of the centennial generation tend to get involved early in initiatives that allow them to find solutions to the problems of their environment because, as Ortega y Vilanova says, they are "precocious at using the creation of companies as a tool for social change in areas such as the environment, inequality, and citizen participation" (Vilanova & Ortega, 2017). This is because they fear that they will not be able to find a job that matches their personality, that they will not have professional opportunities, and that they will not be able to achieve their goals, which is why they prefer flexible environments that facilitate a balance between their professional and personal lives (Solís-Rodríguez, 2020).

Given that the millennial and centennial generations are different in the social, economic and technological context in which they live, it is important to study their perspectives and motivations for entrepreneurship (Solís-Rodríguez, 2020).

As for the professional development expectation, in coincidence with the bliography consulted, which describes the characteristics of the "Millenials" and "Gen Z", the results obtained showed that the majority of the young people have as an expectation of future development to have their own business.

This generation of young people, when not finding work or what their employers demand, exclude themselves and find answers in new value propositions that have as their basis self-employment. However, reality shows that a person creates a business by vocation or by necessity, success and failure do not depend so much on the reason for starting the business but rather on the way of creating and managing it.

On the other hand, half of the students choose to work as employees because they feel more secure and consider it less risky than starting their own business.

Nevertheless, the labor market will suffer an unpredictable impact in the future due to the ways in which today's young people have to face their work life, which differs significantly from the previous generations. Market conditions have already changed to such an extent that in order to start a business one has to first look at the needs of the customer and then at those of the entrepreneur.

Motivation for entrepreneurship has to do with skills, abilities and attitudes to face fears and challenges, as well as understanding people and knowing their environment to cope with the constant changes that could threaten the fulfillment of their entrepreneurial purpose (Solís-Rodríguez, 2020).

As for the skills that could show entrepreneurial potential in the future, three quarters of the group recognized that they have initiative, they are creative and innovative and can generate innovative responses to the complex situations they face, in order to produce original or unusual solutions. In addition, they said they could obtain and manage information in order to make their own decisions.

Regarding working towards the achievement of objectives, they showed, practically in the same proportion, the ability to focus efforts and guide their actions to the expected achievement, since they also expressed having the ability to learn from the mistakes and successes committed to improve from them.

In a smaller percentage, they identified that they value flexibility and time management, and feel confident and motivated to follow up, set objectives, and guide others in team leadership.

In spite of growing up in times of uncertainty and in contexts of vulnerability, most of these young people who attend the Cuatro Vientos Educational Center are enthusiastic and somewhat optimistic about their future, since they maintain expectations of having their own business.

According to De Vincenzi (Programa Educación y Sociedad, 2019), the process of education in new technologies allows young people, the future human capital of work, to reflect, integrate and innovate the methods of future employment or self-employment.

The growing technology that characterizes this new era and the speed of change in today's world, causes these young people a complete uncertainty of the motivations, demands, behaviors, expectations, thoughts, behaviors and concerns that the future work market will have. And this uncertainty is a tool that allows them to recognize their mistakes and continue to search for their projects.

Some Ideas That Arise at the end of This Research

At the end of this research, the possibility of exploring the object of study in greater depth arises.

It is considered that it could be of great importance to reshape the offer of future training provided by the Cuatro Vientos Educational Center, based on what has been expressed by students, teachers and directors of the Institute. Since they are "digital natives", these proposals should be oriented to methodologies and trainings around the appropriation of contents and resources that respond to the demands of the current labor market.

It would also be necessary to assess the conditions of the institutional structure (material, human and budget resources), in order to recognize the strengths, weaknesses, opportunities and threats presented by an institution such as Cuatro Vientos Educational Center, which depends on an NGO since there are more and more young people (millennials and Z's) who, due to their entrepreneurial potential, recognize job training in institutions as a tool that can boost their entry into the labor market, which would impact on the increase in enrollment for years to come.

Based on the previously proposed research, it would be possible to evaluate, if necessary, the possibility of making improvements in the telecommunications infrastructure of the Educational Center, which would allow it to accelerate both the educational and administrative processes, which would result in the quality of the educational offerings of the institution. The current times impose more agile and accessible mechanisms, accompanied by new technologies, given that the production of knowledge is increasingly accelerated.

REFERENCES

Ahituv, N. (2001). The Open Information Society. *Communications of the ACM*, *44*(1), 48–49. doi:10.1145/376134.376158

Andriole, S. (2010). Business Impact of Web 2.0 Technologies. *Communications of the ACM*, *53*(12), 67–79. doi:10.1145/1859204.1859225

Argentina, T. E. C. H. O. (2016). *Argentina - Índice de vulnerabilidad territorial 2016*. http://datos.techo.org/dataset/argentina-indice-de-vulnerabilidad-territorial-2016

Armas, F. (2018). Educar para la vida. *Cuatro Vientos*, (7), 4.

Asociación Rosarina de Ayuda Solidaria (A.R.A.S). (n.d.). *Sobre Nosotros A.R.A.S.* http://www.aras.org.ar

Batalla, M., Monsalvo San Macario, E., González Aguña, A., & Santamaría García, J. M. (2018). Diseño de un método de análisis para el cálculo de la vulnerabilidad como predictor de la fragilidad en salud. *Ene-. Revista de Enfermeria (Barcelona, Spain), 12*(1). http://www.ene-enfermeria.org/ojs/index.php/ENE/article/view/786

Batista, A., Cabrera, L., & Villanueva, F. (2014). Demandas Laborales de la Generación Z. *Repositorio Institucional UADE* (Universidad Argentina de la Empresa). https://repositorio.uade.edu.ar/xmlui/bitstream/handle/123456789/2423/Battista.pdf?sequence=1&isAllowed=y

Bessant, J., & Tidd, J. (2015). *Innovation and Entrepreneurship*. Whiley.

Burton, A. (2020). Improving Social Alignment During Digital Transformation. *Communications of the ACM, 63*(9), 65–71. doi:10.1145/3410429

Cerf, V. (2007). An Information Avalanche. *IEEE Computer, 40*(1), 104–105. doi:10.1109/MC.2007.5

Chen, H. (2010a). Business and Market Intelligence 2.0. *IEEE Intelligent Systems. Part I., 25*(1), 68–81. doi:10.1109/MIS.2010.27

Chen, H. (2010b). Business and Market Intelligence 2.0. *IEEE Intelligent Systems. Part II., 25*(2), 74–82. doi:10.1109/MIS.2010.43

Cipolla-Ficarra, F., & Alma, J. (2015). Banking Online: Design for a New Credibility. In Information Resources Management Association (Ed.), Banking, Finance, and Accounting: Concepts, Methodologies, Tools, and Applications. Hershey: IGI Global.

de Trabajo, M., Empleo y Seguridad, S., & Presidencia de la Nación, A. (2017). *Las Mujeres en el Mercado del Trabajo-Documento de trabajo para el debate en el marco de la CTIO género.* http://trabajo.gob.ar/downloads/igualdad/DocumentoDEGIOT_Sep2017.pdf

Duening, T., Hisrich, R., & Lechter, M. (2014). *Technology Entrepreneurship: Taking Innovation to the Marketplace*. Academic Press.

Gálvez-Muñoz, L., & Rodríguez-Madroño, P. (2011). La desigualdad de género en las crisis económicas. Universidad Complutense Madrid. *Investigaciones Feministas, 2*, 113–132.

García, J. C. S., & Sánchez, B. H. (2016). Influencia del Programa Emprendedor Universitario (PREU) para la mejora de la actitud emprendedora. *Pampa: Revista Interuniversitaria de Estudios Territoriales*, (13), 55-76. https://dialnet.unirioja.es/descarga/articulo/5610764.pdf

Gascó-Hernandez, M. (2019). Building a Smart City: Lessons from Barcelona. *Communications of the ACM, 61*(4), 50–57. doi:10.1145/3117800

Kshetri, N. (2010). Cloud Computing in Developing Economies. *IEEE Computer, 43*(10), 47–55. doi:10.1109/MC.2010.212

López de Toro-Rivera, C. (2014). Características de emprendimiento social de los jóvenes en estudios previos a los universitarios. Universidad Complutense Madrid. *E-Prints Complutense*. https://eprints.ucm.es/27578/

Martínez-Rodriguez, F. M. (2011). Percepción del profesorado de las escuelas taller y casas de oficios en Andalucía acerca del nivel de competencias emprendedoras en su alumnado. *Revista de Educación*, (356), 303-326.

Mattelart, A., & Schmucler, H. (1983). *América Latina en la encrucijada telemática*. Paidós.

Organización Internacional del Trabajo. (2016). *Las mujeres en el trabajo, tendencias 2016*. https://www.ilo.org/global/publications/books/WCMS_483214/lang--es/index.htm

Organización Internacional del Trabajo. (2017). *Desempleo Juvenil en el Mundo*. https://www.ilo.org/global/research/global-reports/world-of-work/lang--es/index.htm

Ortega, I. (2017). El dilema de la generación Z. *El blog de Iñaki Ortega*. http://www.inakiortega.com/2017/04/el-dilema-de-la-generacion-z.html

Pinker, E., Seidmann, A., & Foster, R. (2002). Strategies for Transitioning 'Old Economy' Firms to E-Business. *Communications of the ACM*, *45*(5), 77–83. doi:10.1145/506218.506219

Programa Educación y Sociedad. (2019). *Educación y Sociedad 19 09 2019*. youtube.com/watch?v=F45UM7WgHBc.

Real Academia Española. (2019a). Competencia. In *Diccionario de la Lengua Española*. Retrieved September 4, 2019, from https://dle.rae.es/competencia?m=form

Real Academia Española. (2019b). Generación. In *Diccionario de la Lengua Española*. Retrieved August 20, 2019, from https://dle.rae.es/generaci%C3%B3n?m=form

Real Academia Española. (2020a). Vulnerable. In *Diccionario de la Lengua Española*. Retrieved August 1, 2020, from https://dle.rae.es/vulnerable

Real Academia Española. (2020b). Vulnerabilidad. In *Diccionario de la Lengua Española*. Retrieved August 1, 2020, from https://dle.rae.es/vulnerabilidad?m=form

Rodríguez-Moreno, D., & Gómez-Murillo, A. X. (2014). Las competencias emprendedoras en el departamento de Boyacá. *Apuntes del Cenes*, *33*(58), 217-242. https://www.redalyc.org/articulo.oa?id=4795/479547210009

Rossi-Casé, L., Doná, S., Biganzoli, B., & Garzaniti, R. (2019). Evaluando a los Millennials. Apreciaciones sobre la inteligencia a partir del Test de Raven. *Perspectivas Psicológicas*, *16*(1), 14–25.

Sánchez, J. C. (2013). The impact of an Entrepreneurship Education Program on entrepreneurial competencies and Intention. *Small Business Management*, *51*(3), 447–465. doi:10.1111/jsbm.12025

Schaffer, E. (2006). A Decision Table: Offshore or Not? (When NOT to Use Offshore Resourses). *Interaction*, *8*(2), 32–33. doi:10.1145/1116715.1116737

Schneiderman, B. (2002). Understanding Human Activities and Relationships. *Interaction*, *9*(5), 40–53.

Sobrado-Fernández, L., & Fernández-Rey, E. (2010). Competencias Emprendedoras y Desarrollo del Espíritu Empresarial en los Centros Educativos. *Educación XX1*, *13*(1), 15-38. https://www.redalyc.org/articulo.oa?id=706/70618037001

Solís-Rodríguez, F. T. (2020). *Motivaciones de las Generaciones Millennial y Centennial para la Creación de Nuevas Empresas*. Universidad Autónoma de la Ciudad de Juárez. http://cathi.uacj.mx/20.500.11961/11591

Tambe, P., & Hitt, L. (2010). How Offshoring Affects IT Workers. *Communications of the ACM*, *53*(10), 62–70. doi:10.1145/1831407.1831426

Tobón, S. (2010). Formación integral y competencias. Pensamiento complejo, currículo, didáctica y evaluación (3rd ed.). Bogotá: ECOE.

Vázquez, C., & Mouján-Fernández, J. (2016). Adolescencia y Sociedad. La construcción de Identidad en tiempos de inmediatez. *Revista PSOCIAL*, *2*(1), 38–55.

Vilanova, N., & Ortega, I. (2017). *Generacion Z: todo lo que necesitas sobre los jóvenes que han dejado viejo a los millenials*. Plataforma Editorial.

Villanueva, S. D. (2013). Las competencias dentro del rol profesional: diferencias entre la Educación Superior (universitaria) y las demandas del mercado laboral. *Revista Debate Universitario*, *1*(2), 44-65. http://ppct.caicyt.gov.ar/index.php/debate-universitario/article/viewFile/1605/pdf

Vixie, P. (2011). Arrogance in Business Planning. *Communications of the ACM*, *54*(9), 38–41. doi:10.1145/1995376.1995392

Yingsaeree, C., Treleaven, P., & Nuti, G. (2010). Computational Finance. *IEEE Computer*, *43*(12), 36–43. doi:10.1109/MC.2010.343

ADDITIONAL READING

Asgary, N. H., & Maccari, E. A. (2020). *Entrepreneurship, Innovation and Sustainable Growth: Opportunities and Challenges*. Routledge.

Banks, K. (2016). *Social Entrepreneurship and Innovation: International Case Studies and Pratice*. Kogan Page.

Cipolla-Ficarra, F. V. (2014). Negative Exponent Fraction: A Strategy for a New Virtual Image into the Financial Sector. In Cipolla-Ficarra (Ed.), Advanced Research and Trends in New Technologies, Software, Human-Computer Interaction, and Communicability. Hershey: IGI Global. doi:10.4018/978-1-4666-4490-8.ch024

Gay, C., & Szostak, B. (2019). *Innovation and Creativity in SMEs: Challenges, Evolutions and Prospects*. Wiley. doi:10.1002/9781119513742

Lorenzo, O., Kawalek, P., & Wharton, L. (2018). *Entrepreneurship, Innovation and Technology: A Guide to Core Models and Tools*. Routledge. doi:10.4324/9781351018425

Matthews, C. H. (2015). *Innovation and Entrepreneurship: A Competency Framework*. Routledge. doi:10.4324/9781315813622

Mellor, R. B. (2009). *Entrepreneurship for Everyone: A Student Textbook*. Sage.

Michael, H. Morris, Donald F. Kuratko & Covin, J. (2010). Corporate Entrepreneurship and Innovation: Entrepreneurial Development within Organizations. Mason: South-Western Cengage Learning. Croydon: CPI Group.

Pandit, V. (2015). *We Are Generation Z: How Identity, Attitudes, and Perspectives Are Shaping Our Future*. Brown Books Publishing.

Perna, M. C. (2018). *Answering Why: Unleashing Passion, Purpose, and Performance in Younger Generations*. Greenleaft Book Group Press.

Ramírez-Pasillas, M., Brundin, E., & Markowska, M. (2017). *Contextualizing Entrepreneurship in Emerging Economies and Developing Countries*. Edward Elgar Publishing. doi:10.4337/9781785367533

Zhang, K. (2019). *MOOCs and Open Education in the Global South: Challenges, Successes, and Opportunities*. Routledge. doi:10.4324/9780429398919

KEY TERMS & DEFINITION

Digital Natives: Users that were born with technological devices at their fingertips which constituted their way of connecting with each other.

Millennials: are the first generation that can be considered global. These users more than any other generation in the workforce, can rapidly pick up new information technology and master it.

Z generation: is the generation after the millennials. They are more entrepreneurial, quicker to learn and self-taught, which makes them much more irreverent than their fellow millennials who were educated with much more rigid systems.

Vulnerability: is a broad multidimensional concept that can refer to the person, the family or the population group in which the vulnerability arises. In the context of vulnerability caused by unemployment, constant change and economic uncertainty, etc. The job training proposals for young people are very important.

Labor market: it is an entity that offers opportunities to each of its community members.

Social entrepreneurial: are some the capacities that reinforced the quality of life, reduce the possibility of economic and social vulnerability, and develop tools and attitudes to face the demands of the new society, for example, information and communication technology (ICT).

Chapter 13
The Language of Cinema Fosters the Development of Soft Skills for Inclusion and Interdisciplinary Learning

Annamaria Poli
Università degli Studi di Milano-Bicocca, Italy

Daniela Tamburini
Sperimenta – Centro Studi Cinema e Formazione, Italy

ABSTRACT

This chapter presents research on an Italian education project implemented with immigrant students attending C.P.I.A. courses in Bergamo (Centro Provinciale Istruzione Adulti – Provincial Adult Education Center). This contribution proposes an educational experience characterized by an interactive approach among different disciplines. The title of the project was Cinema as a resource for enhancing interdisciplinary teaching and learning by harnessing knowledge and skills from across different subject areas: from Italian language to geography and history, and from science and maths to the visual arts. Over the four years of the project, film was used in multiple ways as a tool/resource for teaching-learning focused on developing school inclusion. The overall aims of the project were to incorporate the cinema into the construction of an interdisciplinary teaching/learning path, while seeking to integrate theory and praxis within a collaborative professional development and research model. The project activities were designed in keeping with EU recommendations on core competences for ongoing learning. From 2006 to 2018, the European Parliament and Council approved a set of "Recommendations on Key Competences for Lifelong Learning," that is to say, knowledge, skills, and attitudes that will help learners find personal fulfilment and, later in life, find work and take part in society. The project was also informed by recent Italian legislation encouraging the use of cinema in education, particularly Law 14 November 2016, No. 220, containing "Discipline of Cinema and Audiovisual" and the Law 13 July 2015, No. 107, the school reform framework "La BuonaScuola."

DOI: 10.4018/978-1-7998-7010-4.ch013

INTRODUCTION

The research presented in this chapter is part of a broader programme entitled "At School with the Cinema", which was launched in 2014 by the "Riccardo Massa" Department of Human Sciences for Education at the University of Milan Bicocca's and is led by Professor Annamaria Poli, with the collaboration of several schools in the Lombardy region. In the case of the project outlined here –with dott. DanielaTamburiniof Sperimenta - Centro Studi Cinema e Formazione of Milano Italy and the C.P.I.A. school for immigrants in Bergamo.

In 2017, this project was presented at the Setecec conference in Venice, in terms of its research questions, research aims, preliminary outcomes, and initial implementation in an unconventional educational setting with students from different countries around the world. Specifically, the project was conducted at an Italian school for immigrants in Bergamoa provincial centre for adult education, known asC.P.I.A.

C.P.I.A. centres are autonomous state schools located all over Italy, whose specific organization and academic structure is determined by education legislation in the local region. They are the main institutional structure for the coordination and the implementation of educational action targeting the adult population (comprising individuals of 16 years - or in some cases of 15 years - and over) with a view to raising adults' level of education and/or consolidating their key competences for lifelong learning. The C.P.I.A. offers three distinct educational programmes: one aimed at enabling students to complete the compulsory education cycle; another preparing students to obtain a school-leaving diploma in technical, vocational, or artistic studies; and a third level offering Italian language and literacy instruction to adults who are non-nationals.

In the Bergamo C.P.I.A., film was used as a tool and resource for encouraging inclusive education and fostering students' appreciation of cinema. The project was called: *"Film as a resource for enhancing interdisciplinary teaching and learning by harnessing knowledge and skills from across different subject areas: from Italian language to geography and history, and from science and maths to the visual arts."* The aim was to explore how introducing film at school could foster the acquisition of knowledge and competences from a range of disciplines.

1. BACKGROUND

1.1 Competence-led Teaching-learning - key Competences

The concept of competence-led learning emerged in the mid-1990s, in EU policy documents such as the White Paper on teaching and learning drafted by Edith Cresson - then European Commissioner for research, education and training - which reads: *All European countries are attempting to identify 'key skills' and the best ways of acquiring, assessing and certifying them. It is proposed to set up a European system to compare and disseminate such definitions, methods and practices.*[1]

The European Commission adopted the terms "skills" and "key skills" here in preference to "basic skills", which generally refers to basic competence in reading, writing and arithmetic. In contrast, in EU policy documents, "skill" or "competence" came to mean a *combination of knowledge, skills and attitudes appropriate to the context*. At the same time, *key competences are those that support personal fulfilment, active citizenship, social inclusion, and employment.*[2]

1.2 The Regulatory Framework

The aim of this project, which took film as an educational activity fostering the development of competences, was directly informed by the most recent European and Italian legislation.[3]

In terms of EU legislation, we followed the "Recommendation on key competences for lifelong learning" originally approved by the European Parliament and Council of Europe in 2006. This document outlines eight key areas of "European competence". The key European competences are those which all individuals need for their personal fulfilment and development, active citizenship, social inclusion, and employment - that is to say, all the skills and attitudes that will help them to take full part in society.

In terms of Italian legislation on education, it should be noted that since 2007, key citizenship competences modelled on the European competences have been included in the compulsory education curriculum.

Of particular significance is the school reform bill, Law 107 passed on 13 July 2015, known as "La BuonaScuola", which acknowledges and encourages the value of promoting competence by encouraging appreciation of the arts through educational practice.

Furthermore, in response to the widespread demand for quality education in Italian vocational schools, changes were introduced in 2017 that included greater personalization of educational pathways, increased and targeted use of laboratory methods of teaching/learning, with a view to fostering greater integration of competences, abilities, and knowledge, and the grouping of subjects into broad areas of knowledge.

1.2.1 EU Recommendations on the Key Competences for Lifelong Learning

The project was informed by the European Union's recommendations on key competences for lifelong learning. These guidelines are targeted at the secondary education sector.

In 2006 and again in 2018, the European Parliament and Council approved a set of "Recommendations on Key Competences for Lifelong learning": knowledge, skills, and attitudes to help learners find personal fulfilment and, later in life, find work and take part in society. The 2006 document outlined eight macro-skills termed "European skills".[4]

Competences are defined as a combination of knowledge, skills, and attitudes appropriate to the context. Key competences are those, which all individuals need for personal fulfilment and development, active citizenship, social inclusion, and employment.

On 22 May 2018, based on a proposal put forward by the European Commission on 27 January 2018, the Council of Europe adopted a new Recommendation on key competences for lifelong learning replacing the earlier 2006 recommendation.

The new Reference Framework sets out eight key competences:

1. Communication in the mother tongue;
2. Communication in foreign languages;
3. Mathematical competence and basic competences in science and technology;
4. Digital competence;
5. Learning to learn;
6. Social and civic competences;
7. Sense of initiative and entrepreneurship;
8. Cultural awareness and expression.

1.2.2 The Italian Legislative Framework

On 22 August 2007, the Italian Government issued a decree defining the key citizenship competences, which "encompass": traditional "abilities" such as communicating in the mother tongue, foreign languages, digital skills, literacy and basic skills in mathematics and sciences; and horizontal skills such as learning to learn, social and civic responsibility, initiative and entrepreneurship, cultural awareness and creativity. These key competences are based on the EU recommendations outlined above, which are designed to foster the full development of the person, in terms of the construction of self, appropriate and meaningful relationships with others, and positive interaction with the natural and social worlds. The key citizenship competences are: Learning to learn;planning; communicating, collaborating and participating; acting autonomously and responsibly; problem solving; creating connections and relations; acquiring and interpreting information.

As mentioned earlier, the school reform outlined in Law13 July 2015, No. 107,"La BuonaScuola" encourages the promotion of competence via the incorporation of music, art, and cinema into educational practice, through the involvement of museums and other relevant public and private bodies, and the introduction of techniques for the production and dissemination of image, sound, and media in general. Specifically, Article One of "La BuonaScuola" provides for: *7.c) enhancement of competence in the practice and knowledge of music, art, history of art, cinema, and techniques and media for the production and dissemination of image and sound, including through the involvement of museums and other public and private institutions operating in these fields; 7.f) literacy programmes in art and techniques and media for the production and dissemination of images.*

The Law 14 November 2016, No. 220, containing "Discipline of cinema and audiovisual" in the Article One underlines and defines more the importance of promoting and enhancing cinema ad audiovisual media in educational and school contexts: *The Republic, in implementation of Articles 9, 21 and 33 of the Constitution and in the framework of the principles established by Article 167 of the Treaty on the Functioning of the European Union and by the UNESCO Convention on the protection and promotion of the diversity of expressions cultural events, promotes and supports cinema and audiovisual media as fundamental means of artistic expression, cultural training and social communication.*

1.2.3 Legislative Decree No. 61 of 13 April 2017

The school in Bergamo, given that it offers vocational courses of study, is among those impacted by the reform introduced in 2017, which makes provision for and incentivizes the use of laboratory methods. The implementation of profound changes in vocational education has been underway since the 2018/2019 academic year.

These changes, provided for under the terms of Legislative Decree 61 of 13 April 2017, are designed *to revitalize vocational education programs, raising quality and forming citizens of tomorrow, helping girls and boys to develop autonomy, mindfulness, and a sense of responsibility and to acquire tools they need to grow and build a future for themselves via further study or directly in the workplace.*[5]

The new teaching/learning model is based on the personalization of study programmes, frequent and targeted use of laboratory methods, and the full integration of competencies, abilities, and knowledge. The most innovative aspect of the reform is the grouping together of school subjects by broad areas of knowledge.

In order to achieve these objectives, the school and education system will invest greater financial and professional resources. Consequently, key outcomes of the reform will include a greater number of teachers of technical-practical subjects; greater attention to overcoming issues with inclusion, the protection of human rights, and the promotion of equal opportunity; a greater emphasis on school autonomy; and significantly increased investment in laboratories and specialized equipment.

The project we now present was part of the teaching/learning program for the socio-historical area of knowledge (cinema and intercultural) and was aimed at situating personal experience within a system of rules based on mutual recognition of the rights enshrined in the Constitution to protect the person, society, and the environment.

2. CINEMA AS AN EDUCATIONAL TOOL

The virtuous relationship to be established between cinema and vocational secondary education also underpinned our project from a pedagogical viewpoint, especially in terms of identifying connections between the aesthetic dimension characterizing film and the educational/didactic dimension of schooling. Ensuring that this relationship is positive and generative requires thinking about the way in which cinema is understood, practiced, and promoted in the educational/school context.

The use of film, and images more generally, in educational institutions has not always fostered the development of related, appropriate educational knowledge. This is because, although the educational potential of images has been recognized historically (Franza, 1993; Bertolini,1988; Massa, 2005;Rezzara, 2004)[6], the fear persists that their power of attraction or, one might say, of seduction, might prevent teachers from using them with the lucidity, competence, and positive purpose that is usually brought to bear on the reading of books.

Hence, teachers attempt to approach the language of cinematographic images using the same criteria, and even the same instruments, that they use to teach their own subjects. This prevents teachers from developing a proper understanding of the specific nature of the language of film, and its potential to serve as a meaningful educational dispositive.

The introduction of film into schools coincides with the introduction of an approach to teaching/learning that is no longer solely focused on content, thus challenging the previously established mode of knowledge transmission which typically favoured conformity to rigidly preordained models.

However, it is crucial to acknowledge that cinema, while attractive, does not always automatically impart lessons for life. A film is not rendered more or less educational by the topic it deals with, nor by its artistic style or quality, nor by its relevance to the school subjects it illustrates or - in the best-case scenario - adds to. Rather, it contributes to personal growth as a function of the educational approach brought to bear on it: cinema aids learning when the focus is not on the information represented in a film but on the - cognitive and emotional - relationship that arises between the material viewed and the spectator, opening up, almost naturally, the dialogical dimension that is typical of education. It is therefore crucial for teachers to learn how to bring images into schools in a way that is mature and caring, and that takes into account the needs of their particular students and the specific educational setting.

When films were first shown in schools, or groups of students taken to see films in cinemas, this was generally with the aim - via the film itself and the commentary following it - of getting students to engage with, and become more interested in - a topic from a given subject area, based on a view of cinema as offering a reasonably faithful copy of reality. In other cases, it was used as a vehicle for illustrating a set of socially shared behavioural models to be emulated, with the aim of forming or even "shaping" the students' consciences. In both cases, cinema was understood as a pre-packaged form of everyday reality/ discourse on which to base behaviours that were the opposite to subjective; this meant overlooking the aspect of cinema with the greatest educational power, its expressive force and emotional and subjective dimensions, and consequently the potential to interpret a film in different ways. Via the powerful medium of projection that is cinema, a "viewing" takes place that entails a relationship with the viewed object, which in turn offers new and complex keys to interpreting reality (Casetti, 2005).

In practice, these approaches to using film in schools shows that cinema may be engaged with at different levels, which can even evolve over time, including in non-educational contexts. Not all cinema is necessarily educational, and much depends - as earlier stated - on the individual subject's reaction to the viewing of a film. Cinematic images, rather than being viewed as ways of escaping "from" something, should be recognized as ways of escaping "towards" something better, and more significant (Bettelheim, 1990). But to appropriately deploy film in educational settings and view it as an essentially educational instrument, it is first necessary to understand it as a tool for engaging in critical-educational readings of the individual internalized worldviews that shape our understanding of the worldand of ourselves (Morin, 2002, 2016)[7] This implies bringing more intense scrutiny to bear on the reflective/interpretative aspect of cinema, which is ever present but not necessarily always the focus of attention. Here, we may seek and find the signs and meanings displayed in a film, thus coming to gain/hold knowledge of them, in a continuous iterative cycle of representations and co-construction of meaning (Franza&Mottana, 1997). Films generate a series of symbols and meanings - whose authors are not only the film directors and actors but also the spectators - thereby producing an "aggregate set" of data, elements, memories, images (including mental), facts and concepts, which in turn enable us to process and understand, not alone the film, but also the way in which we watch and interpret it, as well as the times in which we live.

Over time, cinema has also become an inexhaustible depositary for conscious historical memory, via the simultaneously virtual and handcrafted narration of cultural contexts, of diverse forms of expression, customs, settings, and accounts of lived experience, and of times past, present and future, thereby allowing us to become familiar with the complexity that characterizes our contemporary era, in which we are not only inhabited by concrete reality, but also by the imaginary (D'Incerti, Santoro &Varchetta, 2007).

In schools and educational settings, therefore, working with film encourages and fosters the development of multiple levels of critical reflection, starting from the analysis of the specific language of film which comprises complex communication processes. Thus, cinema not only helps students to assimilate target learning contents, but also and above all to attain personal and human growth, as well as enhanced capacity to understand the events to which we are exposed today, as a result of focusing on the processing of images and the imaginary, which are increasingly all-pervasive in contemporary life. Furthermore, the empathic participation in cinematographic narratives typically experienced by spectators leads them, by analogy and by difference, to develop their own self-narratives. This is why cinema may be defined as a "highly educational" tool (Franza, 2018).

2.1 The Autobiographical Approach. Individual Life Stories as Processes of Self-Construction

Cinema is taken here to bear educational value when it is understood as a generative stimulus that fosters students' capacity for inference and memory, as well as a locus for investigating the relationship between reality and fiction, the role of emotions in knowledge acquisition processes, and the development of the reflective and self-reflective skills and competences underpinning coherent self-representation. Hence, bringing this kind of educational perspective to bear in this project led us to adopt an autobiographical approach.

Autobiographical perspectives were originally informed by constructivist theories of knowledge[8] and in psychology have largely been developed within the interactive-constructivist paradigm. (Bruner, 1961; Vygotskij, 1966; Wertsch, 1985; Smorti, 1994)[9].Beginning with the research corpus on *narrative thinking*[10](Bruner, 1986, 1990, 2002), contributions to the autobiographical approach came from a diverse range of disciplines leading to the development of autobiographical perspectives within the fields of education, professional development, and care. In the field of adult education, it is essential to cite the work of Duccio Demetrio (Demetrio, 1995) who pioneered autobiographical methodologies in Italy as a mode of self-reflection centred on the reconstruction and rebuilding of personal identity via the exploration of past selves and mindful return to the inner dimension. The key focus is not only, or not necessarily, on reconstructing the stories that are progressively narrated, but rather on the way in which the facts are reconstructed, because the elements of the narrative can take an expressive form that is representative of the narrator's individuality. Constructing a self-narrative triggers a process of active meaning-making, underpinned by inner operational models of which the subject becomes gradually more aware (Demetrio, 1995).

2.2 Film as a Tool for Intercultural Dialogue

Among the multifaceted dimensions of cinema, we should not overlook the fact that it is a social product that draws together narratives, identity, and lived experience into a continuous dialogical encounter, implying that there can be many alternative cultural approaches to drawing out its educational value. This dimension, which simultaneously transcends and includes the geographical, historical and cultural differences among the contexts to which its characteristic form of narration is applied, entails and encourages an intercultural approach to viewing film: an approach that takes into account the specific settings, modes of communication, and different cultures expressed by the film itself, as well as by individual students viewing it - as a function of their personal cultural backgrounds - and by the class as a whole (male and female students, class group and teachers).

Listening to the students' reflections after they have viewed a film also entails encouraging the formation of a class group whose educational goals are not solely content-related but include the acquisition of cultural skills for inclusion and the creation of spaces for open-ended dialogue.

The educational actions undertaken to this end included creating an encouraging atmosphere improving the ability of homogeneous groups to express themselves, or to enhancing processes of dialogue and cooperation (among heterogeneous groups), making crucial use of cinema to get students to work collaboratively and thus to break down the distance between spontaneously forming subgroups based on shared ethnic background to prevent them from becoming places of closedness.by choosing a key topic around which to organize the discussion, within a narrative framework designed to help the students, using images from the film as a stimulus, to identify their own point of view in order to (temporarily) distance themselves from it (decentre) as they explored the different perspectives present in the class.

3. CINEMA AND DIDACTICS

Cinema is present in Italian educational and school settings to a very limited extent. Despite the introduction, many years ago, of legislation paving the way for the introduction of film and film studies into the educational sector and schools, cinema is still not fully valued, and in some cases is not even taken into account, as a possible educational resource or field of studies.

Historically speaking, the key reference documents were a Memorandum of Understanding with the Department of Entertainment and Directive No. 365 of 12 June 1997 on the subject of "Education in artistic and audio-visual languages". A political move that defined, based on key socio-educational research outcomes, a national plan for introducing the teaching and use of audio-visual languages at all levels of schooling.

Currently, the key policy documents are Law No. 107 of 13 July 2015, known as "La BuonaScuola", and elements of the National Cinema for Schools Plan (Piano Nazionale Cinema per la Scuola), which call for research and intervention in the teaching/learning of film in schools and educational settings.[11] These documents have informed experimental teacher professional development and education projects over the past number of years.

However, despite this background, if some valuable research projects have been conducted, and some excellent teaching/learning paths and laboratories for film and media studies have been developed, this is mainly thanks to an extremely small number of teachers who are competent in the field of film and have actively promoted film and engaged in targeted experimentation and inquiry.

Unfortunately, 20 years on, such models are still scarce in Italy and only in rare cases have educational outcomes and gains in subject-specific learning brought about by the use of film been disseminated.

The norm at all levels of schooling continues to be to view film as a form of pure entertainment, or even worse, as a means of covering for absent teachers. Other than this, the main use of cinema in educational settings and schools is the "cineforum": this involves showing the students a film, or selection of films, chosen by the teacher as a function of their themes, without any in-depth study or analysis of the language and communication techniques that are peculiar to cinema.

The reform cited above explicitly states that schools are called to: *encourage the promotion of competence via the incorporation of music, art, and cinema into educational practice, through the involvement of museums and other relevant public and private bodies, along with techniques for the production and dissemination of image, sound, and media in general.*[12]This means that learning about the arts will now be based on studying the history of the medium and its language from the aesthetic and creative point of view and this goal is to be fully pursued at all levels of schooling. The aim is therefore to ensure that future generations of students will benefit from new resources and theoretical and practical knowledge providing them with literacy in the arts and media based on knowledge of the techniques required to master and appreciate the beauty and effectiveness of artistic and audio-visual language. But how may film be used in educational practice as a resource for teaching other school subjects or initiating interdisciplinary teaching-learning paths?

All of this may be implemented only if appropriate methods are applied to educate the students' gaze to the mindful viewing/reading of the language of images and, especially, of the concept of film underpinning a given cinematographic work.

Drawing out the pedagogical and epistemological value of cinematographic culture implies teaching students how to watch a film and/or a multimedia work more generally, triggering all the key cognitive processes that a new language can generate.

When students are cognitively engaged by a film, this can bring to light previously latent expressive and creative abilities. In the words of Maria Vita Nicolosi*school has the goal of forming and not only informing, of stimulating metacognition, including by means of complex aids* (Nicolosi, 2002)that interactively engage and educate the student in critical and divergent thinking. Notably, films should not be studied and analysed using the same method that one would apply to literary texts: the elements composing cinematographic language are numerous, complex and reciprocally connected by virtue of links between technique and language. Mastery of all these elements enables the development of creative, critical, and aesthetic thinking.

When discussing cinema in schools, it should be emphasized that new film projects can take at least two distinct educational paths based on different underlying assumptions. These are: the teaching/learning with images or the teaching/learning about images (Costa, 2011). Both are challenging to implement and require specific competences if they are to have positive impact and yield successful teaching-learning outcomes.

Teaching cinema also means exploring it from a range of historical perspectives, given that the history of film encompasses the historical evolution of cinematographic technology and equipment, filming techniques, the narrative styles of screenwriters, directors and actors, production and distribution strategies, economic factors and much more. Introducing cinema into Italian schools means promoting knowledge of a branch of international cultural heritage and the mindful use of the communicative aspects of film and the language of images in general.

Incorporating film into educational practice is already known to yield a series of key benefits, including: facilitating active learning, stimulating participation in group activities, enhancing student engagement with proposed activities, offering teachers new educational tools that leverage the language of cinema and the digital multimedia, fostering interdisciplinary learning, and promoting explicit knowledge and mastery of the language of images.

4. THE PROJECT AT BERGAMO C.P.I.A.

The main issue that needed to be addressed was the relational challenges experienced by the students with their class group, teachers, and the school environment in general, especially in the early part of the school year. These challenges were due to their diverse cultural backgrounds, as well as to the difficulties and uncertainties associated with their reasons for coming to Italy (often traumatic in nature), their experiences during their migratory journeys, and their encounter with a host culture not always or immediately perceived as welcoming. We expected that helping these students to develop to their relational skills, at both the interpersonal and group (class group and teachers) levels, would indirectly foster a harmonious inclusion process outside of school.

We set out to facilitate the development of relational competences from the design stage of the project, in close collaboration with the teachers, by focusing our intervention on actions that facilitated the students in representing themselves and listening to one another.

Responding to the C.P.I.A. students' specific need to consolidate a personal identity that was in continuity with their past but at the same time flexible enough to accommodate the different culture context of the present took the form of collecting and sharing participants' individual life stories, as a key step towards getting to know one another. We hypothesized that learning to take into account the subjectivity and point of view of both narrator and listeners would foster relational exchange and bonding. The opportunity to relive their memories by expressing them, and being listened to and understood by the other students, would also enable the participants - with the help of automatic writing techniques - to rethink and reconstruct their self-identities, that is to say, to reconstruct, narrate, and share with others their interpretation of self and not simply their narrative of self. In practice, this exercise in self-narration using cinematographic images as initial prompts, allowed the students to develop clearer definitions of self, of their cultural background, and the diverse cultures represented among them, while also becoming more aware of the group's communicative and expressive competences and resources. The teachers also benefited from the opportunity to become more familiar with the students' cognitive styles and relational models.

The researchers observed the students' individual learning styles and shared them with the teachers with a view to informing the design of personalized learning paths and modes of communication.

The students were observed both while they were watching the selected film material and during their subsequent participation in cooperative learning and group activities in which they were led to experience a particular way of relating both to images they had viewed - i.e., familiarizing with the language of film -, and to their classmates and teachers, while focusing simultaneously on the filmic representation and their personal experience in relation to how both of these might be interpreted.

Attending to these related aspects allowed us to simultaneously pursue diverse educational goals, namely, fostering students' capacity for self-narrative, building up the class group, as well as more strictly educational and communication-related objectives, while taking into account the participants' plural - and therefore specific - needs and characteristics.

The more specifically educational focus of the intervention entailed a continuous loop of observation and feedback, designed to foster reflection on the meaning of undergoing education and professional development in a country that is physically distant from the students' countries of origin, but at the same time close to their aspirations of personal fulfilment. We hypothesized that working on this aspect would continue to help the C.P.I.A. students throughout the school year; by stimulating them to more intentionally pursue competence-led learning, with knock-on benefits for their personal and professional inclusion into Italian society.

To this end, we conducted a series of educational and teaching-learning activities structured around the shared viewing of films chosen for their relevance to the proposed discussion topic, lessons on the theme of filmic language and images that offered theoretical and applied knowledge concerning both the different ways of reading a film, as illustrated by analysing the contents of a series of film sequences, and methods of drafting a screenplay and making a filmic product starting from an initial concept. The project's final outputs were a series of individual video-interviews, students' written productions, and a film produced jointly by the entire class.

4.1 The Main Phases in the Intervention

As a first step, we prepared for the intervention by working in synergy with the school's teachers: over a series of meetings, we presented our main educational and research objectives and discussed how we envisaged implementing the project in practice, seeking to establish how we could concurrently also; help the students' achieve their curricular learning objectives. At these meetings, we set out to identify themes and subject areas with particular potential to facilitate the teaching-learning of the competences we were targeting by working on film, ultimately deciding to link the cinema project to the Italian language and history syllabuses. As the guiding theme for the project, we selected the two interrelated terms: "Origins" and "History".

The second phase began with the administration of a questionnaire designed to identify, with a view to leveraging, the participants' prior competences. Next, the students took part in six two-hour sessions of actual project work, at which workshops on the language of film were alternated with classes on the history of cinema and its origins, exercises in developing screenplay and group work focused on sharing and developing the participants' reflections on the film materials they had viewed. During the first sessions, we explored the main characteristics of cinematographic culture in the early years following the invention of cinema, subsequently taking a more in-depth look at the theme of how film originated, its relationship with the worldviews that it represents as well as with the world we live in, seeking to identify connections, differences, and similarities. Based on film sequences shown in class followed by guided discussion sessions, the students' compiled questionnaires and completed a set of practical exercises designed to refine and reinforce their cognitive understanding of film.

During the third phase of the project, the material from the earlier phases was drawn on to write up a series of individual interviews in which the students narratedselected aspects of their life stories.

Each student has writing and reading in Italian language the text of some answers regarding a few questions. The questions referred on their origins and their first relation with the Italian culture and the Italian language. They exposed their work without difficulties and with a good level of cooperative learning. Representing the stories of their origins helped the students to also express their aspirations for the future, and the class ultimately drew inspiration from this to produce a set of video interviews. Ashort moviepresenting the students participants of this learning experience with cinema in their classroom as a final exercise in sharing the experience of taking part in the project.

5. RESULT

During the 2016-2017 school year, the teaching-learning path, composed of structured activities, implemented with the students at Bergamo C.P.I.A. provided the participants with a background in cinema per se. As well as an appreciation of cinema as a tool for learning about history, and in particular about European culture in the period spanning the nineteenth and twentieth centuries and about the Italian language.

The project covered many aspects of film as a discipline in its own right: from the history of cinema and early key players to the history of cinematographic technology, from filming technique to the language of images, the study of screenplay and the analysis of filmic structure.

Meanwhile, cinema as a resource for the teaching/learning of other subjects was mainly presented to the students in the context of learning about the Italian language and narrative structure in general.

Inviting students to explore the theme of their own "origins" helped to introduce the topic of the origins of cinemaand at the same time to promote learning focused on the value of historical knowledge and in particular, the genesis of the revolutionary technological innovation that is cinema from an expressive-narrative point of view.

6. CONCLUSION AND FUTURE RESEARCH DIRECTIONS

This contribution proposed an educational experience characterized by an interactive approach among different disciplines. The use of cinema has allowed the design of activities for an interactive teaching and learning system in which digital technologies have played a decisive role.

The results obtained to date from the educational project implemented at Bergamo C.P.I.A. have been positive. The introduction of cinema in this school for the first time was well received and popular among the students and the teachers.

The project has been extendedin other new learning paths and didactic experiences and it has been repeated in the following two school years. New cinema-based activities and creative teaching-learning paths have been developed with other groups of students.

The future research opportunities at Bergamo C.P.I.A. school immigrantson this same topic included the development of other interdisciplinary activities for the teaching and learning. The researcher group purposed and implemented issues of programs from the creative perspective regarding the implementation of cinema laboratory and the production of short movies by students editing.

REFERENCES

Bertolini, P. (1988). *L'esistere pedagogico. Ragioni e limiti di una pedagogia come scienza fenomenologicamente fondata*. La Nuova Italia.

Bettelheim, B. (1990). *La Vienna di Freud*. Feltrinelli Editore.

Bruner, J. S. (1961). The act of discovery. *Harvard Educational Review*, *31*, 21–32.

Bruner, J. S. (1990). *Acts of meaning* (Vol. 3). Harvard University Press.

Bruner, J. S. (2002). *Making stories: Law, literature* (Vol. 23). Life.

Bruner, J. S., & Minds, A. (1986). *Possible Worlds*. Harvard University Press.

Casetti, F. (2005). *L'occhio del Novecento: cinema, esperienza, modernità*. Bompiani.

Costa, A. (2011). *Saper vedere il cinema*. Giunti.

D'Incerti, D., Santoro, M., & Varchetta, F. (2007). *Nuovi schermi di formazione: i grandi temi del management attraverso il cinema*. Guerini.

Demetrio, D. (1995). Raccontarsi: l'autobiografia come cura di sé. Milano: Cortina.

Franza, A. M. (1993). *Giovani satiri e vecchi sileni: frammenti di un discorso pedagogico*. Unicopli.

Franza, A. M. (2018). *Teoria della pratica formativa. Apprendimento dall'esperienza e clinica della formazione*. Franco Angeli.

Franza, A. M., & Mottana, P. (1997). *Dissolvenze: le immagini della formazione*. Clueb.

Massa, R. (1997). *Cambiare la scuola. Educare o istruire?* Laterza.

Massa, R. (Ed.). (2005). *La Clinica della formazione*. Franco Angeli.

Morin, E. (2002). *Seven complex lessons in education for the future*. UNESCO.

Morin, E. (2016). Il cinema o l'uomo immaginario. Milano: Cortina.

Nicolosi, V. M. (2002). *Sguardo o visione?* Nicola Calabria Editore.

Rezzara, A. (Ed.). (2004). *Dalla scienza pedagogica alla clinica della formazione: sul pensiero e l'opera di Riccardo Massa* (Vol. 9). FrancoAngeli.

Smorti, A. (1994). *Ilpensieronarrativo. Costruzione di storie e sviluppo della conoscenza sociale*. Giunti.

Vygotskji, L. S. (1966). *Pensiero e linguaggio*. GiuntiBarbera.

Wertsch, J. V. (1985). *Vygotskij and the social formation of mind*. Harvard University Press.

KEY TERMS AND DEFINITIONS

Cinema Education: Education towards the cinematographic heritage, culture of cinema and the analysis of images moving language. The educational aims on cinema and its use at school and in the educational contexts are dedicated to development the teaching and the learning by harnessing knowledge and skills from across different subject areas.

Cooperative Learning: The Cooperative learning is a method that involves students in a group work, thanks the interaction of students, the knowledge connections and learning work origin the construction of new knowledge.

Immigrant Students: Students from other countries and other cultures who attend school in a country other than their country of origin.

Interdisciplinary Approach: It is the teaching and learning mode referred to the ability to relate knowledge to each other.

Language of Film: The multimedia dimension of film is based on a complex structure composed with a plurality of more or less specific audiovisual codes.

ENDNOTES

1 http://aei.pitt.edu/82945/1/1996_Issue_5_Le_Magazine.pdf

2 https://eur-lex.europa.eu/legal-content/EN/TXT/PDF/?uri=CELEX:52018SC0014&from=EN

3 https://ec.europa.eu/assets/eac/education/experts-groups/2011-2013/teacher/teachercomp_en.pdf

4 The recommendation of the European Parliament and Council of Europe concerning key competences for lifelong learning was first issued on 18 December 2006. Council Recommendation of 22 May 2018 on key competences for lifelong learning, in the Official Journal of the European Union C189, 4.6.1994, p. 1. The text is availableon website https://ec.europa.eu/education/education-in-the-eu/council-recommendation-on-key-competences-for-lifelong-learning_en

5 https://www.gazzettaufficiale.it/eli/id/2017/05/16/17G00069/sg

6 A. M. Franza and R. Massa developed the clinical-educational approach (clinicadellaformazione in Italian), an educational dispositive that leverages and amplifies the emotional, communicative, and relational dimensions of educational action, while paying particular attention to the process underlying it. Franza pioneered the incorporation of cinema into the clinical-educational dispositive as an educational tool for learning to recognize and explore educational experience that facilitates the identification of the patterns, dynamics, procedures, and strategies deployed by the teacher in relating to him/herself and to others.

7 In*Seven complex lessons in education for the future*,claimed that intellectual understanding is characterized by a process of learning together, or rather by *com-prehending*together that comprises multiple variables. It follows that film can offer a valuable educational tool precisely thanks to the complexity of its language.

8 Constructivism, as a model of learning, describes the individual as an 'epistemic agent' with a personalized vision of the world shaping a subjective interpretation of reality. Hence, the educator's focus shifts from the performative dimension to the cognitive paths involved in the learning process.

9 The interactive constructivist (or co-constructivist) approach is a further school of thought whose main exponents were J. Bruner, Vygotskij,Wertsch, and Smorti.

10 According to J. Bruner, narrative approaches to education can foster learning focused on the significance of knowledge for personal identity.

11 See the previous section on the Italian legislative framework.

12 Idem.

Chapter 14
Comparative Analysis of ACO Algorithms for the Solution of the Travelling Salesman Problem

Gloria Lola Quispe
Facultad de Ingeniería, Universidad Nacional de Jujuy, Argentina

Maria Fernanda Rodríguez
Facultad de Ciencias Económicas, Argentina

José Daniel Ontiveros
Facultad de Ingeniería, Universidad Nacional de Jujuy, Argentina

ABSTRACT

Metaheuristics are non-deterministic algorithms. Metaheuristic strategies are related to design. This chapter presents an introduction on metaheuristics, from the point of view of its theoretical study and the foundations for its use. Likewise, a description and comparative study of the ant colony-based algorithms is carried out. These are ant system (AS), ant colony system (ACS), and max-min ant system (MMAS). These results serve to deliver solutions to complex problems and generally with a high degree of combinatorics for those there is no way to find the best reasonable time. An experimentation and analysis of the results of the ACO algorithms (optimization by ants colonies) is also carried out. For the evaluation of the algorithms, comparisons are made for instances of the TSPLIB test instance library. Therefore, it is deepened in the resolution of the travelling salesman problem (TSP), and a comparative analysis of the different algorithms is carried out in order to see which one adjusts better.

DOI: 10.4018/978-1-7998-7010-4.ch014

1. INTRODUCTION

1.1 Problems and Complexity

When solving problems, it can be observed that not all of them present the same degree of difficulty. Thus, given any problem, how is determined whether it is easy of difficult? Or even more so, what does it mean a problem is easy or difficult? This subject is treated by a brach of mathematics called algorithmic complexity. Algorithmic complexity establishes a classification of the different types of problems by their degree of difficulty according to the computational complexity of the simplest algorithm that ensures their resolution. The problems can be classified into two large groups:

- Intractable problems: include those that are formally undecidable (Minsky, 1967), there is a demonstrationthat there is no algorithm that allows to solve them in all cases. Intractable problems also include all those problems for which an algorithm is known that could solve them, but for which the amount of computational time required to this, makes them inaccessible even for "reasonable" sizes. This is independent of the computational capacity available. It can formally be said that there is no algorithm that allows solving it in a series of steps that is a polynomial function of the input size of the problem.
- Treatable problems: these are problems of class P that can always be solved using an algorithm that involves several steps that is a polynomial function of the input size of the problem.

In summary, it can be said that problems of class P can be solved in polynomial time and intractable ones cannot be solved in polynomial time.

Additionally, an extra classification can be established for those decidable but intractable problems, for which there is at least the possibility of calculating, in a number of steps that is a polynomial function of the size of the problem, if a solution belongs to its solutions. These problems together with those of class P form class NP.

Problems of the class NP are those that can be solved using an imaginary machine called a Non-Deterministic Turing Machine (NDTM), in several polynomial steps. Many of the problems in the NP class are quite common problems, appearing regularly in different areas of engineering and include, but are not limited to, set partitioning problems, network design, planning, optimization, information retrieval, etc. (Garey & Johnson, 1979).

Of all the problems of the NP class, a set of them called NP-complete can be distinguished, which are the most difficult to solve. Cook's Theorem (Cook, 1971) allows us to determine whether a given NP problem belongs to the NP-complete class. The property of the NP-complete class is that every problem of the NP class can be polynomially transformed into it.

However, optimization problems are not generally found in the NP class and therefore may not be NP-complete. Therefore, in general, it is not possible to check whether an optimal solution has been achieved in several steps that is a polynomial function of the size of the problem. In most cases it is only possible to verify this by comparing it with the entire set of solutions to the problem. If the set of solutions grows exponentially with the size of the problem, it is evident that the verification cannot be carried out in polynomial time. These optimization problems are in a class of problems called NP-hard.

From all that has been said above, it is indisputable that for NP-hard optimization problems there is no algorithm in polynomial time that allows determining the optimal solution to the problem. For this reason, approximate methods are used by means of heuristics that allow us to approach an optimal solution generating feasible solutions to the problem that are of practical use.

1.2 Combinatorial Optimization

Combinatorial Optimization is a branch of Optimization in Applied Mathematics and Computer Science (William et al., 1997), related to Operations Research, Theory of Algorithms and Theory of Computational Complexity.

A combinatorial optimization problem can be expressed as a system of equations and related mathematical expressions that describe the essence of the problem.

This type of problem has the following characteristics:

- Sometimes it is difficult to find a possible solution.
- At the same time, there is an extremely high number of possible solutions.
- Of all the solutions, some are optimal.

In this same environment, the combinatorial optimization algorithms appear that solve instances of hard NP type problems by reducing the effective size of the space and exploring the search space efficiently.

The general model that represents a combinatorial optimization problem is as follows (Papadimitriou & Steiglitz, 1982) (equations 1.1 and 1.2):

$$\text{Optimse}\, f(x)$$

$$\text{Subect to :}$$

$$g_i(x) > 0 \; for\, i:1..m \tag{1.1}$$

$$h_j(x) > 0 \; for\, j:1..n \tag{1.2}$$

Where?

- $f(x)$: It is known as the objective function and represents a value that must be optimized in its maximum or minimum expression.

- $h(x)$ y $g(x)$: they are called the constraints of the problem and specify the conditions that any viable solution must have.

Informally, optimizing means more than just improvement; however, in the scientific context, optimization is the process of trying to find the best possible solution for a given problem. Many optimization problems of theoretical and / or practical importance consist in the search for a better configuration of a set of variables to achieve certain objectives. Problems naturally fall into two categories: those in which the solutions are coded with a real value of the variables, and those in which the solutions are coded with discrete variables. Among the latter, there is a class of problems called Combinatorial Optimization Problems (POC). Combinatorial optimization problems are present in various fields such as economics, commerce, engineering, industry or medicine. However, these problems are often exceedingly difficult to solve in practice. The study of this class of problems takes place in the field of Computer Science theory, since many of them belong to the class of NP-Complete problems (problems for which it is not known or perhaps there is no algorithm that solves them in polynomial time) (Garey & Johnson, 1979).

Among the classic combinatorial optimization problems we can mention:

- Commercial Traveler
- Coloring of Graphs
- Partition of Sets
- Quadratic Assignment
- Generalized allocation
- Linear Ordering
- Diversity
- Vehicle routing

1.3 Exact and Approximate Algorithms

The existing algorithms that allow solving Combinatorial Optimization problems can be classified into exact algorithms and approximate algorithms (Osman & Kelly, 1996).

Exact Algorithms

Exact algorithms try to find an optimal solution and show that the solution obtained is in fact the global optimum; These algorithms include techniques such as backtracking, branching and pruning, dynamic programming, and so on. (Papadimitriou & Steiglitz, 1982).

Approximate Algorithms

Because exact algorithms show poor performance for many problems, multiple types of approximate algorithms have been developed that provide high-quality solutions to these combinatorial problems (although not necessarily optimal) in a short computational time.

Approximate algorithms can be classified into two main types:

- Construction algorithms: they are based on generating solutions from scratch by adding components to each solution step by step. A well-known example is greedy construction heuristics (Brassard & Bratley, 1996). Their big advantage is speed, as they are normally very fast and often return reasonably good solutions. However, such solutions cannot be guaranteed to be optimal with respect to small changes at the local level. Consequently, a typical improvement is to refine the solution obtained by the voracious heuristic using a local search.

- Local search algorithms: they repeatedly try to improve the current solution with moves to neighboring solutions (in the hope that they are better). The simplest case is the iterative improvement algorithms: if a better solution s' is found in the neighborhood of the current solution s', it replaces the current solution and the search is continued starting from s'; if no better solution is found in the neighborhood, the algorithm ends up at a local optimum. Unfortunately, iterative improvement algorithms can stagnate in low-quality solutions (local optimum very far from global optimum). To enable further improvement in the quality of solutions, research in this field in the last two decades has focused on the design of general-purpose techniques to guide the construction of solutions or the local search in the various heuristics. These techniques are commonly called metaheuristics and are described in the next chapter.

1.4 Heuristics in Optimization

In Mathematical Optimization (and in Operative Research), the term heuristic applies to a procedure for solving optimization problems with a different conception: a heuristic is a procedure that seeks good solutions (that is, almost optimal) at a reasonable computational cost, although without the need for their feasibility or optimality. In some cases, without being able to determine how close to the optimum a particular feasible solution is found (Hernández, Hernández, 2013).

1.5 Heuristics in AI

In Artificial Intelligence (AI) the qualifier heuristic is used in a very generic sense, to apply it to all those aspects that have to do with the use of knowledge in the dynamic task performance.

It is spoken of heuristics to refer to a technique, method or intelligent procedure, capable to carry out a task that is not the product of a rigorous formal analysis, but of expert knowledge about the task (Moreno Perez, 2004).

In particular, the term heuristic is used to refer to a procedure that tries to provide solutions to a problem with a good performance, in relation to the quality of the solutions and the resources used.

1.6 AI's Strategies

In solving specific problems, successful heuristic procedures have emerged, from whichattempts have been made to extract what is essential in their successin order to apply it to other problems or in more extensive contexts.

As it has clearly happened in diverse fields of AI, especially with the expert systems, this line of reach has contributed to the scientific development of the heuristics field and to expand the application of its results (Melián et al., 2003).

In this way, both, specific techniques and computational resources have been obtained, as well as general design strategies for heuristic problem-solving procedures (Moreno Perez, 2004).

1.7 Metaheuristic Concepts

Metaheuristics are methods that integrate local procedures and high-level strategies to create a rocess capable of escaping from local optimum and performing a robust search in the search space (Glover & Kochenberger, 2003).

A metaheuristic is a set of concepts that can be used to define heuristic methods applicable to a wide variety of problems (Osman & Kelly, 1996).

A metaheuristic can be seen as a general algorithmic framework, that can be applied to different optimization problems with minimal changes to be adapted to a specific problem (Leguizamon, 2012).

Metaheuristic algorithms areapproximate general-purpose search and optimization algorithms. They are iterative procedures that guide a subordinate heuristic intelligently combined different concept to explore and exploit the search space displaced (Herrera, 2012).

Specifically, in AI, metaheuristics are general strategies for building algorithms, which areabove the heuristics, and go somewhat further. It can integrate as an expert system to facilitate its generic use while improving its performance.

The rest of the article is organized as follows: in section 2, a description of the type of problem is made, in section 3, the development of the metaheuristics is presented, in section 4, the proposed problem is described, section 5 contains the conclusions and finally in section 6 references are indicated.

2 CLASS OF PROBLEMS

2.1 NP-hard Problems

In theory of computational complexity, the complexity class NP-hard (or NP-complex, or difficult NP) is the set of decision problems contained in problems Hsoas every problem L in NP can be polynomially transformed into H.

This classtype can be described as the one containing the decision problems that are at least as difficult as an NP problem. This statement is justified because we can find an algorithm A that solves one of the H-problems in polynomial times, so it is possible to construct an algorithm that works in polynomial time for any NP Problem by fist executing the reduction of this problem in H and then executing algorithm A.

Unless NP=P, NP-hard problems do not have polynomial algorithms, so an algorithm that solves exactly.

In theory of computational complexity, the NP-complete complexity class is the subset of the decision problems in NP such that any problem in NP can be reduced in each of the NP-complete problems.

It can be said that the problems of NP-complete are the most difficult ones of NP and most likely are not part of the complexity class P.

2.2 NP-complete Problems

In theory of computational complexity, the NP-complete complexity class is the subset of the decision problems in NP such that any problem in NP can be reduced in each of the NP-complete problems.

It can be said that the problems of NP-complete are the most difficult ones of NP and most likely are not part of the complexity class P.

The reason is that if there was solution for an NP-complete problem, all the problems of NP would also have a polynomial time solution. If it is shown that an NP-complete problem, let us call it A, cannot be solved in polynomial time, the rest of the NP-complete problems cannot be solved in polynomial time either. This is because ifone of the NP-complete problems other than A, say X, can be solved in polynomial time, then it could be solved in polynomial time by definition of NP-complete.

There may be problems in NP and not being NP-complete ones for which there is a polynomial solution, even without the existence of a solution for A (Garey & Johnson, 1979).

The relation between P, NP-hard and NP-complete problems can be seen in figure 1.

Figure 1. Euler's diagram of the problem families P, NP, NP-complete, and NP-hard

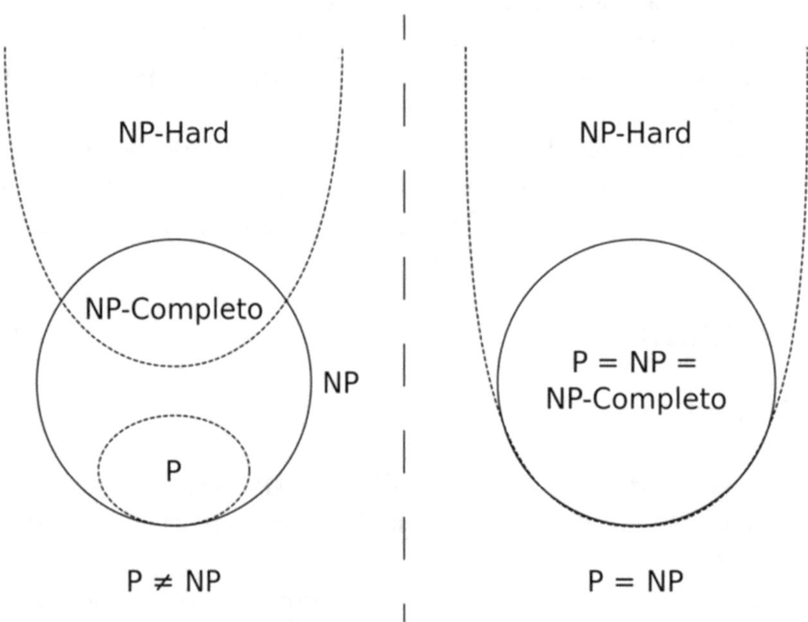

2.3 Travelling Salesman Problem

2.3.1 Problem Description

The Traveling Salesman Problem (TSP) or Traveler's problem, answers the following question: Given a list of cities and the distances between each pair of them, what is the shortest possible route? who visits each city exactly once and returns to the city of origin? This is an NP-hard problem within combinatorial optimization, especially important in operations research and in computer science.

The problem was first formulated in 1930 and is one of the most studied optimization problems. It is used as a test for many optimization methods. Although the problem is computationally complex, many heuristics and exact methods are known, so that some instances from one hundred to thousands of cities can be solved.

TSP has various applications even in its simplest formulation, such as: planning, logistics, and microchip manufacturing. A little modified, it appears as a sub-problem in many areas, such as DNA sequence. In this application, the concept of "city" represents, for example, customers, solder points or DNA fragments and the concept of "distance" represents travel time or cost, or a measure of similarity between DNA fragments.

2.3.2 History

The origin of the traveling salesman problem is unclear. An 1832 guide for travel agents mentions the problem and includes examples of travels through Germany and Switzerland but does not contain a mathematical treatment of it.

The traveling salesman problem was defined in the 1800s by the Irish mathematician W. R. Hamilton and by the British mathematician Thomas Kirkman. Hamilton's Icosian Game was a recreational puzzle based on finding a Hamilton cycle. Everything seems to indicate that the general form of the TSP was studied, for the first time by mathematicians in Vienna and Harvard, during the 1930s. Standing out Karl Menger, who defined the problems, considering the obvious brute force algorithm, and observing the non-optimality of the nearest neighbor heuristic. Shortly after, Hassler Whitney of Princeton University introduced the name "traveling salesmanproblem" (Applegate et al., 2006).

During the years 1950 to 1960, the problem was increasing its popularity between the circle of scientists of Europe and the United States. A notable contribution was that of George Dantzig, Delbert Ray Fulkerson, and Selmer M. Johnson of the RAND Corporation in Santa Monica, who expressed the problem as Integer Linear Programming and developed the Shear Planes method to solve it. With this new method, they solved an instance with 49 cities, optimally, by building a route and proving that there was no route that could be shorter. In the following decades, the problem was studied by many researchers, mathematicians, computer scientists, chemists, physicists, etc.

Richard M. Karp showed in 1972 that the Hamilton Cycle Problem was an NP-complete problem, which implies that the TSP is an NP-hard problem. This has its mathematical explanation for the obvious computational difficulty to find optimal routes.

Great progress was made in the late 70s and early 80s, where Grötschel, Padberg, Rinaldi and others handled exact solutions for instances with 2392 cities, using Cutting Plans and Branching and Dimensioning.

In the 1990s, Applegate, Bixby, Chvátal, and Cook developed the Concorde program, which is used in many of the recent solution registries. Gerhard Reinelt published the TSPLIB in 1991, a collection of test instances of varying difficulty, which is used by many research groups to compare results. In 2006, Cook et al., Obtained an optimal tour for 85,900 cities given by a microchip design problem, currently TSPLIB is the longest resolved instance. For many other instances with millions of cities, the solution can be found by guaranteeing that the solution contains 2-3% of the optimal path.

2.3.3 Formulation

The traveling salesman problem is one of the most widely studied combinatorial optimization problems. His statement is simple: a traveller seeks the shortest way through m cities. In other words, a person must visit a set of m cities, starting in a given city and ending in the same city; after having visited all of them only once. This means that you never return to a city you have already visited, except the first one.

This problem can be modelled by a graph, whose nodes represent each city and the arcs the distance between a pair of them, forming, in this way, a Hamiltonian cycle.

The goal is to find the optimal sequence of visits, which can be evaluated according to different criteria, for example, the minimization of cost or time, the maximization of speed.

The TSP can be symmetric or asymmetric. In the first case, given a set of m nodes and distances for each pair of nodes, the distance from node i to node j is the same as the distance from node j to node i. While in the case of asymmetric TSP, the distance from node i to node j is different from the distance from node j to node i (Reinelt, 1995).

2.3.4 Mathematical TSP Model

A TSP model is defined by the number of cities n and the distance matrix ||d_ij ||. The definition of a route prohibits connecting a city to itself by assigning a remarkably high penalty to the diagonal elements of the distance matrix. A TSP model is symmetric if $d_{\_ij} = d_{\_ji}$ for all i and j. Otherwise, the TSP model is asymmetric.

This is how it is define d $x_{ij} = \begin{cases} 1, if\ city\ j\ is\ reached\ from\ city\ i \\ 0, otherwise \end{cases}$

The TSP model is given as (equation 4.1)

$$Minimize\ z = \sum_{i=1}^{n}\sum_{j=1}^{n} d_{ij}x_{ij}, d_{ij} = \infty\ for\ all\ i = j \tag{2.1}$$

Suject to the following restrictions

- $\sum_{i=1}^{n} x_{ij} = 1\ for\ j = 0, \ldots., n; i \neq j$.
- $\sum_{j=1}^{m} x_{ij} = 1\ for\ i = 1, \ldots., n; j \neq i$
- $x_{ij} = (0,1)$

e solution is a round trip through the cities.

The constraints define a regular assignment model, where $x_{ij} = 1$ if node (city) $i$is connected to a node (ciudad) j, and zero otherwise. If the allocation model solution turns out to be a tour (last constraint), then it is automatically optimal for the TSP.

If $i = j$ a large value must be assigned for the distance d_{ij} to ensure that this will not be a viable route. This value is represented by an M in the model (Taha, 2012).

2.3.5 Applications

TSP has been applied to a wide variety of problems ranging from vendor routes to genetics. Some of the most important applications of the traveling salesman problem are briefly discussed below (Martinez, 2011):

Logistics: The most direct and abundant applications of TSP are in the field of logistics. The flow of people, goods, and vehicles around a series of cities or clients fits perfectly with the philosophy of the TSP, as the first scholars of the problem demonstrated. Among the multiple logistics applications of the traveler's problem, the following stand out:

- Vendors and tourists. Although travel for pleasure or business is rarely considered as a TSP, most vendors and tourists use some route planner to determine the best way to visit the points they want and return to the point of origin (note that tourists want to visit monuments or emblematic places and then return to the hotel). These schedulers generally include some TSP resolution algorithm.
- School routes. School routes represent one of the first applications of the TSP. Currently, many companies dedicated to the transport of people purchase TSP resolution software that allows them to reduce expenses in a significant way.
- Mail delivery. - Although mail delivery is generally better suited to a problem of arc routes, sometimes mail delivery can be modeled as a TSP. These are the cases in which the houses are far from each other or when only some of them should be visited (it will be the case of parcel companies). This scheme is applicable to the distribution of any other type of merchandise.

Industry: The applications in industry are not as numerous as in logistics, but the application of the problem in this area has also led to a significant reduction in costs. Among the applications to the industry we find:

- Sequencing of tasks. Given a machine that must perform a series of tasks in the shortest possible time and regardless of their order, and assuming that it takes time tij to get the machine ready to perform task j if the last task performed was task i . In this case, a TSP can be applied considering that each task is one of the nodes to be visited, that all the tasks have to be performed to produce the product and that the distance between them is the time tij. The source and destination node will be the state of the machine when the product starts or ends. Since the time used to carry out each task does not depend on the order, it will not be necessary to include these times in the model, since the sum of all is constant regardless of the order. A variation of this model was studied by (Gilmore & Gomory, 1964).

Production of electronic circuits: The use of TSP to produce electronic circuits focuses on two aspects: the optimal order of drilling the boards and the optimal paths needed to connect the chips to each other.

- Drilling problems. Integrated circuits are found in many electronic devices, so the production of the boards on which these circuits are mounted is a daily problem. Said plates must be pierced a relatively large number of times. The resulting holes are used to insert the corresponding chips. Generally, automatic drills are those that perform, one after another, the corresponding perforations. If these machines are not programmed correctly, the time it takes to travel the plate from one hole to another can increase significantly, leading to economic losses (if it takes too long to produce each plate, fewer plates will be produced in the same time) . Therefore, the application of TSP in this field consists of, taking as cities each of the positions where a drilling must be made and the distances between them as the time it takes for the machine to move from one to another, minimizing the time it loses the drill to move from one position to another. The city of origin and destination will be an additional point that represents where the drill remains while the plates are changed. Note that if the time it takes to drill is much higher than the travel time, it will not make sense to propose a TSP, since the decrease in time will be almost imperceptible. These applications have been studied for years (Lin & Kernighan, 1973) and have already been used by large companies, such as Siemens and IBM, leading to improvements of approximately 10% of the total performance of production lines.

- Chip connection. This type of example occurs frequently in the design of computers and other digital devices. Inside many of these devices there are boards that have chips that must be connected to each other by cables. To avoid interference problems and due to the small size of the chips, no more than two wires can be put on a single pin. The idea is therefore to minimize the amount of cable required to connect all the points. Clearly this model can be modeled as a TSP taking the pins as the cities and the amount of cable needed to join them as the distance between them. Note that in the absence of the restriction of only two wires per chip, this problem should be modeled as the search for the least-spanning tree, a problem for which there are efficient algorithms.

3 METAHEURISTICS

Metaheuristics integrate local procedures and high-level strategies in a variety of ways to create a process capable of escaping from local optimum and performing a robust search in the search place (Glover et al., 2003).

While metaheuristics represent a family of approximate optimization techniques with an important degree of development in the last two decades. They provide acceptable solutions in reasonable times to solve difficult and complex problems (Leguizamón, 2012). Among the metaheuristic techniques that have obtained the greatest success in the scientific community are:

- Taboo Search (Dorigo & Stützle, 2003): Metaheuristic technique based on a local or neighborhood search.
- Genetic Algorithms: Introduced by Holland in 1970, they are algorithms that are inspired by biological evolution and natural selection (Holland, 1975). These algorithms make evolve a population of individuals in the likeness of natural biological evolution. They serve to solve optimization problems that can be encoded by finite strings in a finite alphabet. They introduce a valuation function of the different individuals, called “fitness”, based on the objective function of the problem. This type of algorithms has been highly successful in different fields considered difficult problems.
- Simulated Tempering (Simulated Annealing): (Dréo et al., 2003): Search for theglobal optimum in a large search space determined in the mental heating process.
- Grasp (Resend and Ribeiro, 2006): acronym for Greedy Randomized Adaptative Search Procedure. Metaheuristic that presents two phases, a first one of construction that originates a good solution,

although not optimal, and another one, from this one, with a local search where neighborhoods are examined to arrive at a local optimum in the same iteration. This process continues until a termination criterion is reached.

- Optimization based on Ants Colony (Dorigo & Stutzle, 2004): Biological inspired algorithms that are based on the behavior of natural ant colonies to solve combinational problems.

3.1 Algorithms Base on ACO Metaheuristics

Various algorithms that follow ACO metaheuristics have been proposed in the literature. Among the main ACO algorithms available for NP-hard combinatorial optimization problems are:

- Ant System
- Max-Min Ant System
- Ant Colony System

The Ant System (AS), was the first ACO algorithm proposed in the literature. Initially, three different variants were presented: ant-density, ant-quantity, and ant-cycle, which differed in the way they updated the pheromone traces. In the first two, the ants deposited pheromone while building their solutions (that is, they applied a step-by-step online pheromone update). While, in ant-cycle, the pheromone update was carried out once all the ants had built a solution and the amount of pheromone deposited by each ant was established based on the quality of the solution. This last variant was the one that obtained the best results and is therefore the one known as AS (Dorigo, 1996).

3.1.1 Ant System. Basic Algorithm

It was the first ant colony optimization algorithm, developed by M. Dorigo, V. Maniezzo, A. Colorni in 1991 (Dorigo et al., 1996) (Dorigo M. & Stutzle T., 2004). This algorithm was carried out to solve the traveling salesman problem, a more traditional and studied combinatorial optimization problem, looking for the shortest route to travel to a set of cities.

The algorithm tries to simulate the behavior of natural ants. This must be able to accept the tasks performed by the ant and simulate the behavior of the whole. Three variants of the algorithm were carried out according to the way in which the pheromone deposit was carried out in the medium.

- Density: The pheromone deposit was carried out during the journey (online step-by-step pheromone update). The amount of pheromone deposited was always constant.
- Quantity: The pheromone was deposited during the tour (step-by-step online update of pheromone). The amount of pheromone deposited was related to the heuristic desirability of the stretch.
- Cycle: The pheromone deposit is carried out once a solution is finished (online pheromone update).

This last variant is the one that provided the best results and the one known by Ant System. This is characterized by the fact that the pheromone update is carried out once all the ants have completed their solutions, and it is carried out as follows: first, all the pheromone traces are reduced by a constant factor, being implemented from this way the evaporation of pheromone. Next, each ant in the colony deposits an amount of pheromone that is a function of the quality of its solution. Initially, the Ant System (AS) or Hormigas System (SH) did not use any action in the background, but it is relatively easy, for example, to add a local search procedure to refine the solutions generated by the ants.

Many variations of the algorithm have been made, mainly in the action functions on the pheromone treatment.

Your pseudocode could be the following:

The ants use the pheromone deposit to remember their behavior, that is, to accumulate the knowledge that they acquire about the problem to be solved. At first, all the arches present the same probability and for this it is considered appropriate to introduce a small pheromone value, an amount that makes it possible that unexplored paths also have the probability of being traveled. As identified in the algorithm, there are two fundamental processes in its execution:

Choice of Momement

An ant*k* chooses to go to the next node with a probability that is given with the formula (Dorigo et al., 1996):

$$P_{rs}^{k} = \begin{cases} \dfrac{[r_{rs}]^{\alpha} \times [\eta_{rs}]^{\beta}}{\sum_{\mu \in N_r^k} [r_{rs}]^{\alpha} \times [\eta_{rs}]^{\beta}} \; si\, s \in \mathrm{N}_{\mathrm{k}}(r) \\ 0, in\, another\, case \end{cases}$$

Where:

are the nodes reachable by ant*k* from node *r.*

α y β are parameters that weigh the importance of the heuristic used and the pheromone values detected.

r_{rs}, represents the pheromone trails bet ween the points r y s.

η_{rs}, r represents the value of the chosen heuristic function, desirability.

- Each ant *k* stores the route taken so as not to repeat visits to the same node.

As it can be seen, defining values of the parameters α y βcan

vary the results quite a bit. If we makeα = 0, it means that we only give importance to the chosen heuristic function, while a value of β = 0 only considers the pheromone traces detected by the ant. The latter causes that the probability of building optimal premises is greatly strengthened, which is not it must occur for the algorithm to function properly.

Pheromone Update It has two Threads

- Evaporation. The pheromone traces are reduced by a constant value. This is what the evaporation of the pheromone from the natural system represents. The different arches suffer a decrease in their pheromone value that comes from the expression

$$r_{rs} \leftarrow (1-\rho) \times r_{rs}$$

, being ρ Î (1,0] the evaporation factor.

- Deposition. Next, the pheromone deposit is made in the path followed by the ant depending on the solution obtained.

$$r_{rs} \leftarrow r_{rs} + \Delta r_{rs}^{k}, \forall a_{rs} \in S_{k}$$

$$\Delta r_{rs}^{k} = f\left(C\left(S_{k}\right)\right)$$

Where, $\Delta r_{rs}^{k} = f\left(C\left(S_{k}\right)\right)$ is the amount of pheromone that is deposited, a function of the quality of the solution obtained. The quality of a solution is usually represented by the inverse of the distance traveled.

This has been the basis for many models developed to make this type of algorithm more efficient. Below are reports of those who, based on this model, have achieved greater success.

3.1.2 Ant Colony System

Algorithm that arises from the extension of the previous algorithms and the use of learning techniques such as Q-learning (Gambardella & Dorigo, 1995) (Dorigo & Gambardella, 1996), published by Dorigo and Gambardella in 1997 (Dorigo & Gambardella, 1997), where the modification of the algorithm is carried out in four main facets

- The transition of states, offering a balance between the exploration and exploitation of the accumulated knowledge. It is modified to explicitly allow browsing. The rule used is called the proportional pseudo-random rule.

k an ant in node r, q_0 (0£ q_0£ 1) a parameter and qa random value in [0,1], the next node*s* is chosen randomly by the following probability distribution

Yes *q* £ *q0*

$$P_{rs}^{k} = \begin{cases} 1, si\, s = arg\, max_{\mu\epsilon N_k(r)} \left\{\tau_{ru\times}\eta_{ru}^{\beta}\right\} \\ 0, in\, another\, case \end{cases}$$

Yes *q* >*q0*

$$P_{rs}^{k}=\begin{cases}\dfrac{[r_{rs}]^{\alpha}\times[\eta_{rs}]^{\beta}}{\sum_{\mu\in N_r^k}[r_{rs}]^{\alpha}\times[\eta_{rs}]^{\beta}} si\, s\in \mathrm{N}_{\mathrm{k}}(r)\\ 0, in\, another\, case\end{cases}$$

- The global pheromone update, since they perform a global update on the best path found in each iteration.
- To carry out the update, the ant system only considers a specific ant, the one that generated the best global solution, S best-global (although in some initial works it was also considered an update based on the best ant of the iteration, in the Ant colony system almost always applies the upgrade by means of the best overall). The pheromone upgrade is done by first evaporating the pheromone traces in all connections used by the best global ant (it is important to note that, in the ant colony system, pheromone evaporation only applies to the solution connections, which is also used to deposit pheromone) as follows:

$$r_{rs}\leftarrow(1-\rho)\times r_{rs},\forall a_{rs}\in S_{mejor-global}$$

Then, pheronome is deposited usingthe rule:

$$r_{rs}\leftarrow r_{rs}+\rho\times f\left(C\left(S_{mejor-global}\right)\right),\forall a_{rs}\in S_{mejor-global}$$

- Local pheromone update. As the ants go through the arches, what they do is reduce the pheromone, thus favoring exploration. The objective is to make the arches visited less attractive, seeking non-convergence on the same route. Itsmathematical representationwould be the following:

$$r_{rs}\leftarrow(1-\varphi)\times r_{rs}+\varphi*\tau_{0}$$

Donde ϕ Î (0,1] es un segundo parámetro de decremento de feromona.

As can be seen, the local update rule includes both pheromone evaporation and pheromone deposition. Since the amount of pheromone deposited is very small (in fact, τ_0 is the value of the initial pheromone trace and was chosen in such a way that, in practice, it corresponds to the lower limit of the pheromone trace, that is, with choosing the pheromone update rules of the ant colony system no pheromone trace can fall below τ_0), the application of this rule makes the pheromone traces between the connections traversed by the ants decrease.

Thus, this leads to a further exploration technique of the ant colony system since the connections traversed by a large number of ants are becoming less attractive to the rest of the ants that traverse them in the current iteration, which clearly helps that not all ants follow the same path.

- Use of a candidate list. List where cities are ordered by visit preference.

Additionally (optional), a local search algorithm can be applied to improve the ant solutions before updating the pheromone traces. The algorithm also adds a local search, using the 3-opt method proposed by Bock in 1958, performing an arc exchange to reduce the length found. This method makes three cuts on the road and exchanges the destination cities and thus not reverse the direction of the cities visited. The algorithm designed according to this model is the following:

3.1.3 Max-Min Ant System

It arises from the observation of the behavior of previously mentioned algorithms (Stützle & Hoos, 2000). This Algorithm modifies the strategy when making the pheromone deposit and only allows the update to the ants that achieve good results. It was presented by Tomas Stützle and Holger Hoos (Stützle & Hoos, 1996). This strategy can give rise to a premature convergence in a non-optimal result, but it was considered appropriate that the best results exert a greater influence on the algorithm used. To avoid the excessive increase in the value of pheromone in non-optimal routes and therefore convergence in these routes, the concept of maximum and minimum was introduced, which referred to the values that the routes could reach in terms of amount of pheromone deposited . The minimum level limits the level of exploration, so that it always has execution possibilities.

$$r_t^{min} \leq r_{rs,t+1} \leq r_t^{max}$$

The algorithm introduced another new concept, it was the possibility of re-initializing the deposited deferomone values, imposing a new exploration of the search space.

It extends the Ant System in the following aspects:

- An update of the offline pheromone traces is applied, like how it is done in the Ant Colony System. After all the ants have built their solution, each trace of pheromone evaporates:

$$r_{rs} \leftarrow (1-\rho) \times r_{rs}$$

The pheronome is then deposited following this formula:

$$r_{rs} \leftarrow r_{rs} + f\left(C\left(S_{mejor}\right)\right) \forall a_{rs} \in S_{mejor}$$

The best ant that is allowed to add pheromone may be the one with the best solution from the iteration or the best overall solution. The experimental results show that the best performance is obtained by gradually increasing the frequency of choosing the best overall for the pheromone update.

Besides, the solutions offered by ants are usually improved using local optimizers prior to pheromone upgrade.

- The possible values for the pheromone traces are limited to the range [τ_{min}, $_{max}$]. Therefore, the probability of an algorithm stalling is decreased by giving each existing connection a probability, albeit a rather small one, of being picked. In practice, there are heuristics to set the values of τmin and τmax. It can be seen that, because of the evaporation of the pheromone, the maximum level of pheromone in the traces is limited to τ max = 1 / (ρ×*C*(*S**)), where *S** is the optimal solution.

Based on this result, the best global solution can be used to estimate τ_{max} subsitituting *S** por $S_{better-global}$ in the equation forτ*max. Forτ*min*, it is normally only necessary to choose its value such that it is a constant factor less than τmax.

To increase the exploration of new solutions, the MMAS occasionally uses re-initializations of pheromone traces.

- Instead of initializing the pheromone traces to a small amount, the MMAS initializes them to an estimate of the maximum allowed for a trace (the estimate can be obtained by generating a solution S 'with a voracious heuristic and replacing said solution S' in the equation of r^*_{max}).

This leads to an additional component of diversification in the algorithm, since at the beginning the relative differences between the pheromone traces will not be very marked, which is not the case when the pheromone traces are initialized to a very small value.

3.2 Comparative Study of the Max − Min Ant System, Ant System, Ant Colony System Algorithms

Table 1. Parameter Values

	AS	ACS	MMAS
Instance	Eil51.tsp	Eil51.tsp	Eil51.tsp
n(cities)	51	51	51
Optimum	426	426	426
Executions	25	25	25
Time(s)	20	20	20
M	10 £ m £ Cities	10 £ m £ Cities	10 £ m £ Cities
A	1	1	1
B	3	2	2
Q	10	1	100
ρ	0,7	0,7	0,1

This experiment was performed for the eil51 instance obtained from the TSPLIB test instance library. Table 1 shows the values of the parameters that were used for the comparison of the algorithms. The parameter m varies according to the set of proposed values and the rest of the parameters remain constant.

Table 2. Variation of "m"

				AS					ACS					MMAS	
m	**Better**	**Worst**	**Prom.**	**Desv. Est.**	**Prom. Iter.**	**Better**	**Worst**	**Prom.**	**Desv. Est.**	**Prom. Iter.**	**Better**	**Worst**	**Prom.**	**Desv. Est.**	**Prom. Iter.**
10	448	462	453,00	4,1182	1266,00	443	468	453,20	6,7498	781,00	429	441	435,10	4,0607	559,00
20	439	458	448,50	4,7381	531,00	440	452	448,10	3,3896	550,00	431	438	434,80	2,3579	525,00
30	442	458	451,50	5,1623	299,00	437	452	446,40	5,9169	220,00	431	437	433,60	2,1500	439,00
40	442	453	446,90	3,2078	525,00	434	454	448,60	5,8685	589,00	429	437	432,20	2,6381	280,00
50	442	455	449,80	3,6276	198,00	435	451	445,60	4,2941	477,00	429	438	432,10	2,7367	262,00

Table 2 shows the AS algorithm obtains the best solution (Best=439) when m is equal to 20. ACS obtains the best solution (Best=434) for m equal to 40. MMAS finds better solutions (Better=429) for m = 10, m = 40 and m = 50, since they are equal, the averages for choosing one of the m are considered.

In Figure 2 it can be observed that the AS algorithm improves up to 20 antswhen increasing the number of ants, then it moves away from the optimal value until stabilized, ACS obtains better values by

Figure 2. Comparison of AS, ACS, MMAS algorithms

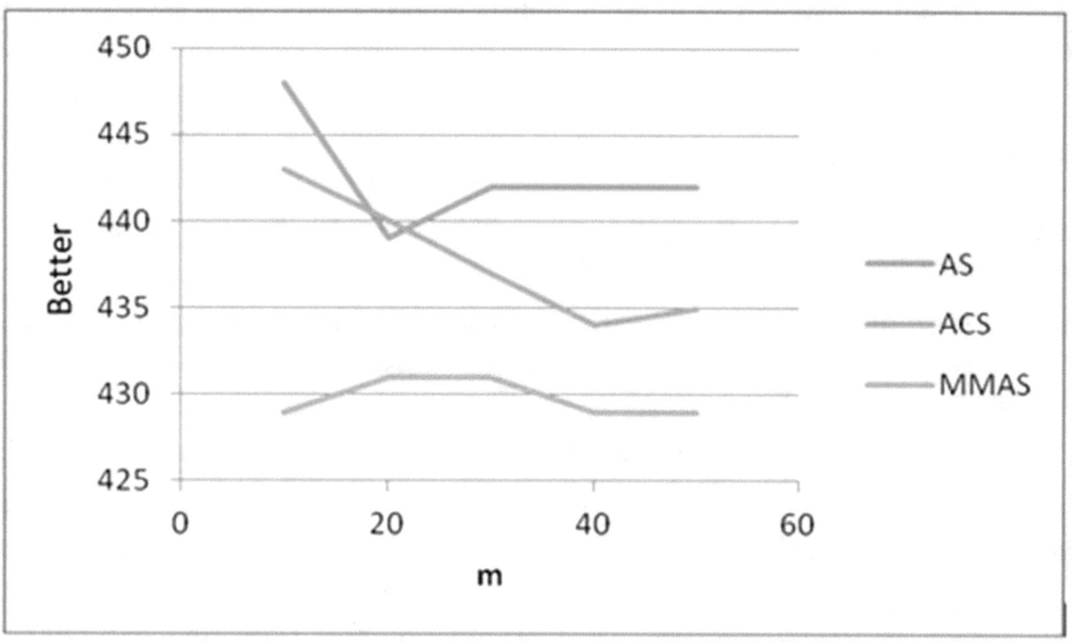

increasing ants up to 40 then increases by 1 unit and MMAA achieves better values for m = 10,40 and 50. Of the three Algorithms, MMAS is the one that has a better performance since its obtained values are very close to the optimum.

The AS Algorithm is one of the first algorithms used to solve the Travelling Salesman Problem (TSP), it has good results for small instances of the problem. The ACS variant performs AS for large instances because it stablished a balance between the exploration of new routes and the exploitation of problem information, the MMAS model also presents good results for large instances but thanks to modification of limits to pheromones its solutions are of better quality.

4. CONCLUSION

As it has been seen in the previous sections the algorithms to be selected depends on the type of problem, its way of implementing and convergence, due to some algorithms are easier to implement than others and converge in a smaller number of interactions.

For this reason, this research study intended to achieve a contribution to knowledge for TSP optimization problems solved with different variants of ACO algorithms, that is why it has been done a comparative analysis of different algorithms to find out which one of them suit better to the resolution of travelling salesman problem. In future research lines it is expected to continue implementing TSP, using the algorithm that best suits to the problem.

The research proposal described in this work aims to help all professionals in charge of providing solutions to different problems of the reality, and those interested in metaheuristics because there is currently a wide variety of algorithms for the development and implementation of different problems, but find the approximation algorithm for each of the them is difficult.

Explore the performance of Ant Colonies algorithms in solving optimization problems other than those used in this work.

REFERENCES

Applegate, D. L., Bixby, R. M., Chvátal, V., & Cook, W. J. (2006). *The Traveling Salesman Problem: A Computational Study*. Princeton University Press.

Arito, F. L. A. (2010). *Optimization Algorithms based on Ant Colonies applied to the Quadratic Allocation Problem and other related problems* (Unpublished degree thesis). National University of Saint Louis. Argentine.

Brassard, G., & Bratley, P. (1996). *Fundamentals of Algorithmics*. Prentice Hall.

Cook, S. (1971). The Complexity of Theorem Proving Procedures. In *Proceedings Third Annual ACM Symposium on Theory of Computing* (pp. 151-158). Shaker Heights, OH: ACM. 10.1145/800157.805047

Dorigo, M., & Gambardella, L. M. (1996). A study of some properties of Ant-Q. In *IV International Conference on Parallel Problem from Nature*. Berlin, Germany: Springer-Verlag. 10.1007/3-540-61723-X_1029

Dorigo, M., & Gambardella, L. M. (1997). Ant Colony System: A cooperative learning approach to the traveling salesman problem. *IEEE Transactions on Evolutionary Computation*, *1*(1), 53–66. doi:10.1109/4235.585892

Dorigo, M., Maniezzo, V., & Colorni, A. (1996). The Ant System: Optimization by a colony of cooperating agents. IEEE Transactions on Systems, Man and Cybernetics - Part B, 26(1), 1-41.

Dorigo, M., & Stützle, T. (2003). The ant colony optimization metaheuristic: Algorithms, applications and advances. Handbook of Metaheuristics, 57, 251-285.

Dorigo, M., & Stützle, T. (2004). *Ant colony optimization*. The MIT Press. doi:10.7551/mitpress/1290.001.0001

Dréo, J., Pétrowski, A., Siarry, P., & Taillard, E. (2003). *Metaheuristics for hard optimization*. Springer.

Gallego Rendón, R. A., & Ríos Porras, C. A. (2004). *Hincapíe Isaza, R. A. Heuristic. Techniques applied to the traveling postman problem (TSP)*. Colombia Scientia Et Technica. Technological University of Pereira.

Gambardella, L., & Dorigo, M. (1995). Ant-Q: Are inforcement learning approach to the traveling salesman problem. *12th International Conference on Machine Learning*, 252-260. 10.1016/B978-1-55860-377-6.50039-6

Garey, M. R., & Johnson, D. S. (1979). *Computers and Intractability: A Guide to the Theory of NP-Completeness*. W. H. Freeman.

Gilmore, P. C., & Gomory, R. E. (1964). Sequencing a one state-variable machine: A solvable case of the traveling salesman problem. *Operations Research*, *12*(5), 655–679. doi:10.1287/opre.12.5.655

Glover, F. G., & Kochenberger, G. A. (2003). *Handbook of Metaheuristics (International Series in Operations Research & Management Science)*. Kluwer Academic Publishers New York.

Hernández, J C. (2003). *Metaheurístics applied to bioinformatics*. University Corporation for Internet Devolopment A.C. (CUDI).

Herrera, F. (2012). *Introduction to Metahuristic Algorithms*. University of Granada.

Holland, J. H. (1975). Adaptation in Natural and Artificial Systems. University of Michigan Press.

Leguizamón, G. (n.d.). *Introduction to Metaheuristics*. Document presented in Postgrade course. University of San Luis.

Lin, S., & Kernighan, B. W. (1973). An effective heuristic algorithm for the traveling-salesman problem. *Operations Research*, *21*(2), 498–516. doi:10.1287/opre.21.2.498

Martinez, A. C. (2011). *Cooperation in Traveler's Problems (TSP) and Vehicle Routes (VRP): An Overview*. University of Santiago de Compostela.

Melián, B., Moreno Pérez, J. A., & Moreno Pérez, J. M. (2003). Metaheuristics: a global visión. *Iberoamerican Journal of Artificial Intelligence, 19*, 7-28.

Minski, M. L. (1967). *Computation: Finite and Infinite Machines*. Prentice-Hall Inc.

Moreno Pérez, J. A. (2004). *Metaheuristics: an updated review. Working Document presented in DEIOC*. University of La Laguna.

Osman, I. H., & Kelly, J. P. (1996). *Meta-Heuristics: Theory and Applications*. Kluwer Academic Publishers. doi:10.1007/978-1-4613-1361-8

Papadimitriou, C. H., & Steiglitz, K. (1982). Combinatorial Optimization: Algorithms and Complexity. Prentice Hall.

Ramos, S. A. (2010). *The Traveler's Problem: Concepts, Variations and Alternative Solutions*. Models and Optimization I. UBA.

Reinelt, G. (1995). *TSPLIB 95. Tech. report*. Universität Heidelberg, Institutfür Angewandte Mathematik.

Resende, M. G. C., & Ribeiro, C. C. (2003). Greedy Randomized Adaptive Search Procedures. In *Handbook of Metaheuristics* (pp. 219–249). Springer. doi:10.1007/0-306-48056-5_8

Stützle, T., & Hoos, H. (1996). Improvements on the Ant System*: Introducing Max-Min Ant System. International Conference on Artificial Neural Networks and Genetic Algorithms, Viena*, Austria.

Stützle, T., & Hoos, H. (2000). Max - Min ant system. *Future Generation Computer Systems*, *16*(8), 889–914. doi:10.1016/S0167-739X(00)00043-1

Taha, H. (2012). *Traveler agent problem. Operations Research* (9th ed.). Pearson Education.

William, J. C., William, H. C., William, R. P., & Alexander, S. (1997). *Combinatorial Optimization* (1st ed.). Wiley-Interscience.

KEY TERMS AND DEFINITIONS

ACO Algorithms: The ant colony optimization (ACO) is a probabilistic technique for solving computational problems that can be reduced to finding the best paths or routes in graphs.

ACS: The Ant Colony System, uses a more aggressive action choice rule than AS, pheromone evaporation and pheromone deposit is applied only to the bows of the best overall tour, and each time an ant uses a bow it decreases a certain amount of pheromone from that bow.

AS: The ant system, the pheromone upgrade takes place after all the ants have built a solution and the amount of pheromone deposited by each ant is established depending on the quality of the solution.

Metaheuristics: Are classes of approximate methods that are designed to solve difficult combinatorial optimization problems, in which classical heuristics are neither effective nor efficient.

MMAS: The MAX - MIN Ant System is an improved algorithm based on the ideas from AS.

TSP: Aims to find a complete route that connects all the nodes of a network, visiting them only once and returning to the starting point.

TSPLIB: is a library of examples of TSP instances (and related problems) from various sources and of various types.

Chapter 15
A Survey on the Techniques to Improve the Visibility of Geospatial Resources on the Web

Saif Ansari
University Institute of Technology, Rajiv Gandhi Proudyogiki Vishwavidyalaya, India

Piyush Kumar Shukla
University Institute of Technology, Rajiv Gandhi Proudyogiki Vishwavidyalaya, India

Rajeev Pandey
University Institute of Technology, Rajiv Gandhi Proudyogiki Vishwavidyalaya, India

Rohit Agrawal
University Institute of Technology, Rajiv Gandhi Proudyogiki Vishwavidyalaya, India

ABSTRACT

Geographical information has become ubiquitous. The demand to access geospatial data on the web is growing in numerous knowledge domains and disciplines. For the sharing of geospatial data, geoportals acts as entryways to the SDI (spatial data infrastructure) from where the data is disseminated. Because these geoportals are limited to geoinformation communities only, they exhibit challenges in terms of indexing by web search engines. Thus, the geospatial resources need a boost in terms of visibility over the internet (web). In this chapter, a discussion on the present state of geospatial resources on the web and comparison of various methods that have been employed for increasing the discoverability of geographical resources is presented. Therefrom, by discussion, the chapter concludes with a conjecture regarding scope for the further improvement in the methods that have been reviewed, along with depicting the need for the presence of geospatial resources on the internet.

DOI: 10.4018/978-1-7998-7010-4.ch015

INTRODUCTION

Due to the frequent usage of geographical information in various fields of study and subject areas, the requirement for suitable geospatial data has become essential (Katumba & Coetzee, 2017). The comfort at which data can be created is leading to a constant increase in the volume of geospatial data that is publically available on the web (Bone, Ager, Bunzel, & Tierney, 2016). However, the challenges to finding the geographical resources on the web remain the same because of the limitations of geoportals to geo communities solely.

This restriction on the availability of geospatial resources has led to the birth of several implementations regarding enhancement of the geo-resources discoverability. The major problem is that the people aware of geo communities know where to search for the spatial data, but same doesn't apply to the ones who aren't aware of these communities & try to find geospatial data on the web (Katumba & Coetzee, 2017). Moreover, at present geoportals are primarily build on the Open Geospatial Consortium (OGC) Catalogue Service for the Web (CSW) that caters HTTP binding (Katumba & Coetzee, 2017). It was designed to enable "the discovery and retrieval of spatial data and services metadata"; However, the geoportals was not designed to be crawled by web crawlers (Lopez-Pellicer, Florczyk, Nogueras-Iso, Muro-Medrano, & Zarazaga, 2010) and is thus the portion of the "Deep Web", i.e. online content inaccessible to web crawlers (Katumba & Coetzee, 2017).

To overcome this barrier of geospatial resources discoverability on the internet, separate geo-web crawling framework & geospatial search engines have been developed. Different techniques like SEO, metadata vocabularies (schema.org & Dublin core) for enhancing geo-resources visibility, thesauri & ontologies in mitigating semantic heterogeneity problems, focused deep web crawler for isolated land map services, GSE based on single-level crawler, javascript, for downloading shapefiles, also taxonomy, folksonomy & semantic annotations have been employed for locating geospatial data on the web.

Furthermore, the chapter advances towards the problems that have been encountered when Geospatial resources were judged on the scale of visibility with other web resources for common users on the web. With the growing demand for geospatial data & sources on the web, the chapter also throws light on how spatial resources are important for users and organisation in out of geocommunities. Moreover, the geoportals that act as entryways for the users, why they have been in deep web instead of being on the surface web accessible to common web users? Various techniques performed by different authors of these six research papers for the advancement of geospatial data discoverability have been examined. Furthermore, the chapter ends with the conclusion signifying about the scope of improvement for the discoverability of geospatial resources in today's scenario.

BACKGROUND

Understandng the Terminologies

In this section, we will see the key terms that are mentioned in the research papers that we are going to review further.

A. Search Engine Optimization Techniques for increasing the discoverability of websites

Ever since the evolution of the World Wide Web has begun. The WWW has seen the gradual increase in numbers of web search engine users, along with the avalanche of websites & web pages. Since then, web visibility has become a major point of concern to various organizations. To come in the first list results has always been the competition for the websites of the same disciplines. Various services are being offered by several organizations for tuning the web pages with the search engine that is by making them crawler friendly (Katumba & Coetzee, 2017).

Commercial Organizations often look for these SEO services to increase their visibility for their better outreach among their targeted audience. They often are prepared to pay search engine providers to make them visible better than their competitors (Katumba & Coetzee, 2017). Although there is another legit way created by search engine providers for the ones who are not willing to pay, they can get it done "Organically" that is through the SEO techniques: On-page & off-page SEO (Malaga, 2010,).

The adoption of metadata vocabularies such as schema.org and Dublin core cannot be ignored when it comes to increasing the visibility of web resources (Ochoa, May 2012). The vocabularies annotate text content in HTML, and that's how they are able to make it semantically advanced. Crawlers are able to "understand" it and, further are able to support it during the time of indexing (Katumba & Coetzee, 2017).

B. SKOS, Ontologies and Thesauri

Cross-language issues come when users look out for Geospatial resources. Some due to historical, cultural while other due to differences in the social background within or amongst states that use different languages still belonging to the same country (Maharashtra, Tamilnadu & Gujarat) (Vockner & Mittlböck, 2014). Due to the use of different languages across the various regions of a country geospatial databases, various descriptions & world views witnesses hindrance during the process of data sharing (Vockner & Mittlböck, 2014).

To prevail over semantic heterogeneity issues, a possible solution of (multilingual) ontologies and thesauri has been suggested. According to Gruber (Gruber, 1995), he defines ontology as a "formal, explicit specification of a shared conceptualisation". Further simplifying what Gruber meant about ontology is that it can be seen as some real-world object representation. On the other side, Thesauri are controlled vocabularies containing relationships whereas the SKOS (simple knowledge organization system) supports the usage of knowledge organization systems (KOS) for example classification schemes, thesauri, subject heading systems and taxonomy built on search query terms within the model of the semantic web containing more than 5000 concepts (Vockner & Mittlböck, 2014).

C. WMS (Web Map Services)

It is a standard protocol for serving geo-referenced maps over the internet. It publishes map images produced by map server & data retrieved from the GIS database (Zhang & Li, 2005) (Florczyk, Nogueras-Iso, Zarazaga-Soria, & Béjar, 2012). Considering the increase in the volume of land cover data & maps, WMS has facilitated open data access & data production to web users. Along with the assistance in crowd-sourcing sampling and validation (Hou, Chen, & Wu, 2016).

D. Folksonomy, Logsonomy & Semantic annotations

A folksonomy is used for providing easiness in the search and discovery of online information. It is formed when users attach their customised or already propagated keywords (tags) to their online content such as videos, pictures and written content as blogs (Trant, 2008). The tagging enhances the chances of online content to be easily found from the sea of the web. There are many tagging platforms available nowadays that can be used for fetching search engine friendly keywords online (Lee, 2008).

i. Logsonomy refers to log data of a web search engine. Folksonomy is constructed from the corpus of keywords obtained from web log data that is "Logsonomy" (Jäschke, 2008).
ii. Semantic annotations

With the help of semantic annotations, the understanding capability of crawler increases as it looks for search keywords. Since tagging causes lots of redundancy & inconsistency because of lack of any rules. So, it's better to let the users' document attach meaningful descriptions with the use of ontologies to OGC compliant data and services. Semantic annotations establish a connection between resources, its ontology and metadata (Katumba & Coetzee, 2015).

E. Georesource Crawler & GSE

Today's work of web crawler is mainly focused on traversing every web page and indexing them automatically for the web search engines. They follow the process of iteration until they explore every single web page on the WWW and index them for search engines. Now, GeoWeb resource crawler aims at discovering geospatial resources on the Web, such as the OGC web service (OWSs), Keyhole Markup Language (KML) files, and Environmental Systems Research Institute, Inc (ESRI) Shapefiles based on the available web crawling concept (Huang & Chang, 2016).

On the other side, Geospatial search engine is a web application with a crawler. It puts together a searchable database of geospatial layers & servers, for finding new geospatial resources while updating an already existing database (Bone, Ager, Bunzel, & Tierney, 2016).

2. LITERATURE REVIEW

This section discusses the previous work of different authors, along with the comparison table explaining about the effectiveness of their research based on the Nine parameters.

To overcome the issues of discoverability of geospatial data on the web, several measures have already taken off:

With the help of metadata vocabularies along with SEO techniques, it is observed in paper (Katumba & Coetzee, 2017) that the pages marked up with metadata vocabularies such as (Schema.org and Dublin Core) were a novel substitute for bettering the discoverability of geospatial resources on the Internet paper (Katumba & Coetzee, 2017).

The resources are dispersed on the web & it is relatively difficult for a user to find geo-resources of their interests considering its limitations up to geo communities only. Considering this challenge, a separate Geoweb crawler based on distributed computing concept was introduced in the paper (Huang

& Chang, 2016) to find geospatial files. An extensile framework of Web crawling that could find different types of GeoWeb resources, such as Open Geospatial Consortium (OGC) web services, Keyhole Markup Language (KML) and Environmental Systems Research Institute, Inc (ESRI) Shapefiles. The GeoWeb Crawler implemented was able to cater to all the geo-resources in terms of both variety and volume (Huang & Chang, 2016).

Semantic heterogeneity issue is another challenge while looking for geographical information. The Geoportal, web-based application comprised of organised directories, search tools, support, & rules act as a gateway to discover geo spatial data. However, these geoportals lack in terms of when dealing with different languages. Because of the diverse interpretations of features based upon social and cultural background, conflicts arise (Vockner & Mittlböck, 2014). In the paper (Vockner & Mittlböck, 2014) an enhanced query interface was presented to augment discovery in geoportals.

For potentially sharing of land cover data discovery of LCWMs come in help. Various LCWMSs are spread on the surface web but, what about those which are dispersed in the deep web? Today's generation crawlers are easily able to locate those are on the surface web, but deep web searching requires extra efforts (Hou, Chen, & Wu, 2016*)*. The services hidden in Javascript code stays solid as a rock when it comes for GeoWeb resources discoverability. To overcome this issue in the paper (Hou, Chen, & Wu, 2016) we can see a proposal for a focused deep web crawler. The crawler is created in a way that it will primarily work towards finding more LCWMSs from the surface web & deep web, i.e. data hidden in JavaScript code.

The foundation of Geoportals was not done in a way that it'll be crawler friendly. The data that is catalogued in geoportals are difficult to discover & index for search engines dues to its limitation to geo communities and current technological limitations. Another barrier to geospatial data discovery is a mismatch. The mismatch that occurs between geospatial metadata content and the search terms that general users apply online when searching for geospatial data (Katumba & Coetzee, 2015).

In (Katumba & Coetzee, 2015) with the help of folksonomies and semantic annotations is employed to eliminate the mismatch between search terms and spatial content on the Internet. Analysis of search query expressions leads to the construction of taxonomy of search terms, during searching for spatial data on the web. The use of taxonomy helps general purpose search engine to find spatial data. Taxonomy shows how HTML pages with standard spatial metadata, can be documented so that they are discoverable by general purpose web search engines. Paper (Katumba & Coetzee, 2015) shows the use of the taxonomy constructed in semantic annotation of web resources, i.e. HTML pages with geospatial metadata on the Internet.

There is a constant increase in data with a growing number of web resources. However, the challenge to discover geospatial resources on the internet is still amiss. The paper (Bone, Ager, Bunzel, & Tierney, 2016) presents a Geospatial Search Engine (GSE) that is publically available. It utilises a web crawler built upon Google search engine for searching geospatial data. The seeding mechanism of crawler unites search terms fed by web users with previously defined keywords that determine geospatial data services (Bone, Ager, Bunzel, & Tierney, 2016). To do away with the servers that go offline and updating map server layers and metadata a regular procedure runs.

The major benefit with this Geospatial based search engine is that it integrates already available methods to cater an effective search engine to general users so that they can easily be able to find a large number of geospatial resources (Bone, Ager, Bunzel, & Tierney, 2016).

Follow the Comparison tables on the next page:

Table 1. Comparison Table 1

Authors' Name and Performance Comparison of their Research Papers
Parameters Samy Katumba *et al.* (2017) **Chih-Yuan Huang *et al.*** (2016) **Bernhard Vockner *et al.*** (2014)
Purpose Use of Metadata Vocabularies Developing a Geoweb Crawler Cross-Language Information to increase the visibility of to find Geospatial resources retrieval for providing more
Used SEO techniques: Metadata Vocabularies GeoWeb Crawling Framework Thesauri, Ontologies & **Technique** such as Schema.org & Dublin core SKOS in Mitigating marked up with Microdata Semantic heterogeneity problems
Test Performed Wilcoxon Signed Rank Test **- -**
Efficiency High with Google Crawl within Five hops High with meaningful Search Engine to find Geospatial data keywords & worst with slangs
Application Geoportals, Administration, financial analyses, Contextual-based Geo resources communities & scientific researches
Accuracy High for Google Search Engine, Higher in providing number High in rendering Low with Bing Search Engine of Geo datasets & resources Multilingual resource compared to present crawlers retrieval
Methodology Relevance Based Evaluation Distributed Computing Concept, Wikitionary as thesauri, & Ranking Based Evaluation Map Reduce Concept for crawler Geo SPARQL, Apache Solr & Bloom Filter for omitting & semantic text matching redundant URL algorithms for semantic enhancement
Platform/ SPSS Statistical Software, - Geoplatform.net, **Tools used** Google & Bing Webmaster Tools Microsoft Translater, Bing Markup Validator Python to extract user- defined keywords of metadata sets
Search Google & Bing Google Search Engine Geoplatform.net **Engine Used for** was used for evaluation **Evaluation**

Problems

The pain point here is the presence of Geospatial resources on the internet. The geo-resources were not at all put on WWW by keeping an account of being crawler friendly, and that's why it's causing issues even in this era when it comes to discovering the Geospatial data on WWW (Katumba & Coetzee, 2017). It's not just that a single issue we are dealing with when it comes to the discoverability of Geospatial resources. It is more than that. Some of them are mentioned below from the papers on which survey has been done:

Understanding Geoportals and SDIs scenario:

Geoportals acts as entryway while users look out for the geospatial data on the web. There are various geoportals that have been established. The portals act as broking agents between users and providers. Amongst the several issues, this review mainly throws light on the issue of geographical information discovery.

Table 2. Comparison Table 2

Authors' Name and Performance Comparison of their Research Papers
Parameters Christopher Bone ***et al*** (2016) **Dongyang Hou** ***et al.*** (2016) **Samy Katumba** ***et al*** (2017)
Purpose Developing a Geospatial A focused deep web crawler Employing taxonomy, Search Engine (GSE) for finding LCWMSs from deep web folksonomy & semantic i.e. JavaScript code along with the annotations design of search engine that retrieves δισχοϖερεδ ΛΧΩΜΣσ
Used Technique Built using Single level crawler, Focused-deep web crawler, Taxonomy, Javascripts & Open source Javascript invocation rules folksonomy & χομπονεντσ συχη ασ οπεν λαψερ & παρσιν γ ενγινε σεμαντιχ αννοτατιονσ
Test Performed - User Experiment & Bing Webmaster Experiment
Efficiency Moderate. Scope of Higher than the ExtractorJS- Scope of improvement Crawler modification approach. Scope of improvement for bigger search query & including ontology in proposed crawler for future. sets & for different languages
Application Locating Shapefiles Isolated land cover Locating Geospatial available for downloading web map services data on the web in Geospatial Resources (LCWMSs)
Accuracy Catalogs a Fair number Succeeded in finding Results contribute in Of geoservices. a larger number of WMS enhancing discovery τηαν φοχυσεδ χραωλερ−βασεδ οφ γεοσπατιαλ δατα
Methodology Calibrating procedure for Pre-defined javascript detection, Taxonomy based the weighting of keywords, Rule matching and on logsonomy & Utility Function to keywords-matching approach to facilitate semantic process search engine results annotations & Dublin Core for ref. description
Platform/ Preview service by Implementation of Search Engine Bing Webmasters tool **Tools Used** Global Risk Data Platform is based on Microsoft.net φραμεωορκ

Currently, if a scientist wants to search geographical data on the web, his search will normally begin with finding an SDI or a data portal. The data portals are the web sites/services that data providers host, like India's geospatial data portal (https://bhuvan.nrsc.gov.in/bhuvan_links.php) & India's biodiversity Portal (https://indiabiodiversity.org/) (Huang & Chang, 2016). Primarily, SDIs are the registry & catalogue services that provide a platform for users and providers to fetch and share the geographical information. SDIs make it possible for the users and providers to come on the same ground. The users can discover service entries, while providers on their own can manage services from SDIs (Huang & Chang, 2016).

1. Now, the current situation of a typical web user is that he is unaware in terms of searching the SDIs or data portals that will furnish the services for his requirements (Huang & Chang, 2016). Even though the data in portals are hosted by various organisations, none of data portals or SDIs can cater complete data index on the GeoWeb. Also, between each portal or SDI, the problem of heterogeneity exists in UIs and data (Huang & Chang, 2016).

Just because of these barriers, the procedures like accessing and understanding data requires spending more time learning to the data users. If we talk about SDI, the complicated registry and absence of payment would be a few reasons behind bringing down the inclination of providers towards registering their data (Huang & Chang, 2016). Generally, these would lead to the discovery of GeoWeb resources inadequate. Also, we cannot ignore the fact that resources out of geodata portals/SDIs are of great significance, too (Huang & Chang, 2016).

To understand the problem of discoverability better, we have analysed the problem in a Longtail model. Now, the long tail theory (Chris, 2006) states that the volume of data in the tail equals to the volume of data in the head. As we know, Geospatial Data & SDIs are being handled by various government units or research institutes. Considering them as "head" in the long tail & assuming small data portals those are being hosted by scientists or other third party providers as "tail".

Figure 1. The GeoWeb Long tal

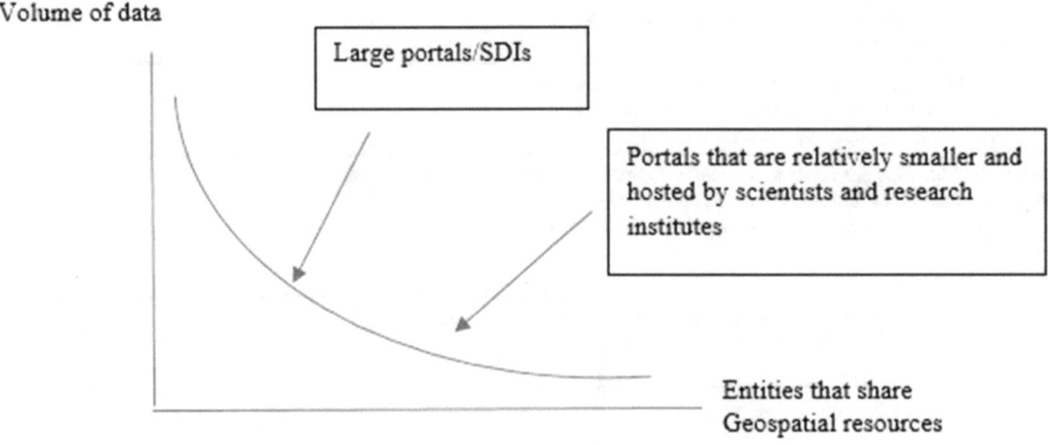

Volume of data

We came to know that, the resources in the tail are not indexed by the data portals or SDIs in the head, and that's why they're usually difficult to be discoverable to the users. Not ignoring data scientists, who may not every time know where to look for the geospatial data.

2. This particular issue deals with problems of semantic heterogeneity and established user's search strategies and preferences (Vockner & Mittlböck, 2014). Semantic interoperability that deals with the meaning of terminologies have been treated minimally. Cross-language information retrieval has been a point to ponder on when it comes to improving the visibility of Geospatial resources. In most of the instances, SDI communities cannot share resources in all languages, keeping English as LCD (lowest common denominator) (Vockner & Mittlböck, 2014).

In the current scenario, if you see, searching for geographic information in geoportals rely on the usual querying of title, abstract, and keyword metadata sections combined with spatial and temporal filters. Semantic heterogeneity problems arise due to the keywords that are inbuilt confined by the natural languages' ambiguities. Moreover, when we deal with different languages because of different interpretations of features contingent upon cultural and social prospects, conflicts do arise (Vockner & Mittlböck, 2014).

3. Technological barriers, along with business & legal aspects, have made the geospatial data in a geoportal "invisible" to the common web users and to publically available search engines (Katumba & Coetzee, 2017). For discovering geospatial resources, the ones who're interested need to be aware of from where to access the geoportal (Katumba & Coetzee, 2017). Web users in geo communities know this, but the same doesn't imply for the ones who are not aware of these geocommunities & have the requirement of geospatial data in their respective field of work (Katumba & Coetzee, 2017).

Moreover, at present geoportals are primarily build on the Open Geospatial Consortium (OGC) Catalogue Service for the Web (CSW) that caters HTTP binding (Katumba & Coetzee, 2017). It was designed to enable "the discovery and retrieval of spatial data and services metadata"; to be crawled by web search engines and is thus part of the "Deep Web", i.e. resources inaccessible to Web crawlers (Katumba & Coetzee, 2017).

4. The web is divided into two parts as surface and deep web. Surface web relates to static pages whilst deep web relates to dynamic pages. The resources that are sunken in deep web requires extra efforts to be found (Hou, Chen, & Wu, 2016). This concept of the deep web is found when we talk about land cover web map services (LCWMSs). Many LCWMs cater land cover data of the global, national or local region. Based on Service-Oriented Architecture, LCWMSs records are stored in catalogues. These LCWMSs can be easily located with the help of search queries in related catalogues (Hou, Chen, & Wu, 2016).

The LCWMSs, those spread on the surface web, can be discovered via hyperlinks associated with static pages (Piccinini, Casanova, Leme, & Furtado, 2014) (Dixit, Bhatia, & Yadav, 2015,). However, in terms of the deep web, the contents are hidden in javascript code & that's why such resources of LCMWSs are hard to discover by just visiting hyperlinks (Piccinini, Casanova, Leme, & Furtado, 2014) (Manvi, Dixit, & Bhatia, 2013). Also, many LCWMSs exist as isolated "information islands", and they're not well connected. Hence are difficult to get discovered by simple keyword matching or visiting hyperlinks.

5. When talking about metadata creation for Geospatial resources, it's typically written without the idea of how users will search the actual documented data (Katumba & Coetzee, 2015). Another barrier to geospatial data discovery is a mismatch. The mismatch that occurs between geospatial metadata content and the search terms that general users apply online when searching for geospatial data (Katumba & Coetzee, 2015).

The requirement comes up for developing and disseminating spatial metadata, which would be discoverable by general-purpose search engines and users likewise.

Figure 2. Surface Web Vs Deep Web

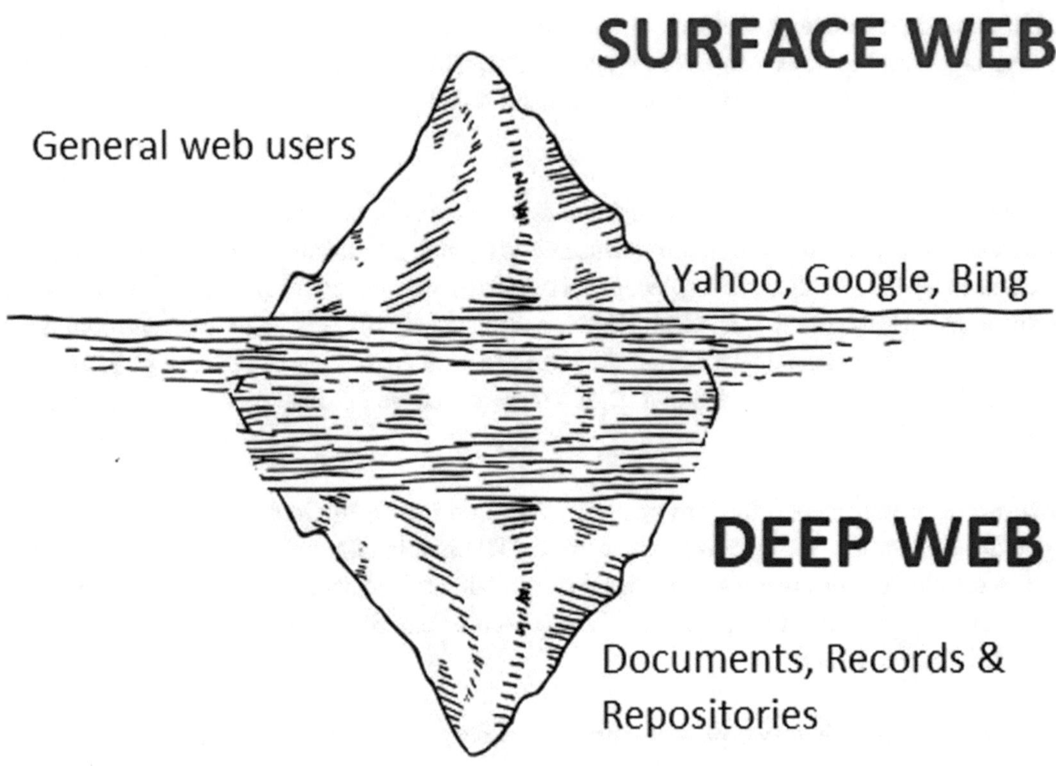

CONCLUSION AND FUTURE RESEARCH DIRECTIONS

The requirement for Geospatial data is increasing. However, the availability of Geospatial resources is limited to geo communities only. Publically, the discoverability of Geospatial resources is still a challenge to look for. Various methods such as using SEO techniques infused with metadata vocabularies have shown some enhancement in terms of visibility of Geospatial resources with a search engine like Google. A focused deep web crawler has been employed to locate data inside Javascript code that has remained untouched by present-day crawlers. For Cross-language barrier folksonomy, taxonomy and semantic annotations have been utilised to eliminate the mismatch between search terms and spatial content on the Web. Semantic heterogeneity issue was another challenge while looking for geographical information, which was overcome with the help of SKOS, thesauri and ontologies.

Furthermore, a separate GeoWeb crawler was developed that provided results in a minimum of five hops. Besides, a GSE (Geospatial search engine) was built on a single level crawler that catalogued a fair number of Geospatial resources., Even after these different implementations show some positive results on one side however demand work in some other aspects. Hence, we can conclude this survey with this conjecture that there remains a scope regarding the further improvement in the current scenario of Geospatial resources visibility.

REFERENCES

Bone, C., Ager, A., Bunzel, K., & Tierney, L. (2016). *A geospatial search engine for discovering multi-format geospatial data across the web.* doi:10.1080/17538947.2014.966164

Chris, A. (2006). *The Long Tail: Why the Future of Business is Selling Less of More.* Hyperion.

Dixit, A., Bhatia, K., & Yadav, J. (2015). Design and implementation of domain based semantic hidden Web crawler. *Int. J. Innov. Adv. Comput. Sci, 4*, 73–84.

Florczyk, A., Nogueras-Iso, J., Zarazaga-Soria, F., & Béjar, R. (2012). Identifying orthoimages in Web Map Services. *Computers & Geosciences, 47*, 130–142. doi:10.1016/j.cageo.2011.10.017

Gruber, T. (1995). Toward principles for the design of ontologies used for knowledge sharing. *International Journal of Human-Computer Studies, 43*(5-6), 907–928. doi:10.1006/ijhc.1995.1081

Hou, D., Chen, J., & Wu, H. (2016). Discovering Land Cover Web Map Services from the Deep Web with JavaScript Invocation Rules. *International Journal of Geo-Information, 5*(7), 105. doi:10.3390/ijgi5070105

Huang, C.-Y., & Chang, H. (2016). GeoWeb Crawler: An Extensible and Scalable Web Crawling Framework for Discovering Geospatial Web Resources. *ISPRS International Journal of Geo-Information, 5*(8), 136. doi:10.3390/ijgi5080136

Jäschke, R. &. (2008). Logsonomy: A Search Engine Folksonomy. *Proceedings of the Second International Conference on Weblogs and Social Media, ICWSM.*

Katumba, S., & Coetzee, S. (2015). Enhancing the online discovery of geospatial data through taxonomy, folksonomy and semantic annotations. *South African Journal of Geomatics, 4*(3), 339. Advance online publication. doi:10.4314ajg.v4i3.14

Katumba, S., & Coetzee, S. (2017, September). Employing Search Engine Optimization (SEO) Techniques for Improving the Discovery of Geospatial Resources on the Web. *ISPRS International Journal of Geo-Information, 6*(9), 284. doi:10.3390/ijgi6090284

Lee, S. (2008). *OntoSonomy: Ontology-based Extension of Folksonomy.* Academic Press.

Lopez-Pellicer, J., Florczyk, J., Nogueras-Iso, J., Muro-Medrano, P., & Zarazaga, J. (2010). Exposing CSW catalogues as Linked data. Geospatial Thinking, Lecture Notes in Geoinformation and Cartography (LNG&C), 183–200.

Malaga, R. (2010). Search Engine Optimization-Black and White Hat Approaches. *Advances in Computers, 78*, 1–39. doi:10.1016/S0065-2458(10)78001-3

Manvi, M., Dixit, A., & Bhatia, K. (2013). Design of an ontology based adaptive crawler for hidden Web. In *Proceedings of the International Conference on Communication Systems and Network Technologies* (pp. 659–663). Gwalior: IEEE. 10.1109/CSNT.2013.140

Ochoa, E. (2012). *An Analysis of the Application of Selected Search Engines Optimization (SEO) Techniques and their Effectiveness on Google's Search Ranking Algorithm.* California State University.

Piccinini, H., Casanova, M., Leme, L., & Furtado, A. (2014). Publishing deep web geographic data. *Geoimformatica*, *18*(4), 769–792. doi:10.100710707-013-0201-3

Trant, J. (2008). *Studying social tagging and folksonomy: A review and framework.* Special Issue on Digital and UserGenerated Content.

Vockner, B., & Mittlböck, M. (2014). Geo-Enrichment and Semantic Enhancement of Metadata Sets to Augment Discovery in Geoportals. *ISPRS International Journal of Geo-Information*, *3*(1), 345–367. doi:10.3390/ijgi3010345

Zhang, C., & Li, W. (2005). The roles of web feature and web map services in real-time geospatial data sharing for. *Cartography and Geoginformation Science*, *32*(4), 269–283. doi:10.1559/152304005775194728

KEY TERMS & DEFINITIONS

Geospatial Metadata: –or Geographic metadata– is a type of metadata for geographic data and information about objects or phenomena, for instance, that are associated with a location relative to our planet.

Spatial Data Infrastructure: (SDIS) is a solid set of technologies, rules, human team, standard tasks, and other activities necessary in order to acquire, process, distribute, use and preserve spatial data.

Geo Portals: is a web portal with geographic information and services, for instance, geographic information systems (GIS) for the navigation.

Surface Web: –or visible web– is the content on the World Wide Web (WWW) that is available to the general users with an universal access and free.

Deep Web: is inaccessible to "generic" search engines and users. The content is not indexed by "normal" and "big" search engines, for instance, Google.

Search Engine Optimization: (SEO) is a group of best software engineering techniques and methods that improving the quantity and quality of a web page from search engines or the website traffic to a website.

Chapter 16
Developing Augmented Reality Multi-Platform Mobile Applications

Susana Isabel Herrera
Universidad Nacional de Santiago del Estero, Argentina

Paola Daniela Budan
Universidad Nacional de Santiago del Estero, Argentina

Federico Rosenzvaig
Universidad Nacional de Santiago del Estero, Argentina

Pablo Javier Najar Ruiz
Universidad Nacional de Santiago del Estero, Argentina

María Inés Morales
Universidad Nacional de Santiago del Estero, Argentina

Marilena del Valle Maldonado
Universidad Nacional de Santiago del Estero, Argentina

Carlos Antonio Sánchez
Universidad Nacional de Santiago del Estero, Argentina

ABSTRACT

This chapter presents advances in the software engineering field related to the efficient development of multi-platform mobile applications that require access to the device hardware for 3D marker-based augmented reality functions. After presenting the theoretical background that supports the proposed solutions, the complex problem of the development of AR multi-platform mobile applications is introduced. The problem about how to choose a framework for developing multi-platform applications is described, and a general model for developing mobile applications with AR is proposed. The advances were applied to the field of m-learning. A linear algebra educational practice was designed using MADE-mlearn, and an augmented reality mobile app called AlgeRA was developed using MobileRA methodology. The instantiation of the general model for the development of AlgeRA is reported. It includes the development environment, the programming libraries (to manage 3D objects repositories, patterns readers, rendering of images) and the 3D model.

DOI: 10.4018/978-1-7998-7010-4.ch016

1. INTRODUCTION

Advances of the research project “Mobile Computing: application development and forensic analysis” of the Research Institute of Computer Science and Information Systems (IIISI), Universidad Nacional de Santiago del Estero (UNSE), are presented in this article.

The research team addresses problems related to the efficient development of multi-platform mobile applications (Fennema et al., 2017), that is, mobile apps that can be run in the most frequently used operating system (OS): Android and iOS. The team works with complex applications that require access to the hardware resources of the mobile device (camera, GPS and accelerometer), in search of an efficient development based on the optimization of time and number of developers. For this purpose, the use of different frameworks that allow create mobile applications, hybrid and native, for various OS from a single web project, has been studied.

Advances of the group in the field of Software Engineering (Budan et al., 2018) are applied to two domains relevant to society: health (Córdoba, 2016) and education (Rosenzvaig et al., 2018; Herrera et al., 2017; Herrera & Sanz, 2014; Herrera et al., 2014). In this case, the design of AlgeRA application, originated from the MADE-mlearn (Herrera et al., 2013) design of an m-learning practice for the Linear Algebra course, is presented. The application uses Augmented Reality (AR) to exemplify Systems of Linear Equations; it also has tools for collecting, in groups and collaboratively, field data for modelling such Systems.

The findings are considered useful for software engineering practitioners developing these types of applications, mainly in the field of education. The general conceptual model provides a map that shows which are the main elements to be considered while developing this kinds of applications. And also an example of how to instantiate this general model into a concrete model is given with AlgeRA.

The chapter is organized as follows: Section 2 describes the referential frameworks necessary to understand the problem and the design of the application. Section 3 briefly describes the design of an m-learning practice of Linear Algebra, which uses AR. Then, in Section 4 the development of AlgeRA application is presented while the problem of the development of this type of types is considered. The MobileRA methodology was used for the development. A comparison of the different multi-platform mobile frameworks is made; and a general conceptual model for developing multi-platform mobile applications using AR is proposed. Also, the instantiation of the general model for the development of AlgeRA is described, as well as the 3D model used. Finally, the preliminary results and conclusions of the study are presented in Section 5.

2. Referential Frameworks

In order to facilitate the understanding of the concepts inherent in this work, a brief description of each is provided below.

2.1 M-learning and MADE-mlearn

M-learning is mainly regarded as a new mode of learning that arises from the mediation of mobile technologies in the learning process. It is related to other forms of the continuum “face-to-face education - distance education”, for example, to e-learning and u-learning (Zangara, 2014).

The main m-learning characteristics are: the ecosystem, modes of interaction, approaches to practice implementation (where collaboration stands out), the relationship with everyday life, and general issues of learning which are important for designing m-learning practices.

M-learning experiences developed both internationally (Oró et al., 2013; De Witt et al., 2014) as well as locally (Arce, 2013; Herrera et al., 2015; Thomas et al., 2015), are becoming more and more diverse and apply to every educational level with a special emphasis at higher education.

Given the diversity of experiences in recent years, some authors have proposed frameworks that constitute guidelines for the analysis of m-learning applications (Park, 2011; Navarro et al., 2015). These frameworks allow the classification of m-learning applications from a pedagogical and/or technological approach.

Undoubtedly, one of the most important results of the m-learning research group of UNSE consists in having produced a systemic and ecological framework for the analysis, design and evaluation of m-learning experiences, called MADE-mlearn (Herrera et al., 2013), as well as the development of several m-learning applications.

MADE-mlearn was made from a socio-cultural ecology approach (Pachler, Bachmair & Cook, 2010). For the analysis, design and evaluation, it considers a set of 80 items that are organized in subcharacteristics characteristics, categories and axis.

From a top-down focus, the framework has four analysis axes according to the basic aspects to be considered in the analysis and design of a new or existing m-learning project (see Fig.1):

- Name and Purpose. It encompasses a set of characteristics identifying the experience, scope, objectives and expected results.
- Context. It encompasses a set of characteristics that allow teachers define the ecosystem of the experience. From the Vygotskian perspective (Vigotsky, 1979), the context could improve the learning process. Both (Pachler, Bachmair & Cook, 2010) and (Woodill, 2011), consider that it is important to study the technological and cultural context in order to design an m-learning project.
- Development and Implementation Mode. It encompasses a set of characteristics that identify the interaction mode of the experience and the learning theories that support it.
- Results. It covers a minimum set of characteristics that allows clarifying the experience results.

These four axis involve five categories:

- Characteristics of axis Name and Purpose are grouped into Category 1-Identification.
- Characteristics of axis Context are grouped into Category 2-Ecosistem. Sub-characteristics refer to m-learning ecosystem described in (Herrera, Fennema & Sanz, 2012). Types of content are included in this category.
- Characteristics of axis Development and Implementation Mode are grouped into categories 3-Interaction Mode and 4-Theoretical Foundations of Teaching and Learning.
    - Interaction Mode refers to the classification mentioned in section I and takes into account the benefits of Collaborative Computed Supported Learning (CSCL).
    - Theoretical foundations of learning consider broad approaches such as behaviourism, cognitivism and constructivism (Pozo, 2008). And then, some more specific ones, such as accumulative learning, significant learning, sociocultural learning, and collaborative learning.
- Characteristics of axis Results are grouped into Category 5-Obtained Results.

Fig. 1 shows the general model of the framework where axes-categories relationships can be clearly seen. In turn, each category has its characteristics which include a set of sub-characteristics. More details can be seen in (Herrera et al., 2013).

Figure 1. Framework for the Analysis, Design and Assessment of m-learning Experiences (MADE-mlearn)

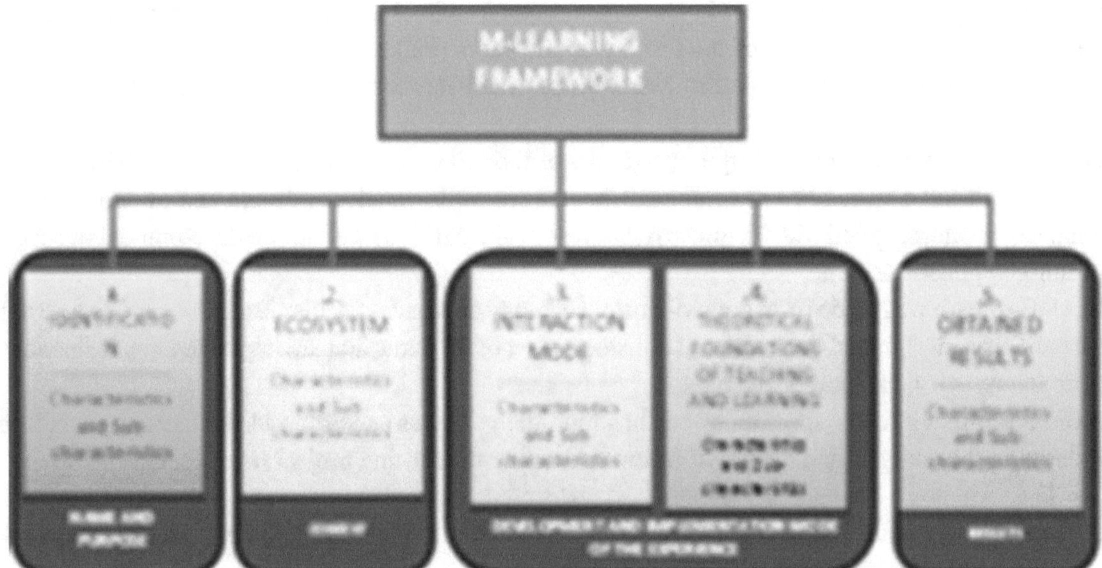

Several mobile apps for m-learning have been developed by UNSE research group and various practices of m-learning were designed and implemented in rural primary schools, and secondary schools, as well as for undergraduate and postgraduate degree programs, covering the study areas of Technologies, Programming and Mathematics (Herrera et al., 2015; Herrera et al., 2014). Currently, practices of m-learning with AR are being studied (Herrera et al., 2017-b). Among the apps, the following stand out: Educ-Mobile and ImaColab.

Educ-Mobile application (Herrera & Sanz, 2014) is an educational, collaborative and mobile game. It consists of three synchronous games. Students form teams of 2 or 3 members and select a leader. It´s a competition among groups that involves following different paths with stations with questions to be solved. The questions are both individual (multiple-choice) and group questions (clues-riddles). Points are accumulative and the winning team is picked based on the team total score and the time spent playing. Fig. 2 shows the application main-menu screen. It uses QR codes detect user position and was developed with Android Studio. It was used in several educational practices.

ImaColab (Herrera et al., 2017-a) is a responsive web application, developed in PHP, JavaScript and Twitter Bootstrap. It consists of a collaborative group educational game based on images captured in everyday life that represent elements or situations indicated by the teacher. It is a competition based on student scores with a solid foundation and feedback from teachers. The application calculates the best image of each group; and, finally, the best image of the entire practice.

Figure 2. Player main screen of Educ-Mobile

It has been used to teach different disciplinary areas at different educational levels. In (Maldonado et al., 2018) various m-learning practices carried out with *ImaColab* were presented, implemented in the areas of Programming, Systems and Organizations Theory, English, Technology and Informatics. In them, the intrinsic motivation of the students and the achievement of learning results were studied. The results were positive in the various practices carried out, confirming the adaptability of *ImaColab*.

2.2 Architectures of Mobile Applications and Multi-Platform Development

In relation to its architecture, a mobile system is usually dependent on a client application that connects to an application server in Internet (Challiol, 2017). This server, in turn, uses the services of a location provider and the information provided by different points of interest. More deeply, alternative architectures that can be taken at the time of developing a mobile application were studied and analyzed in (Najar et. al., 2014). They are:

- Web architecture: the application resides completely on the web server and is accessed through the phone browser. It can be accessed by most devices. Interaction with peripheral devices can be difficult, therefore other technologies should be used, for example, the use of QR codes to determine the localization context.

- Client-server or hybrid architecture: part of the application resides on the client and part on the server. The client application queries the server application through the use of Web Services. Features of the OS and device installation features are taken into account. It allows interaction with the device peripherals (cameras, bluetooth, GPS) that will allow determine the data of the context in which the mobile is located. They are known as native applications developed for each mobile OS.
- Client architecture: the application resides completely in the client, while the information or databases reside on the device. They are also considered native applications.

Since this research is interested in applications that allow interaction between users, it does not include client architectures.

It should be considered that, according to studies by Najar et. al. (2014), hybrid architectures are more efficient than the web, considering the response time and also battery consumption. However, as it has been mentioned before, developing native apps for each OS is expensive since more resources are required. That is why, at present, the development of mobile applications tends to multi-platform development. According to Delía (2017), multi-platform applications can be classified into:

- Mobile Web applications: designed to run within a Web browser, developed with standard web technologies (HTML, CSS, and JavaScript), they do not need to adapt to any operating environment and are platform-independent. However, their response times lag due to the client-server interaction; they are less attractive than native applications since they are not installed on the device, which involves previous access to a browser. In addition, the security restrictions on the code execution by means of a browser limit the access to all the capabilities of the device.
- Hybrid applications: they use web technologies (HTML, Javascript and CSS) but they are not run by a Web browser. Instead, they run in a web container (webview), as part of a native application installed on the mobile device. Hybrid applications allow code reuse across different platforms, access to the device hardware, and distribution through the app stores. In relation to native apps, they have the following disadvantages: i) the user experience is handicapped by not using native components in the interface, and ii) runtime is somewhat slowed by the burden associated with the web container. There is a diversity of frameworks that allow the development of hybrid applications: *PhoneGap, Apache Cordova, CocoonJS, Ionic, SenchaTouch.*
- Interpreted applications: are implemented using a base language which is translated for the most part into native code, while the rest is interpreted at runtime. These applications are implemented independently of platforms using different technologies and languages, such as Javascript, Java, Ruby and XML, among others. One of the main advantages of this type of application is that completely native user interfaces are obtained. However, developers experience a total dependency on the chosen development environment. The frameworks better known to generate these applications are *Appcelerator Titanium* and *NativeScript.*
- Cross-compilation applications: are compiled natively creating a specific high-performance version for each target platform. Examples of development environments for generating applications by cross-compiling are *Applause*, *Xamarin*, *QT*, *Embarcadero Delphi 10 Seattle* and *RubyMotion.*

2.3 Frameworks for Developing Multi-Platform Applications

A brief description of the frameworks studied in the research project is given below. The first three generate hybrid applications and the last two generate cross-compilation applications.

- *Apache Cordova*. It is a framework of mobile open-code development that allows the use of standard web technologies for multi-platform development, avoiding the language of native development of mobile platforms (Wargo, 2015).
- *PhoneGap*. It allows the development of multi-platform applications using HTML y *JavaScript*. It is a free distribution and license-free of Apache Cordova (PhoneGap, 2013). It enables the creation of hybrid applications using a series of APIs that allow control the characteristics of the devices such as the accelerometer, camera, notifications or geolocation (Genbetadev, 2016). PhoneGap allows the connection of a mobile device to a web application, using two main components: Webview and Plugins (Natily, 2013).
- *Ionic*. It is a free and open-code tool for the development of hybrid applications based on HTML5, CSS and JS. It is built with Sass and optimized with AngularJS (Ionic, 2016). It is oriented to the development of mobile hybrid applications. Because Ionic is a HTML5 framework, it needs a native wrap like Cordova or Phonegap to run as a native application.
- *QT*[1]. It allows the development of native applications for various platforms and has extensive support for the developer. The API library has methods to access databases using SQL, as well as the use of XML, thread management, network management, an API unified platform for file manipulation, and a variety of methods for file handling, in addition to traditional data structures.
- *Xamarin* (Hermes, 2015): It is a platform for the development of native mobile applications for Android, iOS, and Windows using C# language. User interfaces of the applications written in C#/Xamarin are native, resulting in an improvement in performance at run time. Applications written in C# /Xamarin allow an approach of multiplatform development where the encoding of business logic is shared. However, user interfaces must be scheduled independently for each target platform.

As Delía (2017) states, the choice as of which framework to use will depend on the type of application to be developed and the OS of the device which will run it.

2.4 Augmented Reality

AR is a technology that adds to the perception and interaction with the real world, since it provides an augmented real environment with additional information generated by the computer or a mobile device. It enables the development of interactive applications that combine reality with synthetic information, such as 3D images, sounds, videos, texts and tactile sensations, in real time, and in accordance with the point of view of the person watching the scene (Salazar Mesia et al., 2015-a).

There are two basic types of AR:

- Geolocation-based AR, which indicates the positioning of the mobile device by means of sensors. By just holding the mobile in the field of vision, nearby points of interest can be displayed by virtue of the information taken through several mobile sensors, such as GPS and compass.

- Mark-based AR, which recognizes patterns of information activators, such as a barcode, QR or a symbol, in the video image that is received from a camera. When a particular pattern is recognized in its position, a digital image is superimposed on the screen. This is the first type of AR which had its origins in something very simple: tags.

The list of programs and applications to develop AR is endless and increases every day. Here follow some very useful ones in the field of education (Blázquez Seville, 2017): Aurasma, Layar, Aumentaty, Geo, Google Goggles. There are also other types of AR applications or programs that do not allow the generation of layers, but they do give access to information generated by the authors of the technology. In iOS and Android it is possible to work with *Frield Trip, Aumentaty 3D, Wallame, Blippar, Smartify, Wikitude, Mixare, Landscapar*, among others.

AR can take different forms, allowing different possibilities in the classroom. Its applications range from the display of 3D models to the incorporation of additional information to printed educational materials and resources, or the creation of geolocated routes that allow associating information to places (Reynoso, 2016). Numerous works that have been carried out using the above-mentioned technologies are applied to teaching in such areas as engineering, architecture, urban planning, medicine, art and history, languages learning, natural sciences, chemistry and physics, and geography (Cabero Almenara et al., 2016). While these educational applications are underway at all educational levels, it is at higher education where they have had a stronger impact, evidenced by the following experiences: Tool for the Teaching of basic programming concepts using augmented reality (EPRA) (Salazar Mesia et al. 2015-b); M-learning and augmented reality, integrated technologies to support the teaching of calculus (Pedraza & Valbuena, 2014); Augmented reality applied to the teaching of Medicine (Cabero Almenara et al., 2017).

3. Design of the m-Learning Practice "M-learning for Systems of Linear Equations"

As mentioned above, the practice was designed using MADE-mlearn (see section 2.1). All features of the framework were completed, except for the axis "Results". This allowed the determination of the practice objectives, context, resources, AlgeRA requirements, among other aspects. The design was carried out by an interdisciplinary group of teacher-researchers: the head of the subject Linear Algebra, three people dedicated to AR and 3D-object design, five specialists in the development of mobile applications, and the project leader. Approximately four working meetings were conducted to complete MADE-mlearn tables.

The general objective of the practice was defined as: to develop in the student the ability to represent everyday-life situations by means of linear equations systems. The specific objectives were: a) to exemplify, by using AR, linear equations systems that represent everyday-life situations, b) to model the behavior of a traffic network by using linear equation systems.

In order to fulfil these objectives, the designed practice consists of 2 main activities. The first is carried out individually, and the second in groups. Each one responds to each objective a) and b) respectively.

The activity related to objective 2) takes place in the classroom without computers. A paper with a QR code is given to the student who reads it using the mobile phone. In this way, the student is shown an everyday-life system whose functioning models a linear equation system (a description is provided in the next section).

The activity related to objective b) consists of carrying out a group survey of a traffic network operation. To do this, students use a mobile application that allows them to conduct the survey in a coordinated and accurate way, using their mobile phones with GPS. Students are placed at relevant points (indicated by the teacher in the App) where, simultaneously, they film the vehicular flow.

Then, based on the surveyed points and the flow of vehicles, students build synchronously, face-to-face and in groups, the mathematical model of the system and represent it with Matlab. In addition, practice is completed with the students pondering upon the variation of the model when there are certain particular situations pointed out by the teacher.

4. Development of Multi-Platform Mobile Applications With AR: AlgeRA

As a result of the design of "M-learning for linear equation systems" practice, the need to develop the mobile app AlgeRA was defined. However, the development of multiplatform mobile applications poses a complex problem.

This section presents the development of AlgeRA application, taking it as a Case Study of the complexity of multiplatform mobile application development with AR. For the development of this application, the methodology MobileRA was used. This is a software development methodology that is specific for mobile apps with RA. It was created for the Mobile Computing Research Group of UNSE. In the following subsection MobileRA is briefly described. After that, in 4.2 the user stories obtained in the Exploration Phase, are presented. Later, in 4.3 the general problems of this type of development are exposed. Section 4.4 presents the choice of framework for developing multi-platform applications, taking into account the characteristics and requirements of the application to be developed. Section 4.5 describes general issues that should be considered for the development of mobile applications that use AR based on the reading of marks and 3D objects (regardless of the multi-platform requirement). And finally, section 4.6 presents the 3D model designed for AlgeRA.

4.1 MobileRA methodology

MobileRA is a software methodology for the development of multiplatform mobile applications that use Augmented Reality (Budan et al., 2018). It is an agile methodology and is an adaptation of Mobile-D methodology.

MobileD, http://agile.vtt.fi/mobiled.html, is an agile methodology for the development of mobile applications. Although this methodology is used successfully by software engineering practitioners (Rahimian & Ramsin, 2008), there are problems inherent to the use of augmented reality that make it difficult to use this methodology in these cases. That is why the UNSE research group proposed to implement two very important modifications to it (see Fig. 3): "a priori contextualization" stage and a cross-sectional activity called the "procedural evaluation of development tools". These new procedural components are described below; more details and justifications of them can be found in (Budan et al., 2018).

The exploration phase presents the project plan and the basic concepts inherent to it. It encompasses the identification of stakeholders and system development needs, a requirements ranking, initial project planning, and baseline planning. Within it, the "a priori contextualization" stage proposes to examine the requirements in depth, to determine the most appropriate tools for the generation of multiplatform applications, according to the domain of the problem. By tools we understand both the programming languages and the standards that have been used for documentation.

For its part, the "process evaluation activity of development tools" recommends evaluating, for each iteration, if the development tool manages to satisfy the requirement considered. It is an activity transversal to all iterations, in which the same criteria can be used as those used in the a priori contextualization stage. Although it is a time-consuming activity, it saves failures that could occur due to not selecting a tool with the appropriate support for handling sensors, camera activation, etc.

Figure 3. Methodological Adaptation of Mobile-D: Mobile-RA

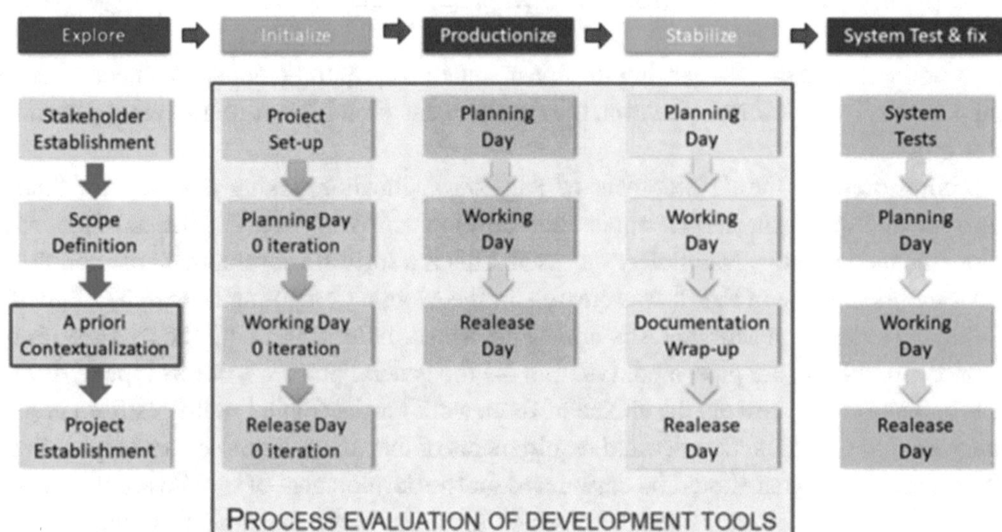

4.2 AlgeRA: Scope and Requirements

AlgeRA provides support for the two main activities of the practice: a) to exemplify Systems of Linear Equations, b) to model everyday situations using Systems of Linear Equations. From now on, the first functionality will be referred to as "Exemplification" while the second as "Field work for modelling". In the future, the application will be incorporating other features which allow the development of m-learning practices related to other topics in Linear Algebra. For this reason, AlgeRA is defined as a mobile application that uses AR for learning of Linear Algebra.

AlgeRA will have three user profiles: teacher, coordinator student and student. Teachers can create different instances of the practice and the groups of students who participate in it. The students are those running the two features previously mentioned.

Exemplification will allow students to observe the behavior of a System of Linear Equations in an everyday-life situation: a sprinkler system. The students will read a label that will allow them to see a 3D object which shows, dynamically, the behavior of a 6-sprinkler irrigation system. They will see, according to the movement from their mobile phone, how the underground network is displayed, and the equations that model the behavior of such system. Moreover, the example will present alternative situations if certain sprinklers are closed, for instance; in this case, the example will show how the mathematical model changes.

Fieldwork for modelling will allow each group to carry out the modelling of the traffic flow system. The application will also allow them to see the group members and the points in which each student has to survey the traffic flow. Students go to their given location. The Coordinator student can see the location of each student online. The students indicate, by using the application, when they are in their positions. The coordinator sends a command that activates the camera of each member's mobile device. When the time of the survey is over, the cameras turn off.

It is worth mentioning that the application does not perform the modelling itself but surveys, in a coordinated fashion, the data students will use to build the model.

The functional requirements of the mentioned features are set out below.

- Exemplification: requirements

R1_Prac1. Based on a statement given by the teacher and a brief theoretical overview, AlgeRA should display examples of the behavior of linear equations.

R2_Prac1. Based on certain given codes, AlgeRA should allow the student view examples of sprinkler irrigation with AR.

R3_Prac1. In order to activate AR the AlgeRA marker must be a QR code.

R4_Prac1. AlgeRA should allow build the model of linear equations assuming exceptions, for example, what happens in case a sprinkler is closed.

- Fieldwork for modelling: requirements

R1_Prac2. AlgeRA should allow the use of phone cameras synchronized to obtain information in a given time interval.

R2_Prac2. AlgeRA should wait for the teacher or coordinator to provide the students with the coordinates of the place they have to go.

R3_Prac2. AlgeRA should wait for the teacher to verify that students are all in right location and synchronized.

R4_Prac2. The teacher or coordinator should be provided with information that allow them to determine whether students are actually at the points indicated and ready to film. To this purpose a map with the actual location of all active points would be useful.

R5_Prac2. When a student taking part in the experience arrives at the point indicated by the teacher, he should send some kind of message to the teacher or coordinator of the type "I'm ready".

R6_Prac2. The experience or fieldwork begins once every student has sent the message "I'm ready".

R7_Prac2. The teacher or coordinator can restart the experience or repeat it as many times as they want.

R8_Prac2.The video made by each student should be stored in a repository of Video Objects.

R9_Prac2.The videos are only the data source so that teacher shows students how to manipulate these data to obtain information and knowledge outside the application.

R10_Prac2. The application should allow the configuration of the synchronized recording experiment to be flexible. For example, the number of locations to make the videos, the coordinates, etc. could be changed.

R11_Prac2. The application should allow the recording of the following information: date of videos, start and finish times, and some descriptive data that may arise from future refinements.

4.3 Problems of Multiplatform Mobile Development With AR

Cross-platform mobile applications can be executed in different mobile operating systems. They are classified, according to Delia (see section 2.2.) into: responsive web applications, hybrid applications, interpreted applications and applications generated by cross-compilation.

On the other hand, AR is a technology that incorporates content - in the form of text, image, audio, video, 3D models - into the perception of the user's real world. These "augmentation" of reality help persons to understand what happens around them. There are two types of AR (see section 2.4): geolocated and markers based.

UNSE research group has been working since 2017 on the optimization of the development of multiplatform mobile applications and on the use of RA for the visualization of 3D objects using markers. They have worked with several frameworks for multiplatform development (see sections 2.3 and 4.3).

To develop mobile applications with AR based on 3D objects, it is necessary to incorporate libraries of specific functions: for the reading of markers (QR codes or patterns), for AR (superimposition of camera images with other visual resources), for accessing repositories of 3D models (recovery and rendering of 3D models), among others.

3D objects - or 3D models - are complex resources that have special characteristics: dimension, shape, texture, special effects, animation, etc. To work with them, several specific software is required: creation, animation, storage, recovery and rendering software. Each of these software provides their own libraries that must be integrated into software projects. In this way, 3D objects are manipulated from the application development tools.

Achieving the correct visualization of 3D models from a mobile application is not easy. In most cases, the use of so many software tools produce loss of some object properties. This and other types of problems appears while developing this application. So UNSE research team has identified the following main problems while developing mobile multiplatform apps with 3Dmodels-AR:

- How to determine which multiplatform development framework to use?
- Which are the software libraries involved and how do they interact with each other?
- What are the elementary characteristics that should be considered in the construction and storage of 3D objects for their effective use in cross-platform mobile applications with RA?

In the following sections these questions are treated, considering AlgeRA as a case study.

4.4 Comparison of Development Frameworks

When comparing frameworks for the development of multi-platform applications, it can be concluded that it is necessary to inquire into a specific domain since a framework is not always more suitable than another.

In the particular case of the AlgeRA development, it was necessary to determine which framework would be most appropriate for the development of an application using AR based on markers with recognition of 3D objects obtained by accessing to a repository.

In this sense, the frameworks were evaluated taking into account the following aspects:

- Development of a native multi-platform application

- Proper management of hardware for mobile devices: camera, GPS, accelerometer.
- AR library support: Vuforia, ARToolkit, LoyAr, among others.
- Optimal use of the device resources.
- Appropriate size of the generated application.
- Support for the reading of QR code
- Access to repositories to get the 3D object from the marker.
- Technology that the development tool allows to use: web services, local databases, use of resources such as native or third- party libraries.

Considering these aspects, the frameworks that have been selected for the development of AlgeRA are Xamarin and QT. The general features which have been compared to make this selection are the following: Xamarin is based on C#, and allows developing for iOS, Android and WindowsPhone. QT is a multi-platform, object-oriented framework under GPL license, generally used to develop software using graphical user interface in native C++ programming language.

More details of this comparative study were published in (Rosenzvaig et al., 2018).

4.5 Model for the Development of AR Mobile Applications

In general, in order to develop AR mobile applications based on 3D objects and markers, different parameters that represent such characteristics should be considered. The main ones are:

- The platform or OS for which it will be developed.
- The type of architecture needed.
- The type of AR trigger or activator to be used.
- The SDK of AR necessary for the application development.

On this basis, a model for the development of the AR mobile application is proposed in Fig. 4.

The application should be multi-platform (Android and iOS), in order to reach the largest number of users. When using 3D objects, it is advisable to use markers as AR activators, which require handling QR-code -or patterns- reader libraries. A good performance in accessing the device hardware (camera, GPS) requires a native application. It also requires access to a repository of 3D objects. As a result, for the visualization of 3D objects, the use of image-rendering libraries is needed. Most importantly is to choose which AR library best responds to the described environment. All these components are shown in Fig. 4.

In the case of the AlgeRA multiplatform application, a specific model has been generated for it, by instantiating the model in Fig. 4. The technologies that participate in the AlgeRA model are the following (see Fig. 5):

- Xamarin Forms 3.4: an open source cross-platform framework from Microsoft for building iOS, Android, & Windows apps with .NET from a single shared codebase;
- Java Developer Kit (JDK) v 8;
- API Android SDK v 9;

Figure 4. Model of components involved in a mobile application with AR based on markers and 3D objects

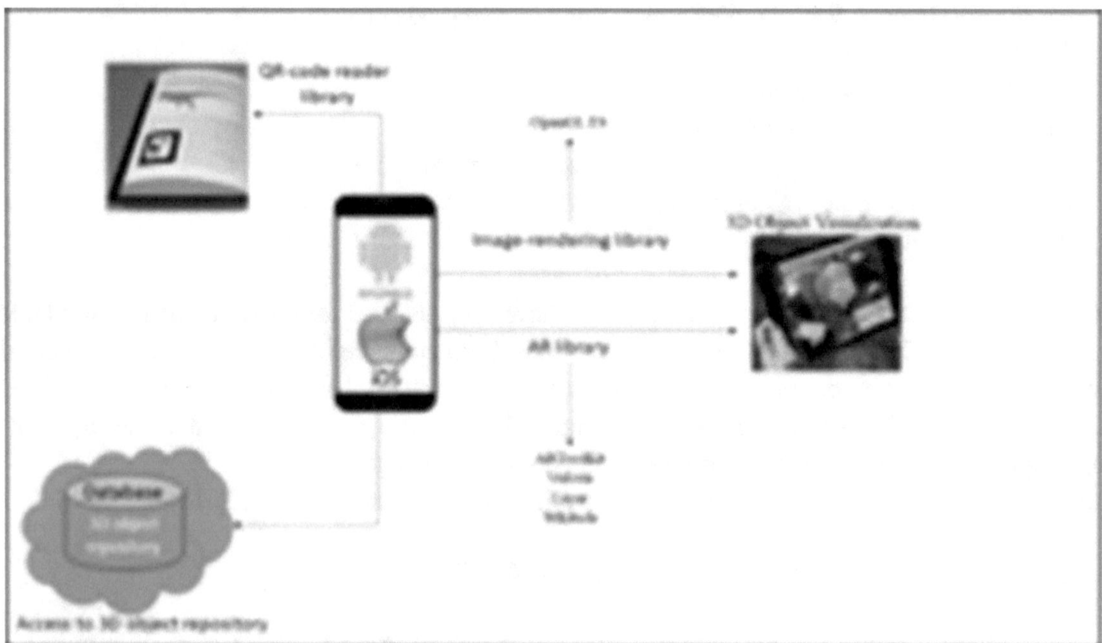

- Xamarin Wikitude SDK v 8: a software library and framework for mobile apps used to create augmented reality experiences. The SDK supports any kind of location based use case as well as use cases which require image recognition and tracking technology;
- Blender animated 3D models, hosted in the www.algera.com.ar repository;
- Business rules are encapsulated in webservices. AlgeRA is an *N-tier* data application. Busines rules and Data Base are separated into different *tiers*. Both are stored at www.algera.com.ar.

AlgeRA application uses the Wikitude library to render the 3D model. To use the camera and the focus on the scoreboard, the application recognizes this and triggers a query to the repository. The query returns the 3D model to use. Then the AR library takes care of rendering the model on the marker. As long as the camera remains focused on the marker, and it is recognized, the model is rendered. This allows that as changing the focus view, the user can observe the 3D model from different perspectives.

4.6 3D Model of AlgeRA

In general, the study of characteristics of 3D models por AR encompasses not only those of the object to be built but also the characteristics that derive from its storage and rendering using alternative tools (like Sketchfab and Wikitude libraries).

The 3D object for AlgeRA was developed with *Blender 2.79*. It consists of an "Sprinkler irrigation system" that can be represented using a system of linear equations. Fig. 6 shows an image of this 3D animated model. It is uploaded en Sketchfab site: https://sketchfab.com/3d-models/sistema-riego-8fae08a98f0a46f98f75314c287e8a4e.

Figure 5. Model of components involved in AlgeRA

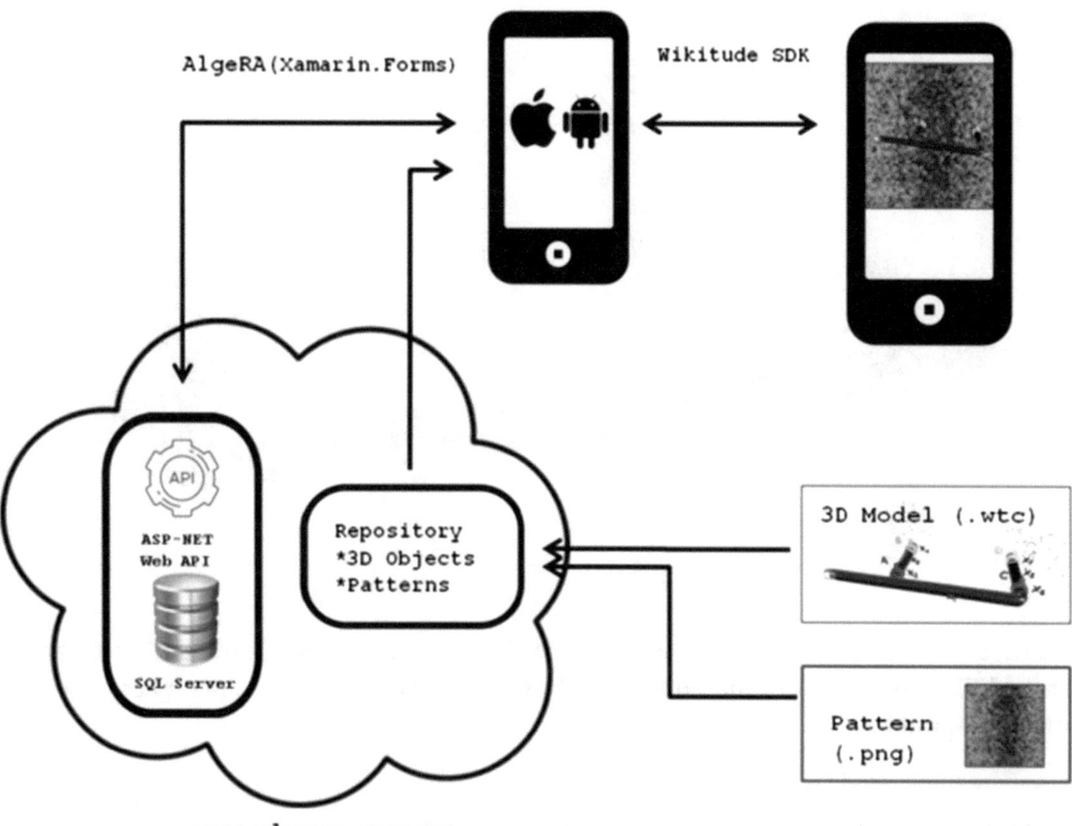

The irrigation system is made up of a series of models: the pipe, the four sprinklers (A, B, C, D), the seven variables with index (x1, x2, x3, x4, x5, x6, and x7) and also of the water flow represented by 200 small spheres, grouped into four groups of 50, one group for each sprinkler. The sprinklers represent a system of four equations that uses the named variables.

Depending on the values assumed by the variables of the equations at a given moment, there is a change in the flow of the irrigation system. That change is represented by the open/close of the sprinklers.

As for the animation itself, from the beginning the four sprinklers are activated for 8 seconds showing the flow of water; then sprinklers A and D are deactivated while sprinklers B and C remain on. The total duration of the animation is 28 seconds. Then it is repeated as long as the example with augmented reality is used.

The file containing the animation has the extension WT3 (the only extension recognized by the Wikitude rendering software). The file size is 1.95 megabytes (small enough to be loaded into the memory of a cell phone).

All the models that are part of the irrigation system were modeled with what is called meshes; that is, their structure is a collection of vertices, edges that connect those vertices, and planes formed by those edges. This is what gives it the structural form that one can visualize.

Regarding the visual aspect of their surface; colors are added to models through what is called materials.

Figure 6. 3D model of AlgeRA: sprinkler irrigation system

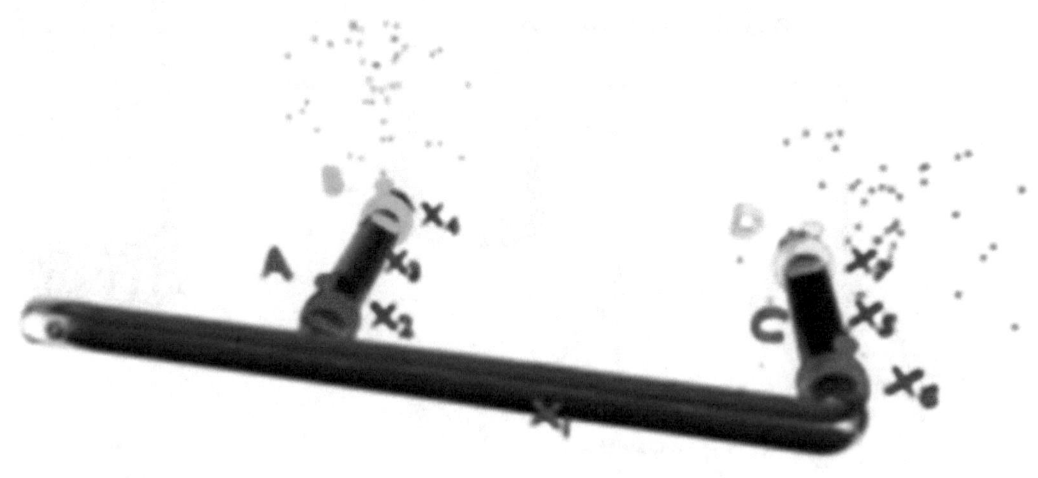

Finally, almost all the models used are static (they do not present animation) except for the water that is animated. This consists of creating an animation where the trajectory of the water spheres is described to simulate a sprinkler.

5. PRELIMINARY RESULTS AND CONCLUSIONS

This article presents preliminary results of the applied research carried out at UNSE in relation to the efficiency of the development and maintenance of mobile applications. In this case, multi-platform applications are included since, in the field of education, practices should reach the largest number of students who have mobile devices with different OS.

Not only the requirement of a multi-platform has been dealt with, but also the need to develop applications with efficient access to the device hardware to allow the use of the camera, GPS, accelerometer, which, in turn, will allow the implementation of AR applications. In addition, such applications require accessing to 3D objects repositories and managing AR, pattern readers, image-rendering libraries, among others technologies.

Up to the present, the various frameworks for multi-platform mobile development have been analyzed and Xamarin Forms has been chosen.

A general conceptual model that makes it easy to consider all the components that participate in this type of applications was produced. This general conceptual model provides a map that shows which are the main elements to be considered while developing multi-platforms mobile applications with AR.

To give an example of how to instantiate that general model into a concrete model, an m-learning practice for Linear Algebra was designed using MADE-mlearn and a multi-platform mobile app, AlgeRA, was developed. The instantiation of the general model shows which are the concrete elements that have been considered in AlgeRA: Xamarin Forms, Wikitude AR SDK, Blender 3D animated objects. The paper also shows the characteristics of 3D models used in AR mobile applications.

The findings are considered useful for software engineering practitioners developing these types of applications, mainly in the field of education. The general model, as well as its instantiation, may be considered as a guide for the development of multi-platform mobile applications.

REFERENCES

Arce, R. A. (2013). *Mobile learning: aprendizaje móvil como complemento de una estrategia de trabajo colaborativo con herramientas Web 2 y entorno virtual de aprendizaje WebUNLP en modalidad de blended learning. In Primeras Jornadas Nacionales de TIC e Innovación en el Aula*. Universidad Nacional de La Plata.

Blazquez Sevilla, A. (2017). Realidad Aumentada en Educación. *Archivo Digital UPM,* 1-35. http://oa.upm.es/45985

Budán, P., Rosenzvaig, F., Najar, P., Saavedra, E., Herrera, S., & Morales, M. (2018). Mobile-RA: Método Ágil para el Desarrollo de Aplicaciones Móviles Multiplataforma. In *VI Congreso Nacional de Ingeniería Informática y Sistemas de Información* (pp. 1009-1022). Universidad Tecnológica Nacional.

Cabero Almenara, J., Barroso Osuna, J. & Obrador, M. (2017). Realidad aumentada aplicada a la enseñanza de la medicina. *Elsevier La revista Educación Médica*, *18*(3), 203-208.

Cabero Almenara, J., García Jiménez, F., & Barroso Osuna, J. (2016). La producción de objetos de aprendizaje en "Realidad Aumentada": La experiencia del SAV de la Universidad de Sevilla. *IJERI International Journal of Educational Research and Innovation*, *6*, 110–123.

Challiol, C., Lliteras, A., & Gordillo, S. (2017). Diseño de Aplicaciones Móviles basadas en Posicionamiento: un Framework Conceptual. In XXIII Congreso Argentino de Ciencias de la Computación, (pp. 682-691). Buenos Aires: Universidad Nacional de La Plata.

Córdoba, M., Budan, P., & Najar, P. (2016). Sistema Alternativo de Comunicación para Niños con Parálisis Cerebral Infantil. In Investigaciones en Facultades de Ingeniería del NOA. Jujuy: Universidad Nacional de Jujuy.

Delía, L. (2017). *Desarrollo de aplicaciones móviles multiplataforma. Especialista en Ingeniería de Software*. Universidad Nacional de La Plata.

DeWitt, D., Siraj, S., & Alias, N. (2014). Collaborative mLearning: A Module for Learning Secondary School Science. *Journal of Educational Technology & Society*, *17*(1), 89–101.

Fennema, M., Herrera, S., Palavecino, R., Budán, P., Rosenzvaig, F., Najar Ruiz, P., Carranza, A., & Saavedra, E. (2017). Aproximaciones para el desarrollo multiplataforma y mantenimiento de Aplicaciones Móviles. In *XIX Workshop de Investigadores en Ciencias de la Computación*, (pp. 446-450). Buenos Aires: Universidad Nacional de La Plata.

Genbetadev. (2016). *PhoneGap*. Retrieved August 18, 2016 https://www.genbetadev.com/frameworks/phonegap

Hermes, D. (2015). *Xamarin Mobile Application Development: Cross-Platform C# and Xamarin. Forms Fundamentals*. Editorial Apress. doi:10.1007/978-1-4842-0214-2

Herrera, S., Morales, M., Palavecino, R., Irurzun, I., Maldonado, M., & Carranza, A. (2017). M-learning con Realidad Aumentada. In *XIX Workshop de Investigadores en Ciencias de la Computación*, (pp. 1280-1284). Buenos Aires: Universidad Nacional de La Plata.

Herrera, S., Morales, M.I., Fennema, M. C. & Sanz, C.V. (2014). *Aprendizaje basado en dispositivos móviles. Experiencias en la Universidad Nacional de Santiago del Estero*. Santiago del Estero: Editorial EDUNSE.

Herrera, S., Palavecino, R., Sanz, C., & Carranza, J. (2017-a). Aprendizaje de Estructuras de Datos mediante m-learning. In I Simpósio Ibero-Americano de Tecnologias Educacionais, (pp. 267-277). Araranguá: Universidade Federal de Santa Catarina.

Herrera, S., Sanz, C., & Fennema, M. (2013). MADE-mlearn: Un marco para el análisis, diseño y evaluación de experiencias de m-learning en el nivel de postgrado. *Revista Iberoamericana de Tecnología en Educación y Educación en Tecnología*, *10*, 7–15.

Herrera, S. I., Fennema, M. C., Morales, M. I., Palavecino, R. A., Goldar, J. E., & Zuain, S. V. (2015). Mobile technologies in engineering education. *Presentado en International Conference on Interactive Collaborative Learning (ICL)*, Florencia, Italia. 10.1109/ICL.2015.7318197

Herrera, S. I., Fennema, M. C., & Sanz, C. V. (2012). Estrategias de m-learning para la formación de posgrado. In *VII Congreso de Tecnología en Educación y Educación en Tecnología*, Buenos Aires: Universidad Nacional de La Plata.

Herrera, S. I., & Sanz, C. (2014). Collaborative m-learning practice using Educ-Mobile. In *2014 International Conference on Collaboration Technologies and Systems (CTS)*, (pp. 363–370). 10.1109/CTS.2014.6867590

Ionic. (2016). *Ionic Framework*. Retrieved August 13, 2016. https://ionicframework.com/docs/guide/preface.html

Maldonado, M., Herrera, S., Irurzun, I., Carranza, J., Palavecino, R., Macedo, A., & Suárez, C. (2018). M-learning: Aprendizaje en Diversos Niveles Educativos Usando ImaColab. In *VI Congreso Nacional de Ingeniería Informática y Sistemas de Información*, (pp. 408-418). Argentina: Universidad Tecnológica Nacional.

Najar, P., Ledesma, E., Rocabado, S., Herrera, S., & Palavecino, R. (2014). Eficiencia de aplicaciones móviles según su arquitectura. In *XX Congreso Argentino de Ciencias de la Computación*. Buenos Aires: Universidad Nacional de La Plata.

Natili, G. (2013). *A guid to building cross-platform apps using the W3C standards based Cordova/PhoneGap framework*. Editorial Packt Publishing.

Navarro, C., Molina, A., Redondo, M., & Juarez-Ramírez, M. (2015). Framework para Evaluar Sistemas M-learning: Un Enfoque Tecnológico y Pedagógico. Revista VAEP-RITA, 3(1), 38-45.

Oró, M. G., Lanna, L. C. & Casas, K. O. (2013). Cambios en el uso y la concepción de las TIC, implementando el Mobile Learning. RED. *Revista de Educación a Distancia*, (37), 1-19.

Pachler, N., Bachmair, B., & Cook, J. (2010). *Mobile learning: structures, agency, practices*. Editorial Springer. doi:10.1007/978-1-4419-0585-7

Park, Y. (2011). A Pedagogical Framework for Mobile Learning: Categorizing Educational Applications of Mobile Technologies into Four Types. *International Review of Research in Open and Distance Learning*, *12*(2), 78–102. doi:10.19173/irrodl.v12i2.791

Pedraza, L. E. & Valbuena S. D. (2014). M-learning y realidad aumentada, tecnologías integradas para apoyar la enseñanza del cálculo. *Revista de investigaciones UNAD*, *13*(2), 29-39.

Pozo, J. (2008). *Aprendices y maestros: La psicología cognitiva del aprendizaje*. Editorial Alianza.

Rahimian, V., & Ramsin, R. (2008). *Designing an agile methodology for mobile software development: A hybrid method engineering approach*. Paper presented at Second International Conference on Research Challenges in Information Science, Marrakech, Morocco. 10.1109/RCIS.2008.4632123

Reinoso, R. (2016). Realidad Aumentada Posibilidades y Usos en Educación. In Recursos Educativos Aumentados una oportunidad para la Inclusión (Ed.), *VIII International Conference of Adaptive and Accessible Virtual Learning Environment*, (pp. 8-25). Cartagena de Indias: Universidad de Cartagena.

Rosenzvaig, F., Budan, P., Herrera, S., Najar, P., Saavedra, E., Sánchez, C., & Fennema, C. (2018). Desarrollo de aplicaciones móviles multiplataforma que usan realidad aumentada. *XIII Jornadas de Ciencia y Tecnología de Facultades de Ingeniería del Noroeste Argentino*, *4*, 247–252.

Salazar Mesía, N., Gorga, G., & Sanz, C. (2015-a). Plan de evaluación del material educativo digital EPRA. Propuesta de indagación sobre la motivación intrínseca. In *XXI Congreso Argentino de Ciencias de la Computación*, (pp. 414-423). Junín: Universidad Nacional del Noroeste de la Provincia de Buenos Aires.

Salazar Mesía, N., Gorga, G., & Sanz, C. (2015-b). EPRA: Herramienta para la Enseñanza de conceptos básicos de programación utilizando realidad aumentada. In *X Congreso de Tecnología en educación y Educación en Tecnología*, (pp. 426-435). Buenos Aries: Universidad Nacional de La Plata.

Thomas, P., Cristina, F., Dapoto, S., & Pesado, P. (2015). Dispositivos Móviles: Desarrollo de Aplicaciones Orientadas a Educación. In *XVII Workshop de Investigadores en Ciencias de la Computación*, (pp. 388-391). Buenos Aries: Universidad Nacional de La Plata.

Vigotsky, L. (1979). *El desarrollo de los procesos psicológicos superiores*. Editorial Crítica.

Wargo, J. (2015). *Apache Cordova 4 Programming*. Editorial Addison-Wesley Professional.

Woodill, G. (2011). *The mobile learning edge*. Editorial Mc Graw Hill.

Zangara, A. (2014). Apostillas sobre los conceptos básicos de educación a distancia o...una brújula en el mundo de la virtualidad. Maestría en Educación a Distancia, Vol 4. Buenos Aires: Facultad de Informática de la Universidad Nacional de La Plata.

KEY TERMS AND DEFINITIONS

AlgeRA: A MADE-mlearn application that aims provides support for the following two activities: a) to exemplify Systems of Linear Equations, b) to model everyday situations using Systems of Linear Equations.

Augmented Reality: A technology that adds to the perception and interaction with the real world, since it provides an augmented real environment with additional information generated by the computer or a mobile device.

Educ-Mobile: An educational, collaborative and mobile game. It consists of three synchronous games. Students form teams of 2 or 3 members and select a leader. It´s a competition among groups that involves following different paths with stations with questions to be solved. The questions are both individual (multiple-choice) and group questions (clues-riddles). Points are accumulative and the winning team is picked based on the team total score and the time spent playing.

Framework: A set of procedures and tools to realize a task in order manner.

ImaColab: A responsive web application. It consists of a collaborative group educational game based on images captured in everyday life that represent elements or situations indicated by the teacher. It is a competition based on student scores with a solid foundation and feedback from teachers. The application calculates the best image of each group; and, finally, the best image of the entire practice.

M-Learning: A mode of learning that arises from the mediation of mobile technologies in the learning process.

MADE-M-Learn: A systemic and ecological framework for the analysis, design and evaluation of m-learning experiences, that include the application for m-learning development.

Multi-Platform Mobile Applications: Mobile apps that can be run in the most frequently used operating system.

ENDNOTE

1 https://www1.qt.io/developers/

Chapter 17
Results of the Research in the Comparison and Analysis of Historical Artifacts' Photographic Images Catalogued in Online Databases:
The Case of a Roman Stele From Ravenna

Marco Tedaldi
University of Bologna, Italy

ABSTRACT

In the field of archaeology, when a discovery is made, the comparison of images is often used to catalogue a find and give it an interpretation. The image on an exhibit is always subject to analysis, comparisons, graphic reconstructions, which can define it, classify it, and most of all, understand it as a whole. The problem arises when the discovered find proposes a completely new and unpublished image. It therefore requires an in-depth study in all its elements. Photographic images, online databases, and archive collections of museums provide some valid help for solutions or interpretations; and the theories that come out of this comparison can then shed light on the meaning of an image present in a find, when there is no direct confirmation.

INTRODUCTION

One of the areas where new technologies have been developed since the rise of multimedia and virtual reality, since the end of the last century, is cultural heritage. As it is well known, Italy has around 70% of the world's cultural heritage. Much of it makes up the UNESCO World Heritage Site. Many are the

DOI: 10.4018/978-1-7998-7010-4.ch017

scholars of the history of art who have contributed to motivate that interest towards the new generations through their publications (Ess, 2001; Veltman, 2006; Oliveira, 2017). However, less than 4% of all workers in Italy are dedicated to the task of conserving the cultural and natural heritage of the territory (Cipolla-Ficara, 2011; Cipolla-Ficarra, 2010; Ferkiss, 1994). Many of her young university professionals from the cultural property sector, being in such a rich country from an artistic point of view, must work in other diverse tasks in order to survive on a daily basis.

However, universities have trained excellent professionals from a theoretical point of view, for example (Ess, 2001; Smith, 2004; Lazarinis, 2010; Oliveira, 2017). They are capable of obtaining great results in their theoretical investigations and conclusions with modest equipment, from a technological point of view. Also, they know how to revalue the techniques of pencil drawing, watercolor, painting, etc., for historical reconstructions. Digital cameras have enhanced direct observation capabilities. This is a technique that within usability engineering requires laboratories connected to simple (video recorders) or sophisticated recording equipment (software or ad hoc applications) to store the data of the movements of the eyes, hands, body position, etc. (Nektarios & Xenos, 2012; Vote, et al., 2002). The purpose is to obtain results of the behaviors of the end users in front of certain contents in the interactive systems.

Some private university education centers in Europe use such usability equipment or labs as a promotional means to attract the attention of future students. However, it is not the technological equipment, the size of the laboratory or the volume of cement used for its construction, the qualitative parameters of education, creativity and technological innovation. Now, this denaturation is transmitted to professionals who act as heads of laboratories.

For example, cultural heritage and social networking are a kind of magnet for astronomers, physicists, geologists, geographers, geodesists, engineers, computer scientists, mathematicians, chemists, etc. (Azuma, 1997; Rasheed & Nordin, 2015; Harrell & Lim, 2017; Marshall & Shipman, 2017; Koo, et al., 2020). However, some professionals continually repeat the same theoretical concepts and practical cases, such as the use of new technologies for the 3D viewing of objects within museums, virtual visits, the architectural context in augmented reality, reconstructions with mixed reality, the comparison of collections between various emblematic museums in the countries, the need to bring culture closer to children, grandparents, the disabled, etc. But all these research works lack original content and research towards that fundamental variables of the latest generation interactive systems. In this chapter it is demonstrated how it is possible to obtain high results of content in archaeology, resorting to field research, consultation in libraries and online databases: EDCS (Epigraphik-Datenbank Clauss / Slaby. See: http://db.edcs.eu/epigr/hinweise/hinweis-it.html), ARACHNE (German Archaeological Institute (DAI) and the Institute of Archeology – University of Colonia. See: https://arachne.uni-koeln.de/drupal), and PATER (Catalogo del Patrimonio culturale dell'Emilia-Romagna – Cultural heritage catalog of Emilia-Romagna Region. See: https://bbcc.ibc.regione.emilia-romagna.it). The steps followed in this regard are detailed below, in one of the towns with a great cultural background that has survived to this day, such as the city of Ravenna.

The city of Ravenna, a municipality in northern Italy, is currently located eight kilometers from the coasts of the Adriatic Sea and within a completely different landscape from the one that saw the origin of this city. The current situation in Ravenna is indeed the result of a long process of change which gradually took place over time, due both to the action of the rivers and to environmental reclamations. In ancient times, the territory of the lower Po valley that includes Ravenna was largely configured as marshy and rich in river courses, difficult to cross and unsuitable for hosting large settlements, an environmental constant that saw the formation of a series of lagoons on the coastal side of the region.

The oldest settlement of the future city of Ravenna was to rise along a line of sandy bumps that divided the sea from the coastal lagoons and from that complex of islets formed by the course of some rivers, that is a branch of the Po called *Padenna* and its tributaries (Cirelli, 2008; Mauro, et al, 2001), the *Flumisello* and the *Lamisa*[1]. According to ancient sources, the Ravenna settlement reflected such environmental conditions of its territory also in its urban planning, configuring itself as a lagoon city distributed over several islands and connected to each other by wooden bridges[2], an aspect that perfectly describes the environment in which it stood.

From its foundation[3] until the appearance of other coastal settlements of a certain competitive importance, Ravenna would play a key role for the connection of maritime traffic with the network of *Emporia* (commercial ports) distributed along the river routes of the Po inland and it guaranteed the coastal passage between the south and the northeast of the peninsula (Cirelli, 2008). This strategic importance inevitably brought Ravenna into contact with the growing Roman power, which from the IInd Century BC started to expand again towards the northern territories of the peninsula, and to be involved in its affairs. From a first phase of commercial exchanges, Ravenna definitively passed into the full Republican period within the system of cities allied with Rome[4]. Throughout time, it then became a fully-fledged Romanized settlement from a cultural, artistic and political point of view, just as other cities did. However, this transformation was definitively consolidated only in the early Imperial age, with the elevation of Ravenna to the role of military port of the Roman fleet used to control the Adriatic and the entire Eastern Mediterranean (Cirelli, 2008).

With the end of the I^st^ Century BC and after the events of Actium, the Augustus-to-be Octavian decided to divide his fleet into two parts, in order to be able to intervene both on the Western and Eastern Mediterranean. To make it possible, Octavian identified two ports suitable for hosting his fleets: Miseno, in today's Campania, would become the port for the fleet in defence of the Western sea while Ravenna, overlooking the Adriatic coast, would have guaranteed the same defence for the Oriental sea[5]. With the construction of the quay to contain the warships, not far from Ravenna, the urban network was also expanded, giving life to a suburb that housed the crews (*classiarii*) and their families, together with all those workers involved in maintenance of boats (*fabri navalis*). This inhabited area, which will expand in subsequent periods[6], would acquire the name of Classe in the late empire, precisely in direct reference to the presence of the fleet (*classis*) established by Augustus[7] (see figure 1).

With the beginning of the Imperial phase, Ravenna reshaped its urban layout by equipping itself with new buildings and received a whole series of stately and celebratory artworks straight from the capital itself. They were aimed at monumentally emphasizing the new "balance" which was re-established immediately after the civil war. Along with the official art of the State also came all those artistic aspects belonging to the popular matrix of the Roman world, described as "Plebeian art": always there in Rome, it took the form of the reproduction of popular artworks directly inspired by the cultured models of the elite, but obviously with lower artistic results (Bianchi-Bandinelli R., 1970). This artistic form was suitable for those low-key and less rich clients, but also tried to maintain and reproduce in his works all those symbols and contents present in high-level artworks, to communicate the same messages.

Its diffusion outside Rome also came to be defined as "provincial art", when the local components themselves tried to copy the original models of official art from Rome, together with the addition of elements artistic or symbolic of autochthonous origin and always with those typical results of Roman popular art (Bianchi-Bandinelli R., 1970).

This dualism of Roman art (Bianchi-Bandinelli R., 1970) also manifested itself in Ravenna, as highlighted by the sculptural finds found in its territory and especially in the funerary steles (Mansuelli,

Figure 1. A reconstruction of how both Ravenna and Classe looked like in the late Empire

1971). Right among the funerary steles we have the testimony of these influences of "Plebeian" popular artistic matrix that came from Rome, the appearance of these steles occurring in conjunction with the period of great changes that involved Ravenna between the end of the I^st^ Century BC and all the I^st^ Century AD. It is during this period that most, if not all, funerary steles with a certain monumental and sculptural tenor were found.

The FIND

This whole series of events, which led to the transformation of Ravenna and its port in the Imperial Age, are necessary to introduce the object of this study, a Roman funerary stele that carries within it the image of a classiario (see figure 2 and 3): a soldier who served in the Classis Ravennatis, the fleet of the Augustan foundation.

The enormous value of the stele lies precisely in the image it proposes, as it is the only find that shows the appearance of a full-length soldier of the imperial classis in armed clothing, therefore a completely new representation: consequently, this is an image containing elements without any equivalent or completely identical comparison, except in some details.

Here's a series of targets aimed at describing the image present in the stele: defining the type of find based on its appearance and classifying it through the reconstruction of the missing parts with graphic apparatuses and its comparison with other similar finds, then reading all those elements (epigraphic and

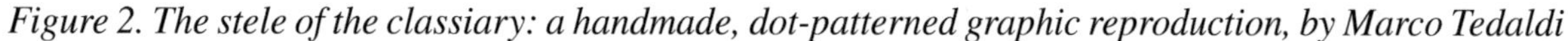

Figure 2. The stele of the classiary: a handmade, dot-patterned graphic reproduction, by Marco Tedaldi

figurative) which are still legible and useful to identify the subject of the monument and the contents related to it.

Keeping in mind the visible elements, both dative and of clear contextual reference, and starting from the assumption that Roman art spread its messages through models and symbols: a series of comparisons with other monuments will surely provide a starting point to find common elements.

To obtain some of these results, graphic contributions and direct juxtapositions between the images of the finds will not be enough, therefore it will also be essential to formulate a series of hypotheses in the absence of information directly comparable with anything new.

In addition, it is necessary to highlight the importance of having an infinity of images stored in digital catalogs that thanks to remote access, through the Internet (e.g., EDCS, ARACHNE and PATER) or in the same libraries or state archives (*Archivio di Stato,* in Italian), these tasks of collection and comparison of images are facilitated in this present research. In our case, it is not necessary to resort to sophisticated

Figure 3. The stele of the classiary as it is today

search mechanisms for the information or quality of the final image. Although there is a constant evolution from capture to storage in 2D or 3D image format, as can be seen in the current literature. Some works that refer to digital photography, algorithms in database search, access to information from the internet, 3D reconstructions, among others, and which are briefly summarized in the following references (Rasheed & Nordin, 2015; Bolter, Engberg & Mcintyre, 2013; Koller, Frischer & Humphreys, 2009; Vote, 2002; Koo, et al. 2020; Mccarthy, et al. 2020).

The Discovery

The stele was occasionally found in 2005, during a series of archaeological surveys near Classe, inside a late imperial sewer pipe passing near an ancient burial area.

Being a large stone block, the stele monument had followed the same fate as other similar finds present in Ravenna, that is the reuse as a building material within a subsequent structure (Mansuelli, 1971). The clear lack of the upper part of the stele also confirms its destination: this had been deliberately removed to create a support block for the structural failure of the sewer pipe, which is why it was found inside this structure rather than in the necropolis8. We should imagine that the stele, deprived of its function long after its construction, was moved from its original location to be then adapted as a building material.

The surviving part of the stele is configured as a single block of marble, just over a meter high and finished with architectural elements as frames. Furthermore, there is part of an epigraph and a representation in relief on it. The figure inside is clearly referable to that of a soldier in arms, while the still legible part of the inscription confirms a reference to the imperial classis: for this reason, the stele was given the name of stele of the classiary.

Classification of the Find

If we are within a state archive, in some of the main cities such as Bologna, Rome, Turin, Venice, etc., the classification of the stored material (e.g. PATER, in Emilia-Romagna Region) facilitates the task of establishing the dates of the same. This is because much of the information (e.g., maps, charts, photos, etc.) is digitized. A digitization that has followed international parameters, models, systems, etc., as can be seen in the following cases (Koller, Frischer & Humphreys, 2009; Mccarthy, et al., 2020). In our study it is necessary to perform a classification task.

Once the historical context of origin and discovery of the find has been defined, it is necessary to classify it and possibly to give an initial dating to it, based on the common characteristics with other finds found in the area.

If we take a look at all the Roman funerary steles documented for the Ravenna area, we realize that they are divided, in terms of appearance and characteristics, into two distinct types: on the one hand we find the "architectural" steles, characterized by a large block of parallelepiped stone and decorated with sculptural reliefs, both figurative and architectural (usually to define *aedicules* culminating in *a tympanum*), on the other hand we have a more documented series of simple poorly decorated stone slabs, usually with engravings, called a "framed" slab or "anarchietectonic" steles (Mansuelli, 1971). See figure 4.

According to this very clear subdivision, due to its features (and although mutilated of its top) it is natural to insert the stele of the classiary in the category of architectural steles, namely the most monumental ones (Mansuelli, 1971). In a direct comparison with other finds of the same model and territorial provenance, it is possible (figure 5) to suppose that the stele of the classiary also culminated, in its upper part, with a tympanum decoration: through a graphic reconstruction it is possible to imagine what its original appearance was before it underwent reuse.

This first classification allows a dative circumscription of the stele to the first Imperial period: the architectural steles of Ravenna are mainly inserted in a time span that goes from the end of the Ist Century BC until the beginning of the IInd Century AD, and only the framed slab model would maintain its presence even later, until the end of the IIIrd Century AD. The reason why in the territory of Ravenna the finds of architectural steles do not go beyond the beginning of the IInd Century AD is to be attributed to a substantial change in the laws and to the society of the period (Mansuelli, 1971).

The funerary stele at its origins was configured as a simple element, aimed at indicating only the point of the burial of a deceased person. Later, it also started to tell the life through images, symbols and epigraphs, assuming not just a monumental function but also to commemorate the dead (Bianchi-

Figure 4. An example of architectural stele on the left and an example of a framed slab stele on the right

Bandinelli R., 1970; Von Hesberg, 1992). In the context of the Roman arts the "Plebeian" current, inspired by the great official monuments, was also fully expressed through the creation of funerary signs, spreading the models in all the territories that were subjected to Rome (Bianchi-Bandinelli R., 1970): Ravenna too was involved but only manifested the phenomenon starting from the end of the Ist Century BC, as evidenced by the finds (Mansuelli, 1967; Mansuelli, 1971). In the territory of the Roman Cispadana, where Ravenna was also included, there is indeed no trace of stone funerary finds of a certain tenor before the changes that occurred within the Imperial period. In the Cispadana region this inclination to erect monumental and architectural steles for burial is a phenomenon of the Augustan age and did not end with the full Julio-Claudian age, but the absence of architectural steles in Ravenna starting from the IInd Century AD should be sought right in the social changes already underway with Augustus (Mansuelli, 1967; Mansuelli, 1971). When all those cultural pressures concerning the burials' monumentality arrived in Ravenna, and then throughout the Cispadana, a whole series of prohibitions issued by the Augustan authority began to take hold in the capital to repress the cult of personality, prohibitions that also involved the monuments. These restrictions of imperial authority would then be perceived and gradually extended, after years, to the rest of the peninsula, and starting from the Middle Imperial Age they would also be felt in the provinces (Mansuelli, 1967; Mansuelli, 1971; Bianchi-Bandinelli, 1970).

This reason explains why in Ravenna we have proof of monumental steles up to the beginning of the IInd Century AD, as the interest in celebrating themselves through sumptuous monuments by the various local social categories was a novelty and enjoyed a certain tolerance from the authorities. From the IInd Century AD the archaeological findings themselves confirmed the arrival of the change taking

Figure 5. A reconstruction of the stele's incomplete part (the tympanum), built on a similar architectural model; the side acroteria were depicted too. In the architectural steles they are almost always there and the preferred shape was the lions' one, while in the framed slab steles they were replaced with other animal figures such as dolphins or plant elements such as palmettes (Mansuelli, 1971)

place in the burial sector: as a matter of fact, the findings of steles show only framed slab models. By configuring themselves as simple tables, they based their message mostly in the epigraphic sector, while the figurative part was reduced to simple engravings, often symbolic or to frame the text (rare examples with small and not very incisive sculptural representations), therefore they were suitable for that context of sobriety required by law for funerary monuments[9] (Mansuelli, 1967; Von Hesberg, 1992).

The classification with the architectural steles can insert the stele of the classiary in a fairly defined time bracket, which goes from the beginning of the Imperial period to the beginning of the IInd Century AD, a period where we have no widespread evidence of these steles in Ravenna.

ANALYSIS OF THE EPIGRAPHIC AND FIGURATIVE ELEMENTS

The Roman funerary steles use two essential means to convey their message, the epigraphic one and the figurative one (Mansuelli, 1967; Von Hesberg, 1992).

Between the two, epigraphs certainly play an essential role in order to understand the meaning of a particular monument, as they directly convey the information (they are enough even without the figuration, as in some cases this one is absent in the framed slab stele). Conversely, an image without any written elements connected to it, in the absence of other comparative references can also be indecipherable and not enough to convey a message.

A message that follows the classic paradigms of human communication (Oliveira, 2017; Veltman, 2006, Ess, 2001) for its decoding by users of the most varied interactive systems, whose contents are related to history, archeology, painting, sculpture, etc. Some content that involves resorting to various disciplines to develop such systems, starting with the analysis and design of the same, where image and text usually interrelate with each other, to facilitate the transmission of content, over time and the interested parties to understand those messages (Bolter, Engberg & Mcintyre, 2013; Cipolla-Ficarra, 2011; Cipolla-Ficarra, 2010).

As far as the stele of the classiary is concerned, we are facing this case: the surviving epigraph is essential because it identifies exactly the subject of the representation, a subject that could also be interpreted in another way if this was absent, a case that we will then analyse.

The Epigraph

The conditions of conservation of the stele of the classiary show us a partially illegible and incomplete epigraph; it is distributed along various registers delimited by the architectural parts: starting from the surface of the epistyle, it continues along the spaces above and below the cornices, and then ends on the plinth (see figure 6).

Figure 6. The epigraph parts still legible on the stele

Keeping in mind only the legible elements, from the epigraph we are still able to acquire a series of important information to identify the subject portrayed.

Starting from the top, by the second and third register we can obtain the name of the deceased person, a *Moni(a)tus or Moni(e)tus Capito*, therefore the beneficiary to whom the monument was dedicated. After the name, in the third register the military rank he held in life is reported in abbreviated form: it was that of opt. (*optio*), so it was a graduate with specific duties. Assisting an officer, generally a *centurion*, and therefore being his aide and substitute when necessary was among the tasks of the *optio* (Cascarino, 2008). Within the Roman navy each ship was considered like a terrestrial cohort and therefore it was subject to the direct command of a centurion, consequently the optio had to fill the role of "second officer" in the governance of a boat (Le Bohec, 1989). In this case, the boat on which this optio served was a *liburna*, as seen from the third register, while the name of this, *Aurata* (the "Golden"), is reported in the last register. The *liburna* is one of the smallest, fastest and most manoeuvrable war boats present in the classis, and therefore suitable for patrolling the Adriatic Sea; this could be both a bireme or a trireme as well as a crew of numerous rowers and soldiers. Mentioning the name of the ship on where crew members served, in the epigraphs of funerary monuments dedicated to them, seemed to be a well-documented custom throughout the duration of the classis[10] (Mansuelli, 1967; Susini, 1973). The epigraph on the *stele of the classiary* concludes by reporting who erected and dedicated this monument, that is a family member and heir *Cogn(at)us Heres F. (Fecit)* of the deceased person. Most of the funerary monuments, including the stelae, were indeed erected posthumously after the beneficiary's death, consequently it was the responsibility of family members or acquaintances to take care of them. This is an important fact if we analyse it mostly in reference to the representation on the stele, because we do not know if this was performed according to precise instructions given by the beneficiary when he was alive[11], or if this is an image resulting from the will of the family members. In any case, the richness of the details of the image on the stele, as well as some clues maybe hinting at some afterthoughts during the work, has to be linked to the client anyway.

Also in this case the epigraph proves to be fundamental for providing immediate information on the deceased person, such as his identity or what he did in life, but does not provide, as in many other cases, an absolute element of dating for the find (Mansuelli, 1967; Von Hesberg, 1992; Hope, 2001).

In the cases of the Northern Italian steles we seldom have absolute chronologies from the epigraphic compartment and it is often only the presence or absence of some elements, such as the formularies, to provide us with some help for a temporal collocation of these finds. Following this reasoning, a chronological indicator for the stele of the classiary could be the absence of the abbreviated formula *D(is) M(anibus)*, limiting its realization to before the IInd Century AD, but in a non-absolute way[12]. This abbreviated formula with *D M* would become mandatory on funeral monuments only at the end of the Ist Century AD and it is absent for most of the Ravenna architectural steles, while it is widely attested for all the other framed slab steles of the IInd Century AD onwards (Susini, 1973; Mansuelli, 1967).

From a chronological point of view, even with the epigraph we can roughly insert the stele of the classiary in a fairly limited period: not prior to the establishment of the *classis* for the subject it identifies and before the usual introduction of the *D M* formula in funerary monuments, which took place around the end of the Ist Century AD (assuming it's valid).

The Figurative Sector

At the center of the body of *the stele of the classiary* appears the figure of a man (see figure 7), with uncovered head and standing, frontally with a formal attitude, only the right leg shows a movement towards the observer; on the bust he wears a *loricae musculata* bordered by scaled plates and from which the *pteruges* emerge, along the waist passes the *cingulum* on which a *pugio* is fixed on the right side; on the opposite side, supported with a *balteus* and held still with one hand, we have the *gladius* even if only perceptible by a few details, while with the right hand it holds a spear or a pilum; on the left shoulder there are folds that identify a cloak, at the feet he wears military shoes, the *caligae*.

This soldier figure was obtained by directly excavating the central plane of the stele, around the figure a niche was therefore defined, with an irregular profile and delimited only at the top by the frame that runs around the central plane; in the frame a cut can be clearly seen, as well as an interruption of its lower profile to allow the realization of the whole figure and the cavity[13].

From the point of view of the artistic rendering, the figure has a fairly natural and well-proportioned anatomy, although the head is slightly large and the body stocky. The author was also careful in balancing by unloading the weight of the body on the legs, keeping one slightly behind the other. The physiognomy of the deceased man and his face are reminiscent of the portraiture models of the Julio-Claudian period (Kleiner, 1977; Kleiner, 1987), especially perceptible in the hair, made compact and very adherent to the head so as to form a sort of hemispherical cap. The absence of a definition of the pupil through engraving, a typical particularization of later portraiture of the Antonine period (Mansuelli, 1967; Mansuelli, 1971), also confirms the stele dating to before the IInd Century AD. The relief is completed with a multitude of details, all obtained through shallow incisions, the different volumes of the shapes are rendered through very soft passages of light on the surface.

The stylistic elements and forms present in the portrait date the *stele of the classiary* back to the Ist Century AD and more likely in the first half, in the period of the Julio-Claudian dynasty.

THE PRESENCE OF OFFICIAL ART IN THE RAVENNA OF THE FIRST IMPERIAL PERIOD

To further validate a dating of the *stele of the classiary* to the Ist Century AD it is necessary to consider local elements of official art found and belonging to that period, which may have influenced or inspired in some way the elements and the production of the figure represented on the stele under analysis, considering what has been said for the "Plebeian" art.

As a matter of fact, the *stele of the classiary* represents the product of the "Plebeian" art that arrived in Ravenna together with the official artworks of the capital, and the result of a popular client who possessed the means to have funerary monuments of good value: the funerary monument had become a concrete expression to participate in the self-celebratory process within the Roman society and aiming at emulating the higher classes of the period (Bianchi-Bandinelli, 1970; Mansuelli, 1967; Von Hesberg, 1992). In order to do this, it was necessary to use the same symbols, inspired by (or, even better, copied from) official monuments.

As far as the imperial period of Ravenna is concerned, we have few fragments from official monuments. Over time, due to the continuity of life of the city and various needs, these monuments suffered the demolition and were dismantled to make reuse material for other buildings, in the ages that followed (Cirelli, 2008; Mansuelli, 1971). The quality of some fragments proves that the new phase of construction progress in Ravenna, which took place at the beginning of the Empire with the promotion of Augustus, must have had a certain impact on the local society.

Although, at present, there are numerous methodologies of building reconstructions carried out in three dimensions to facilitate the tasks of the archaeologist (Cipolla-Ficarra, 2011; Cipolla-Ficarra, 2010; Lazarinis, 2010; Vote, 2002), in our case study we focus on the material exhibited in museums. Surely, of the preserved fragments the ones that best represent this intense building phase are the reliefs of the *Gens Julia*, a series of relief panels preserved in the National Museum of Ravenna. These reliefs, based on their historical and stylistic value, can be considered the most significant testimony of cultured art

Figure 7. A detail of the classiary figure on the stele

of the *Julio-Claudian* era found in Northern Italy. The two surviving panels, which are to be considered together, celebrate a scene of apotheosis of the Julio-Claudian family, through a deified representation of its members (see figure 8). The figures, arranged evenly along the register as if following a procession, attend a sacrifice ceremony, in honor of *Divus Augustus*.

These preserved elements must have been slabs to be applied to a load-bearing support and probably made up the front frieze of a monumental altar, based on the typology of the *Ara Pacis* built by Augustus in Rome (Kleiner, 1977; Kleiner, 1987; Zanker, 1988), an architectural model that was maintained even with subsequent emperors, such as the emperor Claudius14. During the reign of Claudius, the city of Ravenna received a strengthening of the port and was given a gift of new buildings, including the *Porta Aurea*, a monumental entrance to the city consisting of two archways, which was later demolished during the XVIth Century[15] (Mansuelli, 1971).

The official initiative and its artistic donations must have greatly influenced the imagination of the local population: it is no accident that most of the architectural steles found locally are to be attributed to the period of the impressive urban interventions promoted by the emperor Claudius. It follows that the influence exercised by the central power encouraged the production of monumental funerary steles by the local population, a phenomenon to be limited to this phase and which will not recur in the same way in the following centuries.

Elements in the Stele Ascribable to the Official art of Ravenna

The stylistic elements and some details in the depiction of the *classiary* suggest a Julio-Claudian style influence, attributable to representations present in some official monuments of Ravenna at the beginning of the Empire. Just a detail of the weapons of the classiary seems to confirm the direct influence of one of these monuments, and that this was known to the client and the workshop who produced the stele. As a matter of fact, this precise symbolic reference could be found in the cuirass, a *loricae musculata*, worn by the *classiary*. The *loricae musculata* was made with great attention to its details and for this reason it must be the copy of a real element because the Romans were related to the canons of realism (Bianchi-Bandinelli, 1970), but an idealization of its forms typical of the Julio-Claudian age is not excluded –because it tends to the canons of classicism (Mansuelli, 1967; Zanker, 1988). In any case, the presence of this type of cuirass must be read as an added value and an important symbolic element if we consider the ancient world.

The loricae musculata or anatomical armor was configured first of all as a protection for the torso; of Hellenistic derivation and also adopted by the Romans[16], in its most advanced models, it enveloped the entire torso completely, reproducing the details of the chest muscles with a natural shape through relief. These are the latter models that spread mainly between the Republican and the Imperial Ages, especially among the higher ranks of the army, to the point of identifying only the officers. It was these same models that spread mainly between the Republican and the Imperial Ages, especially among the highest ranks of the army, ending up identifying only the officers: not only for the costs of material and production, but also because they lent itself to be enriched with highly symbolic elements of high aesthetic value, compared to other types of armors[17] (Cascarino, 2008).

This armor also had a symbolic and parade value: it was not just any object, but the use of the loricae musculata also by soldiers and naval officers in combat areas seemed to be seen in some depictions of naval battles, present on finds belonging to the Augustan period, even if most of the Roman soldiers (Alston, 1999; Goldsworthy, 1996) used models of armor with a definitely more practical use[18] (Cascarino, 2008). We have to assume that the naval combat of the time, especially in boarding action, had to assume very similar dynamics to those of land combat, therefore most of the armaments of the soldiers embarked should not differ much, for practicality, from that used and spread by soldiers in the legions, and surely even the classiarii had to have the same training because they were not excluded from tasks on the ground[19] (Le Bohec, 1989). Considering the meaning that this cuirass can express and its material cost[20], the theory that the presence of the loricae musculata, in the figure of the classiary, had symbolic reasons and was a model to be used only on official occasions, cannot be excluded: in this regard, the *relief with praetorians of the Louvre*, dating back to the period of Claudius, portrays the praetorian guard in a parade outfit rather than with a realistic combat armament, as they show rich armaments probably to validate their role as imperial guard. Of particular importance is the praetorian guard wearing a loricae musculata also surmounted by the cingulum, therefore completely similar to the representation of the classiary if compared[21] (see figure 9).

Whether it was practical or parade weaponry, the *loricae musculata* also had symbolic value, and in the *stele of the classiary* it could be translated into a heroic and celebratory sense if directly connected to the monument of the Gens Iulia of Ravenna: if we take a look at the detail of the scaled borders of the classiary's armor, especially those present in the lower abdomen, these are completely similar to those that appear in the armor of the character in arms present in the panels of the *Gens Iulia*. Not only are they similar in shape, but also they alternate and are repeated on two orders in the exact same way (see

Figure 8. The most important between the two Gens Iulia panels, now in the National Museum of Ravenna

figure 9). The *stele of the classiary* artist who created this particular of the cuirass was very precise and careful in rendering this detail. Perhaps he copied directly from the monument of the *Gens Iulia*, or he reproduced the real *loricae musculata* that the *classiary* wore, identical in these elements for emulative reasons to the figure in arms of the panels of the altar.

The figure in arms in the reliefs of the *Gens Iulia* is not a random figure but should be attributed to Marco Vipsanio Agrippa (Mansuelli, 1971), the great general who promoted Azio's victory. Depicted in an armed dress, he appears among the members of the *Gens Iulia* because he was the husband of the daughter of Augustus and his great collaborator. During the civil wars Agrippa had the vital task of commanding Octavian's fleet deployed against Marco Antonio and Cleopatra in the famous naval battle of Actium in 31 BC, a battle that ended in favor of the future Augustus. The restored order and peace were attributed to Octavian, but the architect of Actium's success was to be found in Agrippa: in the periods immediately following this battle, which decided the fate of the Roman world, Agrippa's character had to appear as the military hero par excellence in the collective imagination, especially among the soldiers of the fleet: in the mind of a soldier of the imperial classis, who lived around the end of the I[st] Century BC or in the full I[st] Century AD, a figure like Agrippa (who died in 12 BC) was supposed to be a source of inspiration, even after his death. If so, being able to recall the image of this illustrious character and the monument on which he was portrayed, through the same type of armor and other similarities, could be a source of pride for the classiary, and perhaps would explain the desire to represent himself entirely in arms (Von Hesberg, 1992).

By looking carefully at the figure of the *classiary*, the links with the reliefs of the *Gens Iulia* are also highlighted in other details: showing oneself bareheaded, the haircut of the same type as the male characters present, the identical position and the rendering of the folds of the cloak (*paludamentum*) of

Figure 9. A comparison of details: the stele of the classiary in the upper part, the Gens Iulia loricated figure in the lower one, the praetorian guard of the decoration from the Louvre on the right

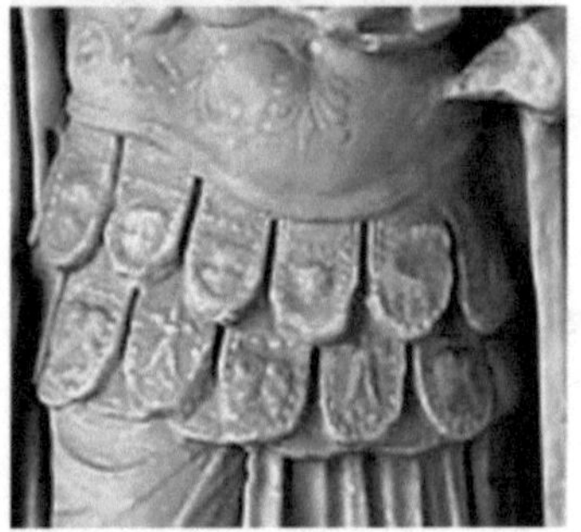

the shoulder like that of the central character of the panel, identified as the deified Augustus (Mansuelli, 1971).

This key to reading the details present in the stele of the classiary is linked to those aspects that identify the "Plebeian" art (Bianchi-Bandinelli R., 1970): copying, being inspired by and recalling the details of the reliefs of the altar of Ravenna could indicate how both the artist and the client knew this monument and its symbolic importance. In this case, the importance of digital photography is highlighted for the tasks of analyzing details in sculptures. Digital photography continues to offer a wide spectrum of information to formulate hypotheses by archaeologists and other related disciplines. This information is based on the theory, practice and technique of digital photography, whether in color or black and white (Lazarinis, 2010; Bolter, Engberg & Mcintyre, 2013).

IDENTIFICATION OF THE BASIC PATTERNS BEHIND THE PRODUCTION OF THE STELE

It seems clearer to determine the models used or known by the workshop for the realization of the figure on the *stele of the classiary*.

As far as the steles belonging to soldiers are concerned, those of the same period or posthumous to the *stele of the classiary*, as well as coming from provincial areas (related to *Soldatenkuntst* or the "art of soldiers"), it is possible to notice that the most widespread model of representation among these steles is that with the deceased in full figure and standing, in the act of showing himself (Franzoni, 1987). Among the variables we can see the soldier either in arms or in civilian clothes, with part of his kit worn or placed in the background as if hanging in a sort of list[22]. The whole and standing representation probably seems to be the most widespread and loved among the soldiers because it allows to show all the military or rank attributes (Franzoni, 1987).

In our case, *the stele of the classiary* easily fits into this category, not only for the subject represented but also for the iconographic model. For the situation of the finds in Ravenna, not only the stele of the classiary is configured as a rarity for the subject of the representation, but also for how it is represented: if we analyse all steles found in the territory historically subject to Ravenna, the majority of those that show a representation of the dead do it through the portrait or the bust, therefore we see whole figurations only in very rare cases (Mansuelli, 1967; Mansuelli, 1971; Susini, 1973).

Among these few steles with the full figure of the deceased person, one very useful for a comparison of style, rendering of volumes, position of the body and proportions, seems to be the *stele of Festio*[23], preserved in the Civic Museum on Palazzo dei Diamanti in Ferrara and for its elements dating back to the I^st^ Century AD, It shows the figure of a child modelled in a very similar way to the figure of the *classiary*, if compared. This similarity is an important element as it could link the production of these two steles to the same workshop and proves that it produced stele models with whole figures of this type.

Another one of these steles, always useful for comparison by subject and type of iconography, incredibly belongs to the framed slap steles: the stele of *Aemilius Severus*[24], datable between the IInd and IIIrd Century AD (Mansuelli, 1967), exceptionally proposes for that period a bas-relief with full figure of the deceased, in this case a *centurion* but in civilian clothes. This figure, made in a sober manner and with few details, in a period where representations were almost completely absent from the steles, shows us that the soldiers' tendency was always to be portrayed in full if they chose to represent themselves (Franzoni, 1987)).

These few artifacts found, together with the stele of the classiary, document the local workshop's knowledge of stele models depicting whole and standing figures of deceased persons even in the Ravenna area (Susini, 1973).

Also the client behind the realization of the stele of the classiary must have considered the possibilities provided by the whole figure, a choice made during construction right in reference to this advantage, as demonstrated by the cut of the lower part of the frame present on the surface of the stele, made to hold the image[25].

Other Aspects Related to the Workshop's Work on the Representation

Once again with reference to the workshop's work, in addition to the solution of the cut of the frame on the prefabricated block, made by the artist to obtain the entire figure of the stele, other irregularities or expedients used to make some of these objects are noticed: the weapon which looks like a spear, held by the figure with the right hand, was made by using the irregular profile of the niche and bends internally towards the top following the line. It is also placed on the bevelled stump of the underlying frame, making this an element almost "real" of space[26]; in the realization of the gladius, the artist limited the presence of this object with the depth of the relief and the left hand that holds it, although there was all the space to represent it in its entirety.

The gladius, worn on the left in a position common to the officers for the Roman sphere[27] (Cascarino, 2008), did not receive the same attention to detail as the pugio, which is clearly visible on the right side and attached to the belt (*cingulum*). We understand that the gladius is present on the left side only thanks to a few elements: from its suspension shoulder strap (*balteus*) which, like a broad band, runs transversely along the *loricae musculata*[28] and from the fact that the *classiary* grasps a spherical, round element with the left hand, this is the final knob placed on the handle of the weapon.

With a few tricks, the artist was then able to convey the presence of the *gladius* without actually depicting it, by proposing a frontal vision of it and defined only with the depth of relief. If we take a look at the stele from the side we will see that the element of the *gladius* pommel, together with the hand placed on the handle, almost seem to come out of the plane where the rest of the figure is located (see figure 10). We do not know why the artist opted for such a solution, albeit always realistic, but in its frontal position the *gladius* only provides its presence without any kind of detail, unlike the other objects.

If we compare a stele like that of the signiferous *Pintaius*[29], datable to the I[st] Century AD, we notice that not only his figure is placed in a condition of extreme frontality, showing all the details of his person, but is also represented with his arms open outwards, similar to a "praying" attitude, right to show in detail the objects he holds: among these the *gladius*, held by the pommel, is rotated outwards to allow a detailed view. On the other hand, in *the stele of the classiary* the figure's arm carries the *gladius* adherent to the body, albeit with a non-rigid movement.

The choice and elaboration of the models, added to the skills of the workshops, seem to lead to very different results in the realization of certain details, probably difficult to render in a natural way: in the case of the stele of the *aquiliferous Lucius Sertorius Firmus*[30], from the I[st] Century AD, the position of the arm and hand that grasps the *gladius*, placed along the left side, and the representation of this movement make the figure assume an unnatural and partly static position, enough to influence the inclination of the shoulders. In the stele of *Marcus Favonius Facilis*[31], a Roman officer of the I[st] Century AD, we see the same setting and movement of the arm seen for the Pintaius stele, but in this case it is the skill and quality of the artist's work that makes the difference, which translates into the natural and harmonic rendering of a complex gesture, like that of tilting the gladius in order to allow its view.

In the case of the *stele of the classiary* it is possible that his artist deliberately chose to avoid that complex movement that showed the *gladius*, in favour of a definitely simpler solution to implement and with favourable results, even if it leaves a certain imbalance between the spaces.

The position of the *gladius* (an element almost always present, even in representations in civilian clothes) and how this is held seems to be one of the elements most subject to possible variations in the representation of soldiers, through solutions that, for example, can reward the naturalness of the position of the arm or the details of the weapon held by the hand. Unlike other elements that are almost always static (such as the *pugio*, which is depicted along the side and close to the body as it's attached to the belt), the *gladius* can be represented as suspended from the shoulder strap or firmly attached to the belt, oriented inwards or outwards, seen from the front or placed along the side, held by the handle or the pommel. All these solutions are generally seen in the figures who carry the *gladius* on the left because they also involve the hand position, which otherwise would be free, as opposed to the right hand which usually holds another object (a stick, a weapon or a rank symbol to give examples).

DEFINITION OF THE SUBJECT DEPICTED ON THE STELE BASED ON THE ICONOGRAPHY

In the previous paragraphs we have classified the *stele of the classiary* as a type of find, analyzing its epigraphic and figurative elements also to date it, then we have identified some of the models underlying its creation and the clues that testify to the interventions of the workshop and the client. In the last part we will try to clarify whether the figure in the *stele of the classiary* would have been attributable to an *optio* in an armed outfit only through the iconographic aspect (in the hypothetical lack of the epigraph), then we will verify if there are those attributes of rank handed down from historiography and sufficient to identify it.

The Attributes That Define the Optio in Relation to the Image on the Stele

According to ancient documents, the *optio* was the direct subordinate of the centurion, with the task of assisting and replacing him when necessary[32] (Cascarino, 2008). As for other graduates, the *optio* needed some attributes in his equipment that could allow easy and immediate recognition. Some of these rank attributes could be the helmet, recognizable above all by two large feathers placed on the sides linked to the ancient heritage[33], or the shield, which was smaller or oval, but most of all it was the stylus (astile) that highlighted its role: a stick surmounted by a metal knob, used to keep the soldiers in compact formation. The rest of the armament had to be configured similarly to that of the other soldiers, for a practical matter (Cascarino, 2008).

Consequently, to recognize the representation of an optio it is necessary to refer to the elements just described. However, if we look at the figure on the *stele of the classiary*, there is no trace of these elements: the figure appears with its head covered and the shield is also absent, and instead of seeing a astile, tightened in the right hand we find what appears to be a spear or a throwing javelin (*pilum*).

Interpretative Problems and Theories About the Image Depicted in the Stele

The image on the *stele of the classiary* is clearly that of a soldier, but we know that it is an *optio* only thanks to the epigraph, because in the representation all those elements that allow us to recognize it as such are missing. Previously we considered that, for practical and employment reasons, a navy *optio* had to be armed and recognizable in the same way as a legion *optio*; moreover, we considered the possibility that the image on the stele of the *classiary* could represent an official vestment or from the parade of the subject. From the figurative elements that can be found here and in relation to the grade attributes that identify the *optio*, it is impossible to understand that the figure mentioned in the epigraph on the stele is the one we're looking at. At this point we cannot even rule out the theory that there is an element unknown to us in the representation that can still identify this subject as an *optio*; in this case, it seems we should focus mostly on the weapon held in the right hand.

Unlike the case of the classiary, in other funerary steles belonging to optiones we always have the version of these ones in civilian clothes. Nevertheless, the astile is always present and seems to be an inseparable element to underline the degree, as we can see in some examples such as the funerary *stele of Caecilius Avitus*, (*optio* della *legio* XX) dating back to the IInd Century AD or the stele of *Publius Aelius Mestrius*, (optio in the legio II *Adiutrix*), datable between the I[st] Century AD and the IInd Century

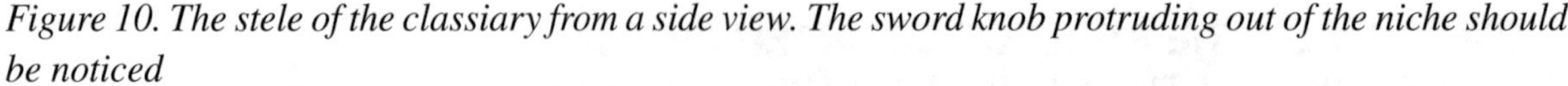

Figure 10. The stele of the classiary from a side view. The sword knob protruding out of the niche should be noticed

AD. In these examples of stele the figure of the *astile* reflects all the characteristics it must possess: it is configured just like a stick that culminates on the top with a sphere, probably metallic.

In the case of the *classiary*, we do not know whether the object it holds can be directly considered a variant of the *astile*: the only element in common that can be seen, when compared with the steles of *Caecilius Avitus or Publius Aelius Mestrius*[34], is the height of these objects, in all cases seem to correspond to the height of a man (see figure 11). The presence of spherical elements could also be another point in common, but in the case of the classiiary we have even two of them and they are not positioned on the top (the object ends with the tip of a spear), but are placed just above the half of the shaft, in a point where we usually find the weights in the throwing javelins (Cascarino, 2008), so they could be weights for a *pilum*.

As an alternative to the simple practical use as weights, the presence in the object of these two spheres could be explained as an element for the recognition of the degree (as supposed before, an element unknown to us), or it could have an ornamental or parade function (therefore it would be considered as an object of official use, as previously supposed for the *loricae musculata*).

Figure 11. A comparison between the figure of the classiary with the one of optio Caelius Avitus, holding the astile

Obviously in both cases, due to lacking of both written evidence and a direct image comparison, we're still hypothetical.

For example, we can consider multiple functions for the same object if we consider it through its ambivalence, both as a weapon and as a symbol. As a matter of fact, if we carefully observe the object, this could be defined as the fusion of two very distinct elements: starting from the base up to the first sphere we have an astile, from the second sphere to the top a *pilum* with a spherical plumbing. Still supposing, the two spheres could be suitable bases to contain decorations or emblems: for instance in a detail of the *relief of the Chancellery*, datable to the I^st^ Century AD, where a *praetorian* guard soldier holds a *pilum* with a ball lead finely decorated with the figure of an eagle, therefore it could be a weapon with some possible ceremonial value (see figure 12).

If the object held in the hand of the class was in effect a simple weapon, that is a *pilum*, we do not know if the presence of two spheres (plumbings) had a particular impact on its use or some other practical function. Most of the documented *pila* have other types of seals or a single sphere, for this reason the idea of a weapon with a symbolic purpose can be evaluated.

A direct comparison that can confirm the existence of this poorly documented object could come from the funerary altar of the veteran soldier *Caio Metellio Costante*[35], datable to the IInd Century AD and coming from the territory of Reggio Emilia, therefore from not far away. The image of the deceased person on the altar holds in the right hand an object very similar to that held by the classiary: except for some details, such as the length and diameter of the shaft, slightly higher, or the presence of a point also at the base, this weapon also has the two superimposed spherical elements, positioned just above the middle of the shaft. Of the two spherical elements, the upper one is evident in its spherical shape, while the lower one is more difficult to define not only for the signs of aging, but also because it would seem

Figure 12. The object held by the classiary on the left, the detail of the pilum filling in the Chancery decoration on the right

to be surmounted by a ring with a drapery, that defines the curved sides of the sphere by falling down. Below the lower sphere, a narrowing of the lower part of the shaft is visible as if it was inserted directly into the sphere element. Such detail could indicate that the weapon was composed of several parts.

Even if the depiction of *Caio Metellio's* weapon gives us some more details, it still seems to be configured in the same way as that of the classiary, and could prove the existence of weapons with this characteristic plumbing. In a juxtaposition of the images we can see how in both cases the spheres are at the same height: if we draw a line they are located below the armpit of the figures, proving that these spheres had to be placed according to a precise rule and measure (see figure 13).

On the other hand, for the slight difference in length that can be seen for the upper part, which sees the weapon of the shorter classiary, the reason should be sought in that space problem, already encountered previously for the realization of the figure. The weapon in the right hand from the *classiary* ends with its tip on the top profile of the niche (delimited in turn by the frame), a compromise that led the artist to resize it in order to contain it. As a consequence of the space and the crushing of the weapon, the position of the hand holding it below the spheres also suggests that the artist had to deal with the limited space and had to find a solution even in this case: if the hand had been above the spheres, as in the position of *Caio Metellio* (with that slight twist of the arm and hand around the shaft, deduced from the models of the official art and used for the characters armed with spears), he would have occupied with the hand that little space between the upper sphere and the tip of the spear, hence compromising the reading of the weapon.

In the case of the *classiary*, the solution of placing the hand under the spheres, even if simpler and of lesser visual effect, solves the problem given by space without distorting the balance of the figure, and it aligns itself with other models of representations anyway.

CONCLUSIONS

This work highlights the importance of image analysis, stored in specialized and freely accessible databases. It is a work that simultaneously to the archaeological value represents a global vision from the point of view of the social sciences. This vision is achieved through the correct use of the direct observation technique and the comparison that has allowed to obtain novel results and with reduced costs, considering that the analysis corpus belongs to a millenary civilization. Besides, on the basis of the elements analysed on the *stele of the classiary* from Ravenna, we can definitely draw some conclusions and new interpretations on the work through a series of theories that could be confirmed in the future, if other finds are found comparable or completely similar in iconography.

An attempt was made to define some of these figurative elements based on a comparison with other finds, but it is clear that the only iconography present on the *stele of the classiary* is not attributable to an optio according to the data we possess, so it is only thanks to the epigraph that we can identify the subject portrayed on the stele.

With the exception of some common and only partially comparable elements, we can affirm that we are looking at a completely new and unprecedented image in the panorama of depictions of the Roman world, as it does not find any direct confirmation for all the elements present. As ascertained, the figure is attributable to the Roman military world for the presence of weapons, nevertheless it is not perceived by observing the rank occupied in the army or by its belonging to a specific unit, such as the fleet: only the epigraph is fundamental for its identification

Although it is possible to determine a classification of the find, its artistic style and the elements related to the production workshop, we can compare the *stele of the classiary* with other finds of the territory but not for the type of representation, mostly found in the finds of the provincial area rather than the local one.

Above all, we tried to read the image of the *classiary* by giving a meaning to its set of weapons and attributes, in order to explain why these did not reflect what we would have expected to see for an *optio*, not only through a material interpretation of the individual objects, but also through a symbolic one. An interpretation that sees in the image of the *classiary* not only a figure of the soldier in arms, but also a figure with the aim of transmitting a strong symbolic and celebratory meaning. Lastly, these results represent the need to have high professional training, from the theoretical, practical and technical perspective (use of new technologies but based on previously acquired knowledge, through reading and research) to make interesting discoveries, in the context of cultural heritage. The verification of the initial hypotheses and the conformation of the progressive conclusions in each of the steps followed, can serve as a model to generate innovative content. Content of archaeological excellence to be enhanced through the augmented reality of the latest generation interactive systems, accessible from museums or from school, home, library, etc., through the Internet.

Figure 13. The comparison between the image of the classiary and the one of veteran Caio Metellio. The similarity between the weapons both figures hold in their right hands should be noticed.

ACKNOWLEDGMENT

A special thanks to Prof. Dr. Francisco V. Cipolla Ficarra for his encouragement, Sara Carlini for assistance and help in translation and my family for support, especially my wife Elena, my mom Emma for his perseverance towards me and my daughters Siria and Olivia.

REFERENCES

Alston, R. (1999). Ties that bind: soldiers and societies. In A. Goldsworthy & I. Haynes (Eds.), *The Roman Army as Community. Academic Press.*

Azuma, R. (1997). A Survey of Augmented Reality. *Presence (Cambridge, Mass.), 6*(4), 355–385. doi:10.1162/pres.1997.6.4.355

Bianchi-Bandinelli, R. (1970). *Rome, la fin de l'art antique: l'art de l'Empire romain de Septime Sévère à Théodose*. Gallimard.

Bolter, J., Engberg, M., & Mcintyre, B. (2013). Media Studies, Mobile Augmented Reality, and Interaction Design. *Interaction, 20*(1), 37–45. doi:10.1145/2405716.2405726

Cascarino, G. (2008). L'esercito romano. Armamento e organizzazione.: Vol. II. *Da Augusto ai Severi*. Il Cerchio.

Cipolla-Ficarra, F. (2010). *Human-Computer Interaction, Tourism and Cultural Heritage*. Springer.

Cipolla-Ficarra, F. (2011). *Human-Computer Interaction, Tourism and Cultural Heritage*. Springer. doi:10.1007/978-3-642-18348-5

Cirelli E. (2008). *Ravenna: archeologia di una città*. Borgo San Lorenzo (Fi), All'Insegna del Giglio.

Ess, C. (2001). Culture, Technology, Communication: Towards an Intercultural Global Village. New York University Press.

Ferkiss, V. (1994). *Nature, Technology, and Society: The Cultural Roots of the Current Environmental Crisis*. New York University Press.

Franzoni C. (1987). *Habitus atque habitudo militis: monumenti funerari di militari nella Cisalpina romana*. Roma: L'Erma di Bretschneider.

Goldsworthy, A. (1996). *The Roman Army at War, 100 BC-AD 200*. Clarendon Press.

Harrell, D., & Lim, C. (2017). Reimagining the Avatar Dream: Modeling Social Identity in Digital Media. *Communications of the ACM, 60*(7), 50–61. doi:10.1145/3098342

Hope, V. M. (2001). *Constructing Identity: the Roman funerary monuments of Aquileia, Mainz and Nîmes*. Oxford: British Archaeological Report: International Series.

Kleiner, D. (1977). *Roman Group Portraiture: the funerary reliefs of the late Republic and early Empire*. Garland.

Kleiner, D. (1987). *Roman Imperial Funerary Altars with Portraits*. G. Bretschneider.

Koller, D., Frischer, B., & Humphreys, G. (2009). Research challenges for digital archives of 3D cultural heritage models. *ACM Journal on Computing and Cultural Heritage, 2*(3), 1–17. doi:10.1145/1658346.1658347

Koo, S., Kim, J., Kim, C., Kim, J., & Cha, H. S. (2020). Development of an Augmented Reality Tour Guide for a Cultural Heritage Site. *ACM Journal on Computing and Cultural Heritage, 12*(4), 1–24. doi:10.1145/3317552

Lazarinis, F. (2010). *Handbook of Research on Technologies and Cultural Heritage: Applications and Environments*. IGI Global.

Le Bohec Y. (1989). *L'armée romaine sous le Haut-Empire*. Paris: Picard éditeur.

Mansuelli, G. A. (1967). *Le stele romane del territorio ravennate e del basso Po*. Longo Editore.

Mansuelli, G. A. (1971). *Urbanistica e architettura della Cisalpina romana fino al III secolo*. Latomus.

Marshall, C., & Shipman, F. (2017). Who Owns the Social Web? *Communications of the ACM*, *60*(5), 36–42. doi:10.1145/2996181

Mauro, M., & ... . (2001). *Ravenna romana*. Adriapress.

Mccarthy, J., Sebo, E., Wilkinson, B., & Sheehan, F. (2020). Open Workflows for Polychromatic Reconstruction of Historical Sculptural Monuments in 3D. *ACM Journal on Computing and Cultural Heritage*, *13*(3), 1–16. doi:10.1145/3386314

Nektarios, K., & Xenos, M. (2012). Usability Evaluation of Augmented Reality Systems. *Intelligent Decision Technologies*, *6*(2), 139–149. doi:10.3233/IDT-2012-0130

Oliveira, A. (2017). *The Digital Mind: How Science is Redefining Humanity*. MIT Press. doi:10.7551/mitpress/9780262036030.001.0001

Rasheed, N. A., & Nordin, M. J. (2015). A Survey of Computer Methods in Reconstruction of 3D Archaeological Pottery Objects. *International Journal of Advanced Research*, *3*(3), 712–714.

Smith, L. (2004). *Archaeological Theory and the Politics of Cultural Heritage*. Routledge. doi:10.4324/9780203307991

Susini, G. (1973). *The Roman Stonecutter*. Blackwell.

Veltman, K. (2006). *Understanding New Media: Augmented Knowledge and Culture*. University of Calgary Press. doi:10.2307/j.ctv6gqs2k

Von Hesberg, H. (1992). *Römische Grabbauten*. Wissenschaftliche Buchgesellschaft.

Vote, E., Feliz, D. A., Laidlaw, D. H., & Joukowsky, M. S. (2002). Discovering Petra: Archaeological Analysis in VR. *IEEE Computer Graphics and Applications*, *22*(5), 38–50. doi:10.1109/MCG.2002.1028725

Zanker, P. (1988). *The Power of Images in the Age of Augustus*. University of Michigan Press. doi:10.3998/mpub.12362

ADDITIONAL READING

Bianchi-Bandinelli, R. (1965). Il ritratto nella antichità. In Enciclopedia dell'arte antica classica e orientale, volume VI. Roma: Istituto della Enciclopedia italiana.

Bollini, M. (1990). La fondazione di Classe e la comunità classiaria. In G. Susini (Ed.), *L'evo antico*. Marsilio.

Cannon, A., Bartel, B., Bradley, R., Chapman, R. W., Curran, M. L., Humphreys, S. C., Morris, I., Quilter, J., Rothschild, N. A., & Runnels, C. (1989). The historical dimension in mortuary expressions of status and sentiment. *Current Anthropology*, *30*(4), 437–457. doi:10.1086/203764

Fasold, P. (1998). *Bestattungsitte und kulturelle Identität. Grabanlagen und Grabbeigaben der frühen römischen Kaiserzeit in Italien und den nordwest Provinzen*. Rheinland-Verlag.

Franchini, F. (2011). Opinabilità dell'archeologia: dubbi e certezze sull'ultima stele rinvenuta a Classe. In Il romagnolo: mensile di storia e tradizione della provincia ravennate, monthly newspaper. Madonna dell'Albero (Ra), Il romagnolo.

Hope, V. M. (2003). Remembering Rome: memory, funerary monuments and the Roman soldier. In H. Williams (Ed.), *Archaeologies of remembrance: death and memory in past societies* (pp. 113–140). Kluwer Academic/Plenum Publishers. doi:10.1007/978-1-4419-9222-2_6

Larsen, P., & Logan, W. (2018). *World Heritage and Sustainable Development: New Directions in World Heritage Management*. Routledge. doi:10.4324/9781315108049

Maioli, M. G. (1990). La topografia della zona di Classe. In G. Susini (Ed.), *L'evo antico*. Marsilio.

Mansuelli, G. A. (1967). Geografia e storia di Ravenna antica. In Corsi di cultura sull'arte ravennate e bizantina. Faenza-Ravenna: F.lli Lega.

Ortalli, J. (1997). Monumenti e architetture sepolcrali di età romana in Emilia Romagna. In *Mirabella Roberti M., Monumenti sepolcrali romani in Aquileia e nella Cisalpina: atti della XXVI Settimana di studi aquileiesi*. Editreg.

Oxholm, G., & Nishino, K. (2013). A flexible approach to reassembling thin artifacts of unknown geometry. *Journal of Cultural Heritage*, *14*(1), 51–61. doi:10.1016/j.culher.2012.02.017

Pasi-Rondinelli, M. (2006-2007). La zona archeologica di Classe: e il ritrovamento dell'eccezionale Stele funeraria del Classiario. In Rumagna: aspetti della storia, della cultura, della tradizione, periodical newspaper. Lugo-Ravenna: Walberti.

Rosetti E. & Pivato S., Matteucci C., (1995). *La Romagna: geografia e storia*. Imola: University press Bologna.

Rusell, R. (1975). *The armour of Imperial Rome*. Scribner.

Scarpellini D., (1987). *Stele romane con imagines clipeatae in Italia*. Roma: L'Erma di Bretschneider.

Susini, G. (1965). Le officine lapidarie romane di Ravenna. In Corsi di cultura sull'arte ravennate e bizantina. Faenza-Ravenna: F.lli Lega.

Susini, G. (1968). Un catalogo classiario ravennate. In Studi romagnoli. Faenza-Ravenna: F.lli Lega.

Veltman, K. (1997). Frontiers in Electronic Media. *Interaction*, *4*(4), 32–64. doi:10.1145/259330.259353

Weapons and Warfare - History and Hardaware of Warfare. (2015). *1: Montanus Capito, Optio of the liburna "Aurata"; second half of 1st century*, In *Misenum*, from https://weaponsandwarfare.com/2015/10/11/misenum/

Weber, G. W. (2014). Another Link between Archaeology and Anthropology: Virtual anthropology. *Digital Applications in Archaeology and Cultural Heritage*, *1*(1), 3–11. doi:10.1016/j.daach.2013.04.001

Woodwark, J. (1991). Reconstructing History with Computer Graphics. *IEEE Computer Graphics and Applications*, *11*(1), 18–20. doi:10.1109/38.67693

KEY TERMS & DEFINITIONS

Cultural Heritage: "It is the legacy of physical artefacts ad intangible attributes of a group or society that are inherid from past generations, maintained in the present and bestowed for the benefit of future generations." (UNESCO definition)

Digital Cultural Heritage: A collection of images, textual, video, etc., information with a remote access through Internet (e.g., EDCS, ARACHNE and PATER). The digital content and materials present and describe human knowledge and cultural manifestations. Although there is a constant evolution from capture to storage in 2D or 3D image format, for example.

Architectural Steles: a large block of parallelepiped stone and decorated with sculptural reliefs, both figurative and architectural (usually to define aedicules culminating in a tympanum). On the other hand, a series of simple poorly decorated stone slabs, usually with engravings, called a "framed" slab or "anarchietectonic" steles.

Stele of the Classiary: is a type of epigraphic and figurative elements also to date it. Some models underlying its creation and the clues that testify to the interventions of the workshop and the client.

Reconstruction from Multiple Digital Images: is to infer the 2D / 3D geometry and structure of objects, scenes, people, etc., from one or multiple 2D / 3D images, for example, 2D / 3D digital photography, 2D / 3D scanner, 3D printer, etc.

Ineractive System: It is a computer device made up by a CPU (Central Processing Unit) and peripheral, whose functioning requires a constant interaction with end user. Currently these systems tend to their miniaturization and / or invisibility, the mobility and wireless connectability among them.

ENDNOTES

1 The ancient path of these rivers can still be seen in the names of some streets of today's urban plan. Over time, these rivers were also the cause of the progressive silting of the lagoon with the sedimentation phenomenon, a reason that led to the displacement of the current beach line and the closure of the various river outlets to the sea; furthermore, we must also consider the process of subsidence, a typical phenomenon for the Ravenna area, that is the natural lowering of the ground towards the aquifer, a problem that also directly affects buildings.

2 Strab., *Geogr.*, V, 1, 7.

3 Ancient historians already had conflicting opinions on the origins of Ravenna and to which territory and people they should have been linked to. According to Strabo, it was a colony of Greeks (of Pelasgians or Thessalians) in the territory of the Umbrians and the colony passed over time under these; on the other hand, the geographer Tolomeo placed Ravenna in the territory of the Galli Boi and attributed its Celtic origin, a presence also remembered by his contemporary Appiano.

The most ancient archaeological finds would place the origin of Ravenna between the IV and III centuries BC.

4 Cicero defines the city of Ravenna as *foederata*, that is an ally of Rome and not as its colony; Pro Balbo, 22, 50.

5 Tac., *Ann.*, IV, 5.

6 During Trajan's Dacian campaigns (101-106 AD), the *Classis Ravennatis* was involved in the transport of troops and provisions; thousands of soldiers settled in the port area and began contributing to the formation of this suburban nucleus. Furthermore, Trajan also donated a large aqueduct to the city.

7 The name of Classe was kept even after the movement of the imperial fleet from Ravenna to Constantinople in 330 AD and for the subsequent Byzantine period (the town is even depicted with its name in the VIth Century AD mosaics of the Basilica of Sant'Apollinare Nuovo in Ravenna).

8 The discovery and identification of burial areas is very complicated for Ravenna. Already in ancient times, the environmental conditions of the territory made it difficult to identify areas suitable for this function, as the building land was limited, and for this reason few necropolises are identified and documented.

9 These steles were suitable for a larger clientele being relatively simpler to produce, because they gave more prominence to the text rather than to the images, which is why there are more findings for this type of stele; the only enriching element that can be seen in these steles is the choice of materials: the architectural steles are almost always blocks of Istrian stone, while those with a framed slap, especially starting from the IInd Century AD, they are made of marble, much more suitable for making thin and sturdy slabs.

10 This made it possible to draw up a list of boats, by type and name, which served in the *Classis Ravennatis*.

11 In the Ancient and Roman world, it was normal to think about how to make the personal burial monument when someone was still alive; even an important person like Augustus did the same for the construction of his mausoleum.

12 For example, in the stele of *Ulcia Glapirya* (Appendix - Figure 14), preserved in the National Museum of Ravenna, it is the antonine hairstyle present in the portrait of the deceased person that provides an element of dating to the IInd Century AD, but in the stele there is not the usual formula *D M* that is seen starting from this century, so there may be exceptions.

13 This could indicate two important things, regarding the work of the workshop that made the stele. The first one is that the figure must have been made starting from the top downwards, since the figure goes beyond the lower part of the frame; the second one is that there were two phases of production of the work: from a prefabricated block with the only architectural parts (from a ready-made model) the figure was subsequently executed, because this cuts the pre-existing frame. Afterthoughts or changes wished by the client already under realization: the prefabricated block chosen, most likely, should not have been designed for a full figure, but only for a portrait, like most of the architectural steles found in the area.

14 A dating of the Ravenna altar would attribute it to the period of Claudius, and therefore included in the building interventions promoted in the city that took place during his reign; a clue for this dating would come from the central figure attributed to Augustus as he is barefoot, a sign that he has already ascended to the divine after death.

15 Some Renaissance artists, such as Palladio, made drawings of *Porta Aurea* (Appendix – Figure 15) before its demolition, for this reason we know its two-arched aspect; fragments of the monumental gate are preserved in the National Museum of Ravenna, including the stone clipei (round discs decorated in relief) that decorated it (Appendix – Figure 16), also a clear example of the artistic value that came from the Roman capital in the early Imperial period.

16 The *loricae musculata* was widely adopted by the Italic peoples and consequently by the Romans; usually composed of two parts held together by laces, straps or hinges, it would pass from simple flat or slightly curved metal plates, from musculature rendered with sketch and incisions, to more elaborate products with cantilevered reliefs that imitate classical statuary.

17 Highly decorated models are widely documented by the iconography of the Imperial period, especially for the loricated images of the emperors. Used for parades and certainly expensive, they could be decorated with embossed figures or metal applications to convey messages like an artistic work. Many remains of statues of emperors, without the head, are recognizable through the *loricae* they wore.

18 These artworks are the commemorative *frieze of the battle of Actium* (Appendix – Figure 17) and the fragment of a relief from the *Temple of Fortuna Primigenia in Praeneste* (Appendix – Figure 18). In both reliefs, especially in the second one, many of the soldiers depicted in anatomical armor could be of Hellenic origin, in some cases a differentiation perhaps intended precisely to distinguish the Ptolemaic allies from the Roman troops of Marco Antonio and Octavian. In any case, the reliefs attest to a use of these armor also in the naval field.

19 On this point too there are many elements to keep in mind. We know that some legions were formed precisely by the direct recruitment of the *classiarii* of the navy of Miseno and Ravenna: As per the events related to the civil war of 68-69 AD for the conquest of the imperial title which ended in favor of Vespasian, it is believed that his success was also obtained through the use of the *classiarii* on land; following this event, many of them formed two legions, the I *Adiutrix* and II *Adiutrix*, which were stationed in Pannonia (Tac., Hist., III, 41). This shows us that the classiarii were trained in ground combat, and even in times of peace they were employed not only for logistical tasks, but also for police and control of the internal territory. Therefore, their armament had to follow that of the legionaries: for example, in one of the reliefs that make up the arch of Constantine in Rome, coming from a work referable to the period of Marcus Aurelius (IInd Century AD), a soldier is depicted wearing a *loricae segmentata* and holding a shield with symbologies linked to the sea and attributable to legions I and II *Auditrix* (Appendix – Figure 19); in a funerary stele dedicated to a soldier called *Septimus*, *optio* of the *legio* I *Adiutrix*, datable between the end of the IInd Century AD and the early IIIrd Century AD, there is a scene of a melee in relief, a Roman soldier fighting in the foreground wearing a *loricae musculata* (Appendix – Figure 20); also in these examples we have other evidence linking this type of armament to the navy, if compared with the images present in the friezes mentioned in note 16.

20 Along with anatomical armors of metal alloy, it is not excluded that there were economic models in shaped leather.

21 It must be considered that the *Classis Ravennatis*, like the *Classis Misenensis*, was elevated over time to the rank of *Praetoria*, in defense of the emperor, and was renamed *Classis Praetoria Ravennatis Pia Vindex*, around the second half of the I[st] Century AD probably at the behest of the emperor Domitian.

22 In some funerary steles of soldiers, the unworn equipment is often shown framed or suspended in the background as hung. An example could be the stele of *Severius Acceptus*, from the IInd Century AD (Appendix – Figure 21).

23 Image to the annexes (Appendix – Figure 22).

24 Image to the annexes (Appendix – Figure 23).

25 To give examples, if one had opted for a half-length figuration, similar to most of the local cases, the figure on the *stele of the classiary* could have appeared as the stele of the *centurion Marco Celio* (Appendix – Figure 24) in Bologna or the stele of *Caius Largennius* (Appendix – Figure 25) in Lucca.

26 The expedient of making the figure interact with some architectural elements and the surrounding space is often found in steles. This gave the idea that the depicted figure was alive and really in front of the observer. An example, also very similar to the case of the *classiary* as the figure's setting, is the stele of *Licaius* auxiliary soldier of the *cohors* I *Pannoniorum* (dating back to the age of Claudius, Ist Century AD), where the spear of the deceased person follows the profile of the niche but then comes out in a realistic way, instead of being contained within the architecture (Appendix – Figure 26).

27 The *gladius* is worn on the opposite side from, for example, troop soldiers. Usually the soldiers belonging to the cohorts are represented in the artworks with the *gladius* on the right side, there are different interpretations on this positioning of the *gladius* especially for the legionaries, this can be linked to a practical factor for combat as well as to a custom determined by other factors.

28 An arrangement very similar to the raffiguration of the soldier in the stele of *Septimus*, *optio* of the *legio* I *Adiutrix* (Appendix – Figure 20).

29 Image to the annexes (Appendix – Figure 27).

30 Image to the annexes (Appendix – Figure 28).

31 Image to the annexes (Appendix – Figure 29).

32 Polib., VI, 24, 2.; we also have other similar information from Varro.

33 This helmet, for the period of the *classiary*, could have been of the Gallic type "I": in brass and datable between the Ist Century AD and the IIIrd Century AD we have an artifact from the site of *Mogontiacum*, and it was owned by a soldier named *L. Lucretius Celeris*, who also belonged to the *legio* I *Adiutrix*; on this helmet perhaps a longitudinal crest could have been fixed, but above all there are the seats to fix the two feathers on the sides, which could indicate that it was an *Optio* (Appendix – Figure 30). Also interesting is the stele belonging to a soldier, *Caius Castricius Victor* of the *legio* II *Adiutrix* (datable to the Ist Century AD) where there seems to be a helmet with two feathers on the sides, but the relief is not clear (Appendix – Figure 31).

34 Image to the annexes (Appendix – Figure 32).

35 Image to the annexes (Appendix – Figures 33, 34 and 35)

APPENDIX: EXAMPLES

Figure 14.

Figure 15.

Figure 16.

Figure 17.

Figure 18.

Figure 19.

Figure 20.

Figure 21.

Figure 22.

Figure 23.

Figure 24.

Figure 25.

Figure 26.

Figure 27.

Figure 28.

Figure 29.

Figure 30.

Figure 31.

Figure 32.

Figure 33.

Figure 34.

Figure 35.

Conclusion

Throughout the pages it has been possible to verify the past, present and future of those areas that we consider fundamental for qualitative web engineering in the third millennium. Each of the works presented forms a compass rose for all those who have got lost with the siren song from the depths of the web. The correct and democratizing initial process of the 20th century Internet has been almost totally distorted, with the rise of the social networks, in the 21st century. For example, a trivial and fun idea, a priori, such as generating a virtual community among young students, through the dissemination of their photographs, some personal data, sentimental issues, etc., today has become an entire international corporation, which is included in the triad of world-wide billionaires. That is, together with one of the main software companies (a pioneer in operating systems for personal computers), and the largest representative of electronic commerce and potential manager of the Internet of Things (IoT). Simply put, we are referring to Facebook, Microsoft, and Amazon.

Social media applications are using and updating all the evolutionary components and attributes of computing, such as: interface design, algorithms for compression and decompression of multimedia files. And free access to databases through the different operating systems for the latest generation mobile telephony, the viewing with high definition of real and virtual images in 2D / 3D, among many other resources, which continue to draw the attention of millions of users and software developers, all over the planet. The only problem is the distorted quantification of the communication quality that the large pioneering multinationals in the ICT (Information and Communication Technology) sector try to emulate.

Many universities and their corresponding R&D (Research and Development) laboratories have become mere mercantilist agents, leaving aside the epistemological principles of science and the social and development value of education, from the theoretical and practical point of view. In this sense, it is enough to consider the cult of visual narcissism and the statistics derived from publications in online databases, subsidized directly and indirectly by the taxpayers, through taxes in the EU and UK, to name a geographical area. Some examples are: the cult of Hirsch's index (H-index), Egghe's index (G-index), I10-index (H-10), etc., in Google Scholar and the Web of Science, the counter in the databases university institutions based in Germany, USA, etc.: Digital Bibliography and Library Project (DBLP), the ordered list (descending order) of the supposed main experts or scientists of a nation (www.guide2research.com), among many other escamotages (retractions), some derived from manipulation of information on the web. The common denominator can be summed up in the prevailing slavery in certain research teams in the formal sciences, the incorrect algorithms that do not differentiate between counters and accumulators, the statistics rigged in advance, the press offices related to the same individuals or experts, the persuaders dynamics, influencers of social networks, the loss of power of the traditional media (basically, press, radio, and TV) within fully aligned real and / or virtual communities, among other components.

The purpose is to show and raise awareness, in the face of the potential social damage of criminals or digital criminals.

The main objective is to generate false realities on the Internet such as fake news that negatively affect the real fabric of production, education, health, etc., of local and global communities, with the need to resort to fact checking, for example. They are very easy to detect through simple heuristic evaluation techniques and methods. Their results put us in front of groups of individuals (Garduñians) or persuasive agents whose mission is to create mirages of reality; generate immutable systems and structures on the web, over time; slow down the solution of the technological gap among the members of the community, and enhance a "glocal" (global + local) social gap (many of these investigations, experiments, etc., are aimed at solving questions thousands of kilometers away, which are indisputably alien to the dwellers of the community, who fund such research). An example are international events (workshops, congresses, symposiums, webinars, etc.) among friends from R&D projects, related to web engineering, information retrieval, advanced visual interfaces, etc. This is briefly the context observed and verified, since the beginning of the democratizing process of the Internet. Consequently, quality on the web remains the great unfinished business in the 21st century, especially in the quantic-nanotechnological-self-sufficient era.

One of the traditional ways of addressing the issue of software quality components in an interactive system is through the use of the notion of the iceberg, with the classic division into internal factors (mode of access to online data, organization of content, etc.) and external factors (use of fonts, colors, illustrations, etc. in the interfaces; ease in obtaining high communication between different types of end users, etc.). To these factors must be added the temporal context, the spatial context, and the human or social factor. The latter is the case of group formation. The human or social factor, depending on behavior, generates a new factor, which can encompass the entire structure or architecture of the system. It is the "G" factor (G = Garduña), which reduces the quality of operation of all computerized systems and their connections (internet, intranet, extranet and ethernet).

The iceberg of the web, currently and graphically, is usually divided into three large areas or sectors: World Wide Web or *surface*, *deep* and *dark*. On the *surface* is the part that is visible and accessible to all end users since it does not require any password, such as websites, Wikipedia, search engines (Ask, Bing, Google, Naver, etc.), e-commerce (Amazon, Alibaba, eBay, etc.), the various social networking applications (LinkedIn, Facebook, Flickr, Instagram, Pinterest, etc., which at the beginning did not require the use of passwords), among others. In the area called *deep*, its existence is verified but it is not freely accessible as it is necessary to enter a password (as currently required by some social media applications). Some examples related to citizens are information academy, medical records, criminal records, financial reports, business intranets, etc.

The *dark* area is made up of portals that use public networks but that require special software or browser to access them and are not found in the main online search engines, in order to guarantee anonymity. In this area, the main users are financial, political, religious among other individuals, who in isolation or in groups, legal and illegal, manage the glocal power of finance, religion, politics, education, health, etc. However, in our days, in that iceberg it is necessary to represent the G factor inside. It acts as a kind of elevator that goes up and down, through the three main areas of the iceberg: surface, deep and dark.

This elevator represents a set of central forces that move freely and immune, influencing each of the systematic and structural aspects of the web. In other words, these forces occupy the central part of the web and expand without limits, throughout the network, changing the spherical shape of the Internet, which traditionally simulated the globe, to an ellipsoid torus. Since the end of the 20th century, these forces have drilled or pierced the sphere, from the two poles, generating a vertical internal space, with

Figure 1. Classic representation of quality in software and all its derivations, including web engineering

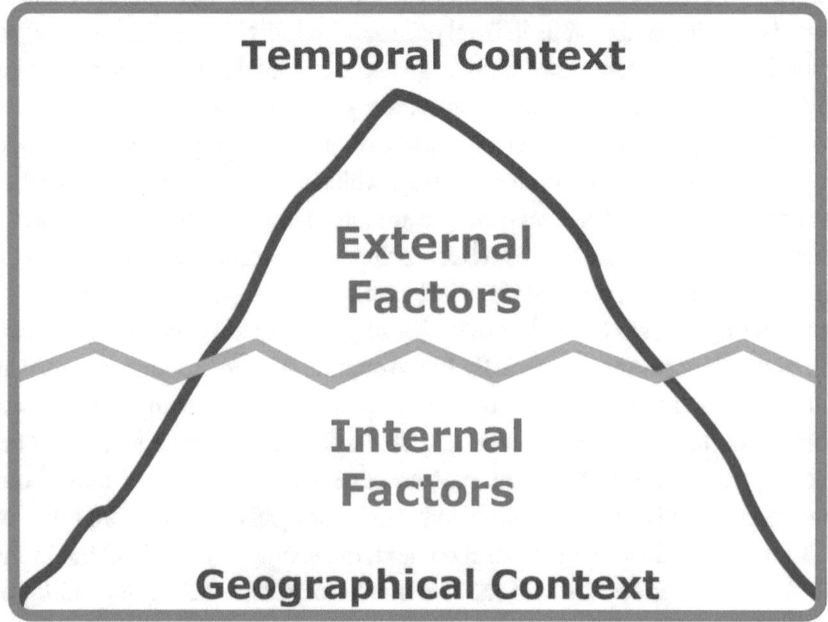

an elliptical hyperboloid geometric shape. This new way of representing the real web has its epicenter at the poles of the former sphere, which ideally represented the global village of the communication defined by McLuhan, the worldwide web by Tim Berners-Lee, etc.

This change in shape is a consequence of the spread of high-resolution screens (basically, the latest generation mobile telephony), the rise of social networks and the concentration of information in databases (mainly, search engines). Three elements that are almost essential for daily life, inside and outside the city. Schematically, the dark area gradually absorbs the deep area, and vice versa. This abnormal phenomenon is directly related to an eternal dilemma for humanity in the face of new information and communication technologies, which in Latin is usually summarized with the rhetorical question: ***"Quis cutodiet ipsos custodes?"*** (Who will watch the watchmen?") From the Roman poet Juvenal in his Satires (Satire VI, lines 347–348). The answer is ***nobody***.

Such a statement can be seen in the collection of examples in the annexes, which in a tragicomic way is summarized in the following comic figure. It is an image that synthesizes the free growth of the negative or anomalous human factor in the new technologies; the loss of the epistemology of the sciences related to computer and systems engineering, software and all its derivations; the infinite expansion of the limits of human-computer interaction, web engineering, information retrieval, etc., from the agents of the formal sciences, such as mathematics and physics, to name a couple of examples.

Now, not everything in computing is human-computer interaction, web engineering, information retrieval, etc. In the same way, not all human knowledge is digitized or found on the Internet. Currently and in this context, end users are in a state of total helplessness. They are only allowed to have the three

Figure 2. The web, the global village, etc. in the collective imagination of humanity. Sphere with nodes and links that interrelate all human beings, artificial intelligence and the various technological components connected to the network.

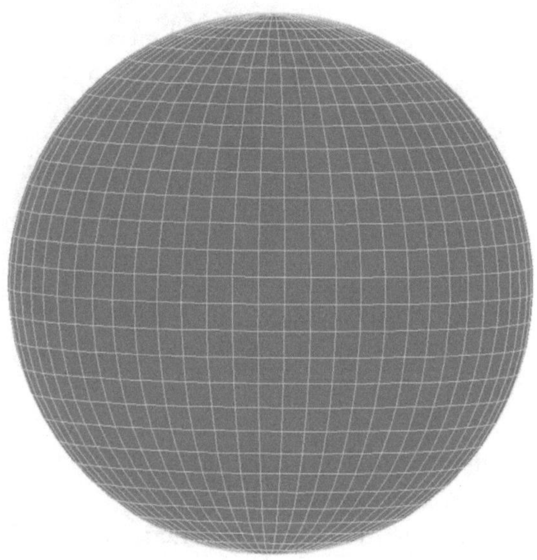

positions of Mafalda (www.quino.com.ar) in figure 5. These positions represent a direct and immutable reference to the ancient culture of the Far East, but today applicable to the rest of the planet.

However, the present research work does not intend to change the world or implement a new international "general data protection regulation", in the face of an unalterable reality that lasts for millennia. The pedagogical intention is to draw attention to the loss of quality in the multimedia contents of interactive communications, for example, since little by little, the origins of the Internet have been distorted. A fact that can cause irreversible damage in future generations, such as: the inability to work independently, the development of free will, the promotion of creative capacity, the motivation towards scientific knowledge, the ability to perform mental calculations, the interest in serious reading, among many other skills and experiences, innate or acquired by the human being. Exceptionally, the positive aspects of graphic arts creativity have been maintained from interactive multimedia to mixed reality, both in design and in content, moving away from commercial clichés such as: "human emotions", "user friendly","user experience","cognitive neuroscience", "accessibility", "gamification", "collaborative learning", etc.

Now, isolating itself from these human factors and focusing on the technical aspect of web engineering, the future can be represented as a horizontal line with a positive angular coefficient that represents growth in constant evolution, with revolutionary peaks, coming from the hardware. The acronym IoE (Internet of Everything) together with artificial intelligence and quantum computing will mark a new milestone on the Internet. It is the voluntary or programmed connection of "everything", through the smartphone, such as NFC (Near Filed Communication). However, new lines of research aim to overcome

Figure 3. Deformation of the web in the face of negative human factors

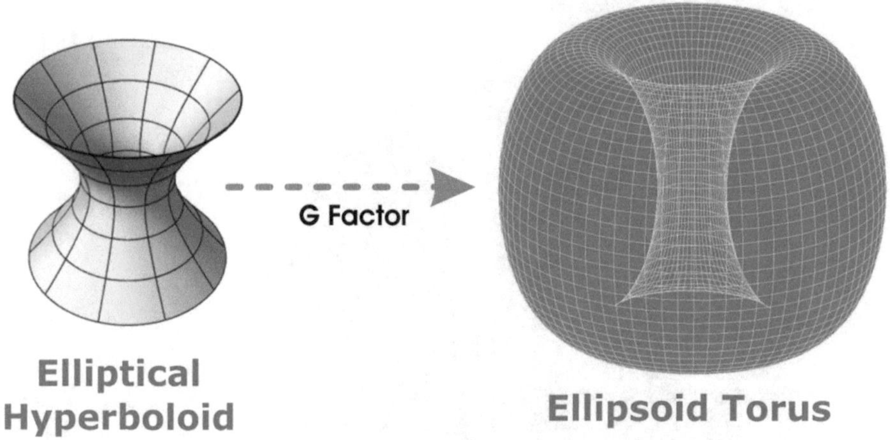

audiovisual and tactile contact to communicate through the brain, as are numerous studies carried out within neurology and the brain-computer interface (BCI).

Some studies that undoubtedly move away from the science fiction of visualizing in 3D, the dreams of the subconscious of people, artificial intelligence, supercomputers, etc. such as HAL 9000 (Heuristically Programmed Algorithmic Computer) from the novel (and film) "2001: A Space Odyssey" (Arthur C. Clarke). Science fiction and comics continue to be an inspiring source for creativity in audiovisual arts, 3D animation, innovative design, etc. Therefore, the roles of Web Architect, Web Designer, Web Master, Web community, etc., will remain valid and in persistent progression. The main objective of all of them is to get away from the standardization or automation in the creation of portals or websites, through the corporations that control the storage of information, through search engines. If the latter were to happen, it would entail the loss of wealth derived from the identity and idiosyncrasy of each of the online portals.

In the development of applications for the web, quality attributes (coherence, efficiency, flexibility, robustness, readability, portability, etc.) coming from software engineering, continue to be essential to improve applications related to interfaces, databases, dynamic information media, etc. Therefore, programming languages such as Java, JavaScript, Python, C, C ++, PHP, Swift, Visual Basic .Net, SQL, among others, will continue to be essential in the evolution of web engineering.

However, in this process of continuity we should focus on the technical aspects of programming, leaving aside: the elaboration of models, metamodels, approaches, ontologies, taxonomies, methodological guidelines, paradigms, protocols, platforms, semantics or other types of works, which usually only remain in the realization of a state of the art, bibliography review or update (many without considering the space-time-technological context of the time), or a work-in-progress, etc. All of them will be left unfinished in the end. That is, from the point of view of the epistemology of the sciences, they are a set of sketches, written according to the style guides of computing, HCI, UX, artificial intelligence, etc., but that only serve to increase the counter of the total publications of their authors and / or co-authors in

Figure 4. Gardunians's elevator that goes up and down, through the web iceberg

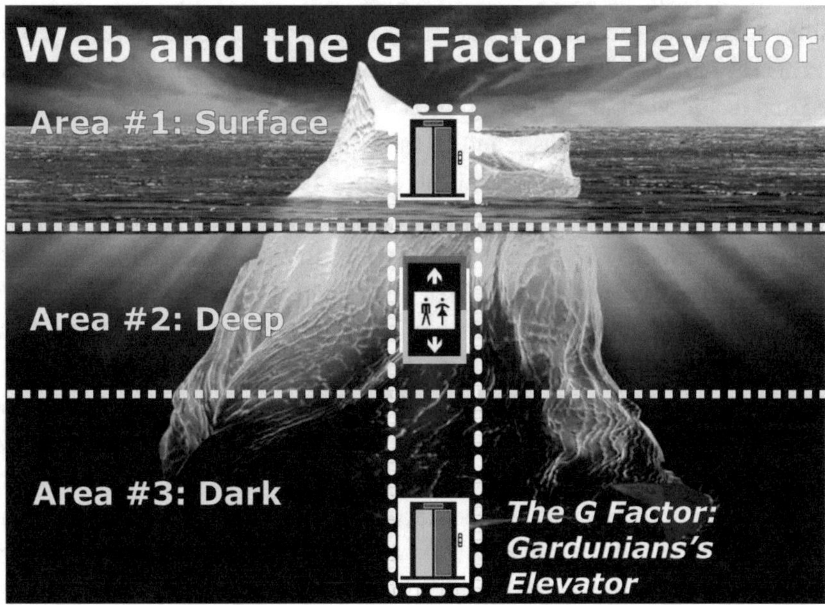

online databases (basically German, American and Dutch), since they do not provide reliable or 100% verified results, as well as new visions, challenges or horizons in the long term, in the central aspects of web engineering, multimedia, augmented reality, mixed reality, recommender systems, etc.

Besides, many individuals at the top of those lists, alone or autonomously, are not able to configure a server, a firewall, program in Assembler, C, Delphi, Java, JavaScript, PHP, SQL, etc., or use applications for multimedia publishing (Corel Draw, Dreamweaver), computer graphics and animation (Rhino, Maya, Lumion 3D Rendering, SolidWorks, etc.), audiovisual editing (Adobe Premiere Pro, Lightworks, Avidemux, etc.) and a long etc. Although they belong to the group of European lifelong civil servants, such as full professors, associate professors, etc., of masters, doctorates, post-doctorates, etc. This is

Figure 5. An international comic character such as Mafalda, perfectly illustrates with his various positions the state of the art of the user in front of the large Internet corporations and their main online applications, culturally linking with the three wise monkeys from the Far East

the reason why in countless university study centers they promote inter / trans / multi / intra / extra /... disciplinarity among their students of the new technologies.

Before concluding, our eternal gratitude goes to all those who are no longer with us due to the Covid-19 pandemic: Prof. Dr. Kim H. Veltman. Once again, thank you very much for your life teachings, all the help received and the good times we have shared.

Without forgetting or ever forgiving sadism and all the injustices that you have suffered, directly and indirectly, for more than a quarter of a century, in the completion of a doctorate "walking for a long decade", at various Spanish universities and "without a real guide in Spain or any European tutoring". Interestingly, many of those European PhD pseudo-tutors, who only like to appear in the acknowledgments section in student research papers, belong to the field of mathematics and computer science, for example.

In a quarter of a century, its metamorphosis from the field of formal sciences (mathematics or physics) towards human-computer interaction, UX, design, etc. has been seen, not only in the educational field, but also related to medicine. The reason for the anomaly is the intrusion and destruction of the social sciences, coupled with intellectual comfort. That is, to avoid the questions that involve using neurons to solve basic questions or not, related to the field of study itself. Some examples are the analysis of the complexity of algorithms, quantum computing, the development of algorithms for computer security, etc., or trying to find the solution to the main problems of the millennium: Riemann hypothesis, P versus NP problem, Birch and Swinnerton-Dyer conjecture, Hodge conjecture, Navier-Stokes equation, Yang-Mills theory, and Poincaré conjecture –www.bbc.com. Through HCI, UX, Web Enginering, etc., and the network derived from the G Factor, is an easy way to increase publications and see the counters increase rapidly in Hirsch's index (H-index), Egghe's index (G-index), I10-index (H-10), **index** Impact, etc., in Google Scholar, Web of Science, Mendeley, etc.

With the passing of time, keeping up dignity, freedom and resistance to the G Factor, together excepcional professionals (i.e., prof. Dr. Kim H. Veltman), this germ has transformed all dysfunctions into a single function: to form a team of excellence of human beings in the new technologies, distributed in the four cardinal points of the planet. All of them make up the vital "kernel" of our activities, in a modest and honest way, as has been the compilation and realization of this book of research.

Across the time of preparing this compilation of research works we have lost the company and guidance of wise professors such as Enrico Bianco, Mario Bunge, Jennifer Brown, Andrea Carminati, Tomás Maldonado, Teresa Marinovic, Luca Paganelli, Ana Pérez, Marcela Ríos, Federico Rodríguez, Marta Romero, Lucia Serra, Mark Thompson, Kim Veltman and Laura Zamora. Some of them have left us prematurely due to the coronavirus. We want to thank all of them infinitely for their kindness in transmitting their wisdom. In addition, the sign of healthy and true friendship, in the unforgettable moments shared for decades. Our gratitude from the soul and the mind, to all of them for their teachings and samples of kindness received.

We close these pages, with the following set of famous quotes, hoping that they can guide and motivate you in everyday life: "*The two most important days in your life are the day you are born and the day you find out why*" (Mark Twain); "*Logic will get you from A to Z; Imagination will get you everywhere*" (Albert Einstein); "*If you obey all the rules you will miss the fun*" (Katherine Hepburn); "*The best and most beautiful things in the world cannot be seen or even touched. They must be felt with the heart*" (Helen Keller); "*You cannot shake hands with a clenched fist*" (Indira Gandhi); "*To improve is to change; to be perfect is to change often*" (Winston Churchill); and "*You may never know what results come of your actions, but if you do nothing, there will be no results*" (Mahatma Gandhi).

Appendix: The "G" Factor in the Web, New Technologies, and Education

ABSTRACT

The appendix presents the first notions related to the G factor and the intersection with education and new information and communication technologies (NICT). A set of new terms are also introduced to describe this international phenomenon –in English (Gardunia, Gardunians, Gardunially, and Gardunying), whose origin is in medieval Spain, the members and the method used in its operation or way of acting. There is a brief historical description of the term and its use in the new millennium. At the end, a series of true cases are included, which interrelate university education, emerging technologies and the use of interactive systems with the didactic purpose of analyzing the actions and their consequences.

INTRODUCTION

The letter "G" refers to the Spanish term Garduña (it is not a G value or the dimensionless magnetic moment in physics, for example). The Garduña or *Gardunia* (a new term in English) is a mythical criminal secret society of medieval Europe, based in Toledo (Spain). Its structure has had a great diffusion in the old and new world, until today. This grouping is the origin of the terms *camorra, 'ndrangheta, mafia, sacra corona unita (SCU), etc.*, in Italy. That is to say, secular, criminal and illegal European associations, with international ramifications, and their members are called Gardunians.

A small example related to new technologies, training, work, future generations, etc., can be the opaque, manipulative and immutable line in time, where a nuclear engineer is invited to grant the best multimedia European awards (Möbius –www.moebiuslugano.ch), in Switzerland or children's education / digital schools / museums mobile, etc., in Italy. The power of decision and influence of the Gardunians, with "nuclear energy", goes from Lugano (Switzerland), passing through the Italian cities of Como, Milan, Bergamo, Pisa, Rome until reaching Bari (headquarters of the SCU), and vice versa. This long geographical journey should be read under the magnifying glass of the transparency of the truth, with which a supposed network of educational help from the Gardunians from the north to the underdeveloped south is observed, having their haven in Switzerland, for the evasion of taxes, for example. That is, money and influences of people that circulate through the SCU and *cielinos* (in Spanish) / CL – Communion and Liberalization (Pinotti, 2010; De Alessandri, 2010). It's a classic example of gardunying and gardunially.

Gardunying is the Gardunians' *destructive action* to demolish structures and systems, through endless human and technological resources. That is, the eternal way that these bipolar, neurotic, xenophobic, pseudo feminist, etc. criminals have, very well camouflaged and experts in lying, of cheating, corrupting, mocking, etc., in a sadistic way of all those who comply with the rules. The term *gardunially* is an adverb of mode and refers to the criminal behavior derived from the psychological profile of the members of the Garduña/Gardunia.

Consequently, the G factor refers to brotherhoods or fraternities, traditionally religious or other types of human, bandits or criminal organizations, not transparent, but distributed throughout the globe (MacKenzie, 1968; Machovec, 1991; House, 2000; Veltman, 2016; Leone, 2018). Sects or internal currents existing within the main group of Western religion (Spilka, 1982; Motilla, 1990). Some examples are: Communion and Liberalization ("*los cielinos*", aimed at the educational elite), Opus Dei, etc. (Pinotti, 2010; De Alessandri, 2010; Qates, Ruf & Driver, 2009).

Now, this does not mean that all the religions of the world have a high index of the Garduña factor. Only the destructive cults. Which skillfully divide their potential followers into the three social classes of nations, with developed economies: high, medium and low. For this reason, there are universities in Madrid, such as the Complutense (Opus Dei), or the Autonomous University of Barcelona (Salesians), in Bellaterra (Barcelona, Spain), etc., where there are two or three departments related to *audiovisual communications, information technologies, etc.,* in the same faculty, for example. That is, one aimed at middle class students and others at the elite. That is, potential *garduñianos* (in Spanish) or Gardunians (a new word, in Engish), inside and outside of Spain.

This repetition and division of the social classes of students and teachers is another of the key elements to detect the presence of the G factor, in the Latin American university structure, with regard to new technologies and education. In Spain: Salamanca, Zaragoza, Lleida, Donostia, Tenerife, Mallorca, Valencia, Barcelona, Madrid, Girona, etc. The reader interested in these topics can consult the following bibliographical references, whose authors are generally former ex-judges or collaborators dedicated to the fight against international organized crime (Aitala, 2018; Leone, 2018, De Alessandri, 2010, Pinotti, F. 2010; Singer & Lalich, 1997).

Through destructive criticism and a myriad of various and illicit strategems, the brotherhood is imposing its rules on the rest of society (Cazeneuve, 1972; Oberschall, 1973; Brown, 1963), particularly, in the entire formative process of the human being. That is, from kindergarten to university. The members resort to a myriad of anthropological, pedagogical, psychological, sociological methods and techniques, etc. (Aitala, 2018; Brown, 1963), making use and abuse of *traditional and new media*. The purpose is to affect the normal and democratic functioning of the latest technologies, through the universal central axis, which is the formation of the human being.

A human being who plays different roles in the face of software and hardware: programmer, systems analyst, graduate in networks and data communication, computer engineer, etc., or simply, end user of interactive systems. Roles where the knowledge and experiences of the formal and factual sciences are interrelated. Therefore, in software engineering there is already the human or social factor, considering the user acting individually or within a group, but it is not considered that function of being a superior being that acts destructively, which is above all norms or rules established in real or virtual communities, be they local and / or international. All this is due to the fact that he or she, supposedly occupies the top of the population hierarchy pyramid, belonging to an atypical fraternity or brotherhood, faithful to the spirit of the bell tower and to the destructive parochialism.

These are the forces that move freely and invincibly, in the three layers of the web. Forces that have taken advantage of global crises, such as those arising from finance in the first decade of the millennium,

Figure 1. An interface that "sacredly" has been in operation since 2001. In 2010, it has been modified to hide the destructive and racist G Factor through its online database. The information on the web still does not reflect the reality of the data that it exposes to users. That is, the heraldic information is practically non-existent

to drill into the central and spherical area of the web, turning it into an ellipsoid torus. Many examples related to the web, university education and new technologies have been presented, for a decade, in annexes or appendixes that have free access online (Cipolla-Ficarra, 2010; Cipolla-Ficarra, 2015).

Below we will see some cases of them that have been modified once the Gardunians have been publicly discovered. The first case analyzed is the GENS portal or website (www.gens.info) –see Annex #1 "Descriptive Statistics for the Communicability Studies" (Cipolla-Ficarra, F., 2010).

Since the beginning of the 21st century, and under the pretext of the origin of the surnames in Italy, it has served to exclude hundreds of thousands of workers for decades, especially if the surnames did not refer to the north of the country. It is a manifest racism because the system works with wrong data from the localities shown on the Italian map as the origin of the surnames, so the racism is based on the distribution of telephone subscribers of the landline network in the Italian territory. The seriousness of this type of portal lies in the promotion of workplace xenophobia. Geographical areas, where real and non-virtual academic merits (i.e., MOOCs –Massive Open Online Courses, from the USA that serve to bulk up the curricula of those who occupy life positions, in European universities) are eclipsed by the G factor, for example.

Today, GENS has modified the interface and hypothetically is dedicated to tourism, travel, traditions, etc., although it continues to maintain its segregationist functions, with its databases that do not represent the heraldic reality. Apparently, something so frivolous for some, has vital consequences for the rest of a community, in the face of emergencies derived from natural or man-made catastrophes. For example, with that website and in the Lombardy of the new millennium, an Anthony Stephen Fauci (https://en.wikipedia.org/wiki/Anthony_Fauci) would never have achieved international significance and the job position he has in the USA, due to his Sicilian ancestors, for example.

At the same time, it is found that the pseudo-quantification derived from descriptive statistics destroys the credibility of online information, and therefore, the quality of communication. The constant problem of the Internet in the face of criminal acts is also verified (visible?), such as the erasure of digital information, the constant change of personal data in online resumes, among an infinity of destructive instruments, methods and techniques, and so it remains without solution. There is still no freely accessible and universal database, with a kind of blacklist of all Gardunians, who sadistically amuse themselves by destroying not only the veracity of online information but also the lives of honest workers.

This website that promotes racial discrimination allows us to discover how the G factor is camouflaged and circulates very well, through the hypothetical informative, educational, cultural and tourist purposes, in each of the three areas that make up the web: surface, deep and dark.

Racism is one of the vital components of this factor, which is added to *lies, deception, envy, pride, ignorance, provocation, mockery, threat, sadism, persecution, plagiarism, personality theft, among other criminal actions* of the Gardunians. They should be criminally suppressed and eradicated from civilized societies. However, it is the opposite since they are absolutely privileged in the face of the legal system.

All this denotes *the high power* of the criminal sects and organizations. That is, they enjoy eternal temporal and spatial immunity. Therefore, the actions of mobbing, bossing, stalking, straining, etc., is the common denominator in their daily behaviors. Invariably, this *modus operandi* is what allows us to affirm that they are actual criminals, since they have a wide and free path of action, unlimited resources to ruin and destroy for life thousands and thousands of excellent professionals of the factual and/or formal sciences, without the pertinent authorities being able to stop them. All of them belong to **religious structures, vertical and monolithic**.

It is a structure that is above the executive, legislative and judicial powers, within democratic communities, in the Western world. Presidents, prime ministers, kings, queens, ministers of education, science, technology, etc., global financial crisis, pandemic, etc. come and go, but they continue and will continue in their perpetual positions and with their destructive functions.

For all of this, it can be confidently stated that universities have bosses or owners, even if they are public institutions. In short, there is an international legal vacuum of institutions that detect this factor to eliminate it.

Today, the codes of ethics that they promote online are an ideal shield. They frequently resort to it to hide their misdeeds as well as pseudo-psychological-religious susceptibility (for example, the promotion of violence in social networks, the spread of hate on the Internet, gender inequality in the labor market, and a long etcetera), the online digital erasure of the evidence, to protect itself in case of being discovered on the web.

Without going into other details of this structure in the educational field, which have been widely explained in (Cipolla-Ficarra, F. et al., 2015), and whose hypotheses, since the beginning of the new millennium, have been verified and confirmed with the passage of time. The following briefly describes the techniques and strategies used from the Gardunian structures to ruin and sink the democratic progress of modernization of science and education, through actions contrary to the realization of scientific events, related to formal and factual sciences, such as conferences, workshops, symposia, parallel sections, etc., in a modest, honest way and without a G factor:

1. Introducing Trojan Horses to scientific, honorary, steering, organizing, etc. committees; proceedings co-editors (i.e., Springer –Lecture Notes in Computer Science) in order to spread rumors, fake news, infamies, offenses, prejudices, etc., inside and outside the working group.
2. Evaluating negatively all the research works that are submitted to the members of the Trojan Horse, in the review process, resorting to a myriad of strategems, such as: idiomatic imprecision, lack of clarity or coherence of the text, the non-reference to certain authors (particularly those who make up the international Garduña), the unfair denigration of work as content for blogs or other minor applications of social networks, etc.
3. Encouraging colleagues in the working group to participate in other committees of national and / or international events, in order to generate conference clones (same committees and topics, for example) and promote the self-destruction of the first group.
4. Sending messages within the group denouncing false events, situations, behaviors, etc.
5. Systematically removing all speaker keynotes from international conferences, workshops, symposiums, etc. and pass them to cloned events.
6. Promoting the holding of similar events, on the same dates, in the same cities or geographic regions. This prevents associations, institutes, etc. International organizations from granting symbolic support (in cooperation, for example) to other events that, even if they are pioneers in certain places, there are already more than one that will take place, coinciding temporally and geographically.
7. Winning the patronage, sponsorship, collaboration, etc., of the same industrial, commercial, cultural, educational, etc. entities. that the members of the group destined to annihilation have obtained instantly.
8. Pursuing, minute by minute, online advertising campaigns, through the international promotion channels of the events That is, at the same time that the call is made to present papers, demos,

posters, etc. For example, if there is a congress with a certain topic, automatically and simultaneously, they make calls for magazines, webinars, etc., with similar and free topics appear.

9. Lying in the online call for the publication of the proceedings of the events, through associations, institutes, federations, publishers, etc. (ACM, IEEE, IFIP, Elsevier, etc.) that after the event will never publish those works. However, they perfectly fulfill the mission of dumping, in the context of destroying international events, related to ICTs, HCI, UX, education, interfaces, interactive design, multimedia, web engineering, software engineering, usability engineering, augmented/mixed/virtual reality, robotics, etc.
10. Spying on the activities within the events through false participants, who are not only not interested in the event's activities, nor in the presentation or publication of their work.
11. Virtually occupying the spaces of the event with jester participants, although in fact they do not attend the conference. For example, sending works that once controlled, approved and corrected, their authors disappear online and in conference rooms. That is, participants (teachers and / or students) who are dedicated to international tourism, whose air tickets, hotel stays, and other expenses related to the event, are paid by the taxes of millions of taxpayers who pay taxes, and who expect the future generations to improve the educational, health, scientific, industrial, commercial, etc. systems.
12. Generating in the social networks, provocative, mocking, offensive web pages, etc. with the same initials of the conferences or the organizing entities, in order to discredit the event and all its members. Some pages that will occupy the first places in the search engines (Google, Yahoo, etc.), in the moments before the closing of the reception of works for their subsequent evaluation. Removing those pages on the current web will require years of legal action.
13. Constantly renewing pressure groups, with young apprentices from the Garduña to maintain constant persecution and extermination.
14. Abusing the traditional means of communication to disseminate the content, activities, etc., of the Gardunians, coming from specialized portals and / or social networks. The narcissism of photographs that can be sold online such as a frustrated actor who has dedicated himself to didactics and special education, or a mathematician who is dedicated to interfaces for disabled children because she wanted to be a doctor, to name a couple of examples, related to academic inbreeding. The latter is another endemic disease of G factor.
15. Manipulating the authorities of the conference organizing committees so that they cyclically accept the works of the same institutions. The objective is to guarantee a steady and international structure, which facilitates rapid obtaining of academic degrees, continuous publications, free trips and stays abroad, R&D agreements and projects, financial grants (with a total of 7 or more figures, of euros or US dollars), among others. That is to say, an organized network aimed at all those who could potentially be included in the group of Gardunians, regardless if they come from public, private and hybrid universities; banking foundations; government institutions, etc.

Only 15 modus operandi or verified destructive strategies have been listed here, out of the more than 2,000 examples detected and documented, between southern Europe and the American continent, over a quarter of a century. Some of the consequences of these items belonging to G factor and all its derivations are the following:

- Existence of complete immunity in the international scientific community;
- Total destruction of groups of relevant work, with a high scientific level, due to envy and ignorance;
- Expansion of narco-education from the Americas (Colombia, Chile, Paraguay, Brazil, Mexico, etc.) to Europe (Portugal, Spain, France, Italy, Greece, Cyprus, etc.) and vice versa;
- Marginalization, workplace and social collapse of intelligent and creative experts;
- Difficulty of publishing online the list of names and surnames of the winners, participants, etc. to the conferences, workshops, symposiums, doctoral consortium, panels, demos, and posters since they would synchronously be victims of an unwanted advertising campaign;
- Disadvantages for holding international events at university venues;

Figure 2. The logo in the figure (bottom) is partially inspired by a fresco, located in the pre-Alpine town of Clusone (Bergamo - Italy), belonging to the artist Giacomo Borlone de Buscáis (15th century), called "The Dance Macabre or Triumph of Death" (https://en.wikipedia.org/wiki/Clusone)

- Inability to freely participate in social networks;
- Damages caused to the harassed persons from the point of view of health, economic-financial, employment, global prestige, family growth, and a very long etcetera.

In other words, these Gardunians set about drilling into the harmonious, democratic and perfect sphere of the 20th century web or global village, to more easily spread their illicit, criminal and fanatic acts, from the hollowed-out center that is the web today. These are activities that enjoy absolute immunity, to the misfortune of millions of human lives, who have to survive through the web. Furthermore, it is an immovable immunity during the centuries, and that is above all the ethical and criminal codes of international law, current and future.

In resume, **the G factor annihilates everything that it cannot have under its control**. All the complaints on the web, are funny to the Gardunians and they dance a macabre dance before the misfortunes suffered by their silent victims throughout their lives.

Logo of the website "*pirateando*" that is a work-in-progress (www.pirateando.net), where presented in a denotative or connotative way: Modus operandis protected by the G factor; Corrupt interrelationships at worldwide level; Nefarious characters with freedom of action; Eradication of human intelligence in academic training; Submission of free will; Contextual alignment, through those of new technologies; Loss of human dignity; Handling in the allocation of scholarships for masters, doctorates, post doctorates, etc.; Condescension towards pre-rigged awards, and very a long etcetera.

A FEW EMERGING EXAMPLES OF THE INTERSECTION BETWEEN DARK WEB, EDUCATION AND "G" FACTOR

Over the last ten years, we have been including examples of the G Factor from the dark web (this last notion has been extensively developed in the chapter Quality and Web Software Engineering Advances and in the Conclusions), in the appendices that are freely accessible in the following references, and whose titles are listed below:

- Descriptive Statistics for the Communicability Studies (Cipolla-Ficarra, 2010).
- Social or Anti-Social Networking? (Cipolla-Ficarra, 2015).

Some of them, we take up and expand to observe the great destructive power of the G Factor, through the web in the field of formal and factual sciences.

The first of them has to do with the use of portals to communicate global events, where a Belarusian mathematician sadistically has fun destroying international events, in the summer period (August, 2012), from Heidelberg – Germany / Trento – Italy (today, in Russia and Switzerland. Computer Science –LNCS/LNAI/LNBI, Springer Nature.), and without prior communication with the managers and organizers. Actually, the *cyber-terrorist* has some *Gardunians* collaborators in the University of Pisa – Italy, University of Amsterdam – the Netherlands, Open University in Milton Keynes – UK; Bar-Ilan University – Israel; University of Russia, etc. See figure 3.

Automatically, the Garduña is activated and begins its macabre dance, another attack at a higher level such as the online Wired magazine in USA (see figures 4 and 5 –www.wired.com). The first international workshop "Human-Computer Interaction, Tourism and Cultural Heritage (HCITOCH 2010): Strategies for a Creative Future with Computer Science, Quality Design and Communicability" (figure 4) was activated in 2010, following the orientation and advice of prof. Dr. Kim H. Veltman (Veltman, 2016).

Figure 3. It is the first time that a publisher in EU has used the DBworld channel to attack its customers (Database – research.cs.wisc.edu)

Nabble | Old Nabble1 | Database World (DBWorld)

Login | Register

[Dbworld] HCITOCH 2012 / ADNTIIC 2012 / SETECEC 2012 proceedings are NOT published by Springer

View: All Messages

1 Messages — Rating Filter: 2 Alert me

[Dbworld] HCITOCH 2012 / ADNTIIC 2012 / SETECEC 2012 proceedings are NOT published by Springer

by Aliaksandr Birukou 3 Aug 20, 2012; 04:39pm

Reply (Restricted by the Administrator) | View Threaded | Show Only this Message

Dear DBWorld members,

Recently, several CFPs of the events **HCITOCH 2012**, ADNTIIC **2012** were distributed in the DBWorld list. Those CFPs, as well as the web sites of the events (including SETECEC **2012** website) contain the information that the proceedings will be published by Springer in Lecture Notes in Computer Science.

I would like to draw to your attention the fact that those events were NOT accepted for the publication in Springer LNCS, therefore, please double-check with the organizers where the proceedings will be published.

Kind regards,

Aliaksandr Birukou
Springer
Editor, Computer Science
...
Tiergartenstrasse 17 | 69121 Heidelberg | Germany
tel +49 (0)6221 / 4878540
e-mail: aliaksandr.birukou@...
visit CCIS webpage: http://www.springer.com/series/7899

Figure 4. First attack from Wired magazine, destroying an international event, at a high professional level from the honor and scientific committee (Summer, 2012)

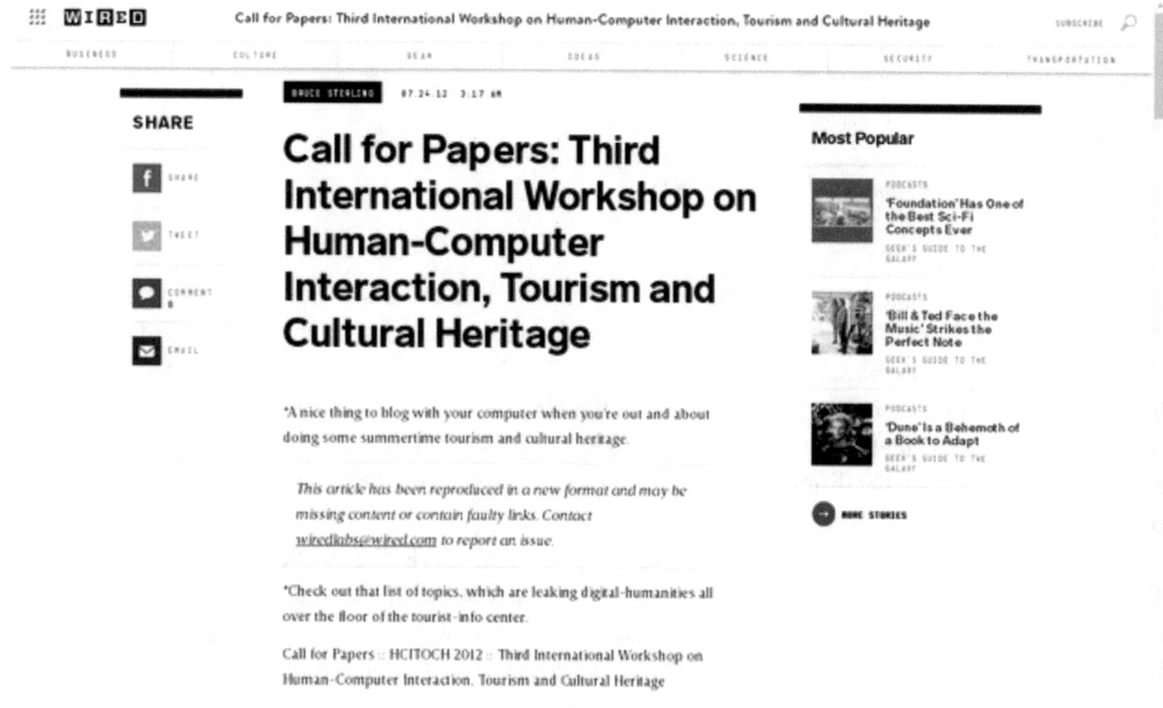

WIRED

Call for Papers: Third International Workshop on Human-Computer Interaction, Tourism and Cultural Heritage

SHARE

Call for Papers: Third International Workshop on Human-Computer Interaction, Tourism and Cultural Heritage

*A nice thing to blog with your computer when you're out and about doing some summertime tourism and cultural heritage.

This article has been reproduced in a new format and may be missing content or contain faulty links. Contact wiredlabs@wired.com to report an issue.

*Check out that list of topics, which are leaking digital-humanities all over the floor of the tourist-info center.

Call for Papers :: HCITOCH 2012 :: Third International Workshop on Human-Computer Interaction, Tourism and Cultural Heritage

Most Popular

'Foundation' Has One of the Best Sci-Fi Concepts Ever

'Bill & Ted Face the Music' Strikes the Perfect Note

'Dune' Is a Behemoth of a Book to Adapt

Figure 5. First International Conference on Multimedia, Scientific Information and Visualization for Information Systems and Metrics (MSIVISM 2014) and second attack from Wired magazine, causing the closure of the university headquarters (University of Maribor, Slovenia), in order to cancel it

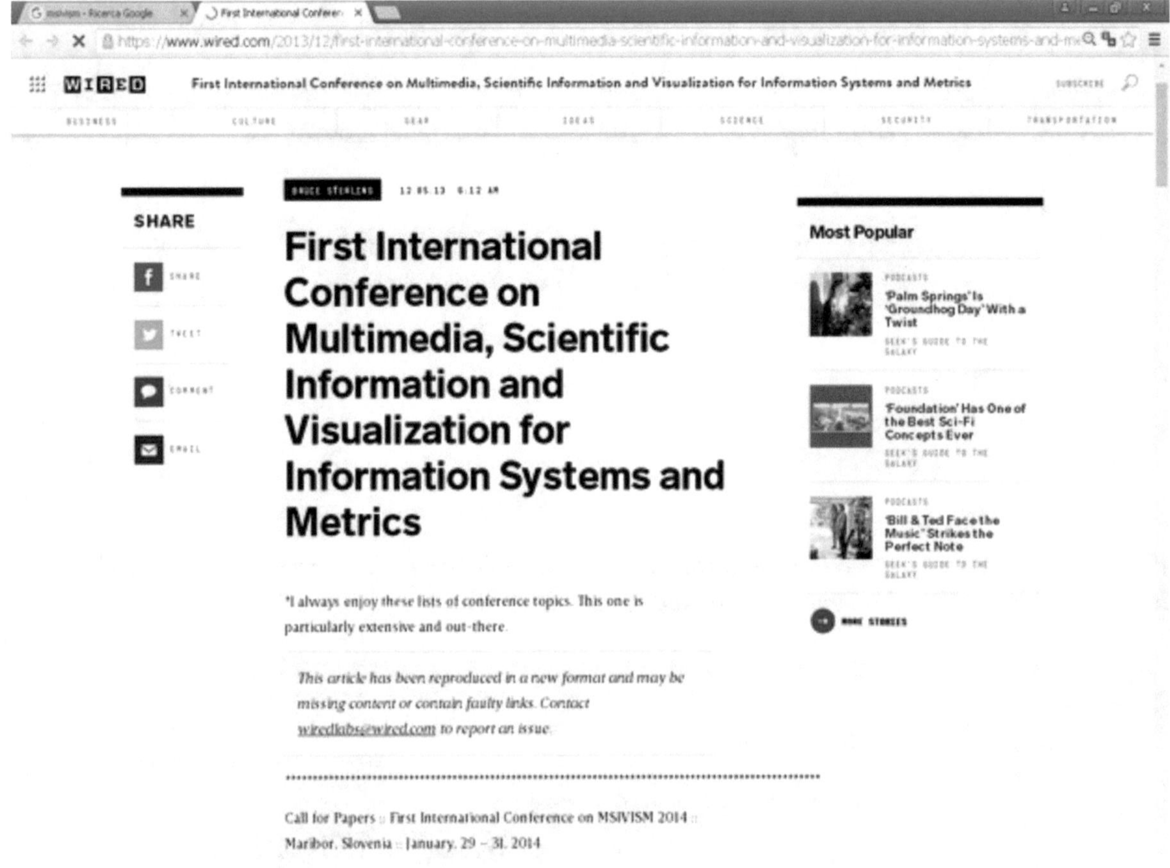

https://www.wired.com/2013/12/first-international-conference-on-multimedia-scientific-information-and-visualization-for-information-systems-and-m

WIRED First International Conference on Multimedia, Scientific Information and Visualization for Information Systems and Metrics

SHARE

First International Conference on Multimedia, Scientific Information and Visualization for Information Systems and Metrics

"I always enjoy these lists of conference topics. This one is particularly extensive and out-there.

This article has been reproduced in a new format and may be missing content or contain faulty links. Contact wiredlabs@wired.com to report an issue.

Call for Papers :: First International Conference on MSIVISM 2014 :: Maribor, Slovenia :: January, 29 – 31, 2014

Most Popular

'Palm Springs' Is 'Groundhog Day' With a Twist

'Foundation' Has One of the Best Sci-Fi Concepts Ever

'Bill & Ted Face the Music' Strikes the Perfect Note

Unfortunately, the author of that note (Bruce Sterling) does not know how to distinguish between "*domains*", "*fields*", and "*specialties*", that is, the fundamental and primary characteristic of each of the disciplines that make up the sciences (Bunge, 1996). It is advisable to consult authors like Mario Bunge before criticizing and destroying equipment with the highest human quality for free. Consequently, an extensive listing connotes and reflects the requirement and also skill necessary to find intersection zones of the disciplines among the different domains, fields, and specialties; which at the same time potentially boosts and merges the formerly different scientific views.

The same author (Bruce Sterling from Wired magazine) returns to the attack in May 2013 (see figure 5). The consequences of this new attack are reflected in the message of the figure 6, where once again, a member of the Garduña comes into play, from Institute of Interactive Systems and Data Science –Graz University of Technology (Graz, Austria). The strategies used by this Austrian character are deception, falsehood, and lies. We can read into the infamous message (figure 6): "*The web site carries the logos of both the University of Maribor and the faculty (FERI). Unfortunately, I believe this might be a fake conference (search on Google for 'fake conference'), based on the following indicators: A similar conference by the same organisations (AInCI and ALAIPO) HCITOCH 2012 was apparently fake ... You*

Figure 6. A "domino effect attack" from Graz University of Technology, in Austria. The author of the email obtains the closure of the headquarters in the University of Maribor. The strategies used by this Austrian character are deception, falsehood, and lies. Fortunately, the truth has been photographed

Subject: Fake Conference in Maribor?
From: Keith Andrews <kandrews@iicm.edu>
Date: 8.12.2013 20:28

...

Dear Borut,

Sorry we missed each other on Thu. I think my talk went down well,
there were certainly plenty of questions.

I wanted to let you know about an upcoming conference in Maribor:

MSIVISM 2014
http://www.ainci.com/MSIVISM/MSIVISM.html

The web site carries the logos of both the University of Maribor and the faculty (FERI).

Unfortunately, I believe this might be a fake conference (search
on google for "fake conference"), based on the following indicators:

o The list of topics covers pretty much the whole of computer science.

...

o A similar conference by the same organisations (AInCI and ALAIPO)
HCITOCH 2012 was apparently fake:
http://comments.gmane.org/gmane.comp.hci.acm-sigchi.announce/9317

You might want to check it out for yourself and reconsider any involvement.

Best regards,

Keith

--

Keith Andrews IICM, Graz University of Technology, Austria

http://www.iicm.tugraz.at/keith "No wild kangaroos in Austria"

Figure 7. The extreme conditions of the Slovenian winter (29-31 Jannuary, 2014) and the attacks received from the Wired magazine and the Institute of Interactive Systems and Data Science –Graz University of Technology (Austria) did not prevent it from being carried out. From 2012 to the present, none of the events organized or promoted by ALAIPO and AInCI have been canceled

might want to check it out for yourself and reconsider any involvement." This is a classical example of the Gardunians behaviour.

At the bottom of the figure 6, there is a local excursion photography (Lido Island, Venice, Italy –September, 2012) with some participants/guided tour (i.e., prof. Dott.ssa Daniela Simionato Putz, prof. Dr. Kim H. Veltman, prof. Dr. David Benyon, prof. Dr. Domer Verber, prof. Dr. Georges Gyory, etc.) of 3rd International Workshop on HCITOCH 2012 (September, 27–28, Venice –Italy), and two from University of Maribor (FERI), in Slovenia. However, the university headquarters of the Slovenian conference (FERI –Faculty of Electrical Engineering and Computer Sciende) at University of Maribor (Maribor, Slovenia) was closed at the last minute. Despite the extremely harsh climatic conditions, *in situ* (see figure 7) and in a short time, it was possible to find another HQ in the rooms of City Hotel of Maribor.

With the thousands of events that exist in the world, the same author from Wired, is dedicated to persecute and destroy the same organizers, not once, but twice. This denotes the presence of a perfectly organized and camouflaged network, within a diverse set of entities and institutions: universities, com-

Figure 8. Since 2012, every time the event's acronym is written (HCITOCH), several images of the links in the Wired magazine appear, indicated by a white bar with red dots. By clicking on the links you go directly to figure 4

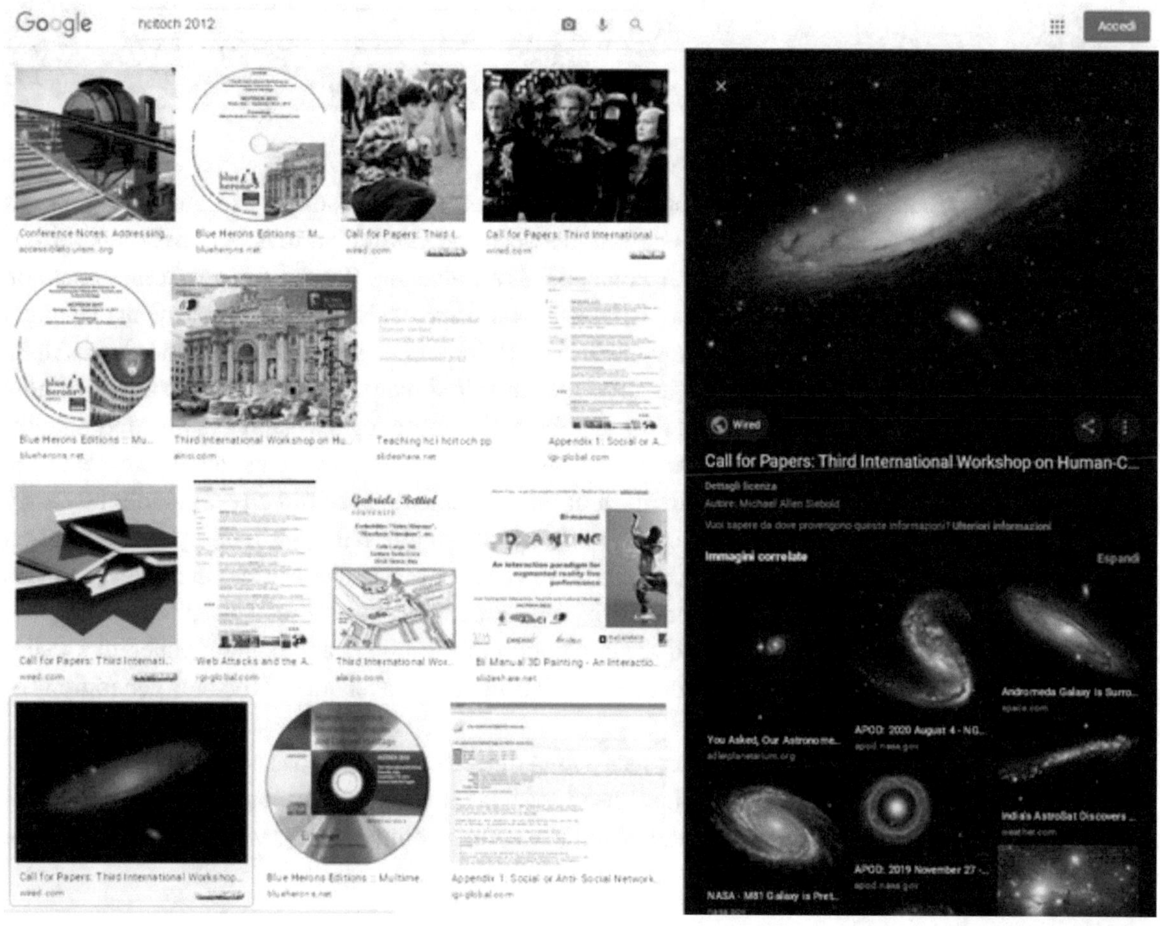

Figure 9. As of 05.12.2013, in search engines such as Google, users when typing in the name of the event, its acronym, the organizers, etc. (MSIVISM, ALAIPO, AInCI, etc.), will automatically see the images of the Wired magazine, which takes them to the defamation of figure 5

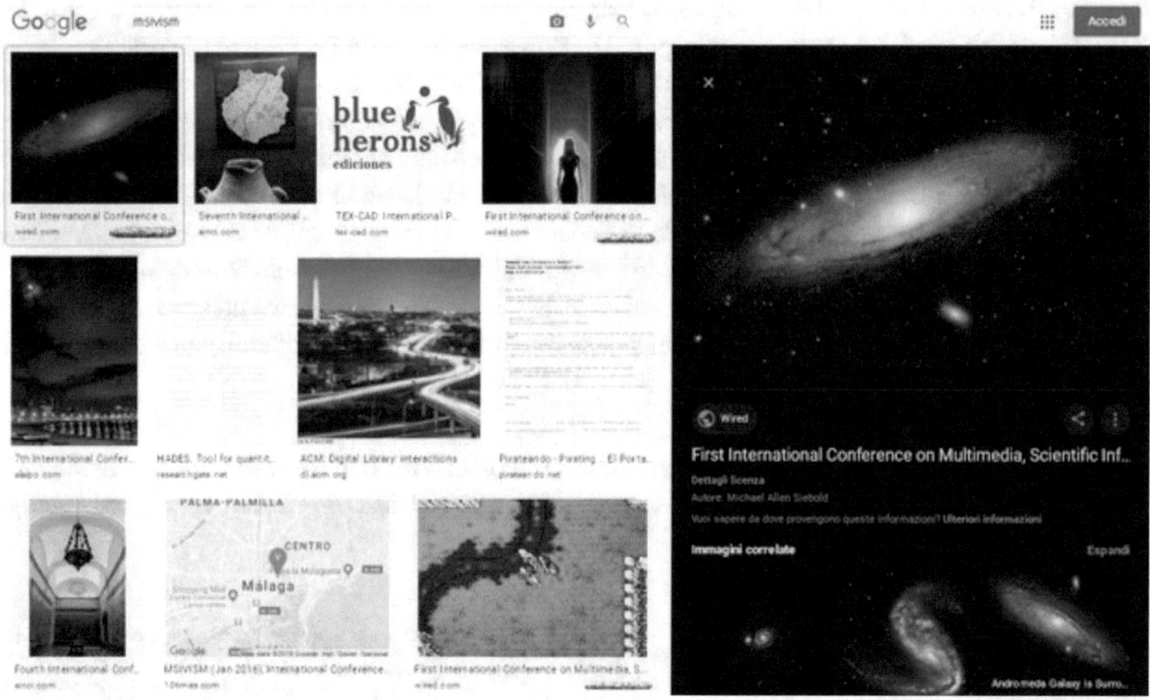

panies, industries, foundations, organizations, associations, etc. In the example in figure 5, which is a reiteration of the attack in figure 4, there is a link between the Gardunian members between various European universities and companies, such as Pompeu Fabra University (Department of Communication and Department of ICT), University of Bergamo (Didactics and Special Education, Department of Human and Social Sciences), Confindustria Bergamo (Industrial Union of Bergamo), Badi, Telefónica – Alpha (Barcelona, Spain), etc., and the author of the messages in Wired magazine. This is an example of how there is no way to stop the Gardunians and they are above the entire legal system existing and imaginable in the future, essentially, when it comes to protecting the reputation and prestige of Internet users.

This phenomenon harms the **democratization** of online content, since directly and indirectly, they are negatively affecting the five basic principles of usability engineering, defined by Jakob Nielsen (Nielsen, 1993), at the beginning of the 90s. In addition, with the passage of time the main premises enunciated by Tomas Maldonado have been verified, with regard to the consequences for users, given the use of new interactive technologies and the corruption of promoters and content generators (Maldonado, 1997). That is how the executioners become victims of the behaviors of the new generations of users of interactive systems.

The infamy of the figures 3, 4, and 5, after such a long time, even today, those nefarious and infamous posts keep on causing damage, since they have been associated with the all events websites (figures 8 and 9). The communication channels with the Wired magazine to eliminate this vilification do not work

Figure 10. This false individual has given himself as surname a plus ultra Gardunian association (AIPO) as owner of an honest and modest association (ALAIPO). The latter, 20 years, have studied the G Factor that derives and expands worldwide, from plus ultra Gardunian association. The end of the link (name – surname, see green bar) is the umpteenth provocative mockery of the Garduña/Gardunia, in order to generate confusion among netizens

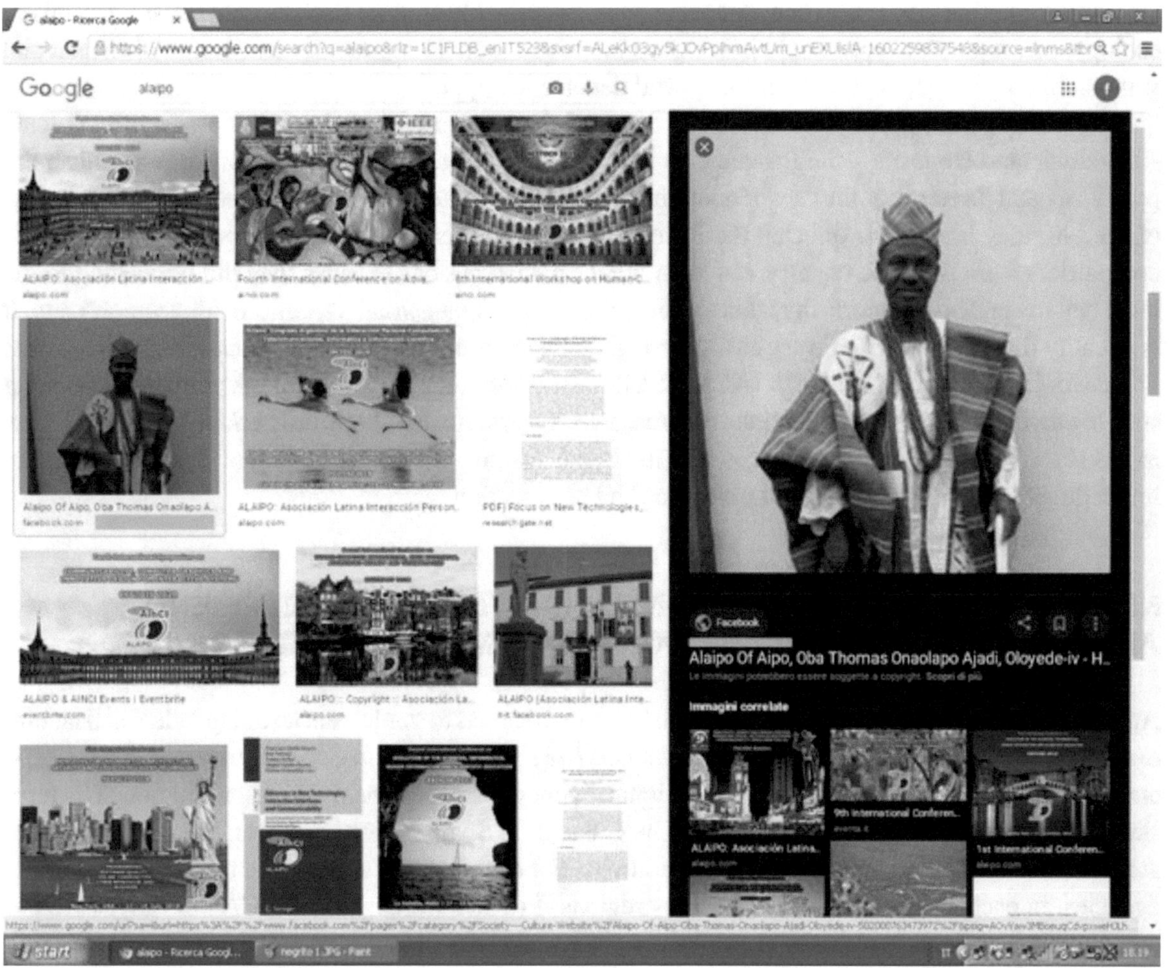

(messages sent to the author, editorial managers and colleagues, without any response). Only the silence of the Garduña/Gardunia is received in response.

The "domino effect" has continued infinitely since then, to the point that false profiles are created on Facebook, joining honest work groups with those top representatives of the Garduña in Spain and other members, inside and outside the Spanish border, such as: AIPO (www.aipo.es), HCI Collab (www.hci-collab.com), EATIS (www.eatis.org), IADIS (www.iadisportal.org), AISTI (www.aisti.eu), etc. Readers interested in updating these unions and interrelationships can consult the following link: www.pirateando.net.

Now, we find the impossibility of quickly correcting defamations on Facebook, as in this case, along with other social network applications, such as Instagram, Twitter, LinkedIn, Pinterest, etc. This ineffectiveness is resolved with the obligation to open branches in each of the countries of the world by the owners of the social network companies, so that users can see those distortions or online offenses corrected in the shortest possible time. Otherwise, in some states severe controls will be imposed on freedom of Internet access. This is a first example of the sadism of the executioners with their victim in other cases, the executioners become victims of the behaviors of the new generations of users of interactive systems. One way to do this is to use in educational portals, fashionable slogans such as anti-racism, feminism, ecology, etc. A Gardunian example is in figure 11, where there is supposedly a rejection of racism and xenophobia. However, the reality of that portal denotes the opposite.

In the first place, if the founders, promotors and main managers of the AIPO association (Lleida – Catalonia and Donostia – the Basque Country, in Spain) are analyzed, as in their roles as university professors and directors of thesis works for masters and doctorates. It can be verified how in the decade of the '90, they have never directed theses to Africans, Americans, Asians, Europeans, etc., and even compatriots from the same country, but from other Spanish regions because they did not belong to the local bell tower, and therefore, they did not share the same language/dialect, culture, idiosyncrasy, etc. It is a reality that can be verified very easily through the names and surnames that appear in the databases of the works published in the 1990s (ACM, IEEE, DBLP, etc.), the formation of the permanent teaching staff in university departments, laboratories, research centers, etc. In other words, *a kind of ethnic cleansing* as shown in figure 1, but which has also led to the shaping and strengthening of Spanish university inbreeding (Penalva-Buitrago, 2011), as described next section.

NEW INFORMATION AND COMMUNICATION TECHNOLOGIES: IBERO-AMERICAN HUMAN INTERRELATIONSHIPS AND THE G FACTOR

An ineffective way to stop inbreeding in Spanish universities was to implement an independent and faculty evaluation agency called ANECA (*Agencia Nacional de Evaluación de la Calidad y Acreditación* –www.aneca.es), in Madrid (2002). In English, National Agency for Assessment and Accreditation. The term 'ineffective' refers to the strong presence of the G Factor in Spain. There have been numerous sabotage actions since the beginning of ANECA's operations. For example, the appearance of similar evaluation agencies, in each of the Spanish autonomous regions. In other words, the ANECA has only served to compile all the scientific material of professors and researchers (Spanish or not) in a large database.

Therefore, the Gardunian teaching staff that already existed in the universities, have been occupying the same places. In other words, zero changes. In addition, with the passing of time, little by little, the Garduña has been incorporating its members into said evaluating structure, as in the rest of the institutions related to education, science, research, NICT, etc. This continues to favor a negative reality in Spanish universities (Penalva-Buitrago, 2011). A brief example is how the Garduña assign the positions of professors in new technologies and education, in Tenerife (after 8 years an associate professor automatically becomes a professor). In figure 11 there is a diagram in this regard, where cultures, modus operandis, Gardunians from both sides of the Atlantic intersect, etc.

Now, to answer the rhetorical question: How is it possible that these realities continue to occur in the new millennium? It is necessary to divide the agents involved in the process, the phases of the method used, and the distorting mechanism of realities. As an *agent*, there is usually a person related to the formal sciences. For example, in the case of the University of La Laguna (Tenerife), he is a retired physicist. He

Figure 11. Synthetic summary of the Gardunian actions for the destruction of human R&D teams, international events, promotion of fratricide, bullying, persecution or stalking, etc., in exchange for lifetime job positions, that is, university professors. In this example there is a link between Spain and the Americas

An Iberoamerican summary of the Gardunian actions in education

1) Detection of the target to destroy: professionals, non-profit associations, fundations, etc.

2) Inclusion in the work team as a Trojan Horse.

3) The camouflaged attack actions begin.

4) Affiliation to the Ibero-American narco-education (e.g., Colombia, Chile, etc.) to increase the international destructive power.

5) Activation of provocative actions.

6) Frontal attack, through associations similar to the ones you have to destroy. She/he gets to lead them quickly thanks to a Gardunia godfather and / or godmother (he/she has absolute control of the local structure and relations with the rest of the national and international Gardunia).

7) Acceleration in the process of publications that are indexed in databases, such as DBLP, IEEE, ACM, etc. by means of escaping organizing local international conferences.

8) Obtaining the life long position (chair / full-time) as a reward for their destructive and fratricidal actions.

has established strong ties for life, in Madrid (Complutense University), Barcelona (Autonomous University of Barcelona) and Bilbao/Donostia (University of the Basque Country). That individual is the central axis that destroys ANECA's functions in Tenerife, in matters related to NICT, HCI, education, artificial intelligence, video games, etc. That is, without his approval, no other candidate can be assumed at that university, at the time of the contest for the position of professor (*mechanism*). The problems generated from physics, mathematics, etc. in web engineering, software engineering, HCI, UX, etc., have already been described in "Quality and Web Software Engineering Advances" chapter.

This is due to the fact that these agents direct projects or theses, with a wide and varied agenda, such as: Automatic and Control, Simulation, Applications of Artificial Intelligence in Control, Simulation, Biomedical Engineering, Education, etc. In addition, they have the power to change the structures of the departments in a public university, a function of the trends of educational marketing, which are in vogue (*method*). Local and national control is non-existent. For example, it is not normal to transform a department of Systems Engineering, Automation, Architecture and Computer Technology, into a department of Computer Science and Systems Engineering, without changing the personnel. As well as placing a former student as rector of the university, obtaining employment contracts from her until the end of his days (figure 9), and a long etcetera. While thousands of young Canarians, with excellent academic records, have to emigrate to the four cardinal points of the planet, in search of a job.

Today, the Gardunians and their young disciples, faced with the demographic decline in the population of Spanish students, try to create virtual networks of collaboration in the Americas. The priority context for them is interactive communication, ICT, HCI, UX, Software Engineering, Systems Engineering, etc., particularly with future students living in economically developing towns, of the American continent, for example. However, these potential students are preferably "captured" in the economic elite of those countries, such as the headquarters of private universities (read pontifical or military universities) where

Figure 12. Publication in the local press of the lack of expert professionals at the University of La Laguna and the supposed need to extend the working life of retired personnel. Newspaper: Tribuna de Tenerife –www.tribunadetenerife.com (01.13.2020)

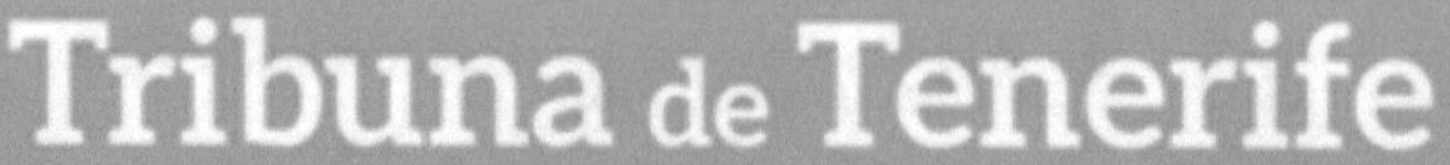

Tribuna de Tenerife

Periódico global de noticias y actualidad de Tenerife, La Palma, La Gomera y El Hierro

La ULL retiene el talento de sus veteranos con el nombramiento de ocho profesores honorarios

Publicado: 13 Enero 2020

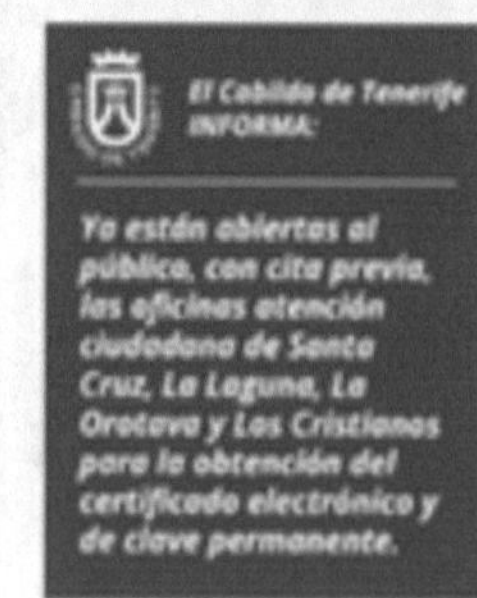

La Universidad de La Laguna ha celebrado hoy 13 de enero un acto de nombramiento de ocho profesores honorarios, en reconocimiento a su dilatada carrera profesional y en el momento en el que pasan a la jubilación. Estos docentes podrán seguir colaborando en actividades docentes e investigadoras, pero sin vínculo contractual alguna y sin remuneración específica. Se trata, en suma, "de seguir contando con los más valiosos y no desperdiciar el talento y la vocación universitaria que les ha guiado toda su vida", destacó la rectora, Rosa Aguilar.

Tres de ellos son exrectores, dado que el reglamento señala que por el mero hecho de haber ejercido la máxima dirección de la universidad tienen la oportunidad de acogerse a esta figura. Así, han sido nombrados profesores honorarios José Gómez Soliño, en el área de Filología; Ángel Gutiérrez Navarro, en Microbiología; y María Luisa Tejedor Salguero, en Edafología.

También han sido designados Gonzalo Lozano Soldevilla, en Zoología; Lorenzo Moreno Ruiz, en Ingeniería de Sistemas y Automática; Manuel Navarro Ibáñez, en Fundamentos de Análisis Económico; Pedro Oromí Masoliver, en Zoología; y Fernando Pérez González, en Análisis Matemático. Estos docentes se mantendrán en la figura de profesores honorarios durante dos años, es decir, hasta noviembre de 2021, prorrogables dos años más, salvo en el caso de Oromí, que acaba de renovar su segundo periodo.

Figure 13. The hypocrisy of the Gardunians on the issue of racism and xenophobia. It is a way of generating false empathy with potential overseas students, professors, researchers, etc., who will be awarded temporary contracts. Besides, they don't want controls (borders, ports, trains, cars, etc.) to limit expansion of narco-education

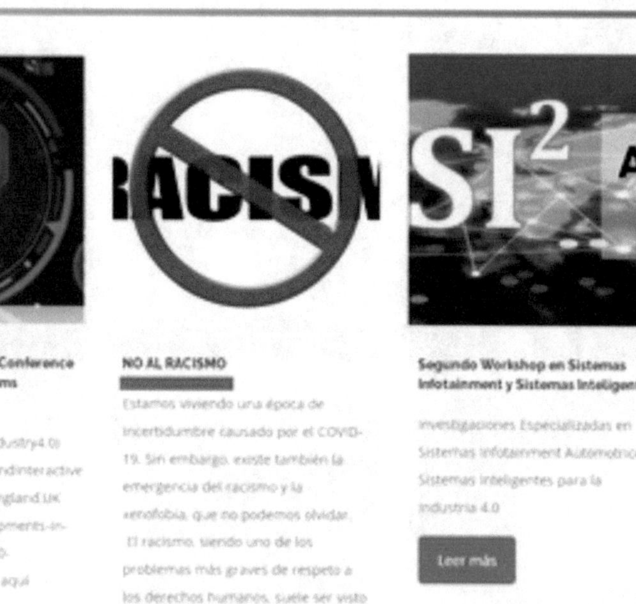

there is a one-way communication from Spain to constantly carry out face-to-face events, webinars, seminars, virtual conferences, etc.

EXCLUSION OF HUMAN AND SOCIAL FACTORS IN THE DATABASES

It is feasible to detect how the Garduña has exercised its **control** in excluding the digital storage of articles, books, newspapers, magazines, etc. that dealt with the issue of racism and xenophobia in the Iberian university environment, detected in the 1990s. For example, the Dialnet database (www.dialnet.es or *dialnet.unirioja.es*) that is based at the University of La Rioja (Spain). The reality indicates that it is partially controlled by the staff of the Informatics and Engineering Systems department at the University of Zaragoza, since the late 1990s. On the web they erroneously maintain that "*it is the largest Hispanic scientific articles library on the Internet.*" The error is due to the fact that not all the articles

Figure 14. University database that has been transformed into a foundation. The objective is to partially accumulate scientific publications such as journals, PhD theses, conference articles, etc., mainly in Spanish

are in Spanish, from the technical and commercial journals/magazines related to the new technologies of the 1990s, as can be seen in figure 14.

The financial crisis of the first decade of the new millennium has implied the closure of technical, scientific, etc., publishers and therefore, millions of pages have been lost that today could be consulted as the history of new technologies in Spain, Europe, America, etc. In other words, the databases on the publishers' servers were home to innumerable contributions made by pioneers of science journalism of the 20th and 21st centuries. Although they were commercial and / or scientific publications, originally on paper, they made up a set of simple and avant-garde contributions, with an eye on the new generations. Supposedly, the Dialnet database had to anticipate and prevent this loss of knowledge in Spain.

One of the hypotheses that circulated in the scientific journalism sector is that it was not a casual phenomenon, but rather a planned one. The goal was not to leave evidence of the racist, xenophobic, anti-feminism, etc. context that existed in the 1990s, in the Spanish academic and scientific environment, for example. Apart from that conjecture that has been verified over time. Besides, Internet was entering the *democratizing* process. The opinion columns of the specialists were not considered profitable by some educational and commercial sectors. For example, practical advice to lower costs in domestic software

Figure 15. Most of the technical articles from the '90s are not stored in the database, when scientific, technical-commercial publishers, etc., had that information online and freely accessible

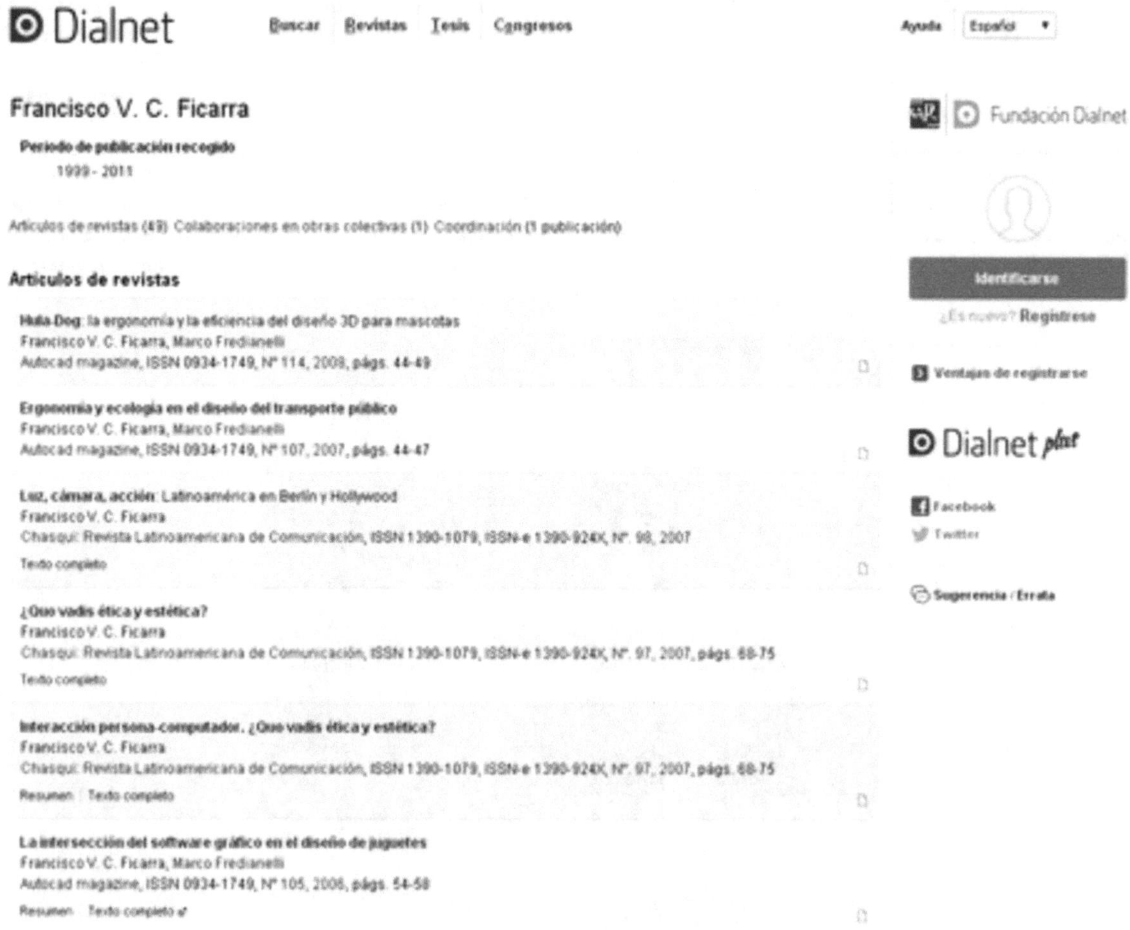

and hardware, through PC computers (preferably clones that worked under the Microsoft environment). That is, not Apple / Macintosh or other brands, whose acquisition costs for the computer, peripherals, certain applications for the multimedia environment, etc., were higher, economically speaking. Or the explanation of techniques and strategies to make the most of the software or other applications available on personal computers, without the need for university courses or most expensive training centres (private colleges, academies, institutes, etc.). Therefore, as it was counterproductive to obtain economic benefits, the members of the Garduña were in charge of immediately closing these publications. Some examples are in figure 16.

An example of the immunity, immobility and expansion of the Gardunians who, after two long decades, are still in the same place, through the section Letters from in Jumping Magazine (Valencia, Spain). Complaint from a reader in Zaragoza (computer scientist and 8 years of high school professor) about a contest for a place at the University of Zaragoza, in the Faculty of Engineering (Department of Computer Science and Engineering Systems Engineering). The contest was awarded to a 22-year-old archaeologist with no computer experience. The post was related to the topic of databases for librar-

Figure 16. Opinion column in Jumping technical magazine with diffusion in Spain and the Americas, where the first issues of the G Factor, ICT and education in Spain were discussed.
Original title in Spanish: ¿Faltan profesionales de I.T. en Europa? –English: Is there a lack of I.T. professionals in Europe? (2000). Author: Francisco V. C. Ficarra. Magazine: Jumping, Vol. 46, pp. 15 (upper area). In Spanish: ¿Arte electrónico o cantamañanas enchufados? –English: Electronic art or phonies with juice and connections? (2001). Author: Francisco V. C. Ficarra. Jumping, Vol. 47, pp. 14 (bottom area). In short, the power of rhetorical questions to warn about the presence of the G Factor. (Top) Articles in Jumping magazine. Headquarter: Valencia, Spain. Original title in Spanish: Últimas tecnologías: Hacia un primer estado de arte –English: Latest technologies: Towards a first state of the art (2001). Author: Francisco V. C. Ficarra. Magazine: Jumping, Vol. 50, pp. 46-52 (bottom area). The opinion section (top right margin). (Bottom) Article in "El Usuario de Multimedia" (Multimedia User) magazine specialized in new technologies and with diffusion in Ibero-American countries (Anaya Multimedia –Madrid, Spain). Title in Spanish: "Escenarios Virtuales, la imaginación humana sin límites" –English: Virtual Scenarios, human imagination without limits (1995). Author: Francisco V. C. Ficarra. Magazine: El Usuario de Multimedia, Vol. 4, pp. 24-29. This Spanish article can be considered as a pioneer in issues related to tangible interfaces in Barcelona/Spain.

ies on the Internet (librarianship), that is, you can see a link with the figure 14, since the staff of that department has always worked at the University of La Rioja. Today, they are in charge of putting out a pamphlet called "Interacción magazine, AIPO", for the neo-enslavement in ICT, aimed at teachers and students in the Americas, through HCI, UX, video games, education, etc. In brief, having opinion columns and replying to the senders of the letters to the editor, leads to the closure of the publication by the Gardunians, in Spain.

These closings demonstrate the enormous power of the Garduña in the face of *freedom of opinion in the written press (technical and / or specialized) in Spain* at the end of the 20th century and the beginning of the new millennium. A power that has gone beyond the analog medium such as paper and that today has been established in the web: surface, deep and dark areas. Sometimes a little book, like *Indignez-vous!* (Time for Outrage!) by **Stéphane Hessel** (Hessel, 2010) is a good example against the G factor. An author who didn't care about counting the Hirsch index or Hirsch number. However, he has achieved more structural and peaceful changes (i.e., end of bipartisanship in Spain), than all those indexes put together by Google and others, where reality is not reflected, due to the G factor.

Definitely, the main objective of the *Gardunians* like the Francoism in the 20th century has been, is and will be: to *destroy intelligence*. It is the common denominator in some Southern European regions. For this reason, from the most varied sectors of society such as the small family industries belonging to the Bergamo metalworking field (i.e., drinks equipment), the criminals, schizophrenics, narcissistics and bipolar Gardunians are intertwined not only with the provincial industrial union, Lions club, churches, local mass and new media, etc., but also, with foundations and associations (i.e., research for rare diseases –taxes evasion), in Lombardy, until they become co-owners / external administrators of public universities through the corrupt departments of human and social sciences, teaching and learning, special education, computer science, etc.

This is a great "Garduian's parable" in which industrial products that seriously damage health are it can be observed in origin, such as facilitating the worldwide diffusion of *sugary*, alcoholic beverages, etc., generating overweight, diabetes, tumors, etc., without counting the serious social (i.e., alcoholism) or environmental problems (i.e., drinks equipment use carbon dioxide). Besides, they resort to the terminology or typical phrases of ICT marketing such as "continuous innovation of products and processes", "best technologies and traditional know-how", "customized and lean job production", "eco-friendly", "creativity", etc.

Furthermore, the control they exercise over universities and local social media, in situations of health emergencies such as a pandemic, have enhanced the fact that a small Lombard province such as Bergamo, has not only been the first European epicenter of the coronavirus but that the total number of victims has exceeded the Netherlands, in the first phase (officially, more than 6,500 deaths in the first semester of 2020; extra officially, more than 18,000 victims). In essence and without regard for peripheral details, *the first European genocide* of the new millennium has been witnessed from the Lombard academic and industrial sphere. Sadly, the Gardunians have managed to silence (Berizzi, 2020) and underestimate the seriousness of the situation (i.e., video "Bergamo is running" –02.28.2020, see Cannavò, Marzocchi and Minnucci, in additional reading section because now the video is disappearing from the web), even on the Internet or the university or the local mass media (TV, radio and newspaper), which has favored the genocide. Perennially, with the Gardunian's actions we can see only old and new tyrannies of the 20th / 21st centuries, and they enjoy absolute immunity from such behavior, as it is no longer just killing the academic intelligence, but thousands and thousands of human lives in all parts of society. Not only are they destructive, but they operate under a false assumption which has and will cost human life. That assumption they share with other tyrannies like those based on religious / sects structures, vertical and monolithic; NSA; PsyOps; FSB datagathering, etc.: "that having all information" means having power over everybody. The irrepressible bureacratic urge to gather all info about everybody on this planet in real time. It may be a great way to make money for retired generals and physicists, but it is false. It will run inevitably against the stone walls of Ashby's Law of requisite variety.

"If you want to control (parts of) Reality you must build and maintain a Model which is at least as complicated as that (part of Reality)." There are three ways to cope with this: (1) destroy people and new ideas, so Reality becomes more simple to control at the center; (2) distribute and share the Model in small local copies: swarms with collective intelligence and local authority, see chapter of Jaap van Till: "Masters of Imagination: From Hierarchies to Connected Swarms"; (3) be much much less ambitious at the centers and encourage creativity and wealth creation with the help of ICT. It should be obvious that the old men and women of the Gardinians did choose (1). But that destruction and sabotage will lead to their own collapse, sooner or later like every outdated empire did.

CONCLUSION

Throughout the appendix, the destructive presence of the G Factor has been verified. The examples have served to detect their presence camouflaged in a myriad of variables that a priori can look trivial, such as searching for information online or lying in the content of the messages. However, in the web each information node is interconnected to other nodes, and the damages caused by false information can be irrepairable, given the legal and technical void to solve them immediately.

In educational structures, the G Factor has multiplied exponentially in recent years, especially with the appearance of the social networks. The consequences of the non-differentiation between the terms freedom and debauchery by users can lead to the loss of access for all to free online information. That is why it is necessary to define Gardunia as a destructive and criminal entity that has spread rapidly throughout our planet. The aim is to obtain the greatest control and in the shortest possible time through the education of future generations and the use of ICT, to cite one example. The members of that invisible but powerful entity, called Gardunians, are above the entire known legal system, and therefore enjoy absolute immunity. All this is irrespective of the fact that in some countries, their local laws can define them as criminal associations to commit crimes.

At the same time, the anchoring of these first new notions (Gardunia, Gardunians, Gardunying, and Gardunially), encompassed in the expression G Factor, serves to indicate the high degree of danger and destruction of this factor, inside and outside the new technologies, education, health, economy, industry, business, etc. Considering also, all the unions and intersections, either with the formal sciences, as well as with the factual sciences. Simultaneously, it is possible to differentiate it from other pejorative terms, with a greater universal use, which are fragmentary and in some cases derivatives of Gardunia. Some of these terms are: 'ndrangueta, camorra, caste, *cielinos*, clan, godfather, godmother, lobby, mafia, masonry, parochialism, sacra corona unita, sect, etc. Linguistics and semiotics, among other disciplines, play a fundamental role in detecting the presence of the G factor.

A G-factor that has managed to destroy in a short time, the exact limits of novel disciplines such as HCI, web engineering, usability engineering, user experience, etc. That is why in our days, from the universities and erroneously HCI = Human Computer Interaction has been diluted in mathematics, physics, chemistry, nuclear engineering, industrial engineering, artificial intelligence, smart city, 5G, cloud computing, IoT, etc. This is a consequence of the lack of control in the educational and scientific structures.

REFERENCES

Aitala, R. (2018). *Il metodo della paura*. Laterza.

Berizzi, P. (2020). Bergamo, il freno delle aziende e gli errori in corsia. Così la città è diventata capitale europea del virus: solo a Wuhan più vittime e contagi. *La Repubblica*. Retrieved September 26, 2020, from https://rep.repubblica.it/pwa/generale/2020/03/21/news/bergamo_il_freno_delle_aziende_e_gli_errori_in_corsia-251938013/

Brown, J. (1963). *Techniques of Persuasion: From Propaganda to Brainwashing*. Penguin Books.

Bunge, M. (1998). *Critical Approaches to Science and Philosophy*. Routledge.

Cazeneuve, J. (1972). *La société de l'ubiquité, communication et diffusion*. Denoël.

Cipolla-Ficarra, F. (2010). *Quality and Communicability for Interactive Hypermedia Systems: Concepts and Practices for Design*. IGI Global. doi:10.4018/978-1-61520-763-3

Cipolla-Ficarra, F. (2015). *Handbook of Research on Interactive Information Quality in Expanding Social Network Communications*. IGI Global. doi:10.4018/978-1-4666-7377-9

Cipolla-Ficarra, F. (2015). *Web Attacks, Security Computer Science and Parochialims of the Cyber Destructors: Concepts and Analysis from Informatics and Social Sciences*. Bergamo: Blue Herons editions.

De Alessandri, E. (2010). *Comunione e liberazione: Assalto al potere in Lombardia*. Bepress.

Hessel, S. (2010). *Indignez-vous!* Montpellier: Indigène éditions.

House, W. (2000). *Charts of Cults, Sects, and Religious Moviments*. Zondervan.

Leone, M. (2018). *Guida alle Società Segrete*. Bolonia: Odoya.

Machovec, F. (1991). Cults and Mental Disorders. *Medical Psychotherapy An International Journal,* (4), 27-33.

MacKenzie, N. (1968). *Secret Societies*. Crescent.

Maldonado, T. (1997). *Critica della ragione informatica*. Feltrinelli.

Motilla, A. (1990). *Sectas y derecho en España: Un estudio en torno a la posición de los nuevos movimientos en el ordenamiento jurídico*. Editoriales de Derecho Reunidas.

Nielsen, J. (1990). *Usability Engineering*. Academic Press.

Oberschall, A. (1973). *Social Conflict and Social Movements*. Prentice-Hall.

Penalva-Buitrago, J. (2011). *Corrupción en la Universidad*. Ciudadela Libros.

Pinotti, F. (2010). *La lobby di Dio. Fede, affari e politica. La prima inchiesta su Comunione e Liberazione e la Compagnia delle opere*. Chiarelettere.

Qates, M., Ruf, L., & Driver, J. (2009). Women of Opus Dei. In *Their Own Words*. The Crossroad.

Singer, M., & Lalich, J. (1997). *Las sectas entre nosotros*. Gedisa.

Spilka, B. (1982). *The Psychology of Religion: An Empirical Approach*. Prentice-Hall.

Veltman, K. (2016). *9 and 11: Day of Fate. Day of Destiny. Day that Changed the World.* VMMI Press.

Wilson, B. (1982). *Religion in Sociological Perspective*. Oxford University Press.

ADDITIONAL READING

Arenal, C. (1974). *La emancipación de la mujer en España*. Júcar.

Barlett, C. (2019). *Predicting Cyberbullying: Research, Theory, and Intervention*. Academic Press.

Bauer, A. (2001). *Grand O. Les vérites du Gran Maître du Grand Orient de France*. Denoël.

Cannavò, S. (2020). Coronavirus, allarme nella Bergamasca già a febbraio. Ma Confindustria pubblicava il video: "Bergamo is running." *Il Fatto Quotidiano*. Retrieved September 27, 2020, from https://www.ilfattoquotidiano.it/in-edicola/articoli/2020/03/20/allarme-gia-a-febbraio-ma-confindustria-bergamo-is-running/5742931/

Cascio, M. (2016). *Umberto Eco e la massoneria*. Tipheret.

Castronovo, V. (2016). *L'Europa e la rinascita dei nazionalismi*. Laterza.

Charaudeau, P. (2014). *Le discours politique: Les masques du pouvoir*. Lambert-Lucas.

Chevalier, J., & Gheerbrant, A. (1994). *A dictionary of symbols*. Blackwell.

Cipolla-Ficarra, F. (2010). *Persuasion On-Line and Communicability*. Nova Publishers.

Cipolla-Ficarra, F. (2019a). Análisis del Discurso Tecnológico como Estrategia del Neocolonialismo. In 14° Congreso Mundial de Semiótica. Buenos Aires: IASS-AIS.

Cipolla-Ficarra, F. (2019b). *Feminismo para Potenciar el Racismo en las Imágenes? Una Metodología de Evaluación en las Redes Sociales Europeas Relacionadas con la Informática. In 14° Congreso Mundial de Semiótica*. IASS-AIS.

De Paz-Sánchez, M. (1983). *Intelectuales, Poetas e Ideólogos en la Francmasonería Canaria del Siglo XIX*. Ecotopia.

Desantes-Fernández, B. (1993). *Inventario de fondos masónicos de Cataluña y Baleares*. Dirección de Archivos Estatales.

Galli, G. (2013). *Hitler e la cultura occulta*. Rizzoli.

Havens, L. (2004). *Psychiatric Movements: From Sects to Science*. Routledge.

Helander, M., Landauer, T., & Prabhu, P. (1997). Handbook of Human Computer Interaction. Amsterdam: Elsevier.

Hirigoyen, M. F., Moore, T., & Marx, H. (2005). *Stalking the Soul: Emotional Abuse and the Erosion of Identity*. DAP.

Kaiser, B. (2019). *Targeted*. HarperCollins.

Madariaga, S. (1967). *Portrait of Europe*. The Bodley Head.

Marzocchi, A. (2020). Coronavirus, il presidente di Confindustria Bergamo: "Errore il video 'Bergamo is running'". E nega pressioni per non istituire la zona rossa. *Il Fatto Quotidiano*. Retrieved September 27, 2020, from https://www.ilfattoquotidiano.it/2020/03/31/coronavirus-il-presidente-di-confindustria-bergamo-errore-il-video-bergamo-is-running-e-nega-pressioni-per-non-istituire-la-zona-rossa/5753746/

Minnucci, M. (2020). "Bergamo is running", quel video stonato di Confindustria. *Collectiva*. https://www.collettiva.it/copertine/italia/2020/03/31/news/_bergamo_is_running_quel_video_stonato_di_confindustria-91259/

Thurlow, C., & Jaworski, A. (2018). *Elite Discourse: The Rhetorics of Status, Privilege and Power*. Routledge. doi:10.4324/9781315100548

Van Dijk, T. A. (1993). *Elite Discourse and Racism*. SAGE. doi:10.4135/9781483326184

Virion, P. (1967). *Bientôt un gouvernement mondial, une super et contre Eglise?* Téqui.

Zimbardo, P. & Hartley, C. (1985). Cults go to High School: A Theoretical and Empirical Analysis of the Inicial Stage in the Recruitment Process. *Cultic Studies Journal,* (2), 91-147.

Compilation of References

Ahituv, N. (2001). The Open Information Society. *Communications of the ACM*, *44*(1), 48–49. doi:10.1145/376134.376158

Akkaya, K., & Younis, M. (2005). A survey on routing protocols for wireless sensor networks. *Ad Hoc Networks*, *3*(3), 325–349. doi:10.1016/j.adhoc.2003.09.010

Al-Fuqaha, A., Guizani, M., Mohammadi, M., Aledhari, M., & Ayyash, M. (2015). Internet of things: A survey on enabling technologies, protocols, and applications. *IEEE Communications Surveys and Tutorials*, *17*(4), 2347–2376. doi:10.1109/COMST.2015.2444095

Allende, S. C. (2018). *Be More Pirate*. Penguin Random House.

Allier, S. (2015). Multitier Diversification in Web-Based Software Applications. *IEEE Computer*, *32*(1), 83–90.

Allu, Y., Douglis, F., Kamat, M., Shilane, P., Patterson, H., & Zhu, B. (2017). Backup to the Future: How Workload and Hardware Changes Continually Redefine Data Domain File Systems. *IEEE Computer*, *50*(7), 64–72. doi:10.1109/MC.2017.187

Al-Sarawi, S., Anbar, M., Alieyan, K., & Alzubaidi, M. (2017). Internet of things (iot) communication protocols: Review. *8th International Conference on Information Technology (ICIT)*, 685–690. 10.1109/ICITECH.2017.8079928

Alston, R. (1999). Ties that bind: soldiers and societies. In A. Goldsworthy & I. Haynes (Eds.), *The Roman Army as Community. Academic Press.*

Andriole, S. (2010). Business Impact of Web 2.0 Technologies. *Communications of the ACM*, *53*(12), 67–79. doi:10.1145/1859204.1859225

Apple. (1992). *Macintosh Human Interface Guidelines*. Addison-Wesley.

Applebaum, A. (2020a). *Twilight of Democracy – The Seductive Lure of Authoritarianism*. London: Penguin Random House.

Applebaum, A. (2020b). The 22-Year-Old Blogger Behind Protests in Belarus. *The Atlantic*. https://www.theatlantic.com/ideas/archive/2020/08/22-year-old-blogger-behind-protests-belarus/615526/

Applegate, D. L., Bixby, R. M., Chvátal, V., & Cook, W. J. (2006). *The Traveling Salesman Problem: A Computational Study*. Princeton University Press.

Appuswamy, R., Graefe, G., Borovica-Gajic, R., & Ailamaki, A. (2019). The Five-Minute Rule 30 Years Later and Its Impact on the Storage Hierarchy. *Communications of the ACM*, *82*(11), 114–120. doi:10.1145/3318163

Arce, R. A. (2013). *Mobile learning: aprendizaje móvil como complemento de una estrategia de trabajo colaborativo con herramientas Web 2 y entorno virtual de aprendizaje WebUNLP en modalidad de blended learning. In Primeras Jornadas Nacionales de TIC e Innovación en el Aula*. Universidad Nacional de La Plata.

Argentina, T. E. C. H. O. (2016). *Argentina - Índice de vulnerabilidad territorial 2016*. http://datos.techo.org/dataset/argentina-indice-de-vulnerabilidad-territorial-2016

Arito, F. L. A. (2010). *Optimization Algorithms based on Ant Colonies applied to the Quadratic Allocation Problem and other related problems* (Unpublished degree thesis). National University of Saint Louis. Argentine.

Armas, F. (2018). Educar para la vida. *Cuatro Vientos*, (7), 4.

Asimov, I. (1957). Profession. In *Astounding Science Fiction*. https://www.abelard.org/asimov.php

Asociación Rosarina de Ayuda Solidaria (A.R.A.S). (n.d.). *Sobre Nosotros A.R.A.S.* http://www.aras.org.ar

Atzori, L., Iera, A., & Morabito, G. (2010). The internet of things: A survey. *Computer Networks*, *54*(15), 2787–2805. doi:10.1016/j.comnet.2010.05.010

Azuma, A. T. (1997). A survey on augmented reality. *Presence (Cambridge, Mass.)*, *6*(4), 355–385.

Azuma, R. (1997). A Survey of Augmented Reality. *Presence (Cambridge, Mass.)*, *6*(4), 355–385. doi:10.1162/pres.1997.6.4.355

Badger L. et al. (2014). US Government Cloud Computing Technology Roadmap. *NIST Special Publication, 1*(2), 85.

Bagchi, S., Siddiqui, M.-B., Wood, P., & Zhang, H. (2020). Dependability in Edge Computing. *Communications of the ACM*, *63*(1), 58–66. doi:10.1145/3362068

Bagga, P. (2013). Real Time Depth Computation Using Stereo Imaging. *JEEE*, *1*(2), 51. doi:10.11648/j.jeee.20130102.13

Baggio, D. L., Emami, S., Escriva, D. M., Ievgen, K., Saragih, J., & Shilkrot, R. (2017). [Packt Publishing Ltd.]. *Mastering Open*, *CV*, 3.

Baier, D., Rese, A., & Schreiber, S. (2015). Analyzing online reviews to measure technology acceptance at the point of scale — the case of IKEA. In E. Pantano (Ed.), *Successful Technological Integration for Competitive Advantage in Retail Settings* (pp. 168–189). IGI Global.

Baker, W. H., & Fallace, L. (2007). Is Information Security Under Control? Investigating Quality in Information Security Management. *IEEE Security and Privacy*, *5*(1), 36–44. doi:10.1109/MSP.2007.11

Balog, A., & Pribeanu, C. (2010). The role of perceived enjoyment in the students' acceptance of an augmented reality teaching platform: A structural equation modeling approach. *Studies in Informatics and Control*, *19*(3), 319–330.

Barabási, A. L. (2016). *Network Science*. Cambridge University Press.

Barker, P. (1991). Interactive Electronic Books. *Interactive Multimedia*, *2*(1), 11–28.

Barker, P. (1993). *Exploring Hypermedia*. Kogan Page.

Baronti, P., Pillai, P., Chook, V. W., Chessa, S., Gotta, A., & Hu, Y. F. (2007). Wireless sensor networks: A survey on the state of the art and the 802.15.4 and zigbee standards. *Computer Communications*, *30*(7), 1655–1695. doi:10.1016/j.comcom.2006.12.020

Basili, V. R., Briand, L., Bianculli, D., Nejati, S., Pastore, F., & Sabetzadeh, M. (2018). Software Engineering Research and Industry: A Symbiotic Relationship to Foster Impact. *IEEE Software*, *35*(5), 44–49. doi:10.1109/MS.2018.290110216

Basili, V. R., & Musa, J. D. (1991). The Future Engineering of Software: A Management Perspective. *IEEE Computer*, *24*(9), 90–96. doi:10.1109/2.84903

Batalla, M., Monsalvo San Macario, E., González Aguña, A., & Santamaría García, J. M. (2018). Diseño de un método de análisis para el cálculo de la vulnerabilidad como predictor de la fragilidad en salud. *Ene-. Revista de Enfermeria (Barcelona, Spain)*, *12*(1). http://www.ene-enfermeria.org/ojs/index.php/ENE/article/view/786

Batista, A., Cabrera, L., & Villanueva, F. (2014). Demandas Laborales de la Generación Z. *Repositorio Institucional UADE* (Universidad Argentina de la Empresa). https://repositorio.uade.edu.ar/xmlui/bitstream/handle/123456789/2423/Battista.pdf?sequence=1&isAllowed=y

Belk, R. (2013). Visual and projective methods in Asian research. *Qualitative Market Research*, *16*(1), 94–107.

Bellekens, B., Spruyt, V., Berkvens, R., & Weyn, M. (2014). A survey of rigid 3d pointcloud registration algorithms. In *AMBIENT 2014: the Fourth International Conference on Ambient Computing, Applications, Services and Technologies, August 24-28, 2014, Rome, Italy* (pp. 8-13). Academic Press.

Benkler, Y., Faris, R., & Roberts, H. (2018). *Network Propaganda –Manipulation, Disinformation, and Radicalization in American Politics*. Oxford University Press.

Bergin, T. J., & Gibson, R. G. (1996). *History of Programming Languages*. ACM Press. doi:10.1145/234286

Berk, A. (1985). *LISP: Language of Artificial Intelligence*. Cengage Learning publisher.

Bermubez Irreño, C. A., & Quiñonez Aguilar, E. D. (2018). Aplicación Práctica Del Proceso De Análisis Jerárquico (AHP), para la Toma de decisiones. *Revista de Ingeniería. Matemáticas y Ciencias de la Informática*, *5*(9), 91–100.

Berners-Lee, T. (2014). World Wide Web needs bill of rights. *BBC News*. https://www.bbc.co.uk/news/uk-26540635

Berners-Lee, T. (1996). WWW: Past, Present, and Future. *IEEE Computer*, *29*(10), 79–85. doi:10.1109/2.539724

Berners-Lee, T. (1999). *Weaving the Web*. HarperCollins.

Berners-Lee, T., Cailliau, R., Luotonen, A., Nielsen, H. F., & Secret, A. (1991). The World-Wide Web. *Communications of the ACM*, *37*(8), 76–82. doi:10.1145/179606.179671

Bertolini, P. (1988). *L'esistere pedagogico. Ragioni e limiti di una pedagogia come scienza fenomenologicamente fondata*. La Nuova Italia.

Berumen, S., & Redondo, F. (2007). La utilidad de lis métodos de decisión multicriterio (como el AHP) en un entorno de competitividad creciente. *Cuadernos Americanos*, *20*(34), 65–87.

Bessant, J., & Tidd, J. (2015). *Innovation and Entrepreneurship*. Whiley.

Bettelheim, B. (1990). *La Vienna di Freud*. Feltrinelli Editore.

Bhagwat, P. (2001). Bluetooth: Technology for short-range wireless apps. *IEEE Internet Computing*, *5*(3), 96–103. doi:10.1109/4236.935183

Bianchi-Bandinelli, R. (1970). *Rome, la fin de l'art antique: l'art de l'Empire romain de Septime Sévère à Théodose*. Gallimard.

Blazquez Sevilla, A. (2017). Realidad Aumentada en Educación. *Archivo Digital UPM,* 1-35. http://oa.upm.es/45985

Bolter, J., Engberg, M., & Mcintyre, B. (2013). Media Studies, Mobile Augmented Reality, and Interaction Design. *Interaction*, *20*(1), 37–45. doi:10.1145/2405716.2405726

Bone, C., Ager, A., Bunzel, K., & Tierney, L. (2016). *A geospatial search engine for discovering multi-format geospatial data across the web*. doi:10.1080/17538947.2014.966164

Book-that-Work. (1996). *CD-Rom Garden Encyclopedia.* Bellevue: Book That *Work*.

Borgia, E. (2014). The internet of things vision: Key features, applications and open issues. *Computer Communications*, *54*, 1–31. doi:10.1016/j.comcom.2014.09.008

Botta, A., de Donato, W., Persico, V., & Pescapé, A. (2016). Integration of cloud computing and internet of things: A survey. *Future Generation Computer Systems*, *56*, 684–700. doi:10.1016/j.future.2015.09.021

Bouissac, P. (1998). *Encyclopedia of Semiotics*. Oxford University Press.

Bovyrin, A. V. (2013). *Development of Multimedia Applications Using the OpenCV and IPP Libraries: studies. course*. NGU N.Lobachevsky.

Brandtzaeg, P., & Folstad, A. (2017). Trust and Distrust in Online Fact-Checking Services. *Communications of the ACM*, *60*(9), 65–71. doi:10.1145/3122803

Brassard, G., & Bratley, P. (1996). *Fundamentals of Algorithmics*. Prentice Hall.

Bruner, J. S. (1961). The act of discovery. *Harvard Educational Review*, *31*, 21–32.

Bruner, J. S. (1990). *Acts of meaning* (Vol. 3). Harvard University Press.

Bruner, J. S. (2002). *Making stories: Law, literature* (Vol. 23). Life.

Bruner, J. S., & Minds, A. (1986). *Possible Worlds*. Harvard University Press.

Buckland, M. (2006). *Emanuel Goldberg and His Knowledge Machine*. Greenwood Publishing Group.

Budán, P., Rosenzvaig, F., Najar, P., Saavedra, E., Herrera, S., & Morales, M. (2018). Mobile-RA: Método Ágil para el Desarrollo de Aplicaciones Móviles Multiplataforma. In *VI Congreso Nacional de Ingeniería Informática y Sistemas de Información* (pp. 1009-1022). Universidad Tecnológica Nacional.

Bulearca, M., & Tamarjan, D. (2010). Augmented reality: A sustainable marketing tool? *Global Business and Management Research*, *2*(2–3), 237–252.

Bunge, M. (1981). *The science: your method and your philosophy*. Siglo XXI.

Burton, A. (2020). Improving Social Alignment During Digital Transformation. *Communications of the ACM*, *63*(9), 65–71. doi:10.1145/3410429

Cabero Almenara, J., Barroso Osuna, J. & Obrador, M. (2017). Realidad aumentada aplicada a la enseñanza de la medicina. *Elsevier La revista Educación Médica*, *18*(3), 203-208.

Cabero Almenara, J., García Jiménez, F., & Barroso Osuna, J. (2016). La producción de objetos de aprendizaje en "Realidad Aumentada": La experiencia del SAV de la Universidad de Sevilla. *IJERI International Journal of Educational Research and Innovation*, *6*, 110–123.

Carlos S., Guzmán B. & Rodríguez M. S. (2007). Computación en la nube, una tecnología emergente en la educación y en el sector empresarial: beneficios y desventajas desde el punto de vista operativo y ambiental. *Revista Iberoamericana para la Investigación y el Desarrollo Educativo*, 1-42.

Carlsson & Gustavsson. (2001). The rise and fall of napster - an evolutionary approach. In Active Media Technology, volume 2252 of Lecture Notes in Computer Science, (pp. 347–354). Springer.

Carra, D., Lo Cigno, R., & Biersack, E. W. (2007). Graph based analysis of mesh overlay streaming systems. Selected Areas in Communications. *IEEE Journal on, 25*(9), 1667–1677.

Cascarino, G. (2008). L'esercito romano. Armamento e organizzazione.: Vol. II. *Da Augusto ai Severi*. Il Cerchio.

Casetti, F. (2005). *L'occhio del Novecento: cinema, esperienza, modernità*. Bompiani.

Cerf, V. (2007). An Information Avalanche. *IEEE Computer, 40*(1), 104–105. doi:10.1109/MC.2007.5

Chafonova, V. G., & Gazeeva, I. V. (2014). Methods of Imaging a Stereo Pair With A Given Parallax Value. *Scientific and Technical Journal of Information Technologies, Mechanics and Optics, 6*(94).

Challiol, C., Lliteras, A., & Gordillo, S. (2017). Diseño de Aplicaciones Móviles basadas en Posicionamiento: un Framework Conceptual. In XXIII Congreso Argentino de Ciencias de la Computación, (pp. 682-691). Buenos Aires: Universidad Nacional de La Plata.

Chang, S. (2018). *Frontiers of Multimedia Research*. ACM and Morgan & Claypool.

Charette, R., & King, J. L. (2018). Winning and Losing in IT. *IEEE Computer, 51*(10), 10–15. doi:10.1109/MC.2018.3971361

Chen, H. (2010a). Business and Market Intelligence 2.0. *IEEE Intelligent Systems. Part I., 25*(1), 68–81. doi:10.1109/MIS.2010.27

Chen, H. (2010b). Business and Market Intelligence 2.0. *IEEE Intelligent Systems. Part II., 25*(2), 74–82. doi:10.1109/MIS.2010.43

Chihi, H., Chainbi, W., & Ghdira, K. (2016). Cloud computing architecture and migration strategy for universities and higher education. *2015 IEEE/ACS 12th International Conference of Computer Systems and Applications (AICCSA)*, 1-8.

Chris, A. (2006). *The Long Tail: Why the Future of Business is Selling Less of More*. Hyperion.

Cicerone, S., Di Stefano, G., & Handke, D. (2005). Self-spanner graphs. *Discrete Applied Mathematics, 150*(1-3), 99–120. doi:10.1016/j.dam.2005.04.004

Cipolla-Ficarra, F., & Alma, J. (2015). Banking Online: Design for a New Credibility. In Information Resources Management Association (Ed.), Banking, Finance, and Accounting: Concepts, Methodologies, Tools, and Applications. Hershey: IGI Global.

Cipolla-Ficarra, F. (1996). *Evaluation and Communication Techniques in Multimedia Product Design for On the Net University Education. In Multimedia on the Net*. Springer. doi:10.1007/978-3-7091-9472-0_14

Cipolla-Ficarra, F. (2010). *Advances in Dynamic and Static Media for Interactive Systems: Communicability, Computer Science and Design*. Blue Herons.

Cipolla-Ficarra, F. (2010). *Human-Computer Interaction, Tourism and Cultural Heritage*. Springer.

Cipolla-Ficarra, F. (2010a). *Persuasion On-Line and Communicability: The Destruction of Credibility in the Virtual Community and Cognitive Models*. Nova Science.

Cipolla-Ficarra, F. (2010b). *Quality and Communicability for Interactive Hypermedia Systems: Concepts and Practices for Design*. IGI Global. doi:10.4018/978-1-61520-763-3

Cipolla-Ficarra, F. (2012). *New Horizons in Creative Open Software, Multimedia, Human Factors and Software Engineering*. Blue Herons.

Cipolla-Ficarra, F. (2014). *Handbook of Research on Interactive Information Quality in Expanding Social Network Communications*. IGI Global.

Cipolla-Ficarra, F. (2017). *Technology-Enhanced Human Interaction in Modern Society*. IGI Global.

Cipolla-Ficarra, F. (2018a). *Expanding Horizonts in Smart Cities, Software Engineering, Mobile Communicability, Cloud Technologies, and Big-data*. Blue Herons.

Cipolla-Ficarra, F. (2019). *Examining New Points of View in Web Engineering, Visual Interfaces, Motion Graphics and Human-Computer Communicability*. Blue Herons.

Cipollla-Ficarra, F. (2017). *Cyber Destructors of the Sciences: Studies in Education, Culture, Employment and New Technologies*. Blue Herons.

Cirelli E. (2008). *Ravenna: archeologia di una città*. Borgo San Lorenzo (Fi), All'Insegna del Giglio.

Classe, A. (1957). The whistled language of La Gomera. *Scientific American*, *196*(4), 111–124. doi:10.1038cientifica merican0457-111

Cline, E. (2011). *Ready Player One*. Crown Publishing Group.

Cobley, P., & Jancz, L. (1999). Introducing Semiotics. Crows Nest: Allen & Unwin Pty.

Cook, S. (1971). The Complexity of Theorem Proving Procedures. In *Proceedings Third Annual ACM Symposium on Theory of Computing* (pp. 151-158). Shaker Heights, OH: ACM. 10.1145/800157.805047

Córdoba, M., Budan, P., & Najar, P. (2016). Sistema Alternativo de Comunicación para Niños con Parálisis Cerebral Infantil. In Investigaciones en Facultades de Ingeniería del NOA. Jujuy: Universidad Nacional de Jujuy.

Corning, P. (2018). *Synergistic Selection – How Cooperation Has Shaped Evolution and the Rise of Humankind*. World Scientific Publishing.

Coskun, V., Ozdenizci, B., & Ok, K. (2013). A survey on near field communication (NFC) technology. *Wireless Personal Communications*, *71*(3), 2259–2294. doi:10.100711277-012-0935-5

Costa, A. (2011). *Saper vedere il cinema*. Giunti.

Crocker, S. D. (2019). The Arpanet and Its Impact on the State of Networking. *IEEE Computer*, *52*(10), 14–23. doi:10.1109/MC.2019.2931601

Csermely, P. (2006). *Weak Links – The Universal key to the Stability of Networks and Complex Systems*. Springer.

D'Incerti, D., Santoro, M., & Varchetta, F. (2007). *Nuovi schermi di formazione: i grandi temi del management attraverso il cinema*. Guerini.

Dahlman, E., Parkvall, S., & Skold, J. (2020). *5G NR: The Next Generation Wireless Access Technology*. Academic Press.

Daponte, P., De Vito, L., Picariello, F., & Riccio, M. (2014). State of the art and future developments of the augmented reality for measurement applications. *Measurement*, *57*, 53–70.

Davies, P. (2019). Life's secret ingredient: A radical theory of what makes things alive. *New Scientist*.

Davis, F. D. (1989). Perceived usefulness, perceived ease of use, and user acceptance of information technology. *Management Information Systems Quarterly*, *13*(3), 319–340.

Dawson-Howe, K. (2014). *A Practical Introduction to Computer Vision with OPENCV*. John Wiley & Sons.

Daymon, C., & Holloway, I. (2002). *Qualitative Research Methods in Public Relations and Marketing Communications*. Routledge.

De Saussure, F. (2011). *Course in General Linguistics*. Columbia University Press.

de Trabajo, M., Empleo y Seguridad, S., & Presidencia de la Nación, A. (2017). *Las Mujeres en el Mercado del Trabajo-Documento de trabajo para el debate en el marco de la CTIO género*. http://trabajo.gob.ar/downloads/igualdad/DocumentoDEGIOT_Sep2017.pdf

Deely, J. (1986). *Frontiers in Semiotics*. Indiana University Press.

Deledalle, G. (2001). *Charles S. Peirce's Philosophy of Signs: Essays in Comparative Semiotics*. Indiana University Press.

Delía, L. (2017). *Desarrollo de aplicaciones móviles multiplataforma. Especialista en Ingeniería de Software*. Universidad Nacional de La Plata.

Demetrio, D. (1995). Raccontarsi: l'autobiografia come cura di sé. Milano: Cortina.

Demirkan, H., & Spohrer, J. (2014). Developing a framework to improve virtual shopping in digital malls with intelligent self-service systems. *Journal of Retailing and Consumer Services*, *21*(5), 860–868.

Dergachov, K., Krasnov, L., Cheliadin, O., & Plakhotnyi, O. (2019). Development of Methods and Means of Color Correction of Web-Cameras in Binocular Systems. Systems of Control, Navigation and Communication. *Collection of Scientific Works, 2*(54), 87-98.

Dergachov, K., Kulik, A., & Zymovin, A. (2019). Environments Diagnosis by Means of Computer Vision System of Autonomous Flying Robots. In Automated Systems in the Aviation and Aerospace Industries (pp. 115-137). IGI Global. doi:10.4018/978-1-5225-7709-6.ch004

DeWitt, D., Siraj, S., & Alias, N. (2014). Collaborative mLearning: A Module for Learning Secondary School Science. *Journal of Educational Technology & Society*, *17*(1), 89–101.

Dideles, M. (2003). Bluetooth: A technical overview. *XRDS*, *9*(4), 11–18. doi:10.1145/904080.904083

Diderot, D., & le-Rond-d'Alembert, J. (1728). Encyclopedia, or a Systematic Dictionary of the Sciences, Arts, and Crafts. *Wikipedia*. Retrieved April 12, 2020 from https://en.wikipedia.org/wiki/Cyclop%C3%A6dia,_or_an_Universal_Dictionary_of_Arts_and_Sciences

Dixit, A., Bhatia, K., & Yadav, J. (2015). Design and implementation of domain based semantic hidden Web crawler. *Int. J. Innov. Adv. Comput. Sci*, *4*, 73–84.

Domina, T., Lee, S. E., & MacGillivray, M. (2012). Understanding factors affecting consumer intention to shop in a virtual world. *Journal of Retailing and Consumer Services*, *19*(6), 613–620.

Dorigo, M., & Stützle, T. (2003). The ant colony optimization metaheuristic: Algorithms, applications and advances. Handbook of Metaheuristics, 57, 251-285.

Dorigo, M., Maniezzo, V., & Colorni, A. (1996). The Ant System: Optimization by a colony of cooperating agents. IEEE Transactions on Systems, Man and Cybernetics - Part B, 26(1), 1-41.

Dorigo, M., & Gambardella, L. M. (1996). A study of some properties of Ant-Q. In *IV International Conference on Parallel Problem from Nature*. Berlin, Germany: Springer-Verlag. 10.1007/3-540-61723-X_1029

Dorigo, M., & Gambardella, L. M. (1997). Ant Colony System: A cooperative learning approach to the traveling salesman problem. *IEEE Transactions on Evolutionary Computation*, *1*(1), 53–66. doi:10.1109/4235.585892

Dorigo, M., & Stützle, T. (2004). *Ant colony optimization*. The MIT Press. doi:10.7551/mitpress/1290.001.0001

Dorling-Kindersley & Zeta. (1998). *CD-Rom Enciclopedia de la Ciencia*. Dorling Kindersley-Zeta.

Doutre, C., & Nasiopoulos, P. (2009). Color Correction Preprocessing for Multiview Video Coding. *IEEE Transactions on Circuits and Systems for Video Technology*, *19*(9), 1400–1406. doi:10.1109/TCSVT.2009.2022780

Dréo, J., Pétrowski, A., Siarry, P., & Taillard, E. (2003). *Metaheuristics for hard optimization*. Springer.

Duening, T., Hisrich, R., & Lechter, M. (2014). *Technology Entrepreneurship: Taking Innovation to the Marketplace*. Academic Press.

Du, M., Liu, N., & Hu, N. (2020). Techniques for Interpretable Machine Learning. *Communications of the ACM*, *63*(1), 68–77. doi:10.1145/3359786

Eco, U. (1979). *Theory of Semiotics*. Indiana University Press.

Eco, U., & Sebeok, T. A. (1984). *The Sign of Three: Dupin, Holmes, Peirce*. Indiana University Press.

Egyed, A., Zeman, K., Hehenberger, P., & Demuth, A. (2018). Maintaining Consistency Across Engineering Artifacts. *IEEE Computer*, *51*(2), 28–35. doi:10.1109/MC.2018.1451666

Eng Keong Lua, J. (2005). A survey and comparison of peer-to-peer overlay network schemes. *IEEE Communications Surveys and Tutorials*, *7*(2), 72–93. doi:10.1109/COMST.2005.1610546

Engelbart, E. (1962). *Augmenting Human Intellect: A Conceptual Framework*. Stanford Research Institute. doi:10.21236/AD0289565

Espasa-Calpe. (1998). *CD-Rom Diccionario de la Lengua Española*. Espasa-Calpe.

Ess, C. (2001). Culture, Technology, Communication: Towards an Intercultural Global Village. New York University Press.

Farris, I., Militano, L., Nitti, M., Atzori, L., & Iera, A. (2016). Mifaas: A mobile IoT federation as a service model for dynamic cooperation of iot cloud providers. *Future Generation Computer Systems*, 126–137.

Farris, I., Militano, L., Nitti, M., Atzori, L., & Iera, A. (2016). Mifaas: A mobile-iot-federation-as-a-service model for dynamic cooperation of iot cloud providers. *Future Generation Computer Systems*, 126–137.

Fecker, U., Barkowsky, M., & Kaup, A. (2008). Histogram-Based Prefiltering for Luminance and Chrominance Compensation of Multiview Video. *IEEE Transactions on Circuits and Systems for Video Technology*, *18*(9), 1258–1267. doi:10.1109/TCSVT.2008.926997

Fennema, M., Herrera, S., Palavecino, R., Budán, P., Rosenzvaig, F., Najar Ruiz, P., Carranza, A., & Saavedra, E. (2017). Aproximaciones para el desarrollo multiplataforma y mantenimiento de Aplicaciones Móviles. In *XIX Workshop de Investigadores en Ciencias de la Computación*, (pp. 446-450). Buenos Aires: Universidad Nacional de La Plata.

Fenton, N. (1994). Software Measurement: A Necessary Scientific Basis. *IEEE Transactions on Software Engineering*, *20*(3), 199–206. doi:10.1109/32.268921

Fenton, N., & Bieman, J. (2014). *Software Metrics: A Rigorous and Practical Approach*. CRC Press. doi:10.1201/b17461

Ferkiss, V. (1994). *Nature, Technology, and Society: The Cultural Roots of the Current Environmental Crisis*. New York University Press.

Florczyk, A., Nogueras-Iso, J., Zarazaga-Soria, F., & Béjar, R. (2012). Identifying orthoimages in Web Map Services. *Computers & Geosciences*, *47*, 130–142. doi:10.1016/j.cageo.2011.10.017

Foucault, M. (1975). *Discipline and Punishment*. Pantheon Books.

Fraigniaud, P., & Gauron, P. (2006). D2b: A de bruijn based content-addressable network. *Theoretical Computer Science*, *355*(1), 65–79. doi:10.1016/j.tcs.2005.12.006

Frantz, T. L., & Carley, K. M. (2005). *A formal characterization of cellular networks*. Available at SSRN 2726808.

Franza, A. M. (1993). *Giovani satiri e vecchi sileni: frammenti di un discorso pedagogico*. Unicopli.

Franza, A. M. (2018). *Teoria della pratica formativa. Apprendimento dall'esperienza e clinica della formazione*. Franco Angeli.

Franza, A. M., & Mottana, P. (1997). *Dissolvenze: le immagini della formazione*. Clueb.

Franzoni C. (1987). *Habitus atque habitudo militis: monumenti funerari di militari nella Cisalpina romana*. Roma: L'Erma di Bretschneider.

Fuller, R. B. (1969). *Operating Manual for Spaceship Earth*. Lasr Muller Publishers.

Fuller, R. B. (1972a). *Synergetics, Explorations in the Geometry of Thinking*. Macmillan.

Fuller, R. B. (1972b). *Utopia or Oblivion: The Prospects for Humanity*. Macmillan.

Gaines, B. (1996). *Convergence to the Information Highway*. University of Calgary Press.

Gallego Rendón, R. A., & Ríos Porras, C. A. (2004). *Hincapíe Isaza, R. A. Heuristic. Techniques applied to the traveling postman problem (TSP)*. Colombia Scientia Et Technica. Technological University of Pereira.

Gálvez-Muñoz, L., & Rodríguez-Madroño, P. (2011). La desigualdad de género en las crisis económicas. Universidad Complutense Madrid. *Investigaciones Feministas*, *2*, 113–132.

Gambardella, L., & Dorigo, M. (1995). Ant-Q: Are inforcement learning approach to the traveling salesman problem. *12th International Conference on Machine Learning*, 252-260. 10.1016/B978-1-55860-377-6.50039-6

Gandhi, D. A., & Ghosal, P. M. (2018). Intelligent Healthcare Using IoT: Extensive Survey. *2018 Second International Conference on Inventive Communication and Computational Technologies (ICICCT)*, 800-802.

García, J. C. S., & Sánchez, B. H. (2016). Influencia del Programa Emprendedor Universitario (PREU) para la mejora de la actitud emprendedora. *Pampa: Revista Interuniversitaria de Estudios Territoriales*, (13), 55-76. https://dialnet.unirioja.es/descarga/articulo/5610764.pdf

Garey, M. R., & Johnson, D. S. (1979). *Computers and Intractability: A Guide to the Theory of NP-Completeness*. W. H. Freeman.

Gascó-Hernandez, M. (2019). Building a Smart City: Lessons from Barcelona. *Communications of the ACM*, *61*(4), 50–57. doi:10.1145/3117800

Genbetadev. (2016). *PhoneGap*. Retrieved August 18, 2016 https://www.genbetadev.com/frameworks/phonegap

Gervautz, M., & Schmalstieg, D. (2012). Anywhere interfaces using handheld augmented reality. *IEEE Computer*, *45*(7), 26–31.

Ghosh, A., Ratasuk, R., Mondal, B., Mangalvedhe, N., & Thomas, T. (2010). Lte-advanced: Next generation wireless broadband technology. *IEEE Wireless Communications*, *17*(3), 10–22. doi:10.1109/MWC.2010.5490974

Gilmore, P. C., & Gomory, R. E. (1964). Sequencing a one state-variable machine: A solvable case of the traveling salesman problem. *Operations Research, 12*(5), 655–679. doi:10.1287/opre.12.5.655

Glover, F. G., & Kochenberger, G. A. (2003). *Handbook of Metaheuristics (International Series in Operations Research & Management Science).* Kluwer Academic Publishers New York.

Godbolt, M. (2020). Optimizations in C++ Compilers. *Communications of the ACM, 63*(2), 41–49. doi:10.1145/3369754

Godoy, P. D., Cayssials, R. L., & Garcia Garino, C. (2016). *Zigbee WSN Round Trip Latency in Function of Channel Occupation and Nodes Configuration.* Paper presented at 3rd IEEE Argencon, Buenos Aires, Argentina.

Godoy, P. D., Cayssials, R. L., & Garcia Garino, C. (2016). A WSN Testbed for Teaching Purposes. *IEEE Latin America Transactions, 14*(7), 3351–3357. doi:10.1109/TLA.2016.7587641

Godoy, P. D., Cayssials, R. L., & García Garino, C. (2018). Communication channel occupation and congestion in wireless sensor networks. *Computers & Electrical Engineering, 72*, 846–858. doi:10.1016/j.compeleceng.2017.12.049

Godoy, P. D., Cayssials, R. L., & Garcia Garino, C. (2019). *A Nomadic Testbed for Teaching Computer Architecture. In Computer Science – CACIC 2018. Communications in Computer and Information Science.* Springer. doi:10.1007/978-3-030-20787-8_6

Goertzel, B. (2006). The Hidden Pattern: A Patternist Theory of Mind. Boca Raton: Brown Walker Press.

Goldsworthy, A. (1996). *The Roman Army at War, 100 BC-AD 200.* Clarendon Press.

Google, L. L. C. (2018). *Google Chrome Remote Desktop.* Retrieved April 2020, from https://remotedesktop.google.com/

Gregory, S. (2019). Requirements Engineering: The Quest for Meaningful Metrics: Time for a Change? *IEEE Software, 36*(6), 7–11. doi:10.1109/MS.2019.2933685

Gruber, T. (1995). Toward principles for the design of ontologies used for knowledge sharing. *International Journal of Human-Computer Studies, 43*(5-6), 907–928. doi:10.1006/ijhc.1995.1081

Gubbi, J., Buyya, R., Marusic, S., & Palaniswami, M. (2013). Internet of things (iot): A vision, architectural elements, and future directions. *Future Generation Computer Systems, 29*(7), 1645–1660. doi:10.1016/j.future.2013.01.010

Guerrero-Liquet, G. C., & Faxas-Guzmán, J. (2015). Análisis de toma de decisión con AHP / ANP de energías renovables en República Dominicana República Dominicana. *Anuario de Jóvenes Investigadores, 8*, 27–29.

Gupta, B., Chaube, A., Negi, A., & Goel, U. (2017). Study on Object Detection using Open CV-Python. *International Journal of Computers and Applications, 162*(8), 17–21. doi:10.5120/ijca2017913391

Habbal, A., Abdullah, S. A., Mkpojiogu, E. O. C., Hassan, S., & Benamar, N. (2017). Assessing Experimental Private Cloud Using Web of System Performance Model. *International Journal of Grid and High Performance Computing, 9*(2), 21–35. doi:10.4018/IJGHPC.2017040102

Hamel, G., & Zannini, M. (2020). *Humanocracy – Creating Organizations as Amazing as the People inside them.* Harvard Business Review Press.

Harper, R. (2016). *Practical Foundations for Programming Languages.* Cambridge University Press. doi:10.1017/CBO9781316576892

Harrell, D., & Lim, C. (2017). Reimagining the Avatar Dream: Modeling Social Identity in Digital Media. *Communications of the ACM, 60*(7), 50–61. doi:10.1145/3098342

Hashmi, M., Hänninen, S., & Maki, K. (2011). *Survey of smart grid concepts, architectures, and technological demonstrations worldwide. In 2011 IEEE PES Conference on Innovative Smart Grid Technologies Latin America.* ISGT LA.

Hehn, Mendez, D., Uebernickel, F., Brenner, W., & Broy, M. (2020). On Integrating Design Thinking for Human-Centered Requirements Engineering. *IEEE Software*, *37*(2), 25–31. doi:10.1109/MS.2019.2957715

Hermes, D. (2015). *Xamarin Mobile Application Development: Cross-Platform C# and Xamarin. Forms Fundamentals.* Editorial Apress. doi:10.1007/978-1-4842-0214-2

Hernández, J C. (2003). *Metaheurístics applied to bioinformatics.* University Corporation for Internet Devolopment A.C. (CUDI).

Herrera, S. I., Fennema, M. C., & Sanz, C. V. (2012). Estrategias de m-learning para la formación de posgrado. In *VII Congreso de Tecnología en Educación y Educación en Tecnología*, Buenos Aires: Universidad Nacional de La Plata.

Herrera, S., Morales, M., Palavecino, R., Irurzun, I., Maldonado, M., & Carranza, A. (2017). M-learning con Realidad Aumentada. In *XIX Workshop de Investigadores en Ciencias de la Computación*, (pp. 1280-1284). Buenos Aires: Universidad Nacional de La Plata.

Herrera, S., Morales, M.I., Fennema, M. C. & Sanz, C.V. (2014). *Aprendizaje basado en dispositivos móviles. Experiencias en la Universidad Nacional de Santiago del Estero.* Santiago del Estero: Editorial EDUNSE.

Herrera, S., Palavecino, R., Sanz, C., & Carranza, J. (2017-a). Aprendizaje de Estructuras de Datos mediante m-learning. In I Simpósio Ibero-Americano de Tecnologias Educacionais, (pp. 267-277). Araranguá: Universidade Federal de Santa Catarina.

Herrera, F. (2012). *Introduction to Metahuristic Algorithms.* University of Granada.

Herrera, S. I., Fennema, M. C., Morales, M. I., Palavecino, R. A., Goldar, J. E., & Zuain, S. V. (2015). Mobile technologies in engineering education. *Presentado en International Conference on Interactive Collaborative Learning (ICL)*, Florencia, Italia. 10.1109/ICL.2015.7318197

Herrera, S. I., & Sanz, C. (2014). Collaborative m-learning practice using Educ-Mobile. In *2014 International Conference on Collaboration Technologies and Systems (CTS)*, (pp. 363–370). 10.1109/CTS.2014.6867590

Herrera, S., Sanz, C., & Fennema, M. (2013). MADE-mlearn: Un marco para el análisis, diseño y evaluación de experiencias de m-learning en el nivel de postgrado. *Revista Iberoamericana de Tecnología en Educación y Educación en Tecnología*, *10*, 7–15.

Heule, M., & Kullmann, O. (2017). The Science of Brute Force. *Communications of the ACM*, *60*(8), 70–79. doi:10.1145/3107239

Hirigoyen, M. F. (2019). *Les Narcisse: Ils ont pris le pouvoir.* La Découverte.

Hoftman, R., Marx, M., & Hancock, P. (2008). Metrics, Metrics, Metrics: Negative Hedonicity. *IEEE Intelligent Systems*, *23*(2), 69–73. doi:10.1109/MIS.2008.31

Holdcroft, D. (1991). *Saussure: Signs, System and Arbitrariness.* Cambridge University Press. doi:10.1017/CBO9780511624599

Holland, J. H. (1975). Adaptation in Natural and Artificial Systems. University of Michigan Press.

Hope, V. M. (2001). *Constructing Identity: the Roman funerary monuments of Aquileia, Mainz and Nîmes.* Oxford: British Archaeological Report: International Series.

Hoschek, W. (2002). A Unified Peer-to-Peer Database Framework for Scalable Service and Resource Discovery (vol. 2536). Springer. doi:10.1007/3-540-36133-2_12

Hou, D., Chen, J., & Wu, H. (2016). Discovering Land Cover Web Map Services from the Deep Web with JavaScript Invocation Rules. *International Journal of Geo-Information*, *5*(7), 105. doi:10.3390/ijgi5070105

Huang, C.-Y., & Chang, H. (2016). GeoWeb Crawler: An Extensible and Scalable Web Crawling Framework for Discovering Geospatial Web Resources. *ISPRS International Journal of Geo-Information*, *5*(8), 136. doi:10.3390/ijgi5080136

Huang, T. L., & Hsu Liu, F. (2014). Formation of augmented-reality interactive technology's persuasive effects from the perspective of experiential value. *Internet Research*, *24*(1), 82–109.

Hubel, D. (1990). *The eye, brain, vision* (Vol. 239). Moscow: Mir.

Internet Architecture Board (IAB). (2020). *RFC 8890 The Internet is for End Users*. https://rfc-editor.org/rfc/rfc8890.pdf

Ionic. (2016). *Ionic Framework*. Retrieved August 13, 2016. https://ionicframework.com/docs/guide/preface.html

IoT Scenarios. (2019). Retrieved from https://iot.ieee.org/iot-scenarios.html

IoT Scenarios. (2020). Retrieved from https://iot.ieee.org/iot-scenarios.html

Ito, M. (2009). *Engineering Play: A Cultural History of Children's Software*. The MIT Press. doi:10.7551/mitpress/7939.001.0001

Jackson, M. (2006). What Can We Expect from Program Verification? *IEEE Computer*, *39*(10), 65–71. doi:10.1109/MC.2006.363

Jäschke, R. &. (2008). Logsonomy: A Search Engine Folksonomy. *Proceedings of the Second International Conference on Weblogs and Social Media, ICWSM*.

Javornik, A. (2016). Augmented reality: Research agenda for studying the impact of its media characteristics on consumer behavior. *Journal of Retailing and Consumer Services*, *30*, 252–261. doi:10.1016/j.jretconser.2016.02.004

Jirotka, M., Grimpe, B., Stahl, B., Eden, G., & Hartswood, M. (2017). Responsible Research and Innovation in the Digital Age. *Communications of the ACM*, *60*(5), 62–68. doi:10.1145/3064940

Joshi, P. (2015). *OpenCV with Python by example*. Packt Publishing Ltd.

Joyanes Aguilar L. (2012). Computación en la Nube. Notas para una estrategia española en cloud computing. *Revista del Instituto Español Estudios Estratégicos,* 89–112.

Kanetkar, Y., & Kanetkar, A. (2020). *Let Us Python Solutions*. BPB Publications.

Kaprow, A. (1991). *New Media Applications in Art and Design*. ACM Siggraph.

Kaptelinin, V., & Czerwinski, M. (2007). *Beyond the Desktop Metaphor: Designing Integrated Digital Work Environments*. The MIT Press. doi:10.7551/mitpress/1584.001.0001

Kapur, S. (2017). *Computer Vision with Python 3*. Packt Publishing Ltd.

Katumba, S., & Coetzee, S. (2015). Enhancing the online discovery of geospatial data through taxonomy, folksonomy and semantic annotations. *South African Journal of Geomatics*, *4*(3), 339. Advance online publication. doi:10.4314ajg.v4i3.14

Katumba, S., & Coetzee, S. (2017, September). Employing Search Engine Optimization (SEO) Techniques for Improving the Discovery of Geospatial Resources on the Web. *ISPRS International Journal of Geo-Information*, *6*(9), 284. doi:10.3390/ijgi6090284

Katz, E., Blumler, J. G., & Gurevitch, M. (1974). Utilization of mass communication by the individual. In J. G. Blumler & E. Katz (Eds.), *The uses of mass communications: Current perspectives on gratifications research* (pp. 19–32). Sage.

Kim, J., & Forsythe, S. (2008). Adoption of virtual try-on technology for online apparel shopping. *Journal of International Marketing*, *22*(2), 45–59.

Kim, K. J., & Shin, D.-H. (2015). An acceptance model for smartwatches: Implications for the adoption of future wearable technology. *Internet Research*, *25*(4), 527–541. doi:10.1108/IntR-05-2014-0126

King, W. R., & He, J. (2006). A meta-analysis of the technology acceptance model. *Information & Management*, *43*(6), 740–755. doi:10.1016/j.im.2006.05.003

Kinney, P. (2003). Zigbee technology: Wireless control that simply works. In Communications design conference (Vol. 2, pp. 1-7). Academic Press.

Kit, E. (1995). *Software Testing in the Real World: Improving the Process*. ACM Press & Addison-Wesley.

Kleiner, D. (1977). *Roman Group Portraiture: the funerary reliefs of the late Republic and early Empire*. Garland.

Kleiner, D. (1987). *Roman Imperial Funerary Altars with Portraits*. G. Bretschneider.

Koller, D., Frischer, B., & Humphreys, G. (2009). Research challenges for digital archives of 3D cultural heritage models. *ACM Journal on Computing and Cultural Heritage*, *2*(3), 1–17. doi:10.1145/1658346.1658347

Koo, S., Kim, J., Kim, C., Kim, J., & Cha, H. S. (2020). Development of an Augmented Reality Tour Guide for a Cultural Heritage Site. *ACM Journal on Computing and Cultural Heritage*, *12*(4), 1–24. doi:10.1145/3317552

Korotaev, V.V., Krasnyaschih, A.V., Yaryshev, S.N., & Viet, N.H. (2014). The Method of Automatic Calibration of the Stereoscopic System. *Scientific and Technical Journal of Information Technologies, Mechanics and Optics, 4*(92).

Koshizuka, N., & Sakamura, K. (2010). Ubiquitous ID: Standards for Ubiquitous Computing and the Internet of Things. *Pervasive Computing, IEEE, 9*(4), 98–101. doi:10.1109/MPRV.2010.87

Koutroumpis, P., Leiponen, A., & Thomas, L. (2017). How Important is IT? *Communications of the ACM*, *60*(7), 62–68. doi:10.1145/3019940

Kramer, K., Dedrick, J., & Sharma, P. (2009). One Laptop Per Child: Vision vs. Reality. *Communications of the ACM*, *52*(6), 66–73. doi:10.1145/1516046.1516063

Krylovetsky, A. A., & Protasov, S. I. (2010). Algorithms for Image Analysis in Real-Time Stereo Vision Systems. *Bulletin of the Voronezh State University*, (2), 9-18.

Kshetri, N. (2010). Cloud Computing in Developing Economies. *IEEE Computer*, *43*(10), 47–55. doi:10.1109/MC.2010.212

Kulik, A., Dergachov, K., & Radomskyi, O. (2015). Binocular Technical Vision for Wheeled Robot Controlling. *Transport Problems*, *10*(1), 55–62. doi:10.21307/tp-2015-006

Laganière, R. (2014). *OpenCV Computer Vision Application Programming Cookbook* (2nd ed.). Packt Publishing Ltd.

Landow, G. (2006). Hypertext 3.0: Critical Theory and New Media in an Era of Globalization. Charles Village: Johns Hopkins University Press

Landow, G. (1991). *Hypermedia and Literary Studies*. The MIT Press.

Lazarinis, F. (2010). *Handbook of Research on Technologies and Cultural Heritage: Applications and Environments*. IGI Global.

Le Bohec Y. (1989). *L'armée romaine sous le Haut-Empire*. Paris: Picard éditeur.

Lee, S. (2008). *OntoSonomy: Ontology-based Extension of Folksonomy*. Academic Press.

Lee, Y. (2009). *Journey to Data Quality*. The MIT Press.

Lee, Y., Kozar, K. A., & Larsen, K. R. (2003). The technology acceptance model: Past, present, and future. *Communications of the Association for Information Systems*, *12*(1), 50. doi:10.17705/1CAIS.01250

Leguizamón, G. (n.d.). *Introduction to Metaheuristics*. Document presented in Postgrade course. University of San Luis.

Lei, Q., Jiang, Y., & Yang, M. (2014). Evaluating open IaaS cloud platforms based upon NIST Cloud Computing Reference Model. *17th IEEE International Conference on Computational Science and Engineering CSE 2014, Jointly with 13th IEEE International Conference on Ubiquitous Communications IUCC 2014, 13th International Symposium on Pervasive Systems*, 1909-1914. 10.1109/CSE.2014.350

Lin, H. F., & Chen, C. H. (2017). Combining the Technology Acceptance Model and Uses and Gratifications Theory to examine the usage behavior of an Augmented Reality Tour-sharing Application. *Symmetry*, *9*(7), 113. doi:10.3390ym9070113

Lin, S., & Kernighan, B. W. (1973). An effective heuristic algorithm for the traveling-salesman problem. *Operations Research*, *21*(2), 498–516. doi:10.1287/opre.21.2.498

LogMeIn, Inc. (2016). *Hamachi, Create virtual private networks on-demand*. Retrieved April 2020, from https://www.vpn.net/

López de Toro-Rivera, C. (2014). Características de emprendimiento social de los jóvenes en estudios previos a los universitarios. Universidad Complutense Madrid. *E-Prints Complutense*. https://eprints.ucm.es/27578/

Lopez-Pellicer, J., Florczyk, J., Nogueras-Iso, J., Muro-Medrano, P., & Zarazaga, J. (2010). Exposing CSW catalogues as Linked data. Geospatial Thinking, Lecture Notes in Geoinformation and Cartography (LNG&C), 183–200.

Lorenzo, M. J. (2017). *Endless Loop: The History of the BASIC Programming Language (Beginner's All-purpose Symbolic Instruction Code)*. SE Books.

Lu, M. (2020). Exploring Visual Information Flows in Infographics. In *CHI 2020 - Conference on Human Factors in Computing Systems* (pp. 1-12). New York: ACM Press.

Lu, C. W., Li, S. C., & Wu, Q. (2011). Interconnecting ZigBee and 6LoWPAN wireless sensor networks for smart grid applications. In *2011 Fifth International Conference on Sensing Technology* (pp. 267-272). IEEE.

Lucas, K., & Sherry, J. L. (2004). Sex differences in video game play: A communication-based explanation. *Communication Research*, *31*(5), 499–523. doi:10.1177/0093650204267930

Magharei, N., Rejaie, R., & Yang, G. (2007). Mesh or multiple-tree: A comparative study of live p2p streaming approaches. In *INFOCOM 2007. 26th IEEE International Conference on Computer Communications*. IEEE.

Makikawa, F., Tsuchiya, T., & Kikuno, T. (2010). Balance and proximity-aware skip graph construction. *Networking and Computing (ICNC), 2010 First International Conference on*, 268 –271. 10.1109/IC-NC.2010.59

Malaga, R. (2010). Search Engine Optimization-Black and White Hat Approaches. *Advances in Computers*, *78*, 1–39. doi:10.1016/S0065-2458(10)78001-3

Maldonado, M., Herrera, S., Irurzun, I., Carranza, J., Palavecino, R., Macedo, A., & Suárez, C. (2018). M-learning: Aprendizaje en Diversos Niveles Educativos Usando ImaColab. In *VI Congreso Nacional de Ingeniería Informática y Sistemas de Información*, (pp. 408-418). Argentina: Universidad Tecnológica Nacional.

Malhotra, N. K. (2010). *Marketing Research: An Applied Orientation, 6/E*. Pearson Education.

Mallon, J., & Whelan, P. F. (2005). Projective Rectification from the Fundamental Matrix. *Image and Vision Computing*, *23*(7), 643–650. doi:10.1016/j.imavis.2005.03.002

Mandelbrot, B. B. (1982). *The Fractal Geometry of Nature. W. H. Freeman and Company.*

Mansuelli, G. A. (1967). *Le stele romane del territorio ravennate e del basso Po*. Longo Editore.

Mansuelli, G. A. (1971). *Urbanistica e architettura della Cisalpina romana fino al III secolo*. Latomus.

Manvi, M., Dixit, A., & Bhatia, K. (2013). Design of an ontology based adaptive crawler for hidden Web. In *Proceedings of the International Conference on Communication Systems and Network Technologies* (pp. 659–663). Gwalior: IEEE. 10.1109/CSNT.2013.140

Marshall, C., & Shipman, F. (2017). Who Owns the Social Web? *Communications of the ACM*, *60*(5), 36–42. doi:10.1145/2996181

Marston, S., Li, Z., Bandyopadhyay, S., Zhang, J., & Ghalsasi, A. (2011). Cloud computing - The business perspective. *Decision Support Systems*, *51*(1), 176–189. doi:10.1016/j.dss.2010.12.006

Martin, B. & Ringham, F. (2006). *Key Terms in Semiotics*. London: Bloomsbury 3PL.

Martinez, A. C. (2011). *Cooperation in Traveler's Problems (TSP) and Vehicle Routes (VRP): An Overview*. University of Santiago de Compostela.

Martínez-Rodriguez, F. M. (2011). Percepción del profesorado de las escuelas taller y casas de oficios en Andalucía acerca del nivel de competencias emprendedoras en su alumnado. *Revista de Educación*, (356), 303-326.

Massa, R. (1997). *Cambiare la scuola. Educare o istruire?* Laterza.

Massa, R. (Ed.). (2005). *La Clinica della formazione*. Franco Angeli.

Mathwick, C., Malhotra, N. K., & Rigdon, E. (2001). Experiential value: Conceptualization, measurement, and application in the catalog and Internet shopping environment. *Journal of Retailing*, *77*(1), 39–56. doi:10.1016/S0022-4359(00)00045-2

Mattelart, A., & Schmucler, H. (1983). *América Latina en la encrucijada telemática*. Paidós.

Mauro, M., & … . (2001). *Ravenna romana*. Adriapress.

Mccarthy, J., Sebo, E., Wilkinson, B., & Sheehan, F. (2020). Open Workflows for Polychromatic Reconstruction of Historical Sculptural Monuments in 3D. *ACM Journal on Computing and Cultural Heritage*, *13*(3), 1–16. doi:10.1145/3386314

McCullough, B. (2018). *How the Internet Happened From Netscape to the iPhone*. W. W. Norton.

McLuhan, M., & Powers, B. (1989). *The Global Village: Transformations in World Life and Media in the 21st Century*. Oxford University Press.

McQuail, D. (1984). With the benefit of hindsight: Reflections on uses and gratifications research. *Critical Studies in Media Communication*, *1*(2), 177–193.

Medina, P., Cruz, E., & Gomez, R. (2012). Selección de proveedor de WMS utilizando método AHP. *Sciences et Techniques (Paris)*, *17*(52), 65–72.

Melián, B., Moreno Pérez, J. A., & Moreno Pérez, J. M. (2003). Metaheuristics: a global visión. *Iberoamerican Journal of Artificial Intelligence, 19*, 7-28.

Mell, P., & Grance, T. (2011). The NIST Definition of Cloud Computing Recommendations of the National Institute of Standards and Technology. *Nist Special Publication.*, *145*, 7.

Menczer, F., Fortunato, S., & Davis, C. A. (2020). *A First Course in Network Science*. Cambridge University Press.

Meng, S., Cong Shi, D.H.X.Z., & Yu, Y. (2005). Gnutella 0.6. Volume 3841 of LNCS. Springer.

Meyer, J. (2008). Typology and acoustic strategies of whistled languages: Phonetic comparison and perceptual cues of whistled vowels. *Journal of the International Phonetic Association*, *38*(1), 69–94. doi:10.1017/S0025100308003277

Michel Cosnarda, L. L., & Chanda, R. (2007). Virtual organizations in arigatoni. *Electronic Notes in Theoretical Computer Science*, *171*(3), 55–75. doi:10.1016/j.entcs.2006.11.035

Micronet. (2004). *CD-Rom Enciclopedia Universal*. Madrid: Micronet.

Minichino, J., & Howse, J. (2015). *Computer Vision with Python*. Packt Publishing Ltd.

Minnaar, J. & de Moree, P. (2020). *Corporate Rebels – make work more fun.* Eindhoven: Corporate Rebels Nederland B.V.

Minski, M. L. (1967). *Computation: Finite and Infinite Machines*. Prentice-Hall Inc.

Miorandi, D., Sicari, S., Pellegrini, F. D., & Chlamtac, I. (2012). Internet of things: Vision, applications and research challenges. *Ad Hoc Networks*, *10*(7), 1497–1516. doi:10.1016/j.adhoc.2012.02.016

Misic, J. (2008). Analysis of Slave–Slave Bridging in IEEE 802.15.4 Beacon-Enabled Networks. *IEEE Transactions on Vehicular Technology*, *57*(3), 1846–1863. doi:10.1109/TVT.2007.909263

Misra, P., & Enge, P. (2006). Global Positioning System: Signals, Measurements, and Performance (2nd ed.). Ganga-Jamuna Press.

Moffett, M. W. (2019). *The Human Swarm – How Our Societies Arise, Thrive and Fall.* London: Head of Zeus.

Moreno Pérez, J. A. (2004). *Metaheuristics: an updated review. Working Document presented in DEIOC*. University of La Laguna.

Morin, E. (2016). Il cinema o l'uomo immaginario. Milano: Cortina.

Morin, E. (2002). *Seven complex lessons in education for the future*. UNESCO.

Moss, A. (2019). *20 Augmented Reality Stats to Keep You Sharp in 2019*. Retrieved from https://techjury.net/stats-about/augmented-reality/

Muntinga, D. G., Moorman, M., & Smit, E. G. (2011). Introducing COBRAs: Exploring motivations for brand-related social media use. *International Journal of Advertising*, *30*(1), 13–46. doi:10.2501/IJA-30-1-013-046

Najar, P., Ledesma, E., Rocabado, S., Herrera, S., & Palavecino, R. (2014). Eficiencia de aplicaciones móviles según su arquitectura. In *XX Congreso Argentino de Ciencias de la Computación*. Buenos Aires: Universidad Nacional de La Plata.

Natili, G. (2013). *A guid to building cross-platform apps using the W3C standards based Cordova/PhoneGap framework*. Editorial Packt Publishing.

Navarro, C., Molina, A., Redondo, M., & Juarez-Ramírez, M. (2015). Framework para Evaluar Sistemas M-learning: Un Enfoque Tecnológico y Pedagógico. Revista VAEP-RITA, 3(1), 38-45.

Negroponte, N. (1995). *Being Digital*. Knopf.

Nektarios, K., & Xenos, M. (2012). Usability Evaluation of Augmented Reality Systems. *Intelligent Decision Technologies*, *6*(2), 139–149. doi:10.3233/IDT-2012-0130

Nelson, T. (1974). *Computer Lib / Dream Machines*. Microsoft Press – Pearson Education.

Nelson, T. (1993). *Literary Machines*. Mindful Press.

Nicolosi, V. M. (2002). *Sguardo o visione?* Nicola Calabria Editore.

Nielsen, J. (1990). *Hypertext and Hypermedia*. Academic Press.

Nielsen, J., & Mack, R. (1994). *Usability Inspection Methods*. Willey. doi:10.1145/259963.260531

Norman, D. (1988). *The Design of Everyday Things*. Basic Books.

Nöth, W. (1995). *Handbook of Semiotics*. Indiana University Press.

O'Neil, C. (2016). *Weapons of Math Destruction: How Big Data Increases Inequality and Threatens Democracy*. Crown.

Ochoa, E. (2012). *An Analysis of the Application of Selected Search Engines Optimization (SEO) Techniques and their Effectiveness on Google's Search Ranking Algorithm.* California State University.

Okai, E., Feng, X., & Sant, P. (2018). Smart Cities Survey. *IEEE 20th International Conference on High Performance Computing and Communications; IEEE 16th International Conference on Smart City; IEEE 4th International Conference on Data Science and Systems (HPCC/SmartCity/DSS),* 1726-1730. 10.1109/HPCC/SmartCity/DSS.2018.00282

Oliveira, A. (2017). *The Digital Mind: How Science is Redefining Humanity*. MIT Press. doi:10.7551/mitpress/9780262036030.001.0001

Olsson, T., Lagerstam, E., Kärkkäinen, T., & Väänänen-Vainio-Mattila, K. (2013). Expected user experience of mobile augmented reality services: A user study in the context of shopping centres. *Personal and Ubiquitous Computing*, *17*(2), 287–304. doi:10.100700779-011-0494-x

Organización Internacional del Trabajo. (2016). *Las mujeres en el trabajo, tendencias 2016*. https://www.ilo.org/global/publications/books/WCMS_483214/lang--es/index.htm

Organización Internacional del Trabajo. (2017). *Desempleo Juvenil en el Mundo*. https://www.ilo.org/global/research/global-reports/world-of-work/lang--es/index.htm

Oró, M. G., Lanna, L. C. & Casas, K. O. (2013). Cambios en el uso y la concepción de las TIC, implementando el Mobile Learning. RED. *Revista de Educación a Distancia*, (37), 1-19.

Ortega, I. (2017). El dilema de la generación Z. *El blog de Iñaki Ortega*. http://www.inakiortega.com/2017/04/el-dilema-de-la-generacion-z.html

Osman, I. H., & Kelly, J. P. (1996). *Meta-Heuristics: Theory and Applications*. Kluwer Academic Publishers. doi:10.1007/978-1-4613-1361-8

Otlet, P. (1935). *Monde: Essaid'universalisme*. Brussels: Editions Mundaneum. Retrieved April 12, 2020 from https://fr.wikisource.org/wiki/Fichier:Otlet_-_Monde_-_1935.djvu

Pachler, N., Bachmair, B., & Cook, J. (2010). *Mobile learning: structures, agency, practices*. Editorial Springer. doi:10.1007/978-1-4419-0585-7

Pandit, V. (2015). *We Are Generation Z: How Identity, Attitudes, and Perspectives Are Shaping Our Future*. Brown Books Publishing.

Pantano, E., & Naccarato, G. (2010). Entertainment in retailing: The influences of advanced technologies. J. Retail. *Consumer Services*, *17*(3), 200–204. doi:10.1016/j.jretconser.2010.03.010

Papadimitriou, C. H., & Steiglitz, K. (1982). Combinatorial Optimization: Algorithms and Complexity. Prentice Hall.

Papert, S. (1993). *Mindstorms Children Computers and Powerful Ideas*. Basic Books.

Park, J. B., & Kak, A. C. (2003, September). A Truncated Least Squares Approach to the Detection of Specular Highlights in Color Images. In *2003 IEEE International Conference on Robotics and Automation (Cat. No. 03CH37422)* (Vol. 1, pp. 1397-1403). IEEE.

Park, Y. (2011). A Pedagogical Framework for Mobile Learning: Categorizing Educational Applications of Mobile Technologies into Four Types. *International Review of Research in Open and Distance Learning*, *12*(2), 78–102. doi:10.19173/irrodl.v12i2.791

Paul, P. V., & Saraswathi, R. (2017). The Internet of Things — A comprehensive survey. *2017 International Conference on Computation of Power, Energy Information and Commuincation (ICCPEIC)*, 421-426. 10.1109/ICCPEIC.2017.8290405

Pedraza, L. E. & Valbuena S. D. (2014). M-learning y realidad aumentada, tecnologías integradas para apoyar la enseñanza del cálculo. *Revista de investigaciones UNAD*, *13*(2), 29-39.

Pendyala, V., Shim, S., & Bussler, C. (2015). The Web that Extends Beyond the World. *IEEE Computer*, *48*(5), 18–25. doi:10.1109/MC.2015.150

Perez, C. (2009). After the crisis: creative construction. *Open Democracy News Analysis*. http://www.opendemocracy.net

Perez, C. (2003). *Technological Revolutions and Financial Capital - The Dynamics of Bubbles and Golden Ages*. Edward Elgar Publishing Ltd.

Perkins, C. E., & Royer, E. M. (1999). Ad-hoc on-demand distance vector routing. *Proceedings WMCSA'99. Second IEEE Workshop on Mobile Computing Systems and Applications*, 90–100. 10.1109/MCSA.1999.749281

Petrock, V. (2019). *Virtual and Augmented Reality Users 2019*. Retrieved from https://www.emarketer.com/content/virtual-and-augmented-reality-users-2019

Piccinini, H., Casanova, M., Leme, L., & Furtado, A. (2014). Publishing deep web geographic data. *Geoimformatica*, *18*(4), 769–792. doi:10.100710707-013-0201-3

Pinker, E., Seidmann, A., & Foster, R. (2002). Strategies for Transitioning 'Old Economy' Firms to E-Business. *Communications of the ACM*, *45*(5), 77–83. doi:10.1145/506218.506219

Poe, M. (2010). *History of Communication Media & Society from the Evolution of Speech to the Internet*. Cambridge University Press. doi:10.1017/CBO9780511976919

Pomerantsev, P. (2019). *This Is Not Propaganda – Adventures in the War Against Reality*. Faber & Faber.

Popper, K. (1972). *Objective Knowledge: An Evolutionary Approach*. Oxford University Press.

Popper, K. (1978). *The Three Worlds - The Tanner Lectures On Human Values*. University of Michigan Press.

Portman, E. (2016). *Towards Cognitive Cities: Advances in Cognitive Computing and its Application to the Governance of Large Urban Systems*. Springer. doi:10.1007/978-3-319-33798-2

Poushneh, A., & Vasquez-Parraga, A. Z. (2017). Discernible impact of augmented reality on retail customer's experience, satisfaction and willingness to buy. *Journal of Retailing and Consumer Services*, *34*, 229–234. doi:10.1016/j.jretconser.2016.10.005

Pozo, J. (2008). *Aprendices y maestros: La psicología cognitiva del aprendizaje*. Editorial Alianza.

Pressman, R., & Lowe, D. (2009). *Web Engineering: A Practitioner's Approach*. McGraw-Hill.

Pressman, R., & Maxim, B. (2015). *Software Engineering: A Practitioner's Approach*. McGraw Hill Education.

Programa Educación y Sociedad. (2019). *Educación y Sociedad 19 09 2019*. youtube.com/watch?v=F45UM7WgHBc.

Protasov, S.I., Kurgalin, S.D., & Krylovetsky, A.A. (2011). Use of a Web Camera as a Source Steeropar. *Bulletin of the Voronezh State University*, (2), 80-86.

Radley, A. (2013a). Computers as Self. In *Fourth International Workshop on Computer Interaction, Tourism and Cultural Heritage* (pp. 124–135). Bergamo: Blue Herons editions.

Radley, A. (2013b). Lookable User Interfaces and 3D. In *Fourth International Workshop on Computer Interaction, Tourism and Cultural Heritage* (pp. 47–65). Bergamo: Blue Herons editions.

Radley, A. (2015). *Computers as Self, BluePrints Visions and Dreams of Technopia*. Radley Books.

Radley, A. (2015). *Self as Computer*. Radley Press. doi:10.4018/978-1-4666-7377-9.ch011

Raggett, D. (2015). The Web of Things: Challenges and Opportunities. *IEEE Computer*, *48*(5), 26–32. doi:10.1109/MC.2015.149

Rahimian, V., & Ramsin, R. (2008). *Designing an agile methodology for mobile software development: A hybrid method engineering approach*. Paper presented at Second International Conference on Research Challenges in Information Science, Marrakech, Morocco. 10.1109/RCIS.2008.4632123

Ramos, S. A. (2010). *The Traveler's Problem: Concepts, Variations and Alternative Solutions*. Models and Optimization I. UBA.

Raphael Chand, L. L., & Cosnard, M. (2007). Improving resource discovery in the arigatoni overlay network. In Architecture of Computing Systems. Volume 4415 of LNCS. Springer.

Rasheed, N. A., & Nordin, M. J. (2015). A Survey of Computer Methods in Reconstruction of 3D Archaeological Pottery Objects. *International Journal of Advanced Research*, *3*(3), 712–714.

Ratnasamy, S., Francis, P., Handley, M., Karp, R., & Shenker, S. (2001). A scalable content-addressable network. *Computer Communication Review*, *31*(4), 161–172. doi:10.1145/964723.383072

Rauschnabel, P. A. (2018). Virtually enhancing the real world with holograms: An exploration of expected gratifications of using augmented reality smart glasses. *Psychology and Marketing*, *35*(8), 557–572. doi:10.1002/mar.21106

Rauschnabel, P. A., Brem, A., & Ivens, B. S. (2015). Who will buy smart glasses? Empirical results of two pre-market-entry studies on the role of personality in individual awareness and intended adoption of Google Glass wearables. *Computers in Human Behavior*, *49*(8), 635–647. doi:10.1016/j.chb.2015.03.003

Rauschnabel, P. A., He, J., & Ro, Y. K. (2018). Antecedents to the adoption of augmented reality smart glasses: A closer look at privacy risks. *Journal of Business Research*, *92*, 374–384. doi:10.1016/j.jbusres.2018.08.008

Rauschnabel, P. A., Rossmann, A., & Tom Dieck, M. C. (2017). An adoption framework for mobile augmented reality games: The case of Pokémon Go. *Computers in Human Behavior, 76*(6), 276–286. doi:10.1016/j.chb.2017.07.030

Rauschnabel, P. A., & Ro, Y. K. (2016). Augmented reality smart glasses: An investigation of technology acceptance drivers. *International Journal of Technology Marketing, 11*(2), 123–148. doi:10.1504/IJTMKT.2016.075690

Ray, P. (2018). A survey on Internet of Things architectures. *Journal of King Saud University - Computer and Information Sciences, 30*(3), 291-319.

Real Academia Española. (2019a). Competencia. In *Diccionario de la Lengua Española*. Retrieved September 4, 2019, from https://dle.rae.es/competencia?m=form

Real Academia Española. (2019b). Generación. In *Diccionario de la Lengua Española*. Retrieved August 20, 2019, from https://dle.rae.es/generaci%C3%B3n?m=form

Real Academia Española. (2020a). Vulnerable. In *Diccionario de la Lengua Española*. Retrieved August 1, 2020, from https://dle.rae.es/vulnerable

Real Academia Española. (2020b). Vulnerabilidad. In *Diccionario de la Lengua Española*. Retrieved August 1, 2020, from https://dle.rae.es/vulnerabilidad?m=form

RealVNC Limited. (2019). *RealVNC Connect*. Retrieved April 2020, from https://www.realvnc.com

Reeves, B., & Nass, C. (1996). *The Media Equation: How People Treat Computers, Television, and New Media Like Real People and Places*. Cambridge University Press.

Reinelt, G. (1995). *TSPLIB 95. Tech. report*. Universität Heidelberg, Institutfür Angewandte Mathematik.

Reinoso, R. (2016). Realidad Aumentada Posibilidades y Usos en Educación. In Recursos Educativos Aumentados una oportunidad para la Inclusión (Ed.), *VIII International Conference of Adaptive and Accessible Virtual Learning Environment*, (pp. 8-25). Cartagena de Indias: Universidad de Cartagena.

Reisman, S. (2020). Viva la Revolucion? *IEEE Computer, 53*(8), 71–73. doi:10.1109/MC.2020.2993622

RemoteIoT Inc. (2018). *Remote Access Raspberry Pi*. Retrieved June 2018, from https://remoteiot.com/

Report, G. S. (2016). *Virtual and Augmented Reality: Understanding the race for next computing platform*. https://www.goldmansachs.com/insights/pages/technology-driving-innovation-folder/virtual-and-augmented-reality/report.pdf

Rese, A., Baier, D., Geyer-Schulz, A., & Schreiber, S. (2017). How augmented reality apps are accepted by consumers: A comparative analysis using scales and opinions. *Technological Forecasting and Social Change, 124*, 306–319. doi:10.1016/j.techfore.2016.10.010

Resende, M. G. C., & Ribeiro, C. C. (2003). Greedy Randomized Adaptive Search Procedures. In *Handbook of Metaheuristics* (pp. 219–249). Springer. doi:10.1007/0-306-48056-5_8

Rezzara, A. (Ed.). (2004). *Dalla scienza pedagogica alla clinica della formazione: sul pensiero e l'opera di Riccardo Massa* (Vol. 9). FrancoAngeli.

Rheingold, H. (1985). *Tools for Thought*. MIT Press.

Risson, J., & Moors, T. (2006). Survey of research towards robust peer-to-peer networks: Search methods. *Computer Networks, 50*(17), 3485–3521. doi:10.1016/j.comnet.2006.02.001

Robbins, J. (2018). *Learning Web Design: A Beginner's Guide to HTML, CSS, JavaScript, and Web Graphics*. O'Reilly Media.

Rodríguez-Moreno, D., & Gómez-Murillo, A. X. (2014). Las competencias emprendedoras en el departamento de Boyacá. *Apuntes del Cenes*, *33*(58), 217-242. https://www.redalyc.org/articulo.oa?id=4795/479547210009

Rosenzvaig, F., Budan, P., Herrera, S., Najar, P., Saavedra, E., Sánchez, C., & Fennema, C. (2018). Desarrollo de aplicaciones móviles multiplataforma que usan realidad aumentada. *XIII Jornadas de Ciencia y Tecnología de Facultades de Ingeniería del Noroeste Argentino*, *4*, 247–252.

Rossi-Casé, L., Doná, S., Biganzoli, B., & Garzaniti, R. (2019). Evaluando a los Millennials. Apreciaciones sobre la inteligencia a partir del Test de Raven. *Perspectivas Psicológicas*, *16*(1), 14–25.

Russell, B. (1963). *Skeptical Essays*. Philosophical Library.

Saaty, T. (1980). *The Analytical Hierarchical Process* (Vol. J). Wiley.

Salazar Mesía, N., Gorga, G., & Sanz, C. (2015-a). Plan de evaluación del material educativo digital EPRA. Propuesta de indagación sobre la motivación intrínseca. In *XXI Congreso Argentino de Ciencias de la Computación*, (pp. 414-423). Junín: Universidad Nacional del Noroeste de la Provincia de Buenos Aires.

Salazar Mesía, N., Gorga, G., & Sanz, C. (2015-b). EPRA: Herramienta para la Enseñanza de conceptos básicos de programación utilizando realidad aumentada. In *X Congreso de Tecnología en educación y Educación en Tecnología*, (pp. 426-435). Buenos Aries: Universidad Nacional de La Plata.

Samie, F., Bauer, L., & Henkel, J. (2016). IoT technologies for embedded computing: A survey. *Hardware/Software Codesign and System Synthesis (CODES+ ISSS), 2016 International Conference on*, 1–10. 10.1145/2968456.2974004

Sánchez, J. C. (2013). The impact of an Entrepreneurship Education Program on entrepreneurial competencies and Intention. *Small Business Management*, *51*(3), 447–465. doi:10.1111/jsbm.12025

Savage, N. (2017). Weaving the Web. *Communications of the ACM*, *60*(6), 20–22. doi:10.1145/3077334

Schaffer, E. (2006). A Decision Table: Offshore or Not? (When NOT to Use Offshore Resourses). *Interaction*, *8*(2), 32–33. doi:10.1145/1116715.1116737

Schermann, J., Cito, J., & Leitner, P. (2018). Continuous Experimentation: Challenges, Implementation Techniques, and Current Research. *IEEE Software*, *35*(2), 26–31. doi:10.1109/MS.2018.111094748

Schneiderman, B. (2002). Understanding Human Activities and Relationships. *Interaction*, *9*(5), 40–53.

Scholz, J., & Smith, A. N. (2016). Augmented reality: Designing immersive experiences that maximize consumer engagement. *Business Horizons*, *59*(2), 149–161. doi:10.1016/j.bushor.2015.10.003

Sebesta, R. (2016). *Concepts of Programming Languages*. Pearson Education.

Seemiller, C., & Grace, M. (2018). *Generation Z: A Century in the Making*. Routledge. doi:10.4324/9780429442476

Selfridge, O. (2006). Learning and Education: A Continuing Frontier for AI. *IEEE Intelligent Systems*, *21*(3), 16–23. doi:10.1109/MIS.2006.54

Shankar, V., Kleijnen, M., Ramanathan, S., Rizley, R., Holland, S., & Morrissey, S. (2016). Mobile shopper marketing: Key issues, current insights, and future research avenues. *Journal of Interactive Marketing*, *34*, 37–48. doi:10.1016/j.intmar.2016.03.002

Shannon, C. E., & Weaver, W. (1963). *Mathematical Theory of Communication*. University of Illinois Press.

Shao, F., Yu, M., Jiang, G. Y., & Yang, R. E. (2010, May). Color Correction for Multi-View Video Based On Color Variation Curve. In *2010 International Conference on Intelligent Computation Technology and Automation* (Vol. 1, pp. 970-973). IEEE. 10.1109/ICICTA.2010.350

Shapiro, L. G., & Stockman, G. C. (2001). *Computer Vision*. Prentice Hall.

Shen, C., & Srivastava, M. (2017). Exploring Hardware Heterogeneity to Improve Pervasive Context Inferences. *IEEE Computer*, *50*(6), 19–26. doi:10.1109/MC.2017.174

Shin, H., Yang, U., & Sohn, K. (2012). Local Color Correction with Three Dimensional Point Set Registration for Underwater Stereo Images. *Optical Engineering (Redondo Beach, Calif.)*, *51*(4), 047002. doi:10.1117/1.OE.51.4.047002

Sieckenius-de-Souza, C. (2004). *The Semiotic Engineering of Human-Computer Interaction*. MIT Press.

Smith, L. (2004). *Archaeological Theory and the Politics of Cultural Heritage*. Routledge. doi:10.4324/9780203307991

Smock, A. D., Ellison, N. B., Lampe, C., & Wohn, D. Y. (2011). Facebook as a toolkit: A uses and gratification approach to unbundling feature use. *Computers in Human Behavior*, *27*(6), 2322–2329. doi:10.1016/j.chb.2011.07.011

Smorti, A. (1994). *Ilpensieronarrativo. Costruzione di storie e sviluppo della conoscenza sociale*. Giunti.

Sobrado-Fernández, L., & Fernández-Rey, E. (2010). Competencias Emprendedoras y Desarrollo del Espíritu Empresarial en los Centros Educativos. *Educación XX1*, *13*(1), 15-38. https://www.redalyc.org/articulo.oa?id=706/70618037001

Solís-Rodríguez, F. T. (2020). *Motivaciones de las Generaciones Millennial y Centennial para la Creación de Nuevas Empresas*. Universidad Autónoma de la Ciudad de Juárez. http://cathi.uacj.mx/20.500.11961/11591

Sommerville, I. (2016). *Software Engineering*. Pearson Education.

Sorokin, M. I. (2017). Pattern Recognition Methods on Images. *Alley of Science*, *2*(9), 895–906.

Spagnolli, A., Guardigli, E., Orso, V., Varotto, A., & Gamberini, L. (2014). *Measuring user acceptance of wearable symbiotic devices: validation study across application scenarios. In Symbiotic Interaction*. Springer International Publishing.

Stubbs, K., Hinds, P., & Wettergreen, D. (2007). Autonomy and Common Ground in Human-Robot Interaction: A Field Study. *IEEE Intelligent Systems*, *22*(2), 42–50. doi:10.1109/MIS.2007.21

Stützle, T., & Hoos, H. (1996). Improvements on the Ant System*: Introducing Max-Min Ant System. International Conference on Artificial Neural Networks and Genetic Algorithms, Viena*, Austria.

Stützle, T., & Hoos, H. (2000). Max - Min ant system. *Future Generation Computer Systems*, *16*(8), 889–914. doi:10.1016/S0167-739X(00)00043-1

Suh, W. (2005). *Web Engineering: Principles and Techniques*. IGI Global. doi:10.4018/978-1-59140-432-3

Sun, J., Staab, S., & Kunegis, J. (2018). Undestanding Social Networks Using Transfer Learning. *IEEE Computer*, *51*(6), 52–60. doi:10.1109/MC.2018.2701640

Susini, G. (1973). *The Roman Stonecutter*. Blackwell.

Taha, H. (2012). *Traveler agent problem. Operations Research* (9th ed.). Pearson Education.

Tambe, P., & Hitt, L. (2010). How Offshoring Affects IT Workers. *Communications of the ACM*, *53*(10), 62–70. doi:10.1145/1831407.1831426

Teilhard-de-Chardin, P. (1976). *The Phenomenon of Man*. HarperCollins.

Thomas, P., Cristina, F., Dapoto, S., & Pesado, P. (2015). Dispositivos Móviles: Desarrollo de Aplicaciones Orientadas a Educación. In *XVII Workshop de Investigadores en Ciencias de la Computación*, (pp. 388-391). Buenos Aries: Universidad Nacional de La Plata.

Till, J. van. (2015a). *The Four Network Effects*. https://theconnectivist.wordpress.com/2015/03/25/np9-engines-for-the-new-power-the-four-network-effects/

Till, J. van. (2015b). *Formal definition of Internet*. https://theconnectivist.wordpress.com/2015/09/01/what-is-internet/

Till, J. van. (2016). *The Financial System is Unstable*. https://theconnectivist.wordpress.com/2016/03/03/the-financial-system-is-unstable/

Till, J. van. (2019). *The Fifth Network Effect*. https://theconnectivist.wordpress.com/2019/08/26/what-can-we-do-8-the-fifth-network-effect-the-law-of-p2p-cooperation-and-scaling-up/

Tobón, S. (2010). Formación integral y competencias. Pensamiento complejo, currículo, didáctica y evaluación (3rd ed.). Bogotá: ECOE.

Trant, J. (2008). *Studying social tagging and folksonomy: A review and framework*. Special Issue on Digital and User-Generated Content.

Turing, A. (1936). On Computable Numbers, with an Application to the Entscheudungsproblem. *Proceedings of the London Mathematical Society*, *2*(42), 230–265. Retrieved April 6, 2020, from https://web.archive.org/web/20141222015347/http://draperg.cis.byuh.edu/archive/winter2014/cs320/Turing_Paper_1936.pdf

Turing, A. (1950). Computing Machinery and Intelligence. *Mind*, *49*(236), 433–460. doi:10.1093/mind/LIX.236.433

Valiron, B., Ross, N. J., Selinger, P., Alexander, D. S., & Smith, J. M. (2015). Programming the Quantum Future. *Communications of the ACM*, *58*(8), 52–61. doi:10.1145/2699415

van Till, J. (2020). *Blog about Audry Tang, interview articles in NRC and FD*. https://theconnectivist.wordpress.com/2020/06/24/digital-democracy-in-taiwan-basic-8-for-synthecracy/

Vázquez, C., & Mouján-Fernández, J. (2016). Adolescencia y Sociedad. La construcción de Identidad en tiempos de inmediatez. *Revista PSOCIAL*, *2*(1), 38–55.

Veltman, K. (2013). Historical Interfaces for Cultures. In *Fourth International Workshop on Computer Interaction, Tourism and Cultural Heritage* (pp. 1–31). Bergamo: Blue Herons editions.

Veltman, K. (2016). Means of Certain Knowledge, Levels of Knowledge and Interfaces. In *Seventh International Workshop on Computer Interaction, Tourism and Cultural Heritage* (pp. 1-75). Bergamo: Blue Herons editions.

Veltman, K. (2000). *Frontiers in Conceptual Navigation for Cultural Heritage*. Ontario Library Association.

Veltman, K. (2001). *Syntactic and semantic interoperability: New approaches to knowledge and the semantic web*. The New Review of Information Networking.

Veltman, K. (2006). *Understanding New Media*. University of Calgary Press. doi:10.2307/j.ctv6gqs2k

Veltman, K. (2014). *The Alphabets of Life*. Virtual Maastricht McLuhan Institute.

Venkatesh, V., & Bala, H. (2008). Technology acceptance model 3 and a research agenda on interventions. *Decision Sciences*, *39*(2), 273–315. doi:10.1111/j.1540-5915.2008.00192.x

Venkatesh, V., & Davis, F. D. (2000). A theoretical extension of the technology acceptance model: Four longitudinal field studies. *Management Science*, *46*(2), 186–204. doi:10.1287/mnsc.46.2.186.11926

Venkatesh, V., Morris, M. G., Davis, G. B., & Davis, F. D. (2003). User acceptance of information technology: Toward a unified view. *Management Information Systems Quarterly*, *27*(3), 425–478. doi:10.2307/30036540

Verhoef, P. C., Kannan, P. K., & Inman, J. J. (2015). From multi-channel retailing to omni-channel retailing: Introduction to the special issue on multi-channel retailing. *Journal of Retailing*, *91*(2), 174–181. doi:10.1016/j.jretai.2015.02.005

Vigotsky, L. (1979). *El desarrollo de los procesos psicológicos superiores*. Editorial Crítica.

Vilanova, N., & Ortega, I. (2017). *Generacion Z: todo lo que necesitas sobre los jóvenes que han dejado viejo a los millenials*. Plataforma Editorial.

Villanueva, S. D. (2013). Las competencias dentro del rol profesional: diferencias entre la Educación Superior (universitaria) y las demandas del mercado laboral. *Revista Debate Universitario, 1*(2), 44-65. http://ppct.caicyt.gov.ar/index.php/debate-universitario/article/viewFile/1605/pdf

Vincentelli, A. S. (2015). Let's get physical: Adding physical dimensions to cyber systems. *Low Power Electronics and Design (ISLPED), 2015 IEEE/ACM International Symposium on*, 1–2.

Vixie, P. (2011). Arrogance in Business Planning. *Communications of the ACM*, *54*(9), 38–41. doi:10.1145/1995376.1995392

Vockner, B., & Mittlböck, M. (2014). Geo-Enrichment and Semantic Enhancement of Metadata Sets to Augment Discovery in Geoportals. *ISPRS International Journal of Geo-Information*, *3*(1), 345–367. doi:10.3390/ijgi3010345

Von Hesberg, H. (1992). *Römische Grabbauten*. Wissenschaftliche Buchgesellschaft.

Vote, E., Feliz, D. A., Laidlaw, D. H., & Joukowsky, M. S. (2002). Discovering Petra: Archaeological Analysis in VR. *IEEE Computer Graphics and Applications*, *22*(5), 38–50. doi:10.1109/MCG.2002.1028725

Vygotskji, L. S. (1966). *Pensiero e linguaggio*. GiuntiBarbera.

Walrad, C. (2017). Standards for the Enterprise IT Profession. *IEEE Computer*, *50*(3), 70–73. doi:10.1109/MC.2017.68

Want, R. (2006). An introduction to RFID technology. *IEEE Pervasive Computing*, *5*(1), 25–33. doi:10.1109/MPRV.2006.2

Wargo, J. (2015). *Apache Cordova 4 Programming*. Editorial Addison-Wesley Professional.

Wauters, T., Coppens, J., De Turck, F., Dhoedt, B., & Demeester, P. (2006). Replica placement in ring-based content delivery networks. *Computer Communications*, *29*(16), 3313–3326. doi:10.1016/j.comcom.2006.05.008

Wehrle, K., & Steinmetz, R. (2005) What is this Peer-to-Peer about? Volume 3485 of LNCS. Springer-Verlag.

Weiser, M. (1991). The Computer for the 21st Century, Scientific American Special Issue on Communications, Computers and Networks. *YouTube*. Retrieved 5 August 2020, from https://www.youtube.com/watch?v=7jwLWosmmjE

Wells, H. G. (1936). *World Brain*. Methuen.

Werbach, K. (Ed.). (2020). *After the Digital Tornado –Networks, Algorithms, Humanity*. Cambridge University Press.

Wertsch, J. V. (1985). *Vygotskij and the social formation of mind*. Harvard University Press.

Westfall, L. (2010). *The Certified Software Quality Engineer Handbook*. Quality Press.

Wiener, N. (1950). *The Human Use of Human Beings; Cybernetics and Society*. Houghton Mifftin Company.

William, J. C., William, H. C., William, R. P., & Alexander, S. (1997). *Combinatorial Optimization* (1st ed.). Wiley-Interscience.

Wolfram, S. (2020). A Project to Find the Fundamental Theory of Physics. Oxfordshire: Wolfram Media.

Woodill, G. (2011). *The mobile learning edge*. Editorial Mc Graw Hill.

Xu, W. (2019). Toward Human-Centered AI: A Perspective from Human-Computer Interaction. *Interaction*, *26*(4), 42–46. doi:10.1145/3328485

Yassein, M. B., Mardini, W., & Khalil, A. (2016). Smart homes automation using z-wave protocol. *International Conference on Engineering MIS (ICEMIS)*, 1–6.

Yingsaeree, C., Treleaven, P., & Nuti, G. (2010). Computational Finance. *IEEE Computer*, *43*(12), 36–43. doi:10.1109/MC.2010.343

Zanella, A., Bui, N., Castellani, A., Vangelista, L., & Zorzi, M. (2014). Internet of things for smart cities. *IEEE Internet of Things Journal*, *1*(1), 22–32. doi:10.1109/JIOT.2014.2306328

Zangara, A. (2014). Apostillas sobre los conceptos básicos de educación a distancia o…una brújula en el mundo de la virtualidad. Maestría en Educación a Distancia, Vol 4. Buenos Aires: Facultad de Informática de la Universidad Nacional de La Plata.

Zanichelli. (1997). *CD-Rom Enciclopedia Zanichelli.* Bologna: Zanichelli.

Zanker, P. (1988). *The Power of Images in the Age of Augustus*. University of Michigan Press. doi:10.3998/mpub.12362

Zhang, C., & Li, W. (2005). The roles of web feature and web map services in real-time geospatial data sharing for. *Cartography and Geoginformation Science*, *32*(4), 269–283. doi:10.1559/152304005775194728

Zhang, Z. (2004). Camera Calibration with One-Dimensional Objects. *IEEE Transactions on Pattern Analysis and Machine Intelligence*, *26*(7), 892–899. doi:10.1109/TPAMI.2004.21 PMID:18579947

Zhou, K., Liu, T., & Zhou, L. (2015). Industry 4.0: Towards future industrial opportunities and challenges. *12th International Conference on Fuzzy Systems and Knowledge Discovery (FSKD)*, 2147-2152. 10.1109/FSKD.2015.7382284

Zhuge, H. (2015). The Future Interconnection Environment. *IEEE Computer*, *38*(4), 27–33. doi:10.1109/MC.2005.142

Zyda, M. (2009). Computer Science in the Conceptual Age. *Communications of the ACM*, *52*(12), 66–72. doi:10.1145/1610252.1610272

About the Contributors

Rohit Agrawal is an Assistant Professor in the Department of Computer Science & Engineering, University Institute of Technology RGPV, Bhopal (M.P.) since January 2016. He has six years of academic experience. He did M.tech in Computer Science & Engineering in 2013 from Jaypee University.

Saif Ansari is currently in the final year of Dual Degree Integrated Post Graduation Programme(B. E+M.tech) in Computer Science and Engineering from University Institute of Technology RGPV, Bhopal (M.P), India. His research areas are primarily in the sphere of Web analytics, Web content, Search Engine Optimization (SEO), Content Management, UX Design & Website Development.

Paola Budan is a Magister in Computer Sciences (graduated from the South´s National University, Argentina), Technology Teaching Specialist (from the National University of Santiago del Estero, Argentina), and Bachelor in Information Systems (from the National University of Santiago del Estero, Argentina). Currently, she is a PhD Student at the South´s National University and her research area is Artificial Intelligence. She works as Adjunct Professor at the National University of Chaco Austral (Argentina) in Artificial Intelligence and Syntaxes and Semantics of the Languages. She is Professor Assistant at the National University of Santiago del Estero in Databases and Compilers topics, among others. She is a Researcher at the Exact Sciences and Technologies Faculty of UNSE and she was part of "Development of Mobile Applications with Augmented Reality for Learning and Disability" workgroup. Currently, she is co-Director in the investigation research called "Modeling complex systems using Intelligent Reasoning" in the National University of Santiago del Estero.

Veronica Castañeira has an Engineer Degree in Information Systems, graduated from the Interamerican Open University (Universidad Abierta Interamericana), Rosario regional site (Santa Fe, Argentina) in 2019. Tutor of students in the Information Systems Engineering career at the Interamerican Open University (Universidad Abierta Interamericana), in subjects corresponding to the socio-professional area. Co-author of two researches, one of them in the framework of the VII International Congress of Entrepreneurship (2019) organized by the Association for Training, Research and Development of Entrepreneurship (by its acronym in Spanish AFIDE: Asociación para la Formación, Investigación y Desarrollo del Emprendimiento, in Spanish) and the other one in the framework of the Eighth Argentine Conference on Human-Computer Interaction, Telecommunications, Informatics and Scientific Information (HCITISI 2019) organized by the Latin Association of Human-Computer Interaction (by its acronym in Spanish ALAIPO: Asociación Latina Interacción Persona-Ordenador). Member of the Scientific Committees of ALAIPO (www.alaipo.com) and AINCI (www.ainci.com) from 2020. Member of CHI Argentina – First

Chapter of Argentina Human-Computer Interaction (www.argentina-chi.net). Sales Support Specialist with 6 years of experience in solution configuration of proposals for clients in Latin America.

Oleksandr Cheliadin is a PhD student of the Department of Aircraft Control Systems of the National Aerospace University KhAI, Kharkov, Ukraine.

Miguel Cipolla-Ficarra is a professor and research. PhD. Area: Power Electronic Engineering (1996). B.A. Electronic Engineering – Telecommunications (1990). B.A. Electric Engineering (1999). Professor in European universities, technical and professional colleges (1987 – present). Software project manager: design, development and implementation of algorithms. Product manager, application engineer and technical sales engineer in international projects. Director of laboratory in F&F Multimedia Communic@tions Corp. Technical manager in AInCI (International Association of Interactive Communication –www.ainci.com) and ALAIPO (Latin Association International of Human-Computer Interaction –www.alaipo.com). Main research interests: interfaces, interactive systems, telecommunication, computer sciences, networks, industrial design, programmation, automation, motors on microprocessor, ecological energy, e-commerce and computer aided education. Co-director of the Foundation & Academy Maria Ficarra.

Kostyantin Dergachov is head of the Department of Aircraft Control Systems of the National Aerospace University KhAI, Kharkov, Ukraine.

İrem Erdoğmuş was born in 1976 in Istanbul, and completed her bachelor degree on Political Science and International Relations at Boğaziçi University, Faculty of Economics and Administrative Sciences in 1998. She started her academic career as a research assistant at Marmara University, Department of Business Administration in 1999. She completed her Ph.D in Marketing at Boğaziçi University, Social Sciences Institute in 2005. Currently, she teaches at Marmara University, Department of Business Administration as a full time professor of marketing. Her research and teaching areas include brand management, services marketing, international marketing, emerging markets, and social media marketing. She has book chapters in national and international books, and articles in national and international journals, some of which include European Journal of Marketing, International Marketing Review, and Journal of Fashion Marketing Management.

Maria Valeria Ficarra is a lawyer. B.A. Union lawyer (2003). Master in International Legal Practice (2008). Public Relations in Barcelona (Spain): ALAIPO, AINCI, Fundation & Academy Maria Ficarra. Main research interest are labour and international law, legal and business strategies, problem-solving tecniques, leadership, psychology, sociology, globalization and communication.

Carlos García Garino is Full Professor, Facultad de Ingeniería and Director of Information and Communication Technologies Institute (ITIC) at Nacional de Cuyo, Mendoza, Argentina. Currently is Vice President of Mendoza ICT Pole. Has got a Ph. D. from Technical University of Catalonia (UPC) and Civil Engineering degree from University of Buenos Aires. His research lines include Distributed Computing, Computer Networks and Computational Mechanics.

Pablo D. Godoy received the Electronic Engineering degree from Universidad Tecnológica Nacional, Argentina, in 2008, and the PhD degree at the Universidad de Mendoza, Argentina, in 2016. Currently he is a Professor at Computer Science Department of the Faculty of Engineering, Professor in the Physics Department of Faculty of Exact and Natural Sciences (FCEN), and researcher at the ITIC Research Institute, Universidad Nacional de Cuyo. His current research interests are remote laboratories, computer networks and computer architecture.

Hugo Rolando Haurech has received an Electronics Engineer in 2001. Since then and until 2005 he dedicated himself to teaching in the areas of electronics and electromechanics. In 2006 he was hired to be part of the National University of Misiones where he works in the area of computer science in tasks related to server infrastructure, data networks and security. Masters in Information Technology.

Susana Herrera is a Doctor in Computer Science (graduated from the National University of La Plata, Argentina), Master in Software Engineering (from the Polytechnic University of Madrid, Spain), University Teaching Specialist (from the National University of Cuyo, Argentina), Bachelor in Information Systems (from the National University of Santiago del Estero, Argentina). She works as Associate Professor and Researcher in Computer Science at the Faculty of Exact Sciences of the National University of Santiago del Estero. She has conducted numerous research projects on topics related to Mobile Computing, Mobile Learning and Technologies for People with Disabilities. She belongs to the Research Institute of Informatics and Information Systems (Argentina). Currently, she conducts research on the subject "Mobile Applications with Augmented Reality for Learning and Disability" and she makes a scientific stage at the University Paris 8, France, until July 2020.

Leonid Krasnov is an Assistant Professor of the Department of Aircraft Control Systems of the National Aerospace University KhAI, Kharkov, Ukraine.

Marilena Maldonado is a Master in Software Engineering (from the Polytechnic University of Madrid, Spain), University Teaching Specialist (from the National University of Cuyo, Argentina), Computer Engineer (from the Catholic University of Santiago del Estero, Argentina). She works as Adjunct Professor and Researcher in Computer Science at the Faculty of Exact Sciences of the National University of Santiago del Estero. Currently, she is part of the Mobile Computing group and develops research on the topic "Development of Mobile Applications with Augmented Reality for Learning and Disability".

Osvaldo L. Marianetti received the Electronics and Electrical Engineering degree from the Universida de Mendoza, Argentina in 1985. He graduated as specialist in Educational Informatics from the UNED, Spain. In 1996 he received the Master's in Teleinformatics degree from the Universidad de Mendoza in 2006. He is currently a professor at the Universidad de Mendoza and the Universidad Nacional de Cuyo. Its current research interests are configurable hardware systems, sensor networks and remote laboratories.

Diego Marzorati has an Engineer Degree in Information Systems, graduated from the Interamerican Open University (Universidad Abierta Interamericana), Rosario regional site (Santa Fe, Argentina) in 2019. Co-author of two researches, one of them in the framework of the VII International Congress of Entrepreneurship (2019) organized by the Association for Training, Research and Development of Entrepreneurship (by its acronym in Spanish AFIDE: Asociación para la Formación, Investigación y Desarrollo del Emprendimiento, in Spanish) and the other one in the framework of the Eighth Argentine Conference on Human-Computer Interaction, Telecommunications, Informatics and Scientific Information

(HCITISI 2019) organized by the Latin Association of Human-Computer Interaction (by its acronym in Spanish ALAIPO: Asociación Latina Interacción Persona-Ordenador). Member of CHI Argentina – First Chapter of Argentina Human-Computer Interaction (www.argentina-chi.net). Sales Manager with 12 years of experience in software solutions marketing and international trading. Responsibilities: Create and execute a strategic sales plan that expands customer base and extends global reach. Meet with potential clients and grow long-lasting relationships by understanding their needs.

María Morales is a graduate in Mathematics (graduated from the National University of Santiago del Estero, Argentina), Professor of Mathematics, Physics and Cosmography (graduated from the Manuel Belgrano Superior National Normal School of Santiago del Estero, Argentina). Currently she works as Associate Professor at the Faculty of Exact Sciences and Technologies of the National University of Santiago del Estero in charge of the chairs of Linear Algebra and Mathematics Technology. She is a researcher at the Faculty of Exact Sciences and Technologies of the National University of Santiago del Estero where she has participated in different investigations related to mobile computing and its application in the educational field. She is currently a member of the research project "Mobile applications with augmented reality for learning and disability".

Pablo Najar Ruiz has a Bachelor in Information Systems from the National University of Santiago del Estero, Argentina. He is an external researcher of the Research Institute of Informatics and Information Systems (Argentina) since 2012. Currently, he collaborates with the Mobile Computing Group on the topic "Development of Mobile Applications with Augmented Reality for Learning and Disability". He is also a practitioner of the field of Information Technologies. He conducts his own IT enterprise; he is the project leader of several IT projects of applications development.

José Ontiveros graduated from the National University of Jujuy, as a Computer Engineer, awarded by the Faculty of Engineering. He was a collaborator in the activities of the Argentine Congress of Computer Science in 2010. He took communication courses at UNJu, as well as training in free software courses, participating in the conferences of the Faculty of Engineering, for three consecutive years. He was awarded a scholarship in the research initiation scholarship projects of the Faculty of Engineering of the National University of Jujuy. He participated as an exhibitor in the Science and Technology Conference of the Faculties of Engineering of NOA.

Rajeev Pandey is an Assistant Professor in Department of Computer Science and Engineering, University Institute of Technology RGPV, Bhopal (M.P.) since July 2007. He has 12 years of academic experience. He received his Bachelor"s degree in Computer Science and Engineering from IET, DR. B.R.A. University, Agra (U.P.). He has done M.E. in Computer Science and Engineering in 2004 & PhD in 2010 from DR. B.R.A. University, Agra (U.P.), India.

Aleksandr Plakhotnyi is a PhD student of the Department of Aircraft Control Systems of the National Aerospace University KhAI, Kharkov, Ukraine.

Annamaria Poli graduated in Architecture at the Politecnico of Milano, Italy, in 1991, she obtained a PhD degree in Bioengineering in 2007. She is currently researcher and professor of Cinema and Visual Art at Department of Human Sciences for Education "Riccardo Massa", Università degli Studi di

Milano-Bicocca, Italy. Current research interests: Cinema and visual art in educational contexts, Media and Digital Technologies at school, human visual perception and image language, Cinema and visual disabilities, Emerging Interactive Technologies for teaching and learning, Computer Graphics in design of visual communication, Arts and Creativity. In 2000-2001 visiting professor at Stanford University, San Francisco (CA). She is curator of expositions, author of several papers and experimental works on Cinema and digital technologies at school and in the educational contexts, the visual color perception and the visual color disabilities.

Silvia Poncio has an Engineer Degree in Information Systems. Interamerican Open University in Rosario (Santa Fe, Argentina). Master in Educational Psychoinformatics. Lomas de Zamora University (Buenos Aires, Argentina). Master in Innovation and Entrepreneurship. University of Salamanca. (Salamanca. Spain). Experience Summary: Member of the Scientific Committees of ALAIPO (www.alaipo.com), AINCI (www.ainci.com) and Blue Herons editions (www.blueherons.net) from 2013 to present; AFIDE. University of Salamanca. Spain (asociacionafide.com). Presentation at AFIDE International Congresses AFIDE. Member of CAETI (caeti.uai.edu.ar) General Coordinator of the PNFS Timely Information Hub. Ministry of Education of Santa Fe. 2014-2019. Co-Chairs International Conferences: Seventh Argentine Conference on Human-Computer Interaction, Telecommunications, Informatics and Scientific Information (HCITISI 2018). Córdoba, Argentina; Ninth International Conference on Advances in New Technologies, Interactive Interfaces and Communicability (ADNTIIC 2018) Design, E-commerce, E-learning, E-health, E-tourism, Web 2.0 and Web 3.0. Córdoba (Huerta Grande), Argentina; Eighth Argentine Conference on Human-Computer Interaction, Telecommunications, Informatics and Scientific Information (HCITISI 2019), Córdoba (Huerta Grande), Argentina; Tenth International Conference on Advances in New Technologies, Interactive Interfaces and Communicability (ADNTIIC 2019) in Córdoba, Argentina. Keynotes Relator/Speaker in HCITISI and ADNTIIC conferences from 2017 to present. Member of CHI Argentina – First Chapter of Argentina Human-Computer Interaction (www.argentina-chi.net).

Alejandra Quiroga received a Bachelor's Degree in Computer Sciences in 1983 (Bahia Blanca, Argentina). She has a Educational Bachelor in 1988 (Buenos Aires, Argentina), a Master's Degree in Computer Engineering in 2004 (Sweden), and PhD in Computer Science in 2018 (Argentina). She is currently a teaching assistant in Argentina and post-doctoral student in Australia. Her current research subjects are education, user-centered design, computer graphics, software engineering, semantic web, and cloud computing. New fields of interest are computer vision, artificial intelligence, and robotics.

Gloria Lola Quispe has a degree in Information Systems from the Faculty of Engineering of the National University of Jujuy. She is also an Information Systems Engineer graduated from the same University. She is currently pursuing a Master's Degree in Information Systems Engineering and a specialty in Information Systems Engineering. She is a researcher at the National University of Jujuy. She is currently a teacher in the chair of Mathematical Analysis (I) of the Engineering Faculty of the UNJu. She was a collaborator of Congresses of the Science and Technology conference of the NOA engineering faculties, and she was awarded a scholarship in projects for initiation in R&D. Member of CHI Argentina – First Chapter of Argentina Human-Computer Interaction (www.argentina-chi.net).

Alan Radley is Scientific Director of the Kim Veltman Perspective Institute. Alan has worked at Logica PLC as a Senior Data Scientist for the ESA/NASA XMM Astronomical Satellite Observatory; and he also worked as a senior project manager at General Dynamics on the Bowman Communications Network for NATO, plus he was chief optical engineer for the HROS instrument on the Gemini Astronomical Observatory in Hawaii. Alan has been the author and co-editor of 5 handbooks on computing and he is the author of: "Self as Computer: Blueprints Visions and Dreams of Technopia" plus "The Science of Cybersecurity: A Treatise on Communications Security" and much-heralded associated website. Alan holds a Ph.D. in Physics from University College London plus a Master of Science degree in Spacecraft Technology and Satellite Communications. Alan is a Fellow of the Royal Society of Arts.

D. La Red is an expert in Statistics and Computing, 1979, Northeast National University, Argentine; Master's degree in Computer Science and Informatic, 2001, Northeast National University, Argentine, under an agreement with the University of Cantabria, Spain; University Teaching Specialist, 2003, Northeast National University, Argentine; PhD in Systems and Computer Engineering, 2011, University of Malaga, Spain; Professor of the Northeast National University, National Technological University and Chaco Austral National University, Argentina; research areas: operating systems, data communications, decision-making systems, aggregation operators, data mining, academic performance.

Fernanda Rodríguez has a BA in Letters in English from the National University of Salta. She has a Master's Degree in Applied Linguistics, Specialist in Teaching English as a Foreign Language. She also has a Specialization in Educational Research graduated from Professor and Researcher from the faculties of Humanities and Social Sciences, Economics and Engineering of the National University of Jujuy. The United States Embassy awarded her the "Teacher Ambassadors" Scholarship. She teaches at the Faculty of Humanities and Sciences and Socials, as well as at the Faculty of Engineering at the San Pedro de Jujuy headquarters, as well as at the Faculty of Economic Sciences.

Federico Rosenzvaig has a Bachelor in Information Systems from the National University of Santiago del Estero, Argentina. He currently works as Adjunct Professor at the Universidad del Chaco Austral (Argentina) and as Professor Assistant at Faculty of Exact Sciences of the National University of Santiago del Estero. He is in charge of the Simulation and Communications chairs. He is a researcher at the Faculty of Exact Sciences and Technologies of the National University of Santiago del Estero. As a practitioner of Information Technologies, he is a systems administrator and an application developer. He has developed web applications with ASP.Net and Java technologies. Currently, he is part of the Mobile Computing group and develops research on the topic "Development of Mobile Applications with Augmented Reality for Learning and Disability". He also researches on Artificial Intelligence in Argumentation branch.

Eric Roth has an Engineer Degree in Information Systems, graduated from the Interamerican Open University (Universidad Abierta Interamericana), Rosario regional site (Santa Fe, Argentina) in 2019. Co-author of two researches, one of them in the framework of the VII International Congress of Entrepreneurship (2019) organized by the Association for Training, Research and Development of Entrepreneurship (by its acronym in Spanish AFIDE: Asociación para la Formación, Investigación y Desarrollo del Emprendimiento, in Spanish) and the other one in the framework of the Eighth Argentine Conference on Human-Computer Interaction, Telecommunications, Informatics and Scientific

Information (HCITISI 2019) organized by the Latin Association of Human-Computer Interaction (by its acronym in Spanish ALAIPO: Asociación Latina Interacción Persona-Ordenador). Member of CHI Argentina – First Chapter of Argentina Human-Computer Interaction (www.argentina-chi.net). Analyst and Co-Assistant in computer systems and networks, in the JyM Comunicaciones company, as well as external advisor. Working as a technician in the cell phone workshop for 8 years. Also, as a network and security technician in the DyC Multishop company.

Sergio Ariel Salinas received the Information System Engineer degree from the UTN University, Mendoza, and the Ph.D. in Computer Science from UNICEN University, Buenos Aires, Argentina. He is currently an associate professor at the Department of Information System Engineering of the UTN University where he teaches courses of Discrete Mathematics. Additionally, he is a professor at the Department of Computer Science of the UNCuyo University where he teaches Logic. He is currently finishing a Master in Business Administration at UTN University and a Master in Business Intelligence and Analytics at HNU University, Germany. His research interests include decentralized communication systems, peer-to-peer networks, ad hoc networks, Internet of Things, machine learning, and business analytics.

Carlos Sánchez is an Information Systems Analyst, graduated from the National University of Santiago del Estero; and final student of the Bachelor's Degree in Information Systems at the same university. He belongs to the Research Institute of Informatics and Information Systems (Argentina) since 2018. He performs everything concerning to the development and research of 3D resources (modeling, animating, visual aspect and export) for multiplatform mobile applications.

Pelin Serefhan was born in 1994 in Istanbul, and completed her bachelor degree on Industrial Design at Anadolu University, Faculty of Architecture and Design in 2017. She started her academic career as an industrial designer at Korkmaz Kitchen Appliance in 2017. She completed her master in Production Management and Marketing at Marmara University, Social Sciences Institute in 2019 and made her graduation project on the impact of augmented reality technology on users.

Piyush Kumar Shukla received his Bachelor"s degree in Electronics & Communication Engineering, LNCT, Bhopal in 2001, M. Tech (Computer Science & Engineering) in 2005 from SATI, Vidisha and Ph.D. (Computer Science & Engineering) in 2013 from RGPV, Bhopal. M.P. India. He is Member of ISTE (Life Member), IEEE, ACM, IACSIT, IAENG. Currently he is working as an Assistant Professor (Grade 8,000/-) in Department of Computer Science & Engineering, UIT-RGPV Bhopal. He is also I/C of PG Program (Dual Degree Integrated PG-Programs) in DoCSE, UIT, RGPV, Bhopal, Madhya Pradesh. He has published more than 60 Research Papers in various International & National Journals & Conferences, including 04 papers in SCIE Journals & more than 10 papers in Scopus Journals. He has also published an Indian patent. He is guiding 04 students in PhD Program and also has been awarded 02 candidates in PhD under his guidance.

Daniela Tamburini graduated in Pedagogy at the UniversitàCattolicadelSacroCuore of Milan and obtained a Master in Development of Clinical Skills in Educational and Training Professions at the UniversitàDegliStudi of Milano-Bicocca. She has taught in several public and private institutions including the ScuolaMagistraleSalesiana and at the UniversitàdegliStudi di Milano-Bicocca, Department of

Sociology (Laboratories of Cinematic Language and Communications Systems). She works on research projects developing particular applications of the Clinica di Formazione in educational, training and school fields. Since 2012she has been the director of Sperimenta, the Centro Studi di Cinema e Formazione in Milan. Some of her publications: Tamburini D. (2017), "School-Cinema". A Research Experience That Combines Educational Theories, Educational Processes and Educational Technologies, in A cura di Cipolla-Ficara F., Optimizing Human-Computer Interaction With Emerging Technologies, IGI Global, USA; ibid., (2010), Film Language and Training Communication, in Adolescents and Media: cinema, television and the role of the school, Milan, Italy: Centro Filippo Buonarroti. She also collaborates with the UniversitàdegliStudi di Milano-Bicocca as a consultant within the research project "A school with cinema for the enhancement of learning and teaching".

Marco Tedaldi has obtained a Bachelor's degree in Cultural Property Conservation (University of Bologna, 2011) with a classical historical-artistic specialization (Faculty of Conservation of Cultural Heritage, in Ravenna). His main areas of interest are Ancient and Renaissance History and Digital Photography which he applies in the field of historical reconstruction, as well as through new information technologies for the search for historical and illustrative material. Currently he is dedicated to teaching to the public and the reproduction of ancient objects, through the constant research of images and documents preserved in specialized databases. Among the new areas of interest that he would like to develop are those related to experimental archeology, new imaging technologies, 3D reconstruction aimed at understanding all those aspects that cannot be directly verified in ancient objects that have been preserved or that have been lost with the passing of time.

Daniel Tedini has a Bachelor's Degree in International Trade. Interamerican Open University in Rosario (Santa Fe., Argentina). Bachelor's Degree in Psychology. Interamerican Open University in Rosario (Santa Fe., Argentina). Degree in Civil Engineer. National University of Rosario (Santa Fe., Argentina). Degree in Information Systems. Interamerican Open University in Rosario (Santa Fe., Argentina). Diploma in Management Development. Interamerican Open University in Rosario (Santa Fe., Argentina). Master in Virtual Learning Environments. National University of Panama (Republic of Panama). Master's Degree in Educational Technology. Interamerican Open University in Rosario (Santa Fe., Argentina). Experience Summary: General IT Coordinator at the Interamerican Open University, campus Rosario (Santa Fe., Argentina). Director of the Information Systems Engineering Career at the Interamerican Open University. Vice Dean of the Information Technology School at the Interamerican Open University. Researcher at the Center for Higher Studies in Information Technology of the Interamerican Open University. Co-authorship in scientific research: Argentina, Brazil, Mexico, Peru, Spain, Uruguay, etc. Topics: Teaching-learning Process in Software; University Entrepreneurial; Cloud Computing; Video Games; etc.

Jaap van Till is an Electronics Engineer, graduated in Pattern Recognition from Delft University, he designed and built factory- and corporate networks. Worked for James Martin Associates, Arthur D. Little and became partner at Stratix Consulting Group. He was network infrastructures professor at Delft University and HAN polytechnic. His interests shifted to: effects of ICT, social networks and FttH networks.

Görkem Vural was born in 1984 in Kırklareli, and completed his bachelor degree on Chemical Engineering at Ankara University, Faculty of Engineering in 2009. He started his professional career as a Commission Member at the Ministry of National Defence, Quality Management Department in 2010. He was assigned as a Quality Control and Technical Specification Expert at Logistics Command in 2016. He completed his MSc in Engineering Management at Marmara University, Institute of Pure and Applied Sciences in 2019. During studying his master's degree, he studied on a project called "Augmented Reality and It's Effects on Experiential Marketing". Currently, he is specializing in Quality and Environmental Management Systems, as an external auditor.

Index

3D object augmented reality 371

A

ACO Algorithms 338, 349, 356, 358
ACS 283, 338, 355, 358
AlgeRA 371-372, 378-387, 390
Anomalous and Predatory Agents 76
ARACHNE 391-392, 395, 418
archaeology 391-392, 418
architectural 265, 391-392, 397-401, 403, 418-419, 421
architectural steles 397-399, 401, 403, 418-419
artificial intelligence 4-5, 10, 16, 29, 35, 39-40, 42-43, 45, 47, 56, 58, 64-65, 70-72, 76, 79, 102, 110, 216, 225, 240-241, 243, 246, 248, 342, 357
artwork 391
as 1-6, 8, 10-18, 20-32, 39, 41-45, 49-60, 62-65, 67-68, 70-71, 79-80, 83-87, 89, 91-92, 94-100, 102-103, 105-106, 108-111, 113-120, 122-127, 129-130, 132, 137, 140, 144-146, 148-149, 151-153, 155-159, 161-167, 169, 173-176, 178, 181-182, 190, 192-194, 196-202, 204-206, 211, 213-216, 218-235, 237-242, 244-250, 252-257, 260-264, 267-279, 282-283, 285-295, 297-299, 302, 305-310, 312-313, 316-319, 324-334, 337-338, 340-352, 355-356, 358-364, 366-369, 372-374, 376-385, 387, 391-394, 396-413, 415, 419-421
augmented reality 45, 52, 54, 77, 216, 285-288, 290, 299-303, 371-372, 377-379, 384-385, 390, 392, 413, 415-416
AUTOMATED THING 233-234
Automated Thing-Automated Action 250
autonomous 29, 34, 53, 58, 71, 154, 189, 196, 228, 240-241, 252-253, 255, 257-258, 261-264, 266, 307, 325

B

Bare Metal 274, 284
Basili 4-5, 27, 30, 35, 77, 79
Berners-Lee 41-42, 44, 53, 73, 113-114, 130
Brand Loyalty 303
brand outcomes 285
broadcast service 194, 202-204, 206-208, 266
Business Management 44, 60, 304, 321

C

Captured by Web-Cameras Stereo-System 154, 191
Cinema Education 324, 336
classiary 395-397, 399-414, 418, 421
cloud computing 30, 133, 136-137, 139, 143, 146, 149-151, 153, 222, 264, 267-268, 271, 282-283, 305, 320
Cloud Laboratories 153
collaborative learning 324, 373, 388
Color Balance of the Left and Right Chambers 191
color correction 154-156, 158-162, 168-170, 173-175, 178-179, 182, 188-191
communicability 1-2, 4-5, 8-10, 18, 29, 32, 34-35, 41, 52, 54, 56, 59-60, 62-63, 71, 73, 76, 79-80, 322
computer networks 99-100, 133, 144, 151, 153, 212, 264, 267
computer science 2, 12, 32, 35, 38, 42, 45, 52, 56, 62, 79, 141, 151-152, 210-211, 308, 340-341, 344, 372
computing resources 239, 267-270, 283
cooperative learning 324, 333-334, 336, 356
creativity 2-3, 6, 12, 16, 28, 40, 42, 45, 55, 57, 248, 309-311, 314, 322, 327, 392
Cultural Heritage 2, 44, 67, 130-131, 332, 391-392, 413, 415-418
Cyber Physical Systems 192, 194, 266
Cyber-physical System 252, 266

D

database 16, 18, 26, 43, 76, 79-81, 136, 140-141, 143, 147-149, 154, 196, 211, 361-362, 391, 396

De Saussure 8, 13, 36
decentralized communication model 192-194, 252
Decentralized communication models 192-193, 196
deep web 51, 360, 363, 367-370
design 4-5, 17-18, 20, 27, 29-30, 32, 34-35, 39, 41, 43-45, 47-48, 52-55, 57-63, 68, 70-71, 73-74, 77-78, 95-96, 104-106, 110, 129, 152, 154, 170-171, 212-215, 218, 222, 225, 227-228, 231-233, 237, 240, 243, 245-247, 250, 265, 298-299, 311, 320, 332-333, 335, 338-339, 342, 345, 348, 369, 372-374, 378-379, 390, 400, 415
design models 52-54, 77
Digital Cultural Heritage 418
digital natives 306, 319, 323
Distributed Intelligence 106, 213, 216, 228-229, 239-241, 243-245, 250
dynamic routing algorithm 258

E

Eco 8-9, 11, 20, 36, 38, 54, 58, 73, 86
EDCS 391-392, 395, 418
education 1-2, 5, 14-15, 17, 23, 28-29, 32, 37, 41, 44, 52, 55, 57-60, 62, 70, 73-74, 76, 88, 94, 96, 103, 118, 130, 151-153, 283, 286, 288, 301, 306, 316-317, 319, 321, 323-328, 330-331, 333, 336-337, 358, 372-373, 378, 386-388, 392
Educ-Mobile 374-375, 388, 390
Effects of Use of Social Media 83, 101
Embodied Virtuality 223-224, 250
entrepreneur 304, 309, 318
entrepreneurship 3, 28, 30, 304, 307, 309-310, 316, 318, 320-323, 326-327
evaluation 1, 3-4, 10, 18, 31, 43, 54, 59, 63, 68, 73, 152, 163-164, 194, 232-233, 273, 275, 289, 338, 373, 379, 390, 416
extraordi 94-96, 101

F

Fenton 3, 36, 38, 53, 73
Focus Group Interview 293, 303
fractal geometry 192, 194, 196, 198, 208-209, 211
framework 32, 39, 117, 124-126, 130, 196, 211, 217-218, 239, 243, 245, 247, 254, 286, 288, 290, 300, 302, 305, 308, 310, 322, 324, 326-327, 330, 337, 343, 360, 363, 369-371, 373-374, 377-379, 382-384, 387-390

G

G factor 1, 26, 29-30, 32, 41, 43, 50, 59, 61, 63, 70, 79-80
Geo Portals 359, 370
geocommunities 360, 367
geospatial data discoverability 359-360
geospatial metadata 363, 367, 370
graphic 26-27, 43-45, 52-53, 55, 60, 95, 391, 394-395, 397

H

HCI 3, 17, 29-30, 32, 41, 43, 49, 53, 58, 62, 78-80
human factors 2, 9, 11, 34-35, 40, 45, 57, 72, 74, 76
Hypervisor 272, 283

I

ICT 4, 53, 64, 80, 83-89, 91-96, 98-101, 105-106, 193, 323
ImaColab 374-375, 388, 390
image 13, 17, 45, 55-56, 58, 90, 98, 101, 109, 116, 123, 127, 139, 155-169, 174-175, 177-182, 190-191, 285, 296-297, 305, 307, 322, 327, 331, 374, 378, 382, 384, 390-391, 394, 396, 400-401, 405, 407, 409, 411, 413-414, 418, 421
Immigrant Students 324, 336
immune 72, 83, 93-94, 101
Immune to propaganda 83, 94, 101
in-depth interview 290, 292-293, 303
Ineractive System 418
Inert Thing-Controlled Action 250
infographics 41, 45-49, 74
Information and Communications Technologies 304
information technologies 2, 32, 71, 189-190, 267
innovation 1-4, 6, 11, 13, 28, 30-31, 33-34, 36, 39, 42, 44, 52, 57, 95, 309-311, 314, 316-317, 320, 322-323, 334, 387, 392
INTELLIGENT THING 234
Intelligent Thing-Intelligent Action 250
Interdisciplinary Approach 324, 336
Internet 1, 3-4, 12, 16, 26, 28, 32, 34, 37, 42, 44-45, 48, 50-52, 56, 60, 63-64, 68-70, 72, 74, 79-80, 83-85, 87-89, 91, 93-94, 96-104, 106, 108, 110, 119-120, 122, 129, 131, 142-143, 146-150, 192, 194, 209-210, 212-213, 217-219, 221-223, 225-231, 234, 236, 243-245, 252-253, 255, 257-258, 263-268, 300-301, 305, 316, 357, 359-364, 375, 395-396, 413, 418
internet architecture 83, 99-101
Internet of Things 45, 69, 88, 108, 192, 194, 210, 212-

213, 217-219, 222-223, 225-226, 228-231, 236, 243-245, 252-253, 264-266
Invisible High-Quality Factors 1, 32, 39

J

Joint Rectification of the Left and Right Chambers 191

L

labor market 3, 304-307, 316-319, 323
language of film 324, 328-329, 333-334, 336
linguistics 5, 8, 13, 25, 32, 36

M

MADE-mlearn 371-374, 378, 386, 388, 390
MADE-M-Learn 390
McLuhan 2, 11, 37, 39, 92, 131-132, 221
metadata 359-363, 367-368, 370
Metaheuristics 338, 342-343, 348-349, 356-358
millennials 55, 62, 306-308, 312, 319, 321, 323
m-learning 371-375, 378-380, 386, 388-390
MMAS 338, 354-356, 358
mobile applications 69, 286-287, 294, 371-372, 375-379, 382-383, 386-387, 390
multimedia 2, 5, 11, 15, 17, 24, 30, 35, 38, 43-45, 47-49, 51-58, 64-65, 67-68, 70-73, 75, 77, 79, 189, 316, 331-332, 336, 391
Multi-platform mobile application development 371
multi-platform mobile applications 371-372, 379, 387, 390
Musa 5, 27, 35, 77, 79

N

natural languages 10, 13, 16, 25, 39, 367
New Media 45, 60, 74, 131, 217, 286, 288, 416
Nomadic Laboratories 133, 149, 153

O

observation 8, 30, 42, 180, 218, 257, 333, 353, 391-392, 413
Omnipresent 267, 283
Online Experiments 153
optio 400-401, 409, 411, 413, 417, 420-421

P

P2P 83, 89, 92, 193-196, 209, 211
PATER 391-392, 395, 397, 418
perceived ease of use 287, 300, 303
Perceived Usefullness 303
photography 58, 109, 391, 396, 406, 418
Pierce 8-9, 11, 18, 20, 39
Plebeian art 393
predatory agents 62-63, 76
Pressman 3-4, 25, 27, 37, 42-43, 54, 57-58, 74
PROGRAMMABLE THING 234
Programmable Thing-Programmable Action 250
programming languages 1, 3-5, 13, 15, 23-25, 27-30, 32, 34-37, 39, 57, 69, 71, 77, 192, 379

Q

quality 1-6, 8, 11-13, 17-18, 20, 25-30, 32-35, 37-39, 41-43, 45, 52, 54-59, 64, 68, 71-73, 76, 78-79, 123, 155, 162, 164, 169-171, 177, 181-189, 193, 237-239, 244, 252-253, 256, 263, 306-308, 317, 319, 323, 326-328, 342, 349, 351, 356, 358, 370, 396, 402, 408

R

Ravenna 391-394, 397-399, 401-407, 413, 415-420
reconstruction 174, 188, 330, 394, 397, 399, 416, 418
Reconstruction from Multiple Digital Images 418
remote control 153, 221
Remote Experiments 133, 153
remote laboratories 133-137, 146, 148-150, 152-153
Remote Learning 133, 153
Remote Teaching 133, 153
Rome 43, 52, 189, 393-394, 397-398, 403, 415, 417, 419-420

S

Scalable Communication System 252
sculpture 400
Search Engine Optimization 69, 361, 369-370
semiosis 9, 17, 20, 41, 43, 53-54, 62, 64, 67, 71, 76, 90
Semiosis of Digital Metamorphosis 76
Semiotics 5, 8, 11, 25, 32, 35-39, 54, 58-59, 73-74, 77
Situated Intelligence 213, 216, 218, 225-226, 228-229, 235-240, 242-244, 251
smart cities 69, 73, 193-194, 212, 245, 252-253, 257, 266
Smart City 212, 223, 245, 253, 260, 263, 266, 316, 320
smart grid 211, 265
Social entrepreneurial 308, 323
social networking 7, 69, 392
software engineering 1-2, 4-6, 24, 26, 29, 32, 35-37,

39, 41-43, 53-54, 57, 60-62, 64, 73-74, 76, 78-80, 370-372, 379, 387
soldier 394, 397, 402, 405, 407, 409, 411, 413, 417, 420-421
spatial data 359-360, 363, 367, 370
Spatial Data Infrastructure 359, 370
Spatial data infrastructure (SDIs) 359
stele 391, 394-410, 413, 416-421
stele of the classiary 395-397, 399-402, 404-410, 413, 418, 421
Stereoscopic Vision Systems 154, 191
Super Resolution 83, 91, 98-99, 101
surface web 360, 363, 367-368, 370
surveillance 83, 93-94, 97, 101, 219
Swarms 83, 88, 92, 97-99, 101
Synergetic Inter-Accommodation 213, 215, 251
Synergy 86-87, 97, 213-215, 251, 333

T

Technology Acceptance Model 285-287, 300-303
technology risks 285
the language of film 324, 328, 333-334
transitions 83, 86-87, 89, 94, 96, 100-101
TSP 338, 344-348, 355-358
TSPLIB 338, 345, 354, 358

U

ubiquitous 43, 65, 194, 223-224, 254, 265, 267, 283, 301, 359
unicast service 194, 201-202, 206, 266
Uses and Gratifications 285-286, 288, 301, 303

V

Video Stream Images 154, 191
Video Stream Images, Color Correction, Captured by Web-Cameras Stereo-System 154
virtual reality 3, 44-45, 47, 52, 57, 155, 191, 249, 287, 295, 297-298, 303, 391
Virtual Server 274, 284
virtualization 271-272, 282-283
vulnerability 307-309, 317-318, 323

W

Web Communicability 62, 76
web engineering 4-5, 29, 41-43, 45, 48, 50, 52-54, 58, 61-62, 64, 67, 71-76, 78, 80
web interface 133, 135-137, 141, 153
Web Software Engineering 41
weight 273, 276, 278, 283, 289, 402

Z

Z generation 4, 323

Printed in the United States
by Baker & Taylor Publisher Services